MW00380276

GO
MATH!

Volume 2

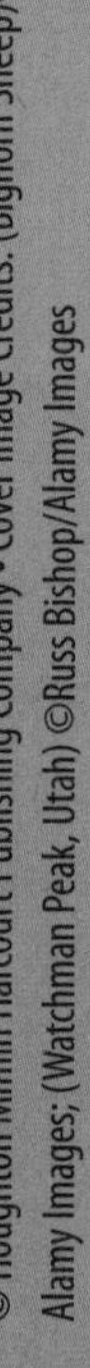

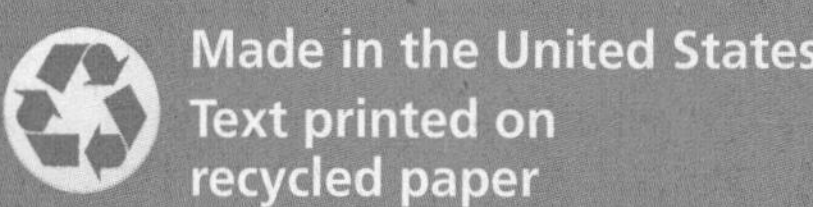
Made in the United States
Text printed on
recycled paper

Printed in the U.S.A.

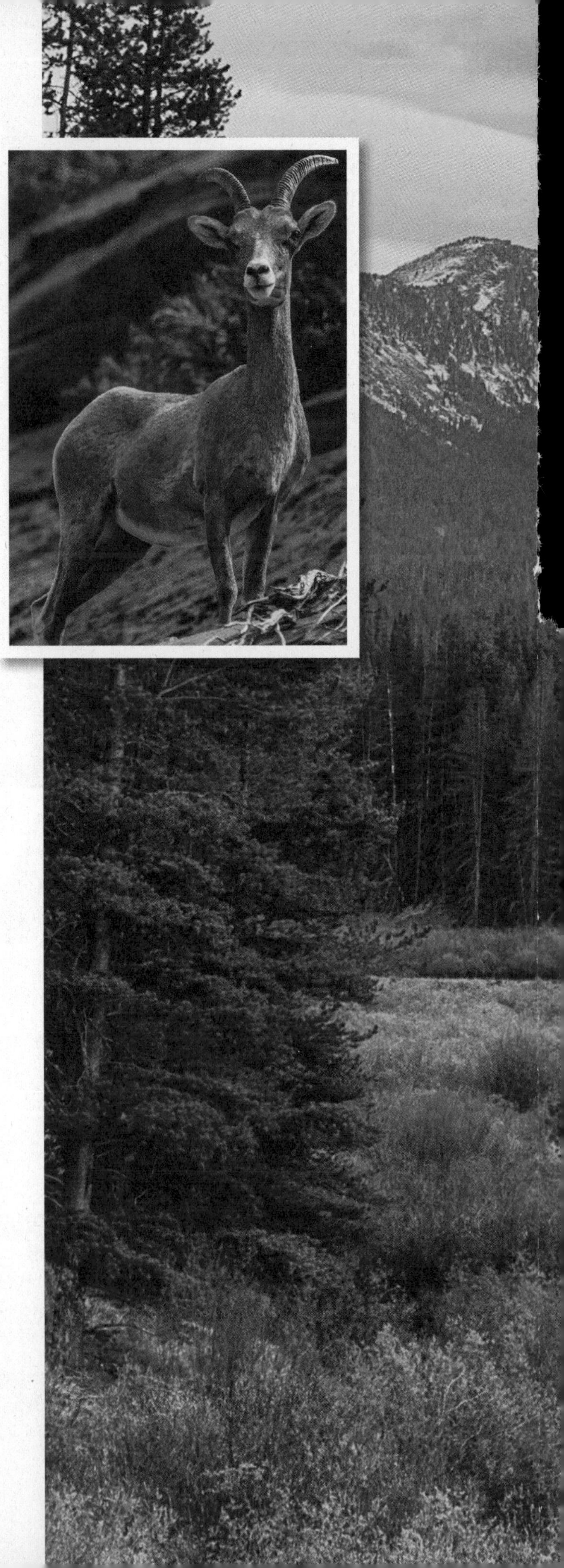

ISBN 978-0-544-43282-6

22 0928 23

4500864542 DEFG

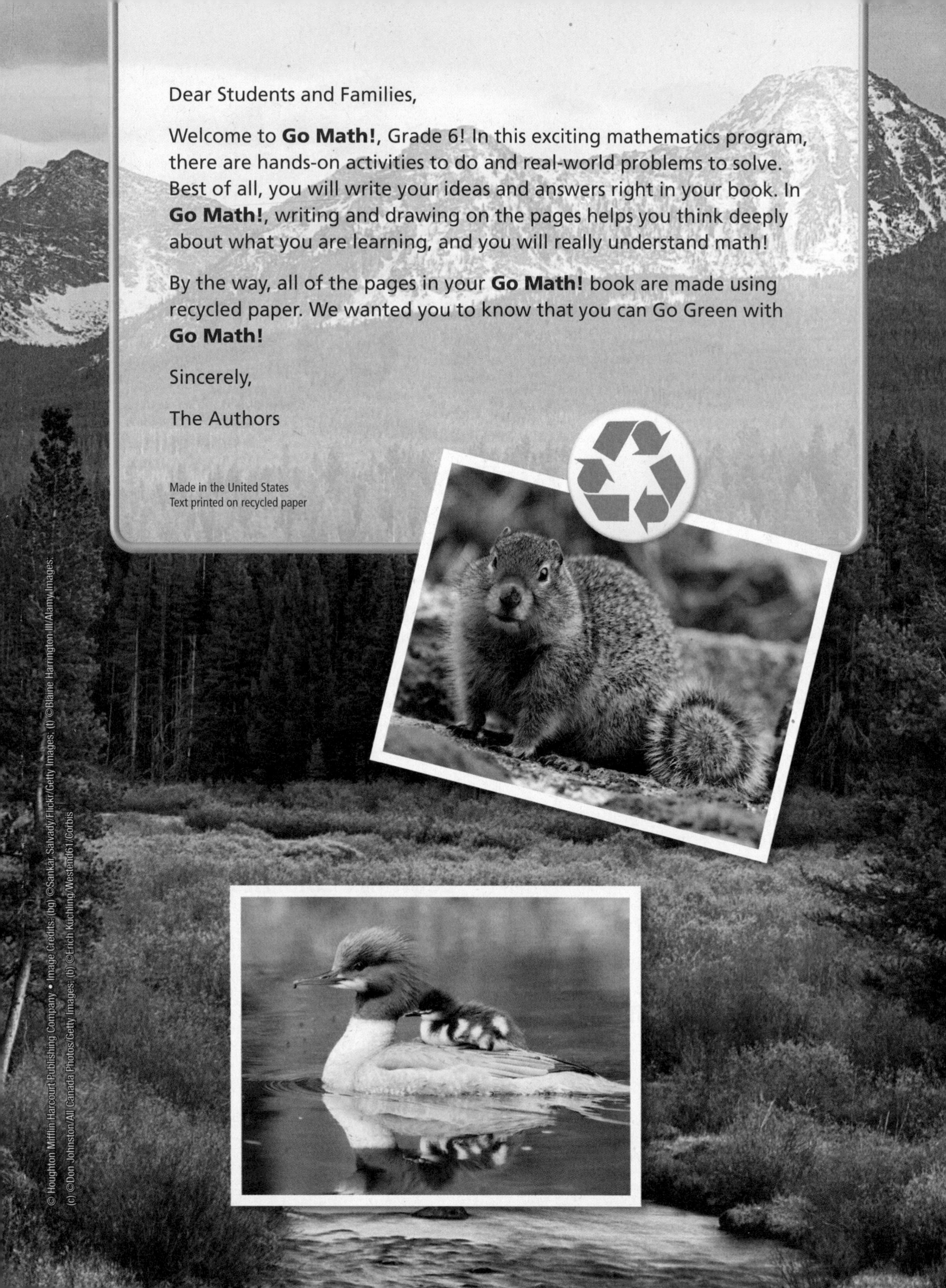

Dear Students and Families,

Welcome to **Go Math!**, Grade 6! In this exciting mathematics program, there are hands-on activities to do and real-world problems to solve. Best of all, you will write your ideas and answers right in your book. In **Go Math!**, writing and drawing on the pages helps you think deeply about what you are learning, and you will really understand math!

By the way, all of the pages in your **Go Math!** book are made using recycled paper. We wanted you to know that you can Go Green with **Go Math!**

Sincerely,

The Authors

Made in the United States
Text printed on recycled paper

Authors

Juli K. Dixon, Ph.D.
Professor, Mathematics Education
University of Central Florida
Orlando, Florida

Edward B. Burger, Ph.D.
President, Southwestern University
Georgetown, Texas

Steven J. Leinwand
Principal Research Analyst
American Institutes for Research (AIR)
Washington, D.C.

Contributor

Rena Petrello
Professor, Mathematics
Moorpark College
Moorpark, CA

Matthew R. Larson, Ph.D.
K-12 Curriculum Specialist for Mathematics
Lincoln Public Schools
Lincoln, Nebraska

Martha E. Sandoval-Martinez
Math Instructor
El Camino College
Torrance, California

English Language Learners Consultant

Elizabeth Jiménez
CEO, GEMAS Consulting
Professional Expert on English Learner Education
Bilingual Education and Dual Language
Pomona, California

VOLUME 1

The Number System

Critical Area Completing understanding of division of fractions and extending the notion of number to the system of rational numbers, which includes negative numbers

Whole Numbers and Decimals 3

Domain The Number System

COMMON CORE STATE STANDARDS 6.NS.B.2, 6.NS.B.3, 6.NS.B.4

Fractions 67

Domain The Number System

COMMON CORE STATE STANDARDS 6.NS.A.1, 6.NS.B.4, 6.NS.C.6c

Critical Area

GO DIGITAL

Go online! Your math lessons are interactive. Use *i*Tools, Animated Math Models, the Multimedia eGlossary, and more.

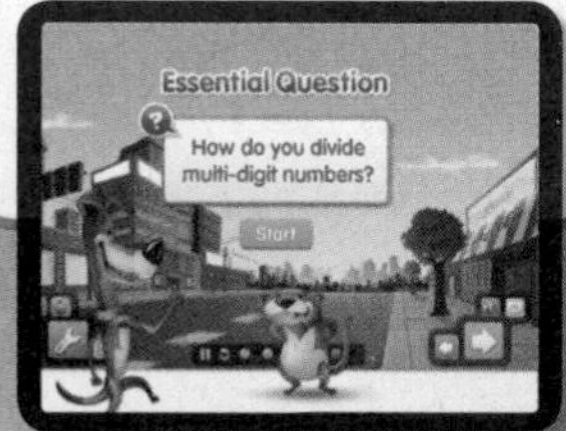

Chapter 1 Overview

In this chapter, you will explore and discover answers to the following **Essential Questions**:

- How do you solve real-world problems involving whole numbers and decimals?
- How does estimation help you solve problems involving decimals and whole numbers?
- How can you use the GCF and the LCM to solve problems?

Chapter 2 Overview

In this chapter, you will explore and discover answers to the following **Essential Questions**:

- How can you use the relationship between multiplication and division to divide fractions?
- What is a mixed number?
- How can you estimate products and quotients of fractions and mixed numbers?

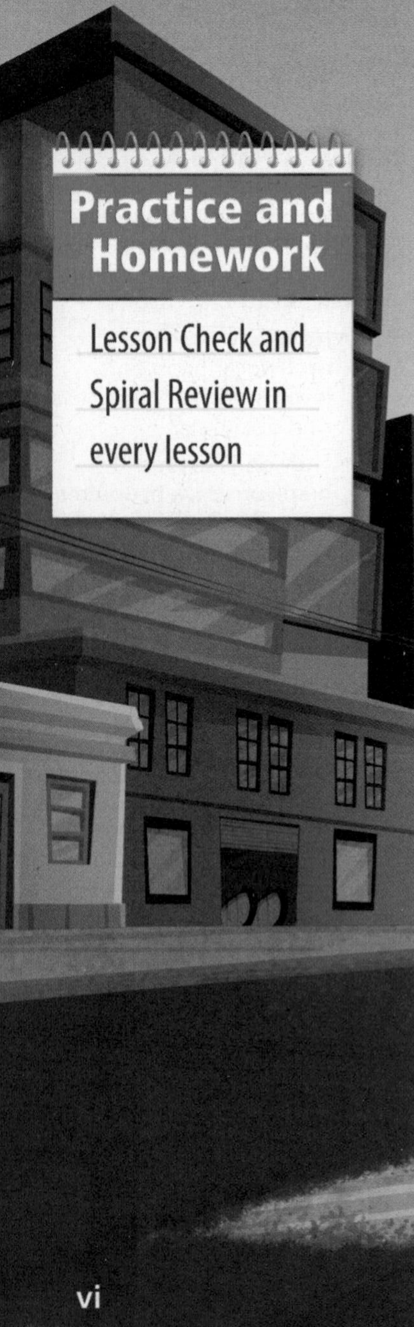

Chapter 3 Overview

In this chapter, you will explore and discover answers to the following **Essential Questions**:

- How do you write, interpret, and use rational numbers?
- How do you calculate the absolute value of a number?
- How do you graph an ordered pair?

Rational Numbers 137

Domain The Number System

COMMON CORE STATE STANDARDS 6.NS.C.5, 6.NS.C.6a, 6.NS.C.6b, 6.NS.C.6c, 6.NS.C.7a, 6.NS.C.7b, 6.NS.C.7c, 6.NS.C.7d, 6.NS.C.8

Ratios and Rates

Critical Area Connecting ratio and rate to whole number multiplication and division and using concepts of ratio and rate to solve problems

Critical Area

GO DIGITAL

Go online! Your math lessons are interactive. Use *i*Tools, Animated Math Models, the Multimedia eGlossary, and more.

Chapter 4 Overview

In this chapter, you will explore and discover answers to the following **Essential Questions**:

- How can you use ratios to express relationships and solve problems?
- How can you write a ratio?
- What are equivalent ratios?
- How are rates related to ratios?

Chapter 5 Overview

In this chapter, you will explore and discover answers to the following **Essential Questions**:

- How can you use ratio reasoning to solve percent problems?
- How can you write a percent as a fraction?
- How can you use a ratio to find a percent of a number?

Personal Math Trainer
Online Assessment and Intervention

Chapter 6 Overview

In this chapter, you will explore and discover answers to the following **Essential Questions**:

- How can you use measurements to help you describe and compare objects?
- Why do you need to convert between units of measure?
- How can you use a ratio to convert units?
- How do you transform units to solve problems?

6 Units of Measure 313

Domain Ratios and Proportional Relationships

COMMON CORE STATE STANDARDS 6.RP.A.3d

Practice and Homework

Lesson Check and Spiral Review in every lesson

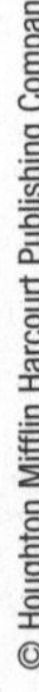

VOLUME 2

Expressions and Equations

Critical Area Writing, interpreting, and using expressions and equations

Algebra: Expressions 355

Domain Expressions and Equations

COMMON CORE STATE STANDARDS 6.EE.A.1, 6.EE.A.2a, 6.EE.A.2b, 6.EE.A.2c, 6.EE.A.3, 6.EE.A.4, 6.EE.B.6

Critical Area

GO DIGITAL

Go online! Your math lessons are interactive. Use *i*Tools, Animated Math Models, the Multimedia eGlossary, and more.

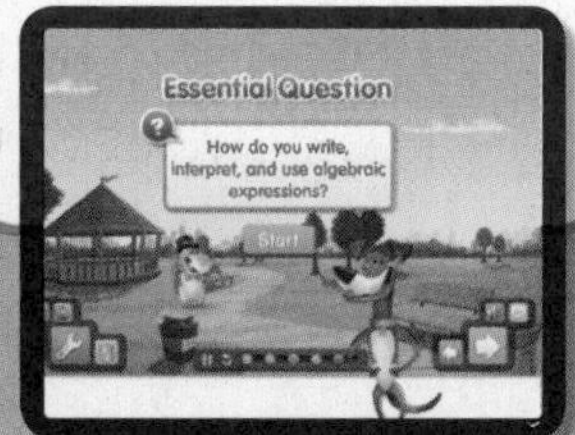

Chapter 7 Overview

In this chapter, you will explore and discover answers to the following **Essential Questions**:

- How do you write, interpret, and use algebraic expressions?
- How can you use expressions to represent real-world situations?
- How do you use the order of operations to evaluate expressions?
- How can you tell whether two expressions are equivalent?

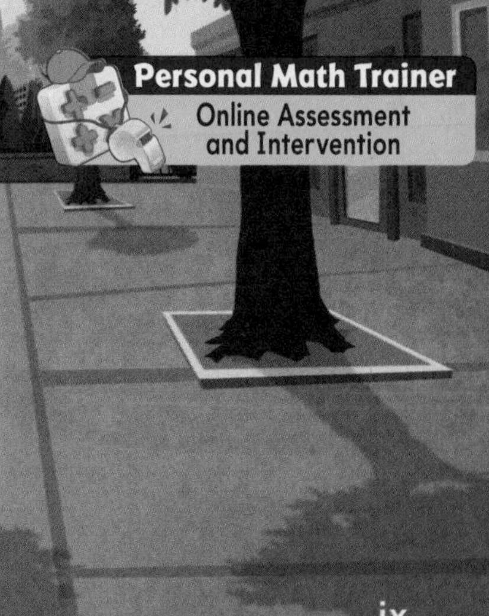

Personal Math Trainer
Online Assessment and Intervention

Chapter 8 Overview

In this chapter, you will explore and discover answers to the following **Essential Questions**:

- How can you use equations and inequalities to represent situations and solve problems?
- How can you use Properties of Equality to solve equations?
- How do inequalities differ from equations?
- Why is it useful to describe situations by using algebra?

Practice and Homework

Lesson Check and Spiral Review in every lesson

Chapter 9 Overview

In this chapter, you will explore and discover answers to the following **Essential Questions**:

- How can you show relationships between variables?
- How can you determine the equation that gives the relationship between two variables?
- How can you use tables and graphs to visualize the relationship between two variables?

8 Algebra: Equations and Inequalities 419

Domain Expressions and Equations

COMMON CORE STATE STANDARDS 6.EE.B.5, 6.EE.B.7, 6.EE.B.8

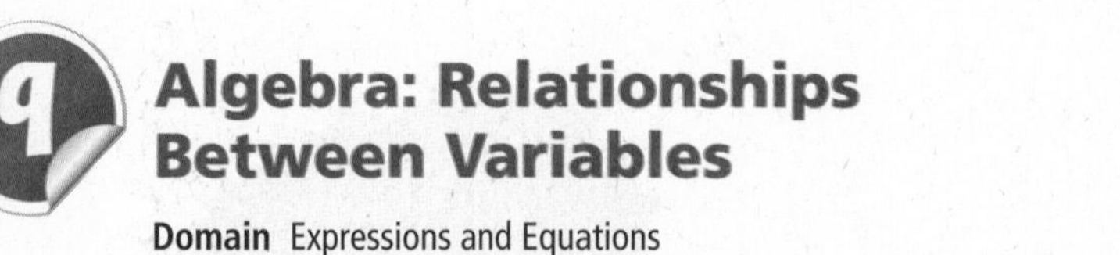

9 Algebra: Relationships Between Variables 489

Domain Expressions and Equations

COMMON CORE STATE STANDARDS 6.EE.C.9

Geometry and Statistics

Common Core

Critical Area Solve real-world and mathematical problems involving area, surface area, and volume; and developing understanding of statistical thinking

10 Area 531

Domain Geometry

COMMON CORE STATE STANDARDS 6.G.A.1, 6.G.A.3

11 Surface Area and Volume 595

Domain Geometry

COMMON CORE STATE STANDARDS 6.G.A.2, 6.G.A.4

Critical Area

GO DIGITAL

Go online! Your math lessons are interactive. Use *i*Tools, Animated Math Models, the Multimedia *e*Glossary, and more.

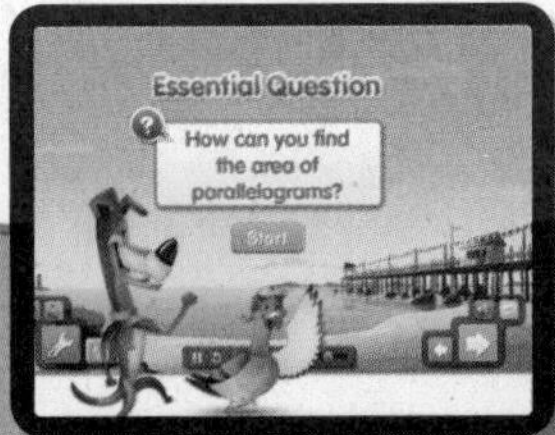

Chapter 10 Overview

In this chapter, you will explore and discover answers to the following **Essential Questions**:

- How can you use measurements to describe two-dimensional figures?
- What does area represent?
- How are the areas of rectangles and parallelograms related?
- How are the areas of triangles and trapezoids related?

Chapter 11 Overview

In this chapter, you will explore and discover answers to the following **Essential Questions**:

- How can you use measurements to describe three-dimensional figures?
- How can you use a net to find the surface area of a three-dimensional figure?
- How can you find the volume of a rectangular prism?

Chapter 12 Overview

In this chapter, you will explore and discover answers to the following **Essential Questions**:

- How can you display data and analyze measures of center?
- When does it make sense to display data in a dot plot? in a histogram?
- What are the differences between the three measures of center?

Practice and Homework

Lesson Check and Spiral Review in every lesson

Chapter 13 Overview

In this chapter, you will explore and discover answers to the following **Essential Questions**:

- How can you describe the shape of a data set using graphs, measures of center, and measures of variability?
- How do you calculate the different measures of center?
- How do you calculate the different measures of variability?

Data Displays and Measures of Center 647

Domain Statistics and Probability

COMMON CORE STATE STANDARDS 6.SP.A.1, 6.SP.B.4, 6.SP.B.5a, 6.SP.B.5b, 6.SP.B.5c, 6.SP.B.5d

Variability and Data Distributions 705

Domain Statistics and Probability

COMMON CORE STATE STANDARDS 6.SP.A.2, 6.SP.A.3, 6.SP.B.4, 6.SP.B.5c, 6.SP.B.5d

Critical Area Expressions and Equations

CRITICAL AREA Writing, interpreting, and using expressions and equations

Great Smoky Mountains National Park is located in the states of North Carolina and Tennessee.

The Great Outdoors

The Moores are planning a family reunion in Great Smoky Mountains National Park. This park includes several campgrounds and over 800 miles of hiking trails. Some trails lead to stunning views of the park's many waterfalls.

Get Started

The Moores want to camp at the park during their reunion. They will have 17 people in their group, and they want to spend no more than $100 on camping fees.

Decide how many and what type of campsites the Moores should reserve, and determine how many nights n the Moores can camp without going over budget. Show your work, and support your answer by writing and evaluating algebraic expressions.

Important Facts

Group Campsite
- Fee of $35 per night
- Holds up to 25 people

Individual Campsite
- Fee of $14 per night
- Holds up to 6 people

Completed by ______________________

Algebra: Expressions

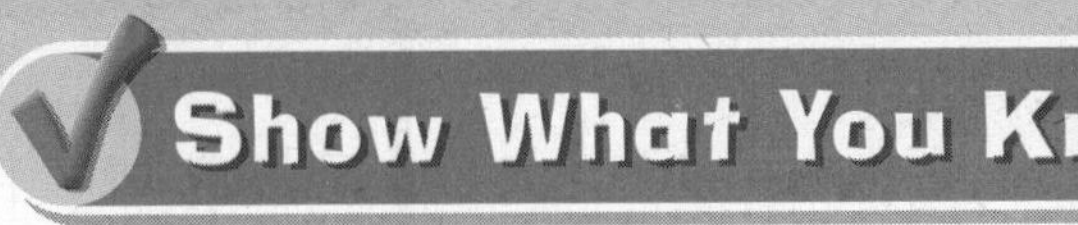

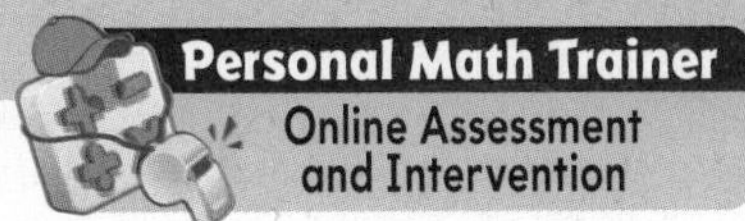

Check your understanding of important skills.

Name ________________

Addition Properties **Find the unknown number. Tell whether you used the Identity (or Zero) Property, Commutative Property, or Associative Property of Addition.** (5.OA.A.1)

1. $128 + \_\_\_\_ = 128$

____

2. $(17 + 36) + 14 = 17 + (\_\_\_\_ + 14)$

____

3. $23 + 15 = \_\_\_\_ + 23$

____

4. $9 + (11 + 46) = (9 + \_\_\_\_) + 46$

____

Multiply with Decimals **Find the product.** (5.NBT.B.7)

5. 1.5×7 ________

6. 5.83×6 ________

7. 3.7×0.8 ________

8. 0.27×0.9 ________

Use Parentheses **Identify which operation to do first. Then, find the value of the expression.** (5.NBT.B.6)

9. $5 \times (3 + 6)$ ______________________

10. $(24 \div 3) - 2$ ______________________

11. $40 \div (20 - 16)$ ______________________

12. $(7 \times 6) + 5$ ______________________

Greg just moved into an old house and found a mysterious trunk in the attic. The lock on the trunk has a dial numbered 1 to 60. Greg found the note shown at right lying near the trunk. Help Greg figure out the three numbers needed to open the lock.

Lock Combination
Top Secret!

1st number: $3x$
2nd number: $5x - 1$
3rd number: $x^2 + 4$

Hint: $x = 6$

Vocabulary Builder

▶ Visualize It

Sort the review words into the bubble map.

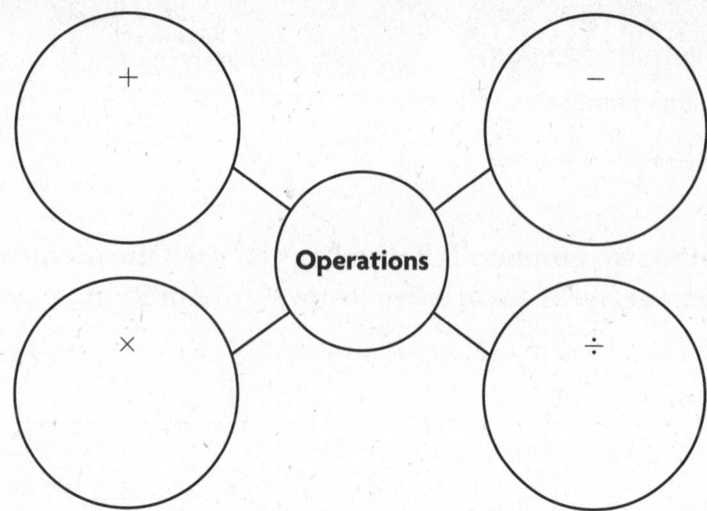

Review Words
addition
difference
division
multiplication
product
quotient
subtraction
sum

Preview Words
algebraic expression
base
coefficient
evaluate
numerical expression
terms
variable

▶ Understand Vocabulary

Complete the sentences using the preview words.

1. An exponent is a number that tells how many times a(n) ______________ is used as a factor.

2. In the expression 4*a*, the number 4 is a(n) ______________.

3. To ______________ an expression, substitute numbers for the variables in the expression.

4. A mathematical phrase that uses only numbers and operation symbols is a(n) ______________.

5. A letter or symbol that stands for one or more numbers is a(n) ______________.

6. The parts of an expression that are separated by an addition or subtraction sign are the ______________ of the expression.

GO DIGITAL
• Interactive Student Edition
• Multimedia eGlossary

Chapter 7 Vocabulary

algebraic expression

expresión algebraica

3

base (arithmetic)

base

6

coefficient

coeficiente

10

difference

diferencia

22

equivalent expressions

expresiones equivalentes

28

evaluate

evaluar

31

exponent

exponente

32

factor

factor

33

A number used as a repeated factor

$\underbrace{5 \times 5 \times 5}_{\text{3 repeated factors}} = 5^3$ ← exponent; 5 = base

An expression that includes at least one variable

$x + 10$　　$3 \times y$　　$3 \times (a + 4)$

variable　variable　variable

The answer to a subtraction problem

$7 - 3 = 4$ ← difference

A number that is multiplied by a variable

Example: $4k$ The coefficient of the term $4k$ is 4.

To find the value of a numerical or algebraic expression

Example: Evaluating $2x + 3y$ when $x = 1$ and $y = 4$ gives $2(1) + 3(4) = 2 + 12 = 14$.

Expressions that are equal to each other for any values of their variables

Example: $2x + 4x = 6x$

A number multiplied by another number to find a product

$2 \times 3 \times 7 = 42$

factors

A number that shows how many times the base is used as a factor

$\underbrace{5 \times 5 \times 5}_{\text{3 repeated factors}} = 5^3$ ← exponent; 5 = base

like terms términos semejantes 49	**numerical expression** expresión numérica 67
order of operations orden de las operaciones 69	**product** producto 80
quotient cociente 84	**sum** suma o total 99
terms términos 101	**variable** variable 105

A mathematical phrase that uses only numbers and operation signs

$3 + 16 \times 2^2$ $4 \times (8 + 5)$ $2^3 + 4$

Expressions that have the same variable with the same exponent

Algebraic Expression	Terms	Like Terms
$5x + 3y - 2x$	$5x$, $3y$, and $2x$	$5x$ and $2x$
$8z^2 + 4z + 12z^2$	$8z^2$, $4z$, and $12z^2$	$8z^2$ and $12z^2$
$15 - 3x + 5$	15, $3x$, and 5	15 and 5

The answer to a multiplication problem

$3 \times 4 = 12$ ← product

A set of rules which gives the order in which calculations are done in an expression

Order of Operations

1. Perform operations in parentheses.
2. Find the values of numbers with exponents.
3. Multiply and divide from left to right.
4. Add and subtract from left to right.

The answer to an addition problem

$2 + 5 = 7$ ← sum

The number that results from dividing

$80 \div 4 = 20$ ↑ quotient

$4\overline{)80}$ with 20 ← quotient

A letter or symbol that stands for an unknown number or numbers

$x + 10$ $3 \times y$ $3 \times (a + 4)$

variable (x) variable (y) variable (a)

The parts of an expression that are separated by an addition or subtraction sign

Example:

$4k + 5$ The expression has two terms, $4k$ and 5.

Going Down the Blue Ridge Parkway

For 2 to 4 players

Materials

- 1 each as needed: red, blue, green, and yellow playing pieces
- 1 number cube
- Clue Cards

How to Play

1. Each player puts a playing piece on START.
2. To take a turn, toss the number cube. Move that many spaces.
3. If you land on these spaces:

   Green Space Follow the directions in the space.

   Yellow Space Explain how to evaluate the expression. If you are correct, move ahead 1 space.

   Blue Space Use a math term to name what is shown. If you are correct, move ahead 1 space.

   Red Space The player to your right draws a Clue Card and reads you the question. If you answer correctly, move ahead 1 space. Return the Clue Card to the bottom of the pile.
4. The first player to reach FINISH wins.

Word Box

- algebraic expression
- base
- coefficient
- difference
- equivalent expressions
- evaluate
- exponent
- factor
- like terms
- numerical expression
- order of operations
- product
- quotient
- sum
- terms
- variable

DIRECTIONS Each player puts a playing piece on START. • To take a turn, toss the number cube. Move that many spaces. • If you land on these spaces: Green Space – Follow the directions in the space. • Yellow Space – Explain how to evaluate the expression. If you are correct, move ahead 1 space. • Blue Space – Use a math term to name what is shown. If you are correct, move ahead 1 space. • Red Space – The player to your right draws a Clue Card and reads you the question. If you answer correctly, move ahead 1 space. Return the Clue Card to the bottom of the pile. • The first player to reach FINISH wins.

START

Take a scenic hike. Move ahead 1.

$4 \times (5 + 1)$

CLUE CARD

5^2

Visit the Natural Bridge. Go back 1.

$48 \div 4^2$

CLUE CARD

2^3

Get a flat tire. Lose 1 turn.

CLUE CARD

FINISH

$4 \times (y + 5)$ for $y = 11$

$x + 7$

CLUE CARD

$7^2 - (x^2 + 5)$ for $x = 2$

Ride along the Great Smoky Mountains Railroad. Take another turn.

$4^2 \times 10 + 6$

CLUE CARD

$2 \times (3^3 + 7)$

Climb Chimney Rock. Trade places with another player.

The Write Way

Reflect

Choose one idea. Write about it.

- Tell how to rewrite this expression so that each base has an exponent.
  $4 \times 4 \times 4 \times 7 \times 7$
- Explain how to evaluate this expression using the order of operations:
  $3 \times (1 + 5^2)$.
- Define the term algebraic expression in your own words. Give an example.
- Jin wrote the following expression. Explain how he can simplify the expression by using like terms. Then write an equivalent expression.
  $2x + x + 9$

Name ______________________________

Exponents

Essential Question How do you write and find the value of expressions involving exponents?

Common Core **Expressions and Equations—6.EE.A.1**
MATHEMATICAL PRACTICES
MP6, MP7, MP8

You can use an exponent and a base to show repeated multiplication of the same factor. An **exponent** is a number that tells how many times a number called the **base** is used as a repeated factor.

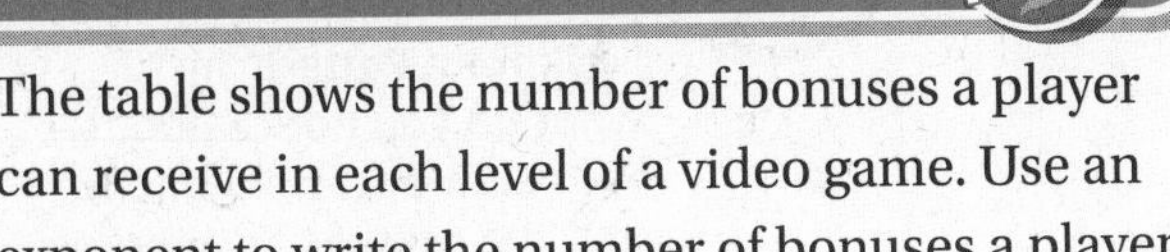

Math Idea

- 5^2 can be read "the 2nd power of 5" or "5 squared."
- 5^3 can be read "the 3rd power of 5" or "5 cubed."

Unlock the Problem — Real World

The table shows the number of bonuses a player can receive in each level of a video game. Use an exponent to write the number of bonuses a player can receive in level D.

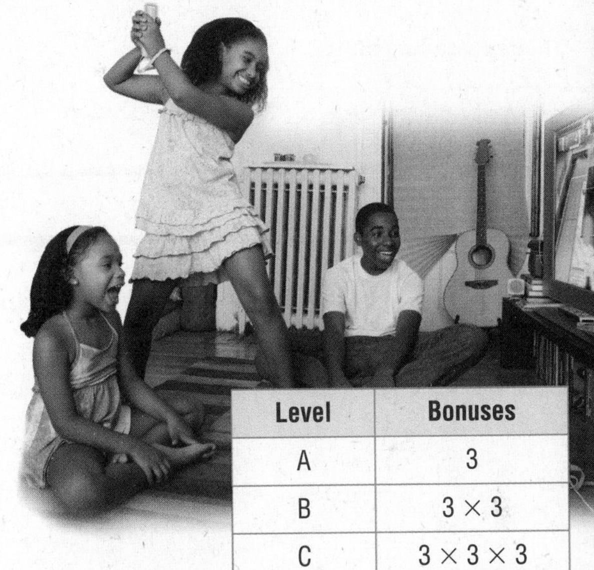

Level	Bonuses
A	3
B	3×3
C	$3 \times 3 \times 3$
D	$3 \times 3 \times 3 \times 3$

Use an exponent to write $3 \times 3 \times 3 \times 3$.

The number ______ is used as a repeated factor.

3 is used as a factor ______ times.

Write the base and exponent. ______

So, a player can receive ______ bonuses in level D.

Math Talk MATHEMATICAL PRACTICES 6

Explain How do you know which number to use as the base and which number to use as the exponent?

Try This! **Use one or more exponents to write the expression.**

A $7 \times 7 \times 7 \times 7 \times 7$

The number ______ is used as a repeated factor.

7 is used as a factor ______ times.

Write the base and exponent. ______

B $6 \times 6 \times 8 \times 8 \times 8$

The numbers ______ and ______ are used as repeated factors.

6 is used as a factor ______ times.

8 is used as a factor ______ times.

Write each base with its own exponent. $6^{\square} \times 8^{\square}$

Example 1 Find the value.

A 10^3

STEP 1 Use repeated multiplication to write 10^3.

The repeated factor is ______. 10^3 = ______ × ______ × ______

Write the factor ______ times.

STEP 2 Multiply.

Multiply each pair of factors, working from left to right.   10 × 10 × 10 = ______ × 10

= ______

B 7^1

The repeated factor is ______. 7^1 = ______

Write the factor ______ time.

MATHEMATICAL PRACTICES 7

Look for a Pattern In 10^3, what do you notice about the value of the exponent and the product? Is there a similar pattern in other powers of 10? Explain.

Example 2 Write 81 with an exponent by using 3 as the base.

STEP 1 Find the correct exponent.

Try 2. 3^2 = 3 × 3 = ______

Try 3. 3^3 = ______ × ______ × ______ = ______

Try 4. 3^4 = ______ × ______ × ______ × ______ = ______

STEP 2 Write using the base and exponent.

81 = ______

1. Explain how to write repeated multiplication of a factor by using an exponent.

______

______

2. THINK SMARTER Is 5^2 equal to 2^5? Explain why or why not.

______

3. MATHEMATICAL PRACTICE 6 **Describe a Method** Describe how you could have solved the problem in Example 2 by using division.

______

______

Name ____________________

Share and Show

1. Write 2^4 by using repeated multiplication. Then find the value of 2^4.

$2^4 = 2 \times 2 \times$ _____ $\times$ _____ $=$ _____

Use one or more exponents to write the expression.

2. $7 \times 7 \times 7 \times 7$ _____

3. $5 \times 5 \times 5 \times 5 \times 5$ _____

4. $3 \times 3 \times 4 \times 4$ _____

Math Talk — MATHEMATICAL PRACTICES 8

Generalize In 3^4, does it matter in what order you multiply the factors when finding the value? Explain.

On Your Own

Find the value.

5. 20^2 _____

6. 82^1 _____

7. 3^5 _____

8. Write 32 as a number with an exponent by using 2 as the base.

_____

Complete the statement with the correct exponent.

9. $5^{\square} = 125$

10. $16^{\square} = 16$

11. $30^{\square} = 900$

12. MATHEMATICAL PRACTICE 8 **Use Repeated Reasoning** Find the values of 4^1, 4^2, 4^3, 4^4, and 4^5. Look for a pattern in your results and use it to predict the ones digit in the value of 4^6.

_____

13. THINKSMARTER Select the expressions that are equivalent to 32. Mark all that apply.

- (A) 2^5
- (B) 8^4
- (C) $2^3 \times 4$
- (D) $2 \times 4 \times 4$

Connect to Science

Bacterial Growth

Bacteria are tiny, one-celled organisms that live almost everywhere on Earth. Although some bacteria cause disease, other bacteria are helpful to humans, other animals, and plants. For example, bacteria are needed to make yogurt and many types of cheese.

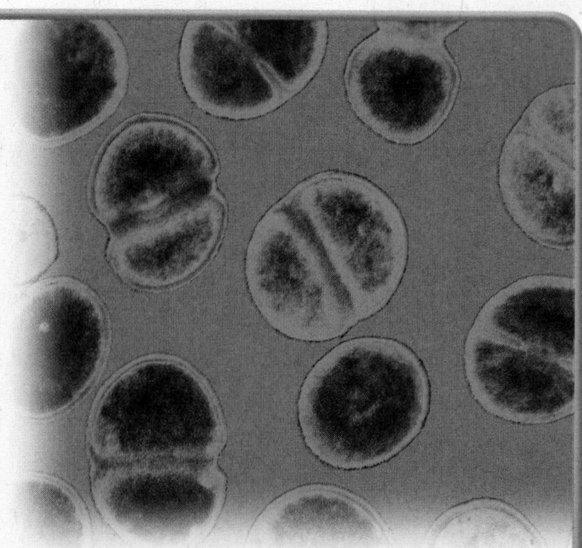

Under ideal conditions, a certain type of bacterium cell grows larger and then splits into 2 "daughter" cells. After 20 minutes, the daughter cells split, resulting in 4 cells. This splitting can happen again and again as long as conditions remain ideal.

Complete the table.

Bacterial Growth	
Number of Cells	**Time (min)**
1	0
$2^1 = 2$	20
$2^2 = 2 \times 2 = 4$	40
$2^3 =$ ___ × ___ × ___ = ___	60
$2^{\square} = 2 \times 2 \times 2 \times 2 = 16$	80
$2^5 =$ ___ × ___ × ___ × ___ × ___ = ___	100
$2^{\square} =$ ___ × ___ × ___ × ___ × ___ × ___ = ___	120
$2^7 = 2 \times 2 \times 2 \times 2 \times 2 \times 2 \times 2 =$ ___	___

Extend the pattern in the table above to answer 14 and 15.

14. GO DEEPER What power of 2 shows the number of cells after 3 hours? How many cells are there after 3 hours?

____

15. THINK SMARTER How many minutes would it take to have a total of 4,096 cells?

____

Name ______________________________

Exponents

COMMON CORE STANDARD—6.EE.A.1
Apply and extend previous understandings of arithmetic to algebraic expressions.

Use one or more exponents to write the expression.

1. 6×6

   6^2

2. $11 \times 11 \times 11 \times 11$

   ____

3. $9 \times 9 \times 9 \times 9 \times 7 \times 7$

   ____

Find the value.

4. 6^4

   ____

5. 1^6

   ____

6. 10^5

   ____

7. Write 144 with an exponent by using 12 as the base.

   ____

8. Write 343 with an exponent by using 7 as the base.

   ____

Problem Solving Real World

9. Each day Sheila doubles the number of push-ups she did the day before. On the fifth day, she does $2 \times 2 \times 2 \times 2 \times 2$ push-ups. Use an exponent to write the number of push-ups Shelia does on the fifth day.

   ____

10. The city of Beijing has a population of more than 10^7 people. Write 10^7 without using an exponent.

   ____

11. WRITE Math Explain what the expression 4^5 means and how to find its value.

   ____

   ____

   ____

Lesson Check (6.EE.A.1)

1. The number of games in the first round of a chess tournament is equal to $2 \times 2 \times 2 \times 2 \times 2 \times 2$. Write the number of games using an exponent.

2. The number of gallons of water in a tank at an aquarium is equal to 8^3. How many gallons of water are in the tank?

Spiral Review (6.RP.A.3a, 6.RP.A.3c, 6.RP.A.3d)

3. The table shows the amounts of strawberry juice and lemonade needed to make different amounts of strawberry lemonade. Name another ratio of strawberry juice to lemonade that is equivalent to the ratios in the table.

Strawberry juice (cups)	2	3	4
Lemonade (cups)	6	9	12

4. Which percent is equivalent to the fraction $\frac{37}{50}$?

5. How many milliliters are equivalent to 2.7 liters?

6. Use the formula $d = rt$ to find the distance traveled by a car driving at an average speed of 50 miles per hour for 4.5 hours.

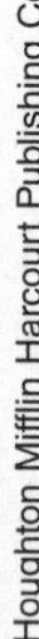

FOR MORE PRACTICE GO TO THE **Personal Math Trainer**

Name ____________________

Evaluate Expressions Involving Exponents

Essential Question How do you use the order of operations to evaluate expressions involving exponents?

Expressions and Equations—6.EE.A.1

MATHEMATICAL PRACTICES
MP4, MP6, MP7

A **numerical expression** is a mathematical phrase that uses only numbers and operation symbols.

$3 + 16 \times 2^2$ $4 \times (8 + 5^1)$ $2^3 + 4$

You **evaluate** a numerical expression when you find its value. To evaluate an expression with more than one type of operation, you must follow a set of rules called the **order of operations**.

Order of Operations
1. Perform operations in parentheses.
2. Find the values of numbers with exponents.
3. Multiply and divide from left to right.
4. Add and subtract from left to right.

Unlock the Problem

An archer shoots 6 arrows at a target. Two arrows hit the ring worth 8 points, and 4 arrows hit the ring worth 4 points. Evaluate the expression $2 \times 8 + 4^2$ to find the archer's total number of points.

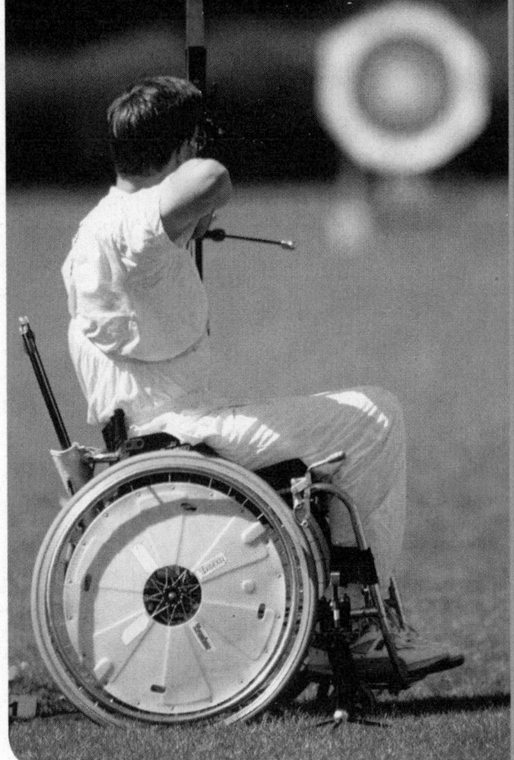

Follow the order of operations.

Write the expression. There are no parentheses.	$2 \times 8 + 4^2$
Find the value of numbers with exponents.	$2 \times 8 +$ ______
______ from left to right.	______ $+ 16$
Then add.	______

So, the archer scores a total of ______ points.

Math Talk MATHEMATICAL PRACTICES 6

Explain In which order should you perform the operations to evaluate the expression $30 - 10 + 5^2$?

Try This! **Evaluate the expression $24 \div 2^3$.**

There are no parentheses.	$24 \div 2^3$
Find the value of numbers with exponents.	$24 \div$ ______
Then divide.	______

Example 1 Evaluate the expression $72 \div (13 - 4) + 5 \times 2^3$.

Write the expression. $72 \div (13 - 4) + 5 \times 2^3$

Perform operations in ______. $72 \div$ ______ $+ 5 \times 2^3$

Find the values of numbers with ______. $72 \div 9 + 5 \times$ ______

Multiply and ______ from left to right. ______ $+ 5 \times 8$

$8 +$ ______

Then add. ______

Example 2

Last month, an online bookstore had approximately 10^5 visitors to its website. On average, each visitor bought 2 books. Approximately how many books did the bookstore sell last month?

STEP 1 Write an expression.

Think: The number of books sold is equal to the number of visitors times the number of books each visitor bought.

number of visitors | times | number of books bought

↓ ↓ ↓

10^5 $\times$ ______

STEP 2 Evaluate the expression.

Write the expression. There are no parentheses. $10^5 \times 2$

Find the values of numbers with ______. ______ $\times 2$

Multiply. ______

So, the bookstore sold approximately ______ books last month.

- MATHEMATICAL PRACTICE 6 **Explain** why the order of operations is necessary.

______

______

______

Name ___________________________

Share and Show

1. Evaluate the expression $9 + (5^2 - 10)$.

$9 + (5^2 - 10)$ — Write the expression.

$9 + (\_\_\_\_ - 10)$ — Follow the order of operations within the parentheses.

$9 + \_\_\_\_$

$\_\_\_\_$ — Add.

Evaluate the expression.

2. $6 + 3^3 \div 9$

3. $(15 - 3)^2 \div 9$

4. $(8 + 9^2) - 4 \times 10$

MATHEMATICAL PRACTICES 7

Look for Structure How does the parentheses make the values of these expressions different: $(2^2 + 8) \div 4$ and $2^2 + (8 \div 4)$?

On Your Own

Evaluate the expression.

5. $10 + 6^2 \times 2 \div 9$

6. $6^2 - (2^3 + 5)$

7. $16 + 18 \div 9 + 3^4$

THINKSMARTER **Place parentheses in the expression so that it equals the given value.**

8. $10^2 - 50 \div 5$
value: 10

9. $20 + 2 \times 5 + 4^1$
value: 38

10. $28 \div 2^2 + 3$
value: 4

Problem Solving • Applications

Use the table for 11–13.

11. MATHEMATICAL PRACTICE 4 **Write an Expression** To find the cost of a window, multiply its area in square feet by the price per square foot. Write and evaluate an expression to find the cost of a knot window.

____

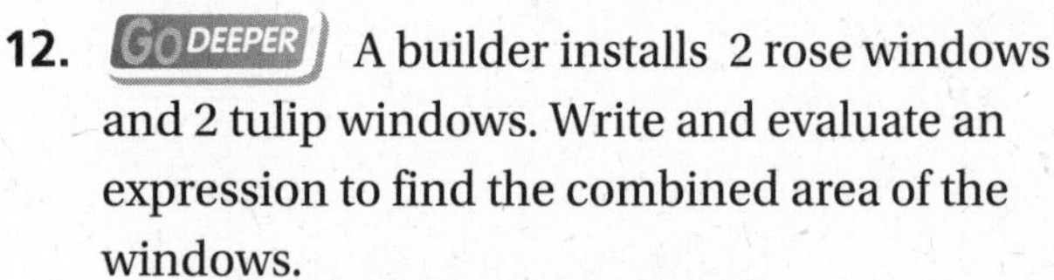

12. GO DEEPER A builder installs 2 rose windows and 2 tulip windows. Write and evaluate an expression to find the combined area of the windows.

____

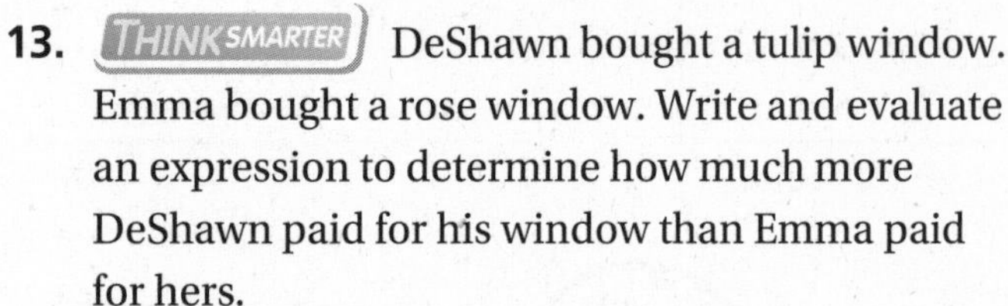

13. THINK SMARTER DeShawn bought a tulip window. Emma bought a rose window. Write and evaluate an expression to determine how much more DeShawn paid for his window than Emma paid for hers.

____

Art Glass Windows		
Type	**Area (square feet)**	**Price per square foot**
Knot	2^2	\$27
Rose	3^2	\$30
Tulip	4^2	\$33

Math on the Spot

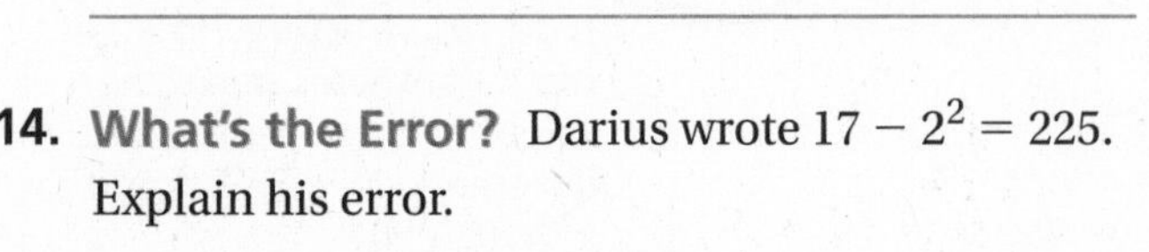

14. **What's the Error?** Darius wrote $17 - 2^2 = 225$. Explain his error.

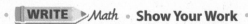

____

____

____

____

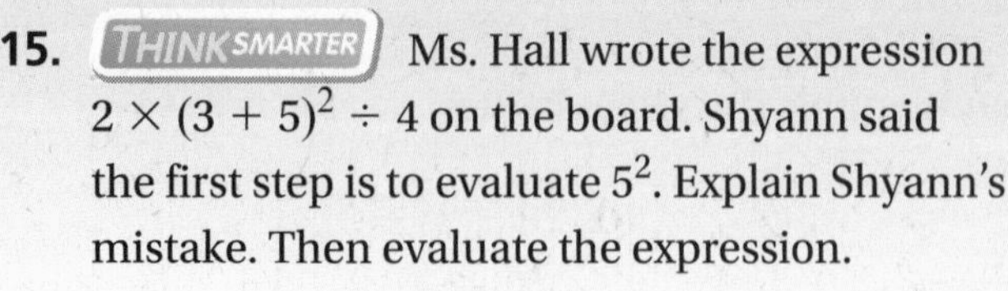

15. THINK SMARTER Ms. Hall wrote the expression $2 \times (3 + 5)^2 \div 4$ on the board. Shyann said the first step is to evaluate 5^2. Explain Shyann's mistake. Then evaluate the expression.

____

____

WRITE Math • Show Your Work

Name ______________________________

Evaluate Expressions Involving Exponents

Common Core **COMMON CORE STANDARD—6.EE.A.1**
Apply and extend previous understandings of arithmetic to algebraic expressions.

Evaluate the expression.

1. $5 + 17 - 10^2 \div 5$

$5 + 17 - 100 \div 5$

$5 + 17 - 20$

$22 - 20$

2

2. $7^2 - 3^2 \times 4$

3. $2^4 \div (7 - 5)$

4. $(8^2 + 36) \div (4 \times 5^2)$

5. $12 + 21 \div 3 + (2^2 \times 0)$

6. $(12 - 8)^3 - 24 \times 2$

Place parentheses in the expression so that it equals the given value.

7. $12 \times 2 + 2^3$; value: 120

8. $7^2 + 1 - 5 \times 3$; value: 135

Problem Solving Real World

9. Hugo is saving for a new baseball glove. He saves \$10 the first week, and \$6 each week for the next 6 weeks. The expression $10 + 6^2$ represents the total amount in dollars he has saved. What is the total amount Hugo has saved?

10. A scientist placed 5 fish eggs in a tank. Each day, twice the number of eggs from the previous day hatch. The expression 5×2^6 represents the number of eggs that hatch on the seventh day. How many eggs hatch on the seventh day?

11. WRITE Math Explain how you could determine whether a calculator correctly performs the order of operations.

Lesson Check (6.EE.A.1)

1. Ritchie wants to paint his bedroom ceiling and four walls. The ceiling and each of the walls are 8 feet by 8 feet. A gallon of paint covers 40 square feet. Write an expression that can be used to find the number of gallons of paint Ritchie needs to buy.

2. A Chinese restaurant uses about 225 pairs of chopsticks each day. The manager wants to order a 30-day supply of chopsticks. The chopsticks come in boxes of 750 pairs. How many boxes should the manager order?

Spiral Review (6.RP.A.3a, 6.RP.A.3c, 6.RP.A.3d, 6.EE.A.1)

3. Annabelle spent $5 to buy 4 raffle tickets. How many tickets can she buy for $20?

4. Gavin has 460 baseball players in his collection of baseball cards, and 15% of the players are pitchers. How many pitchers are in Gavin's collection?

5. How many pounds are equivalent to 40 ounces?

6. List the expressions in order from least to greatest.

   $1^5 \quad 3^3 \quad 4^2 \quad 8^1$

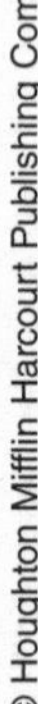

FOR MORE PRACTICE GO TO THE **Personal Math Trainer**

Name ______________________________

Write Algebraic Expressions

Essential Question How do you write an algebraic expression to represent a situation?

Expressions and Equations—6.EE.A.2a

MATHEMATICAL PRACTICES
MP2, MP6, MP7

An **algebraic expression** is a mathematical phrase that includes at least one variable. A **variable** is a letter or symbol that stands for one or more numbers.

$x + 10$	$3 \times y$	$3 \times (a + 4)$
↑ variable	↑ variable	↑ variable

Math Idea

There are several ways to show multiplication with a variable. Each expression below represents "3 times y."

$3 \times y$ $3y$ $3(y)$ $3 \cdot y$

Unlock the Problem

An artist charges $5 for each person in a cartoon drawing. Write an algebraic expression for the cost in dollars for a drawing that includes p people.

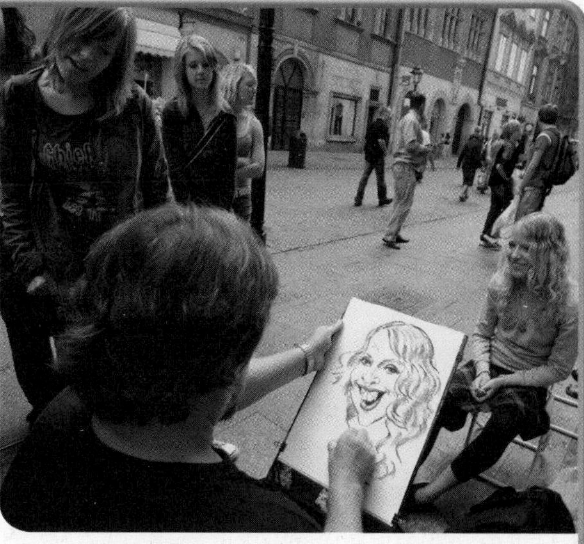

Write an algebraic expression for the cost.

Think: cost for each person | times | number of ________

↓ ↓ ↓

________ × p

So, the cost in dollars is ______.

Math Talk MATHEMATICAL PRACTICES 2

Reasoning Why is p an appropriate variable for this problem? Would it be appropriate to select a different variable? Explain.

Try This! On Mondays, a bakery adds 2 extra muffins for free with every muffin order. Write an algebraic expression for the number of muffins customers will receive on Mondays when they order *m* muffins.

Think: muffins ordered | ________ | extra muffins on Mondays

↓ ↓ ↓

______ + 2

So, customers will receive ____________ muffins on Mondays.

Example 1 The table at the right shows the number of points that items on a quiz are worth. Write an algebraic expression for the quiz score of a student who gets *m* multiple-choice items and *s* short-answer items correct.

Quiz Scoring	
Item Type	**Points**
Multiple-choice	2
Short-answer	5

points for multiple-choice items | ______ | points for short-answer items

↓ ↓ ↓

$(2 \times m)$ $+$ (______)

So, the student's quiz score is ____________ points.

Example 2 Write an algebraic expression for the word expression.

A **30 more than the product of 4 and *x***

Think: Start with the product of 4 and *x*. Then find 30 more than the product.

the product of 4 and *x* ______ × ______

30 more than the product ______ + 4*x*

B **4 times the sum of *x* and 30**

Think: Start with the sum of *x* and 30. Then find 4 times the sum.

the sum of *x* and 30 ______ + ______

4 times the sum ______ × (*x* + 30)

1. When you write an algebraic expression with two operations, how can you show which operation to do first?

____

2. THINK SMARTER One student wrote $4 + x$ for the word expression "4 more than *x*." Another student wrote $x + 4$ for the same word expression. Are both students correct? Justify your answer.

____

____

____

Name ________________________________

Share and Show MATH BOARD

1. Write an algebraic expression for the product of 6 and p.

What operation does the word "product" indicate?

____

The expression is ______ $\times$ ______.

Write an algebraic expression for the word expression.

2. 11 more than e

____

3. 9 less than the quotient of n and 5

____

On Your Own

Math Talk — MATHEMATICAL PRACTICES 6

Explain why $3x$ is an algebraic expression.

Write an algebraic expression for the word expression.

4. 20 divided by c

____

5. 8 times the product of 5 and t

____

6. There are 12 eggs in a dozen. Write an algebraic expression for the number of eggs in d dozen.

____

7. A state park charges a $6.00 entry fee plus $7.50 per night of camping. Write an algebraic expression for the cost in dollars of entering the park and camping for n nights.

____

8. MATHEMATICAL PRACTICE 7 **Look for Structure** At a bookstore, the expression $2c + 8g$ gives the cost in dollars of c comic books and g graphic novels. Next month, the store's owner plans to increase the price of each graphic novel by $3. Write an expression that will give the cost of c comic books and g graphic novels next month.

____

Unlock the Problem

9. Martina signs up for the cell phone plan described at the right. Write an expression that gives the total cost of the plan in dollars if Martina uses it for *m* months.

SPECIAL OFFER
CELL PHONE
PLAN!
Pay a low monthly fee of $50.
Receive $10 off your first month's fee.

a. What information do you know about the cell phone plan?

____

____

b. Write an expression for the monthly fee in dollars for *m* months.

____

c. What operation can you use to show the discount of $10 for the first month?

____

d. Write an expression for the total cost of the plan in dollars for *m* months.

____

10. THINK SMARTER A group of *n* friends evenly share the cost of dinner. The dinner costs $74. After dinner, each friend pays $11 for a movie. Write an expression to represent what each friend paid for dinner and the movie.

____

11. THINK SMARTER A cell phone company charges $40 per month plus $0.05 for each text message sent. Select the expressions that represent the cost in dollars for one month of cell phone usage and sending *m* text messages. Mark all that apply.

- ○ $40m + 0.05$
- ○ $40 + 0.05m$
- ○ 40 more than the product of 0.05 and *m*
- ○ the product of 40 and *m* plus 0.05

Name ______________________

Write Algebraic Expressions

Common Core **COMMON CORE STANDARD—6.EE.A.2a**
Apply and extend previous understandings of arithmetic to algebraic expressions.

Write an algebraic expression for the word expression.

1. 13 less than p

$p - 13$

2. the sum of x and 9

____

3. 6 more than the difference of b and 5

____

4. the sum of 15 and the product of 5 and v

____

5. the difference of 2 and the product of 3 and k

____

6. 12 divided by the sum of h and 2

____

7. the quotient of m and 7

____

8. 9 more than 2 multiplied by f

____

9. 6 minus the difference of x and 3

____

10. 10 less than the quotient of g and 3

____

11. the sum of 4 multiplied by a and 5 multiplied by b

____

12. 14 more than the difference of r and s

____

Problem Solving Real World

13. Let h represent Mark's height in inches. Suzanne is 7 inches shorter than Mark. Write an algebraic expression that represents Suzanne's height in inches.

____

14. A company rents bicycles for a fee of $10 plus $4 per hour of use. Write an algebraic expression for the total cost in dollars for renting a bicycle for h hours.

____

15. WRITE *Math* Give an example of a real-world situation involving two unknown quantities. Then write an algebraic expression to represent the situation.

____

____

Lesson Check (6.EE.A.2a)

1. The female lion at a zoo weighs 190 pounds more than the female cheetah. Let c represent the weight in pounds of the cheetah. Write an expression that gives the weight in pounds of the lion.

2. Tickets to a play cost \$8 each. Write an expression that gives the ticket cost in dollars for a group of g girls and b boys.

Spiral Review (6.RP.A.2, 6.RP.A.3a, 6.RP.A.3c, 6.RP.A.3d, 6.EE.A.1)

3. A bottle of cranberry juice contains 32 fluid ounces and costs \$2.56. What is the unit rate?

4. There are 32 peanuts in a bag. Elliott takes 25% of the peanuts from the bag. Then Zaire takes 50% of the remaining peanuts. How many peanuts are left in the bag?

5. Hank earns \$12 per hour for babysitting. How much does he earn for 15 hours of babysitting?

6. Write an expression using exponents that represents the area of the figure in square centimeters.

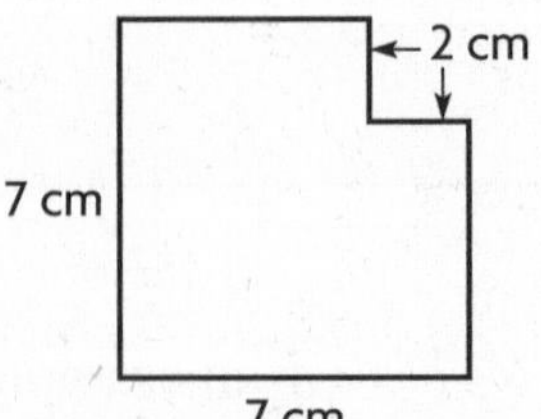

FOR MORE PRACTICE GO TO THE **Personal Math Trainer**

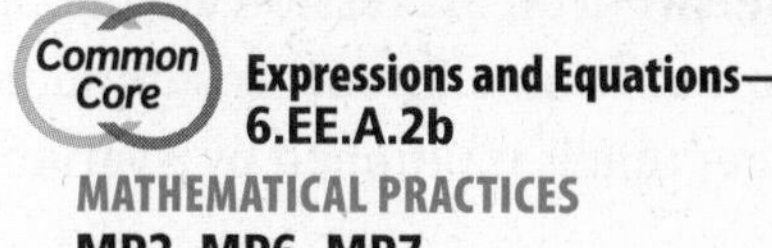

Name ______________________________

Identify Parts of Expressions

Essential Question How can you describe the parts of an expression?

Common Core **Expressions and Equations—6.EE.A.2b**

MATHEMATICAL PRACTICES **MP2, MP6, MP7**

Unlock the Problem (Real World)

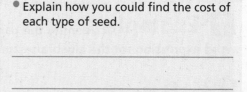

At a gardening store, seed packets cost \$2 each. Martin bought 6 packets of lettuce seeds and 7 packets of pea seeds. The expression $2 \times (6 + 7)$ represents the cost in dollars of Martin's seeds. Identify the parts of the expression. Then write a word expression for $2 \times (6 + 7)$.

- Explain how you could find the cost of each type of seed.

____

____

____

Describe the parts of the expression $2 \times (6 + 7)$.

Identify the operations in the expression.

multiplication and ____________

Describe the part of the expression in parentheses, and tell what it represents.

- The part in parentheses shows the ______ of 6 and ______.
- The sum represents the number of packets of ____________ seeds plus the number of packets of ____________ seeds.

Describe the multiplication, and tell what it represents.

- One of the factors is ______. The other factor is the ______ of 6 and 7.
- The product represents the ______ per packet times the number of each type of ____________ Martin bought.

So, a word expression for $2 \times (6 + 7)$ is "the ____________ of 2 and the ______ of ______ and 7."

- MATHEMATICAL PRACTICE 6 **Attend to Precision** Explain how the expression $2 \times (6 + 7)$ differs from $2 \times 6 + 7$. Then, write a word expression for $2 \times 6 + 7$.

____

____

____

The **terms** of an expression are the parts of the expression that are separated by an addition or subtraction sign. A **coefficient** is a number that is multiplied by a variable.

$4k + 5$ — The expression has two terms, $4k$ and 5. The coefficient of the term $4k$ is 4.

Example

Identify the parts of the expression. Then write a word expression for the algebraic expression.

A $2x + 8$

Identify the terms in the expression. — The expression is the sum of ______ terms.

The terms are ______ and 8.

Describe the first term. — The first term is the product of the coefficient ______ and the variable ______.

Describe the second term. — The second term is the number ______.

A word expression for $2x + 8$ is "8 more than the ____________ of ______ and x."

Math Talk MATHEMATICAL PRACTICES 6

Explain Why are the terms of the expression $2x$ and 8, not x and 8?

B $3a - 4b$

Identify the terms in the expression. — The expression is the ____________ of 2 terms. The terms are ______ and ______.

Describe the first term. — The first term is the product of the ____________ 3 and the variable ______.

Describe the second term. — The second term is the product of the coefficient ______ and the variable ______.

A word expression for the algebraic expression is "the difference of ______ times ______ and 4 ____________ b."

Math Talk MATHEMATICAL PRACTICES 2

Reasoning Identify the coefficient of y in the expression $12 + y$. Explain your reasoning.

Name ______________________________

Share and Show

MATH BOARD

Identify the parts of the expression. Then, write a word expression for the numerical or algebraic expression.

1. $7 \times (9 \div 3)$

The part in parentheses shows the ____________ of ______ and ______.

One factor of the multiplication is ______, and the other factor is $9 \div 3$.

Word expression: ______________________________

2. $5m + 2n$

____

____

____

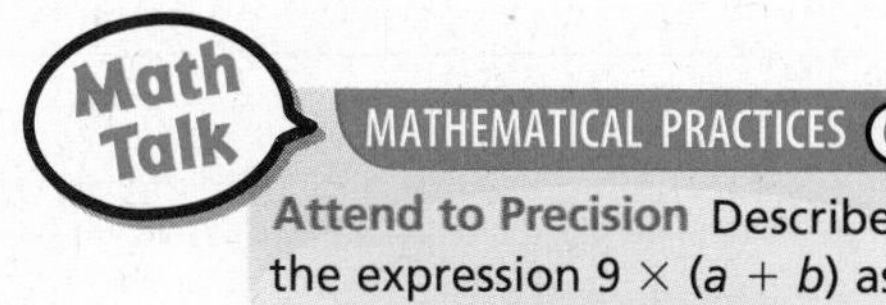

Math Talk
MATHEMATICAL PRACTICES 6
Attend to Precision Describe the expression $9 \times (a + b)$ as a product of two factors.

On Your Own

Practice: Copy and Solve **Identify the parts of the expression. Then write a word expression for the numerical or algebraic expression.**

3. $8 + (10 - 7)$

4. $1.5 \times 6 + 8.3$

5. $b + 12x$

6. $4a \div 6$

Identify the terms of the expression. Then, give the coefficient of each term.

7. $k - \frac{1}{3}d$

____

____

8. $0.5x + 2.5y$

____

____

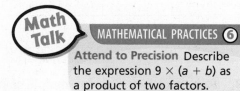

9. MATHEMATICAL PRACTICE 2 **Connect Symbols and Words** Ava said she wrote an expression with three terms. She said the first term has the coefficient 7, the second term has the coefficient 1, and the third term has the coefficient 0.1. Each term involves a different variable. Write an expression that could be the expression Ava wrote.

____

Problem Solving • Applications Real World

Football Scoring

Type	Points
Touchdown	6
Field Goal	3
Extra Point	1

Use the table for 10–12.

10. GO DEEPER A football team scored 2 touchdowns and 2 extra points. Their opponent scored 1 touchdown and 2 field goals. Write a numerical expression for the points scored in the game.

____

11. Write an algebraic expression for the number of points scored by a football team that makes t touchdowns, f field goals, and e extra points.

____

12. Identify the parts of the expression you wrote in Exercise 11.

____

____

____

13. THINKSMARTER Give an example of an expression involving multiplication in which one of the factors is a sum. Explain why you do or do not need parentheses in your expression.

____

____

____

____

14. THINKSMARTER Kennedy bought a pounds of almonds at \$5 per pound and p pounds of peanuts at \$2 per pound. Write an algebraic expression for the cost of Kennedy's purchase.

____

WRITE Math
Show Your Work

Name ______________________

Identify Parts of Expressions

Common Core **COMMON CORE STANDARD—6.EE.A.2a**
Apply and extend previous understandings of arithmetic to algebraic expressions.

Identify the parts of the expression. Then write a word expression for the numerical or algebraic expression.

1. $(16 - 7) \div 3$

The subtraction is the difference of 16 and 7.

The division is the difference divided by 3.

Word expression: the difference of 16 and 7, divided by 3

2. $8 + 6q + q$

Identify the terms of the expression. Then give the coefficient of each term.

3. $11r + 7s$

4. $6g - h$

Problem Solving Real World

5. Adam bought granola bars at the store. The expression $6p + 5n$ gives the number of bars in p boxes of plain granola bars and n boxes of granola bars with nuts. What are the terms of the expression?

6. In the sixth grade, each student will get 4 new books. There is one class of 15 students and one class of 20 students. The expression $4 \times (15 + 20)$ gives the total number of new books. Write a word expression for the numerical expression.

7. WRITE Math Explain how knowing the order of operations helps you write a word expression for a numerical or algebraic expression.

Lesson Check (6.EE.A.2a)

1. A fabric store sells pieces of material for \$5 each. Ali bought 2 white pieces and 8 blue pieces. She also bought a pack of buttons for \$3. The expression $5 \times (2 + 8) + 3$ gives the cost in dollars of Ali's purchase. How can you describe the term $(2 + 8)$ in words?

2. A hotel offers two different types of rooms. The expression $k + 2f$ gives the number of beds in the hotel where k is the number of rooms with a king size bed and f is the number of rooms with 2 full size beds. What are the terms of the expression?

Spiral Review (6.RP.A.3b, 6.RP.A.3c, 6.RP.A.3d, 6.EE.A.2a)

3. Meg paid \$9 for 2 tuna sandwiches. At the same rate, how much does Meg pay for 8 tuna sandwiches?

4. Jan is saving for a skateboard. She has saved \$30 already, which is 20% of the total price. How much does the skateboard cost?

5. It took Eduardo 8 hours to drive from Buffalo, NY, to New York City, a distance of about 400 miles. Find his average speed.

6. Write an expression that represents the value, in cents, of n nickels.

FOR MORE PRACTICE GO TO THE **Personal Math Trainer**

Name ______________________________

Evaluate Algebraic Expressions and Formulas

Essential Question How do you evaluate an algebraic expression or a formula?

Common Core **Expressions and Equations—6.EE.A.2c**
MATHEMATICAL PRACTICES
MP1, MP6, MP8

To evaluate an algebraic expression, substitute numbers for the variables and then follow the order of operations.

Unlock the Problem

Amir is saving money to buy an MP3 player that costs \$120. He starts with \$25, and each week he saves \$9. The expression $25 + 9w$ gives the amount in dollars that Amir will have saved after w weeks.

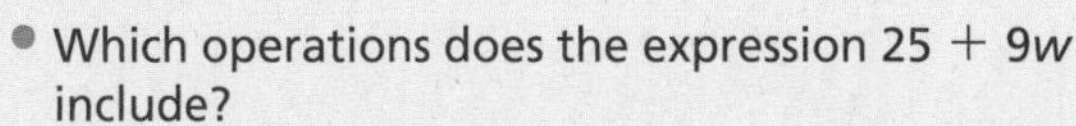

- Which operations does the expression $25 + 9w$ include?

  ____

- In what order should you perform the operations?

  ____

(A) How much will Amir have saved after 8 weeks?

Evaluate the expression for $w = 8$.

Write the expression.	$25 + 9w$
Substitute 8 for w.	$25 + 9 \times$ ____
Multiply.	$25 +$ ____
Add.	____

So, Amir will have saved \$ ____ after 8 weeks.

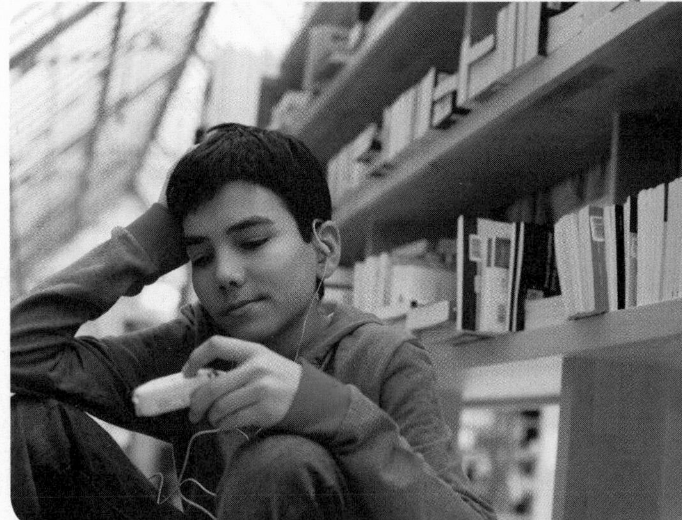

(B) After how many weeks will Amir have saved enough money to buy the MP3 player?

Make a table to find the week when the amount saved is at least \$120.

Week	Value of $25 + 9w$	Amount Saved
9	$25 + 9 \times 9 = 25 +$ ____ $= 106$	
10	$25 + 9 \times 10 = 25 +$ ____ $=$ ____	
11	$25 + 9 \times 11 = 25 +$ ____ $=$ ____	

So, Amir will have saved enough money for the MP3 player after ____ weeks.

MATHEMATICAL PRACTICES 6

Explain What does it mean to substitute a value for a variable?

Example 1 Evaluate the expression for the given value of the variable.

A $4 \times (m - 8) \div 3$ for $m = 14$

Write the expression.	$4 \times (m - 8) \div 3$
Substitute 14 for m.	$4 \times (\_\_\_\_ - 8) \div 3$
Perform operations in parentheses.	$4 \times \_\_\_\_ \div 3$
Multiply and divide from left to right.	$\_\_\_\_ \div 3$
	$\_\_\_\_$

B $3 \times (y^2 + 2)$ for $y = 4$

Write the expression.	$3 \times (y^2 + 2)$
Substitute 4 for y.	$3 \times (\_\_\_\_^2 + 2)$
Follow the order of operations within the parentheses.	$3 \times (\_\_\_\_ + 2)$
	$3 \times \_\_\_\_$
Multiply.	$\_\_\_\_$

ERROR Alert

When squaring a number, be sure to multiply the number by itself.

$4^2 = 4 \times 4$

Recall that a *formula* is a set of symbols that expresses a mathematical rule.

Example 2

The formula $P = 2\ell + 2w$ gives the perimeter P of a rectangle with length ℓ and width w. What is the perimeter of a rectangular garden with a length of 2.4 meters and a width of 1.2 meters?

Write the expression for the perimeter of a rectangle.	$2\ell + 2w$
Substitute 2.4 for ℓ and ____ for w.	$2 \times \_\_\_\_ + 2 \times \_\_\_\_$
Multiply from left to right.	$\_\_\_\_ + 2 \times 1.2$
	$4.8 + \_\_\_\_$
Add.	$\_\_\_\_$

So, the perimeter of the garden is ____ meters.

MATHEMATICAL PRACTICES 6

Compare How is evaluating an algebraic expression different from evaluating a numerical expression?

Name ______________________________

Share and Show

MATH BOARD

1. Evaluate $5k + 6$ for $k = 4$.

Write the expression. ________

Substitute 4 for *k*. $5 \times$ ______ $+ 6$

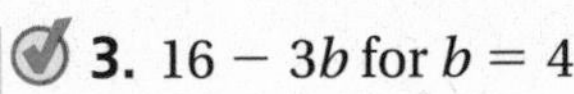

Multiply. ______ $+ 6$

Add. ______

Evaluate the expression for the given value of the variable.

2. $m - 9$ for $m = 13$

3. $16 - 3b$ for $b = 4$

4. $p^2 + 4$ for $p = 6$

5. The formula $A = \ell w$ gives the area A of a rectangle with length ℓ and width w. What is the area in square feet of a United States flag with a length of 12 feet and a width of 8 feet?

Math Talk MATHEMATICAL PRACTICES 8

Use Repeated Reasoning What information do you need to evaluate an algebraic expression?

On Your Own

Practice: Copy and Solve **Evaluate the expression for the given value of the variable.**

6. $7s + 5$ for $s = 3$

7. $21 - 4d$ for $d = 5$

8. $(t - 6)^2$ for $t = 11$

9. $6 \times (2v - 3)$ for $v = 5$

10. $2 \times (k^2 - 2)$ for $k = 6$

11. $5 \times (f - 32) \div 9$ for $f = 95$

12. GO DEEPER The formula $P = 4s$ gives the perimeter P of a square with side length s. How much greater is the perimeter of a square with a side length of $5\frac{1}{2}$ inches than a square with a side length of 5 inches?

Problem Solving • Applications

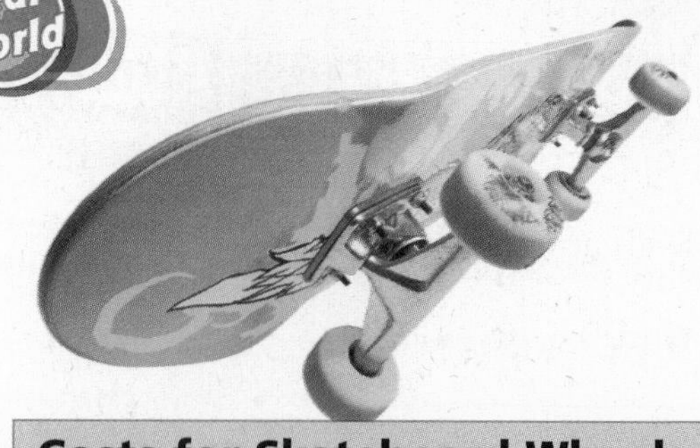

The table shows how much a company charges for skateboard wheels. Each pack of 8 wheels costs \$50. Shipping costs \$7 for any order. Use the table for 13–15.

13. Complete the table.

Costs for Skateboard Wheels		
Packs	$50 \times n + 7$	Cost
1	$50 \times 1 + 7$	\$57
2		
3		
4		
5		

14. A skateboard club has \$200 to spend on new wheels this year. What is the greatest number of packs of wheels the club can order?

____

15. MATHEMATICAL PRACTICE 1 **Make Sense of Problems** A sporting goods store placed an order for 12 packs of wheels on the first day of each month last year. How much did the sporting goods store spend on these orders last year?

____

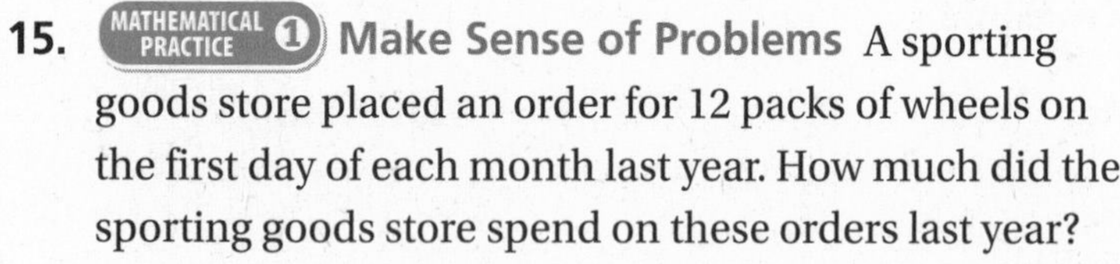

16. THINKSMARTER **What's the Error?** Bob used these steps to evaluate $3m - 3 \div 3$ for $m = 8$. Explain his error.

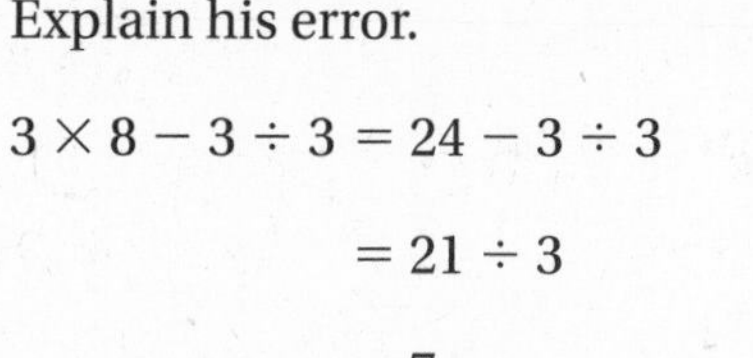

$$3 \times 8 - 3 \div 3 = 24 - 3 \div 3$$
$$= 21 \div 3$$
$$= 7$$

____

____

____

____

WRITE Math • Show Your Work

17. THINKSMARTER The surface area of a cube can be found by using the formula $6s^2$, where s represents the length of the side of the cube.

The surface area of a cube that has a side length of 3 meters is [54 / 108 / 2,916] meters squared.

Name ______________________

Evaluate Algebraic Expressions and Formulas

Common Core **COMMON CORE STANDARD—6.EE.A.2c**
Apply and extend previous understandings of arithmetic to algebraic expressions.

Evaluate the expression for the given values of the variables.

1. $w + 6$ for $w = 11$

   $11 + 6$

   17

2. $17 - 2c$ for $c = 7$

   ____

3. $b^2 - 4$ for $b = 5$

   ____

4. $(h - 3)^2$ for $h = 5$

   ____

5. $m + 2m + 3$ for $m = 12$

   ____

6. $4 \times (21 - 3h)$ for $h = 5$

   ____

7. $7m - 9n$ for $m = 7$ and $n = 5$

   ____

8. $d^2 - 9k + 3$ for $d = 10$ and $k = 9$

   ____

9. $3x + 4y \div 2$ for $x = 7$ and $y = 10$

   ____

Problem Solving Real World

10. The formula $P = 2\ell + 2w$ gives the perimeter P of a rectangular room with length ℓ and width w. A rectangular living room is 26 feet long and 21 feet wide. What is the perimeter of the room?

    ____

11. The formula $C = 5(F - 32) \div 9$ gives the Celsius temperature in C degrees for a Fahrenheit temperature of F degrees. What is the Celsius temperature for a Fahrenheit temperature of 122 degrees?

    ____

12. WRITE Math Explain how the terms *variable, algebraic expression,* and *evaluate* are related.

    ____

Lesson Check (6.EE.A.2c)

1. When Debbie baby-sits, she charges \$5 to go to the house plus \$8 for every hour she is there. The expression $5 + 8h$ gives the amount in dollars she charges. How much will she charge to baby-sit for 5 hours?

2. The formula to find the cost C in dollars of a square sheet of glass is $C = 25s^2$ where s represents the length of a side in feet. How much will Ricardo pay for a square sheet of glass that is 3 feet on each side?

Spiral Review (6.NS.A.1, 6. RP.A.3c, 6.EE.A.1, 6.EE.A.2a)

3. Evaluate using the order of operations.

$$\frac{3}{4} + \frac{5}{6} \div \frac{2}{3}$$

4. Patricia scored 80% on a math test. She missed 4 problems. How many problems were on the test?

5. What is the value of 7^3?

6. James and his friends ordered b hamburgers that cost \$4 each and f fruit cups that cost \$3 each. Write an algebraic expression for the total cost in dollars of their purchases.

FOR MORE PRACTICE GO TO THE **Personal Math Trainer**

Name ________________________________

Mid-Chapter Checkpoint

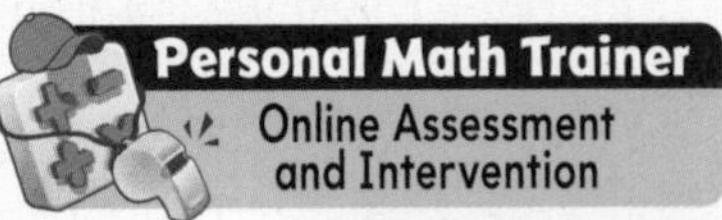

Vocabulary

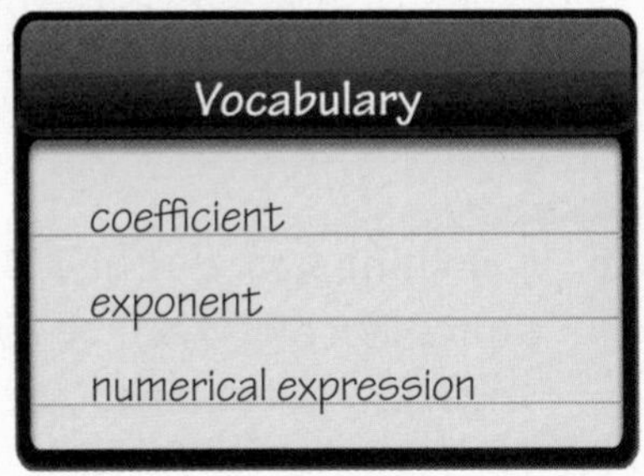

Choose the best term from the box to complete the sentence.

1. A(n) ______________________ tells how many times a base is used as a factor. (p. 357)

2. The mathematical phrase $5 + 2 \times 18$ is an example of a(n) ______________________. (p. 363)

Concepts and Skills

Find the value. (6.EE.A.1)

3. 5^4

4. 21^2

5. 8^3

Evaluate the expression. (6.EE.A.1)

6. $9^2 \times 2 - 4^2$

7. $2 \times (10 - 2) \div 2^2$

8. $30 - (3^3 - 8)$

Write an algebraic expression for the word expression. (6.EE.A.2a)

9. the quotient of c and 8

10. 16 more than the product of 5 and p

11. 9 less than the sum of x and 5

Evaluate the expression for the given value of the variable. (6.EE.A.2c)

12. $5 \times (h + 3)$ for $h = 7$

13. $2 \times (c^2 - 5)$ for $c = 4$

14. $7a - 4a$ for $a = 8$

15. The greatest value of any U.S. paper money ever printed is 10^5 dollars. What is this amount written in standard form? (6.EE.A.1)

____

16. A clothing store is raising the price of all its sweaters by $3.00. Write an expression that could be used to find the new price of a sweater that originally cost d dollars. (6.EE.A.2a)

____

17. Kendra bought a magazine for $3 and 4 paperback books for $5 each. The expression $3 + 4 \times 5$ represents the total cost in dollars of her purchases. What are the terms in this expression? (6.EE.A.2b)

____

18. The expression $5c + 7m$ gives the number of people who can ride in c cars and m minivans. What are the coefficients in this expression? (6.EE.A.2b)

____

19. GO DEEPER The formula $P = a + b + c$ gives the perimeter P of a triangle with side lengths a, b, and c. How much greater is the perimeter of a triangular field with sides that measure 33 yards, 56 yards, and 65 yards than the perimeter of a triangular field with sides that measure 26 yards, 49 yards, and 38 yards? (6.EE.A.2c)

____

Name ______________________

Use Algebraic Expressions

Essential Question How can you use variables and algebraic expressions to solve problems?

Common Core **Expressions and Equations—6.EE.B.6**
MATHEMATICAL PRACTICES
MP1, MP2, MP6

Sometimes you have an unknown number that you need to solve a problem. You can represent a problem like this by writing an algebraic expression in which a variable represents the unknown number.

Unlock the Problem (Real World)

Rafe's flight from Los Angeles to New York took 5 hours. He wants to know the average speed of the plane in miles per hour.

A Write an expression to represent the average speed of the plane.

Use a variable to represent the unknown quantity.

Think: The plane's average speed is equal to the distance traveled divided by the time traveled.

Use a variable to represent the unknown quantity. — Let d represent the ____________ traveled in units of ____________.

Write an algebraic expression for the average speed. — $\frac{d \text{ mi}}{\square \text{ hr}}$

B Rafe looks up the distance between Los Angeles and New York on the Internet and finds that the distance is 2,460 miles. Use this distance to find the average speed of Rafe's plane.

Evaluate the expression for $d = 2{,}460$.

Write the expression. — $\frac{d \text{ mi}}{5 \text{ hr}}$

Substitute 2,460 for d. — $\frac{\square \text{ mi}}{5 \text{ hr}}$

Divide to find the unit rate. — $\frac{2{,}460 \text{ mi} \div \square}{5 \text{ hr} \div 5} = \frac{\square \text{ mi}}{1 \text{ hr}}$

So, the plane's average speed was ____________ miles per hour.

Math Talk MATHEMATICAL PRACTICES 1

Evaluate How could you check whether you found the plane's average speed correctly?

In the problem on the previous page, the variable represented a single value—the distance in miles between Los Angeles and New York. In other situations, a variable may represent any number in a particular set of numbers, such as the set of positive numbers.

Example

Joanna makes and sells candles online. She charges $7 per candle, and shipping is $5 per order.

A Write an expression that Joanna can use to find the total cost for any candle order.

Think: The number of candles a customer buys will vary from order to order.

Let n represent the number of ________ a customer buys, where n is a whole number greater than 0.

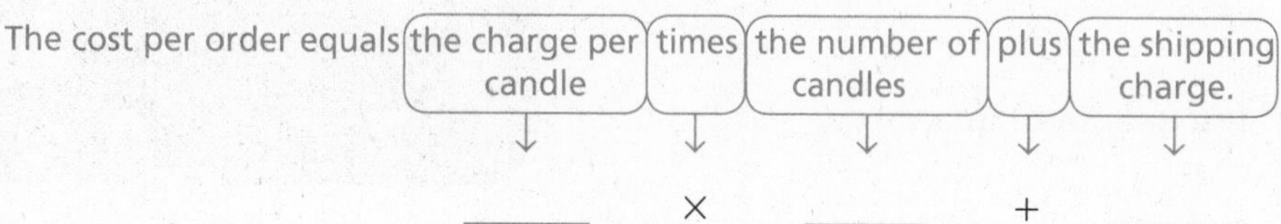

The cost per order equals
the charge per candle
times
the number of candles
plus
the shipping charge.

______ × ______ + ______

So, an expression for the total cost of a candle order is ____________.

B In March, one of Joanna's customers placed an order for 4 candles. In May, the same customer placed an order for 6 candles. What was the total charge for both orders?

STEP 1 Find the charge in dollars for each order.

	March	**May**
Write the expression.	$7n + 5$	$7n + 5$
Substitute the number of candles ordered for n.	$7 \times$ ______ $+ 5$	$7 \times$ ______ $+ 5$
Follow the order of operations.	______ $+ 5$	______ $+ 5$
	______	______

STEP 2 Find the charge in dollars for both orders.

Add the charge in dollars for March to the charge in dollars for May. ______ + ______ = ______

So, the total charge for both orders was ______.

MATHEMATICAL PRACTICES 2

Reasoning Why is the value of the variable n in the Example restricted to the set of whole numbers greater than 0?

Name ______________________________

Share and Show MATH BOARD

Louisa read that the highest elevation of Mount Everest is 8,848 meters. She wants to know how much higher Mount Everest is than Mount Rainier. Use this information for 1–2.

1. Write an expression to represent the difference in heights of the two mountains. Tell what the variable in your expression represents.

2. Louisa researches the highest elevation of Mount Rainier and finds that it is 4,392 meters. Use your expression to find the difference in the mountains' heights.

MATHEMATICAL PRACTICES 2

Reason Quantitatively Explain whether the variable in Exercise 1 represents a single unknown number or any number in a particular set.

On Your Own

A muffin recipe calls for 3 times as much flour as sugar. Use this information for 3–5.

3. Write an expression that can be used to find the amount of flour needed for a given amount of sugar. Tell what the variable in your expression represents.

4. Use your expression to find the amount of flour needed when $\frac{3}{4}$ cup of sugar is used.

5. MATHEMATICAL PRACTICE 2 **Reason Quantitatively** Is the value of the variable in your expression restricted to a particular set of numbers? Explain.

Practice: Copy and Solve **Write an algebraic expression for each word expression. Then evaluate the expression for these values of the variable: $\frac{1}{2}$, 4, and 6.5.**

6. the quotient of p and 4

7. 4 less than the sum of x and 5

Problem Solving • Applications Real World

Use the graph for 8–10.

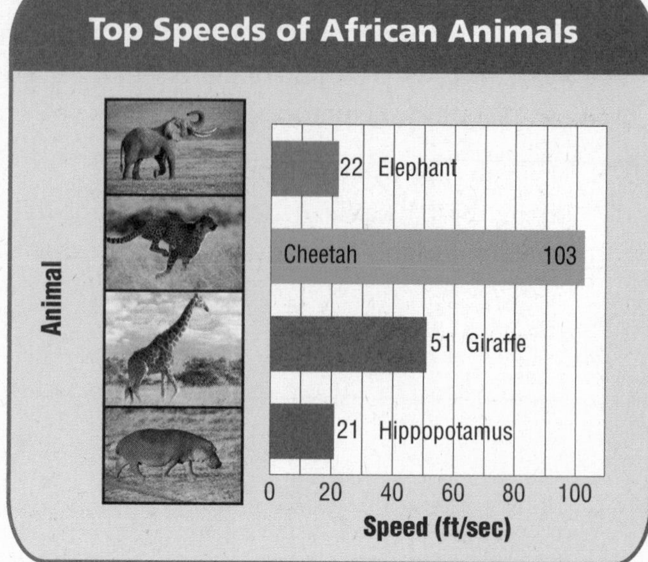

8. Write expressions for the distance in feet that each animal could run at top speed in a given amount of time. Tell what the variable in your expressions represents.

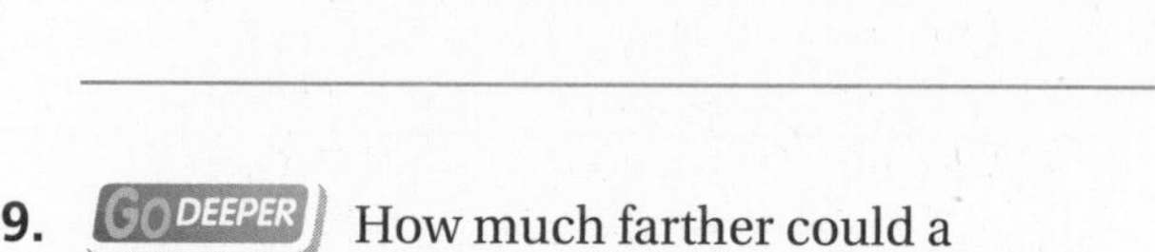

9. GO DEEPER How much farther could a cheetah run in 20 seconds at top speed than a hippopotamus could?

10. THINK SMARTER A giraffe runs at top speed toward a tree that is 400 feet away. Write an expression that represents the giraffe's distance in feet from the tree after s seconds.

Personal Math Trainer

11. THINK SMARTER + A carnival charges \$7 for admission and \$2 for each ride. An expression for the total cost of going to the carnival and riding n rides is $7 + 2n$.

Complete the table by finding the total cost of going to the carnival and riding n rides.

Number of rides, n	$7 + 2n$	Total Cost
1		
2		
3		
4		

WRITE Math • Show Your Work

Name ______________________________

Use Algebraic Expressions

Common Core **COMMON CORE STANDARD—6.EE.B.6**
Reason about and solve one-variable equations and inequalities.

Jeff sold the pumpkins he grew for $7 each at the farmer's market.

1. Write an expression to represent the amount of money in dollars Jeff made selling the pumpkins. Tell what the variable in your expression represents.

   $7p$, where p is the number of pumpkins

2. If Jeff sold 30 pumpkins, how much money did he make?

   ____

An architect is designing a building. Each floor will be 12 feet tall.

3. Write an expression for the number of floors the building can have for a given building height. Tell what the variable in your expression represents.

   ____

4. If the architect is designing a building that is 132 feet tall, how many floors can be built?

   ____

Write an algebraic expression for each word expression. Then evaluate the expression for these values of the variable: 1, 6, 13.5.

5. the quotient of 300 and the sum of b and 24

   ____

6. 13 more than the product of m and 5

   ____

Problem Solving Real World

7. In the town of Pleasant Hill, there is an average of 16 sunny days each month. Write an expression to represent the approximate number of sunny days for any number of months. Tell what the variable represents.

   ____

8. How many sunny days can a resident of Pleasant Hill expect to have in 9 months?

   ____

9. WRITE *Math* Describe a situation in which a variable could be used to represent any whole number greater than 0.

   ____

   ____

Lesson Check (6.EE.B.6)

1. Oliver drives 45 miles per hour. Write an expression that represents the distance in miles he will travel for h hours driven.

2. Socks cost $5 per pair. The expression $5p$ represents the cost in dollars of p pairs of socks. Why must p be a whole number?

Spiral Review (6.RP.A.3c, 6.RP.A.3d, 6.EE.A.1, 6.EE.A.2c)

3. Sterling silver consists of 92.5% silver and 7.5% copper. What decimal represents the portion of silver in sterling silver?

4. How many pints are equivalent to 3 gallons?

5. Which operation should be done first to evaluate $10 + (66 - 6^2)$?

6. Evaluate the algebraic expression $h(m + n) \div 2$ for $h = 4$, $m = 5$, and $n = 6$.

FOR MORE PRACTICE GO TO THE **Personal Math Trainer**

Name ______________________________

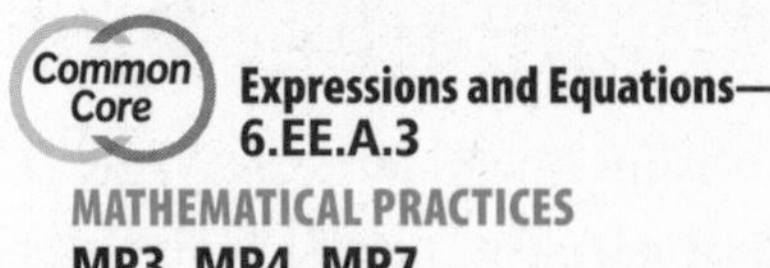

Problem Solving • Combine Like Terms

Essential Question How can you use the strategy *use a model* to combine like terms?

Common Core **Expressions and Equations—6.EE.A.3**
MATHEMATICAL PRACTICES
MP3, MP4, MP7

Like terms are terms that have the same variables with the same exponents. Numerical terms are also like terms.

Algebraic Expression	Terms	Like Terms
$5x + 3y - 2x$	$5x$, $3y$, and $2x$	$5x$ and $2x$
$8z^2 + 4z + 12z^2$	$8z^2$, $4z$, and $12z^2$	$8z^2$ and $12z^2$
$15 - 3x + 5$	15, $3x$, and 5	15 and 5

Unlock the Problem

Baseball caps cost $9, and patches cost $4. Shipping is $8 per order. The expression $9n + 4n + 8$ gives the cost in dollars of buying caps with patches for n players. Simplify the expression $9n + 4n + 8$ by combining like terms.

Use the graphic organizer to help you solve the problem.

Read the Problem

What do I need to find?

I need to simplify the expression __________.

What information do I need to use?

I need to use the like terms $9n$ and ______.

How will I use the information?

I can use a bar model to find the sum of the ______ terms.

Solve the Problem

Draw a bar model to add ______ and ______. Each square represents n, or $1n$.

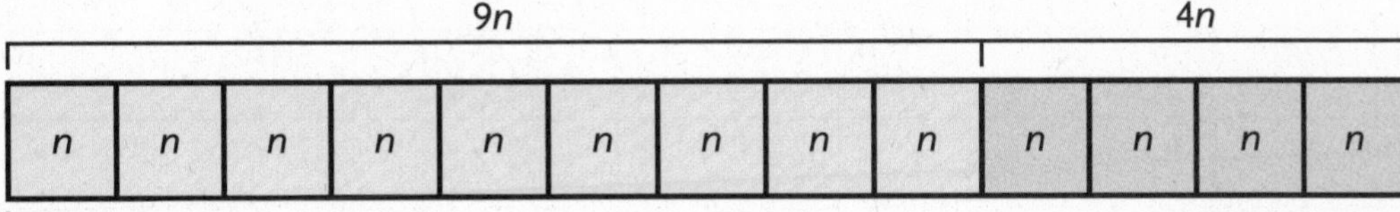

______n

The model shows that $9n + 4n =$ ______.

$9n + 4n + 8 =$ ______ $+ 8$

So, a simplified expression for the cost in dollars is __________.

Math Talk MATHEMATICAL PRACTICES 4

Use Models Explain how the bar model shows that your answer is correct.

Try Another Problem

Paintbrushes normally cost \$5 each, but they are on sale for \$1 off. A paintbrush case costs \$12. The expression $5p - p + 12$ can be used to find the cost in dollars of buying p paintbrushes on sale plus a case for them. Simplify the expression $5p - p + 12$ by combining like terms.

Use the graphic organizer to help you solve the problem.

Read the Problem

What do I need to find?	What information do I need to use?	How will I use the information?

Solve the Problem

So, a simplified expression for the cost in dollars is ____________.

1. MATHEMATICAL PRACTICE 4 **Use Models** Explain how the bar model shows that your answer is correct.

____

____

____

2. Explain how you could combine like terms without using a model.

____

____

____

Name ______________________________

Share and Show

MATH BOARD

1. Museum admission costs \$7, and tickets to the mammoth exhibit cost \$5. The expression $7p + 5p$ represents the cost in dollars for p people to visit the museum and attend the exhibit. Simplify the expression by combining like terms.

First, draw a bar model to combine the like terms.

Next, use the bar model to simplify the expression.

____

So, a simplified expression for the cost in dollars is ______.

2. THINKSMARTER **What if** the cost of tickets to the exhibit were reduced to \$3? Write an expression for the new cost in dollars for p people to visit the museum and attend the exhibit. Then, simplify the expression by combining like terms.

____

3. A store receives tomatoes in boxes of 40 tomatoes each. About 4 tomatoes per box cannot be sold due to damage. The expression $40b - 4b$ gives the number of tomatoes that the store can sell from a shipment of b boxes. Simplify the expression by combining like terms.

____

4. Each cheerleading uniform includes a shirt and a skirt. Shirts cost \$12 each, and skirts cost \$18 each. The expression $12u + 18u$ represents the cost in dollars of buying u uniforms. Simplify the expression by combining like terms.

____

5. A shop sells vases holding 9 red roses and 6 white roses. The expression $9v + 6v$ represents the total number of roses needed for v vases. Simplify the expression by combining like terms.

____

Unlock the Problem

- √ Read the entire problem carefully before you begin to solve it.
- √ Check your answer by using a different method.

WRITE Math
Show Your Work

On Your Own

6. GO DEEPER Marco received a gift card. He used it to buy 2 bike lights for $10.50 each. Then he bought a handlebar bag for $18.25. After these purchases, he had $0.75 left on the card. How much money was on the gift card when Marco received it?

____

Sea snail shells

Scallop shell

7. Lydia collects shells. She has 24 sea snail shells, 16 conch shells, and 32 scallop shells. She wants to display the shells in equal rows, with only one type of shell in each row. What is the greatest number of shells Lydia can put in each row?

____

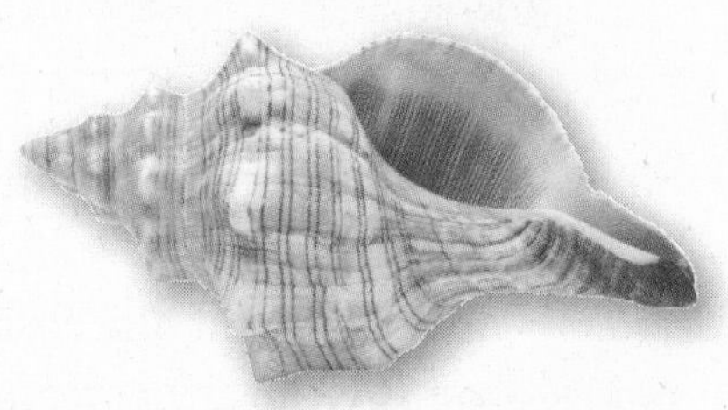

Conch shell

8. THINK SMARTER The three sides of a triangle measure $3x + 6$ inches, $5x$ inches, and $6x$ inches. Write an expression for the perimeter of the triangle in inches. Then simplify the expression by combining like terms.

____

9. MATHEMATICAL PRACTICE 3 **Verify the Reasoning of Others** Karina states that you can simplify the expression $20x + 4$ by combining like terms to get $24x$. Does Karina's statement make sense? Explain.

____

____

____

Personal Math Trainer

10. THINK SMARTER + Vincent is ordering accessories for his surfboard. A set of fins costs $24 each and a leash costs $15. The shipping cost is $4 per order. The expression $24b + 15b + 4$ can be used to find the cost in dollars of buying b fins and b leashes plus the cost of shipping.

For numbers 10a–10c, select True or False for each statement.

10a. The terms are $24b$, $15b$ and 4. ○ True ○ False

10b. The like terms are $24b$ and $15b$. ○ True ○ False

10c. The simplified expression is $43b$. ○ True ○ False

Name ______________________

Problem Solving • Combine Like Terms

Common Core **COMMON CORE STANDARD—6.EE.A.3**
Apply and extend previous understandings of arithmetic to algebraic expressions.

Read each problem and solve.

1. A box of pens costs \$3 and a box of markers costs \$5. The expression $3p + 5p$ represents the cost in dollars to make p packages that includes 1 box of pens and 1 box of markers. Simplify the expression by combining like terms.

   $3p + 5p = 8p$

2. Riley's parents got a cell phone plan that has a \$40 monthly fee for the first phone. For each extra phone, there is a \$15 phone service charge and a \$10 text service charge. The expression $40 + 15e + 10e$ represents the total phone bill in dollars, where e is the number of extra phones. Simplify the expression by combining like terms.

   ____

3. A radio show lasts for h hours. For every 60 minutes of air time during the show, there are 8 minutes of commercials. The expression $60h - 8h$ represents the air time in minutes available for talk and music. Simplify the expression by combining like terms.

   ____

4. A sub shop sells a meal that includes an Italian sub for \$6 and chips for \$2. If a customer purchases more than 3 meals, he or she receives a \$5 discount. The expression $6m + 2m - 5$ shows the cost in dollars of the customer's order for m meals, where m is greater than 3. Simplify the expression by combining like terms.

   ____

5. **WRITE** *Math* Explain how combining like terms is similar to adding and subtracting whole numbers. How are they different?

   ____
   ____
   ____

Lesson Check (6.EE.A.3)

1. For each gym class, a school has 10 soccer balls and 6 volleyballs. All of the classes share 15 basketballs. The expression $10c + 6c + 15$ represents the total number of balls the school has for c classes. What is a simpler form of the expression?

____

2. A public library wants to place 4 magazines and 9 books on each display shelf. The expression $4s + 9s$ represents the total number of items that will be displayed on s shelves. Simplify this expression.

____

Spiral Review (6.RP.A.3c, 6.RP.A.3d, 6.EE.A.1)

3. A bag has 8 bagels. Three of the bagels are cranberry. What percent of the bagels are cranberry?

____

4. How many kilograms are equivalent to 3,200 grams?

____

5. Toni earns \$200 per week plus \$5 for every magazine subscription that she sells. Write an expression that represents how much she will earn in dollars in a week in which she sells s subscriptions.

____

6. At a snack stand, drinks cost \$1.50. Write an expression that could be used to find the total cost in dollars of d drinks.

____

FOR MORE PRACTICE GO TO THE **Personal Math Trainer**

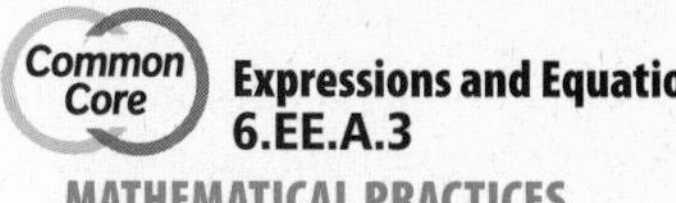

Name ______________________________

Generate Equivalent Expressions

Essential Question How can you use properties of operations to write equivalent algebraic expressions?

Common Core **Expressions and Equations—6.EE.A.3**
MATHEMATICAL PRACTICES
MP4, MP6, MP8

Equivalent expressions are equal to each other for any values of their variables. For example, $x + 3$ and $3 + x$ are equivalent. You can use properties of operations to write equivalent expressions.

$x + 3$	$3 + x$
$4 + 3$	$3 + 4$
7	7

Properties of Addition

Property	Example
Commutative Property of Addition If the order of terms changes, the sum stays the same.	$12 + a = a + 12$
Associative Property of Addition When the grouping of terms changes, the sum stays the same.	$5 + (8 + b) = (5 + 8) + b$
Identity Property of Addition The sum of 0 and any number is that number.	$0 + c = c$

Properties of Multiplication

Property	Example
Commutative Property of Multiplication If the order of factors changes, the product stays the same.	$d \times 9 = 9 \times d$
Associative Property of Multiplication When the grouping of factors changes, the product stays the same.	$11 \times (3 \times e) = (11 \times 3) \times e$
Identity Property of Multiplication The product of 1 and any number is that number.	$1 \times f = f$

Unlock the Problem

Nelson ran 2 miles, 3 laps, and 5 miles. The expression $2 + 3\ell + 5$ represents the total distance in miles Nelson ran, where ℓ is the length in miles of one lap. Write an equivalent expression with only two terms.

Rewrite the expression $2 + 3\ell + 5$ with only two terms.

The like terms are 2 and ______. Use the ____________ Property to reorder the terms. $\quad 2 + 3\ell + 5 = 3\ell +$ ______ $+ 5$

Use the ____________ Property to regroup the terms. $\quad = 3\ell + ($______ $+$ ______$)$

Add within the parentheses. $\quad = 3\ell +$ ______

So, an equivalent expression for the total distance in miles is __________.

Distributive Property

Multiplying a sum by a number is the same as multiplying each term by the number and then adding the products. | $5 \times (g + 9) = (5 \times g) + (5 \times 9)$

The Distributive Property can also be used with multiplication and subtraction. For example, $2 \times (10 - h) = (2 \times 10) - (2 \times h)$.

Example 1 Use properties of operations to write an expression equivalent to $5a + 8a - 16$ by combining like terms.

Use the Commutative Property of Multiplication to rewrite the like terms $5a$ and $8a$. $5a + 8a - 16 = a \times$ ______ $+ a \times$ ______ $- 16$

Use the Distributive Property to rewrite $a \times 5 + a \times 8$. $=$ ______ $\times (5 + 8) - 16$

Add within the parentheses. $= a \times$ ______ $- 16$

Use the Commutative Property of Multiplication to rewrite $a \times 13$. $=$ ______ $- 16$

So, the expression ____________ is equivalent to $5a + 8a - 16$.

Example 2 Use the Distributive Property to write an equivalent expression.

A $6(y + 7)$

Use the Distributive Property. $6(y + 7) = (6 \times$ ______$) + (6 \times$ ______$)$

Multiply within the parentheses. $= 6y +$ ______

So, the expression ____________ is equivalent to $6(y + 7)$.

Math Idea

When one factor in a product is in parentheses, you can leave out the multiplication sign. So, $6 \times (y + 7)$ can be written as $6(y + 7)$.

B $12a + 8b$

Find the greatest common factor (GCF) of the coefficients of the terms. The GCF of 12 and 8 is ______.

Write the first term, $12a$, as the product of the GCF and another factor. $12a + 8b = 4 \times 3a + 8b$

Write the second term, $8b$, as the product of the GCF and another factor. $= 4 \times 3a + 4 \times$ ______

Use the Distributive Property. $= 4 \times ($______ $+ 2b)$

So, the expression ____________ is equivalent to $12a + 8b$.

Math Talk MATHEMATICAL PRACTICES 8

Generalize Give a different expression that is equivalent to $12a + 8b$. Explain what property you used.

Name ______________________________

Share and Show

Use properties of operations to write an equivalent expression by combining like terms.

1. $3\frac{7}{10}r - 1\frac{5}{10}r$ ________

2. $20a + 18 + 16a$ ________

3. $7s + 8t + 10s + 12t$ ________

Use the Distributive Property to write an equivalent expression.

4. $8(h + 1.5)$ ________

5. $4m + 4p$ ________

6. $3a + 9b$ ________

Math Talk MATHEMATICAL PRACTICES 6

Compare List three expressions with two terms that are equivalent to $5x$. Compare and discuss your list with a partner's.

On Your Own

Practice: Copy and Solve **Use the Distributive Property to write an equivalent expression.**

7. $3.5(w + 7)$

8. $\frac{1}{2}(f + 10)$

9. $4(3z + 2)$

10. $20b + 16c$

11. $30d + 18$

12. $24g - 8h$

13. MATHEMATICAL PRACTICE 4 **Write an Expression** The lengths of the sides of a triangle are $3t$, $2t + 1$, and $t + 4$. Write an expression for the perimeter (sum of the lengths). Then, write an equivalent expression with 2 terms.

____

14. GO DEEPER Use properties of operations to write an expression equivalent to the sum of the expressions $3(g + 5)$ and $2(3g - 6)$.

____

Problem Solving • Applications

15. THINK SMARTER **Sense or Nonsense** Peter and Jade are using what they know about properties to write an expression equivalent to $2 \times (n + 6) + 3$. Whose answer makes sense? Whose answer is nonsense? **Explain** your reasoning.

Peter's Work

Expression:	$2 \times (n + 6) + 3$
Associative Property of Addition:	$2 \times n + (6 + 3)$
Add within parentheses:	$2 \times n + 9$
Multiply:	$2n + 9$

Jade's Work

Expression:	$2 \times (n + 6) + 3$
Distributive Property:	$(2 \times n) + (2 \times 6) + 3$
Multiply within parentheses:	$2n + 12 + 3$
Associative Property of Addition:	$2n + (12 + 3)$
Add within parentheses:	$2n + 15$

For the answer that is nonsense, correct the statement.

16. THINK SMARTER Write the algebraic expression in the box that shows an equivalent expression.

$6(z + 5)$ $6z + 5z$ $2 + 6z + 3$

$6z + 5$	$11z$	$6z + 30$

Name ____________________

Generate Equivalent Expressions

COMMON CORE STANDARD—6.EE.A.3
Apply and extend previous understandings of arithmetic to algebraic expressions.

Use properties of operations to write an equivalent expression by combining like terms.

1. $7h - 3h$

   $4h$

2. $5x + 7 + 2x$

3. $16 + 13p - 9p$

4. $y^2 + 13y - 8y$

5. $5(2h + 3) + 3h$

6. $12 + 18n + 7 - 14n$

Use the Distributive Property to write an equivalent expression.

7. $2(9 + 5k)$

8. $4d + 8$

9. $21p + 35q$

Problem Solving Real World

10. The expression $15n + 12n + 100$ represents the total cost in dollars for skis, boots, and a lesson for n skiers. Simplify the expression $15n + 12n + 100$. Then find the total cost for 8 skiers.

11. Casey has n nickels. Megan has 4 times as many nickels as Casey has. Write an expression for the total number of nickels Casey and Megan have. Then simplify the expression.

12. WRITE Math Explain how you would use properties to write an expression equivalent to $7y + 4b - 3y$.

Lesson Check (6.EE.A.3)

1. A ticket to a museum costs \$8. A ticket to the dinosaur exhibit costs \$5. The expression $8n + 5n$ represents the cost in dollars for n people to visit the museum and the exhibit. What is a simpler form of the expression $8n + 5n$?

2. What is an expression that is equivalent to $3(2p - 3)$?

Spiral Review (6.RP.A.3c, 6.NS.B.2, 6.EE.A.2b, 6.EE.A.3)

3. A Mexican restaurant received 60 take-out orders. The manager found that 60% of the orders were for tacos and 25% of the orders were for burritos. How many orders were for other items?

4. The area of a rectangular field is 1,710 square feet. The length of the field is 45 feet. What is the width of the field?

5. How many terms are in $2 + 4x + 7y$?

6. Boxes of cereal usually cost \$4, but they are on sale for \$1 off. A gallon of milk costs \$3. The expression $4b - 1b + 3$ can be used to find the cost in dollars of buying b boxes of cereal and a gallon of milk. Write the expression in simpler form.

FOR MORE PRACTICE GO TO THE **Personal Math Trainer**

Name ______________________________

Identify Equivalent Expressions

Essential Question How can you identify equivalent algebraic expressions?

Common Core **Expressions and Equations—6.EE.A.4**
MATHEMATICAL PRACTICES
MP2, MP3, MP6, MP8

Unlock the Problem Real World

Each train on a roller coaster has 10 cars, and each car can hold 4 riders. The expression $10t \times 4$ can be used to find the greatest number of riders when there are t trains on the track. Is this expression equivalent to $14t$? Use properties of operations to support your answer.

- What is one property of operations that you could use to write an expression equivalent to $10t \times 4$?

____

____

Determine whether $10t \times 4$ is equivalent to $14t$.

The expression $14t$ is the product of a number and a variable, so rewrite $10t \times 4$ as a product of a number and a variable.

Use the Commutative Property of Multiplication. $10t \times 4 = 4 \times$ ______

Use the ______________ Property of Multiplication. $= (4 \times$ ______$) \times t$

Multiply within the parentheses. $=$ ______

Compare the expressions $40t$ and $14t$.

Think: 40 times a number is not equal to 14 times the number, except when the number is 0.

Check by choosing a value for t and evaluating $40t$ and $14t$.

Write the expressions.	$40t$	$14t$
Use 2 as a value for t.	$40 \times$ ______	$14 \times$ ______
Multiply. The expressions have different values.	______	______

So, the expressions $10t \times 4$ and $14t$ are ______________.

Math Talk MATHEMATICAL PRACTICES 6

Explain Why are the expressions $7a$ and $9a$ not equivalent, even though they have the same value when $a = 0$?

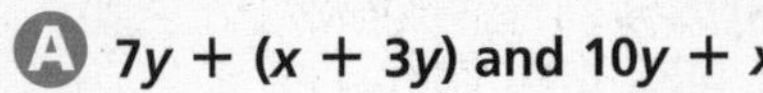 Use properties of operations to determine whether the expressions are equivalent.

A **$7y + (x + 3y)$ and $10y + x$**

The expression $10y + x$ is a sum of two terms, so rewrite $7y + (x + 3y)$ as a sum of two terms.

Use the Commutative Property of Addition to rewrite $x + 3y$.	$7y + (x + 3y) = 7y + (\_\_\_\_ + \_\_\_\_)$
Use the ________ Property of Addition to group like terms.	$= (\_\_\_\_ + 3y) + x$
Combine like terms.	$= \_\_\_\_ + x$

Compare the expressions $10y + x$ and $10y + x$: They are the same.

So, the expressions $7y + (x + 3y)$ and $10y + x$ are ________.

MATHEMATICAL PRACTICES 8

Generalize Explain how you can decide whether two algebraic expressions are equivalent.

 **$10(m + n)$ and $10m + n$**

The expression $10m + n$ is a sum of two terms, so rewrite $10(m + n)$ as a sum of two terms.

Use the Distributive Property.	$10(m + n) = (10 \times \_\_\_\_) + (10 \times \_\_\_\_)$
Multiply within the parentheses.	$= 10m + \_\_\_\_$

Compare the expressions $10m + 10n$ and $10m + n$.

Think: The first terms of both expressions are ________, but the second terms are different.

Check by choosing values for m and n and evaluating $10m + 10n$ and $10m + n$.

Write the expressions.	$10m + 10n$	$10m + n$
Use 2 as a value for m and 4 as a value for n.	$10 \times \_\_\_\_ + 10 \times \_\_\_\_$	$10 \times \_\_\_\_ + \_\_\_\_$
Multiply.	$\_\_\_\_ + \_\_\_\_$	$\_\_\_\_ + \_\_\_\_$
Add. The expressions have different values.	____	____

So, the expressions $10(m + n)$ and $10m + n$ are

________.

MATHEMATICAL PRACTICES 3

Apply How do you know that the terms $10n$ and n from Part B are not equivalent?

Name ___

Share and Show MATH BOARD

Use properties of operations to determine whether the expressions are equivalent.

1. $7k + 4 + 2k$ and $4 + 9k$

Rewrite $7k + 4 + 2k$. Use the Commutative Property of Addition. $7k + 4 + 2k = 4 +$ ___ $+ 2k$

Use the Associative Property of Addition. $= 4 + ($___ $+$ ___$)$

Add like terms. $= 4 +$ ___

The expressions $7k + 4 + 2k$ and $4 + 9k$ are ___.

2. $9a \times 3$ and $12a$

___

3. $8p + 0$ and $8p \times 0$

___

4. $5(a + b)$ and $(5a + 2b) + 3b$

___

MATHEMATICAL PRACTICES 2

Reasoning How do you know that $x + 5$ is not equivalent to $x + 8$?

On Your Own

Use properties of operations to determine whether the expressions are equivalent.

5. $3(v + 2) + 7v$ and $16v$

___

6. $14h + (17 + 11h)$ and $25h + 17$

___

7. $4b \times 7$ and $28b$

___

8. GO DEEPER Each case of dog food contains c cans. Each case of cat food contains 12 cans. Four students wrote the expressions below for the number of cans in 6 cases of dog food and 1 case of cat food. Which of the expressions are correct?

$6c + 12$ $6c \times 12$ $6(c + 2)$ $(2c + 4) \times 3$

___

Problem Solving • Applications Real World

Use the table for 9–11.

Collectible Cards	
Type	**Number per Packet**
Baseball	b
Cartoon	c
Movie	m
Animal	a

9. Marcus bought 4 packets of baseball cards and 4 packets of animal cards. Write an algebraic expression for the total number of cards Marcus bought.

____

10. MATHEMATICAL PRACTICE 3 **Make Arguments** Is the expression for the number of cards Marcus bought equivalent to $4(a + b)$? Justify your answer.

____

____

____

____

WRITE Math • Show Your Work

11. THINKSMARTER Angelica buys 3 packets of movie cards and 6 packets of cartoon cards and adds these to the 3 packets of movie cards she already has. Write three equivalent algebraic expressions for the number of cards Angelica has now.

____

____

12. 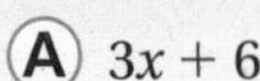 THINKSMARTER Select the expressions that are equivalent to $3(x + 2)$. Mark all that apply.

Ⓐ $3x + 6$

Ⓑ $3x + 2$

Ⓒ $5x$

Ⓓ $x + 5$

Name ______________________

Identify Equivalent Expressions

Common Core **COMMON CORE STANDARD—6.EE.A.4**
Apply and extend previous understandings of arithmetic to algebraic expressions.

Use properties of operations to determine whether the expressions are equivalent.

1. $2s + 13 + 15s$ and $17s + 13$

equivalent

2. $5 \times 7h$ and $35h$

____

3. $10 + 8v - 3v$ and $18 - 3v$

____

4. $(9w \times 0) - 12$ and $9w - 12$

____

5. $11(p + q)$ and $11p + (7q + 4q)$

____

6. $6(4b + 3d)$ and $24b + 3d$

____

7. $14m + 9 - 6m$ and $8m + 9$

____

8. $(y \times 1) + 2$ and $y + 2$

____

9. $4 + 5(6t + 1)$ and $9 + 30t$

____

10. $9x + 0 + 10x$ and $19x + 1$

____

11. $12c - 3c$ and $3(4c - 1)$

____

12. $6a \times 4$ and $24a$

____

Problem Solving Real World

13. Rachel needs to write 3 book reports with b pages and 3 science reports with s pages during the school year. Write an algebraic expression for the total number of pages Rachel will need to write.

____

14. Rachel's friend Yassi has to write $3(b + s)$ pages for reports. Use properties of operations to determine whether this expression is equivalent to the expression for the number of pages Rachel has to write.

____

15. WRITE *Math* Use properties of operations to show whether $7y + 7b + 3y$ and $7(y + b) + 3b$ are equivalent expressions. Explain your reasoning.

____

____

Lesson Check (6.EE.A.4)

1. Ian had 4 cases of comic books and 6 adventure books. Each case holds c comic books. He gave 1 case of comic books to his friend. Write an expression that gives the total number of books Ian has left.

2. In May, Xia made 5 flower planters with f flowers in each planter. In June, she made 8 flower planters with f flowers in each planter. Write an expression in simplest form that gives the number of flowers Xia has in the planters.

Spiral Review (6.RP.A.3c, 6.RP.A.3d, 6.EE.A.2c, 6.EE.A.3)

3. Keisha wants to read for 90 minutes. So far, she has read 30% of her goal. How much longer does she need to read to reach her goal?

4. Marvyn travels 105 miles on his scooter. He travels for 3 hours. What is his average speed?

5. The expression $5(F - 32) \div 9$ gives the Celsius temperature for a Fahrenheit temperature of F degrees. The noon Fahrenheit temperature in Centerville was 86 degrees. What was the temperature in degrees Celsius?

6. At the library book sale, hardcover books sell for $4 and paperbacks sell for $2. The expression $4b + 2b$ represents the total cost for b hardcover books and b paperbacks. Write a simpler expression that is equivalent to $4b + 2b$.

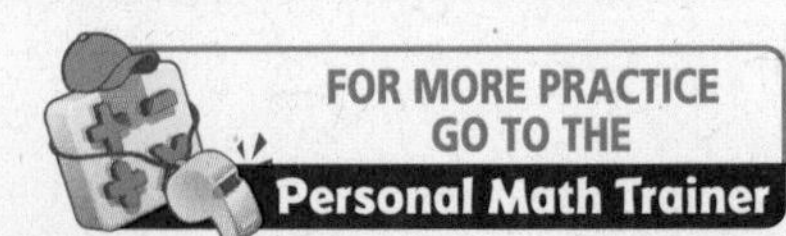

Name ______________________

Chapter 7 Review/Test

Personal Math Trainer
Online Assessment and Intervention

1. Use exponents to rewrite the expression.

$3 \times 3 \times 3 \times 3 \times 5 \times 5$

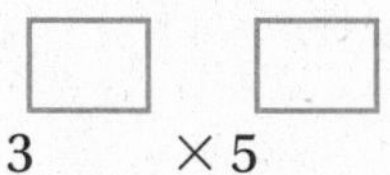

3 $\times$ 5

2. A plumber charges \$10 for transportation and \$55 per hour for repairs. Write an expression that can be used to find the cost in dollars for a repair that takes h hours.

____

3. Ellen is 2 years older than her brother Luke. Let k represent Luke's age. Identify the expression that can be used to find Ellen's age.

Ⓐ $k - 2$

Ⓑ $k + 2$

Ⓒ $2k$

Ⓓ $\frac{k}{2}$

4. Write 4^3 using repeated multiplication. Then find the value of 4^3.

____

5. Jasmine is buying beans. She bought r pounds of red beans that cost \$3 per pound and b pounds of black beans that cost \$2 per pound. The total amount of her purchase is given by the expression $3r + 2b$. Select the terms of the expression. Mark all that apply.

Ⓐ 2

Ⓑ $2b$

Ⓒ 3

Ⓓ $3r$

Assessment Options
Chapter Test

6. Choose the number that makes the sentence true.

The formula $V = s^3$ gives the volume V of a cube with side length s.

The volume of a cube that has a side length of 8 inches is [24 / 64 / 512] inches cubed.

7. Liang is ordering new chairs and cushions for his dining room table. A new chair costs \$88 and a new cushion costs \$12. Shipping costs \$34. The expression $88c + 12c + 34$ gives the total cost for buying c sets of chairs and cushions. Simplify the expression by combining like terms.

____

8. Mr. Ruiz writes the expression $5 \times (2 + 1)^2 \div 3$ on the board. Chelsea says the first step is to evaluate 1^2. Explain Chelsea's mistake. Then, evaluate the expression.

9. Jake writes this word expression.

the product of 7 and *m*

Write an algebraic expression for the word expression. Then, evaluate the expression for $m = 4$. Show your work.

Name ______________________________

10. Sora has some bags that each contain 12 potatoes. She takes 3 potatoes from each bag. The expression $12p - 3p$ represents the number of potatoes p left in the bags. Simplify the expression by combining like terms. Draw a line to match the expression with the simplified expression.

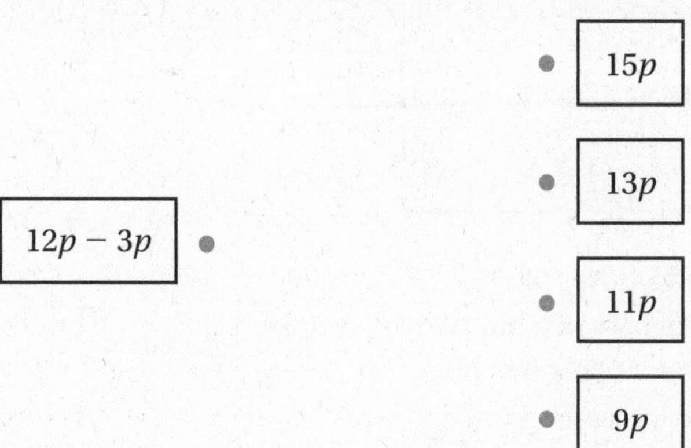

11. GO DEEPER Logan works at a florist. He earns \$600 per week plus \$5 for each floral arrangement he delivers. Write an expression that gives the amount in dollars that Logan earns for delivering f floral arrangements. Use the expression to find the amount Logan will earn if he delivers 45 floral arrangements in one week. Show your work.

12. Choose the word that makes the sentence true.

Dara wrote the expression $7 \times (d + 4)$ in her notebook. She used the

Associative Commutative Distributive	Property to write the equivalent expression $7d + 28$.

13. Use properties of operations to determine whether $5(n + 1) + 2n$ and $7n + 1$ are equivalent expressions.

14. Alisha buys 5 boxes of peanut butter granola bars and 5 boxes of cinnamon granola bars. Let p represent the number of bars in a box of peanut butter granola bars and c represent the number of bars in a box of cinnamon granola bars. Jaira and Emma each write an expression that represents the total number of granola bars Alisha bought. Are the expressions equivalent? Justify your answer.

Jaira	Emma
$5p + 5c$	$5(p + c)$

15. Abe is 3 inches taller than Chen. Select the expressions that represent Abe's height if Chen's height is h inches. Mark all that apply.

- ○ $h - 3$
- ○ $h + 3$
- ○ the sum of h and 3
- ○ the difference between h and 3

16. Write the algebraic expression in the box that shows an equivalent expression.

$3(k + 2)$ | $3k + 2k$ | $2 + 6k + 3$

$6k + 5$	$5k$	$3k + 6$

Name ____________________

17. Draw a line to match the property with the expression that shows the property.

Associative Property of Addition •	• $0 + 14 = 14$
Commutative Property of Addition •	• $14 + b = b + 14$
Identity Property of Addition •	• $6 + (8 + b) = (6 + 8) + b$

Personal Math Trainer

18. THINK SMARTER + A bike rental company charges $10 to rent a bike plus $2 for each hour the bike is rented. An expression for the total cost of renting a bike for *h* hours is $10 + 2h$. Complete the table to find the total cost of renting a bike for *h* hours.

Number of Hours, *h*	$10 + 2h$	Total Cost
1	$10 + 2 \times 1$	
2		
3		
4		

19. An online sporting goods store charges $12 for a pair of athletic socks. Shipping is $2 per order.

Part A

Write an expression that Hana can use to find the total cost in dollars for ordering *n* pairs of socks.

____

Part B

Hana orders 3 pairs of athletic socks and her friend, Charlie, orders 2 pairs of athletic socks. What is the total cost, including shipping, for both orders? Show your work.

20. Fernando simplifies the expression $(6 + 2)^2 - 4 \times 3$.

Part A

Fernando shows his work on the board. Use numbers and words to explain his mistake.

$(6 + 2)^2 - 4 \times 3$

$(6 + 4) - 4 \times 3$

$10 - 4 \times 3$

6×3

18

Part B

Simplify the expression $(6 + 2)^2 - 4 \times 3$ using the order of operations.

Chapter 8

Algebra: Equations and Inequalities

Check your understanding of important skills.

Name ____________________

▶ **Multiplication Properties** **Find the unknown number. Write which multiplication property you used.** (5.NBT.B.6)

1. $42 \times$ _____ $= 42$

____

2. $9 \times 6 =$ _____ $\times 9$

____

▶ **Evaluate Algebraic Expressions** **Evaluate the expression.** (6.EE.A.2c)

3. $4a - 2b$ for $a = 5$ and $b = 3$

____

4. $7x + 9y$ for $x = 7$ and $y = 1$

____

5. $8c \times d - 6$ for $c = 10$ and $d = 2$

____

6. $4s \div t + 10$ for $s = 9$ and $t = 3$

____

▶ **Add Fractions and Decimals** **Find the sum. Write the sum in simplest form.** (5.NF.A.1)

7. $35.68 + 17.84 =$ _______________

8. $24.38 + 25.3 =$ _______________

9. $\frac{3}{4} + \frac{1}{8} =$ _______________

10. $\frac{2}{5} + \frac{1}{4} =$ _______________

The equation $m = 19.32v$ can be used to find the mass m in grams of a pure gold coin with volume v in cubic centimeters. Carl has a coin with a mass of 37.8 grams. The coin's volume is 2.1 cubic centimeters. Could the coin be pure gold? Explain your reasoning.

Vocabulary Builder

▶ Visualize It

Use the review words to complete the tree diagram. You may use some words more than once.

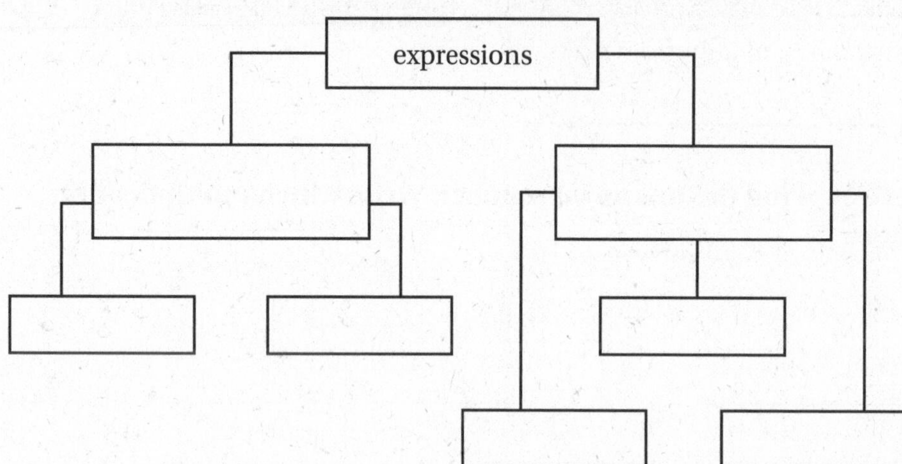

Review Words
algebraic expressions
numbers
numerical expressions
operations
variables

Preview Words
Addition Property of Equality
equation
inequality
inverse operations
solution of an equation
Subtraction Property of Equality

▶ Understand Vocabulary

Draw a line to match the preview word with its definition.

Preview Words

1. Addition Property of Equality •
2. inequality •
3. inverse operations •
4. equation •
5. solution of an equation •
6. Subtraction Property of Equality •

Definitions

- • operations that undo each other
- • a value of a variable that makes an equation true
- • property that states that if you add the same number to both sides of an equation, the two sides will remain equal
- • a mathematical statement that compares two expressions by using the symbol $<$, $>$, $\leq$, $\geq$, or $\neq$
- • property that states that if you subtract the same number from both sides of an equation, the two sides will remain equal
- • a statement that two mathematical expressions are equal

GO DIGITAL
• Interactive Student Edition
• Multimedia eGlossary

Chapter 8 Vocabulary

Addition Property of Equality
propiedad de suma de la igualdad
2

algebraic expression
expresión algebraica
3

Division Property of Equality
propiedad de división de la igualdad
24

equation
ecuación
27

Identity Property of Addition
propiedad de identidad de la suma
40

Identity Property of Multiplication
propiedad de identidad de la multiplicación
41

inequality
desigualdad
43

inverse operations
operaciones inversas
46

An expression that includes at least one variable

$x + 10$ — variable (x)

$3 \times y$ — variable (y)

$3 \times (a + 4)$ — variable (a)

Addition Property of Equality

If you add the same number to both sides of an equation, the two sides will remain equal.

$7 - 4 = 3$

$7 - 4 + 4 = 3 + 4$

$7 + 0 = 7$

$7 = 7$

An algebraic or numerical sentence that shows that two quantities are equal

Examples:

$8 + 12 = 20$ $14 = a - 3$ $2d = 14$

Division Property of Equality

If you divide both sides of an equation by the same nonzero number, the two sides will remain equal.

$2 \times 6 = 12$

$\frac{2 \times 6}{2} = \frac{12}{2}$

$1 \times 6 = 6$

$6 = 6$

The property that states that the product of any number and 1 is that number

Examples:

$475 \times 1 = 475$ $\frac{2}{3} \times 1 = \frac{2}{3}$ $0.7 \times 1 = 0.7$

The property that states that when you add zero to a number, the result is that number

Examples:

$5{,}026 + 0 = 5{,}026$ $\frac{2}{3} + 0 = \frac{2}{3}$

$1.5 + 0 = 1.5$

Opposite operations, or operations that undo each other, such as addition and subtraction or multiplication and division

A mathematical sentence that contains the symbol $<$, $>$, $\leq$, $\geq$, or $\neq$

Examples:

$8 < 11$ $9 > {}^{-}4$ $a \leq 50$ $x \geq 3.2$

Multiplication Property of Equality
propiedad de multiplicación de la igualdad
62

reciprocal
recíproco
89

solution of an equation
solución de una ecuación
94

solution of an inequality
solución de una desigualdad
95

Subtraction Property of Equality
propiedad de resta de la igualdad
98

variable
variable
105

Two numbers are reciprocals of each other if their product equals 1.

Example: $\frac{2}{3} \times \frac{3}{2} = 1$

Multiplication Property of Equality

If you multiply both sides of an equation by the same number, the two sides will remain equal.

$\frac{12}{4} = 3$

$4 \times \frac{12}{4} = 4 \times 3$

$1 \times 12 = 12$

$12 = 12$

A value that, when substituted for the variable, makes an inequality true

A value that, when substituted for the variable, makes an equation true.

Example:

$x + 3 = 5$ $x = 2$ is the solution of the equation because $2 + 3 = 5$.

A letter or symbol that stands for an unknown number or numbers

$x + 10$ — x: variable

$3 \times y$ — y: variable

$3 \times (a + 4)$ — a: variable

Subtraction Property of Equality

If you subtract the same number from both sides of an equation, the two sides will remain equal.

$3 + 4 = 7$

$3 + 4 - 4 = 7 - 4$

$3 + 0 = 3$

$3 = 3$

Pick It

For 3 players

Materials

- 4 sets of word cards

How to Play

1. Each player is dealt 5 cards. The remaining cards are a draw pile.
2. To take a turn, ask any player if he or she has a word or term that matches one of your word cards.
3. If the player has the word, he or she gives the word card to you, and you must define the term.
   - If you are correct, keep the card and put the matching pair in front of you. Take another turn.
   - If you are wrong, return the card. Your turn is over.
4. If the player does not have the word, he or she answers, "Pick it." Then you take a card from the draw pile.
5. If the card you draw matches one of your word cards, follow the directions for Step 3 above. If it does not, your turn is over.
6. The game is over when one player has no cards left. The player with the most pairs wins.

Word Box

- Addition Property of Equality
- algebraic expression
- Division Property of Equality
- equation
- Identity Property of Addition
- Identity Property of Multiplication
- inequality
- inverse operations
- Multiplication Property of Equality
- reciprocal
- solution of an equation
- solution of an inequality
- Subtraction Property of Equality
- variable

The Write Way

Reflect

Choose one idea. Write about it.

- Which of the following is an equation? Tell how you know.
  $8 + 20 =$ $9x + 4$ $6d = 12$ $3(5 + 2^3)$
- Explain how you can use inverse operations to solve this equation and check your solution.
  $a - 7 = 15$
- Suppose you write a math advice column and a reader needs help solving a multiplication equation. Write a letter to the reader explaining how to use the Division Property of Equality to solve the equation.
- Compare and contrast an equation and an inequality. How are they alike? How are they different?

Name ______________________________

Solutions of Equations

Essential Question How do you determine whether a number is a solution of an equation?

Common Core **Expressions and Equations—6.EE.B.5**

MATHEMATICAL PRACTICES MP2, MP3, MP6

An **equation** is a statement that two mathematical expressions are equal. These are examples of equations:

$8 + 12 = 20$ $\quad$ $14 = a - 3$ $\quad$ $2d = 14$

A **solution of an equation** is a value of a variable that makes an equation true.

$x + 3 = 5$ $\quad$ $x = 2$ is the solution of the equation because $2 + 3 \stackrel{?}{=} 5$.

Unlock the Problem (Real World)

In the 2009–2010 season, the women's basketball team of Duke University lost 5 of their 29 games. The equation $w + 5 = 29$ can be used to find the team's number of wins w. Determine whether $w = 14$ or $w = 24$ is a solution of the equation, and tell what the solution means.

Use substitution to determine the solution.

STEP 1 Check whether $w = 14$ is a solution.

Write the equation. $\quad w + 5 = 29$

Substitute 14 for w. $\quad$ _____ $+ 5 \stackrel{?}{=} 29$

Add. $\quad$ _____ $\neq 29$

The equation is not true when $w = 14$, so $w = 14$ is not a solution.

Math Idea

The symbol $\neq$ means "is not equal to."

STEP 2 Check whether $w = 24$ is a solution.

Write the equation. $\quad w + 5 = 29$

Substitute 24 for w. $\quad$ _____ $+ 5 \stackrel{?}{=} 29$

Add. $\quad$ _____ $= 29$

The equation is true when $w = 24$, so $w = 24$ is a solution.

So, the solution of the equation $w + 5 = 29$ is $w =$ _____,

which means that the team won _____ games.

Math Talk — MATHEMATICAL PRACTICES 6

Explain How is an algebraic equation, such as $x + 1 = 4$, different from a numerical equation, such as $3 + 1 = 4$?

Example 1 Determine whether the given value of the variable is a solution of the equation.

A $x - 0.7 = 4.3;\ x = 3.6$

Write the equation. $x - 0.7 = 4.3$

Substitute the given value for the variable. $\_\_\_\_ - 0.7 \stackrel{?}{=} 4.3$

Subtract. Write = or ≠. $\_\_\_\_ \bigcirc\ 4.3$

The equation ________ true when $x = 3.6$, so $x = 3.6$

________ a solution.

B $\frac{1}{3}a = \frac{1}{4};\ a = \frac{3}{4}$

Write the equation. $\frac{1}{3}a = \frac{1}{4}$

Substitute the given value for the variable. $\frac{1}{3} \times \frac{\square}{\square} \stackrel{?}{=} \frac{1}{4}$

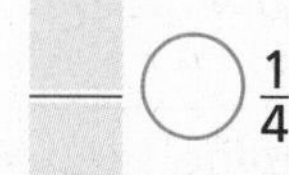

Simplify factors and multiply. Write = or ≠. $\frac{\square}{\square} \bigcirc\ \frac{1}{4}$

The equation ______ true when $a = \frac{3}{4}$, so $a = \frac{3}{4}$

______ a solution.

Example 2 The sixth-grade class president serves a term of 8 months.

Janice has already served 5 months of her term as class president. The equation $m + 5 = 8$ can be used to determine the number of months m Janice has left. Use mental math to find the solution of the equation.

Think: What number plus 5 is equal to 8? ______ plus 5 is equal to 8.

Use substitution to check whether $m = 3$ is a solution.

Write the equation. $m + 5 = 8$

Substitute 3 for m. $\_\_\_\_ + 5 \stackrel{?}{=} 8$

Add. Write = or ≠. $\_\_\_\_ \bigcirc\ 8$

So, $m =$ ______ is the solution of the equation, and

______ months of Janice's term remain.

MATHEMATICAL PRACTICES 3

Apply Give an example of an equation whose solution is $y = 7$. Explain how you know that the equation has this solution.

Name ______________________

Share and Show

Determine whether the given value of the variable is a solution of the equation.

1. $x + 12 = 29; x = 7$

   ____ $+ 12 \stackrel{?}{=} 29$

   ____ ◯ 29

   ____

2. $n - 13 = 2; n = 15$

   ____

3. $\frac{1}{2}c = 14; c = 28$

   ____

4. $m + 2.5 = 4.6; m = 2.9$

   ____

5. $d - 8.7 = 6; d = 14.7$

   ____

6. $k - \frac{3}{5} = \frac{1}{10}; k = \frac{7}{10}$

   ____

Math Talk — MATHEMATICAL PRACTICES 6

Explain why $2x - 6$ is not an equation.

On Your Own

Determine whether the given value of the variable is a solution of the equation.

7. $17.9 + v = 35.8; v = 17.9$

   ____

8. $c + 35 = 57; c = 32$

   ____

9. $18 = \frac{2}{3}h; h = 12$

   ____

10. In the equation $t + 2.5 = 7$, determine whether $t = 4.5$, $t = 5$, or $t = 5.5$ is a solution of the equation.

    ____

11. Antonio ran a total of 9 miles in two days. The first day he ran $5\frac{1}{4}$ miles. The equation $9 - d = 5\frac{1}{4}$ can be used to find the distance d in miles Antonio ran the second day. Determine whether $d = 4\frac{3}{4}$, $d = 4$, or $d = 3\frac{3}{4}$ is a solution of the equation, and tell what the solution means.

    ____

Problem Solving • Applications

Use the table for 12–14.

12. MATHEMATICAL PRACTICE 2 **Connect Symbols and Words** The length of a day on Saturn is 14 hours less than a day on Mars. The equation $24.7 - s = 14$ can be used to find the length in hours s of a day on Saturn. Determine whether $s = 9.3$ or $s = 10.7$ is a solution of the equation, and tell what the solution means.

___

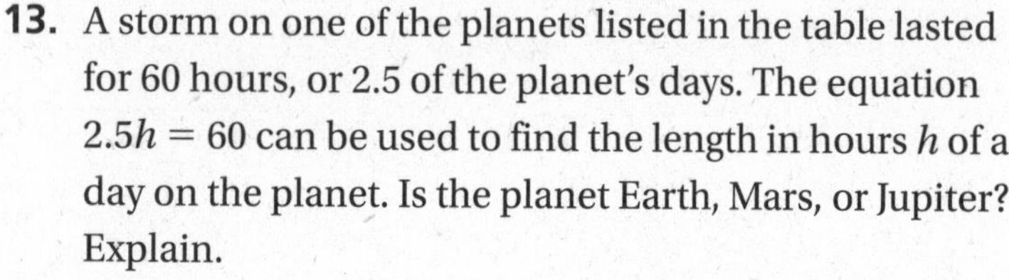

13. A storm on one of the planets listed in the table lasted for 60 hours, or 2.5 of the planet's days. The equation $2.5h = 60$ can be used to find the length in hours h of a day on the planet. Is the planet Earth, Mars, or Jupiter? Explain.

___

___

Length of Day

Planet	Length of Day (hours)
Earth	24.0
Mars	24.7
Jupiter	9.9

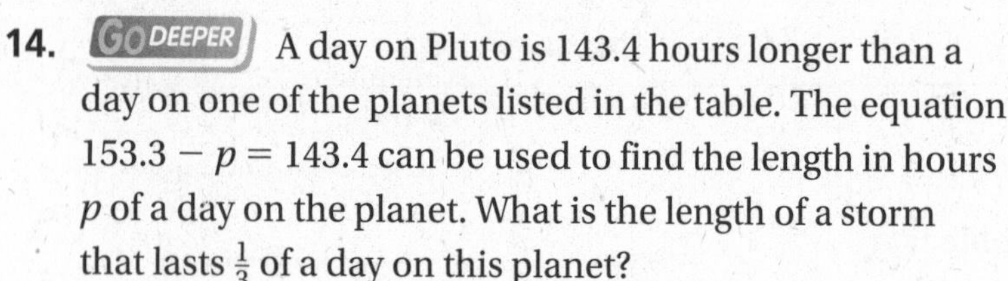

14. GO DEEPER A day on Pluto is 143.4 hours longer than a day on one of the planets listed in the table. The equation $153.3 - p = 143.4$ can be used to find the length in hours p of a day on the planet. What is the length of a storm that lasts $\frac{1}{3}$ of a day on this planet?

___

15. THINK SMARTER **What's the Error?** Jason said that the solution of the equation $2m = 4$ is $m = 8$. Describe Jason's error, and give the correct solution.

___

___

16. THINK SMARTER The marking period is 45 school days long. Today is the twenty-first day of the marking period. The equation $x + 21 = 45$ can be used to find the number of days x left in the marking period. Using substitution, Rachel determines

there are [20 / 24 / 26] days left in the marking period.

Name ____________________

Solutions of Equations

Common Core **COMMON CORE STANDARD—6.EE.B.5**
Reason about and solve one-variable equations and inequalities.

Determine whether the given value of the variable is a solution of the equation.

1. $x - 7 = 15; x = 8$

8 $- 7 \stackrel{?}{=} 15$

1 ≠ 15

not a solution

2. $c + 11 = 20; c = 9$

____

3. $\frac{1}{3}h = 6; h = 2$

____

4. $16.1 + d = 22; d = 6.1$

____

5. $9 = \frac{3}{4}e; e = 12$

____

6. $15.5 - y = 7.9; y = 8.4$

____

Problem Solving

7. Terrance needs to score 25 points to win a game. He has already scored 18 points. The equation $18 + p = 25$ can be used to find the number of points p that Terrance still needs to score. Determine whether $p = 7$ or $p = 13$ is a solution of the equation, and tell what the solution means.

____

____

____

8. Madeline has used 50 sheets of a roll of paper towels, which is $\frac{5}{8}$ of the entire roll. The equation $\frac{5}{8}s = 50$ can be used to find the number of sheets s in a full roll. Determine whether $s = 32$ or $s = 80$ is a solution of the equation, and tell what the solution means.

____

____

____

9. **WRITE** *Math* Use mental math to find the solution to $4x = 36$. Then use substitution to check your answer.

____

____

Lesson Check (6.EE.B.5)

1. Sheena received a gift card for \$50. She has already used it to buy a lamp for \$39.99. The equation $39.99 + x = 50$ can be used to find the amount x that is left on the gift card. What is the solution of the equation?

2. When Pete had a fever, his temperature was 101.4°F. After taking some medicine, his temperature was 99.2°F. The equation $101.4 - d = 99.2$ can be used to find the number of degrees d that Pete's temperature decreased. What is the solution of the equation?

Spiral Review (6.RP.A.3c, 6.EE.A.1, 6.EE.A.4, 6.EE.B.6)

3. Melanie has saved \$60 so far to buy a lawn mower. This is 20% of the price of the lawn mower. What is the full price of the lawn mower that she wants to buy?

4. A team of scientists is digging for fossils. The amount of soil in cubic feet that they remove is equal to 6^3. How many cubic feet of soil do the scientists remove?

5. Andrew made p picture frames. He sold 2 of them at a craft fair. Write an expression that could be used to find the number of picture frames Andrew has left.

6. Write an expression that is equivalent to $4 + 3(5 + x)$.

FOR MORE PRACTICE GO TO THE Personal Math Trainer

Name ______________________________

Write Equations

Essential Question How do you write an equation to represent a situation?

Expressions and Equations—6.EE.B.7

MATHEMATICAL PRACTICES
MP2, MP3, MP4, MP6

CONNECT You can use what you know about writing algebraic expressions to help you write algebraic equations.

Unlock the Problem (Real World)

A circus recently spent $1,650 on new trapezes. The trapezes cost $275 each. Write an equation that could be used to find the number of trapezes t that the circus bought.

- Circle the information that you need to write the equation.
- What expression could you use to represent the cost of t trapezes?

____

Write an equation for the situation.

Think:

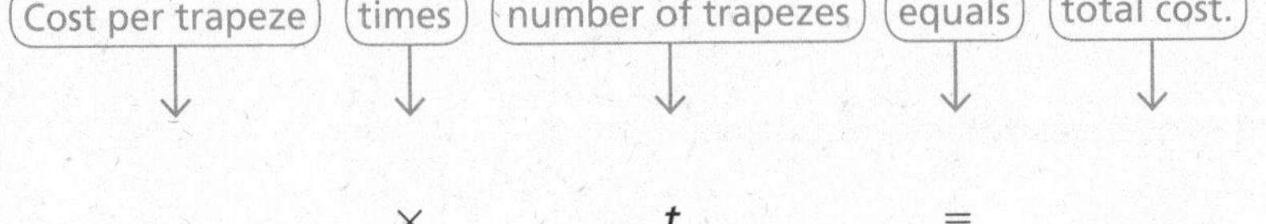

______ $\times$ t $=$ ______

So, an equation that could be used to find the number of trapezes t is ______________________.

Try This! **Ben is making a recipe for salsa that calls for $3\frac{1}{2}$ cups of tomatoes. He chops 4 tomatoes, which fill $2\frac{1}{4}$ cups. Write an equation that could be used to find out how many more cups c Ben needs.**

Think:

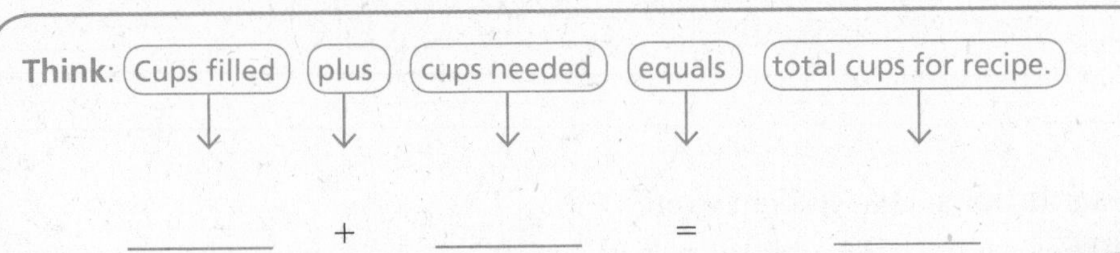

______ $+$ ______ $=$ ______

So, an equation that could be used to find the number of additional cups c is ______________________.

MATHEMATICAL PRACTICES 4

Represent What is another equation you could use to model the problem?

Example 1 Write an equation for the word sentence.

A **Six fewer than a number is 46.33.**

Think: Let n represent the unknown number. The phrase "fewer than" indicates

________.

_____ − _____ = _____

ERROR Alert

The expression $n - 6$ means "6 fewer than n." The expression $6 - n$ means "n fewer than 6."

B **Two-thirds of the cost of the sweater is $18.**

Think: Let c represent the ________ of the sweater in dollars. The word "of" indicates ________.

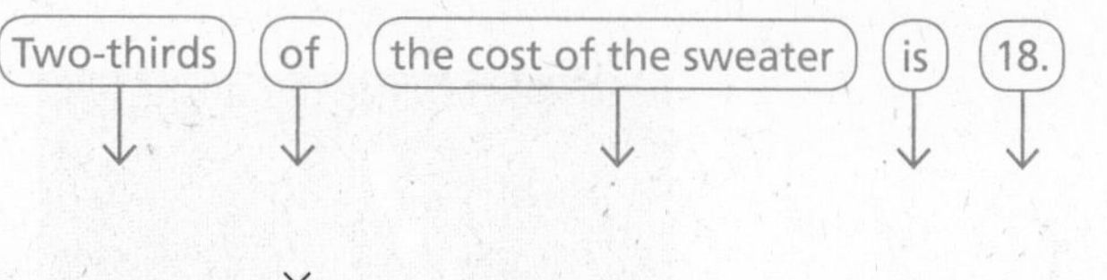

_____ × _____ = _____

Example 2 Write two word sentences for the equation.

A $a + 15 = 24$

- The ________ of a and 15 ________ 24.
- 15 ________ than a ________ 24.

B $r \div 0.2 = 40$

- The ________ of r and 0.2 ________ 40.
- r ________ by 0.2 ________ 40.

1. Explain how you can rewrite the equation $n + 8 = 24$ so that it involves subtraction rather than addition.

____

____

2. MATHEMATICAL PRACTICE 3 **Compare Representations** One student wrote $18 \times d = 54$ for the sentence "The product of 18 and d equals 54." Another student wrote $d \times 18 = 54$ for the same sentence. Are both students correct? Justify your answer.

____

____

Name ____________________

Share and Show

MATH BOARD

1. Write an equation for the word sentence "25 is 13 more than a number."

   What operation does the phrase "more than" indicate? ____________

   The equation is ____________ = ____________ + ____________.

Write an equation for the word sentence.

2. The difference of a number and 2 is $3\frac{1}{3}$.

3. Ten times the number of balloons is 120.

Write a word sentence for the equation.

4. $x - 0.3 = 1.7$

5. $25 = \frac{1}{4}n$

MATHEMATICAL PRACTICES 6

Explain How does an equation differ from an expression?

On Your Own

Write an equation for the word sentence.

6. The quotient of a number and 20.7 is 9.

7. 24 less than the number of snakes is 35.

8. 75 is $18\frac{1}{2}$ more than a number.

9. d degrees warmer than 50 degrees is 78 degrees.

Write a word sentence for the equation.

10. $15g = 135$

11. $w \div 3.3 = 0.6$

Problem Solving • Applications

To find out how far a car can travel on a certain amount of gas, multiply the car's fuel efficiency in miles per gallon by the gas used in gallons. Use this information and the table for 12–13.

Fuel Efficiency

Vehicle	Miles per gallon, city	Miles per gallon, highway
Hybrid SUV	36	31
Minivan	19	26
Sedan	20	28
SUV	22	26

12. Write an equation that could be used to find how many miles a hybrid SUV can travel in the city on 20 gallons of gas.

____

13. A sedan traveled 504 miles on the highway on a full tank of gas. Write an equation that could be used to find the number of gallons the tank holds.

____

14. MATHEMATICAL PRACTICE 2 **Connect Symbols to Words** Sonya was born in 1998. Carmen was born 11 years after Sonya. If you wrote an equation to find the year in which Carmen was born, what operation would you use in your equation?

____

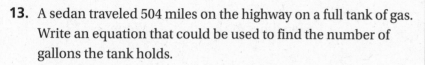

15. GO DEEPER A magazine has 110 pages. There are 23 full-page ads and 14 half-page ads. The rest of the magazine consists of articles. Write an equation that can be used to find the number of pages of articles in the magazine.

____

16. THINK SMARTER **What's the Error?** Tony is traveling 560 miles to visit his cousins. He travels 313 miles the first day. He says that he can use the equation $m - 313 = 560$ to find the number of miles m he has left on his trip. Describe and correct Tony's error.

____

17. THINK SMARTER Jamie is making cookies for a bake sale. She triples the recipe in order to have enough cookies to sell. Jamie uses 12 cups of flour to make the triple batch.

Write an equation that can be used to find out how much flour f is needed for one batch of cookies.

____

WRITE Math
Show Your Work

Name ________________________

Write Equations

Common Core **COMMON CORE STANDARD—6.EE.B.7**
Reason about and solve one-variable equations and inequalities.

Write an equation for the word sentence.

1. 18 is 4.5 times a number.

   $18 = 4.5n$

2. Eight more than the number of children is 24.

   ____

3. The difference of a number and $\frac{2}{3}$ is $\frac{3}{8}$.

   ____

4. A number divided by 0.5 is 29.

   ____

Write a word sentence for the equation.

5. $x - 14 = 52$

   ____

6. $2.3m = 0.46$

   ____

7. $25 = k \div 5$

   ____

8. $4\frac{1}{3} + q = 5\frac{1}{6}$

   ____

Problem Solving Real World

9. An ostrich egg weighs 2.9 pounds. The difference between the weight of this egg and the weight of an emu egg is 1.6 pounds. Write an equation that could be used to find the weight w, in pounds, of the emu egg.

   ____

10. In one week, the number of bowls a potter made was 6 times the number of plates. He made 90 bowls during the week. Write an equation that could be used to find the number of plates p that the potter made.

    ____

11. WRITE *Math* When writing a word sentence as an equation, explain when to use a variable.

    ____

    ____

Lesson Check (6.EE.B.7)

1. Three friends are sharing the cost of a bucket of popcorn. The total cost of the popcorn is \$5.70. Write an equation that could be used to find the amount a in dollars that each friend should pay.

2. Salimah had 42 photos on her phone. After she deleted some of them, she had 23 photos left. What equation could be used to find the number of photos p that Salimah deleted?

Spiral Review (6.RP.A.3d, 6.EE.A.1, 6.EE.A.3, 6.EE.B.5)

3. A rope is 72 feet long. What is the length of the rope in yards?

4. Julia evaluated the expression $3^3 + 20 \div 2^2$. What value should she get as her answer?

5. The sides of a triangle have lengths s, $s + 4$, and $3s$. Write an expression in simplest form that represents the perimeter of the triangle.

6. Gary knows that $p = 2\frac{1}{2}$ is a solution to one of the following equations. Which one has $p = 2\frac{1}{2}$ as its solution?

   $p + 2\frac{1}{2} = 5$ $\quad$ $p - 2\frac{1}{2} = 5$

   $2 + p = 2\frac{1}{2}$ $\quad$ $4 - p = 2\frac{1}{2}$

FOR MORE PRACTICE GO TO THE Personal Math Trainer

Name ____________________

Model and Solve Addition Equations

Essential Question How can you use models to solve addition equations?

Common Core **Expressions and Equations—6.EE.B.7**

MATHEMATICAL PRACTICES
MP4, MP5, MP6

You can use algebra tiles to help you find solutions of equations.

Algebra Tiles

x tile

1 tile

Investigate

Hands On

Materials ■ MathBoard, algebra tiles

Thomas has $2. He wants to buy a poster that costs $7. Model and solve the equation $x + 2 = 7$ to find the amount x in dollars that Thomas needs to save in order to buy the poster.

A. Draw 2 rectangles on your MathBoard to represent the two sides of the equation.

B. Use algebra tiles to model the equation. Model $x + 2$ in the left rectangle, and model 7 in the right rectangle.

- What type of tiles and number of tiles did you use to model $x + 2$?

____

C. To solve the equation, get the x tile by itself on one side. If you remove a tile from one side, you can keep the two sides equal by removing the same type of tile from the other side.

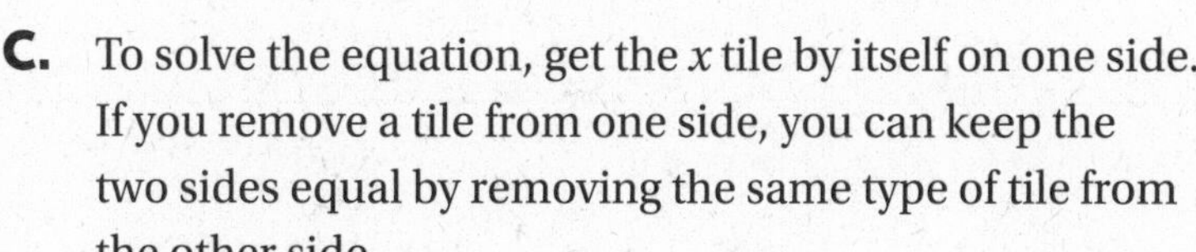

- How many 1 tiles do you need to remove from each side to get the x tile by itself on the left side? ______
- When the x tile is by itself on the left side, how many 1 tiles are on the right side? ______

D. Write the solution of the equation: $x =$ ______.

So, Thomas needs to save $ ______ in order to buy the poster.

MATHEMATICAL PRACTICES 4

Model What operation did you model when you removed the tiles?

Draw Conclusions

1. MATHEMATICAL PRACTICE 5 **Use Appropriate Tools** Describe how you could use your model to check your solution.

____

____

____

2. Tell how you could use algebra tiles to model the equation $x + 4 = 8$.

____

____

3. THINKSMARTER What would you do to solve the equation $x + 9 = 12$ without using a model?

____

Make Connections

You can solve an equation by drawing a model to represent algebra tiles.

Let a rectangle represent the variable. Let a small square represent 1.

Solve the equation $x + 3 = 7$.

STEP 1

Draw a model of the equation.

STEP 2

Get the variable by itself on one side of the model by doing the same thing to both sides.

Cross out _______ squares on the left side and

_______ squares on the right side.

STEP 3

Draw a model of the solution.

There is 1 rectangle on the left side. There are

_______ squares on the right side.

So, the solution of the equation $x + 3 = 7$ is $x =$ _______.

Name ___

Share and Show

MATH BOARD

Model and solve the equation by using algebra tiles or *i*Tools.

1. $x + 5 = 7$ ___

2. $8 = x + 1$ ___

3. $x + 2 = 5$ ___

4. $x + 6 = 8$ ___

5. $5 + x = 9$ ___

6. $5 = 4 + x$ ___

Solve the equation by drawing a model.

7. $x + 1 = 5$ ___

8. $3 + x = 4$ ___

9. $6 = x + 4$ ___

10. $8 = 2 + x$ ___

11. MATHEMATICAL PRACTICE 6 **Describe a Method** Describe how you would draw a model to solve the equation $x + 5 = 10$.

___

___

___

___

Problem Solving • Applications

12. MATHEMATICAL PRACTICE 4 **Interpret a Result** The table shows how long several animals have lived at a zoo. The giraffe has lived at the zoo 4 years longer than the mountain lion. The equation $5 = 4 + y$ can be used to find the number of years y the mountain lion has lived at the zoo. Solve the equation. Then tell what the solution means.

Zoo Animals

Animal	Time at zoo (years)
Giraffe	5
Hippopotamus	6
Kangaroo	2
Zebra	9

13. GO DEEPER Carlos walked 2 miles on Monday and 5 miles on Saturday. The number of miles he walked on those two days is 3 miles more than the number of miles he walked on Friday. Write and solve an addition equation to find the number of miles Carlos walked on Friday.

14. THINK SMARTER **Sense or Nonsense?** Gabriela is solving the equation $x + 1 = 6$. She says that the solution must be less than 6. Is Gabriela's statement sense or nonsense? Explain.

Personal Math Trainer

15. THINK SMARTER+ The Hawks beat the Tigers by 5 points in a football game. The Hawks scored a total of 12 points.

Use numbers and words to explain how this model can be used to solve the equation $x + 5 = 12$.

Name ____________________

Model and Solve Addition Equations

Common Core **COMMON CORE STANDARD—6.EE.B.7**
Reason about and solve one-variable equations and inequalities.

Model and solve the equation by using algebra tiles.

1. $x + 6 = 9$

$x = 3$

2. $8 + x = 10$

____

3. $9 = x + 1$

____

Solve the equation by drawing a model.

4. $x + 4 = 7$

____

5. $x + 6 = 10$

____

Problem Solving Real World

6. The temperature at 10:00 was 10°F. This is 3°F warmer than the temperature at 8:00. Model and solve the equation $x + 3 = 10$ to find the temperature x in degrees Fahrenheit at 8:00.

____

7. Jaspar has 7 more checkers left than Karen does. Jaspar has 9 checkers left. Write and solve an addition equation to find out how many checkers Karen has left.

____

8. WRITE Math Explain how to use a drawing to solve an addition equation such as $x + 8 = 40$.

____

____

Lesson Check (6.EE.B.7)

1. What is the solution of the equation that is modeled by the algebra tiles?

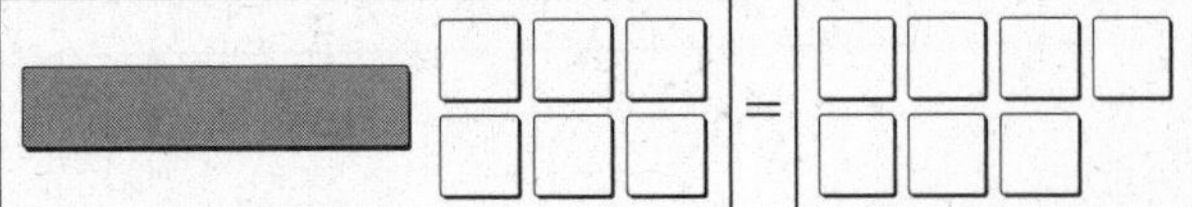

2. Alice has played soccer for 8 more years than Sanjay has. Alice has played for 12 years. The equation $y + 8 = 12$ can be used to find the number of years y Sanjay has played. How long has Sanjay played soccer?

Spiral Review (6.RP.A.3d, 6.EE.A.2a, 6.EE.A.3, 6.EE.B.7)

3. A car's gas tank has a capacity of 16 gallons. What is the capacity of the tank in pints?

4. Craig scored p points in a game. Marla scored twice as many points as Craig but 5 fewer than Nelson scored. How many points did Nelson score?

5. Simplify $3x + 2(4y + x)$.

6. The Empire State Building in New York City is 443.2 meters tall. This is 119.2 meters taller than the Eiffel Tower in Paris. Write an equation that can be used to find the height h in meters of the Eiffel Tower.

FOR MORE PRACTICE GO TO THE **Personal Math Trainer**

Name ______________________________

Solve Addition and Subtraction Equations

Essential Question How do you solve addition and subtraction equations?

Common Core **Expressions and Equations—6.EE.B.7**

MATHEMATICAL PRACTICES
MP2, MP6, MP8

CONNECT To solve an equation, you must get the variable on one side of the equal sign by itself. You have solved equations by using models. You can also solve equations by using Properties of Equality.

Subtraction Property of Equality	
If you subtract the same number from both sides of an equation, the two sides will remain equal.	$3 + 4 = 7$ $3 + 4 - 4 = 7 - 4$ $3 + 0 = 3$ $3 = 3$

Unlock the Problem

The longest distance jumped on a pogo stick is 23 miles. Emilio has jumped 5 miles on a pogo stick. The equation $d + 5 = 23$ can be used to find the remaining distance d in miles he must jump to match the record. Solve the equation, and explain what the solution means.

Solve the addition equation.

To get d by itself, you must undo the addition by 5. Operations that undo each other are called **inverse operations**. Subtracting 5 is the inverse operation of adding 5.

Write the equation. $d + 5 = 23$

Use the Subtraction Property of Equality. $d + 5 - 5 = 23 - $ _____

Subtract. $d + 0 = $ _____

Use the Identity Property of Addition. _____ $= 18$

Check the solution.

Write the equation. $d + 5 = 23$

Substitute _____ for d. _____ $+ 5 = 23$

The solution checks. _____ $= 23$

So, the solution means that Emilio must jump _____ more miles.

Math Talk — MATHEMATICAL PRACTICES 8

Generalize How do you know what number to subtract from both sides of the equation?

When you solve an equation that involves subtraction, you can use addition to get the variable by itself on one side of the equal sign.

Addition Property of Equality

If you add the same number to both sides of an equation, the two sides will remain equal.

$$7 - 4 = 3$$
$$7 - 4 + 4 = 3 + 4$$
$$7 + 0 = 7$$
$$7 = 7$$

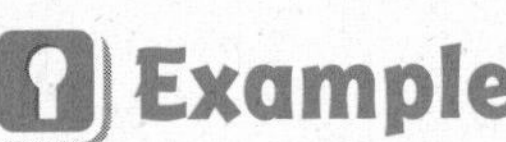

Example

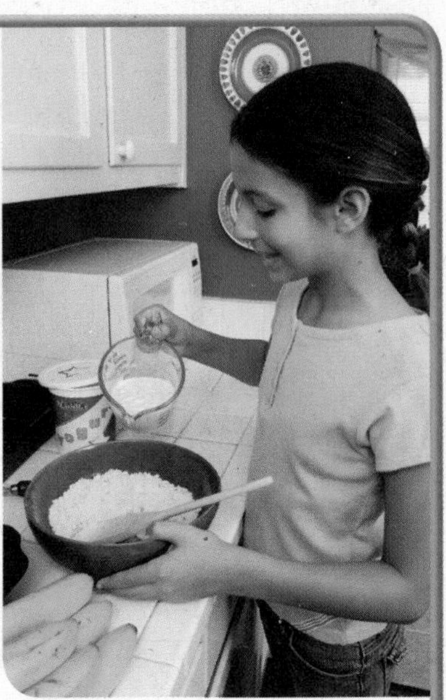

While cooking dinner, Carla pours $\frac{5}{8}$ cup of milk from a carton. This leaves $\frac{7}{8}$ cup of milk in the carton. Write and solve an equation to find how much milk was in the carton when Carla started cooking.

STEP 1 Write an equation.

Let a represent the amount of milk in cups in the carton when Carla started cooking.

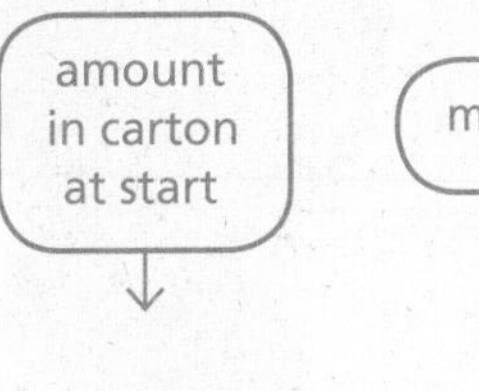

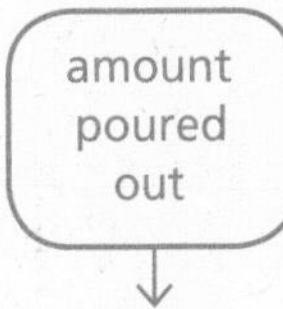

amount poured out
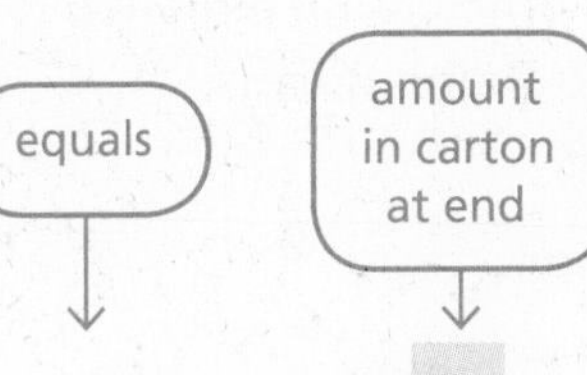

amount in carton at end

$a \quad - \quad \frac{\square}{\square} \quad = \quad \frac{\square}{\square}$

____

STEP 2 Solve the equation.

Think: $\frac{5}{8}$ is subtracted from a, so add $\frac{5}{8}$ to both sides to undo the subtraction.

Write the equation. $a - \frac{5}{8} = \frac{7}{8}$

Use the Addition Property of Equality. $a - \frac{5}{8} + \frac{\square}{\square} = \frac{7}{8} + \frac{\square}{\square}$

Add. $a = \frac{\square}{\square}$

Write the fraction greater than 1 as a mixed number, and simplify. $a =$ ______

So, there were ______ cups of milk in the carton when Carla started cooking.

MATHEMATICAL PRACTICES 6

Explain How can you check the solution of the equation?

Name ________________

Share and Show

MATH BOARD

1. Solve the equation $n + 35 = 80$.

$n + 35 = 80$

$n + 35 - 35 = 80 -$ ______ Use the ______ Property of Equality.

$n =$ ______ Subtract.

Solve the equation, and check the solution.

2. $16 + x = 42$

3. $y + 6.2 = 9.1$

4. $m + \frac{3}{10} = \frac{7}{10}$

5. $z - \frac{1}{3} = 1\frac{2}{3}$

6. $12 = x - 24$

7. $25.3 = w - 14.9$

Math Talk — MATHEMATICAL PRACTICES 8

Generalize What can you do to get the variable by itself on one side of a subtraction equation?

On Your Own

Practice: Copy and Solve **Solve the equation, and check the solution.**

8. $y - \frac{3}{4} = \frac{1}{2}$

9. $75 = n + 12$

10. $m + 16.8 = 40$

11. $w - 36 = 56$

12. $8\frac{2}{5} = d + 2\frac{2}{5}$

13. $8.7 = r - 1.4$

14. The temperature dropped 8 degrees between 6:00 P.M. and midnight. The temperature at midnight was 26°F. Write and solve an equation to find the temperature at 6:00 P.M.

______

15. MATHEMATICAL PRACTICE 2 **Reason Abstractly** Write an addition equation that has the solution $x = 9$.

______

Unlock the Problem — Real World

16. GO DEEPER In July, Kimberly made two deposits into her bank account. She made no withdrawals. At the end of July, her account balance was $120.62. Write and solve an equation to find Kimberly's balance at the beginning of July.

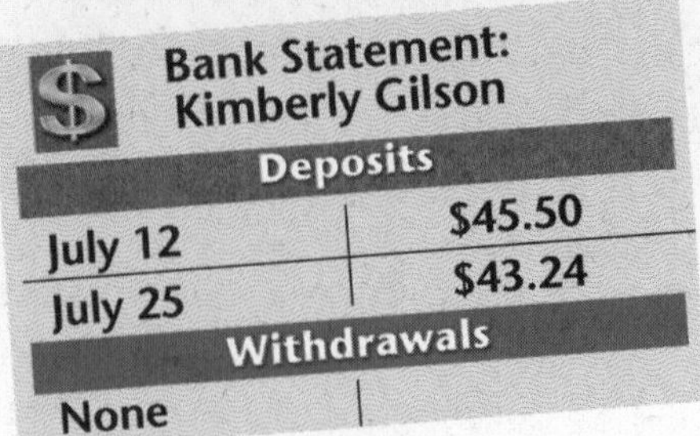

Bank Statement: Kimberly Gilson

Deposits	
July 12	$45.50
July 25	$43.24
Withdrawals	
None	

a. What do you need to find?

____

____

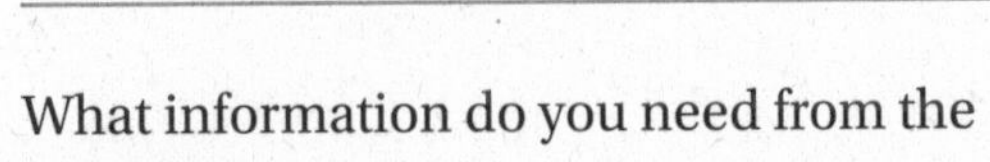

b. What information do you need from the bank statement?

____

____

c. Write an equation you can use to solve the problem. Explain what the variable represents.

____

____

____

____

d. Solve the equation. Show your work and describe each step.

e. Write Kimberly's balance at the beginning of July.

____

17. THINK SMARTER If $x + 6 = 35$, what is the value of $x + 4$? Explain how to find the value without solving the equation.

____

____

____

18. THINK SMARTER Select the equations that have the solution $n = 23$. Mark all that apply.

Ⓐ $16 + n = 39$

Ⓑ $n - 4 = 19$

Ⓒ $25 = n - 2$

Ⓓ $12 = n - 11$

Name ______________________________

Practice and Homework
Lesson 8.4

Solve Addition and Subtraction Equations

Common Core **COMMON CORE STANDARD—6.EE.B.7** *Reason about and solve one-variable equations and inequalities.*

Solve the equation, and check the solution.

1. $y - 14 = 23$

$y - 14 + 14 = 23 + 14$

$y = 37$

____

2. $x + 3 = 15$

____

3. $n + \frac{2}{5} = \frac{4}{5}$

____

4. $16 = m - 14$

____

5. $w - 13.7 = 22.8$

____

6. $s + 55 = 55$

____

7. $23 = x - 12$

____

8. $p - 14 = 14$

____

9. $m - 2\frac{3}{4} = 6\frac{1}{2}$

____

Problem Solving

10. A recipe calls for $5\frac{1}{2}$ cups of flour. Lorenzo only has $3\frac{3}{4}$ cups of flour. Write and solve an equation to find the additional amount of flour Lorenzo needs to make the recipe.

____

11. Jan used 22.5 gallons of water in the shower. This amount is 7.5 gallons less than the amount she used for washing clothes. Write and solve an equation to find the amount of water Jan used to wash clothes.

____

12. WRITE *Math* Explain how to check if your solution to an equation is correct.

____

____

Lesson Check (6.EE.B.7)

1. The price tag on a shirt says \$21.50. The final cost of the shirt, including sales tax, is \$23.22. The equation $21.50 + t = 23.22$ can be used to find the amount of sales tax t in dollars. What is the sales tax?

2. The equation $l - 12.5 = 48.6$ can be used to find the original length l in centimeters of a wire before it was cut. What was the original length of the wire?

Spiral Review (6.RP.A.3d, 6.EE.A.2b, 6.EE.A.4, 6.EE.B.7)

3. How would you convert a mass in centigrams to a mass in milligrams?

4. In the expression $4 + 3x + 5y$, what is the coefficient of x?

5. Write an expression that is equivalent to $10c$.

6. Miranda bought a \$7-movie ticket and popcorn for a total of \$10. The equation $7 + x = 10$ can be used to find the cost x in dollars of the popcorn. How much did the popcorn cost?

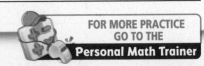

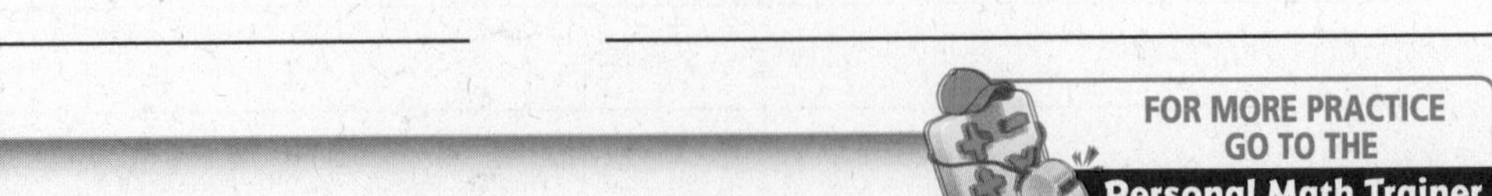

Name ______________________________

Model and Solve Multiplication Equations

Essential Question How can you use models to solve multiplication equations?

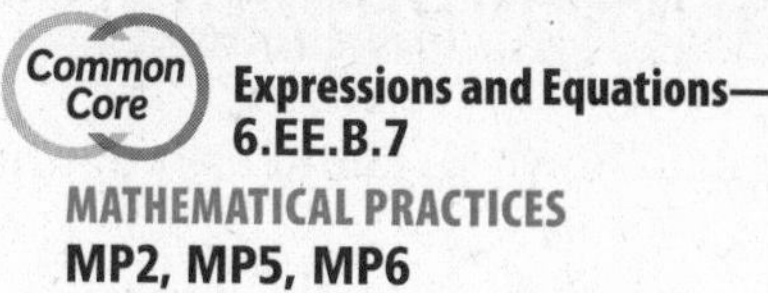

Expressions and Equations— 6.EE.B.7

MATHEMATICAL PRACTICES
MP2, MP5, MP6

You can use algebra tiles to model and solve equations that involve multiplication.

Algebra Tiles

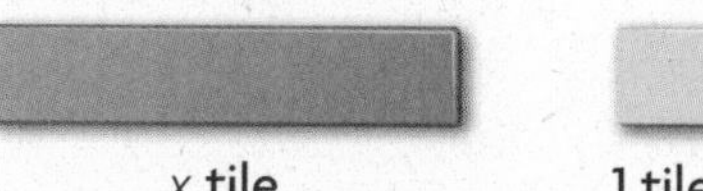

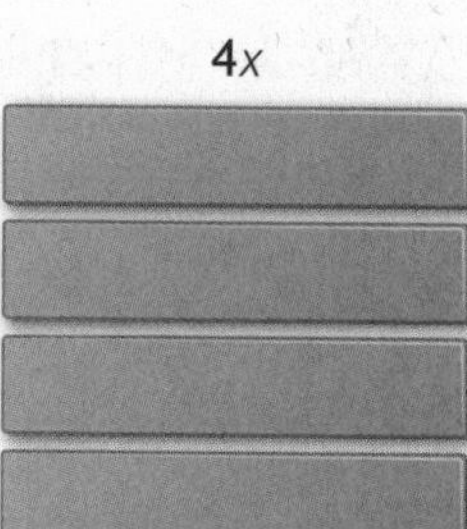

To model an expression involving multiplication of a variable, you can use more than one x tile. For example, to model the expression $4x$, you can use four x tiles.

Investigate

Materials ■ MathBoard, algebra tiles

Hands On

Tennis balls are sold in cans of 3 tennis balls each. Daniel needs 15 tennis balls for a tournament. Model and solve the equation $3x = 15$ to find the number of cans x that Daniel should buy.

A. Draw 2 rectangles on your MathBoard to represent the two sides of the equation.

B. Use algebra tiles to model the equation. Model $3x$ in the left rectangle, and model 15 in the right rectangle.

C. There are three x tiles on the left side of your model. To solve the equation by using the model, you need to find the value of one x tile. To do this, divide each side of your model into 3 equal groups.

- When the tiles on each side have been divided into 3 equal groups, how many 1 tiles are in each group on the right side? ______

D. Write the solution of the equation: $x =$ ______.

So, Daniel should buy ______ cans of tennis balls.

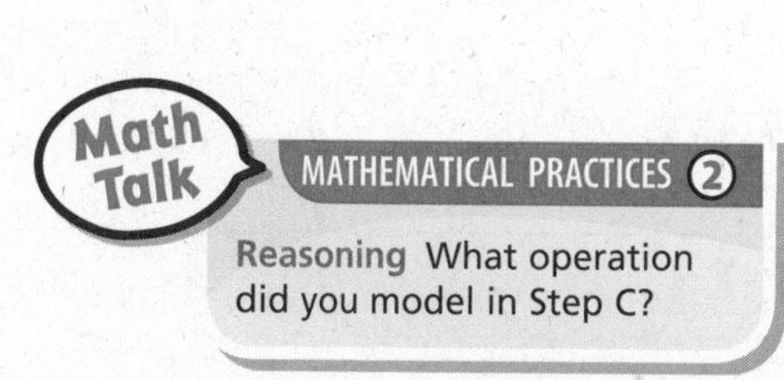

Math Talk
MATHEMATICAL PRACTICES 2
Reasoning What operation did you model in Step C?

Draw Conclusions

1. Explain how you could use your model to check your solution.

____

____

____

2. MATHEMATICAL PRACTICE 6 **Describe** how you could use algebra tiles to model the equation $6x = 12$.

____

3. THINKSMARTER What would you do to solve the equation $5x = 35$ without using a model?

____

Make Connections

You can also solve multiplication equations by drawing a model to represent algebra tiles. Let a rectangle represent x. Let a square represent 1. Solve the equation $2x = 6$.

STEP 1 Draw a model of the equation.

STEP 2 Find the value of one rectangle.

Divide each side of the model into ________ equal groups.

STEP 3 Draw a model of the solution.

There is 1 rectangle on the left side. There are ________ squares on the right side.

So, the solution of the equation $2x = 6$ is $x =$ ______.

Name ______________________________

Share and Show

Model and solve the equation by using algebra tiles.

1. $4x = 16$ ______

2. $3x = 12$ ______

3. $4 = 4x$ ______

4. $3x = 9$ ______

5. $2x = 10$ ______

6. $15 = 5x$ ______

Solve the equation by drawing a model.

7. $4x = 8$ ______

8. $3x = 18$ ______

Problem Solving • Applications

9. MATHEMATICAL PRACTICE 5 **Communicate** Explain the steps you use to solve a multiplication equation with algebra tiles.

______

______

______

______

______

The bar graph shows the number of countries that competed in the first four modern Olympic Games. Use the bar graph for 10–11.

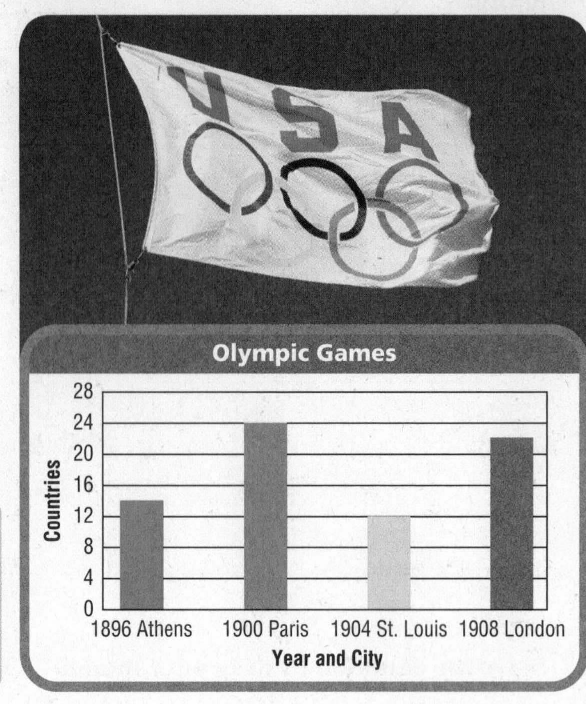

10. GO DEEPER Naomi is doing a report about the 1900 and 1904 Olympic Games. Each page will contain information about 4 of the countries that competed each year. Write and solve an equation to find the number of pages Naomi will need.

____

11. THINK SMARTER **Pose a Problem** Use the information in the bar graph to write and solve a problem involving a multiplication equation.

____

12. The equation $7s = 21$ can be used to find the number of snakes s in each cage at a zoo. Solve the equation. Then tell what the solution means.

____

13. THINK SMARTER A choir is made up of 6 vocal groups. Each group has an equal number of singers. There are 18 singers in the choir. Solve the equation $6p = 18$ to find the number of singers in each group. Use a model.

Name ______________________

Model and Solve Multiplication Equations

Common Core **COMMON CORE STANDARD—6.EE.B.7**
Reason about and solve one-variable equations and inequalities.

Model and solve the equation by using algebra tiles.

1. $2x = 8$ ____ $x = 4$ ____
2. $5x = 10$ ______________
3. $21 = 3x$ ______________

Solve the equation by drawing a model.

4. $6 = 3x$ ______________
5. $4x = 12$ ______________

Problem Solving Real World

6. A chef used 20 eggs to make 5 omelets. Model and solve the equation $5x = 20$ to find the number of eggs x in each omelet. ______________
7. Last month, Julio played 3 times as many video games as Scott did. Julio played 18 video games. Write and solve an equation to find the number of video games Scott played. ______________
8. WRITE Math Write a multiplication equation, and explain how you can solve it by using a model.

____

____

____

Lesson Check (6.EE.B.7)

1. What is the solution of the equation that is modeled by the algebra tiles?

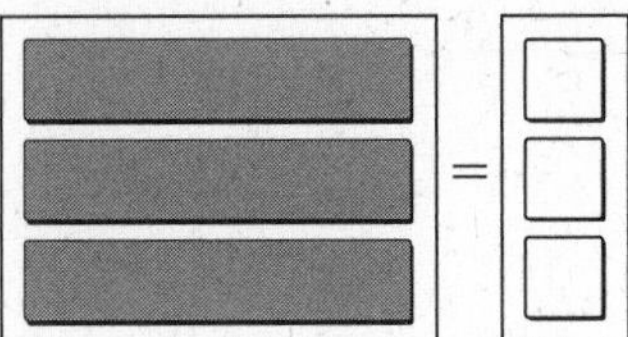

2. Carlos bought 5 tickets to a play for a total of \$20. The equation $5c = 20$ can be used to find the cost c in dollars of each ticket. How much does each ticket cost?

Spiral Review (6.RP.A.3d, 6.EE.A.2c, 6.EE.B.5, 6.EE.B.7)

3. A rectangle is 12 feet wide and 96 inches long. What is the area of the rectangle?

4. Evaluate the algebraic expression $24 - x \div y$ for $x = 8$ and $y = 2$.

5. Ana bought a 15.5-pound turkey at the grocery store this month. The equation $p - 15.5 = 2.5$ can be used to find the weight p, in pounds, of the turkey she bought last month. What is the solution of the equation?

6. A pet store usually keeps 12 birds per cage, and there are 7 birds in the cage now. The equation $7 + x = 12$ can be used to find the remaining number of birds x that can be placed in the cage. What is the solution of the equation?

FOR MORE PRACTICE GO TO THE **Personal Math Trainer**

Name ____________________

Solve Multiplication and Division Equations

Essential Question How do you solve multiplication and division equations?

Expressions and Equations— 6.EE.B.7

MATHEMATICAL PRACTICES
MP1, MP7, MP8

CONNECT You can use Properties of Equality and inverse operations to solve multiplication and division equations.

Division Property of Equality

If you divide both sides of an equation by the same nonzero number, the two sides will remain equal.

$$2 \times 6 = 12$$
$$\frac{2 \times 6}{2} = \frac{12}{2}$$
$$1 \times 6 = 6$$
$$6 = 6$$

Unlock the Problem — Real World

Mei ran 14 laps around a track for a total of 4,200 meters. The equation $14d = 4{,}200$ can be used to find the distance d in meters she ran in each lap. Solve the equation, and explain what the solution means.

- What operation is indicated by $14d$? ____________________

Solve a multiplication equation.

To get d by itself, you must undo the multiplication by 14. Dividing by 14 is the inverse operation of multiplying by 14.

Write the equation. $14d = 4{,}200$

Use the Division Property of Equality. $\frac{14d}{\square} = \frac{4{,}200}{\square}$

Divide. $1 \times d =$ ______

Use the Identity Property of Multiplication. ______ $= 300$

Check the solution.

Write the equation. $14d = 4{,}200$

Substitute ______ for d. $14 \times$ ______ $= 4{,}200$

The solution checks. ______ $= 4{,}200$

So, the solution means that Mei ran ______ meters in each lap.

MATHEMATICAL PRACTICES 8

Use Repeated Reasoning How do you know what number to divide both sides of the equation by?

Example 1 Solve the equation $\frac{2}{3}n = \frac{1}{4}$.

Think: n is multiplied by $\frac{2}{3}$, so divide both sides by $\frac{2}{3}$ to undo the division.

Write the equation. $\frac{2}{3}n = \frac{1}{4}$

Use the ______________ Property of Equality. $\frac{2}{3}n \div \frac{2}{3} = \frac{1}{4} \div \frac{\square}{\square}$

To divide by $\frac{2}{3}$, multiply by its reciprocal. $\frac{2}{3}n \times \frac{3}{2} = \frac{1}{4} \times \frac{\square}{\square}$

Multiply. $n = \frac{\square}{\square}$

Multiplication Property of Equality

If you multiply both sides of an equation by the same number, the two sides will remain equal.

$\frac{12}{4} = 3$

$4 \times \frac{12}{4} = 4 \times 3$

$1 \times 12 = 12$

$12 = 12$

Example 2

A biologist divides a water sample equally among 8 test tubes. Each test tube contains 24.5 milliliters of water. Write and solve an equation to find the volume of the water sample.

STEP 1 Write an equation. Let v represent the volume in milliliters.

Think: The volume divided by 8 equals the volume in each test tube. $\frac{v}{\square} =$ ______________

STEP 2 Solve the equation. v is divided by 8, so multiply both sides by 8 to undo the division.

Write the equation. $\frac{v}{8} = 24.5$

Use the ______________ Property of Equality. ______ $\times \frac{v}{8} =$ ______ $\times 24.5$

Multiply. $v =$ ______________

So, the volume of the water sample is ______________ milliliters.

MATHEMATICAL PRACTICES 7

Look for Structure How can you use the Multiplication Property of Equality to solve Example 1?

Name ___________________________________

Share and Show

1. Solve the equation $2.5m = 10$.

$$2.5m = 10$$

$$\frac{2.5m}{2.5} = \frac{10}{\square}$$ Use the ____________ Property of Equality.

$$m = \_\_\_\_$$ Divide.

Solve the equation, and check the solution.

2. $3x = 210$

3. $2.8 = 4t$

4. $\frac{1}{3}n = 15$

5. $\frac{1}{2}y = \frac{1}{10}$

6. $25 = \frac{a}{5}$

7. $1.3 = \frac{c}{4}$

Math Talk — MATHEMATICAL PRACTICES 8

Generalize What strategy can you use to get the variable by itself on one side of a division equation?

On Your Own

Practice: Copy and Solve **Solve the equation, and check the solution.**

8. $150 = 6m$

9. $14.7 = \frac{b}{7}$

10. $\frac{1}{4} = \frac{3}{5}s$

11. GO DEEPER There are 100 calories in 8 fluid ounces of orange juice and 140 calories in 8 fluid ounces of pineapple juice. Tia mixed 4 fluid ounces of each juice. Write and solve an equation to find the number of calories in each fluid ounce of Tia's juice mixture.

____

12. THINK SMARTER Write a division equation that has the solution $x = 16$.

____

Problem Solving • Applications

What's the Error?

13. THINKSMARTER Melinda has a block of clay that weighs 14.4 ounces. She divides the clay into 6 equal pieces. To find the weight w in ounces of each piece, Melinda solved the equation $6w = 14.4$.

Look at how Melinda solved the equation. Find her error.

This is how Melinda solved the equation:

$$6w = 14.4$$

$$\frac{6w}{6} = 6 \times 14.4$$

$$w = 86.4$$

Melinda concludes that each piece of clay weighs 86.4 ounces.

Correct the error. Solve the equation, and explain your steps.

So, $w =$ ______.

This means each piece of clay weighs ______________.

- MATHEMATICAL PRACTICE 1 **Describe** the error that Melinda made.

____

____

14. THINKSMARTER For numbers 14a–14d, choose Yes or No to indicate whether the equation has the solution $x = 15$.

14a. $15x = 30$ ○ Yes ○ No

14b. $4x = 60$ ○ Yes ○ No

14c. $\frac{x}{5} = 3$ ○ Yes ○ No

14d. $\frac{x}{3} = 5$ ○ Yes ○ No

Name ______________________

Solve Multiplication and Division Equations

COMMON CORE STANDARD—6.EE.B.7
Reason about and solve one-variable equations and inequalities.

Solve the equation, and check the solution.

1. $8p = 96$

$\frac{8p}{8} = \frac{96}{8}$ $p = 12$

2. $\frac{z}{16} = 8$

3. $3.5x = 14.7$

4. $32 = 3.2c$

5. $\frac{2}{5}w = 40$

6. $\frac{a}{14} = 6.8$

7. $1.6x = 1.6$

8. $23.8 = 3.5b$

9. $\frac{3}{5} = \frac{2}{3}t$

Problem Solving Real World

10. Anne runs 6 laps on a track. She runs a total of 1 mile, or 5,280 feet. Write and solve an equation to find the distance, in feet, that she runs in each lap.

11. In a serving of 8 fluid ounces of pomegranate juice, there are 32.8 grams of carbohydrates. Write and solve an equation to find the amount of carbohydrates in each fluid ounce of the juice.

12. WRITE Math Write and solve a word problem that can be solved by solving a multiplication equation.

Lesson Check (6.EE.B.7)

1. Estella buys 1.8 pounds of walnuts for a total of $5.04. She solves the equation $1.8p = 5.04$ to find the price p in dollars of one pound of walnuts. What does one pound of walnuts cost?

2. Gabriel wants to solve the equation $\frac{5}{8}m = 25$. What step should he do to get m by itself on one side of the equation?

Spiral Review (6.RP.A.3d, 6.EE.B.6, 6.EE.B.7)

3. At top speed, a coyote can run at a speed of 44 miles per hour. If a coyote could maintain its top speed, how far could it run in 15 minutes?

4. An online store sells DVDs for $10 each. The shipping charge for an entire order is $5.50. Frank orders d DVDs. Write an expression that represents the total cost of Frank's DVDs.

5. A ring costs $27 more than a pair of earrings. The ring costs $90. Write an equation that can be used to find the cost c in dollars of the earrings.

6. The equation $3s = 21$ can be used to find the number of students s in each van on a field trip. How many students are in each van?

FOR MORE PRACTICE GO TO THE **Personal Math Trainer**

Name ______________________

Problem Solving • Equations with Fractions

Essential Question How can you use the strategy *solve a simpler problem* to solve equations involving fractions?

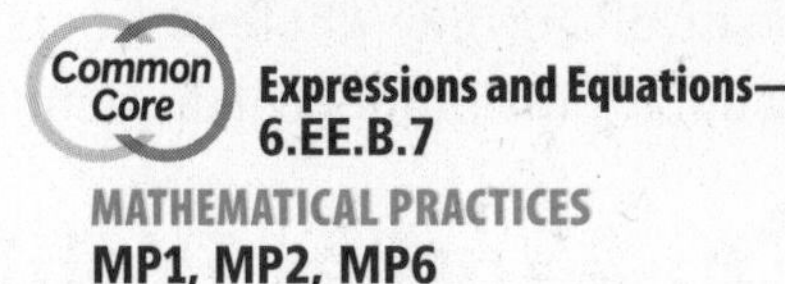

Common Core
Expressions and Equations—6.EE.B.7
MATHEMATICAL PRACTICES
MP1, MP2, MP6

You can change an equation involving a fraction to an equation involving only whole numbers. To do so, multiply both sides of the equation by the denominator of the fraction.

Unlock the Problem

On canoe trips, people sometimes carry their canoes between bodies of water. Maps for canoeing use a unit of length called a *rod* to show distances. Victoria and Mick carry their canoe 40 rods. The equation $40 = \frac{2}{11}d$ can be used to find the distance d in yards that they carried the canoe. How many yards did they carry the canoe?

Use the graphic organizer to help you solve the problem.

Read the Problem

What do I need to find?

I need to find ______________________

______________________.

What information do I need to use?

I need to use ______________________.

How will I use the information?

I can solve a simpler problem by changing the equation to an equation involving only whole numbers. Then I can solve the simpler equation.

Solve the Problem

- Write a simpler equation.

Write the equation.	$40 = \frac{2}{11}d$
Multiply both sides by the denominator.	$11 \times 40 = \_\_\_\_ \times \frac{2}{11}d$
Multiply.	$\_\_\_\_ = 2d$

- Solve the simpler equation.

Write the equation.	$440 = 2d$
Use the Division Property of Equality.	$\frac{440}{\square} = \frac{2d}{\square}$
Divide.	$\_\_\_\_ = d$

So, Victoria and Mick carried their canoe ______ yards.

MATHEMATICAL PRACTICES 1

Evaluate How can you check that your answer to the problem is correct?

If an equation contains more than one fraction, you can change it to an equation involving only whole numbers by multiplying both sides of the equation by the product of the denominators of the fractions.

Try Another Problem

Trevor is making $\frac{2}{3}$ of a recipe for chicken noodle soup. He adds $\frac{1}{2}$ cup of chopped celery. The equation $\frac{2}{3}c = \frac{1}{2}$ can be used to find the number of cups c of chopped celery in the original recipe. How many cups of chopped celery does the original recipe call for?

Use the graphic organizer to help you solve the problem.

Read the Problem	Solve the Problem
What do I need to find?	
What information do I need to use?	
How will I use the information?	

So, the original recipe calls for ______ cup of chopped celery.

- MATHEMATICAL PRACTICE 6 **Describe a Method** Describe another method that you could use to solve the problem.

____

____

Math Talk

MATHEMATICAL PRACTICES 2

Reasoning How do you know that your answer is reasonable?

Name ___________________________

Share and Show

1. Connor ran 3 kilometers in a relay race. His distance represents $\frac{3}{10}$ of the total distance of the race. The equation $\frac{3}{10}d = 3$ can be used to find the total distance d of the race in kilometers. What was the total distance of the race?

First, write a simpler equation by multiplying both sides by the denominator of the fraction.

____

Next, solve the simpler equation.

____

So, the race is ______________ long.

2. THINKSMARTER **What if** Connor's distance of 3 kilometers represented only $\frac{2}{10}$ of the total distance of the race. What would the total distance of the race have been?

____

3. The lightest puppy in a litter weighs 9 ounces, which is $\frac{3}{4}$ of the weight of the heaviest puppy. The equation $\frac{3}{4}w = 9$ can be used to find the weight w in ounces of the heaviest puppy. How much does the heaviest puppy weigh?

____

4. Sophia took home $\frac{2}{5}$ of the pizza that was left over from a party. The amount she took represents $\frac{1}{2}$ of a whole pizza. The equation $\frac{2}{5}p = \frac{1}{2}$ can be used to find the number of pizzas p left over from the party. How many pizzas were left over?

____

5. A city received $\frac{3}{4}$ inch of rain on July 31. This represents $\frac{3}{10}$ of the total amount of rain the city received in July. The equation $\frac{3}{10}r = \frac{3}{4}$ can be used to find the amount of rain r in inches the city received in July. How much rain did the city receive in July?

____

Unlock the Problem

- ✓ Circle the important information.
- ✓ Use the Properties of Equality when you solve equations.
- ✓ Check your solution by substituting it into the original equation.

WRITE Math • Show Your Work

On Your Own

6. GO DEEPER Carole ordered 4 dresses for \$80 each, a \$25 sweater, and a coat. The cost of the items without sales tax was \$430. What was the cost of the coat?

____

7. THINK SMARTER A dog sled race is 25 miles long. The equation $\frac{5}{8}k = 25$ can be used to estimate the race's length k in kilometers. Approximately how many hours will it take a dog sled team to finish the race if it travels at an average speed of 30 kilometers per hour?

____

____

8. MATHEMATICAL PRACTICE 6 **Explain a Method** Explain how you could use the strategy *solve a simpler problem* to solve the equation $\frac{3}{4}x = \frac{3}{10}$.

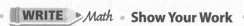

____

____

____

____

9. THINK SMARTER In a basket of fruit, $\frac{5}{6}$ of the pieces of fruit are apples. There are 20 apples in the display. The equation $\frac{5}{6}f = 20$ can be used to find how many pieces of fruit f are in the basket. Use words and numbers to explain how to solve the equation to find how many pieces of fruit are in the basket.

____

____

____

____

WRITE Math • **Show Your Work**

Name ______________________________

Problem Solving • Equations with Fractions

COMMON CORE STANDARD—6.EE.B.7
Reason about and solve one-variable equations and inequalities.

Read each problem and solve.

1. Stu is 4 feet tall. This height represents $\frac{6}{7}$ of his brother's height. The equation $\frac{6}{7}h = 4$ can be used to find the height h, in feet, of Stu's brother. How tall is Stu's brother?

$7 \times \frac{6}{7}h = 7 \times 4$

$6h = 28$

$\frac{6h}{6} = \frac{28}{6}$

$h = 4\frac{2}{3}$

$4\frac{2}{3}$ feet

2. Bryce bought a bag of cashews. He served $\frac{7}{8}$ pound of cashews at a party. This amount represents $\frac{2}{3}$ of the entire bag. The equation $\frac{2}{3}n = \frac{7}{8}$ can be used to find the number of pounds n in a full bag. How many pounds of cashews were in the bag that Bryce bought?

____

3. In Jaime's math class, 9 students chose soccer as their favorite sport. This amount represents $\frac{3}{8}$ of the entire class. The equation $\frac{3}{8}s = 9$ can be used to find the total number of students s in Jaime's class. How many students are in Jaime's math class?

____

4. **WRITE** *Math* Write a math problem for the equation. $\frac{3}{4}n = \frac{5}{6}$. Then solve a simpler problem to find the solution.

____

____

____

Lesson Check (6.EE.B.7)

1. Roger served $\frac{5}{8}$ pound of crackers, which was $\frac{2}{3}$ of the entire box. What was the weight of the crackers originally in the box?

2. Bowser ate $4\frac{1}{2}$ pounds of dog food. That amount is $\frac{3}{4}$ of the entire bag of dog food. How many pounds of dog food were originally in the bag?

Spiral Review (6.RP.A.3d, 6.NS.A.1, 6.EE.A.2a, 6.EE.B.7)

3. What is the quotient $4\frac{2}{3} \div 4\frac{1}{5}$?

4. Miranda had 4 pounds, 6 ounces of clay. She divided it into 10 equal parts. How heavy was each part?

5. The amount Denise charges to repair computers is \$50 an hour plus a \$25 service fee. Write an expression to show how much she will charge for h hours of work.

6. Luis has saved \$14 for a skateboard that costs \$52. He can use the equation $14 + m = 52$ to find how much more money m he needs. How much more does he need?

FOR MORE PRACTICE GO TO THE **Personal Math Trainer**

Name ______________________________

Mid-Chapter Checkpoint

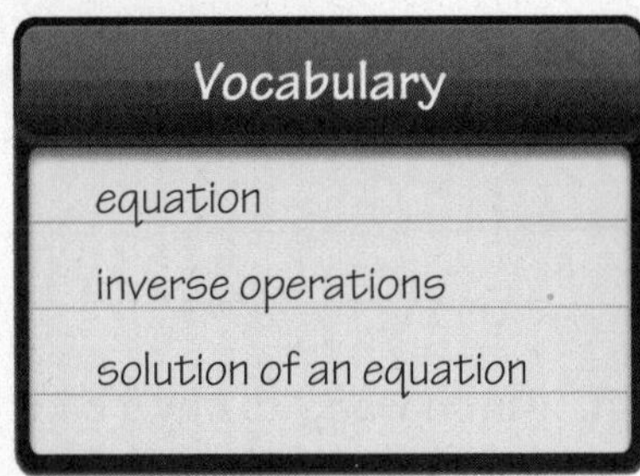

Vocabulary

Vocabulary
equation
inverse operations
solution of an equation

Choose the best term from the box to complete the sentence.

1. A(n) ______________ is a statement that two mathematical expressions are equal. (p. 421)

2. Adding 5 and subtracting 5 are ______________. (p. 439)

Concepts and Skills

Write an equation for the word sentence. (6.EE.B.7)

3. The sum of a number and 4.5 is 8.2.

4. Three times the cost is $24.

Determine whether the given value of the variable is a solution of the equation. (6.EE.B.5)

5. $x - 24 = 58$; $x = 82$

6. $\frac{1}{3}c = \frac{3}{8}$; $c = \frac{3}{4}$

Solve the equation, and check the solution. (6.EE.B.7)

7. $a + 2.4 = 7.8$

8. $b - \frac{1}{4} = 3\frac{1}{2}$

9. $3x = 27$

10. $\frac{1}{3}s = \frac{1}{5}$

11. $\frac{t}{4} = 16$

12. $\frac{w}{7} = 0.3$

13. A stadium has a total of 18,000 seats. Of these, 7,500 are field seats, and the rest are grandstand seats. Write an equation that could be used to find the number of grandstand seats s. (6.EE.B.7)

____

14. Aaron wants to buy a bicycle that costs \$128. So far, he has saved \$56. The equation $a + 56 = 128$ can be used to find the amount a in dollars that Aaron still needs to save. What is the solution of the equation? (6.EE.B.7)

____

15. GO DEEPER Ms. McNeil buys 2.4 gallons of gasoline. The total cost is \$7.56. Write and solve an equation to find the price p in dollars of one gallon of gasoline. (6.EE.B.7)

____

16. Crystal is picking blueberries. So far, she has filled $\frac{2}{3}$ of her basket, and the blueberries weigh $\frac{3}{4}$ pound. The equation $\frac{2}{3}w = \frac{3}{4}$ can be used to estimate the weight w in pounds of the blueberries when the basket is full. About how much will the blueberries in Crystal's basket weigh when it is full? (6.EE.B.7)

____

Name ______________________________

Solutions of Inequalities

Essential Question How do you determine whether a number is a solution of an inequality?

Common Core Expressions and Equations—6.EE.B.5
MATHEMATICAL PRACTICES
MP2, MP3, MP6

An **inequality** is a mathematical sentence that compares two expressions using the symbol $<$, $>$, $\leq$, $\geq$, or $\neq$. These are examples of inequalities:

$8 < 11$ $\quad$ $9 > {}^{-}4$ $\quad$ $a \leq 50$ $\quad$ $x \geq 3.2$

A **solution of an inequality** is a value of a variable that makes the inequality true. Inequalities can have more than one solution.

Math Idea

- The symbol $\leq$ means "is less than or equal to."
- The symbol $\geq$ means "is greater than or equal to."

Unlock the Problem — Real World

A library has books from the Middle Ages. The books are more than 650 years old. The inequality $a > 650$ represents the possible ages a in years of the books. Determine whether $a = 678$ or $a = 634$ is a solution of the inequality, and tell what the solution means.

Use substitution to determine the solution.

STEP 1 Check whether $a = 678$ is a solution.

Write the inequality. $a > 650$

Substitute 678 for a. ________ $\stackrel{?}{>}$ 650

Compare the values. 678 is ________ than 650.

The inequality is true when $a = 678$, so $a = 678$ is a solution.

STEP 2 Check whether $a = 634$ is a solution.

Write the inequality. $a > 650$

Substitute 634 for a. ________ $\stackrel{?}{>}$ 650

Compare the values. 634 ________ greater than 650.

The inequality ________ true when $a = 634$, so $a = 634$ ________ a solution.

The solution $a = 678$ means that a book in the library from the Middle Ages could be ________ years old.

Math Talk MATHEMATICAL PRACTICES 3

Apply Give another solution of the inequality $a > 650$. Explain how you determined the solution.

Example 1 Determine whether the given value of the variable is a solution of the inequality.

A $b < 0.3$; $b = {}^{-}0.2$

Write the inequality. $b < 0.3$

Substitute the given value for the variable. ______ $\overset{?}{<} 0.3$

Compare the values. $^{-}0.2$ is ______ than 0.3.

The inequality ______ true when $b = {}^{-}0.2$, so $b = {}^{-}0.2$ ______ a solution.

B $m \geq \frac{2}{3}$; $m = \frac{3}{5}$

Write the inequality. $m \geq \frac{2}{3}$

Substitute the given value for the variable. $\frac{\square}{\square} \overset{?}{\geq} \frac{2}{3}$

Rewrite the fractions with a common denominator. $\frac{\square}{15} \overset{?}{\geq} \frac{\square}{15}$

Compare the values. $\frac{9}{15}$ ______ greater than or equal to $\frac{10}{15}$.

The inequality ______ true when $m = \frac{3}{5}$, so $m = \frac{3}{5}$ ______ a solution.

Example 2

An airplane can hold no more than 416 passengers. The inequality $p \leq 416$ represents the possible number of passengers p on the airplane, where p is a whole number. Give two solutions of the inequality, and tell what the solutions mean.

Think: The solutions of the inequality are whole numbers ______ than or ______ to 416.

- $p = 200$ is a solution because 200 is ______ than ______.
- $p =$ ______ is a solution because ______ is ______ than 416.

These solutions mean that the number of passengers on the plane could be ______ or ______.

MATHEMATICAL PRACTICES 3

Apply Give an example of a value of p that is not a solution of the inequality. How do you know it is not a solution?

Name ______________________

Share and Show

Determine whether the given value of the variable is a solution of the inequality.

1. $a \geq {}^{-}6$; $a = {}^{-}3$

   ______ $\overset{?}{\geq} {}^{-}6$

   ______

2. $y < 7.8$; $y = 8$

   ______

3. $c > \frac{1}{4}$; $c = \frac{1}{5}$

   ______

4. $x \leq 3$; $x = 3$

   ______

5. $d < {}^{-}0.52$; $d = {}^{-}0.51$

   ______

6. $t \geq \frac{2}{3}$; $t = \frac{3}{4}$

   ______

Math Talk MATHEMATICAL PRACTICES 6

Explain How could you use a number line to check your answer to Exercise 5?

On Your Own

Practice: Copy and Solve **Determine whether $s = \frac{3}{5}$, $s = 0$, or $s = 1.75$ are solutions of the inequality.**

7. $s > {}^{-}1$

8. $s \leq 1\frac{2}{3}$

9. $s < 0.43$

Give two solutions of the inequality.

10. $e < 3$

    ______

11. $p > {}^{-}12$

    ______

12. $y \geq 5.8$

    ______

13. MATHEMATICAL PRACTICE 2 **Connect Symbols and Words** A person must be at least 18 years old to vote. The inequality $a \geq 18$ represents the possible ages a in years at which a person can vote. Determine whether $a = 18$, $a = 17\frac{1}{2}$, and $a = 91.5$ are solutions of the inequality, and tell what the solutions mean.

____

____

Problem Solving • Applications 

The table shows ticket and popcorn prices at five movie theater chains. Use the table for 14–15.

14. GO DEEPER The inequality $p < 4.75$ represents the prices p in dollars that Paige is willing to pay for popcorn. The inequality $p < 8.00$ represents the prices p in dollars that Paige is willing to pay for a movie ticket. At how many theaters would Paige be willing to buy a ticket and popcorn?

____

15. THINK SMARTER **Sense or Nonsense?** Edward says that the inequality $d \geq 4.00$ represents the popcorn prices in the table, where d is the price of popcorn in dollars. Is Edward's statement sense or nonsense? Explain.

____

____

____

Movie Theater Prices

Ticket Price ($)	Popcorn Price ($)
8.00	4.25
8.50	5.00
9.00	4.00
7.50	4.75
7.25	4.50

WRITE Math • Show Your Work

16. MATHEMATICAL PRACTICE 6 **Use Math Vocabulary** Explain why the statement $t > 13$ is an inequality.

____

____

Personal Math Trainer

17. THINK SMARTER+ The minimum wind speed for a storm to be considered a hurricane is 74 miles per hour. The inequality $w \geq 74$ represents the possible wind speeds of a hurricane.

Two possible solutions for the inequality $w \geq 74$ are [71 / 73 / 75] and [80. / 60. / 40.]

Name ______________________

Solutions of Inequalities

COMMON CORE STANDARD—6.EE.B.5
Reason about and solve one-variable equations and inequalities.

Determine whether the given value of the variable is a solution of the inequality.

1. $s \geq {}^{-}1; s = 1$

   $1 \overset{?}{\geq} {}^{-}1$

   solution

2. $p < 0; p = 4$

   ____

3. $y \leq {}^{-}3; y = {}^{-}1$

   ____

4. $u > {}^{-}\frac{1}{2}; u = 0$

   ____

5. $q \geq 0.6; q = 0.23$

   ____

6. $b < 2\frac{3}{4}; b = \frac{2}{3}$

   ____

Give two solutions of the inequality.

7. $k < 2$

   ____

8. $z \geq {}^{-}3$

   ____

9. $f \leq {}^{-}5$

   ____

Problem Solving (Real World)

10. The inequality $s \geq 92$ represents the score s that Jared must earn on his next test to get an A on his report card. Give two possible scores that Jared could earn to get the A.

    ____

11. The inequality $m \leq \$20$ represents the amount of money that Sheila is allowed to spend on a new hat. Give two possible money amounts that Sheila could spend on the hat.

    ____

12. **WRITE** *Math* Describe a situation and write an inequality to represent the situation. Give a number that is a solution and another number that is not a solution of the inequality.

    ____

    ____

Lesson Check (6.EE.B.5)

1. Three of the following are solutions of $g < {}^{-}1\frac{1}{2}$. Which one is not a solution?

$g = {}^{-}4$ $g = {}^{-}7\frac{1}{2}$ $g = 0$ $g = {}^{-}2\frac{1}{2}$

2. The inequality $w \geq 3.2$ represents the weight of each pumpkin, in pounds, that is allowed to be picked to be sold. The weights of pumpkins are listed. How many pumpkins can be sold? Which pumpkins can be sold?

3.18 lb, 4 lb, 3.2 lb, 3.4 lb, 3.15 lb

Spiral Review (6.EE.A.1, 6.EE.A.3, 6.EE.B.7)

3. What is the value of $8 + (27 \div 9)^2$?

4. Write an expression that is equivalent to $5(3x + 2z)$.

5. Tina bought a t-shirt and sandals. The total cost was $41.50. The t-shirt cost $8.95. The equation $8.95 + c = 41.50$ can be used to find the cost c in dollars of the sandals. How much did the sandals cost?

6. Two-thirds of a number is equal to 20. What is the number?

FOR MORE PRACTICE GO TO THE **Personal Math Trainer**

Name ________________________________

Write Inequalities

Essential Question How do you write an inequality to represent a situation?

Common Core **Expressions and Equations—6.EE.B.8**

MATHEMATICAL PRACTICES
MP2, MP4, MP6

CONNECT You can use what you know about writing equations to help you write inequalities.

Unlock the Problem

The highest temperature ever recorded at the South Pole was 8°F. Write an inequality to show that the temperature t in degrees Fahrenheit at the South Pole is less than or equal to 8°F.

- Underline the words that tell you which inequality symbol to use.
- Will you use an equal sign in your inequality? Explain.

____

____

Write an inequality for the situation.

Think:

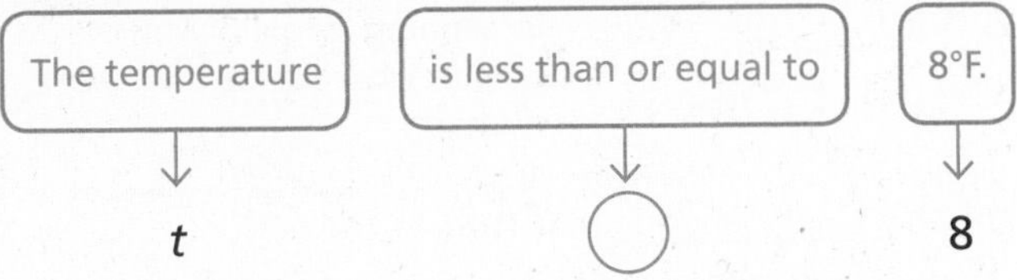

So, an inequality that describes the temperature t in degrees Fahrenheit at the South Pole is ____________.

Try This! **The directors of an animal shelter need to raise more than $50,000 during a fundraiser. Write an inequality that represents the amount of money m in dollars that the directors need to raise.**

Think:

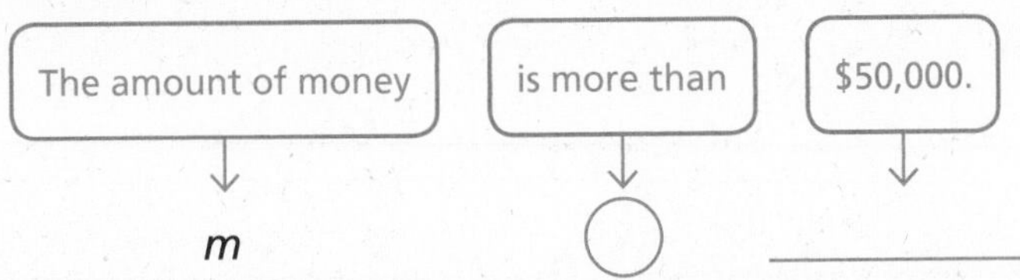

So, an inequality that describes the amount of money m in dollars is ____________.

MATHEMATICAL PRACTICES 6

Explain How did you know which inequality symbol to use in the Try This! problem?

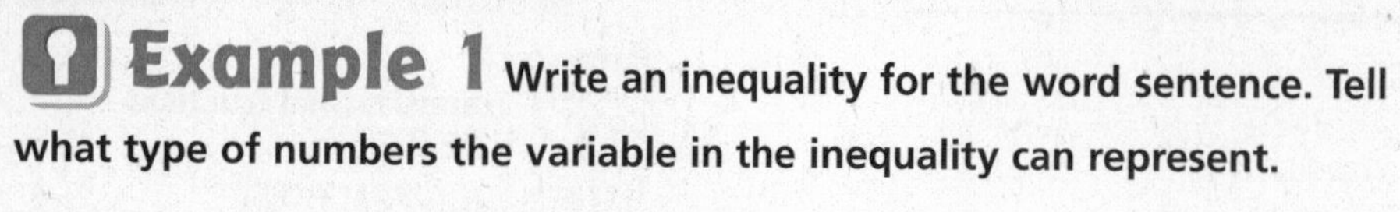

Example 1 Write an inequality for the word sentence. Tell what type of numbers the variable in the inequality can represent.

A **The weight is less than $3\frac{1}{2}$ pounds.**

Think: Let w represent the unknown weight in pounds.

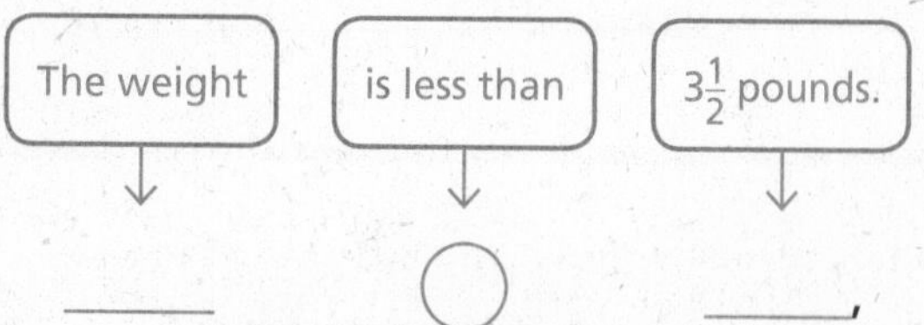

_______ ◯ _______, where w is a positive number

B **There must be at least 65 police officers on duty.**

Think: Let p represent the number of police officers. The phrase "at least" is equivalent to "is __________ than or equal to."

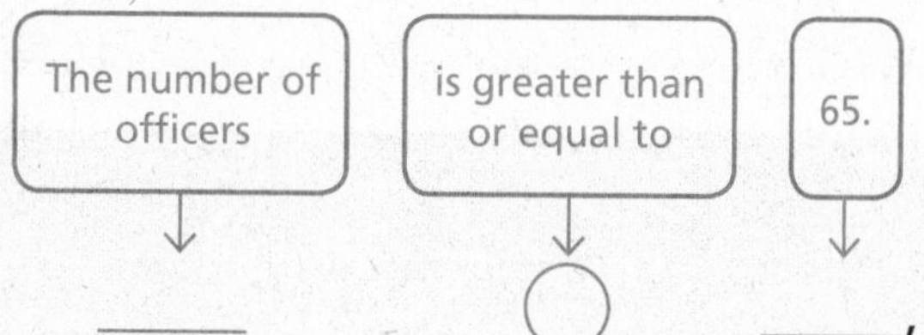

_______ ◯ _______, where p is a __________ number

MATHEMATICAL PRACTICES 2

Reasoning Explain why the value of p must be a whole number.

Example 2 Write two word sentences for the inequality.

A $n \leq 0.3$

- n is __________ than or __________ to 0.3.
- n is no __________ than 0.3.

B $a > {}^{-}4$

- a is __________ than $^{-}4$.
- a is __________ than $^{-}4$.

- THINK SMARTER Which inequality symbol would you use to show that the number of people attending a party will be at most 14? Explain.

____

____

Name ____________________

Share and Show

MATH BOARD

Write an inequality for the word sentence. Tell what type of numbers the variable in the inequality can represent.

1. The elevation e is greater than or equal to 15 meters.

2. A passenger's age a must be more than 4 years.

Write a word sentence for the inequality.

3. $b < \frac{1}{2}$

4. $m \geq 55$

On Your Own

5. MATHEMATICAL PRACTICE 6 **Compare** Explain the difference between $t \leq 4$ and $t < 4$.

6. GO DEEPER A children's roller coaster is limited to riders whose height is at least 30 inches and at most 48 inches. Write two inequalities that represent the height h of riders for the roller coaster.

7. THINK SMARTER Match the inequality with the word sentence it represents.

Inequality	Word sentence
$r > 10$	Walter sold more than 10 tickets.
$s \leq 10$	Fewer than 10 children are at the party.
$t \geq 10$	No more than 10 people can be seated at a table.
$w < 10$	At least 10 people need to sign up for the class.

Connect to Reading

Make Generalizations

The reading skill *make generalizations* can help you write inequalities to represent situations. A generalization is a statement that is true about a group of facts.

Sea otters spend almost their entire lives in the ocean. Their thick fur helps them to stay warm in cold water. Sea otters often float together in groups called *rafts*. A team of biologists weighed the female sea otters in one raft off the coast of Alaska. The chart shows their results.

Weights of Female Sea Otters

Otter Number	Weight (pounds)
1	50
2	61
3	62
4	69
5	71
6	54
7	68
8	62
9	58
10	51
11	61
12	66

Write two inequalities that represent generalizations about the sea otter weights.

First, list the weights in pounds in order from least to greatest.

50, 51, 54, ______, ______, ______, ______, ______,

______, ______, ______, ______

Next, write an inequality to describe the weights by using the least weight in the list. Let w represent the weights of the otters in pounds.

Think: The least weight is ______ pounds, so all of the weights are greater than or equal to 50 pounds. w ◯ 50

Now, write an inequality to describe the weights by using the greatest weight in the list.

Think: The greatest weight is ______ pounds, so all of the weights are ______ than or equal to ______ pounds. w ◯ 71

So, the inequalities ____________ and ____________ represent generalizations about the weights w in pounds of the otters.

8. THINKSMARTER Use the chart at the right to write two inequalities that represent generalizations about the number of sea otter pups per raft.

Sea Otter Pups per Raft

Raft Number	Number of Pups
1	7
2	10
3	15
4	23
5	6
6	16
7	20
8	6

____

____

Math on the Spot

Name ______________________

Write Inequalities

Common Core **COMMON CORE STANDARD—6.EE.B.8**
Reason about and solve one-variable equations and inequalities.

Write an inequality for the word sentence. Tell what type of numbers the variable in the inequality can represent.

1. The width w is greater than 4 centimeters.

   The inequality symbol for "is greater than" is $>$. $w > 4$, where w is the width in centimeters. w is a positive number.

2. The score s in a basketball game is greater than or equal to 10 points.

3. The mass m is less than 5 kilograms.

4. The height h is greater than 2.5 meters.

5. The temperature t is less than or equal to $^-3°$.

Write a word sentence for the inequality.

6. $k < {}^-7$

7. $z \geq 2\frac{3}{5}$

Problem Solving Real World

8. Tabby's mom says that she must read for at least 30 minutes each night. If m represents the number of minutes reading, what inequality can represent this situation?

9. Phillip has a $25 gift card to his favorite restaurant. He wants to use the gift card to buy lunch. If c represents the cost of his lunch, what inequality can describe all of the possible amounts of money, in dollars, that Phillip can spend on lunch?

10. WRITE *Math* Write a short paragraph explaining to a new student how to write an inequality.

Lesson Check (6.EE.B.8)

1. At the end of the first round in a quiz show, Jeremy has at most $^{-}20$ points. Write an inequality that means "at most $^{-}20$".

2. Describe the meaning of $y \geq 7.9$ in words.

Spiral Review (6.EE.A.2a, 6.EE.A.4, 6.EE.B.5, 6.EE.B.7)

3. Let y represent Jaron's age in years. If Dawn were 5 years older, she would be Jaron's age. Which expression represents Dawn's age?

4. Simplify the expression $7 \times 3g$.

5. What is the solution of the equation $8 = 8f$?

6. Which of the following are solutions of the inequality $k \leq {}^{-}2$?

   $k = 0, k = {}^{-}2, k = {}^{-}4, k = 1, k = {}^{-}1\frac{1}{2}$

FOR MORE PRACTICE GO TO THE Personal Math Trainer

Name ___________________________

Graph Inequalities

Essential Question How do you represent the solutions of an inequality on a number line?

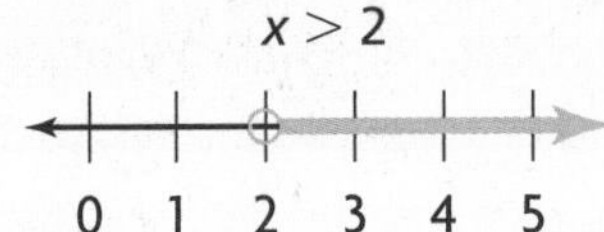

Expressions and Equations—6.EE.B.8

MATHEMATICAL PRACTICES
MP3, MP4, MP6

Inequalities can have an infinite number of solutions. The solutions of the inequality $x > 2$, for example, include all numbers greater than 2. You can use a number line to represent all of the solutions of an inequality.

The number line at right shows the solutions of the inequality $x > 2$.

$x > 2$

0 1 2 3 4 5

The empty circle at 2 shows that 2 is not a solution. The shading to the right of 2 shows that values greater than 2 are solutions.

Unlock the Problem

Forest fires are most likely to occur when the air temperature is greater than 60°F. The inequality $t > 60$ represents the temperatures t in degrees Fahrenheit for which forest fires are most likely. Graph the solutions of the inequality on a number line.

Show the solutions of $t > 60$ on a number line.

Think: I need to show all solutions that are greater than 60.

Draw an empty circle at ______ to show that 60 is not a solution.

Shade to the ____________ of ______ to show that values greater than 60 are solutions.

0 10 20 30 40 50 60 70 80 90 100

Try This! **Graph the solutions of the inequality $y < 5$.**

Draw an empty circle at ______ to show that 5 is not a solution.

Shade to the ____________ of ______ to show that values less than 5 are solutions.

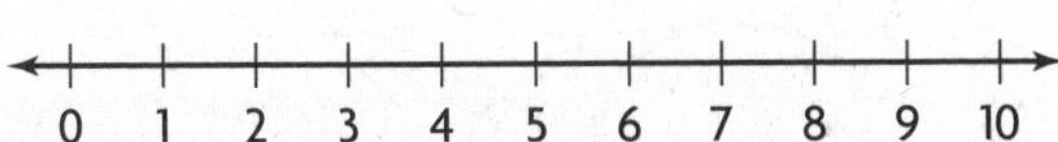

- MATHEMATICAL PRACTICE 6 **Make Connections** Explain why $y = 5$ is not a solution of the inequality $y < 5$.

____

You can also use a number line to show the solutions of an inequality that includes the symbol ≤ or ≥.

The number line at right shows the solutions of the inequality $x \geq 2$.

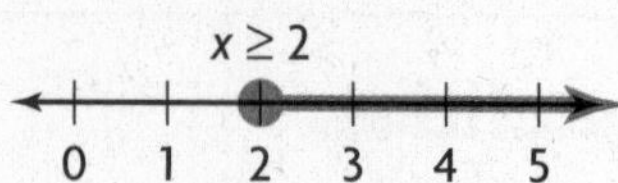

The filled-in circle at 2 shows that 2 is a solution. The shading to the right of 2 shows that values greater than 2 are also solutions.

Example 1 Graph the solutions of the inequality on a number line.

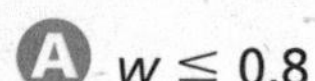

A $w \leq 0.8$

Draw a filled-in circle at _______ to show that 0.8 is a solution.

Shade to the _______________ of _______ to show that values less than 0.8 are also solutions.

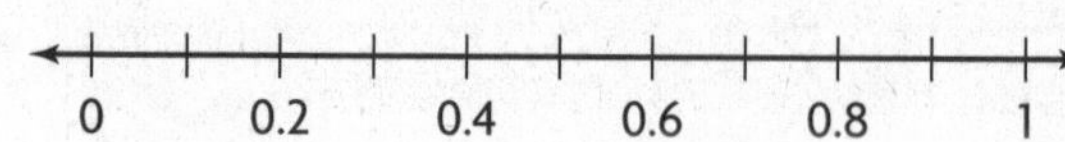

B $n \geq {}^{-}3$

Draw a filled-in circle at _______ to show that ⁻3 is a solution.

Shade to the _______________ of _______ to show that values greater than ⁻3 are also solutions.

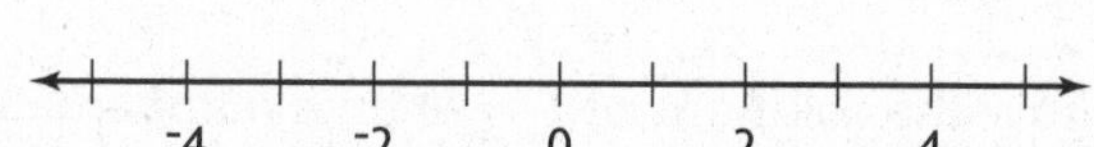

Example 2 Write the inequality represented by the graph.

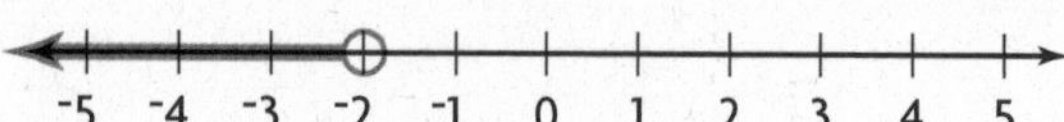

Use x (or another letter) for the variable in the inequality.

The _______________ circle at _______ shows that ⁻2 _______________ a solution.

The shading to the _______________ of _______ shows that values _______________ than ⁻2 are solutions.

So, the inequality represented by the graph is _______________.

MATHEMATICAL PRACTICES 6

Explain How do you know whether to shade to the right or to the left when graphing an inequality?

Name ________________

Share and Show

Graph the inequality.

1. $m < 15$

Draw an empty circle at ______ to show that 15 is not a solution. Shade to the ______ of ______ to show that values less than 15 are solutions.

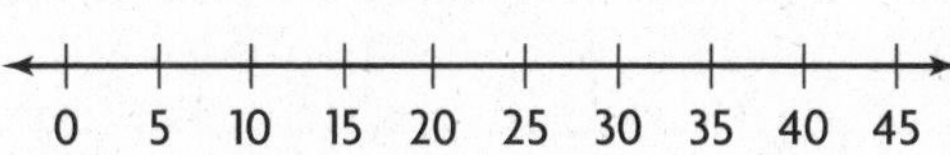

2. $c \geq {}^{-}1.5$

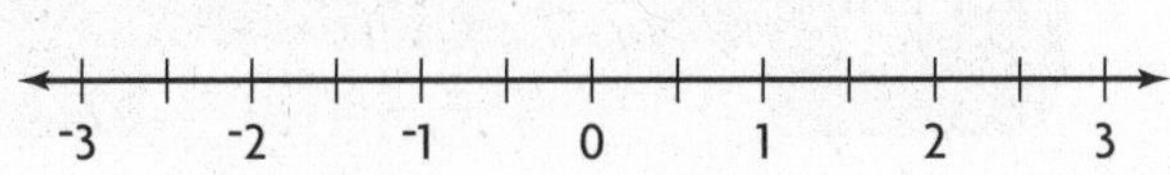

3. $b \leq \frac{5}{8}$

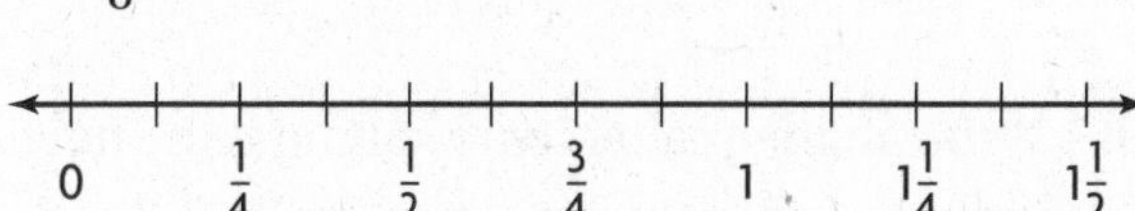

Math Talk MATHEMATICAL PRACTICES 3

Apply Why is it easier to graph the solutions of an inequality than it is to list them?

On Your Own

Practice: Copy and Solve **Graph the inequality.**

4. $a < \frac{2}{3}$

5. $x > {}^{-}4$

6. $k \geq 0.3$

7. $t \leq 6$

Write the inequality represented by the graph.

8.

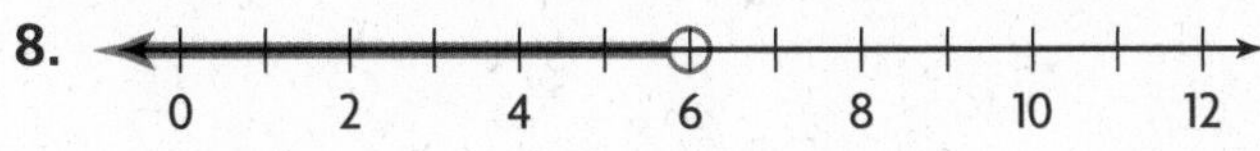

______

9.

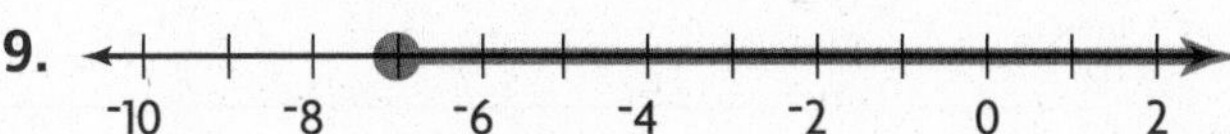

______

10. MATHEMATICAL PRACTICE 4 **Model Mathematics** The inequality $w \geq 60$ represents the wind speed w in miles per hour of a tornado. Graph the solutions of the inequality on the number line.

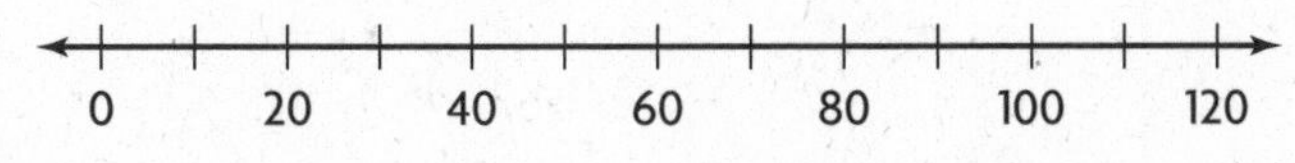

11. GO DEEPER Graph the solutions of the inequality $c < 12 \div 3$ on the number line.

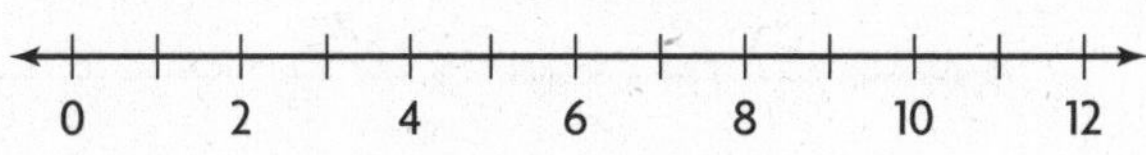

Problem Solving • Applications

The table shows the height requirements for rides at an amusement park. Use the table for 12–16.

Height Requirements	
Ride	Minimum height (in.)
Mighty Mountain	44
Race Track	42
River Rapids	38
Twirl & Whirl	48

12. Write an inequality representing t, the heights in inches of people who can go on Twirl & Whirl.

____

13. Graph your inequality from Exercise 12.

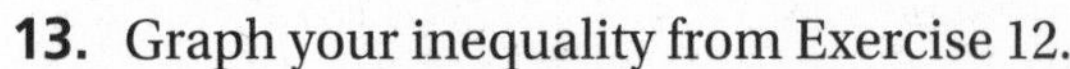

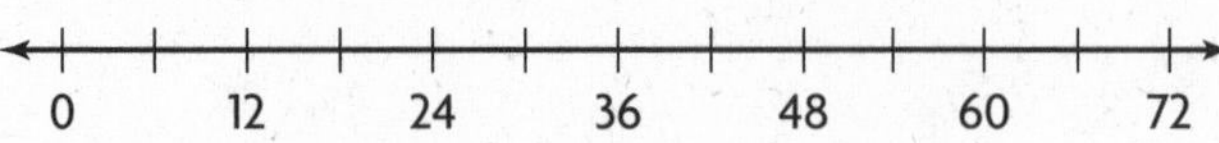

14. Write an inequality representing r, the heights in inches of people who can go on Race Track.

____

15. Graph your inequality from Exercise 14.

0 12 24 36 48 60 72

16. THINK SMARTER Write an inequality representing b, the heights in inches of people who can go on *both* River Rapids and Mighty Mountain. Explain how you determined your answer.

____

____

____

____

17. THINK SMARTER Alena graphed the inequality $c \leq 25$.

Darius said that 25 is not part of the solution of the inequality. Do you agree or disagree with Darius? Use numbers and words to support your answer.

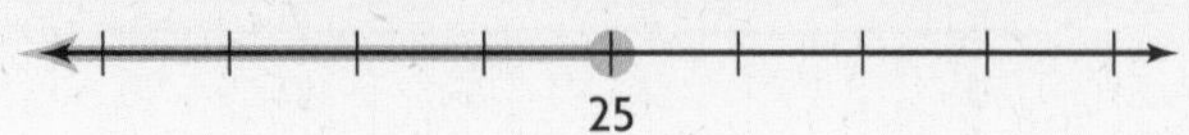

____

____

WRITE Math • Show Your Work

Name ______________________________

Graph Inequalities

Common Core **COMMON CORE STANDARD—6.EE.B.8**
Reason about and solve one-variable equations and inequalities.

Graph the inequality.

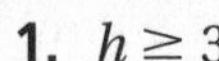

1. $h \geq 3$

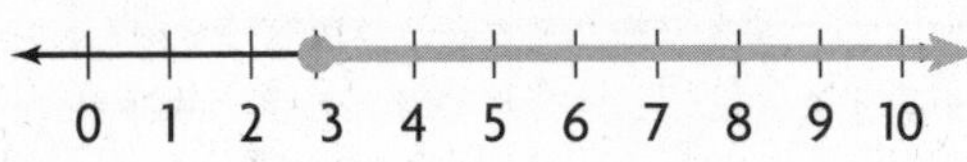

Draw a filled-in circle at <u>3</u> to show that 3 is a solution. Shade to the <u>right</u> of <u>3</u> to show that values greater than 3 are solutions.

2. $x < -\frac{4}{5}$

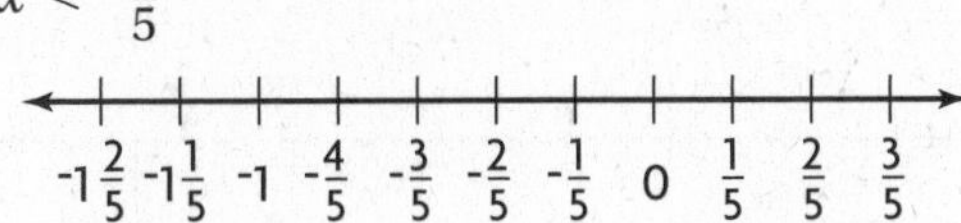

3. $y > {}^{-}2$

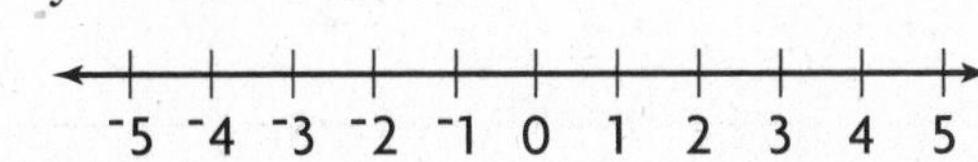

4. $n \geq 1\frac{1}{2}$

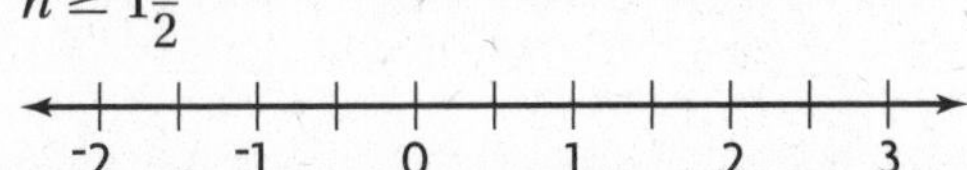

5. $c \leq {}^{-}0.4$

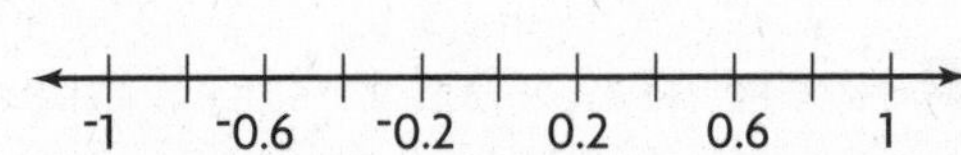

Write the inequality represented by the graph.

6.

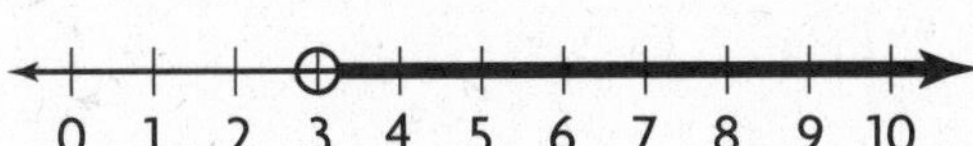

____

7.

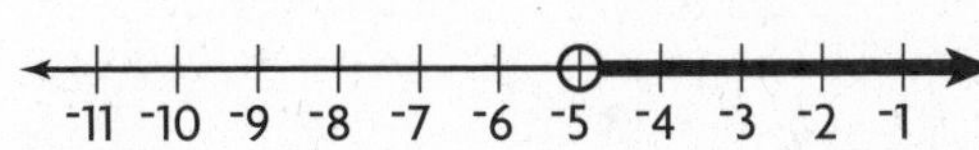

____

Problem Solving

8. The inequality $x \leq 2$ represents the elevation x of a certain object found at a dig site. Graph the solutions of the inequality on the number line.

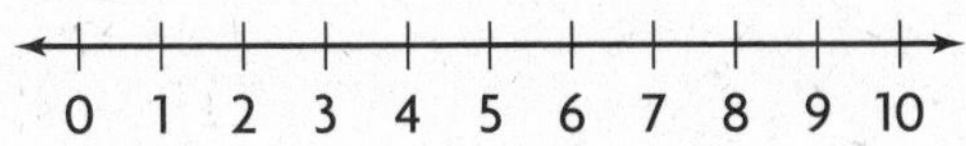

9. The inequality $x \geq 144$ represents the possible scores x needed to pass a certain test. Graph the solutions of the inequality on the number line.

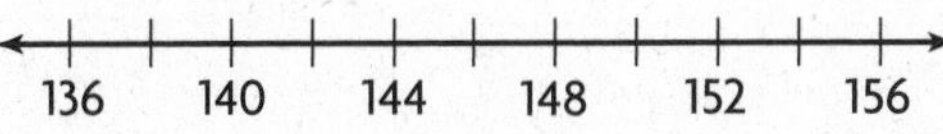

10. **WRITE** *Math* Write an inequality and graph the solutions on a number line.

____

____

Lesson Check (6.EE.B.8)

1. Write the inequality that is shown by the graph.

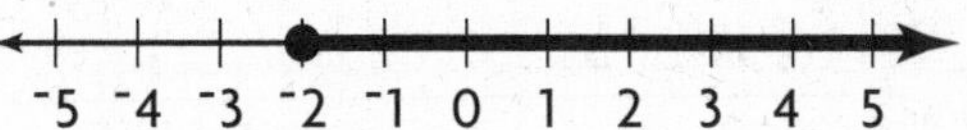

2. Describe the graph of $g < 0.6$.

Spiral Review (6.EE.A.2b, 6.EE.B.5, 6.EE.B.7, 6.EE.B.8)

3. Write an expression that shows the product of 5 and the difference of 12 and 9.

4. What is the solution of the equation $8.7 + n = 15.1$?

5. The equation $12x = 96$ gives the number of egg cartons x needed to package 96 eggs. Solve the equation to find the number of cartons needed.

6. The lowest price on an MP3 song is $0.35. Write an inequality that represents the cost c of an MP3 song.

FOR MORE PRACTICE GO TO THE **Personal Math Trainer**

Name ___

Chapter 8 Review/Test

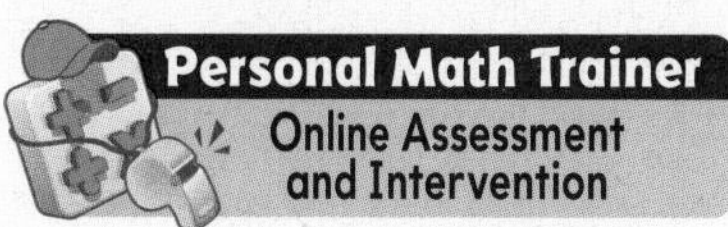

1. For numbers 1a–1c, choose Yes or No to indicate whether the given value of the variable is a solution of the equation.

1a. $\frac{2}{5}v = 10; v = 25$ ○ Yes ○ No

1b. $n + 5 = 15; n = 5$ ○ Yes ○ No

1c. $5z = 25; z = 5$ ○ Yes ○ No

2. The distance from third base to home plate is 88.9 feet. Romeo was 22.1 feet away from third base when he was tagged out. The equation $88.9 - t = 22.1$ can be used to determine how far he needed to run to get to home plate. Using substitution, the coach determines that Romeo needed

to run [66 / 66.8 / 111] feet to get to home plate.

3. There are 84 grapes in a bag. Four friends are sharing the grapes. Write an equation that can be used to find out how many grapes *g* each friend will get if each friend gets the same number of grapes.

___

4. Match each scenario with the equation that can be used to solve it.

Scenario	Equation
Jane's dog eats 3 pounds of food a week. How many weeks will a 24-pound bag last?	$3x = 39$
There are 39 students in the gym, and there are an equal number of students in each class. If three classes are in the gym, how many students are in each class?	$4x = 24$
There are 4 games at the carnival. Kevin played all the games in 24 minutes. How many minutes did he spend at each game if he spent an equal amount of time at each?	$3x = 24$

GO DIGITAL Assessment Options Chapter Test

5. GO DEEPER Frank's hockey team attempted 15 more goals than Spencer's team. Frank's team attempted 23 goals. Write and solve an equation that can be used to find how many goals Spencer's team attempted.

____

6. Ryan solved the equation $10 + y = 17$ by drawing a model. Use numbers and words to explain how Ryan's model can be used to find the solution.

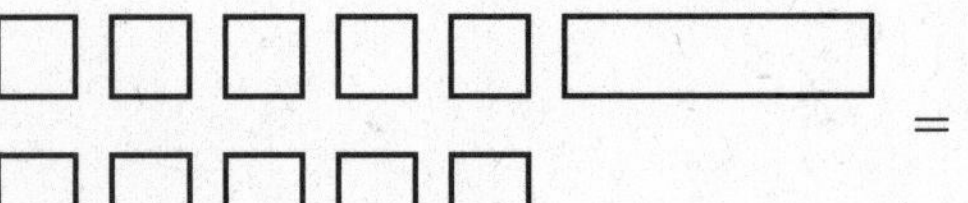 = 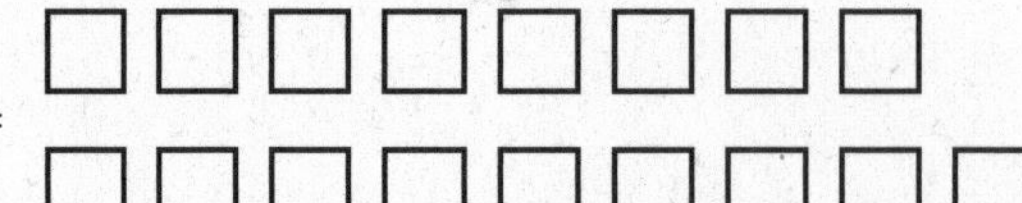

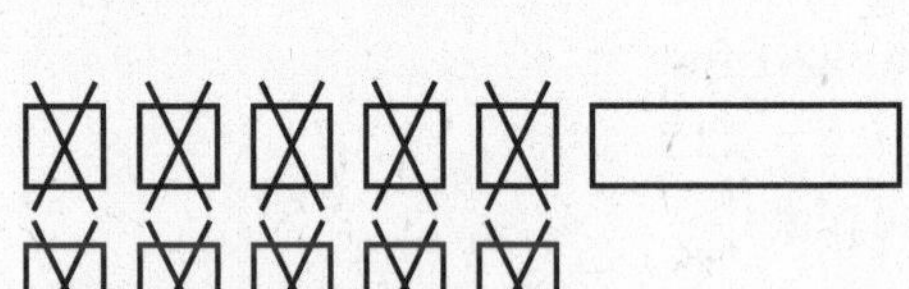 = 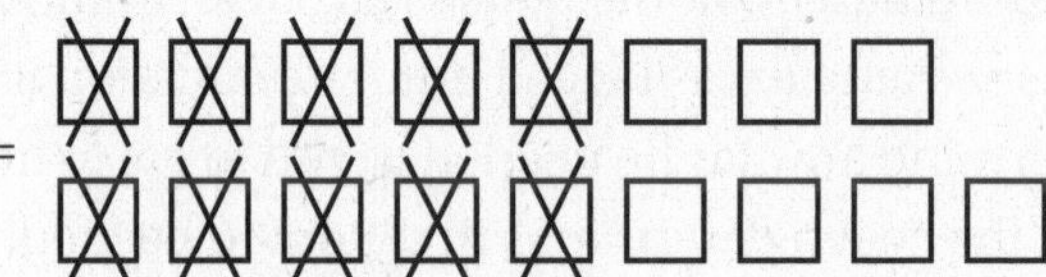

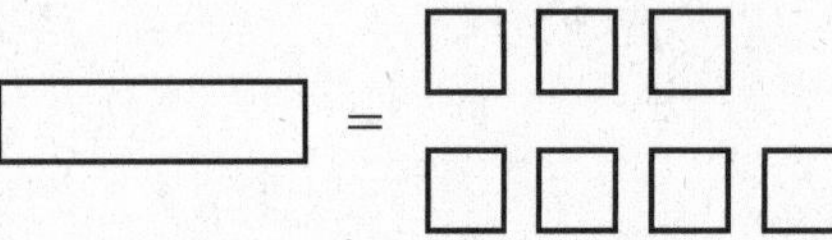

7. Gabriella and Max worked on their math project for a total of 6 hours. Max worked on the project for 2 hours by himself. Solve the equation $x + 2 = 6$ to find out how many hours Gabriella worked on the project.

____

8. Select the equations that have the solution $m = 17$. Mark all that apply.

(A) $3 + m = 21$

(B) $m - 2 = 15$

(C) $14 = m - 3$

(D) $2 = m - 15$

Name ________________________________

9. Describe how you could use algebra tiles to model the equation $4x = 20$.

10. For numbers 10a–10d, choose Yes or No to indicate whether the equation has the solution $x = 12$.

10a. $\frac{3}{4}x = 9$ ○ Yes ○ No

10b. $3x = 36$ ○ Yes ○ No

10c. $5x = 70$ ○ Yes ○ No

10d. $\frac{x}{3} = 4$ ○ Yes ○ No

11. Bryan rides the bus to and from work on the days he works at the library. In one month, he rode the bus 24 times. Solve the equation $2x = 24$ to find the number of days Bryan worked at the library. Use a model.

12. Betty needs $\frac{3}{4}$ of a yard of fabric to make a skirt. She bought 9 yards of fabric.

Part A

Write and solve an equation to find how many skirts x she can make from 9 yards of fabric.

Part B

Explain how you determined which operation was needed to write the equation.

13. Karen is working on her math homework. She solves the equation $\frac{b}{8} = 56$ and says that the solution is $b = 7$. Do you agree or disagree with Karen? Use words and numbers to support your answer. If her answer is incorrect, find the correct answer.

Name ______________________________

14. There are 70 historical fiction books in the school library. Historical fiction books make up $\frac{1}{10}$ of the library's collection. The equation $\frac{1}{10}b = 70$ can be used to find out how many books the library has. Solve the equation to find the total number of books in the library's collection. Use numbers and words to explain how to solve $\frac{1}{10}b = 70$.

15. Andy drove 33 miles on Monday morning. This was $\frac{3}{7}$ of the total number of miles he drove on Monday. Solve the equation $\frac{3}{7}m = 33$ to find the total number of miles Andy drove on Monday.

Personal Math Trainer

16. THINKSMARTER+ The maximum number of players allowed on a lacrosse team is 23. The inequality $t \leq 23$ represents the total number of players t allowed on the team.

Two possible solutions for the inequality are [23 / 25 / 27] and [26. / 24. / 22.]

17. Mr. Charles needs to have at least 10 students sign up for homework help in order to use the computer lab. The inequality $h \geq 10$ represents the number of students h who must sign up. Select possible solutions of the inequality. Mark all that apply.

Ⓐ 7
Ⓑ 8
Ⓒ 9
Ⓓ 10
Ⓔ 11
Ⓕ 12

18. The maximum capacity of the school auditorium is 420 people. Write an inequality for the situation. Tell what type of numbers the variable in the inequality can represent.

____

19. Match the inequality to the word sentence it represents.

$w < 70$ •	• The temperature did not drop below 70 degrees.
$x \leq 70$ •	• Dane saved more than \$70.
$y > 70$ •	• Fewer than 70 people attended the game.
$z \geq 70$ •	• No more than 70 people can participate.

20. Cydney graphed the inequality $d \leq 14$.

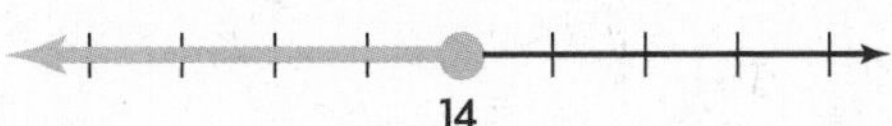

Part A

Dylan said that 14 is not a solution of the inequality. Do you agree or disagree with Dylan? Use numbers and words to support your answer.

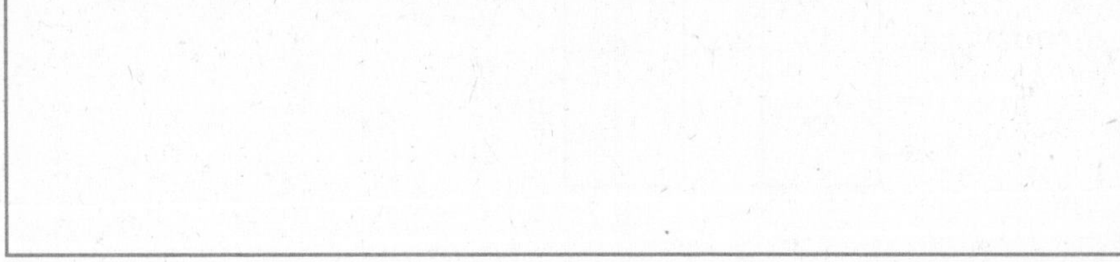

Part B

Suppose Cydney's graph had an empty circle at 14. Write the inequality represented by this graph.

____

Algebra: Relationships Between Variables

Show What You Know

Check your understanding of important skills.

Name ______________________________

▶ **Number Patterns** **Write a rule to explain the pattern. Use the rule to find the missing numbers.** (4.OA.C.5)

1. 127, 123, 119, ■, 111, ■

____

2. 5,832, ■, 648, 216, 72, ■, 8

____

▶ **Identify Points on a Coordinate Grid** **Use the ordered pair to name the point on the grid.** (5.G.A.1)

3. (4, 6) ____________

4. (8, 4) ____________

5. (2, 8) ____________

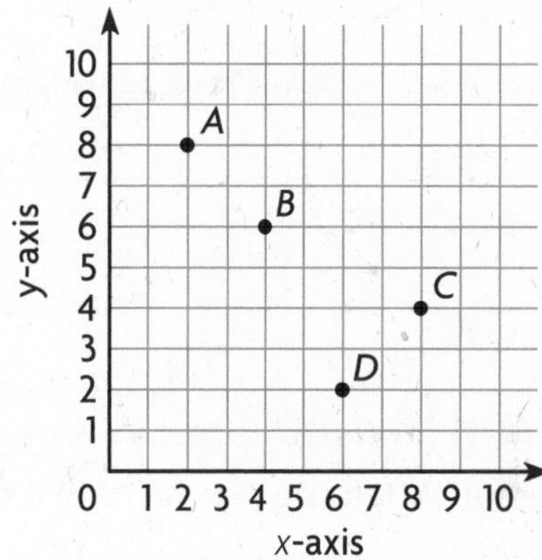

▶ **Evaluate Expressions** **Evaluate the expression.** (5.OA.A.1)

6. $18 + 4 - 7$ ____________

7. $59 - 20 + 5$ ____________

8. $(40 - 15) + 30$ ____________

9. $77 - (59 - 18)$ ____________

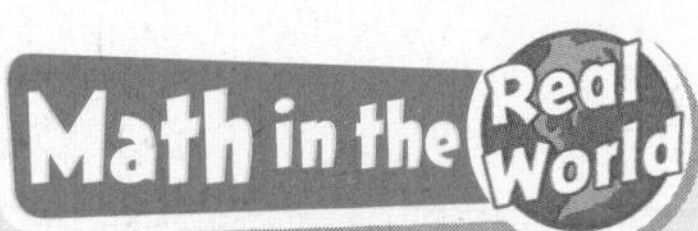

Terrell plotted points on the coordinate plane as shown. He noticed that the points lie on a straight line. Write an equation that shows the relationship between the *x*- and *y*-coordinate of each point Terrell plotted. Then use the equation to find the *y*-coordinate of a point on the line with an *x*-coordinate of 20.

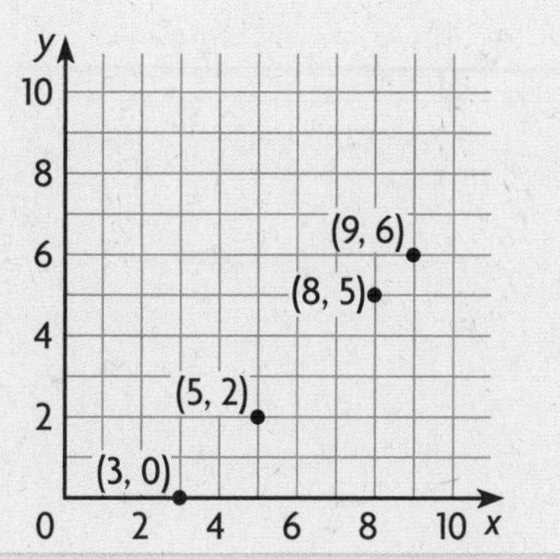

Vocabulary Builder

▶ Visualize It

Use the review words to complete the bubble map.

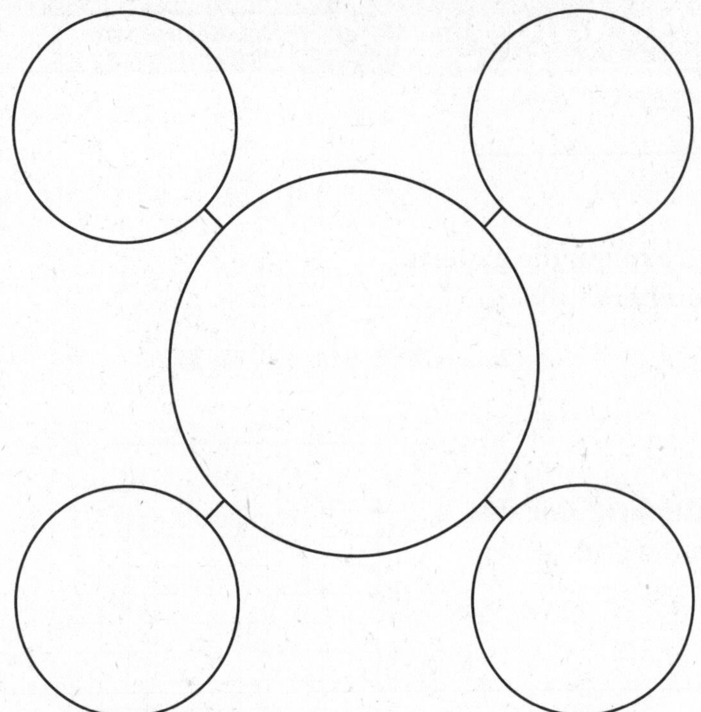

Review Words

- coordinate plane
- ordered pair
- quadrants
- x-coordinate
- y-coordinate

Preview Words

- dependent variable
- independent variable
- linear equation

▶ Understand Vocabulary

Draw a line to match the preview word with its definition.

Preview Words	Definitions
1. dependent variable •	• has a value that determines the value of another quantity
2. independent variable •	• names the point where the axes in the coordinate plane intersect
3. linear equation •	• has a value that depends on the value of another quantity
	• forms a straight line when graphed

- Interactive Student Edition
- Multimedia eGlossary

Chapter 9 Vocabulary

coordinate plane

plano cartesiano

17

dependent variable

variable dependiente

21

independent variable

variable independiente

42

linear equation

ecuación lineal

53

ordered pair

par ordenado

70

quadrants

cuadrantes

82

***x*-coordinate**

coordenada *x*

109

***y*-coordinate**

coordenada *y*

111

A variable whose value depends on the value of another quantity

A plane formed by a horizontal line called the *x*-axis and a vertical line called the *y*-axis

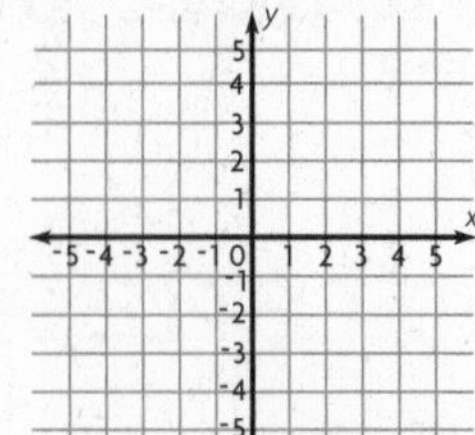

An equation that, when graphed, forms a straight line

Example:

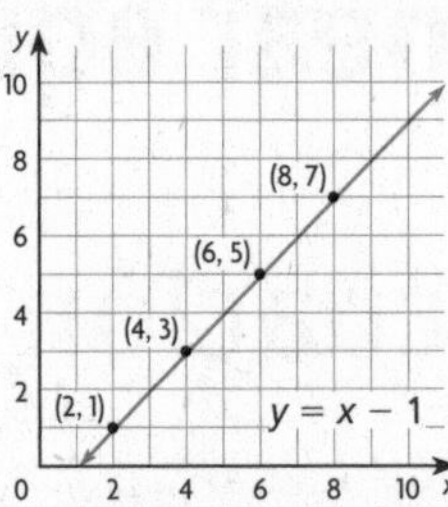

A variable whose value determines the value of another quantity

The four regions of the coordinate plane separated by the *x*- and *y*-axes

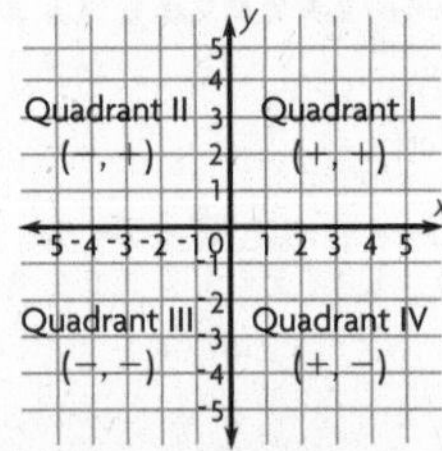

A pair of numbers used to locate a point on a grid.

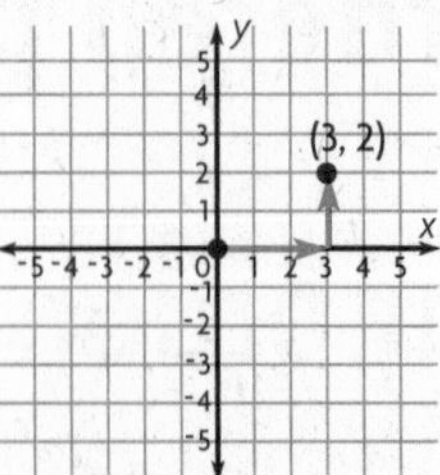

The second number in an ordered pair; tells the distance to move up or down from (0,0)

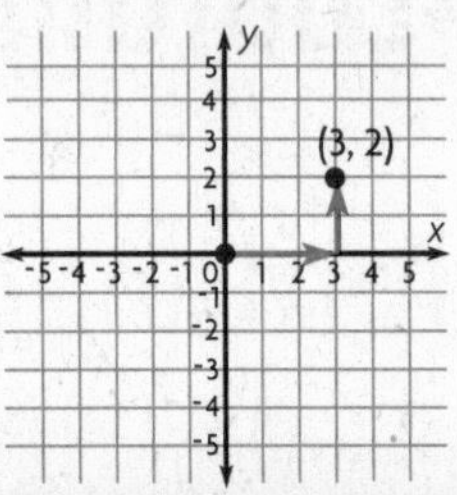

The first number in an ordered pair; tells the distance to move right or left from (0,0)

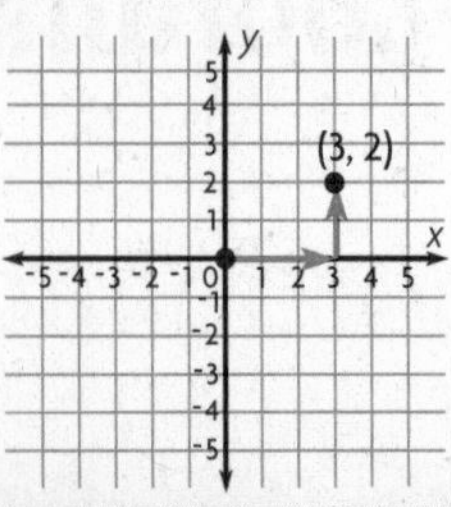

Guess the Word

Word Box
coordinate plane
dependent variable
independent variable
linear equation
ordered pair
quadrants
x-coordinate
y-coordinate

For 3 to 4 players

Materials

- timer

How to Play

1. Take turns to play.
2. Choose a math term, but do not say it aloud.
3. Set the timer for 1 minute.
4. Give a one-word clue about your term. Give each player one chance to guess the term.
5. If nobody guesses correctly, repeat Step 4 with a different clue. Repeat until a player guesses the term or time runs out.
6. The player who guesses the term gets 1 point. If he or she can use the word in a sentence, they get 1 more point. Then that player gets a turn.
7. The first player to score 10 points wins.

The Write Way

Reflect

Choose one idea. Write about it.

- Write and solve a word problem that includes a dependent variable and an independent variable.
- Define *linear equation* in your own words.
- Tell how to determine which of the following ordered pairs makes this linear equation true. $y = x \div 3$

  (2, 6) **(6, 2)** **(27, 9)** **(21, 6)** **(9, 3)**
- Write a note to a friend about something you learned in Chapter 9.

Name ______________________________

Independent and Dependent Variables

Essential Question How can you write an equation to represent the relationship between an independent variable and a dependent variable?

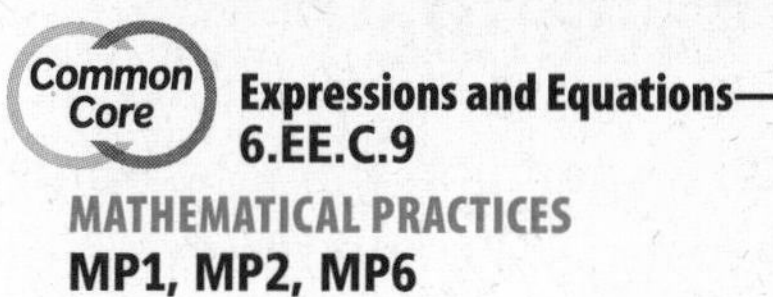

Common Core
Expressions and Equations—6.EE.C.9
MATHEMATICAL PRACTICES
MP1, MP2, MP6

You can use an equation with two variables to represent a relationship between two quantities. One variable is called the *independent variable,* and the other is called the *dependent variable.* The value of the **independent variable** determines the value of the **dependent variable**.

Unlock the Problem

Jeri burns 5.8 calories for every minute she jogs. Identify the independent and dependent variables in this situation. Then write an equation to represent the relationship between the number of minutes Jeri jogs and the total number of calories she burns.

- Why do you need to use a variable?

  ____

- How many variables are needed to write the equation for this problem?

  ____

Identify the independent and dependent variables. Then use the variables to write an equation.

Let c represent the total number of __________ Jeri burns.

Let m represent the number of __________ Jeri jogs.

Think: The total number of calories Jeri burns **depends** on the number of minutes she jogs.

_____ is the dependent variable.

_____ is the independent variable.

Write an equation to represent the situation.

Think: The total calories burned | is equal to | 5.8 | times | the number of minutes jogged.

_____ = 5.8 × _____

So, the equation __________ represents the number of calories c Jeri burns if she jogs m minutes, where _____ is the dependent variable and _____ is the independent variable.

Math Talk MATHEMATICAL PRACTICES 6

Explain how you know that the value of c is dependent on the value of m.

Example

Lorelei is spending the afternoon bowling with her friends. Each game she plays costs \$3.25, and there is a one-time shoe-rental fee of \$2.50.

A Identify the independent and dependent variables in this situation. Then write an equation to represent the relationship between the number of games and the total cost.

Think: The total cost in dollars c depends on the number of games g Lorelei plays.

______ is the dependent variable.

______ is the independent variable.

ERROR Alert

Note that the fee for the shoes, \$2.50, is a one-time fee, and therefore is not multiplied by the number of games.

Think:

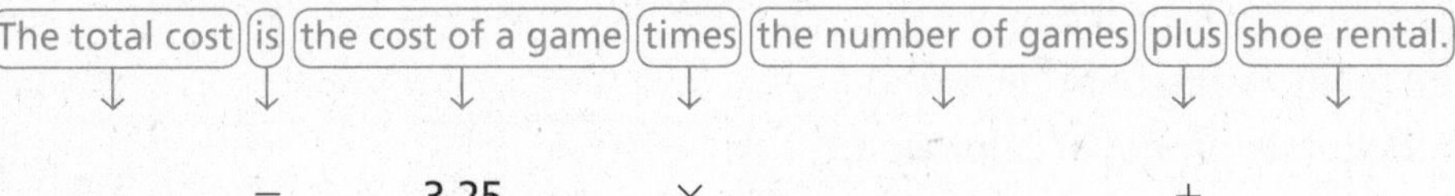

______ = 3.25 × ______ + ______

So, the equation ______________ represents the total cost in dollars c that Lorelei spends if she bowls g games, where ______ is the dependent variable and ______ is the independent variable.

B Use your equation to find the total cost for Lorelei to play 3 games.

Think: Find the value of c when $g = 3$.

Write the equation.	$c = 3.25g + 2.50$
Substitute 3 for g.	$c = 3.25($______$) + 2.50$
Follow the order of operations to solve for c.	$b =$ ______ $+ 2.50 =$ __________

So, it will cost Lorelei __________ to play 3 games and rent shoes.

1. THINK SMARTER **What if** there were no fee for shoe rentals? How would the equation be different?

____

2. MATHEMATICAL PRACTICE 1 **Evaluate Reasonableness** How can you use estimation to check that your answer is reasonable?

____

____

____

Name ______________________________

Share and Show

Identify the independent and dependent variables. Then write an equation to represent the relationship between them.

1. An online store lets customers have their name printed on any item they buy. The total cost c in dollars is the price of the item p in dollars plus $3.99 for the name.

   The __________ depends on the ______________.

   dependent variable: _____

   independent variable: _____

   equation: _____ = __________

2. A raft travels downriver at a rate of 6 miles per hour. The total distance d in miles that the raft travels is equal to the rate times the number of hours h.

   dependent variable: _____

   independent variable: _____

   equation: __________

3. Apples are on sale for $1.99 a pound. Sheila buys p pounds of apples for a total cost of c dollars.

   dependent variable: _____

   independent variable: _____

   equation: __________

Math Talk MATHEMATICAL PRACTICES 1

Analyze Relationships How do you know which variable in a relationship is dependent and which is independent?

On Your Own

Identify the independent and dependent variables. Then write an equation to represent the relationship between them.

4. Sean can make 8 paper birds in an hour. The total number of birds b is equal to the number of birds he makes per hour times the number of hours h.

   dependent variable: _____

   independent variable: _____

   equation: __________

5. Billy has $25. His father is going to give him more money. The total amount t Billy will have is equal to the amount m his father gives him plus the $25 Billy already has.

   dependent variable: _____

   independent variable: _____

   equation: __________

6. MATHEMATICAL PRACTICE 2 **Connect Symbols and Words** Describe a situation that can be represented by the equation $c = 12b$.

   ____

   ____

   ____

7. GO DEEPER Belinda pays $4.25 for each glass she buys. The total cost c is equal to the price per glass times the number of glasses n plus $9.95 for shipping and handling. Write an equation and use it to find how much it will cost Belinda to buy 12 glasses.

   ____

Unlock the Problem

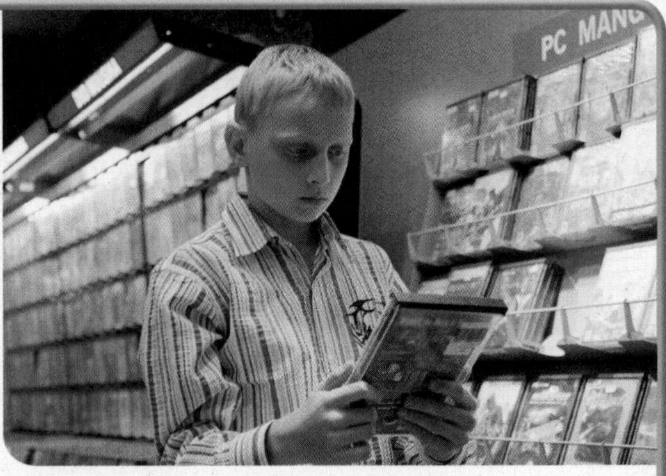

8. Benji decides to save $15 per week to buy a computer program. Write an equation that models the total amount t in dollars Benji will have saved in w weeks.

a. What does the variable t represent?

____

b. Which is the dependent variable? Which is the independent variable? How do you know?

____

c. How can you find the total amount saved in w weeks?

____

d. Write an equation for the total amount that Benji will have saved.

____

9. GO DEEPER Coach Diaz is buying hats for the baseball team. The total cost c is equal to the number of hats n that he buys times the sum of the price per hat h and a $2 charge per hat to have the team name printed on it. Write an equation that can be used to find the cost of the hats.

____

10. THINK SMARTER A steel cable that is $\frac{1}{2}$ inch in diameter weighs 0.42 pound per foot. The total weight in pounds w is equal to 0.42 times of the number of feet f of steel cable. Choose the letter or equation that makes each sentence true.

The independent variable is [f. / w.]

The dependent variable is [f. / w.]

The equation that represents the relationship between the variables is [$w = 0.42f$. / $f = 0.42w$.]

Name ______________________________

Independent and Dependent Variables

Common Core **COMMON CORE STANDARD—6.EE.C.9**
Represent and analyze quantitative relationships between dependent and independent variables.

Identify the independent and dependent variables. Then write an equation to represent the relationship between them.

1. Sandra has a coupon to save \$3 off her next purchase at a restaurant. The cost of her meal *c* will be the price of the food *p* that she orders, minus \$3.

   The ___cost of her meal___ depends on the ___price of her food___.

   dependent variable: ___c___

   independent variable: ___p___

   equation: ___c___ = ___$p - 3$___

2. An online clothing store charges \$6 for shipping, no matter the price of the items. The total cost *c* in dollars is the price of the items ordered *p* plus \$6 for shipping.

   dependent variable: ______

   independent variable: ______

   equation: ______ = ______________

3. Melinda is making necklaces. She uses 12 beads for each necklace. The total number of beads *b* depends on the number of necklaces *n*.

   dependent variable: ______

   independent variable: ______

   equation: ______ = ______________

Problem Solving Real World

4. Maria earns \$45 for every lawn that she mows. Her earnings *e* in dollars depend on the number of lawns *n* that she mows. Write an equation that represents this situation.

   ____

5. Martin sells cars. He earns \$100 per day, plus any commission on his sales. His daily salary *s* in dollars depends on the amount of commission *c*. Write an equation to represent his daily salary.

   ____

6. WRITE *Math* Write a situation in which one unknown is dependent on another unknown. Write an equation for your situation and identify the dependent and independent variables.

   ____

   ____

   ____

Lesson Check (6.EE.C.9)

1. There are 12 boys in a math class. The total number of students s depends on the number of girls in the class g. Write an equation that represents this situation.

2. A store received a shipment of soup cans. The clerk put an equal number of cans on each of 4 shelves. Write an equation to represent the relationship between the total number of cans t and the number of cans on each shelf n.

Spiral Review (6.EE.A.2a, 6.EE.B.7, 6.EE.B.8)

3. The formula $F = \frac{9}{5}C + 32$ gives the Fahrenheit temperature for a Celsius temperature of C degrees. Gwen measured a Celsius temperature of 35 degrees. What is this temperature in degrees Fahrenheit?

4. Write an equation to represent this sentence.

   The difference of a number n and 1.8 is 2.

5. Drew drank 4 cups of orange juice. This is $\frac{2}{5}$ of the total amount of juice that was in the container. Solve $\frac{2}{5}x = 4$ to find the number of cups x of juice in the container. How much juice was in the container?

6. Graph $x \leq {}^{-}4.5$ on a number line.

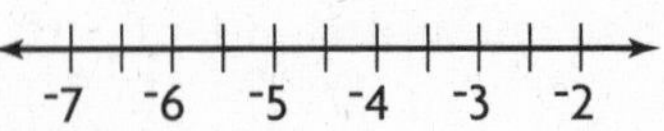

Name ______________________________

Equations and Tables

Essential Question How can you translate between equations and tables?

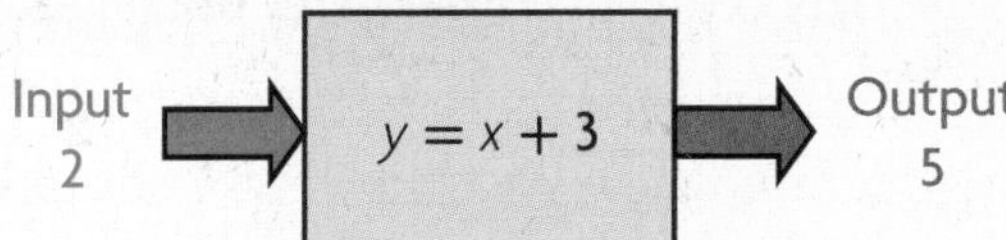

Expressions and Equations—6.EE.C.9

MATHEMATICAL PRACTICES
MP3, MP4, MP5

When an equation describes the relationship between two quantities, the variable x often represents the independent variable, and y often represents the dependent variable.

Input 2 → $y = x + 3$ → Output 5

Input 4 → $y = x + 3$ → Output 7

A value of the independent variable is called the *input* value, and a value of the dependent variable is called the *output* value.

Unlock the Problem — Real World

A skating rink charges $3.00 for each hour of skating, plus $1.75 to rent skates. Write an equation for the relationship that gives the total cost y in dollars for skating x hours. Then make a table that shows the cost of skating for 1, 2, 3, and 4 hours.

Write an equation for the relationship, and use the equation to make a table.

- What is the independent variable? What is the dependent variable?

  ____

  ____

STEP 1 Write an equation.

Think:

The total cost	is	________.	for each	hour	plus	________.
↓	↓	↓	↓	↓	↓	↓
______	=	3	·	______	+	1.75

So, the equation for the relationship is ________________.

STEP 2 Make a table.

Input	Rule	Output
Time (hr), x	**$3x + 1.75$**	**Cost ($), y**
1	$3 \cdot 1 + 1.75$	4.75
2		
3		
4		

Replace x with each input value, and then evaluate to find each output value.

MATHEMATICAL PRACTICES 5

Communicate Explain how you could use the equation to find the total cost of skating for 6 hours.

Example

Jamal downloads songs on his MP3 player. The table shows how the time it takes him to download a song depends on the song's file size. Write an equation for the relationship shown in the table. Then use the equation to find how many seconds it takes Jamal to download a song with a file size of 7 megabytes (MB).

Download Times	
File Size (MB), x	Time (s), y
4	48
5	60
6	72
7	?
8	96

STEP 1 Write an equation.

Look for a pattern between the file sizes and the download times.

File Size (MB), x	4	5	6	8
Time (s), y	48	60	72	96
	↑ $12 \cdot 4$	↑ $12 \cdot 5$	↑ $12 \cdot$ ______	↑ $12 \cdot$ ______

Think: You can find each download time by multiplying the file size by ________.

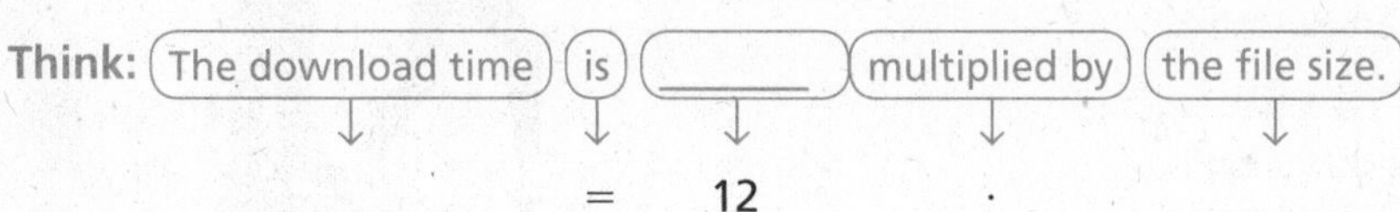

______ = 12 · ______

So, the equation for the relationship is ____________.

STEP 2 Use the equation to find the download time for a file size of 7 megabytes.

Write the equation. $y = 12x$

Replace x with 7. $y = 12 \cdot$ ______

Solve for y. $y =$ ______

So, it takes Jamal ______ seconds to download a 7-megabyte song.

1. Explain how you can check that your equation for the relationship is correct.

____

____

2. MATHEMATICAL PRACTICE 3 **Compare Representations** Describe a situation in which it would be more useful to represent a relationship between two quantities with an equation than with a table of values.

____

____

Name ___________________________________

Share and Show

MATH BOARD

Use the equation to complete the table.

1. $y = x + 3$

Input	Rule	Output
x	$x + 3$	y
6	6 + 3	
8	8 + 3	
10		

2. $y = 2x + 1$

Input	Output
x	y
4	
7	
10	

On Your Own

Write an equation for the relationship shown in the table. Then find the unknown value in the table.

3.

x	8	9	10	11
y	16	18	?	22

____

4.

x	10	20	30	40
y	5	10	15	?

____

5. GO DEEPER The table shows the current cost of buying apps for a cell phone. Next month, the price of each app will double. Write an equation you can use to find the total cost y of buying x apps next month.

____

Cell Phone Apps	
Number of apps, x	Total cost ($), y
3	9
4	12
5	15

6. THINK SMARTER A beach resort charges $1.50 per hour plus $4.50 to rent a bicycle. The equation $c = 1.50x + 4.50$ gives the total cost c of renting a bicycle for x hours. Use numbers and words to explain how to find the cost c of renting a bicycle for 6 hours.

____

____

____

Input	Output
Time (hr), x	Cost ($), c
1	6.00
2	7.50
3	9.00
4	10.50

Connect to Reading

Cause and Effect

The reading skill *cause and effect* can help you understand how a change in one variable may cause a change in another variable.

In karate, a person's skill level is often shown by the color of his or her belt. At Sara's karate school, students must pass a test to move from one belt level to the next. Each test costs \$23. Sara hopes to move up 3 belt levels this year. How will this affect her karate expenses?

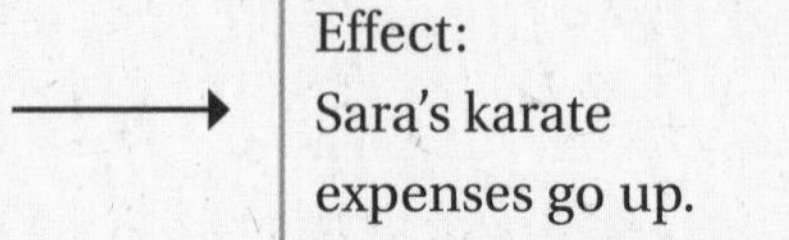

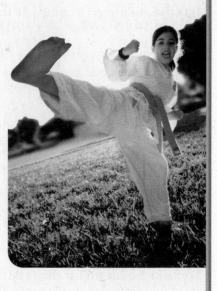

Cause: Sara moves to higher belt levels.	→	Effect: Sara's karate expenses go up.

Write an equation to show the relationship between cause and effect. Then use the equation to solve the problem.

Let x represent the number of belt levels Sara moves up, and let y represent the increase in dollars in her karate expenses.

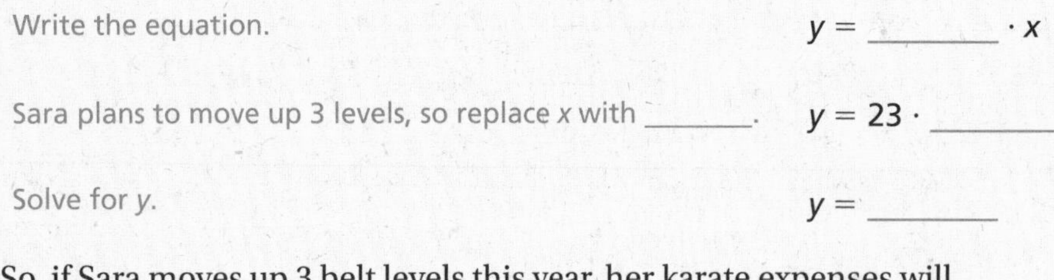

Write the equation. $y =$ ______ $\cdot x$

Sara plans to move up 3 levels, so replace x with ______. $y = 23 \cdot$ ______

Solve for y. $y =$ ______

So, if Sara moves up 3 belt levels this year, her karate expenses will increase by \$______.

Write an equation to show the relationship between cause and effect. Then use the equation to solve the problem.

7. THINK SMARTER Classes at Tony's karate school cost \$29.50 per month. This year he plans to take 2 more months of classes than he did last year. How will this affect Tony's karate expenses?

8. MATHEMATICAL PRACTICE 4 **Write an Equation** A sporting goods store regularly sells karate uniforms for \$35.90 each. The store is putting karate uniforms on sale for 10% off. How will this affect the price of a karate uniform?

Name ______________________________

Equations and Tables

COMMON CORE STANDARD—6.EE.C.9
Represent and analyze quantitative relationships between dependent and independent variables.

Use the equation to complete the table.

1. $y = 6x$

Input	Output
x	y
2	12
5	30
8	48

2. $y = x - 7$

Input	Output
x	y
10	
15	
20	

3. $y = 3x + 4$

Input	Output
x	y
3	
4	
5	

Write an equation for the relationship shown in the table. Then find the unknown value in the table.

4.

x	2	3	4	5
y	16	?	32	40

____

5.

x	18	20	22	24
y	9	10	?	12

____

Problem Solving Real World

6. Tickets to a play cost $11 each. There is also a service charge of $4 per order. Write an equation for the relationship that gives the total cost *y* in dollars for an order of *x* tickets.

____

7. Write an equation for the relationship shown in the table. Then use the equation to find the estimated number of shrimp in a 5-pound bag.

Weight of bag (pounds), x	1	2	3	4
Estimated number of shrimp, y	24	48	72	96

____

8. WRITE ▶Math Write a word problem that can be represented by a table and equation. Solve your problem and include the table and equation.

____

____

Lesson Check (6.EE.C.9)

1. Write an equation that represents the relationship shown in the table.

x	8	10	12	14
y	4	6	8	10

2. There is a one-time fee of $27 to join a gym. The monthly cost of using the gym is $18. Write an equation for the relationship that gives the total cost y in dollars of joining the gym and using it for x months.

Spiral Review (6.EE.B.5, 6.EE.B.6, 6.EE.B.7, 6.EE.C.9)

3. Mindy wants to buy several books that each cost $10. She has a coupon for $6 off her total cost. Write an expression to represent her total cost in dollars for b books.

4. When a coupon of $1.25 off is used, the cost of a taco meal is $4.85. The equation $p - 1.25 = 4.85$ can be used to find the regular price p in dollars of a taco meal. How much does a regular taco meal cost?

5. Which of the following are solutions to the inequality $n > {}^{-}7$?

   $n = {}^{-}7, n = {}^{-}6.9, n = {}^{-}7.2, n = {}^{-}6\frac{1}{2}$

6. Marcus sold brownies at a bake sale. He sold d dollars worth of brownies. He spent $5.50 on materials, so his total profit p in dollars can be found by subtracting $5.50 from his earnings. Write an equation that represents this situation.

FOR MORE PRACTICE GO TO THE **Personal Math Trainer**

Name ______________________________

Problem Solving • Analyze Relationships

Essential Question How can you use the strategy *find a pattern* to solve problems involving relationships between quantities?

Common Core **Expressions and Equations—6.EE.C.9**

MATHEMATICAL PRACTICES
MP1, MP2, MP7, MP8

Unlock the Problem

The table shows the amount of water pumped through a fire hose over time. If the pattern in the table continues, how long will it take a firefighter to spray 3,000 gallons of water on a fire using this hose?

Fire Hose Flow Rate

Time (min)	1	2	3	4
Amount of water (gal)	150	300	450	600

Use the graphic organizer to help you solve the problem.

Read the Problem

What do I need to find?

I need to find ______________________________

______________________________.

What information do I need to use?

I need to use the relationship between ____________ and ______________________.

How will I use the information?

I will find a ____________ in the table and write an ____________________.

Solve the Problem

Use the table above to find the relationship between the time and the amount of water.

Think: Let t represent the time in minutes, and w represent the amount of water in gallons. The amount of water in gallons is ______ multiplied by the time in minutes.

______ = 150 · ______

Use the equation to find how long it will take to spray 3,000 gallons.

Write the equation.	$w = 150t$
Substitute 3,000 for w.	$3{,}000 = 150t$
Solve for t. Divide both sides by 150.	$\frac{3{,}000}{\square} = \frac{150t}{\square}$
	______ $= t$

So, it will take ______ minutes to spray 3,000 gallons of water.

MATHEMATICAL PRACTICES 1

Evaluate How can you check that your answer is correct?

Try Another Problem

Dairy cows provide 90% of the world's milk supply. The table shows the amount of milk produced by a cow over time. If the pattern in the table continues, how much milk can a farmer get from a cow in 1 year (365 days)?

Cow Milk Production				
Time (days), x	2	7	10	30
Amount of milk (L), y	50	175	250	750

Read the Problem

What do I need to find?	What information do I need to use?	How will I use the information?

Solve the Problem

MATHEMATICAL PRACTICES 2

Reasoning Explain how you wrote an equation to represent the pattern in the table.

So, in 365 days, the farmer can get ___________ liters of milk from the cow.

- Explain how you could find the number of days it would take the cow to produce 500 liters of milk.

____

____

____

Name ______________________________

Share and Show 

1. A soccer coach is ordering shirts for the players. The table shows the total cost based on the number of shirts ordered. How much will it cost the coach to order 18 shirts?

First, find a pattern and write an equation.

The cost is ______ multiplied by __________________.

______ = ______ · ______

Next, use the equation to find the cost of 18 shirts.

So, the cost of 18 shirts is ______.

2. THINKSMARTER **What if** the coach spent $375 to purchase a number of shirts? Could you use the same equation to find how many shirts the coach bought? Explain.

____

____

3. GO DEEPER The table shows the number of miles the Carter family drove over time. If the pattern continues, will the Carter family have driven more than 400 miles in 8 hours? Explain.

____

____

____

4. MATHEMATICAL PRACTICE 7 **Look for a Pattern** The Carter family drove a total of 564 miles. Describe how to use the pattern in the table to find the number of hours they spent driving.

____

____

____

Unlock the Problem

- ✓ Find a pattern in the table.
- ✓ Write an equation to represent the pattern.
- ✓ Check your answer.

Soccer Shirts

Number of Shirts, n	2	3	5	6
Cost ($), c	30	45	75	90

Carter Family Trip

Time (hr), x	Distance (mi), y
1	47
3	141
5	235
6	282

On Your Own

5. A group of dancers practiced for 4 hours in March, 8 hours in April, 12 hours in May, and 16 hours in June. If the pattern continues, how many hours will they practice in November?

6. GO DEEPER The table shows the number of hours Jacob worked and the amount he earned each day.

Jacob's Earnings					
Time (hr), h	5	7	6	8	4
Amount earned ($), d	60	84	72	96	48

At the end of the week, he used his earnings to buy a new pair of skis. He had $218 left over. How much did the skis cost?

7. THINK SMARTER **Pose a Problem** Look back at Problem 6. Use the data in the table to write a new problem in which you could use the strategy *find a pattern*. Then solve the problem.

8. MATHEMATICAL PRACTICE 8 **Draw Conclusions** Marlon rode his bicycle 9 miles the first week, 18 miles the second week, and 27 miles the third week. If the pattern continues, will Marlon ride exactly 100 miles in a week at some point? Explain how you determined your answer.

Personal Math Trainer

9. THINK SMARTER + A diving instructor ordered snorkels. The table shows the cost based on the number of snorkels ordered.

Number of Snorkels, s	1	2	3	4
Cost ($), c	32	64	96	128

If the diving instructor spent $1,024, how many snorkels did he order? Use numbers and words to explain your answer.

Name ____________________

Problem Solving • Analyze Relationships

COMMON CORE STANDARD—6.EE.C.9
Represent and analyze quantitative relationships between dependent and independent variables.

The table shows the number of cups of yogurt needed to make different amounts of a fruit smoothie. Use the table for 1–3.

Batches, b	3	4	5	6
Cups of Yogurt, c	9	12	15	18

1. Write an equation to represent the relationship.

The number of cups needed is ___3___ multiplied by the number of batches,

so ___c___ = ___3___ × ___b___ .

2. How much yogurt is needed for 9 batches of smoothie? ____________

3. Jerry used 33 cups of yogurt to make smoothies. How many batches did he make? ____________

The table shows the relationship between Winn's age and his sister's age. Use the table for 4–5.

Winn's age (yr), w	8	9	10	11
Winn's sister's age (yr), s	12	13	14	15

4. Write an equation to represent the relationship. $s =$ ____________

5. When Winn is 14 years old, how old will his sister be? ____________

6. WRITE *Math* Write a problem for the table. Use a pattern and an equation to solve your problem.

Hours, h	1	2	3	4
Miles, m	16	32	48	64

____

____

Lesson Check (6.EE.C.9)

1. The table shows the total cost c in dollars of n gift baskets. What will be the cost of 9 gift baskets?

Cost of Gift Baskets				
Number of baskets, n	3	4	5	6
Cost of baskets ($), c	36	48	60	72

2. The table shows the number of minutes m that Tara has practiced after d days. If Tara has practiced for 70 minutes, how many days has she practiced?

Practice Times				
Days practiced, d	1	3	5	7
Minutes practiced, m	35	105	175	245

Spiral Review (6.EE.A.3, 6.EE.B.7, 6.EE.B.8, 6.EE.C.9)

3. Soccer shirts cost $15 each, and soccer shorts cost $18 each. The expression $15n + 18n$ represents the total cost in dollars of n uniforms. Simplify the expression by combining like terms.

4. What is an equation that represents the relationship in the table?

x	8	10	12	14
y	4	5	6	7

5. The lowest price of an MP3 of a song in an online store is $0.99. Write an inequality that represents the price p in dollars of any MP3 in the store.

6. Marisol plans to make 9 mini-sandwiches for every 2 people attending her party. Write a ratio that is equivalent to Marisol's ratio.

FOR MORE PRACTICE GO TO THE Personal Math Trainer

Name ______________________________

Mid-Chapter Checkpoint

Vocabulary

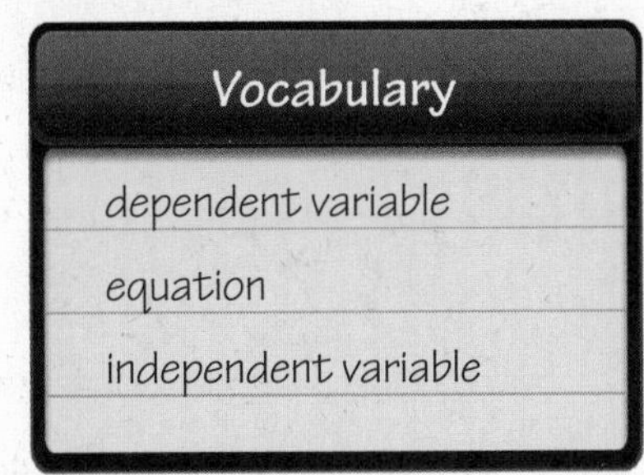

Choose the best term from the box to complete the sentence.

1. A(n) ____________________ has a value that determines the value of another quantity. (p. 491)

2. A variable whose value is determined by the value of another quantity is called a(n) ____________________. (p. 491)

Concepts and Skills

Identify the independent and dependent variables. (6.EE.C.9)

3. Marco spends a total of d dollars on postage to mail party invitations to each of g guests.

   dependent variable: ______

   independent variable: ______

4. Sophie has a doll collection with 36 dolls. She decides to sell s dolls to a museum and has r dolls remaining.

   dependent variable: ______

   independent variable: ______

Write an equation for the relationship shown in the table. Then find the unknown value in the table. (6.EE.C.9)

5.

x	6	7	8	9
y	42	?	56	63

____

6.

x	20	40	60	80
y	4	8	?	16

____

Write an equation that describes the pattern shown in the table. (6.EE.C.9)

7. The table shows how the number of pepperoni slices used depends on the number of pizzas made.

Pepperonis Used				
Pizzas, x	2	3	5	9
Pepperoni slices, y	34	51	85	153

____

8. Brayden is training for a marathon. The table shows how the number of miles he runs depends on which week of training he is in.

Miles Run During Training				
Week, w	3	5	8	12
Miles, m	8	10	13	17

____

9. The band has a total of 152 members. Some of the members are in the marching band, and the rest are in the concert band. Write an equation that models how many marching band members m there are if there are c concert band members. (6.EE.C.9)

____

10. A coach is ordering baseball jerseys from a website. The jerseys cost $15 each, and shipping is $8 per order. Write an equation that can be used to determine the total cost y, in dollars, for x jerseys. (6.EE.C.9)

____

11. Amy volunteers at an animal shelter. She worked 10 hours in March, 12 hours in April, 14 hours in May, and 16 hours in June. If the pattern continues, how many hours will she work in December? (6.EE.C.9)

____

12. GO DEEPER Aaron wants to buy a new snowboard. The table shows the amount that he has saved. If the pattern in the table continues, how much will he have saved after 1 year? (6.EE.C.9)

Aaron's Savings

Time (months)	Money saved ($)
3	135
4	180
6	270
7	315

____

Name ____________________

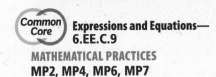

Graph Relationships

Essential Question How can you graph the relationship between two quantities?

Common Core **Expressions and Equations—6.EE.C.9**
MATHEMATICAL PRACTICES
MP2, MP4, MP6, MP7

CONNECT You have learned that tables and equations are two ways to represent the relationship between two quantities. You can also represent a relationship between two quantities by using a graph.

Unlock the Problem

A cafeteria has a pancake-making machine. The table shows the relationship between the time in hours and the number of pancakes the machine can make. Graph the relationship represented by the table.

Pancake Production	
Time (hours)	Pancakes Made
1	200
2	400
3	600
4	800
5	1,000

Use the table values to graph the relationship.

STEP 1 Write ordered pairs.

Let *x* represent the time in hours and *y* represent the number of pancakes made. Use each row of the table to write an ordered pair.

(1, 200) (2, ________) (3, ________) (____, ________) (____, ________)

STEP 2 Choose an appropriate scale for each axis of the graph. Label the axes and give the graph a title.

STEP 3 Graph a point for each ordered pair.

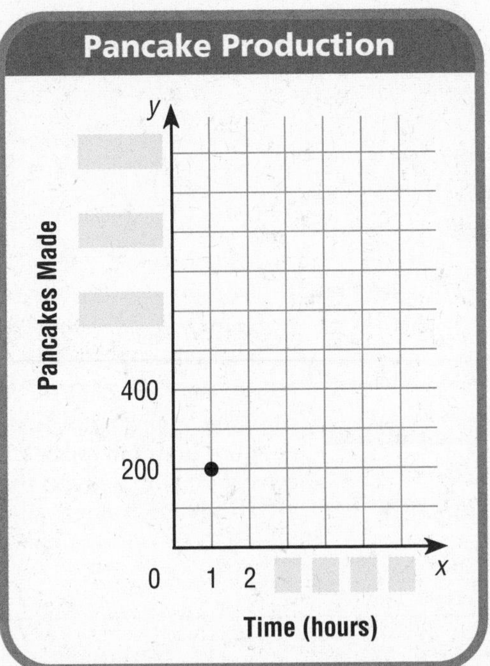

Math Talk MATHEMATICAL PRACTICES 7

Look for Structure What pattern do you notice in the set of points you graphed?

Example

The table shows the relationship between the number of bicycles y Shawn has left to assemble and the number of hours x he has worked. Graph the relationship represented by the table to find the unknown value of y.

Bicycle Assembly	
Time (hours), x	Bicycles Left to Assemble, y
0	10
1	8
2	?
3	4
4	2

STEP 1 Write ordered pairs.

Use each row of the table to write an ordered pair. Skip the row with the unknown y-value.

(0, 10) (1, ______) (3, ______) (______, ______)

STEP 2 Graph a point for each ordered pair on a coordinate plane.

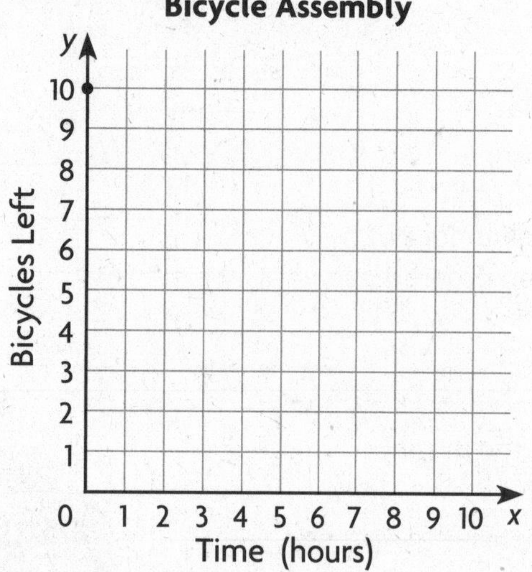

STEP 3 Find the unknown y-value.

The points on the graph appear to lie on a line. Use a ruler to draw a dashed line through the points.

Use the line to find the y-value that corresponds to an x-value of 2. Start at the origin, and move 2 units right. Move up until you reach the line you drew. Then move left to find the y-value on the y-axis.

When x has a value of 2, y has a value of ______.

So, after 2 hours, Shawn has ______ bicycles left to assemble.

Remember

The first value in an ordered pair represents the independent variable x. The second value represents the dependent variable y.

Math Talk MATHEMATICAL PRACTICES 2

Reasoning Describe a situation in which it would be more useful to represent a function with a graph than with a table of values.

- MATHEMATICAL PRACTICE 6 **Describe** another way you could find the unknown value of y in the table.

______

______

Name ________________________________

Share and Show

Graph the relationship represented by the table.

1.

x	1	2	3	4
y	50	100	150	200

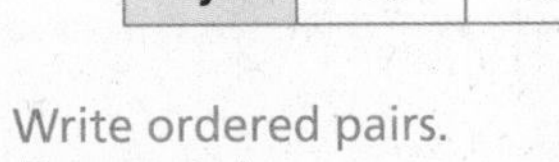

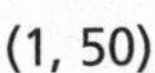

Write ordered pairs. Then graph.

(1, 50)

(2, ________)

(3, ________)

(________, ________)

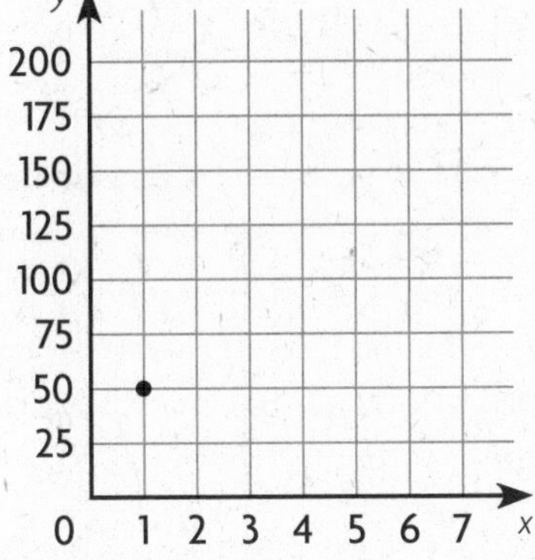

2.

x	20	40	60	80
y	100	200	300	400

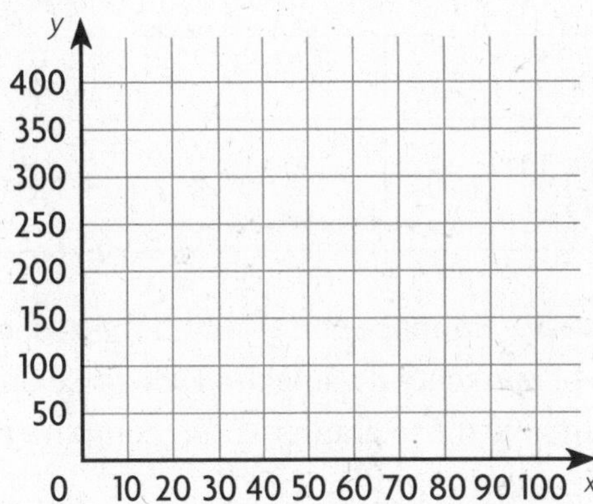

Graph the relationship represented by the table to find the unknown value of *y*.

3.

x	4	5	6	7	8
y	9	7	5		1

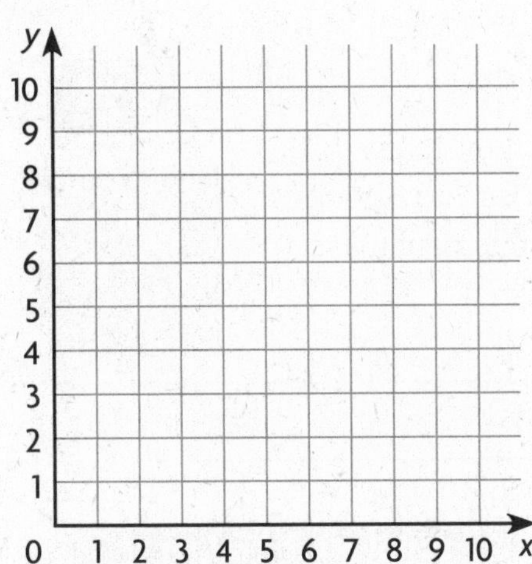

4.

x	1	3	5	7	9
y	3	4	5		7

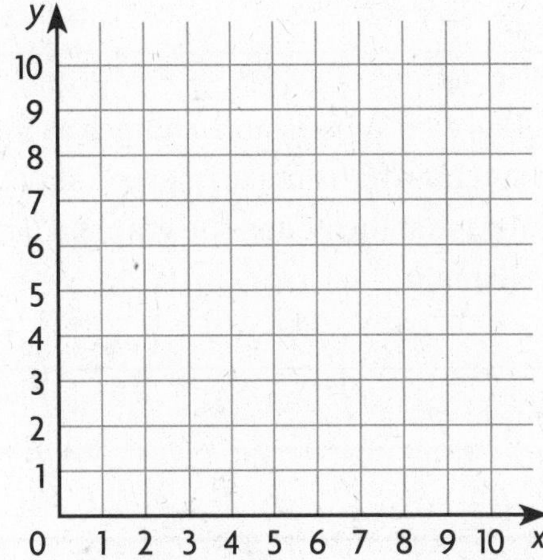

Math Talk

MATHEMATICAL PRACTICES 4

Use Graphs Explain how to use a graph to find an unknown *y*-value in a table.

On Your Own

Practice: Copy and Solve Graph the relationship represented by the table to find the unknown value of *y*.

5.

x	1	3	5	7	9
y	7	6		4	3

6.

x	1	2	4	6	7
y	2	3	5		8

Problem Solving • Applications

The table at the right shows the typical price of a popular brand of corn cereal over time. Use the table for 7–8.

Price of Corn Cereal

Year	Price per box ($)
1968	0.39
1988	1.50
2008	4.50

7. MATHEMATICAL PRACTICE 4 **Use Graphs** Complete the table below to show the cost of buying 1 to 5 boxes of corn cereal in 1988. Then graph the relationship on the coordinate plane at right.

Boxes	1	2	3	4	5
Cost in 1988 ($)	1.50				

Cost of Corn Cereal, 1988

Cost ($)

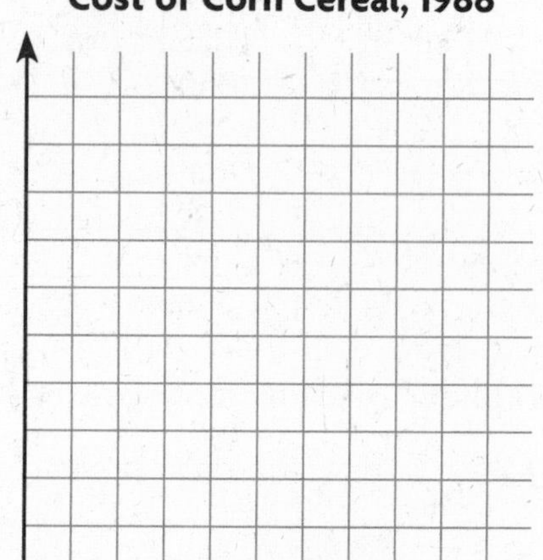

Boxes

8. GO DEEPER Suppose you graphed the cost of buying 1 to 5 boxes of corn cereal using the 1968 price and the 2008 price. Explain how those graphs would compare to the graph you made using the 1988 price.

____

____

____

____

____

9. THINK SMARTER A bookstore charges $4 for shipping, no matter how many books you buy. Irena makes a graph showing the shipping cost for 1 to 5 books. She claims that the points she graphed lie on a line. Does her statement make sense? Explain.

____

____

10. THINK SMARTER + Graph the relationship represented by the table to find the unknown value of y.

x	1	2	3	4
y	2	2.5		3.5

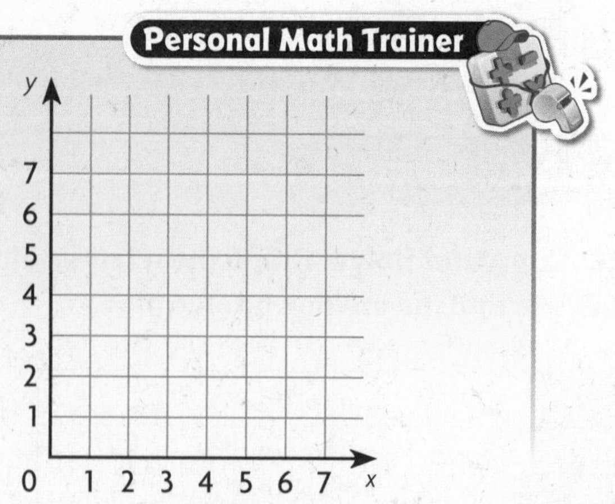

Name ______________________________

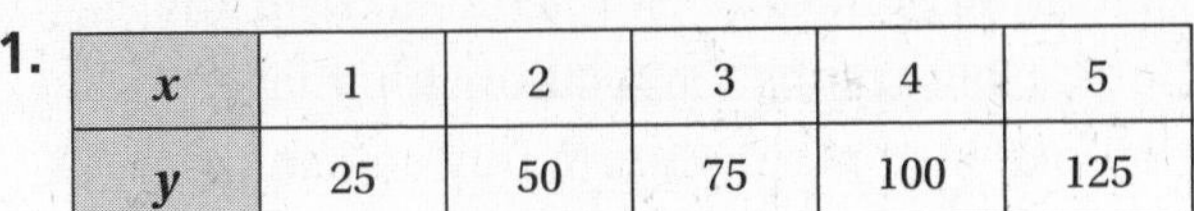

Graph Relationships

Common Core **COMMON CORE STANDARD—6.EE.C.9**
Represent and analyze quantitative relationships between dependent and independent variables.

Graph the relationship represented by the table.

1.

x	1	2	3	4	5
y	25	50	75	100	125

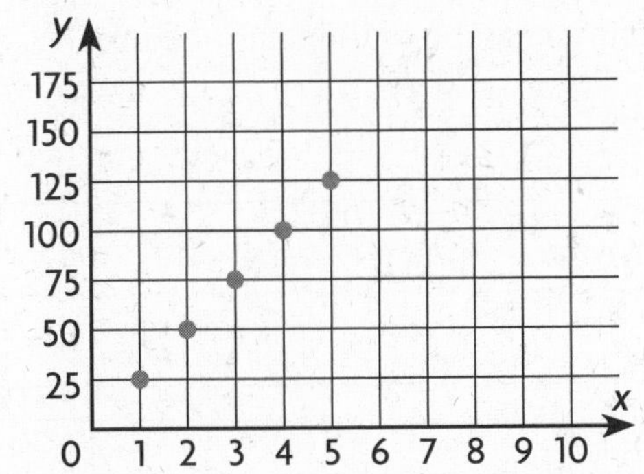

2.

x	10	20	30	40	50
y	350	300	250	200	150

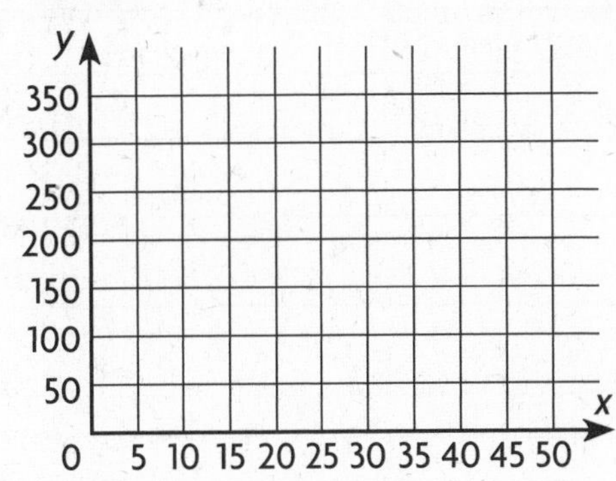

Graph the relationship represented by the table to find the unknown value of y.

3.

x	3	4	5	6	7
y	8	7		5	4

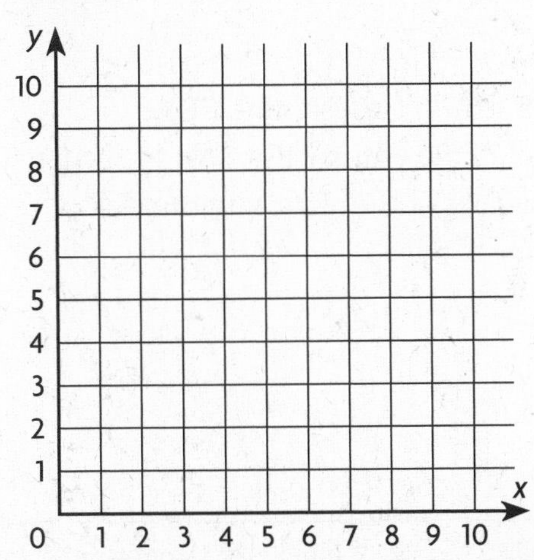

4.

x	1	3	5	7	9
y	1		3	4	5

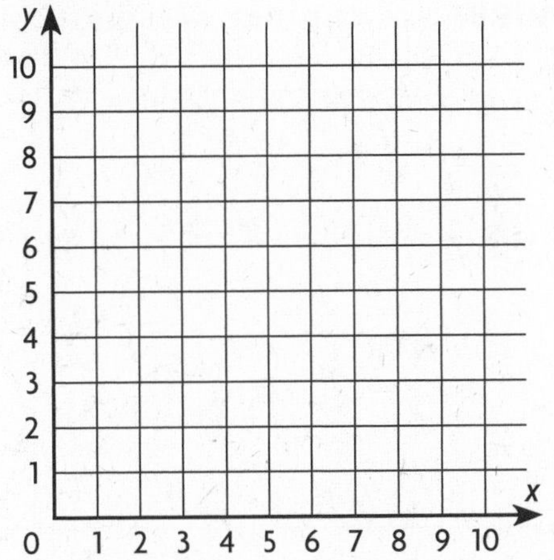

Problem Solving

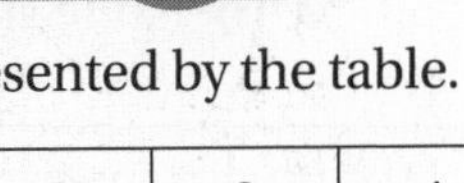

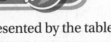

5. Graph the relationship represented by the table.

DVDs Purchased	1	2	3	4
Cost ($)	15	30	45	60

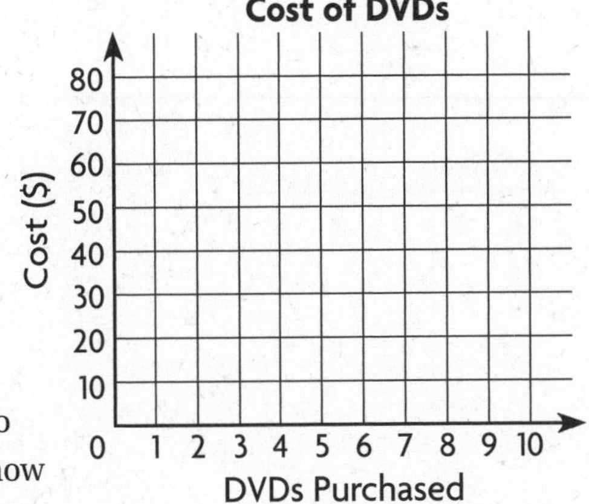

6. Use the graph to find the cost of purchasing 5 DVDs.

____

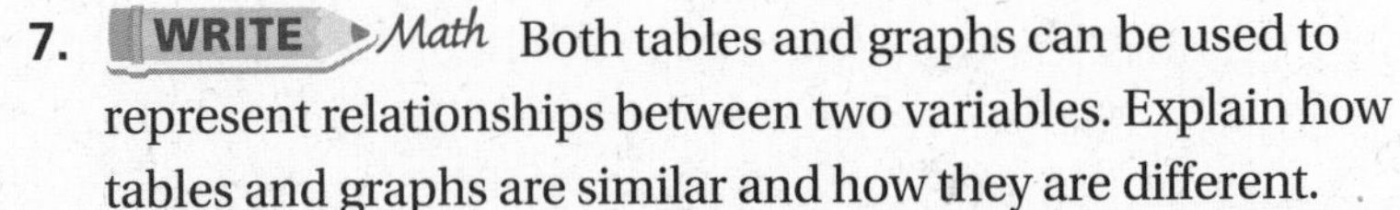

7. WRITE *Math* Both tables and graphs can be used to represent relationships between two variables. Explain how tables and graphs are similar and how they are different.

____

Lesson Check (6.EE.C.9)

1. Mei wants to graph the relationship represented by the table. Write an ordered pair that is a point on the graph of the relationship.

T-shirts purchased, x	1	2	3	4
Cost ($), y	8	16	24	32

2. An online bookstore charges $2 to ship any book. Cole graphs the relationship that gives the total cost y in dollars to buy and ship a book that costs x dollars. Name an ordered pair that is a point on the graph of the relationship.

Spiral Review (6.EE.A.3, 6.EE.B.7, 6.EE.B.8, 6.EE.C.9)

3. Write an expression that is equivalent to $6(g + 4)$.

4. There are 6 girls in a music class. This represents $\frac{3}{7}$ of the entire class. Solve $\frac{3}{7}s = 6$ to find the number of students, s, in the class.

5. Graph $n > {}^{-}2$ on a number line.

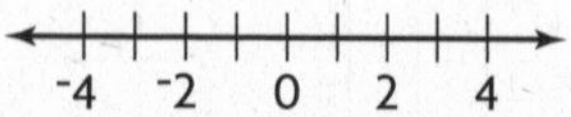

6. Sam is ordering lunch for the people in his office. The table shows the cost of lunch based on the number of people. How much will lunch cost for 35 people?

Number of people, n	5	10	15	20
Cost ($), c	40	80	120	160

FOR MORE PRACTICE GO TO THE **Personal Math Trainer**

Name ____________________

Equations and Graphs

Essential Question How can you translate between equations and graphs?

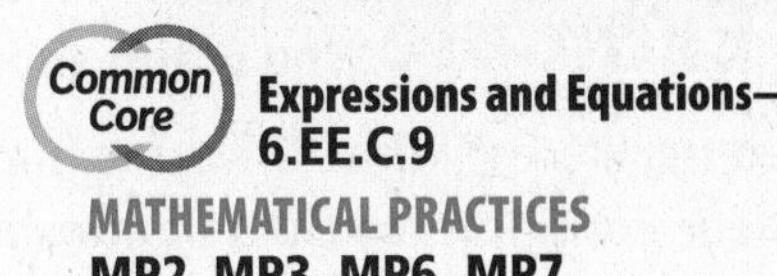

Common Core
Expressions and Equations—6.EE.C.9
MATHEMATICAL PRACTICES
MP2, MP3, MP6, MP7

The solution of an equation in two variables is an ordered pair that makes the equation true. For example, (2, 5) is a solution of the equation $y = x + 3$ because $5 = 2 + 3$.

A **linear equation** is an equation whose solutions form a straight line on the coordinate plane. Any point on the line is a solution of the equation.

Unlock the Problem

A blue whale is swimming at an average rate of 3 miles per hour. Write a linear equation that gives the distance y in miles that the whale swims in x hours. Then graph the relationship.

- What formula can you use to help you write the equation?

____

Write and graph a linear equation.

STEP 1 Write an equation for the relationship.

Think: Distance → equals → rate → multiplied by → time.

_____ = _____ · _____

STEP 2 Find ordered pairs that are solutions of the equation.

Choose several values of x and find the corresponding values of y.

x	$3x$	y	Ordered Pair
1	3 · 1	3	(1, 3)
2	3 ·		(2,)
3	3 ·		(,)
4	3 ·		(,)

STEP 3 Graph the relationship.

Graph the ordered pairs. Draw a line through the points to show all the solutions of the linear equation.

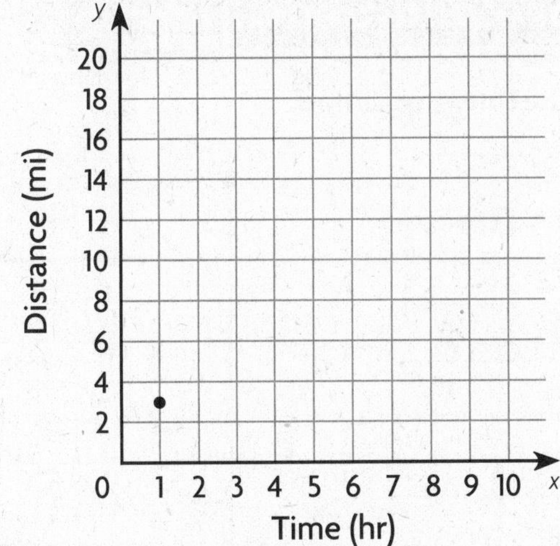

Math Talk MATHEMATICAL PRACTICES 2

Reasoning Explain why the graph does not show negative values of x or y.

Example

The graph shows the number of beaded necklaces *y* that Ginger can make in *x* hours. Write the linear equation for the relationship shown by the graph.

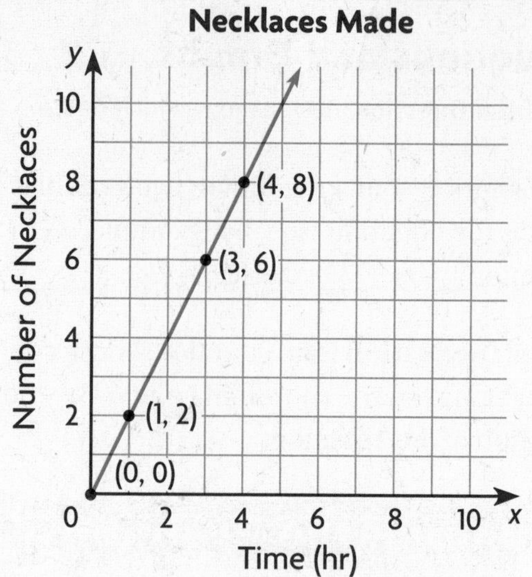

STEP 1 Use ordered pairs from the graph to complete the table of values below.

STEP 2 Look for a pattern in the table.

Compare each *y*-value with the corresponding *x*-value.

x	0	1	3	4
y	0			
	↑ $2 \cdot 0$	↑ $2 \cdot 1$	↑ $2 \cdot$ ______	↑ $2 \cdot$ ______

Think: Each *y*-value is ______ times the corresponding *x*-value.

So, the linear equation for the relationship is $y =$ ______.

1. Explain how to graph a linear equation. ______________________________

____

____

2.  **Compare Representations** Describe a situation in which it would be more useful to represent a relationship with an equation than with a graph.

____

____

Share and Show MATH BOARD

Graph the linear equation.

1. $y = x - 2$

Make a table of values. Then graph.

x	*y*
2	0
4	
6	
8	

2. $y = 3x$

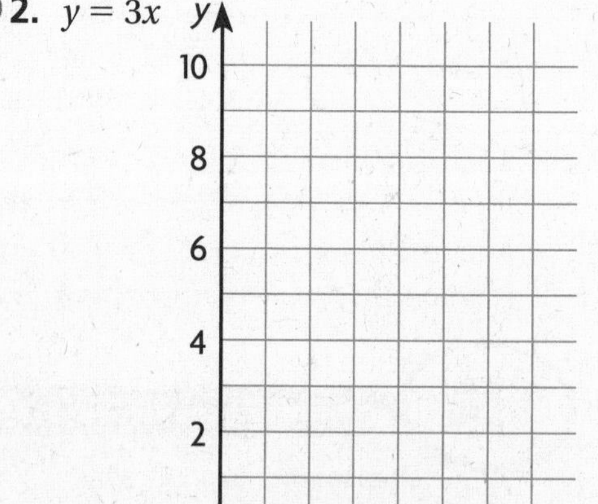

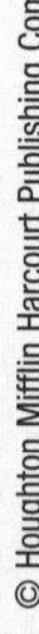

Name ______________________________

Write the linear equation for the relationship shown by the graph.

3.

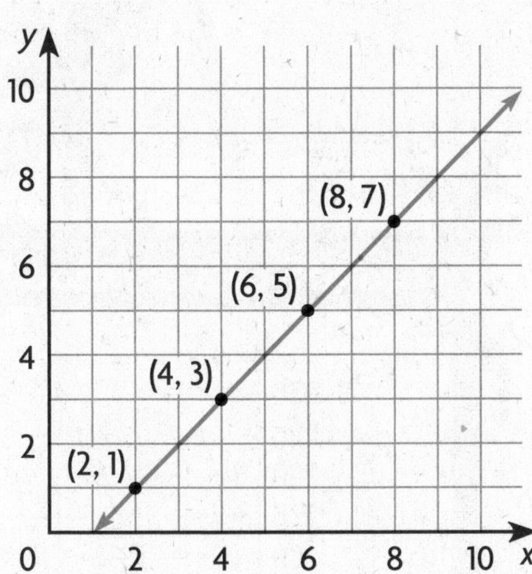

____

4.

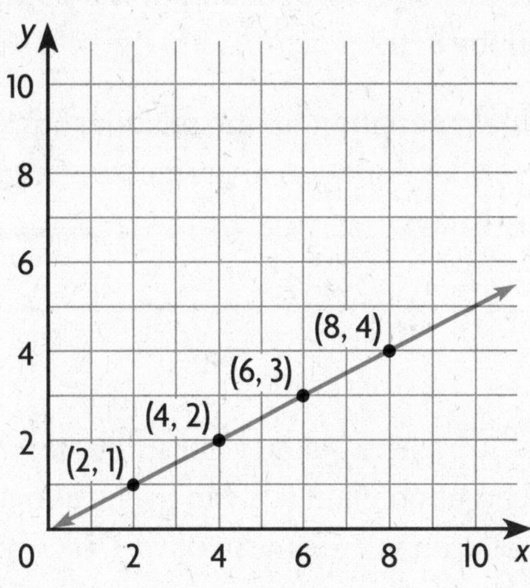

____

Math Talk

MATHEMATICAL PRACTICES 6

Explain how you can tell whether you have graphed a linear equation correctly.

On Your Own

Graph the linear equation.

5. $y = x + 1$

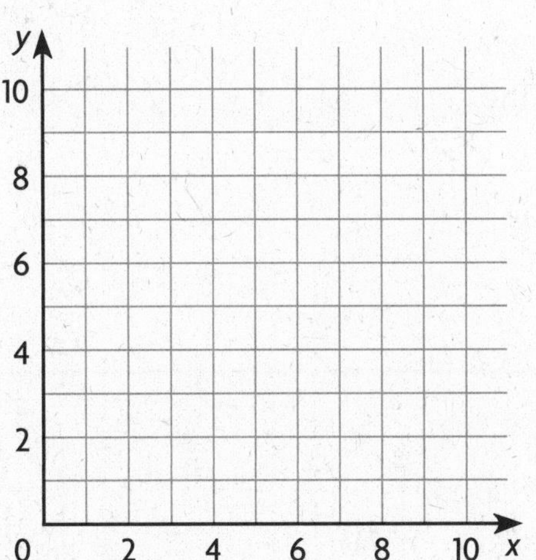

6. $y = 2x - 1$

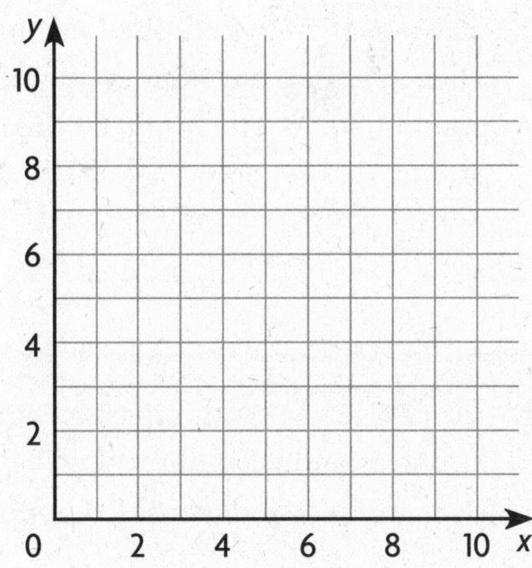

7. MATHEMATICAL PRACTICE 7 **Identify Relationships** The graph shows the number of loaves of bread y that Kareem bakes in x hours. Write the linear equation for the relationship shown by the graph.

____

Loaves of Bread Baked

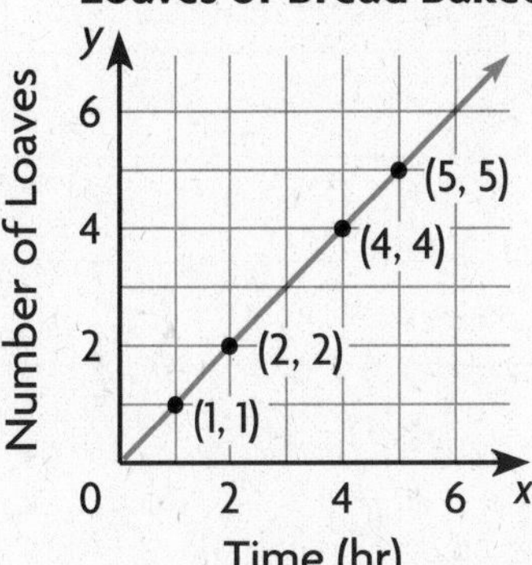

Problem Solving • Applications

The graph shows the growth of a bamboo plant. Use the graph for 8–9.

8. Write a linear equation for the relationship shown by the graph. Use your equation to predict the height of the bamboo plant after 7 days.

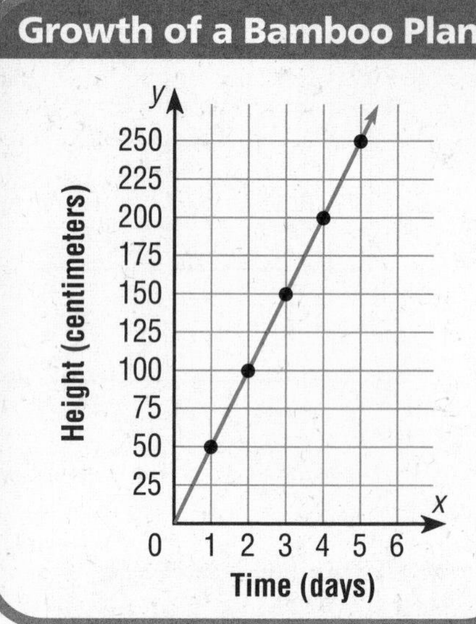

9. THINKSMARTER The height y in centimeters of a second bamboo plant is given by the equation $y = 30x$, where x is the time in days. Describe how the graph showing the growth of this plant would compare to the graph showing the growth of the first plant.

10. GO DEEPER Maria graphed the linear equation $y = x + 3$. Then she used her ruler to draw a vertical line through the point (4, 0). At what point do the two lines intersect?

11. THINKSMARTER Antonio claims the linear equation for the relationship shown by the graph is $y = \frac{1}{2}x + 2$. Use numbers and words to support Antonio's claim.

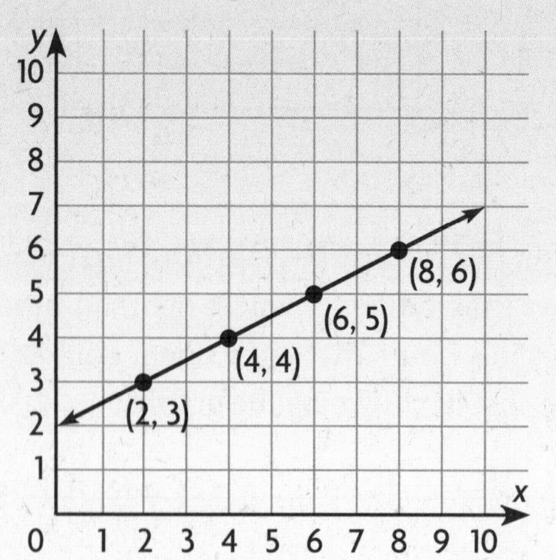

Name ______________________________

Equations and Graphs

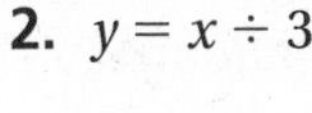

COMMON CORE STANDARD—6.EE.C.9
Represent and analyze quantitative relationships between dependent and independent variables.

Graph the linear equation.

1. $y = x - 3$

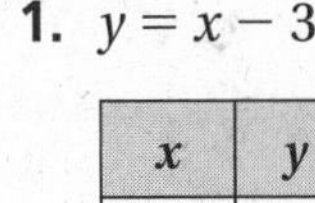

x	y
5	2
6	3
7	4
8	5

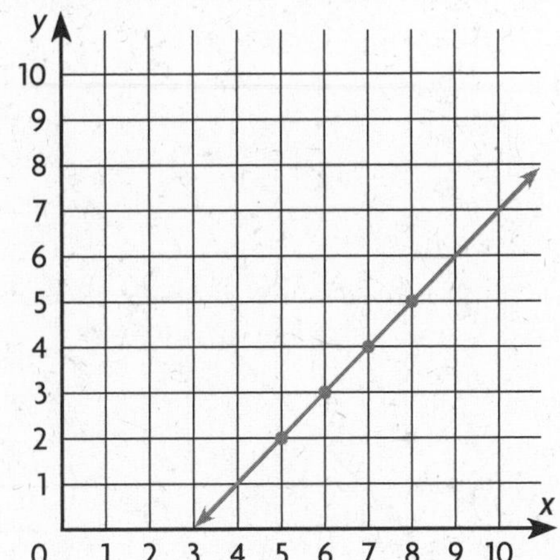

2. $y = x \div 3$

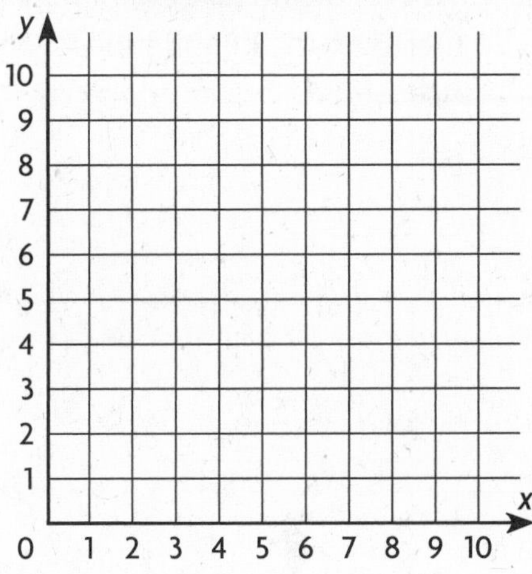

Write a linear equation for the relationship shown by the graph.

3.

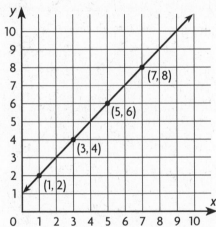

4.

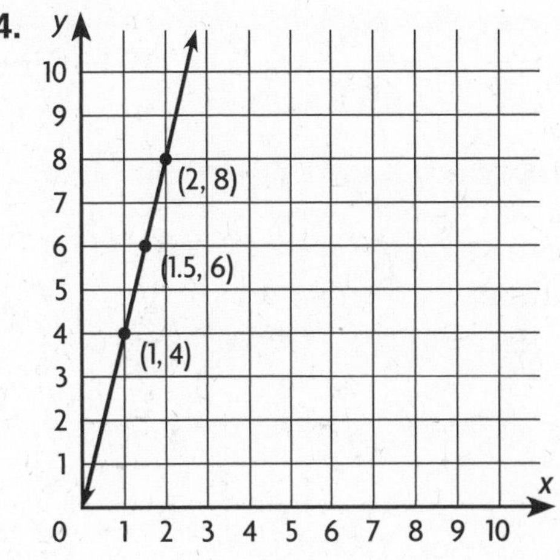

______________________ ______________________

Problem Solving

5. Dee is driving at an average speed of 50 miles per hour. Write a linear equation for the relationship that gives the distance y in miles that Dee drives in x hours.

____

6. Graph the relationship from Exercise 5.

Dee's Distance

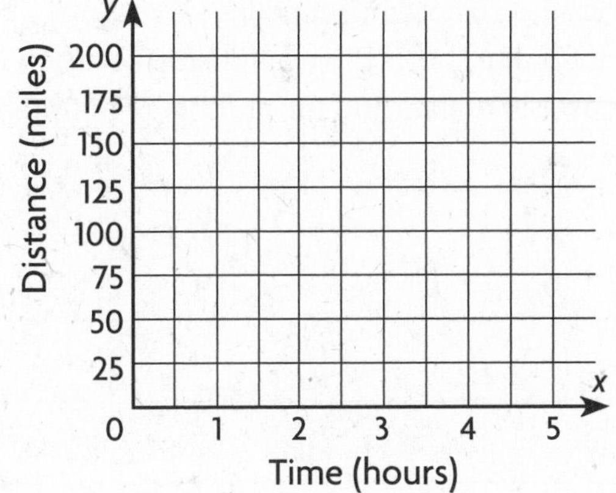

7. WRITE *Math* Explain how to write a linear equation for a line on a graph.

____

Lesson Check (6.EE.C.9)

1. A balloon rises at a rate of 10 feet per second. What is the linear equation for the relationship that gives the height y in feet of the balloon after x seconds?

2. Write the linear equation that is shown by the graph.

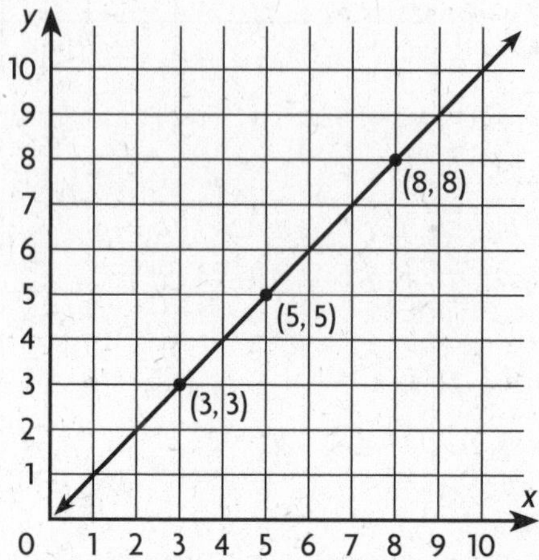

Spiral Review (6.EE.A.4, 6.EE.B.5, 6.EE.C.9)

3. Of the three expressions shown, which two are equivalent?

   $3 + 2(9 + 2n)$ $\quad 7(3 + 4n)$ $\quad 21 + 4n$

4. Which of the following are solutions of $j \geq 0.6$?

   $j = 1, j = {}^{-}0.6, j = \frac{3}{5}, j = 0.12, j = 0.08$

5. Red grapes cost \$2.49 per pound. Write an equation that shows the relationship between the cost c in dollars and the number of pounds of grapes p.

6. It costs \$8 per hour to rent a bike. Niko graphs this relationship using x for number of hours and y for total cost in dollars. Write an ordered pair that is a point on the graph of the relationship.

FOR MORE PRACTICE GO TO THE **Personal Math Trainer**

Name ______________________________

Chapter 9 Review/Test

Personal Math Trainer
Online Assessment and Intervention

1. A box of peanut butter crackers contains 12 individual snacks. The total number of individual snacks s is equal to 12 times the number of boxes of crackers b.

The independent variable is [b. / s.] The dependent variable is [b. / s.]

The equation that represents the relationship between the variables is [$b = 12s$. / $s = 12b$.]

2. A stationery store charges \$8 to print logos on paper purchases. The total cost c is the price of the paper p plus \$8 for printing the logo.

For numbers 2a–2d, select True or False for each statement.

2a. The total cost c depends on the price of the paper. ○ True ○ False

2b. c is the dependent variable. ○ True ○ False

2c. p is the independent variable. ○ True ○ False

2d. The equation that represents the relationship between the variables is $c = 8p$. ○ True ○ False

3. An electrician charges \$75 an hour for labor and an initial fee of \$65. The total cost c equals 75 times the number of hours x plus 65. Write an equation for the relationship and use the equation to complete the table.

Time (hr), x	Cost (\$), c
1	
2	
3	
4	

equation ______________________

GO DIGITAL Assessment Options Chapter Test

4. The community center offers classes in arts and crafts. There is a registration fee of $125 and each class costs $79. The total cost *c* in dollars equals 79 times the number of classes *n* plus 125.

Input	Output
Number of Classes, *n*	Cost ($), *c*
1	204
2	283
3	362
4	441

For numbers 4a–4d, select True or False for each statement.

4a. The registration fee is $120. ○ True ○ False

4b. *n* is the independent variable. ○ True ○ False

4c. *c* is the dependent variable. ○ True ○ False

4d. The cost for 7 classes is $678. ○ True ○ False

5. Ms. Walsh is buying calculators for her class. The table shows the total cost based on the number of calculators purchased.

Number of Calculators, *n*	1	2	3	4
Cost ($), *c*	15	30	45	60

If Ms. Walsh spent a total of $525, how many calculators did she buy? Use numbers and words to explain your answer.

Name ___

6. The table shows the number of cups of lemonade that can be made from cups of lemon juice.

Lemon Juice (cups), j	2	4	5	7
Lemonade (cups), l	14	28	35	49

Mary Beth says the number of cups of lemon juice j depends on the number of cups of lemonade l. She says the equation $j = 7l$ represents the relationship between the cups of lemon juice j and the cups of lemonade l. Is Mary Beth correct? Use words and numbers to explain why or why not.

7. For numbers 7a–7d, choose Yes or No to indicate whether the points, when graphed, would lie on the same line.

7a. (1, 6), (2, 4), (3, 2), (4, 0) ○ Yes ○ No

7b. (1, 1), (2, 4), (3, 9), (4, 16) ○ Yes ○ No

7c. (1, 3), (2, 5), (3, 7), (4, 9) ○ Yes ○ No

7d. (1, 8), (2, 10), (3, 12), (4, 14) ○ Yes ○ No

Personal Math Trainer

8. THINK SMARTER + Graph the relationship represented by the table to find the unknown value.

Time (seconds), x	40	50	60	70
Water in Tub (gal), y	13	11.5		8.5

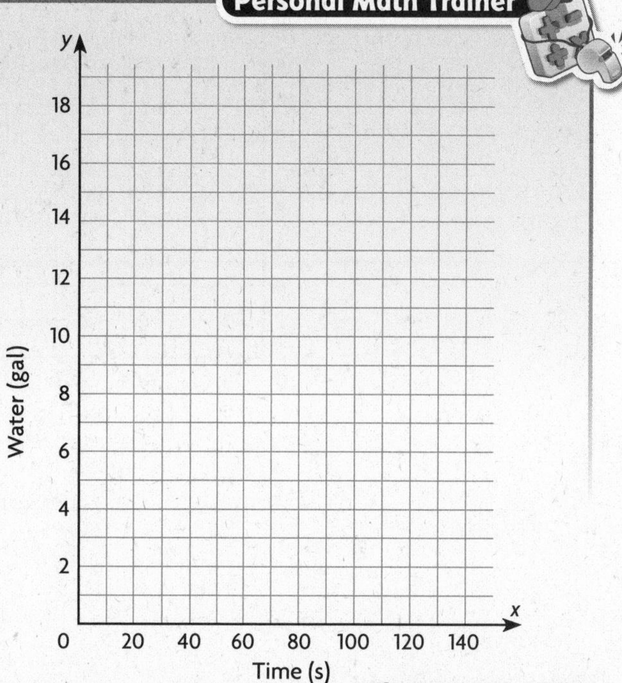

9. Graph the relationship represented by the table.

Time (hr), x	3	4	5	6
Distance (mi), y	240	320	400	480

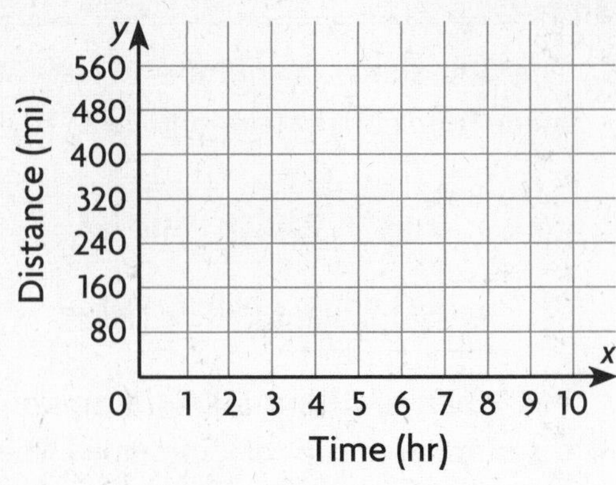

10. Miranda's wages are $15 per hour. Write a linear equation that gives the wages w in dollars that Miranda earns in h hours.

____

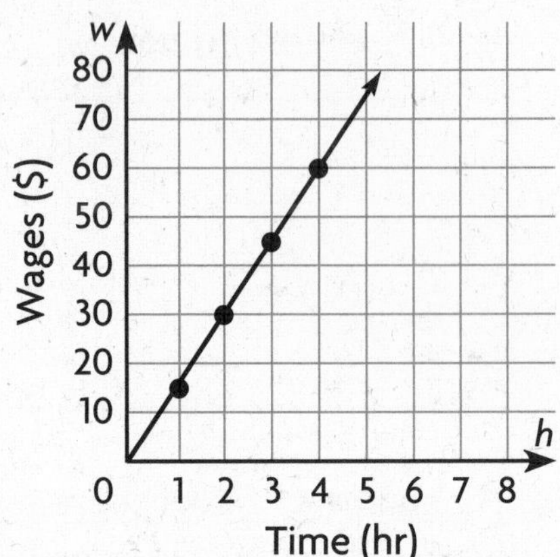

11. GO DEEPER The table shows the number of miles m that Lucinda could walk in h hours.

Hours, h	1	2	3	4
Miles, m	4	8	12	16

Graph the relationship between hours h and miles m. Then write the equation that shows the relationship.

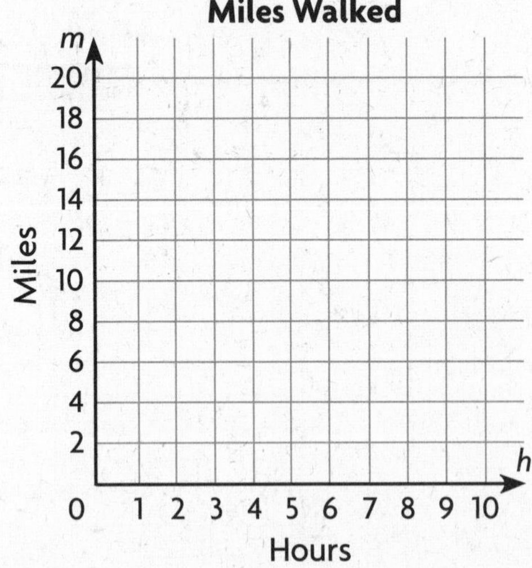

____

Name ________________________________

12. Delonna walks 4 miles per day for exercise. The total number of miles m she walks equals 4 times the number of days d she walks.

What is the dependent variable? ____________

What is the independent variable? ____________

Write the equation that represents the relationship between the m and d.

____

13. Lacy is staying at a hotel that costs \$85 per night. The total cost c in dollars of Lacy's stay is 85 times the number of nights n she stays.

For numbers 13a–13d, select True or False for each statement.

13a. The number of nights n is dependent on the cost c. ○ True ○ False

13b. n is the independent variable. ○ True ○ False

13c. c is the dependent variable. ○ True ○ False

13d. The equation that represents the total cost is $c = 85n$. ○ True ○ False

14. A taxi cab company charges an initial fee of \$5 and then \$4 per mile for a ride. Use the equation $c = 4x + 5$ to complete the table.

Input	Output
Miles (mi), x	Cost (\$), c
2	
4	
6	
8	

15. A grocery display of cans is arranged in the form of a pyramid with 1 can in the top row, 3 in the second row from the top, 5 in the third row, and 7 in the fourth row. The total number of cans c equals 2 times the row r minus 1. Use the equation $c = 2r - 1$ to complete the table.

Row, r	Cans, c
5	
6	
7	
8	

16. The graph shows the number of words Mason read in a given amount of minutes. If Mason continues to read at the same rate, how many words will he have read in 5 minutes?

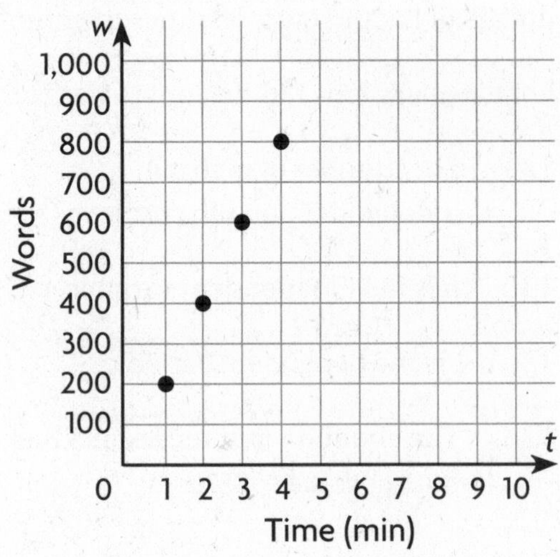

____

17. Casey claims the linear equation for the relationship shown by the graph is $c = 25j$. Use numbers and words to support Casey's claim.

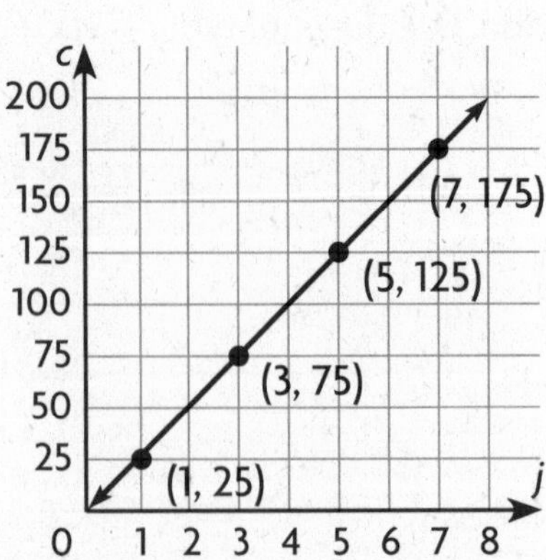

Critical Area

Geometry and Statistics

CRITICAL AREA
Solve real-world and mathematical problems involving area, surface area, and volume.

Developing understanding of statistical thinking

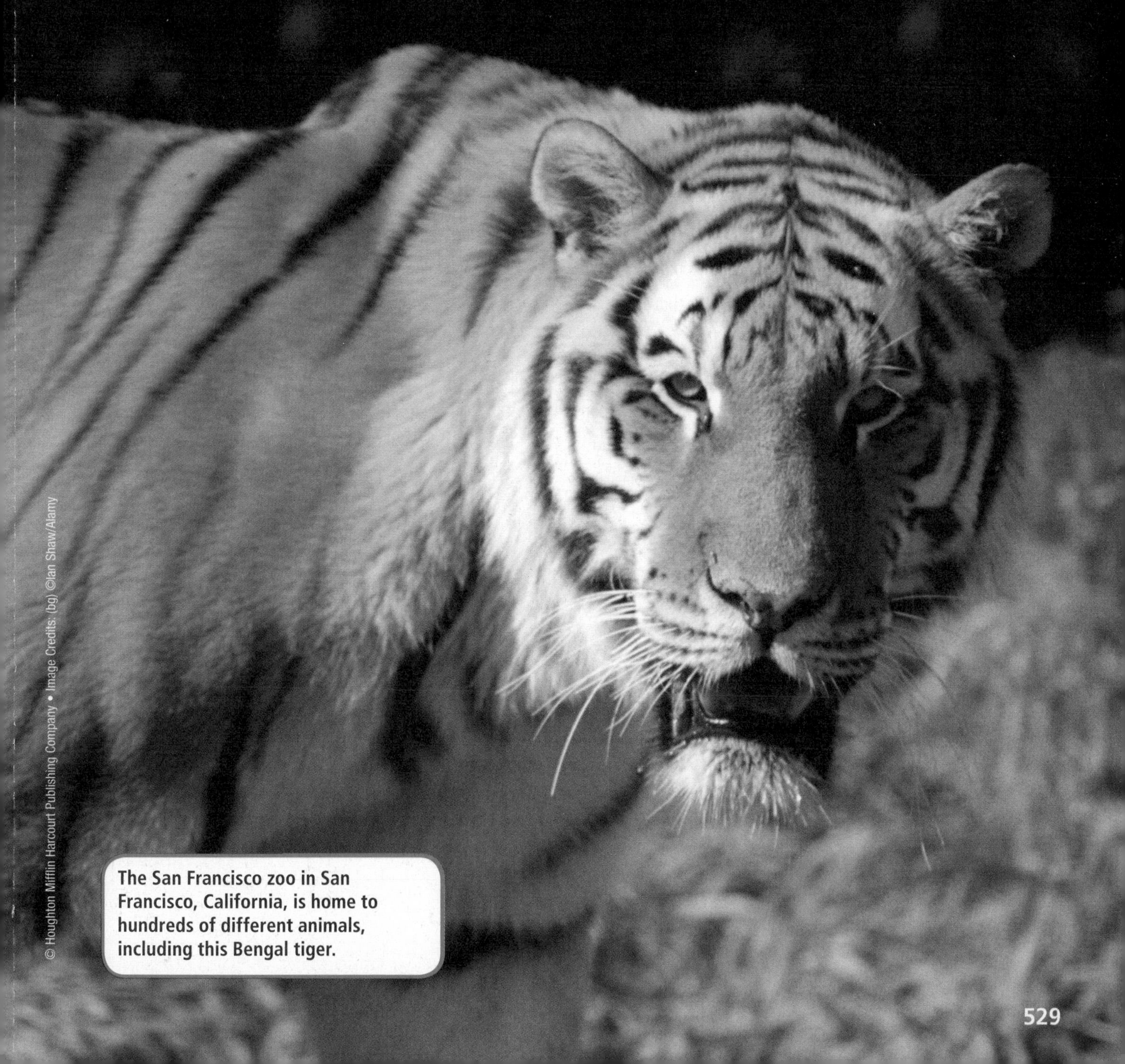

The San Francisco zoo in San Francisco, California, is home to hundreds of different animals, including this Bengal tiger.

This Place is a Zoo!

Planning a zoo is a difficult task. Each animal requires a special environment with different amounts of space and different features.

Get Started

You are helping to design a new section of a zoo. The table lists some of the new attractions planned for the zoo. Each attraction includes notes about the type and the amount of space needed. The zoo owns a rectangle of land that is 100 feet long and 60 feet wide. Find the dimensions of each of the attractions and draw a sketch of the plan for the zoo.

Important Facts

Attraction	Minimum Floor Space (sq ft)	Notes
American Alligators	400	rectangular pen with one side at least 24 feet long
Amur Tigers	750	trapezoid-shaped area with one side at least 40 feet long
Howler Monkeys	450	parallelogram-shaped cage with one side at least 30 feet long
Meerkat Village	250	square pen with glass sides
Red Foxes	350	rectangular pen with length twice as long as width
Tropical Aquarium	200	triangular bottom with base at least 20 feet long

Completed by ______________________

Area

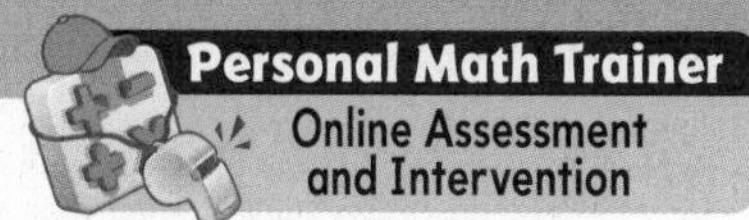

Check your understanding of important skills.

Name ____________________________

Perimeter Find the perimeter. (4.MD.A.3)

1. 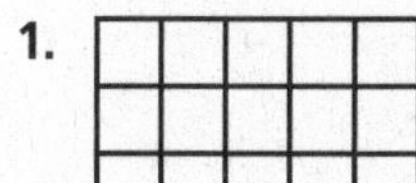

$P =$ ______ units

2. 8 mm, 15 mm, 17 mm

$P =$ ______ mm

Identify Polygons Name each polygon based on the number of sides. (5.G.B.4)

3. 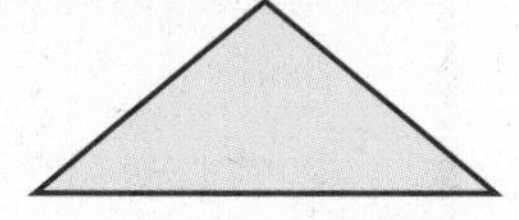

____

4. 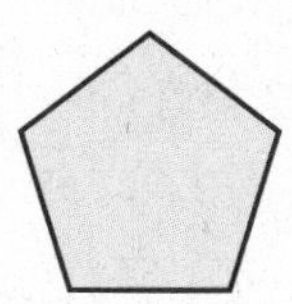

____

5. 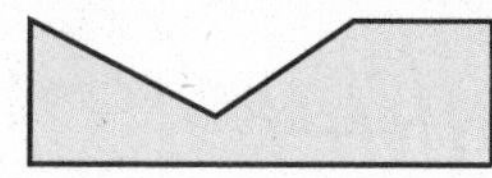

____

Evaluate Algebraic Expressions Evaluate the expression. (6.EE.A.2c)

6. $5x + 2y$ for $x = 7$ and $y = 9$

____

7. $6a \times 3b + 4$ for $a = 2$ and $b = 8$

____

8. $s^2 + t^2 - 2^3$ for $s = 4$ and $t = 6$

____

Ross needs to paint the white boundary lines of one end zone on a football field. The area of the end zone is 4,800 square feet, and one side of the end zone measures 30 feet. One can of paint is enough to paint 300 feet of line. Help Ross find out if one can is enough to line the perimeter of the end zone.

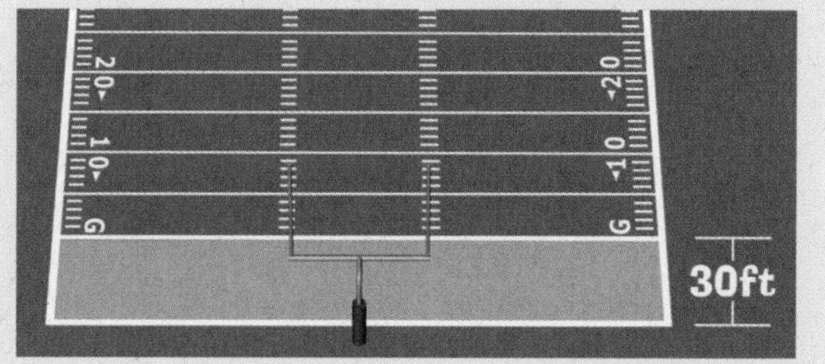

Vocabulary Builder

▶ Visualize It

Complete the bubble map by using the checked words that are types of quadrilaterals.

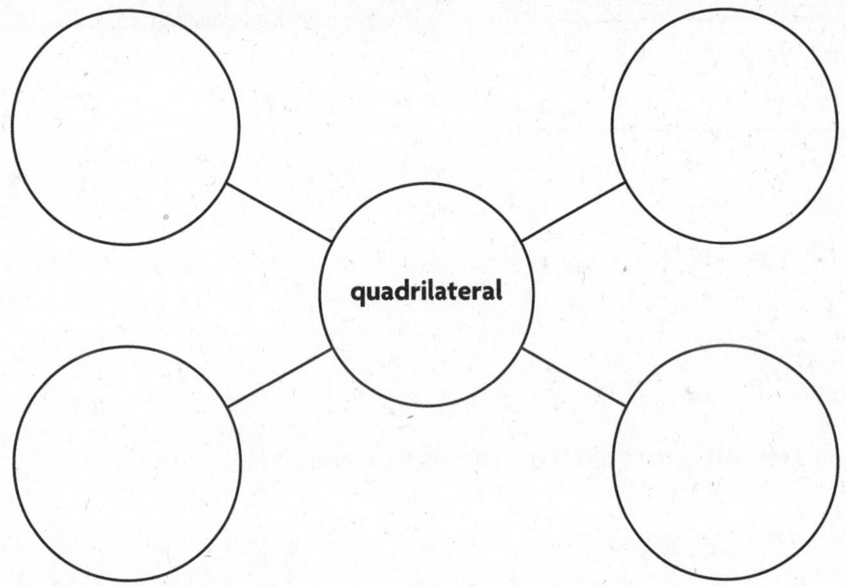

Review Words

- acute triangle
- base
- height
- obtuse triangle
- ✓ polygon
- quadrilateral
- ✓ rectangle
- right triangle
- ✓ square

Preview Words

- area
- composite figure
- congruent
- ✓ parallelogram
- regular polygon
- ✓ trapezoid

▶ Understand Vocabulary

Complete the sentences using the preview words.

1. The ______________________ of a figure is the measure of the number of unit squares needed to cover it without any gaps or overlaps.

2. A polygon in which all sides are the same length and all angles have the same measure is called a(n) ______________________.

3. A(n) ______________________ is a quadrilateral with at least one pair of parallel sides.

4. ______________________ figures have the same size and shape.

5. A quadrilateral with two pairs of parallel sides is called a ______________________.

6. A(n) ______________________ is made up of more than one shape.

GO DIGITAL
- Interactive Student Edition
- Multimedia eGlossary

Chapter 10 Vocabulary

area área 4	**composite figure** figura compuesta 14
congruent congruente 15	**parallelogram** paralelogramo 73
polygon polígono 75	**quadrilateral** cuadrilátero 83
regular polygon polígono regular 90	**trapezoid** trapecio 102

A figure that is made up of two or more simpler figures, such as triangles and quadrilaterals

Example:

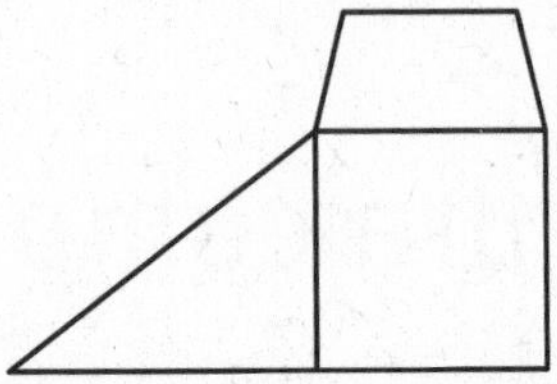

The measure of the number of unit squares needed to cover a surface without any gaps or overlaps

Example:

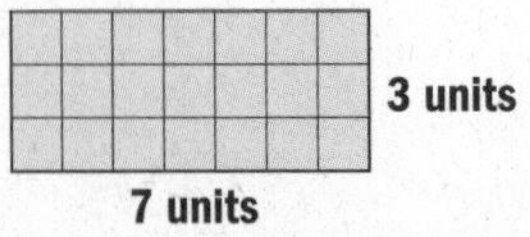

3 units

7 units

Area = 21 square units

A quadrilateral whose opposite sides are parallel and congruent

Example:

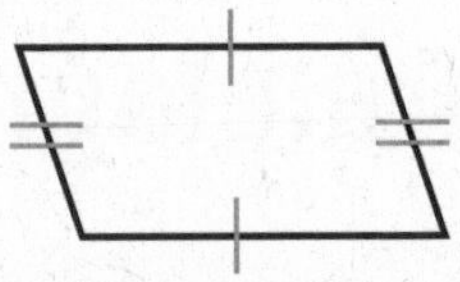

Having the same size and shape

Example:

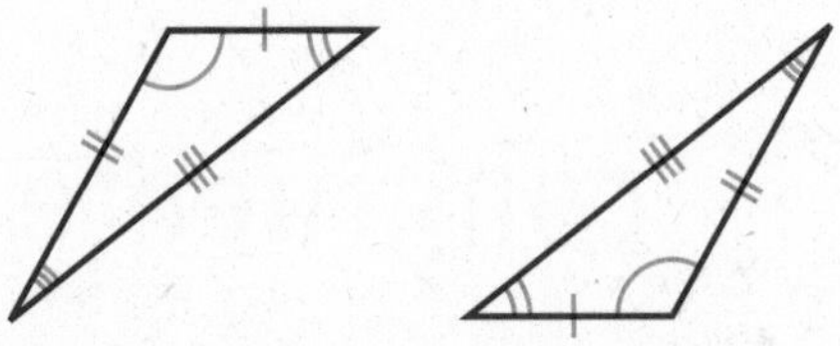

A polygon with four sides and four angles

Example:

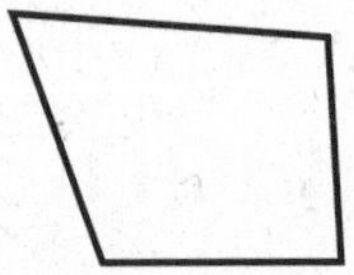

A closed plane figure formed by three or more line segments

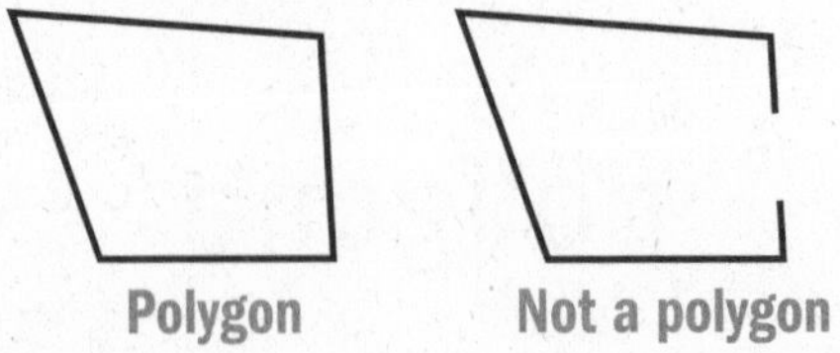

Polygon

Not a polygon

A quadrilateral with at least one pair of parallel sides

Examples:

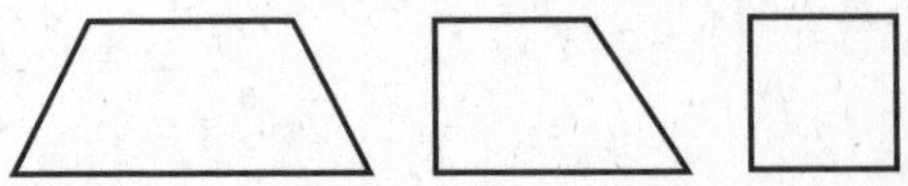

A polygon in which all sides are congruent and all angles are congruent

Example:

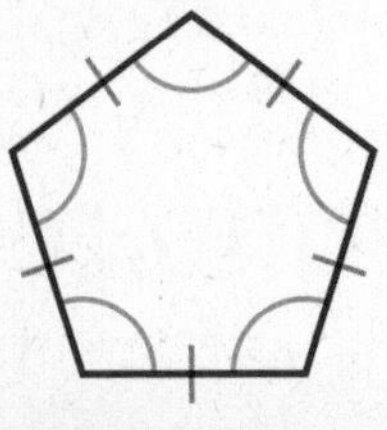

Going to the Philadelphia Zoo

Word Box
area
composite figure
congruent
parallelogram
polygon
quadrilateral
regular polygon
trapezoid

For 2 players

Materials

- 1 each: playing pieces
- 1 number cube

How to Play

1. Each player chooses a playing piece and puts it on START.
2. Toss the number cube to take a turn. Move your playing piece that many spaces.
3. If you land on these spaces:

   Light Green Tell the meaning of the math term or use it in a sentence. If the other player agrees that your answer is correct, jump to the next space with the same term.

   Dark Green Follow the directions printed in the space. If there are no directions, stay where you are.

4. The first player to reach FINISH wins.

DIRECTIONS Each player chooses a playing piece and puts it on START. • Toss the number cube to take a turn. Move your playing piece that many spaces. • If you land on these spaces: Light Green Tell the meaning of the math term or use it in a sentence. If the other player agrees that your answer is correct, jump to the next space with the same term. • Dark Green Follow the directions printed in the space. If there are no directions, stay where you are. • The first player to reach FINISH wins.

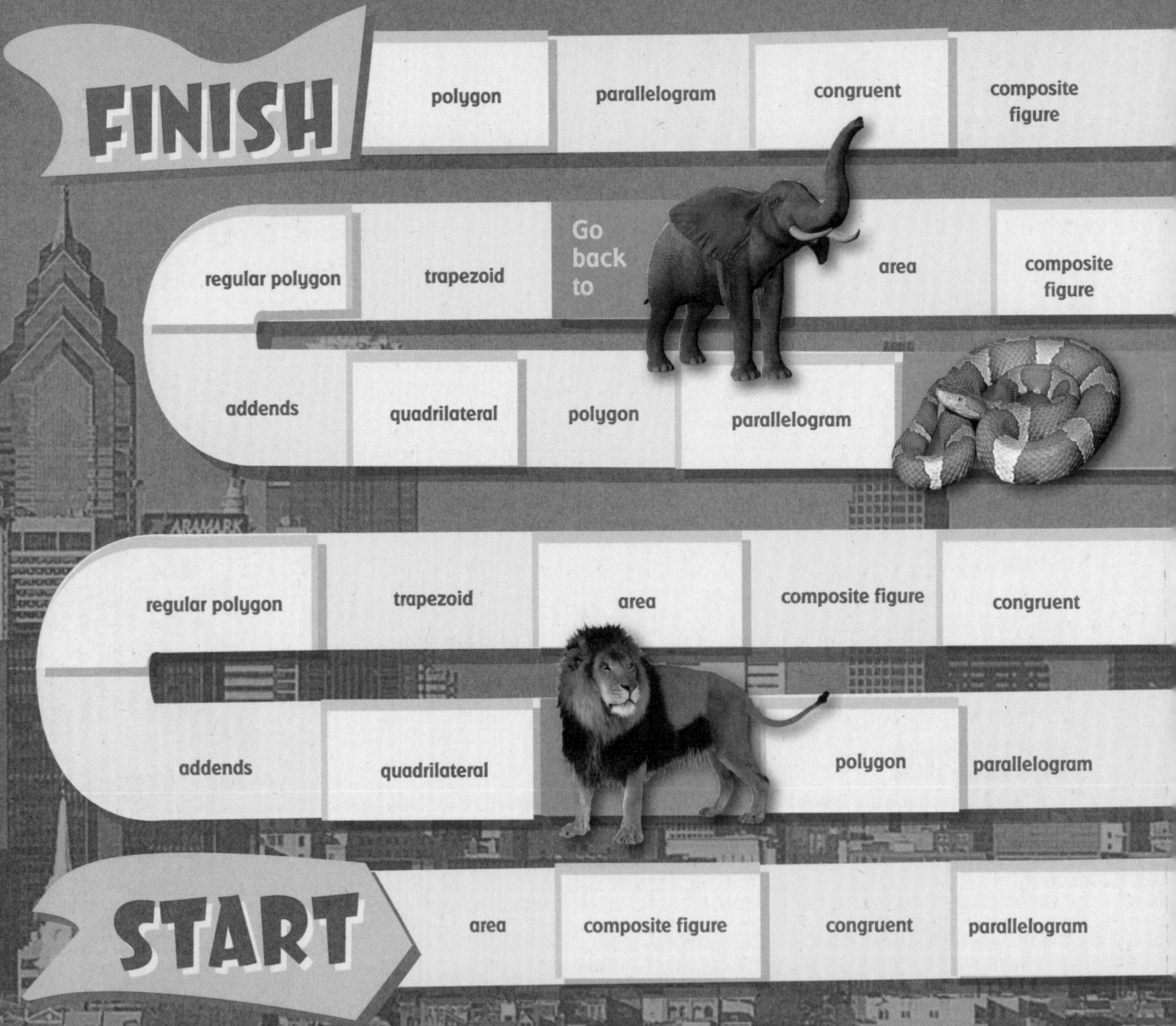

FINISH
polygon
parallelogram
congruent
composite figure

regular polygon
trapezoid
Go back to
area
composite figure

addends
quadrilateral
polygon
parallelogram

regular polygon
trapezoid
area
composite figure
congruent

addends
quadrilateral
polygon
parallelogram

START
area
composite figure
congruent
parallelogram

area | Go back to | trapezoid | regular polygon | Go back to

congruent | parallelogram | polygon | quadrilateral | addends

congruent | composite figure | area | trapezoid | regular polygon

Go back to | parallelogram | polygon | quadrilateral | addends

ZOO

congruent | composite figure | area | trapezoid

polygon | quadrilateral | addends | regular polygon

ZOO

Image Credits: (bg) ©Digital Vision/Getty Images; (elephant) ©Elvele Images Ltd/Alamy; (lion) ©PhotoDisc/Getty Images; (snake) ©Design Pics/Superstock

The Write Way

Reflect

Choose one idea. Write about it.

- Explain how to find the area of a parallelogram.
- Tell how a trapezoid and a quadrilateral are related.
- Write a paragraph that uses the following words

  area **congruent** **regular polygon**
- Describe three real-life objects that are composite figures.

Name ____________________________

Area of Parallelograms

Essential Question How can you find the area of parallelograms?

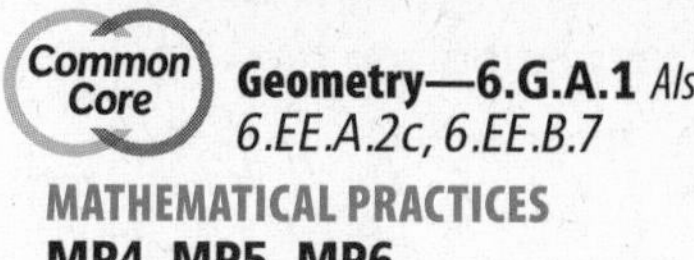

Common Core Geometry—6.G.A.1 *Also 6.EE.A.2c, 6.EE.B.7*

MATHEMATICAL PRACTICES
MP4, MP5, MP6

CONNECT The **area** of a figure is the measure of the number of unit squares needed to cover it without any gaps or overlaps. The area of a rectangle is the product of the length and the width. The rectangle shown has an area of 12 square units. For a rectangle with length l and width w, $A = l \times w$, or $A = lw$.

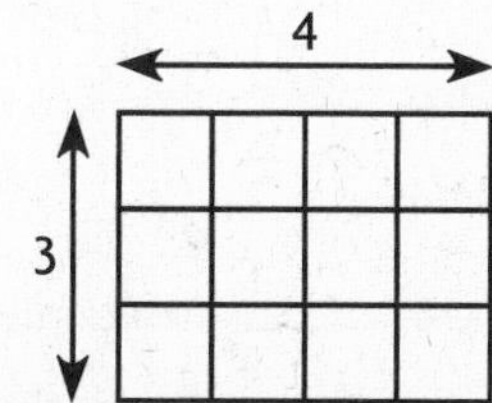

Recall that a rectangle is a special type of parallelogram. A parallelogram is a quadrilateral with two pairs of parallel sides.

Unlock the Problem

Victoria is making a quilt. She is using material in the shape of parallelograms to form the pattern. The base of each parallelogram measures 9 cm and the height measures 4 cm. What is the area of each parallelogram?

Activity Use the area of a rectangle to find the area of the parallelogram.

Materials ■ grid paper ■ scissors

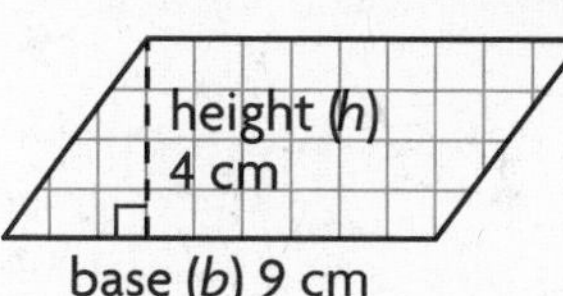

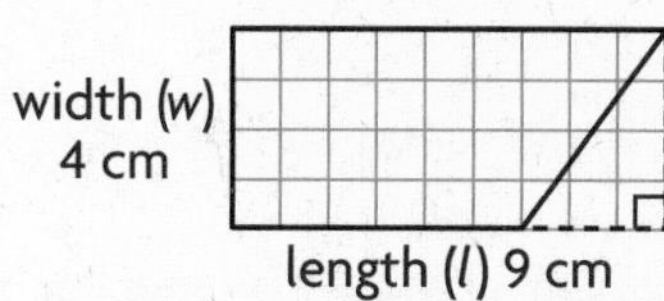

- Draw the parallelogram on grid paper and cut it out.
- Cut along the dashed line to remove a triangle.
- Move the triangle to the right side of the figure to form a rectangle.
- What is the area of the rectangle? ____________
- What is the area of the parallelogram? ____________
- base of parallelogram = ____________ of rectangle

  height of parallelogram = ____________ of rectangle

  area of parallelogram = ____________ of rectangle
- For a parallelogram with base b and height h, $A =$ ____________

Area of parallelogram $= b \times h = 9 \text{ cm} \times 4 \text{ cm} =$ ______ sq cm

So, the area of each parallelogram in the quilt is ______ sq cm.

Math Idea

The height of a parallelogram forms a 90° angle with the base.

MATHEMATICAL PRACTICES 6

Explain how you know that the area of the parallelogram is the same as the area of the rectangle.

Example 1 Use the formula $A = bh$ to find the area of the parallelogram.

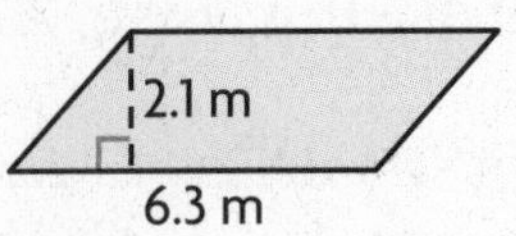

Write the formula. $A = bh$

Replace b and h with their values. $A = 6.3 \times$ ______

Multiply. $A =$ ____________

So, the area of the parallelogram is ________ square meters.

A square is a special rectangle in which the length and width are equal. For a square with side length s, $A = l \times w = s \times s = s^2$, or $A = s^2$.

Example 2 Find the area of a square with sides measuring 9.5 cm.

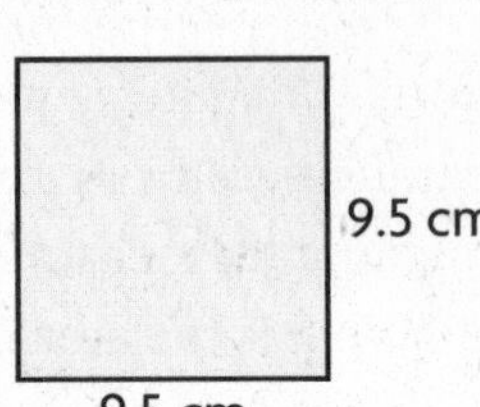

Write the formula. $A = s^2$

Substitute 9.5 for s. Simplify. $A = ($__________$)^2 =$ ________

So, the area of the square is __________ cm^2.

Example 3 A parallelogram has an area of 98 square feet and a base of 14 feet. What is the height of the parallelogram?

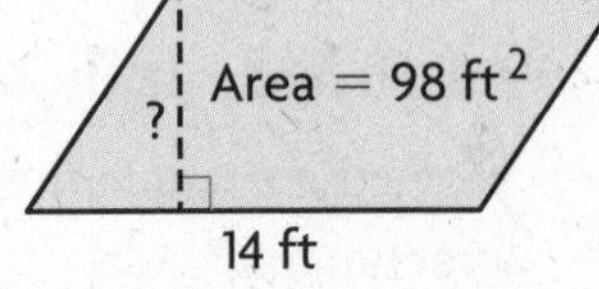

Write the formula. $A = bh$

Replace A and b with their values. ______ = ______ $\times h$

Use the Division Property of Equality. $\frac{98}{\square} = \frac{14h}{\square}$

Solve for h. ______ $= h$

So, the height of the parallelogram is ______ feet.

- MATHEMATICAL PRACTICE 6 **Compare** Explain the difference between the height of a rectangle and the height of a parallelogram.

____

____

____

Name ____________________

Share and Show MATH BOARD

Find the area of the parallelogram or square.

1. $A = bh$

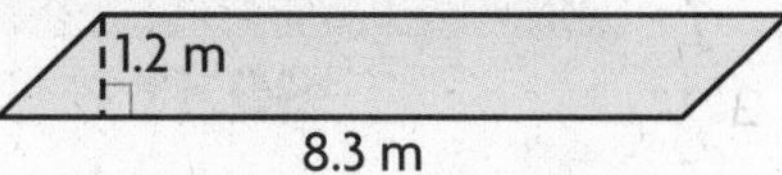

$A = 8.3 \times 1.2$

$A =$ __________ m^2

2.

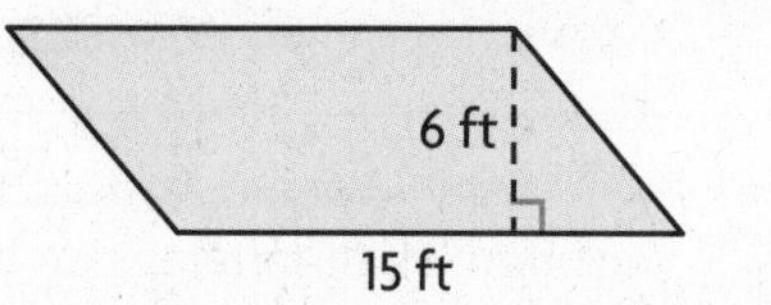

__________ ft^2

3.

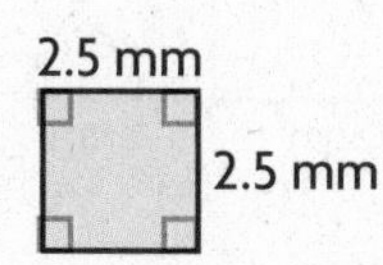

__________ mm^2

4.

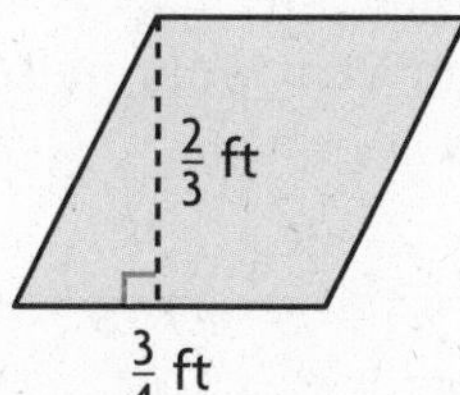

__________ ft^2

Find the unknown measurement for the parallelogram.

5. Area = 11 yd^2

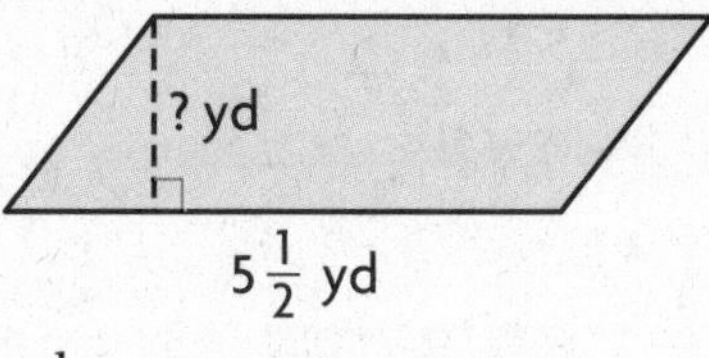

__________ yd

6. Area = 32 yd^2

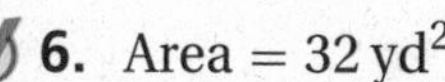

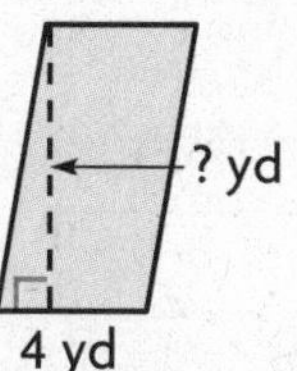

__________ yd

MATHEMATICAL PRACTICES 2

Reasoning Explain how the areas of some parallelograms and rectangles are related.

On Your Own

Find the area of the parallelogram.

7.

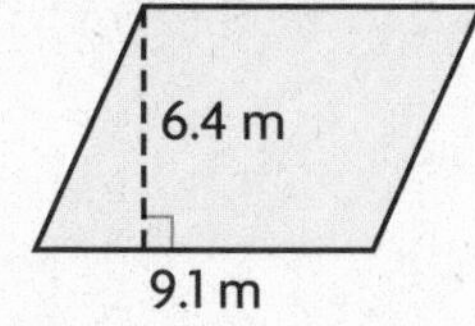

__________ m^2

8.

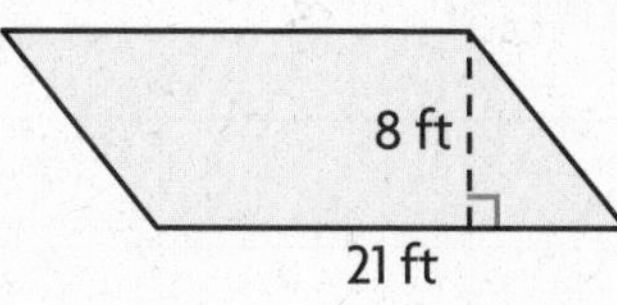

__________ ft^2

Find the unknown measurement for the figure.

9. square

$A =$ __________

$s = 15$ ft

10. parallelogram

$A = 32\ m^2$

$b =$ __________

$h = 8$ m

11. parallelogram

$A = 51\frac{1}{4}$ in.^{2}

$b = 8\frac{1}{5}$ in.

$h =$ __________

12. parallelogram

$A = 121\ mm^2$

$b = 11$ mm

$h =$ __________

13. THINKSMARTER The height of a parallelogram is four times the base. The base measures $3\frac{1}{2}$ ft. Find the area of the parallelogram.

____

Problem Solving • Applications

14. Jane's backyard is shaped like a parallelogram. The base of the parallelogram is 90 feet, and the height is 25 feet. What is the area of Jane's backyard?

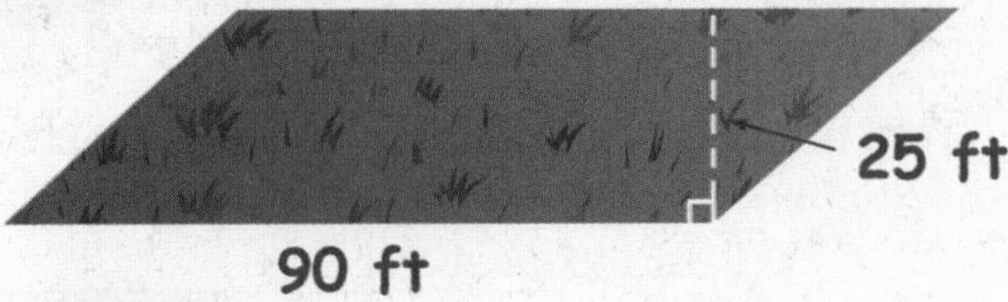

____

15. THINK SMARTER Jack made a parallelogram by putting together two congruent triangles and a square, like the figures shown at the right. The triangles have the same height as the square. What is the area of Jack's parallelogram?

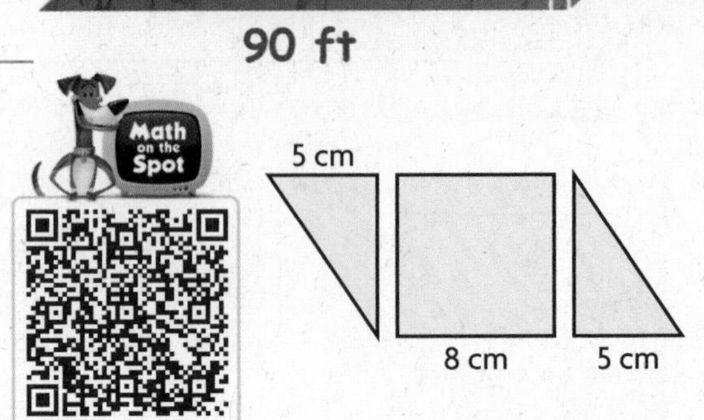

____

16. GO DEEPER The base of a parallelogram is 2 times the parallelogram's height. If the base is 12 inches, what is the area?

____

17. MATHEMATICAL PRACTICE 3 **Verify the Reasoning of Others** Li Ping says that a square with 3-inch sides has a greater area than a parallelogram that is not a square but has sides that have the same length. Does Li Ping's statement make sense? Explain.

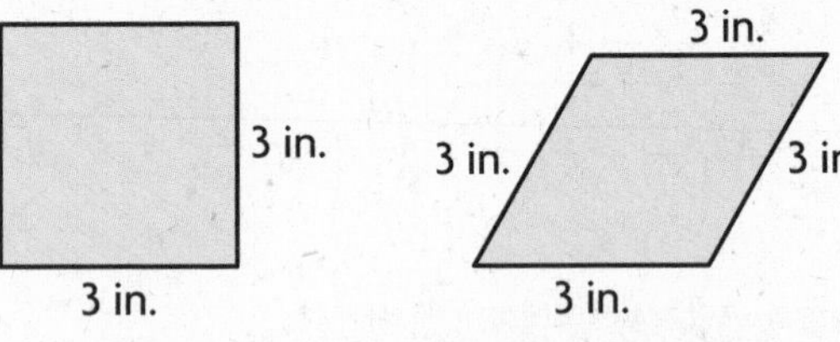

____

____

____

____

____

18. THINK SMARTER Find the area of the parallelogram.

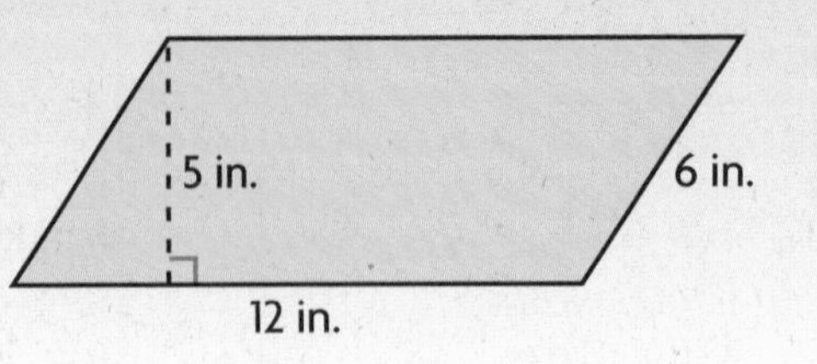

The area is ______ in^2.

Name ______________________

Area of Parallelograms

Common Core

COMMON CORE STANDARD—6.G.A.1
Solve real-world and mathematical problems involving area, surface area, and volume.

Find the area of the figure.

1. 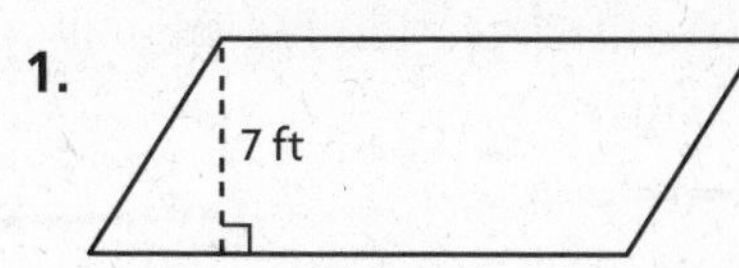

$A = bh$
$A = 18 \times 7$
$A = 126 \text{ ft}^2$

2. 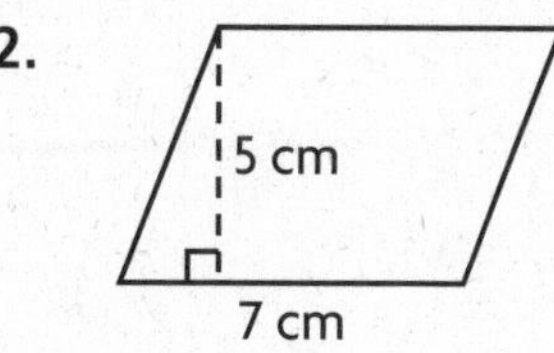

__________ cm^2

Find the unknown measurement for the figure.

3. parallelogram

$A = 9.18 \text{ m}^2$

$b = 2.7 \text{ m}$

$h =$ __________

4. parallelogram

$A =$ __________

$b = 4\frac{3}{10} \text{m}$

$h = 2\frac{1}{10} \text{m}$

5. square

$A =$ __________

$s = 35 \text{ cm}$

6. parallelogram

$A = 6.3 \text{ mm}^2$

$b =$ __________

$h = 0.9 \text{ mm}$

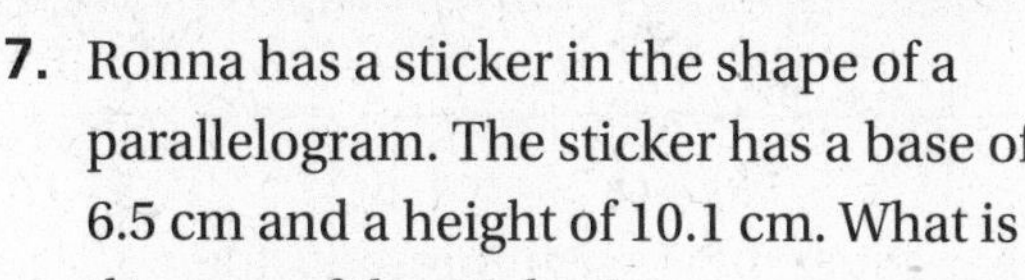

7. Ronna has a sticker in the shape of a parallelogram. The sticker has a base of 6.5 cm and a height of 10.1 cm. What is the area of the sticker?

____

8. A parallelogram-shaped tile has an area of 48 in.². The base of the tile measures 12 in. What is the measure of its height?

____

9. WRITE Math Copy the two triangles and the square in Exercise 15 on page 536. Show how you found the area of each piece. Draw the parallelogram formed when the three figures are put together. Calculate its area using the formula for the area of a parallelogram.

____

____

Lesson Check (6.G.A.1, 6.EE.A.2c, 6.EE.B.7)

1. Cougar Park is shaped like a parallelogram and has an area of $\frac{1}{16}$ square mile. Its base is $\frac{3}{8}$ mile. What is its height?

2. Square County is a square-shaped county divided into 16 equal-sized square districts. If the side length of each district is 4 miles, what is the area of Square County?

Spiral Review (6.EE.B.5, 6.EE.B.8, 6.EE.C.9)

3. Which of the following values of y make the inequality $y < {}^{-}4$ true?

   $y = {}^{-}4$ $\quad y = {}^{-}6$ $\quad y = 0$ $\quad y = {}^{-}8$ $\quad y = 2$

4. On a winter's day, 9°F is the highest temperature recorded. Write an inequality that represents the temperature t in degrees Fahrenheit at any time on this day.

5. In 2 seconds, an elevator travels 40 feet. In 3 seconds, the elevator travels 60 feet. In 4 seconds, the elevator travels 80 feet. Write an equation that gives the relationship between the number of seconds x and the distance y the elevator travels.

6. The linear equation $y = 4x$ represents the number of bracelets y that Jolene can make in x hours. Which ordered pair lies on the graph of the equation?

FOR MORE PRACTICE GO TO THE Personal Math Trainer

Name ______________________________

Explore Area of Triangles

Essential Question What is the relationship among the areas of triangles, rectangles, and parallelograms?

Geometry—6.G.A.1

MATHEMATICAL PRACTICES
MP1, MP3, MP5, MP8

Investigate

Hands On

Materials ■ grid paper ■ tracing paper ■ ruler ■ scissors

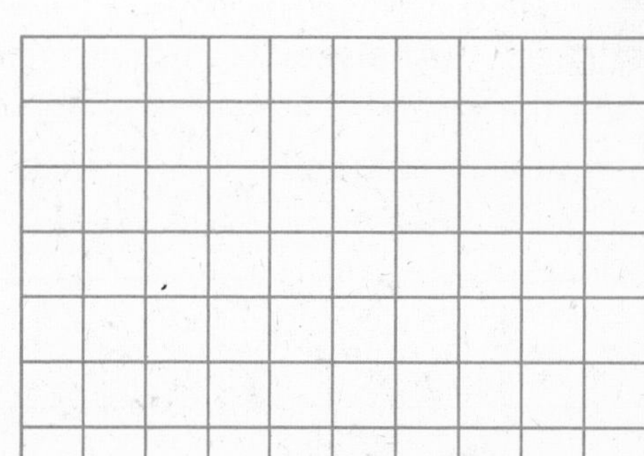

A. On the grid, draw a rectangle with a base of 6 units and a height of 5 units.

- What is the area of the rectangle?

____

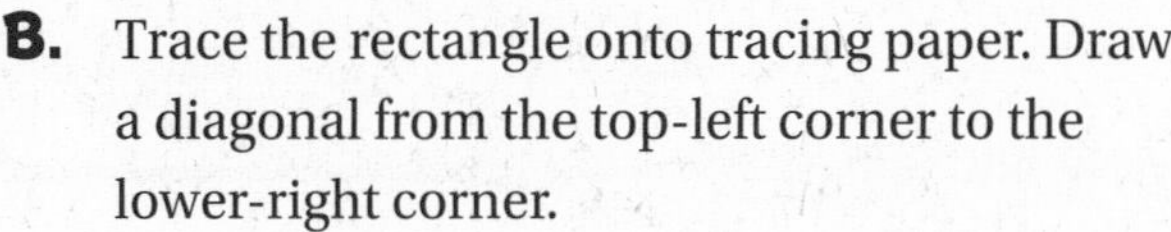

B. Trace the rectangle onto tracing paper. Draw a diagonal from the top-left corner to the lower-right corner.

- A diagonal is a line segment that connects two nonadjacent vertices of a polygon.

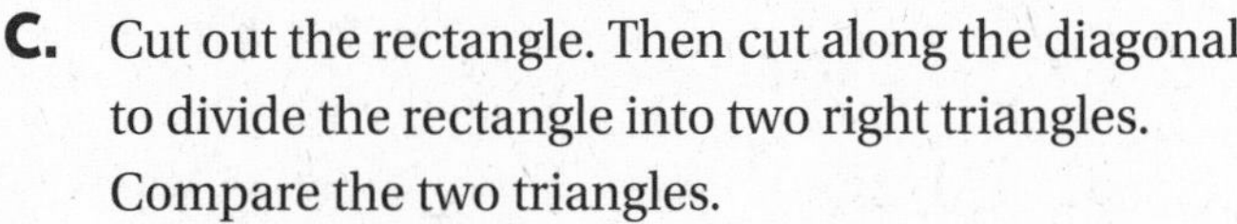

C. Cut out the rectangle. Then cut along the diagonal to divide the rectangle into two right triangles. Compare the two triangles.

- **Congruent** figures are the same shape and size. Are the two right triangles congruent?

____

____

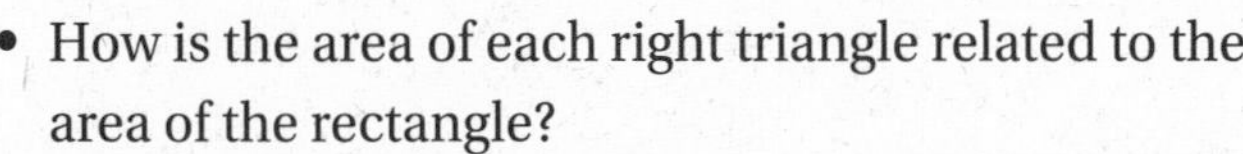

- How is the area of each right triangle related to the area of the rectangle?

____

____

- What is the area of each right triangle?

____

Draw Conclusions

1. Explain how finding the area of a rectangle is like finding the area of a right triangle. How is it different?

____

____

2. MATHEMATICAL PRACTICE 1 **Analyze** Because a rectangle is a parallelogram, its area can be found using the formula $A = b \times h$. Use this formula and your results from the Investigate to write a formula for the area of a right triangle with base b and height h.

____

MATHEMATICAL PRACTICES 3

Apply Explain how you determined the formula for the area of a right triangle.

Make Connections

The area of any parallelogram, including a rectangle, can be found using the formula $A = b \times h$. You can use a parallelogram to look at more triangles.

A. Trace and cut out two copies of the acute triangle.

B. Arrange the two triangles to make a parallelogram.

- Are the triangles congruent? _______
- If the area of the parallelogram is 10 square centimeters, what is the area of each triangle? Explain how you know.

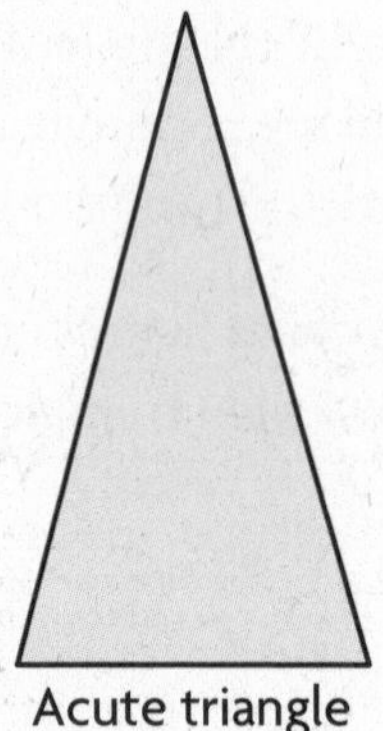

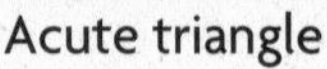

Acute triangle

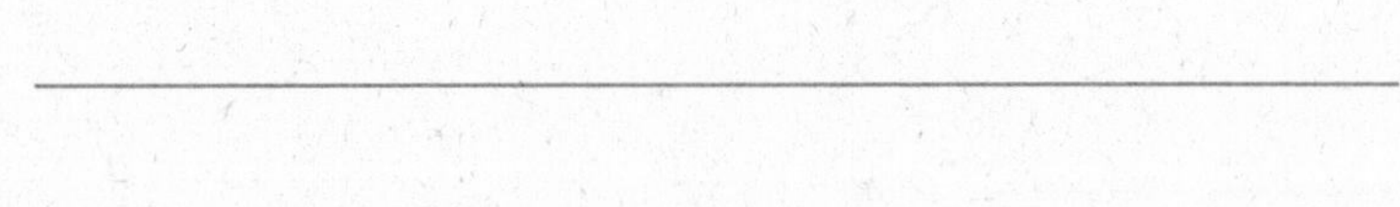

____

____

____

Obtuse triangle

C. Repeat Steps A and B with the obtuse triangle.

3. MATHEMATICAL PRACTICE 8 **Generalize** Can you use the formula $A = \frac{1}{2} \times b \times h$ to find the area of any triangle? Explain.

____

____

Name ______________________

Share and Show

1. Trace the parallelogram, and cut it into two congruent triangles. Find the areas of the parallelogram and one triangle, using square units.

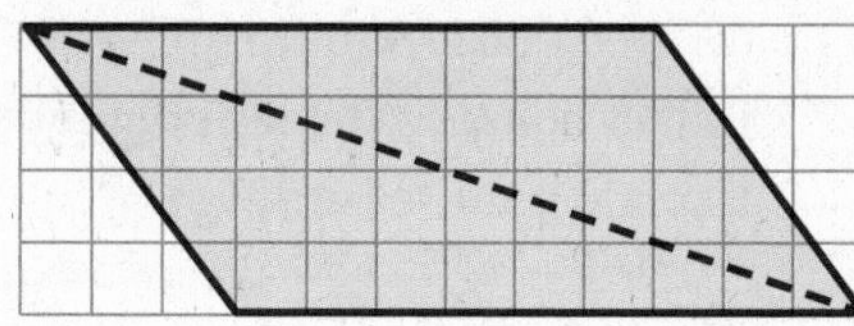

____

Find the area of each triangle.

2. 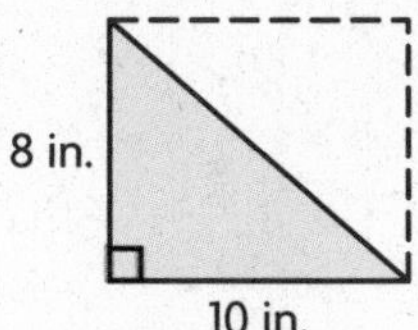

_______ in.^{2}

3. 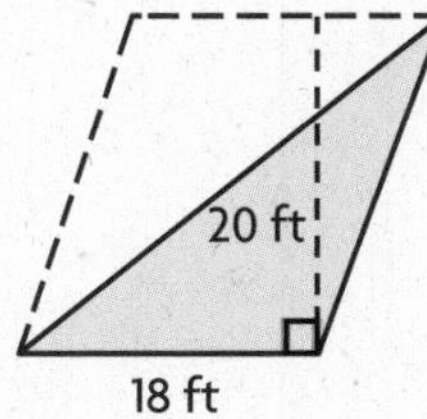

_______ ft^2

4. 

_______ yd^2

5. 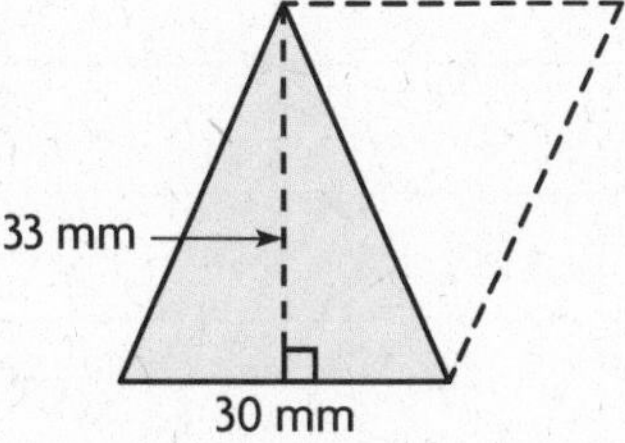

_______ mm^2

6. 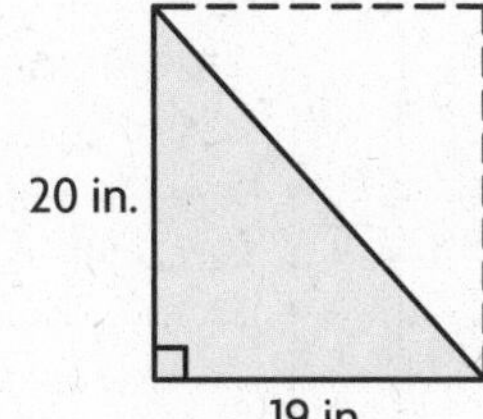

_______ in.^{2}

7. 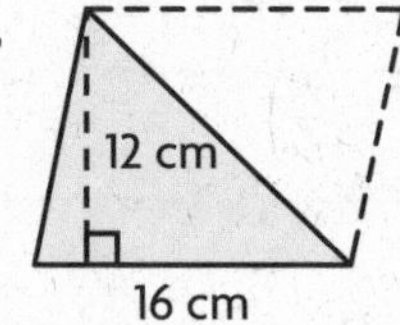

_______ cm^2

Problem Solving • Applications

8. MATHEMATICAL PRACTICE 5 **Communicate** Describe how you can use two triangles of the same shape and size to form a parallelogram.

____

____

____

9. GO DEEPER A school flag is in the shape of a right triangle. The height of the flag is 36 inches and the base is $\frac{3}{4}$ of the height. What is the area of the flag?

____

 Sense or Nonsense?

10. Cyndi and Tyson drew the models below. Each said his or her drawing represents a triangle with an area of 600 square inches. Whose statement makes sense? Whose statement is nonsense? Explain your reasoning.

Tyson's Model

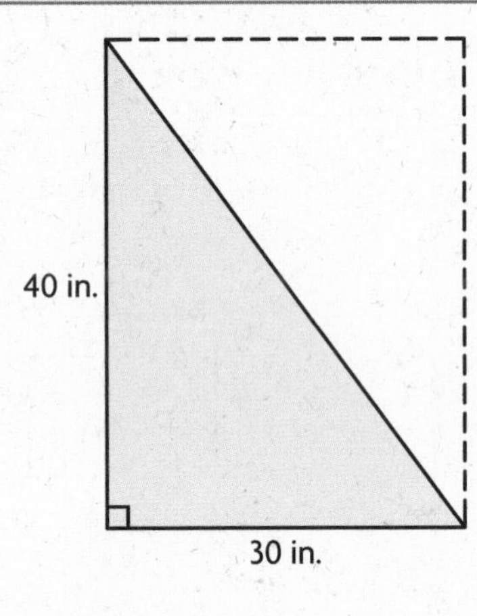

Cyndi's Model

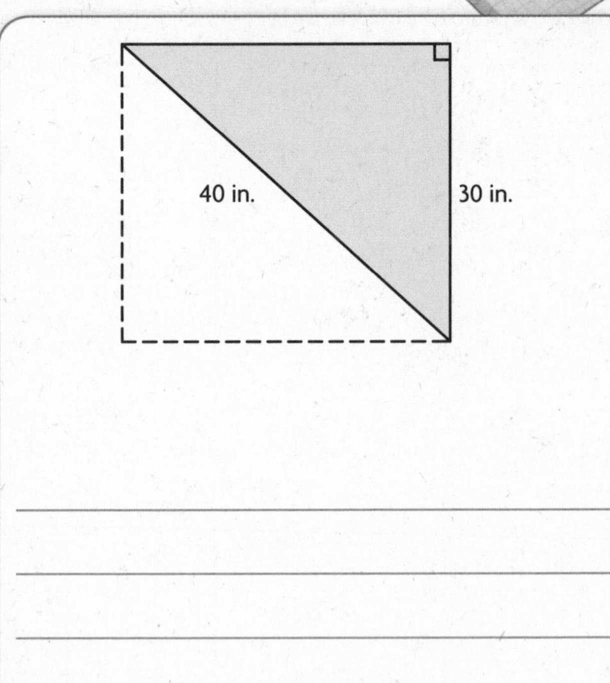

11. THINK SMARTER A flag is separated into two different colors. Find the area of the white region. Show your work.

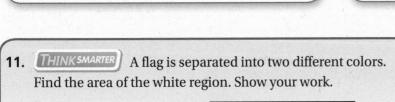

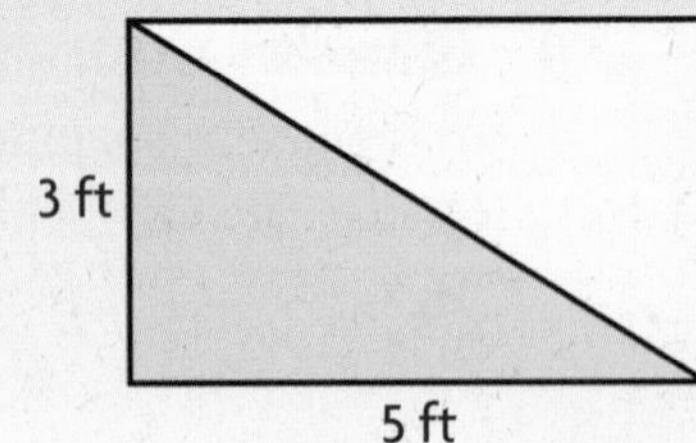

Name ____________________

Explore Area of Triangles

Common Core — COMMON CORE STANDARD—6.G.A.1
Solve real-world and mathematical problems involving area, surface area, and volume.

Find the area of each triangle.

1.
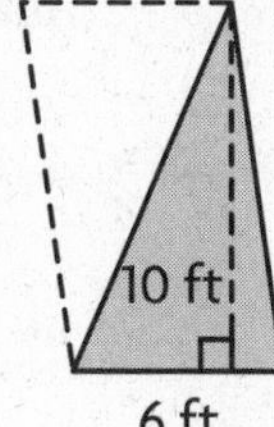

30 ft²

2.
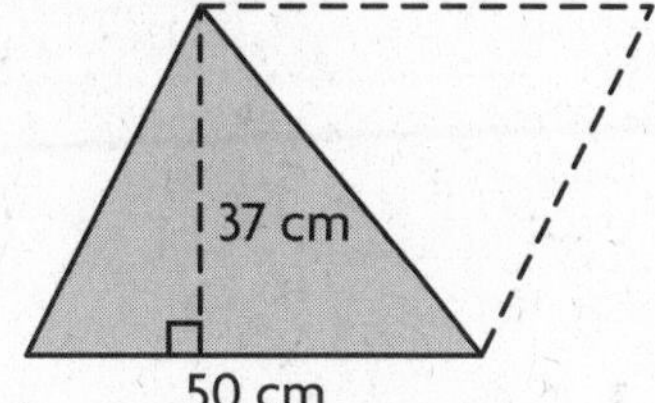

______

3.
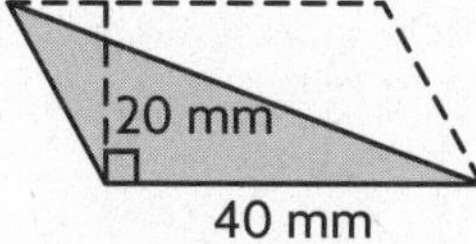

______

4.
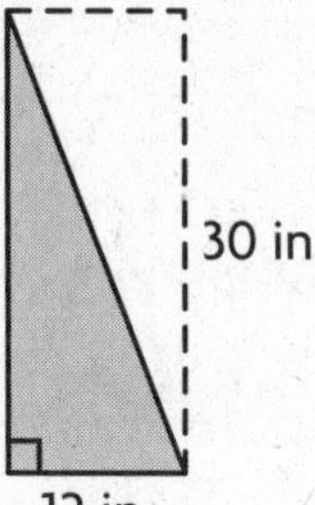

______

5.
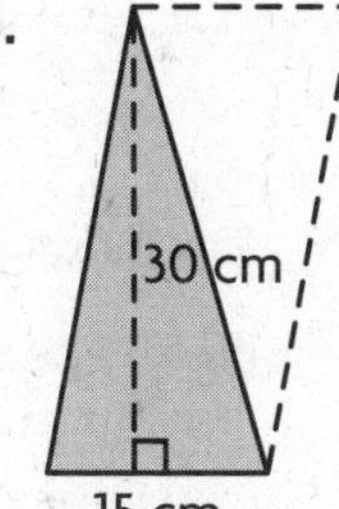

______

6.
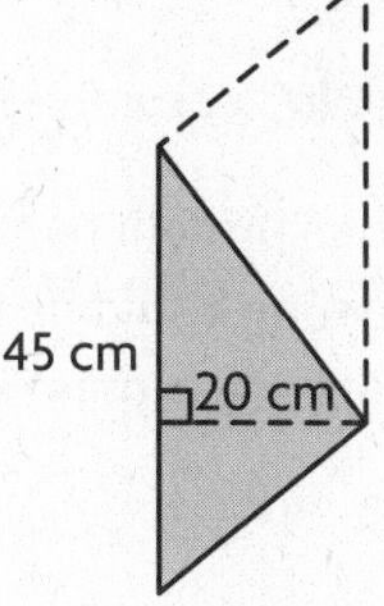

______

Problem Solving Real World

7. Fabian is decorating a triangular pennant for a football game. The pennant has a base of 10 inches and a height of 24 inches. What is the total area of the pennant?

______

8. Ryan is buying a triangular tract of land. The triangle has a base of 100 yards and a height of 300 yards. What is the area of the tract of land?

______

9. WRITE *Math* Draw 3 triangles on grid paper. Draw appropriate parallelograms to support the formula for the area of the triangle. Tape your drawings to this page.

______

______

Lesson Check (6.G.A.1)

1. What is the area of a triangle with a height of 14 feet and a base of 10 feet?

2. What is the area of a triangle with a height of 40 millimeters and a base of 380 millimeters?

Spiral Review (6.EE.A.2c, 6.EE.B.7, 6.EE.B.8, 6.G.A.1)

3. Jack bought 3 protein bars for a total of $4.26. Which equation could be used to find the cost c in dollars of each protein bar?

4. Coach Herrera is buying tennis balls for his team. He can solve the equation $4c = 92$ to find how many cans c of balls he needs. How many cans does he need?

5. Sketch the graph of $y \leq {}^{-}7$ on a number line.

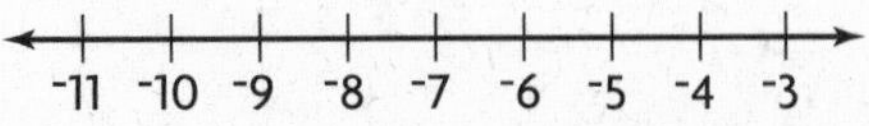

6. A square photograph has a perimeter of 20 inches. What is the area of the photograph?

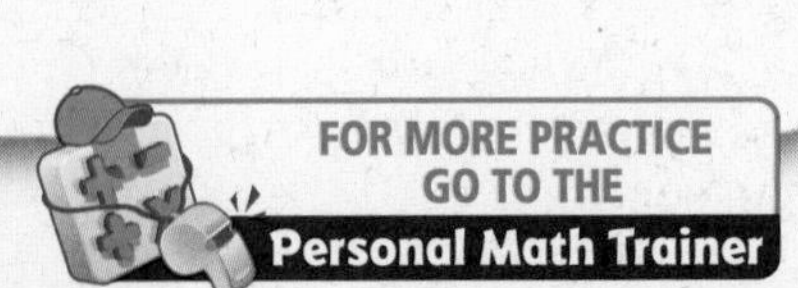

Name ______________________________

Area of Triangles

Essential Question How can you find the area of triangles?

Geometry—6.G.A.1
Also 6.EE.A.2c

MATHEMATICAL PRACTICES
MP3, MP6, MP8

Any parallelogram can be divided into two congruent triangles. The area of each triangle is half the area of the parallelogram, so the area of a triangle is half the product of its base and its height.

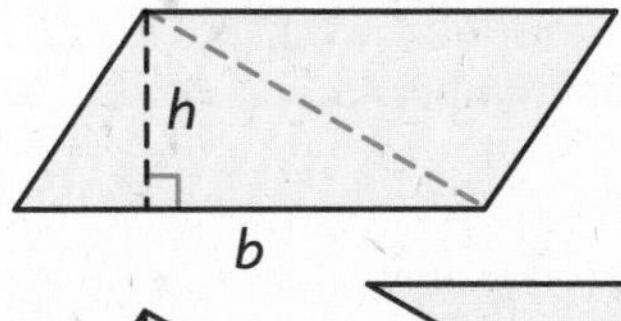

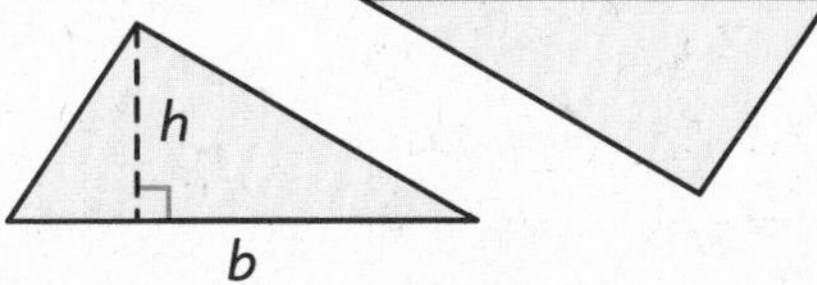

Area of a Triangle

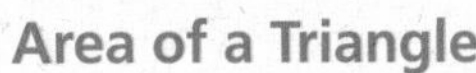

$A = \frac{1}{2}bh$

where b is the base and h is the height

Unlock the Problem

The Flatiron Building in New York is well known for its unusual shape. The building was designed to fit the triangular plot of land formed by 22nd Street, Broadway, and Fifth Avenue. The diagram shows the dimensions of the triangular foundation of the building. What is the area of the triangle?

- How can you identify the base and the height of the triangle?

____

____

____

____

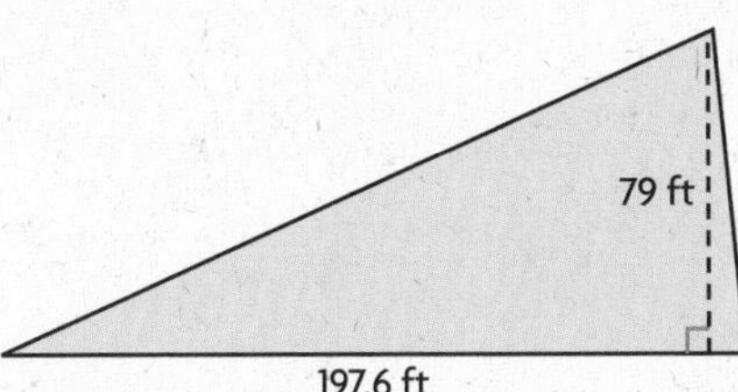

Find the area of the triangle.

Write the formula.	$A = \frac{1}{2}bh$
Substitute 197.6 for b and 79 for h.	$A = \frac{1}{2} \times$ ________ $\times$ ________
Multiply the base and height.	$A = \frac{1}{2} \times$ ________
Multiply by $\frac{1}{2}$.	$A =$ ________

So, the area of the triangle is ____________ ft^2.

MATHEMATICAL PRACTICES 8

Generalize How does the area of a triangle relate to the area of a rectangle with the same base and height?

Example 1 Find the area of the triangle.

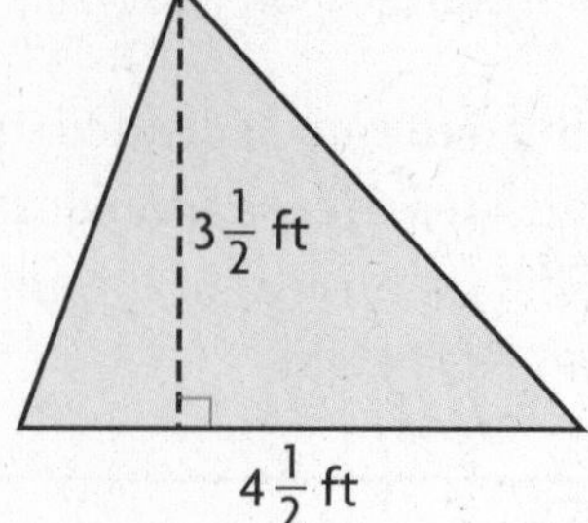

Write the formula. $A = \frac{1}{2}bh$

Substitute $4\frac{1}{2}$ for b and $3\frac{1}{2}$ for h. $A = \frac{1}{2} \times$ ______ $\times$ ______

Rewrite the mixed numbers as fractions. $A = \frac{1}{2} \times \frac{\square}{2} \times \frac{\square}{2}$

Multiply. $A = \frac{\square}{8}$

Rewrite the fraction as a mixed number. $A =$ ______

So, the area of the triangle is ______ ft^2.

Example 2

Daniella is decorating a triangular pennant for her wall. The area of the pennant is 225 in.^{2} and the base measures 30 in. What is the height of the triangular pennant?

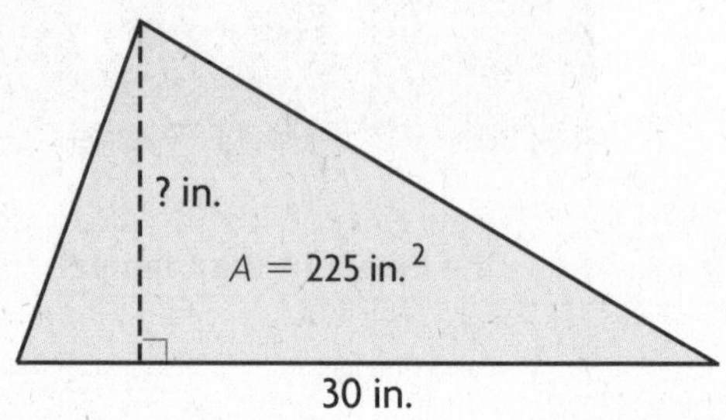

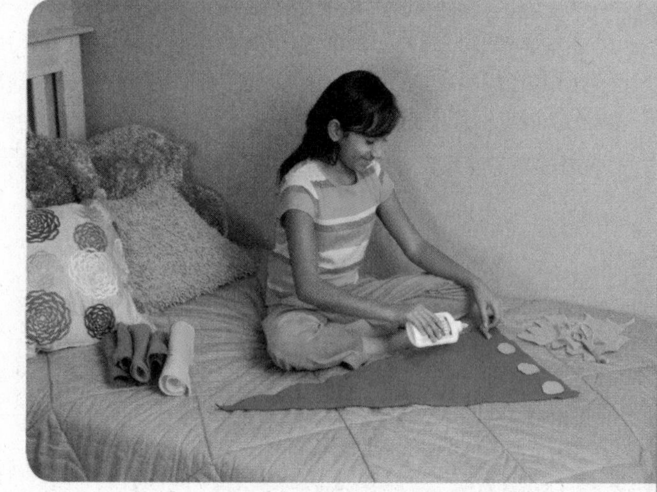

Write the formula. $A = \frac{1}{2}bh$

Substitute 225 for A and 30 for b. ______ $= \frac{1}{2} \times$ ______ $\times h$

Multiply $\frac{1}{2}$ and 30. $225 =$ ______ $\times h$

Use the Division Property of Equality. $\frac{225}{\square} = \frac{\square \times h}{\square}$

Simplify. ______ $= h$

So, the height of the triangular pennant is ______ in.

Name ______________________________

Share and Show

1. FInd the area of the triangle.

$A = \frac{1}{2}bh$

$A = \frac{1}{2} \times 14 \times$ ______

$A =$ ______ cm^2

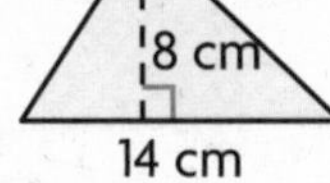

2. The area of the triangle is 132 in.[2] Find the height of the triangle.

$h =$ ______________

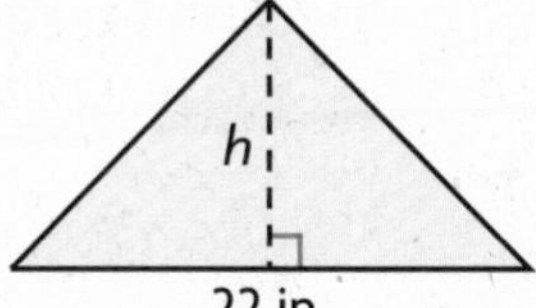

Find the area of the triangle.

3.

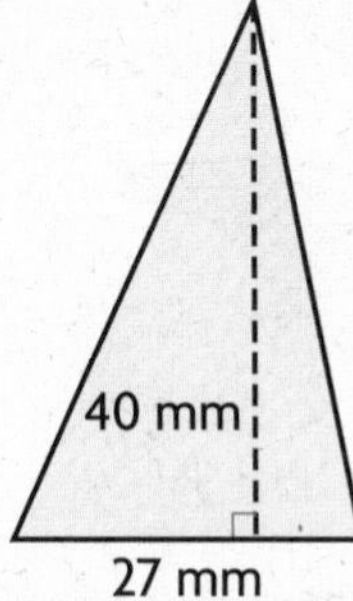

$A =$ ______________

4.

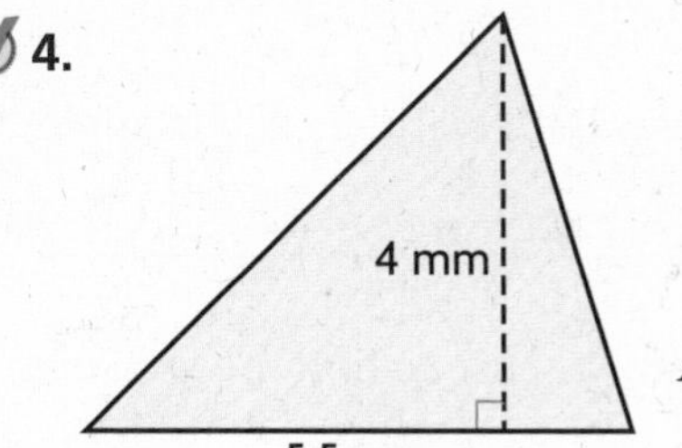

$A =$ ______________

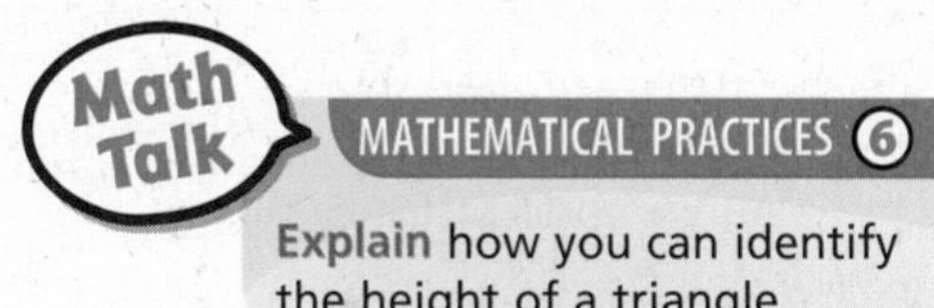

Math Talk
MATHEMATICAL PRACTICES 6
Explain how you can identify the height of a triangle.

On Your Own

THINK SMARTER **Find the unknown measurement for the figure.**

5.

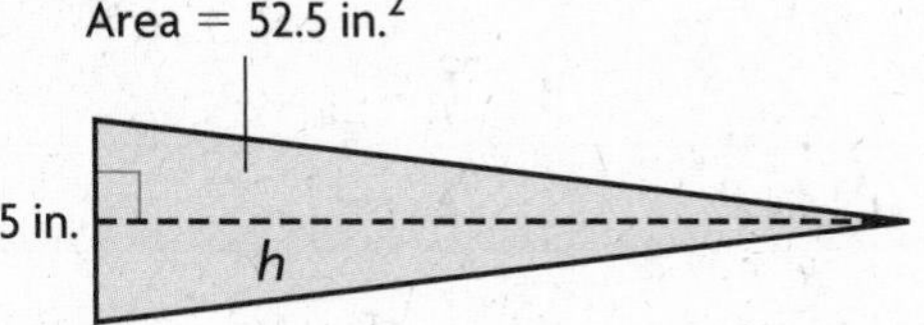

$h =$ ______________

6.

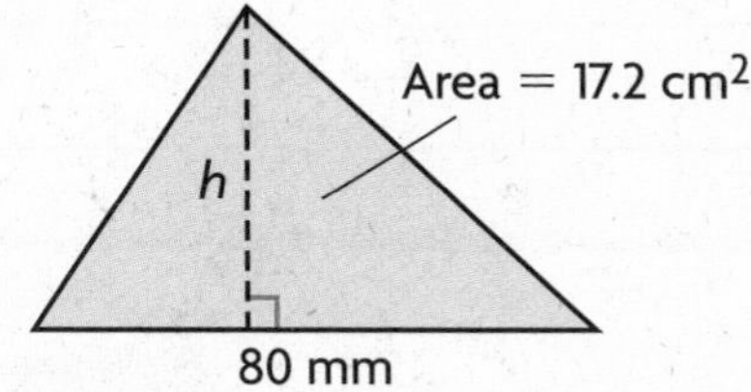

$h =$ ______________

7. MATHEMATICAL PRACTICE 3 **Verify the Reasoning of Others** The height of a triangle is twice the base. The area of the triangle is 625 in.[2] Carson says the base of the triangle is at least 50 in. Is Carson's estimate reasonable? Explain.

____

____

____

Unlock the Problem Real World

8. GO DEEPER Alani is building a set of 4 shelves. Each shelf will have 2 supports in the shape of right isosceles triangles. Each shelf is 14 inches deep. How many square inches of wood will she need to make all of the supports?

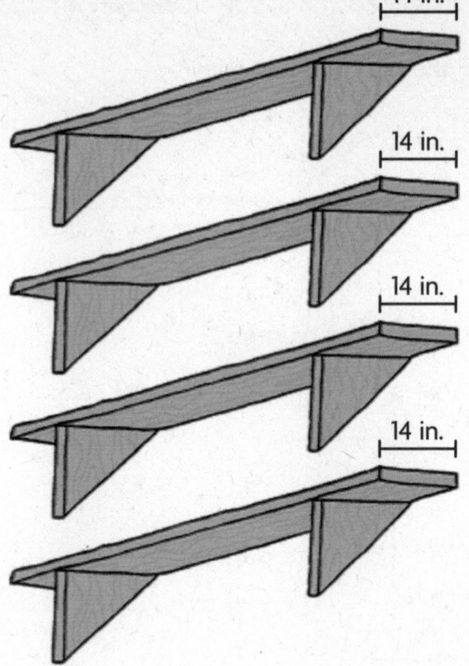

a. What are the base and height of each triangle?

____

b. What formula can you use to find the area of a triangle?

____

c. Explain how you can find the area of one triangular support.

____

____

____

____

d. How many triangular supports are needed to build 4 shelves?

____

e. How many square inches of wood will Alani need to make all the supports?

____

9. THINKSMARTER The area of a triangle is 97.5 cm^2. The height of the triangle is 13 cm. Find the base of the triangle. Explain your work.

____

____

____

____

10. THINKSMARTER The area of a triangle is 30 ft^2. For numbers 10a–10d, select Yes or No to tell if the dimensions given could be the height and base of the triangle.

10a. $h = 3, b = 10$ ○ Yes ○ No

10b. $h = 3, b = 20$ ○ Yes ○ No

10c. $h = 5, b = 12$ ○ Yes ○ No

10d. $h = 5, b = 24$ ○ Yes ○ No

Name ______________________________

Area of Triangles

Common Core **COMMON CORE STANDARD—6.G.A.1**
Solve real-world and mathematical problems involving area, surface area, and volume.

Find the area.

1. 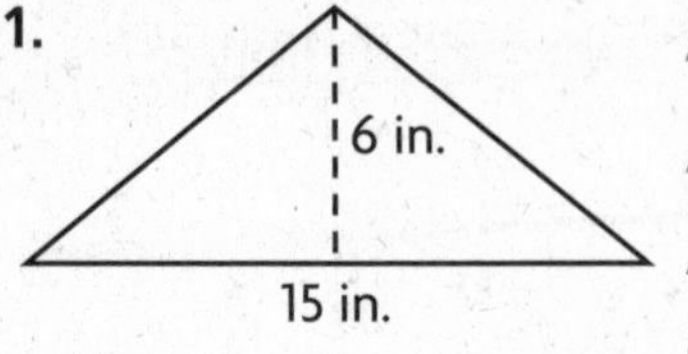

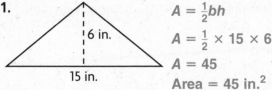

$A = \frac{1}{2}bh$

$A = \frac{1}{2} \times 15 \times 6$

$A = 45$

Area = 45 in.^{2}

2. 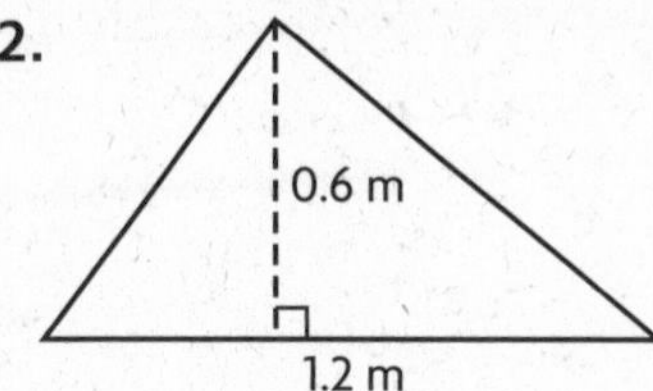

____

3. 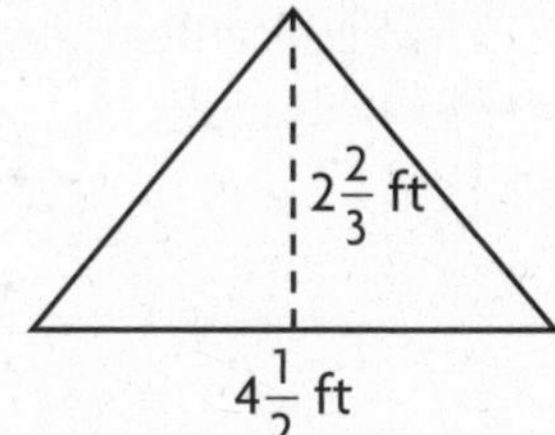

____

Find the unknown measurement for the triangle.

4. $A = 0.225$ mi^2
$b = 0.6$ mi
$h =$ ▢

____

5. $A = 4.86$ yd^2
$b =$ ▢
$h = 1.8$ yd

____

6. $A = 63$ m^2
$b =$ ▢
$h = 12$ m

____

7. $A = 2.5$ km^2
$b = 5$ km
$h =$ ▢

____

Problem Solving Real World

8. Bayla draws a triangle with a base of 15 cm and a height of 8.5 cm. If she colors the space inside the triangle, what area does she color?

____

9. Alicia is making a triangular sign for the school play. The area of the sign is 558 in.^{2}. The base of the triangle is 36 in. What is the height of the triangle?

____

10. WRITE Math Describe how you would find how much grass seed is needed to cover a triangular plot of land.

____

____

Lesson Check (6.G.A.1, 6.EE.A.2c)

1. A triangular flag has an area of 187.5 square inches. The base of the flag measures 25 inches. How tall is the triangular flag?

2. A piece of stained glass in the shape of a right triangle has sides measuring 8 centimeters, 15 centimeters, and 17 centimeters. What is the area of the piece?

Spiral Review (6.EE.B.7, 6.EE.C.9, 6.G.A.1)

3. Tina bought a t-shirt and sandals. The total cost was $41.50. The t-shirt cost $8.95. The equation $8.95 + c = 41.50$ can be used to find the cost c in dollars of the sandals. How much did the sandals cost?

4. There are 37 paper clips in a box. Carmen places more paper clips in the box. Write an equation to show the total number of paper clips p in the box after Carmen places n more paper clips in the box.

5. Name another ordered pair that is on the graph of the equation represented by the table.

People in group, x	1	2	3	4
Total cost of ordering lunch special ($), y	6	12	18	24

6. Find the area of the triangle that divides the parallelogram in half.

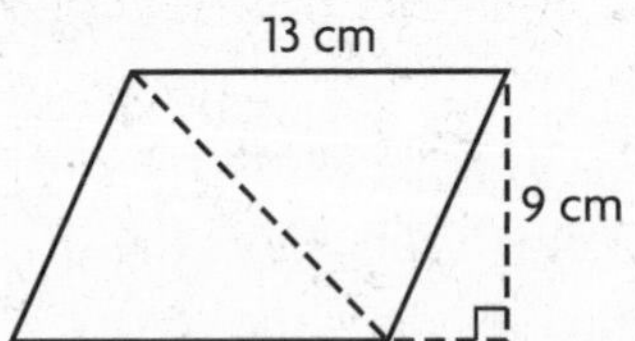

FOR MORE PRACTICE GO TO THE Personal Math Trainer

Name ________________________________

Explore Area of Trapezoids

Geometry—
6.G.A.1

MATHEMATICAL PRACTICES
MP4, MP7, MP8

Essential Question What is the relationship between the areas of trapezoids and parallelograms?

CONNECT A **trapezoid** is a quadrilateral with at least one pair of parallel sides. Any pair of parallel sides can be the *bases* of the trapezoid. A line segment drawn at a 90° angle to the two bases is the *height* of the trapezoid. You can use what you know about the area of a parallelogram to find the area of a trapezoid.

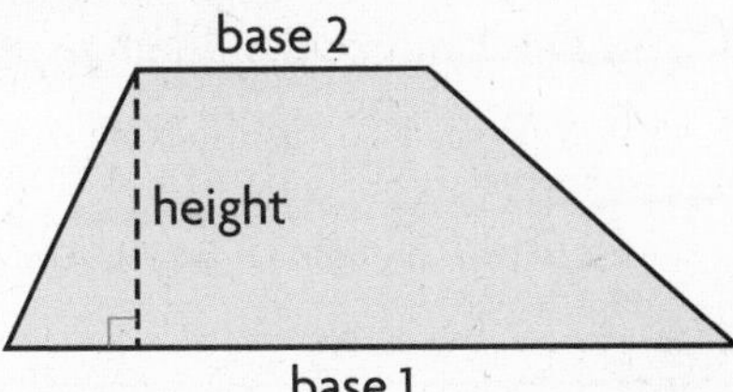

Investigate

Hands On

Materials ■ grid paper ■ ruler ■ scissors

3 units
4 units
6 units

A. Draw two copies of the trapezoid on grid paper.

B. Cut out the trapezoids.

C. Arrange the trapezoids to form a parallelogram, as shown. Examine the parallelogram.

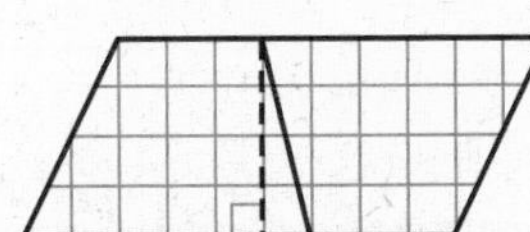

- How can you find the length of the base of the parallelogram?

____

____

- The base of the parallelogram is ______ + ______ = ______ units.
- The height of the parallelogram is ______ units.
- The area of the parallelogram is ______ × ______ = ______ square units.

D. Examine the trapezoids.

- How does the area of one trapezoid relate to the area of the parallelogram?

____

____

- Find the area of one trapezoid. Explain how you found the area.

____

____

Draw Conclusions

1. MATHEMATICAL PRACTICE 7 **Identify Relationships** Explain how knowing how to find the area of a parallelogram helped you find the area of the trapezoid.

____

2. Use your results from the Investigate to describe how you can find the area of any trapezoid.

____

____

____

3. MATHEMATICAL PRACTICE 8 **Generalize** Can you use the method you described above to find the area of a trapezoid if two copies of the trapezoid can be arranged to form a rectangle? Explain.

____

____

Make Connections

You can use the formula for the area of a rectangle to find the area of some types of trapezoids.

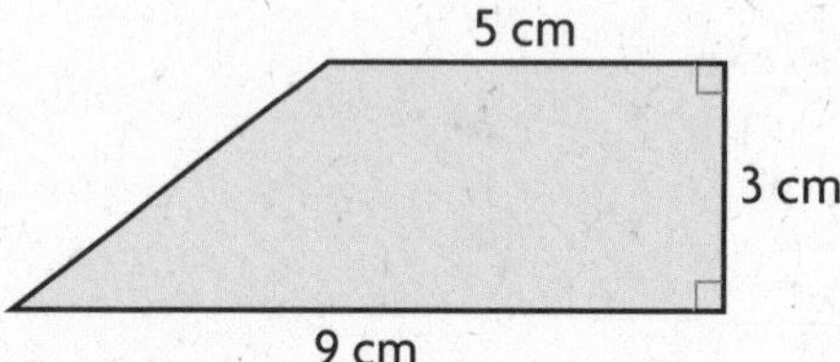

A. Trace and cut out two copies of the trapezoid.

B. Arrange the two trapezoids to form a rectangle. Examine the rectangle.

- The length of the rectangle is ______ + ______ = ______ cm.
- The width of the rectangle is ______ cm.
- The area of the rectangle is ______ × ______ = ______ cm^2.

C. Examine the trapezoids.

- How does the area of each trapezoid relate to the area of the rectangle?

____

- The area of the given trapezoid is $\frac{1}{2}$ × ______ = ______ cm^2.

Name ______________________________

Share and Show MATH BOARD

1. Trace and cut out two copies of the trapezoid. Arrange the trapezoids to form a parallelogram. Find the areas of the parallelogram and one trapezoid using square units.

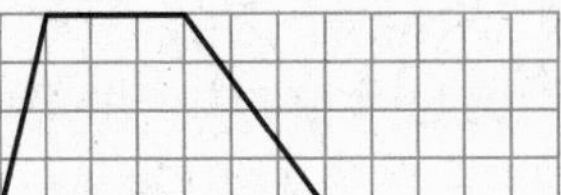

____

Find the area of the trapezoid.

2. 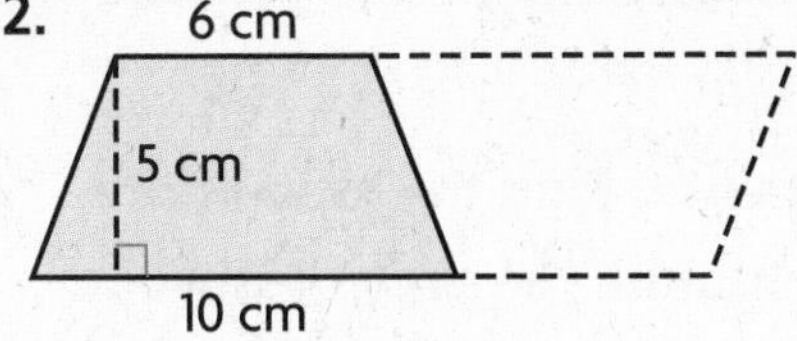

______ cm^2

3. 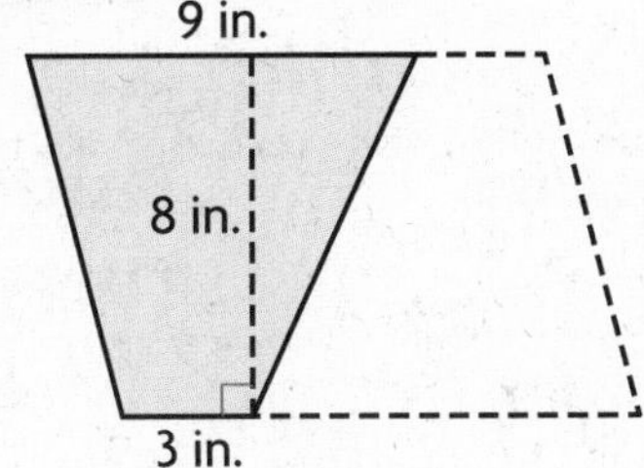

______ $in.^2$

4. 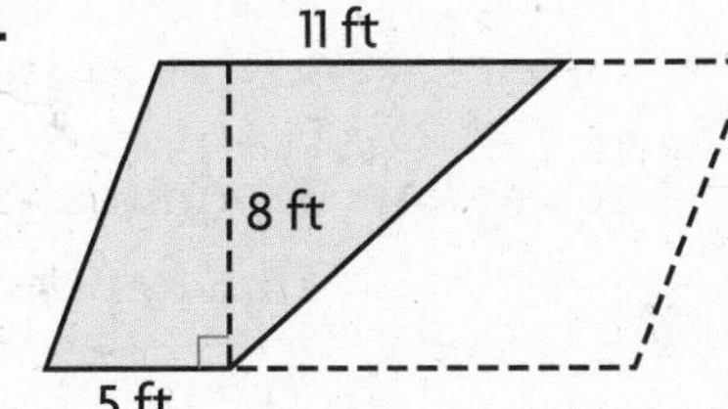

______ ft^2

5. 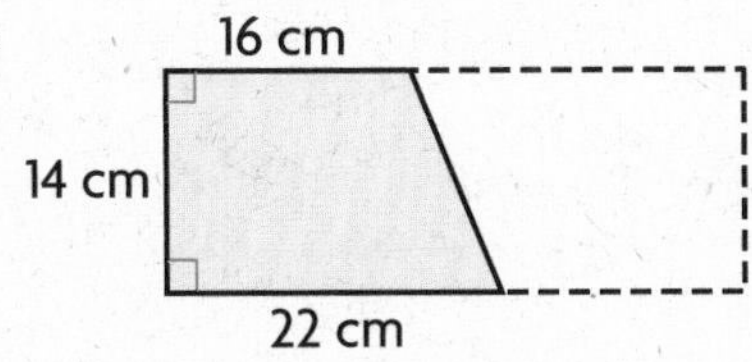

______ cm^2

6. 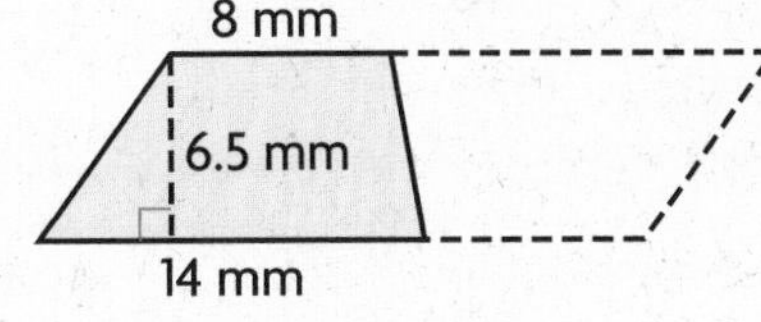

______ mm^2

7. 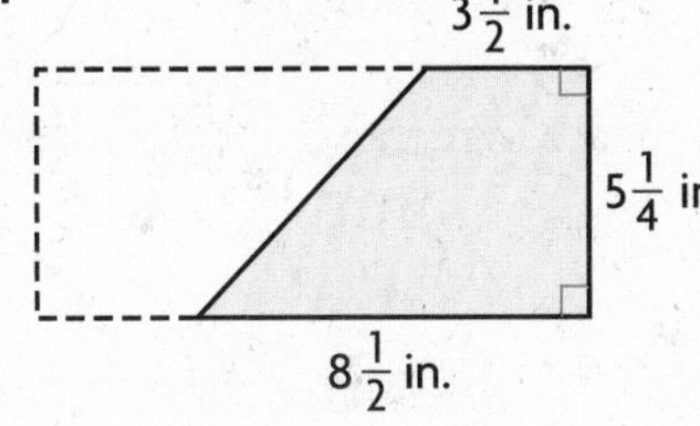

______ $in.^2$

Problem Solving • Applications

8. MATHEMATICAL PRACTICE 4 **Describe a Method** Explain one way to find the height of a trapezoid if you know the area of the trapezoid and the length of both bases.

____

____

____

9. GO DEEPER A patio is in the shape of a trapezoid. The length of the longer base is 18 feet. The length of the shorter base is two feet less than half the longer base. The height is 8 feet. What is the area of the patio?

____

THINKSMARTER What's the Error?

10. Except for a small region near its southeast corner, the state of Nevada is shaped like a trapezoid. The map at the right shows the approximate dimensions of the trapezoid. Sabrina used the map to estimate the area of Nevada.

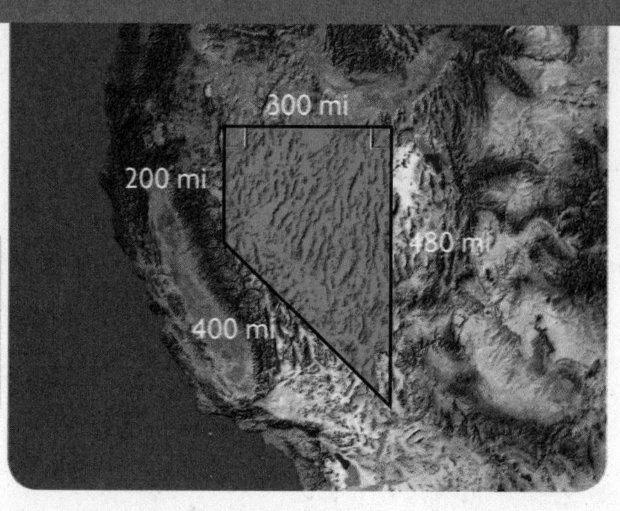

Look at how Sabrina solved the problem. Find her error.

Two copies of the trapezoid can be put together to form a rectangle.

length of rectangle:

$200 + 480 = 680$ mi

width of rectangle: 300 mi

$A = lw$

$= 680 \times 300$

$= 204{,}000$

The area of Nevada is about 204,000 square miles.

Describe the error. Find the area of the trapezoid to estimate the area of Nevada.

11. THINKSMARTER A photo was cut in half at an angle. What is the area of one of the cut pieces?

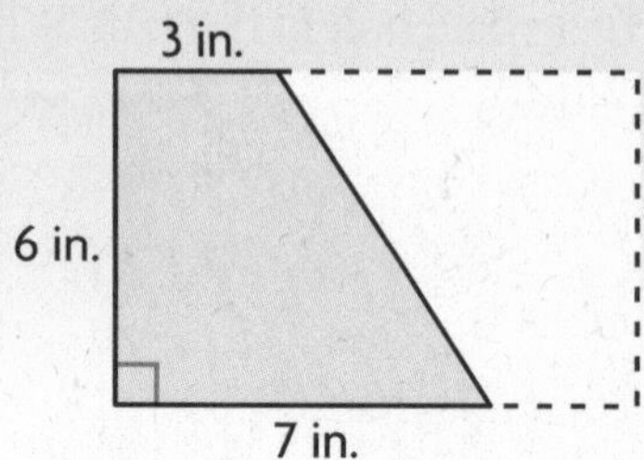

The area is ________.

Name ______________________

Explore Area of Trapezoids

COMMON CORE STANDARD—6.G.A.1
Solve real-world and mathematical problems involving area, surface area, and volume.

1. Trace and cut out two copies of the trapezoid. Arrange the trapezoids to form a parallelogram. Find the areas of the parallelogram and the trapezoids using square units.

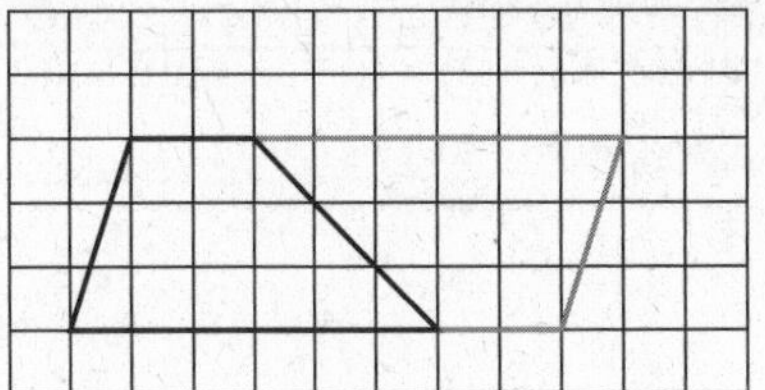

parallelogram: 24 square units; trapezoids:

12 square units

Find the area of the trapezoid.

2. 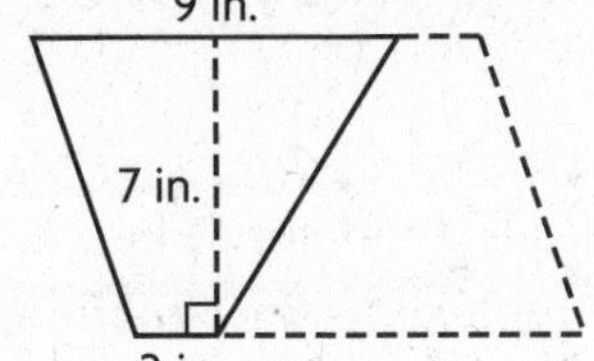

_______ in.^{2}

3. 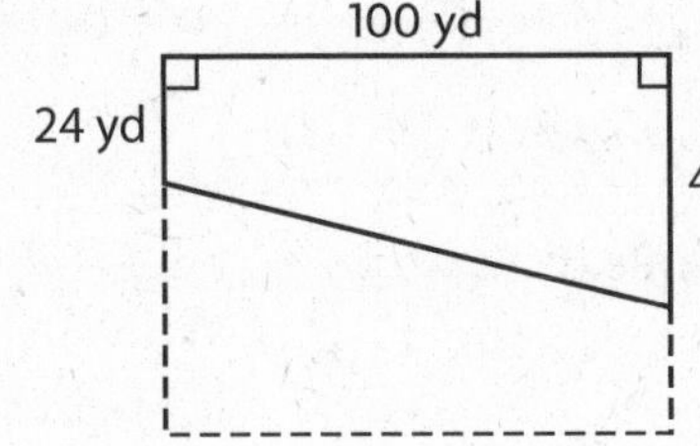

_______ yd^2

4. 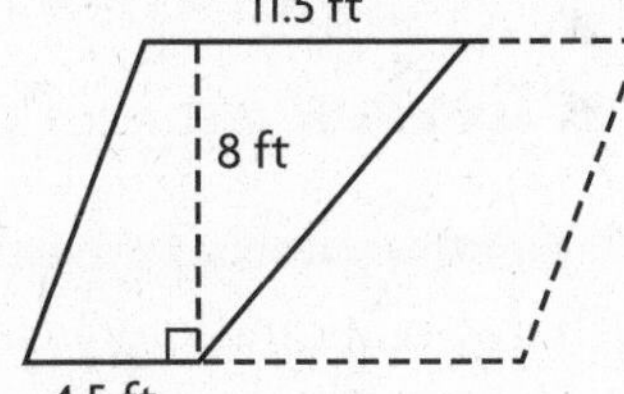

_______ ft^2

Problem Solving Real World

5. A cake is made out of two identical trapezoids. Each trapezoid has a height of 11 inches and bases of 9 inches and 14 inches. What is the area of one of the trapezoid pieces?

____

6. A sticker is in the shape of a trapezoid. The height is 3 centimeters, and the bases are 2.5 centimeters and 5.5 centimeters. What is the area of the sticker?

____

7. **WRITE** *Math* Find the area of a trapezoid that has bases that are 15 inches and 20 inches and a height of 9 inches.

____

Lesson Check (6.G.A.1)

1. What is the area of figure *ABEG*?

A 9 yd B C
7 yd
G F 15 yd E D

2. Maggie colors a figure in the shape of a trapezoid. The trapezoid is 6 inches tall. The bases are 4.5 inches and 8 inches. What is the area of the figure that Maggie colored?

Spiral Review (6.EE.A.2c, 6.EE.B.7, 6.EE.C.9, 6.G.A.1)

3. Cassandra wants to solve the equation $30 = \frac{2}{5}p$. What operation should she perform to isolate the variable?

4. Ginger makes pies and sells them for $14 each. Write an equation that represents the situation, if *y* represents the money that Ginger earns and *x* represents the number of pies sold.

5. What is the equation for the graph shown below?

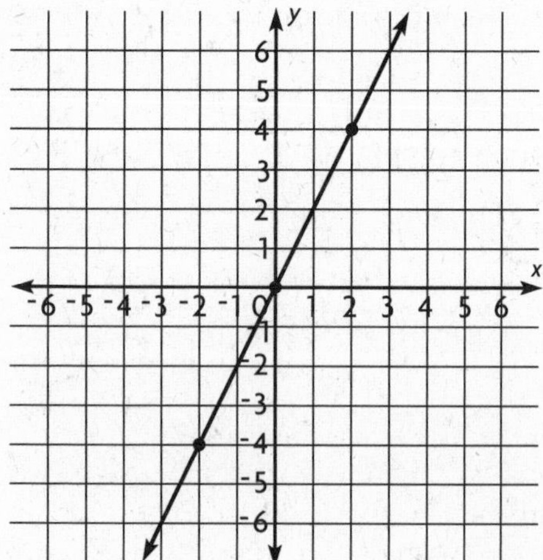

6. Cesar made a rectangular banner that is 4 feet by 3 feet. He wants to make a triangular banner that has the same area as the other banner. The triangular banner will have a base of 4 feet. What should its height be?

Name ______________________________

Area of Trapezoids

Essential Question How can you find the area of trapezoids?

Geometry—6.G.A.1
Also 6.EE.A.2c

MATHEMATICAL PRACTICES
MP1, MP3, MP6

Any parallelogram can be divided into two trapezoids with one pair of parallel sides that are also the same shape and size. The bases of the trapezoids, b_1 and b_2, form the base of the parallelogram. The area of each trapezoid is half the area of the parallelogram. So, the area of a trapezoid is half the product of its height and the sum of its bases.

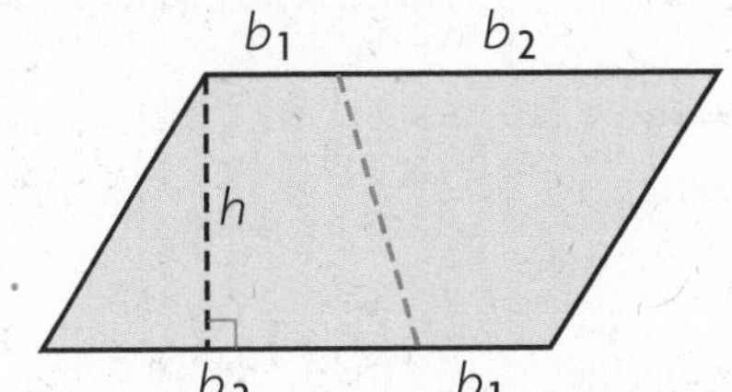

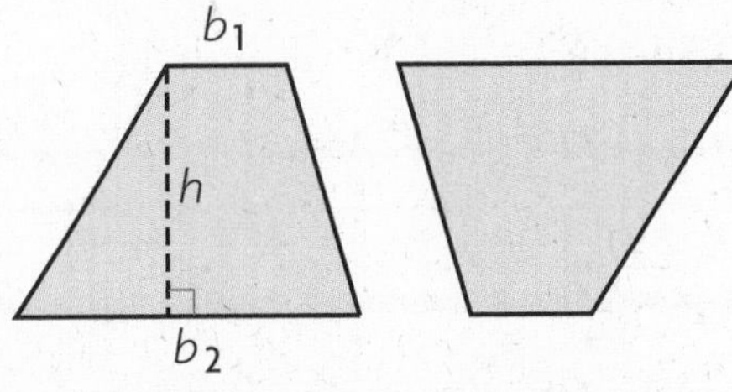

Area of a Trapezoid

$$A = \frac{1}{2}(b_1 + b_2)h$$

where b_1 and b_2 are the two bases and h is the height

Unlock the Problem (Real World)

Mr. Desmond has tables in his office with tops shaped like trapezoids. The diagram shows the dimensions of each tabletop. What is the area of each tabletop?

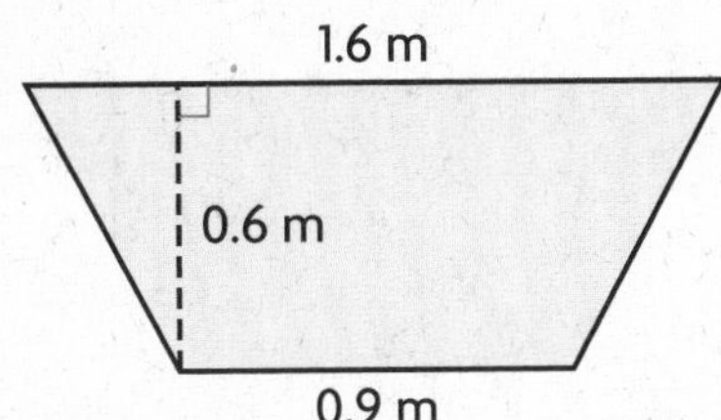

- How can you identify the bases?

____

____

- How can you identify the height?

____

____

Find the area of the trapezoid.

Write the formula. $A = \frac{1}{2}(b_1 + b_2)h$

Substitute 1.6 for b_1, 0.9 for b_2, and 0.6 for h. $A = \frac{1}{2} \times (\_\_\_\_ + \_\_\_\_) \times \_\_\_\_$

Add within the parentheses. $A = \frac{1}{2} \times \_\_\_\_ \times 0.6$

Multiply. $A = \frac{1}{2} \times \_\_\_\_ = \_\_\_\_$

So, the area of each tabletop is ______ m^2.

Math Talk MATHEMATICAL PRACTICES 1

Describe Relationships Describe the relationship between the area of a trapezoid and the area of a parallelogram with the same height and a base equal to the sum of the trapezoid's bases.

Example 1 Find the area of the trapezoid.

Write the formula. $A = \frac{1}{2}(b_1 + b_2)h$

Substitute 4.6 for b_1, 9.4 for b_2, and 3.5 for h. $A = \frac{1}{2} \times (\_\_\_\_ + \_\_\_\_) \times 3.5$

4.6 cm

3.5 cm

9.4 cm

Add. $A = \frac{1}{2} \times \_\_\_\_ \times 3.5$

Multiply. $A = \_\_\_\_ \times 3.5 = \_\_\_\_$

So, the area of the trapezoid is ________ cm².

Example 2 The area of the trapezoid is 702 in.² Find the height of the trapezoid.

Write the formula. $A = \frac{1}{2}(b_1 + b_2)h$

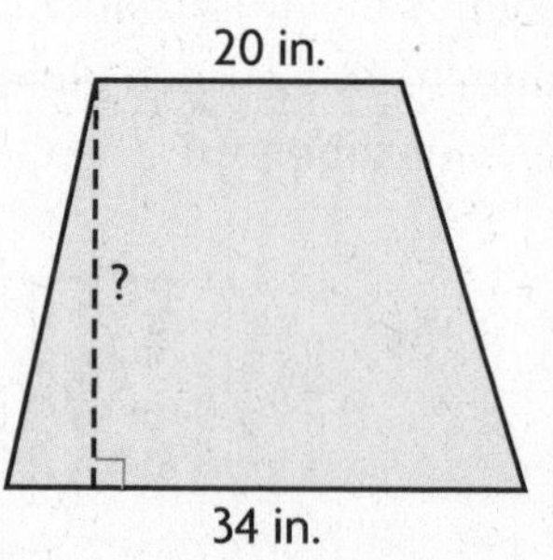

Substitute 702 for A, 20 for b_1, and 34 for b_2. $702 = \frac{1}{2} \times (20 + \_\_\_\_) \times h$

Add within the parentheses. $702 = \frac{1}{2} \times \_\_\_\_ \times h$

Multiply $\frac{1}{2}$ and 54. $702 = \_\_\_\_ \times h$

Use the Division Property of Equality. $\frac{702}{\square} = \frac{\square \times h}{\square}$

Simplify. $\_\_\_\_ = h$

So, the height of the trapezoid is ____ in.

Math Talk MATHEMATICAL PRACTICES 1

Analyze Relationships Explain why the formula for the area of a trapezoid contains the expression $b_1 + b_2$.

- MATHEMATICAL PRACTICE 6 **Attend to Precision** Name all the trapezoids that have more than one pair of parallel sides. Do you have to use the formula for area of a trapezoid to find the area of these types of trapezoids? Explain why or why not.

____

____

____

Name ______________________

Share and Show

1. Find the area of the trapezoid.

$A = \frac{1}{2}(b_1 + b_2)h$

$A = \frac{1}{2} \times ($ ______ + ______ $) \times 4$

$A = \frac{1}{2} \times$ ______ $\times 4$

$A =$ ______ cm^2

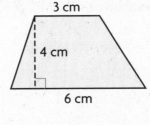

3 cm

4 cm

6 cm

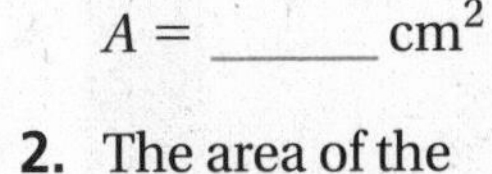

2. The area of the trapezoid is 45 ft^2. Find the height of the trapezoid.

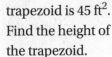

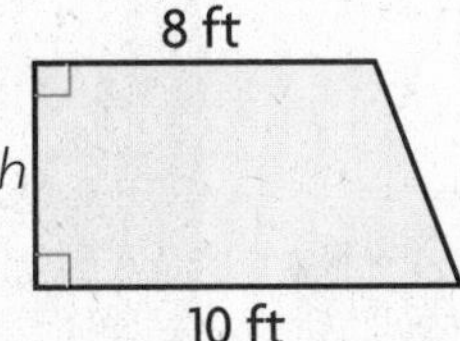

$h =$ ______________

3. Find the area of the trapezoid.

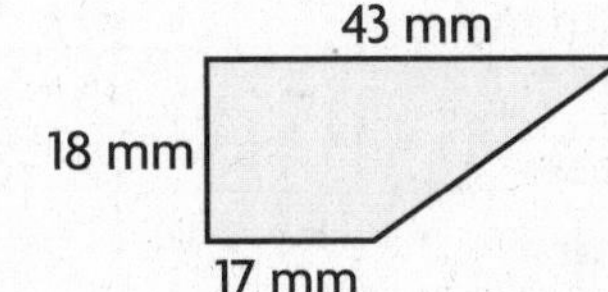

$A =$ ______________

Math Talk

MATHEMATICAL PRACTICES 1

Analyze Two trapezoids have the same bases and the same height. Are the areas equal? Must the trapezoids have the same shape?

On Your Own

Find the area of the trapezoid.

4.

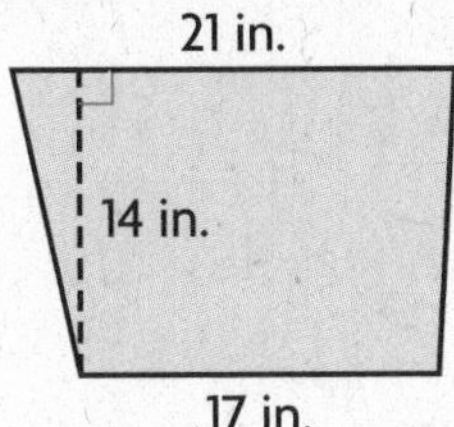

$A =$ ______________

5.

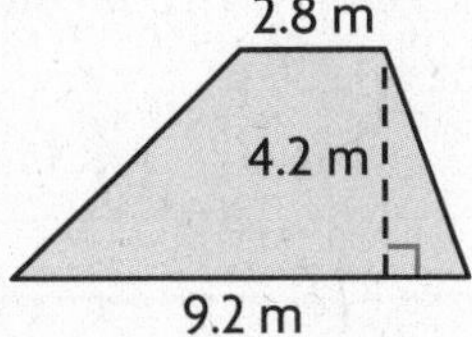

$A =$ ______________

Find the height of the trapezoid.

6.

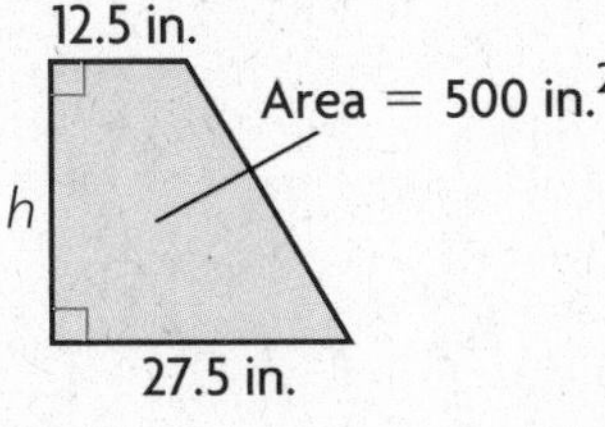

$h =$ ______________

7.

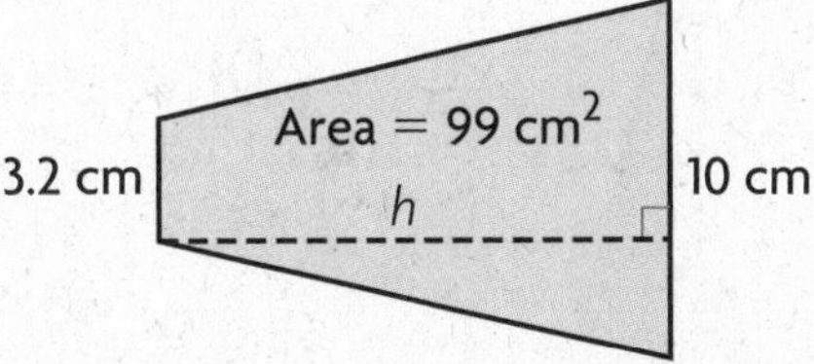

$h =$ ______________

Problem Solving • Applications

Use the diagram for 8–9.

Home Plate

17 in.
8.5 in.
8.5 in.
17 in.
12 in.
12 in.

8. GO DEEPER A baseball home plate can be divided into two trapezoids with the dimensions shown in the drawing. Find the area of home plate.

____

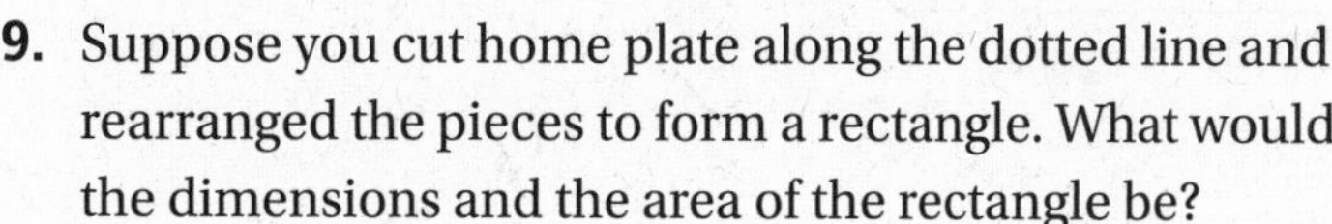

9. Suppose you cut home plate along the dotted line and rearranged the pieces to form a rectangle. What would the dimensions and the area of the rectangle be?

dimensions: _______________

area: _______________

10. THINK SMARTER A pattern used for tile floors is shown. A side of the inner square measures 10 cm, and a side of the outer square measures 30 cm. What is the area of one of the yellow trapezoid tiles?

____

11. MATHEMATICAL PRACTICE 3 **Verify the Reasoning of Others** A trapezoid has a height of 12 cm and bases with lengths of 14 cm and 10 cm. Tina says the area of the trapezoid is 288 cm^2. Find her error, and correct the error.

____

WRITE Math
Show Your Work

12. THINK SMARTER Which expression can be used to find the area of the trapezoid? Mark all that apply.

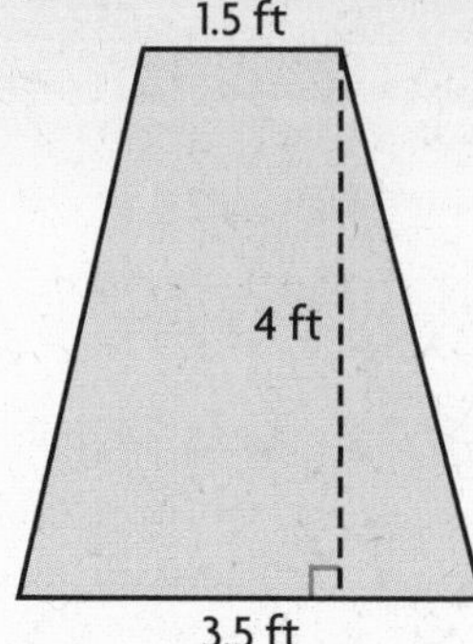

Ⓐ $\frac{1}{2} \times (4 + 1.5) \times 3.5$

Ⓑ $\frac{1}{2} \times (1.5 + 3.5) \times 4$

Ⓒ $\frac{1}{2} \times (4 + 3.5) \times 1.5$

Ⓓ $\frac{1}{2} \times (5) \times 4$

Name ____________________

Area of Trapezoids

Common Core **COMMON CORE STANDARD—6.G.A.1**
Solve real-world and mathematical problems involving area, surface area, and volume.

Find the area of the trapezoid.

1. $A = \frac{1}{2}(b_1 + b_2)h$

$A = \frac{1}{2} \times (\underline{\ 11\ } + \underline{\ 17\ }) \times 18$

$A = \frac{1}{2} \times \underline{\ 28\ } \times 18$

$A = \underline{\ 252\ }\ \text{cm}^2$

11 cm
18 cm
17 cm

2.

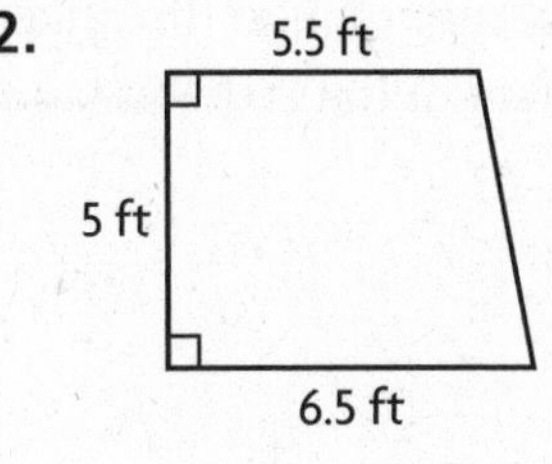

$A =$ ____________

3.

0.2 cm
0.2 cm
0.6 cm

$A =$ ____________

4.

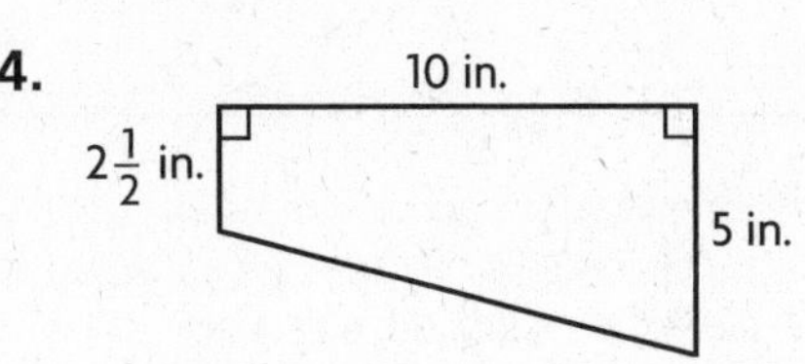

$A =$ ____________

Problem Solving Real World

5. Sonia makes a wooden frame around a square picture. The frame is made of 4 congruent trapezoids. The shorter base is 9 in., the longer base is 12 in., and the height is 1.5 in. What is the area of the picture frame?

____

6. Bryan cuts a piece of cardboard in the shape of a trapezoid. The area of the cutout is 43.5 square centimeters. If the bases are 6 centimeters and 8.5 centimeters long, what is the height of the trapezoid?

____

7. WRITE *Math* Use the formula for the area of a trapezoid to find the height of a trapezoid with bases 8 inches and 6 inches and an area of 112 square inches.

____

Lesson Check (6.G.A.1, 6.EE.A.2c)

1. Dominic is building a bench with a seat in the shape of a trapezoid. One base is 5 feet. The other base is 4 feet. The perpendicular distance between the bases is 2.5 feet. What is the area of the seat?

2. Molly is making a sign in the shape of a trapezoid. One base is 18 inches and the other is 30 inches. How high must she make the sign so its area is 504 square inches?

Spiral Review (6.NS.C.6c, 6.RP.A.3d, 6.EE.A.2c)

3. Write these numbers in order from least to greatest.

   $3\frac{3}{10}$ 3.1 $3\frac{1}{4}$

4. Write these lengths in order from least to greatest.

   2 yards 5.5 feet 70 inches

5. To find the cost for a group to enter the museum, the ticket seller uses the expression $8a + 3c$ in which a represents the number of adults and c represents the number of children in the group. How much should she charge a group of 3 adults and 5 children?

6. Brian frosted a cake top shaped like a parallelogram with a base of 13 inches and a height of 9 inches. Nancy frosted a triangular cake top with a base of 15 inches and a height of 12 inches. Which cake's top had the greater area? How much greater was it?

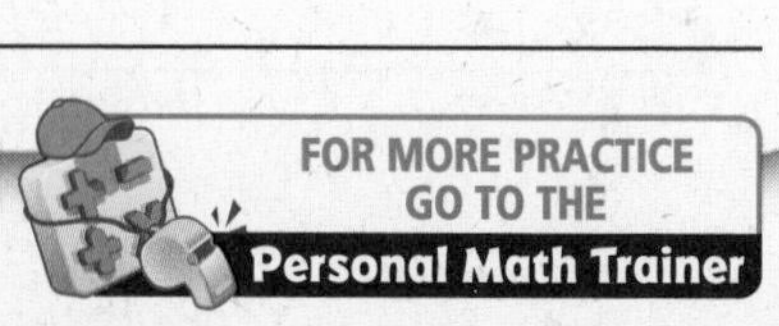

Name ____________________

 # Mid-Chapter Checkpoint

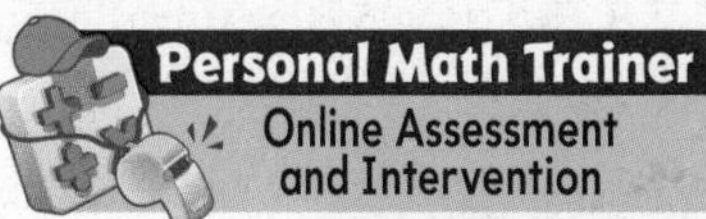

Vocabulary

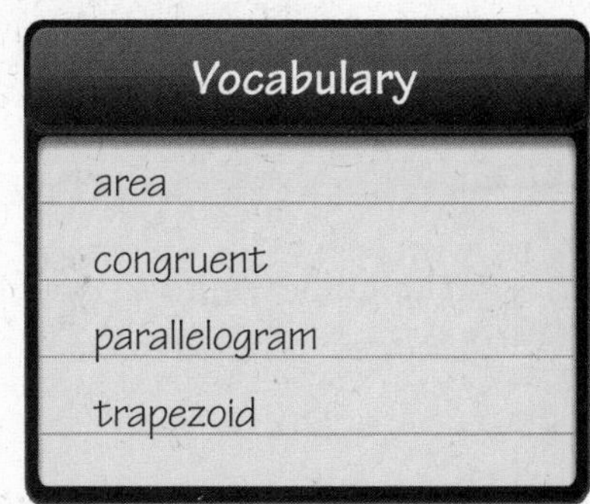

Choose the best term from the box to complete the sentence.

1. A ______________ is a quadrilateral that always has two pairs of parallel sides. (p. 533)
2. The measure of the number of unit squares needed to cover a surface without any gaps or overlaps is called the ______________. (p. 533)
3. Figures with the same size and shape are ______________. (p. 539)

Concepts and Skills

Find the area. (6.G.A.1, 6.EE.A.2c)

4. 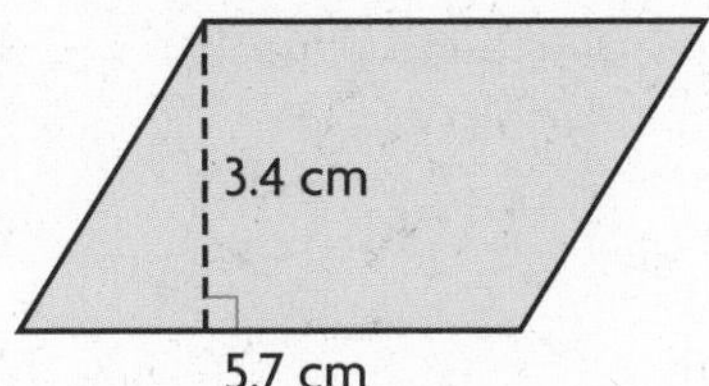

____

5. 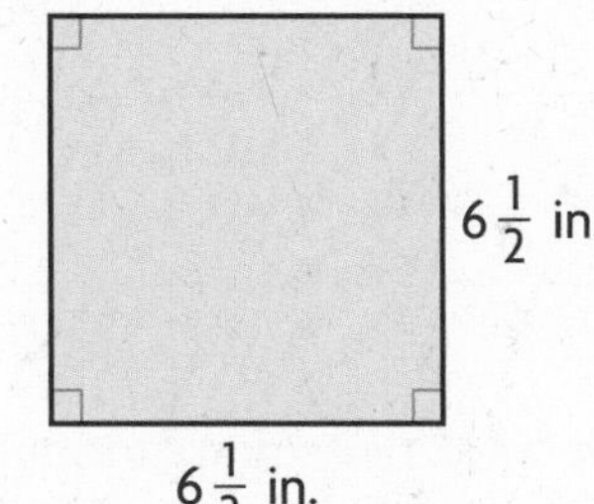

____

6. 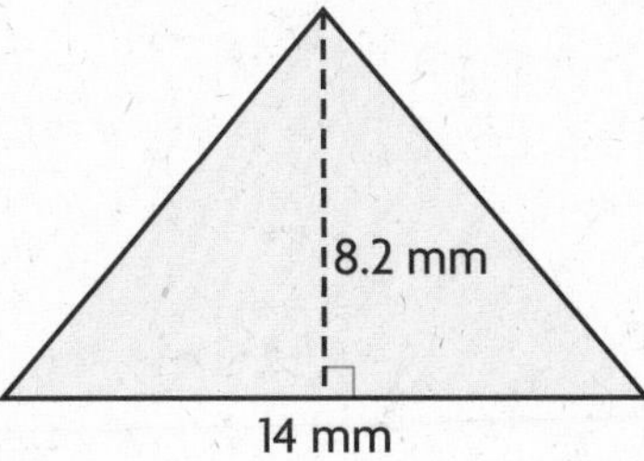

____

7. 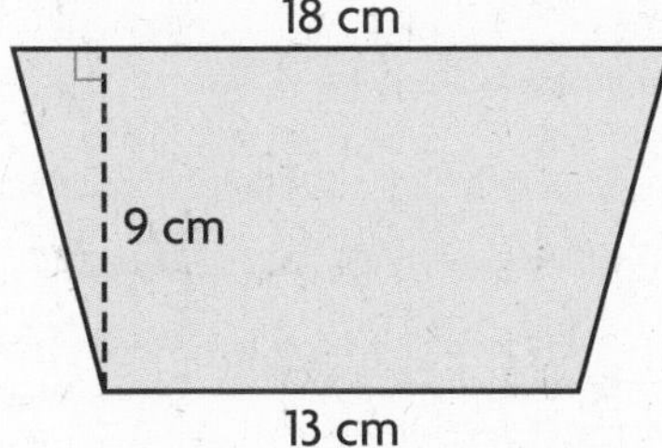

____

8. A parallelogram has an area of 276 square meters and a base measuring 12 meters. What is the height of the parallelogram?

____

9. The base of a triangle measures 8 inches and the area is 136 square inches. What is the height of the triangle?

____

10. The height of a parallelogram is 3 times the base. The base measures 4.5 cm. What is the area of the parallelogram? (6.G.A.1)

______

11. A triangular window pane has a base of 30 inches and a height of 24 inches. What is the area of the window pane? (6.G.A.1)

______

12. The courtyard behind Jennie's house is shaped like a trapezoid. The bases measure 8 meters and 11 meters. The height of the trapezoid is 12 meters. What is the area of the courtyard? (6.G.A.1)

______

13. GO DEEPER Rugs sell for $8 per square foot. Beth bought a 9-foot-long rectangular rug for $432. How wide was the rug? (6.G.A.1, 6.EE.A.2c)

______

14. A square painting has a side length of 18 inches. What is the area of the painting? (6.G.A.1, 6.EE.A.2c)

______

Name ______________________________

Area of Regular Polygons

Essential Question How can you find the area of regular polygons?

Common Core **Geometry—6.G.A.1**
Also 6.EE.A.2C

MATHEMATICAL PRACTICES
MP1, MP6, MP8

Unlock the Problem Real World

Emory is making a patch for his soccer ball. The patch he is using is a regular polygon. A **regular polygon** is a polygon in which all sides have the same length and all angles have the same measure. Emory needs to find the area of a piece of material shaped like a regular pentagon.

Activity

You can find the area of a regular polygon by dividing the polygon into congruent triangles.

- Draw line segments from each vertex to the center of the pentagon to divide it into five congruent triangles.

- You can find the area of one of the triangles if you know the side length of the polygon and the height of the triangle.

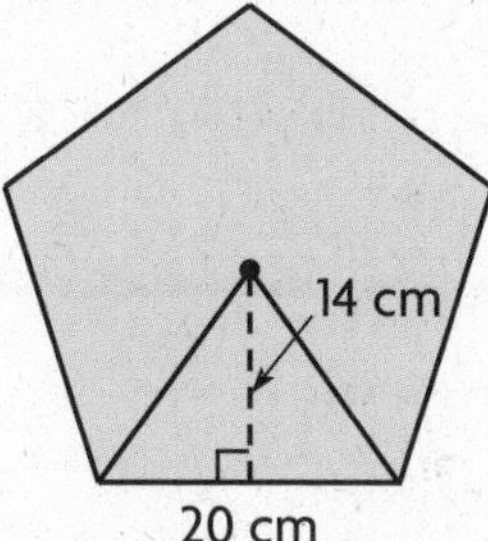

Math Talk MATHEMATICAL PRACTICES 6

Explain How do you determine the number of congruent triangles a regular polygon should be divided into in order to find the area?

- Find the area of one triangle.

Write the formula.	$A = \frac{1}{2}bh$
Substitute 20 for *b* and 14 for *h*.	$A = \frac{1}{2} \times$ ______ $\times$ ______
Simplify.	$A =$ ______ cm^2

- Find the area of the regular polygon by multiplying the number of triangles by the area of one triangle.

$A =$ ______ $\times$ ______ $=$ ______ cm^2

So, the area of the pentagon-shaped piece is ____________.

 **Example** Find the area of the regular polygon.

STEP 1 Draw line segments from each vertex to the center of the hexagon.

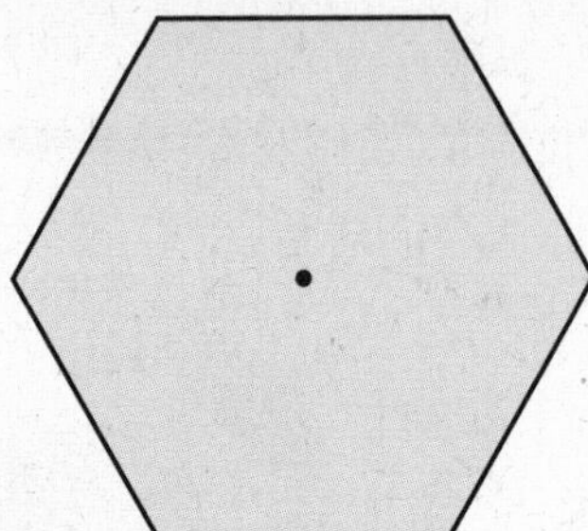

Into how many congruent triangles did you divide the figure? ______

STEP 2 Find the area of one triangle.

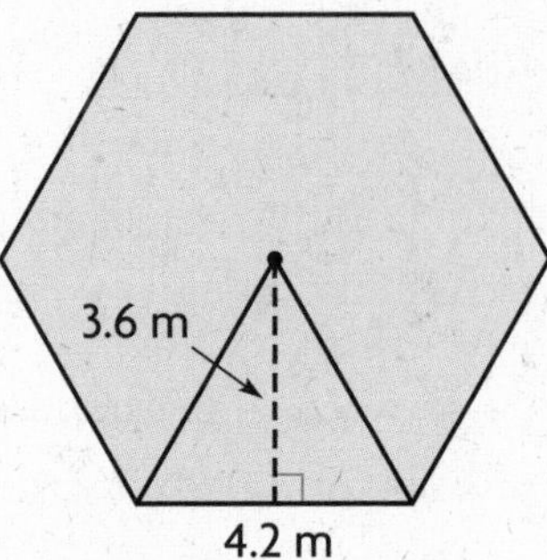

Write the formula. $A = \frac{1}{2}bh$

Substitute 4.2 for *b* and 3.6 for *h*. $A = \frac{1}{2} \times$ ______ $\times$ ______

Simplify. $A =$ ______ m^2

STEP 3 Find the area of the hexagon.

$A =$ ______ $\times$ ______ $=$ ____________ m^2

So, the area of the hexagon is ____________ m^2

1. MATHEMATICAL PRACTICE 8 **Use Repeated Reasoning** Into how many congruent triangles can you divide a regular decagon by drawing line segments from each vertex to the center of the decagon? Explain.

____

____

2. THINKSMARTER In an *irregular polygon,* the sides do not all have the same length and the angles do not all have the same measure. Could you find the area of an irregular polygon using the method you used in this lesson? Explain your reasoning.

____

____

Name ___________________________

Share and Show

Find the area of the regular polygon.

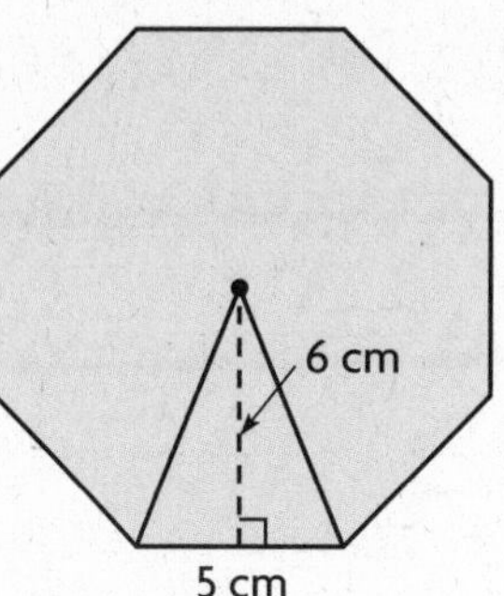

1. number of congruent triangles inside the figure: ______

area of each triangle: $\frac{1}{2} \times$ ______ $\times$ ______ $=$ ______ cm^2

area of octagon: ______ $\times$ ______ $=$ ______ cm^2

2.

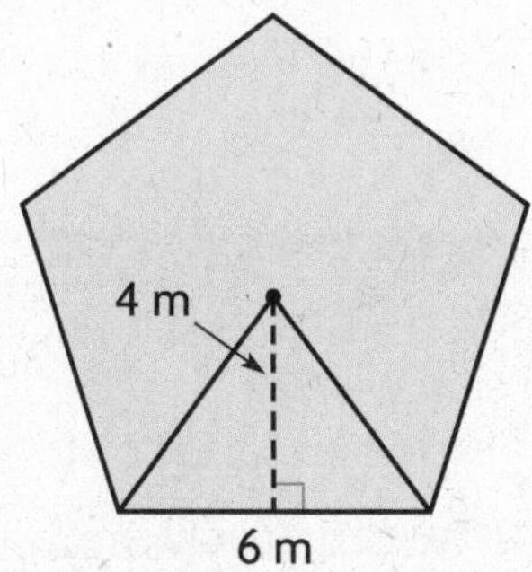

3.

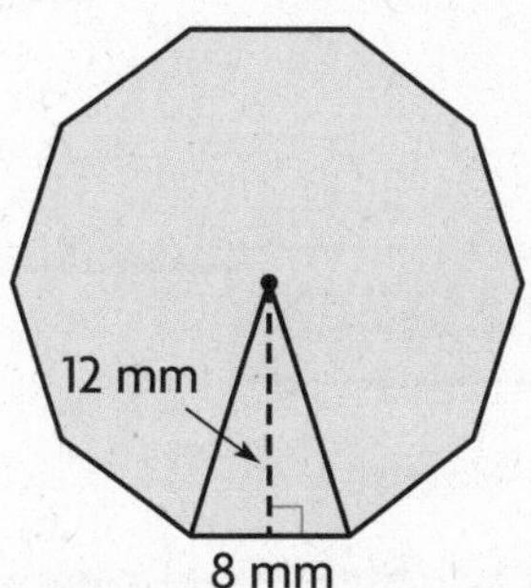

Math Talk — MATHEMATICAL PRACTICES 1

Describe the information you must have about a regular polygon in order to find its area.

On Your Own

Find the area of the regular polygon.

4.

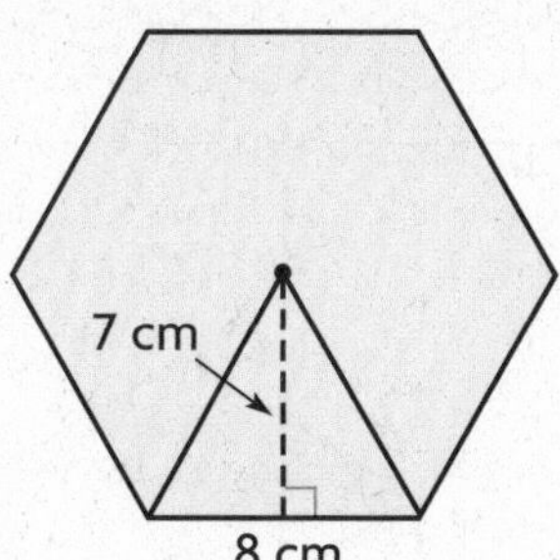

5.

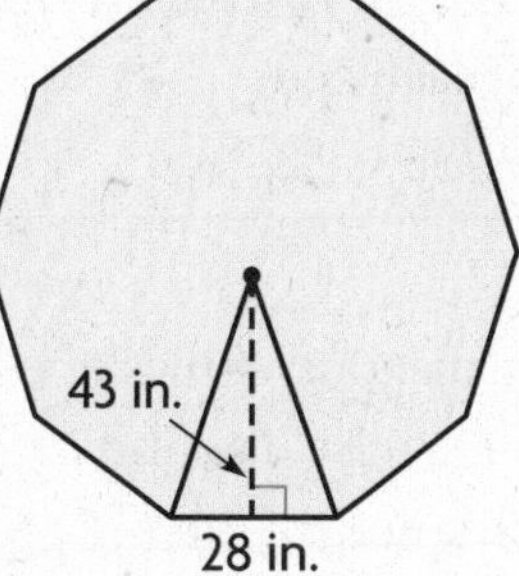

6. MATHEMATICAL PRACTICE 6 **Explain** A regular pentagon is divided into congruent triangles by drawing a line segment from each vertex to the center. Each triangle has an area of 24 cm^2. Explain how to find the area of the pentagon.

7. THINK SMARTER Name the polygon and find its area. Show your work.

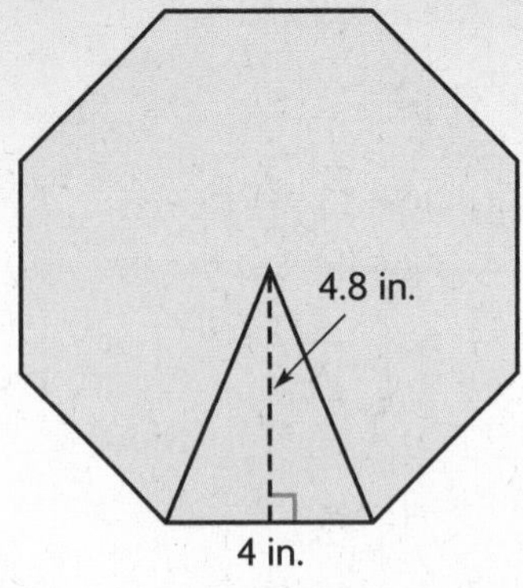

Connect to Science

Regular Polygons in Nature

Regular polygons are common in nature. One of the best-known examples of regular polygons in nature is the small hexagonal cells in honeycombs constructed by honeybees. The cells are where bee larvae grow. Honeybees store honey and pollen in the hexagonal cells. Scientists can measure the health of a bee population by the size of the cells.

8. Cells in a honeycomb vary in width. To find the average width of a cell, scientists measure the combined width of 10 cells, and then divide by 10.

The figure shows a typical 10-cell line of worker bee cells. What is the width of each cell?

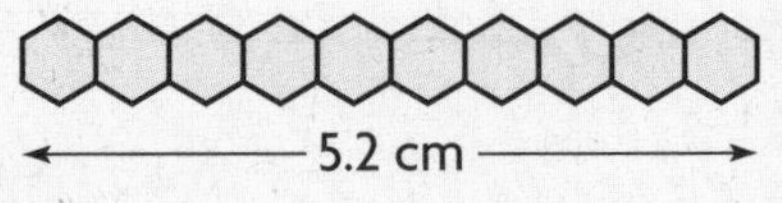

9. THINK SMARTER The diagram shows one honeycomb cell. Use your answer to Exercise 8 to find h, the height of the triangle. Then find the area of the hexagonal cell.

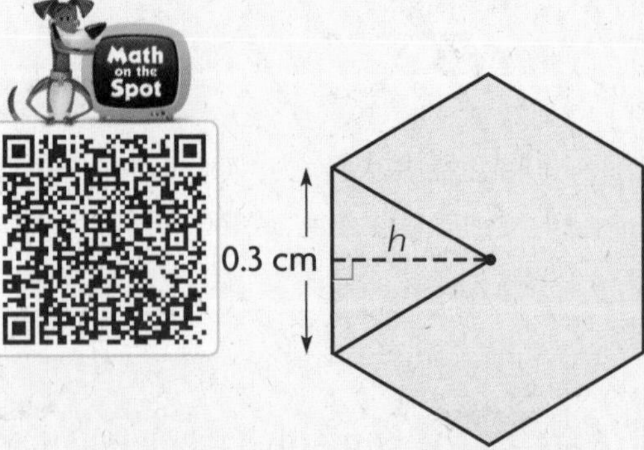

10. GO DEEPER A rectangular honeycomb measures 35.1 cm by 32.4 cm. Approximately how many cells does it contain?

Name ______________________

Area of Regular Polygons

Common Core **COMMON CORE STANDARD—6.G.A.1**
Solve real-world and mathematical problems involving area, surface area, and volume.

Find the area of the regular polygon.

1. 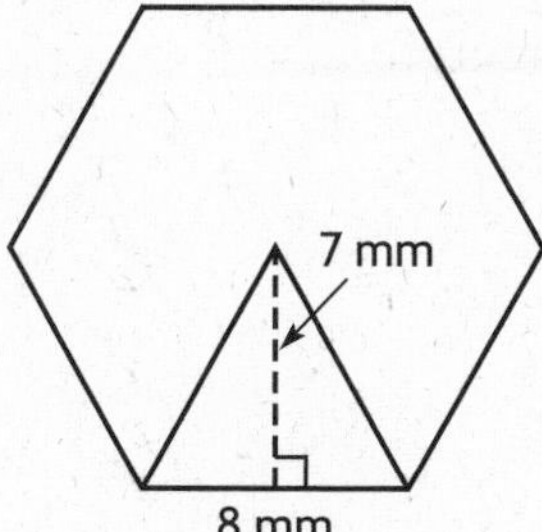

number of congruent triangles inside the figure: 6

area of each triangle: $\frac{1}{2}\times$ 8 $\times$ 7 $=$ 28 mm^2

area of hexagon: 168 mm^2

2. 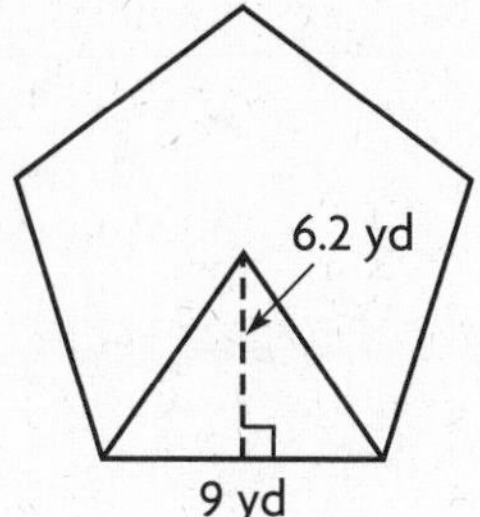

____

3. 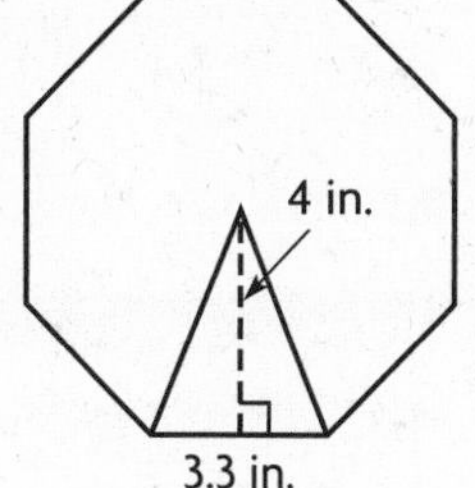

____

Problem Solving Real World

4. Stu is making a stained glass window in the shape of a regular pentagon. The pentagon can be divided into congruent triangles, each with a base of 8.7 inches and a height of 6 inches. What is the area of the window?

____

5. A dinner platter is in the shape of a regular decagon. The platter has an area of 161 square inches and a side length of 4.6 inches. What is the area of each triangle? What is the height of each triangle?

____

6. **WRITE** *Math* A square has sides that measure 6 inches. Explain how to use the method in this lesson to find the area of the square.

____

____

____

Lesson Check (6.G.A.1, 6.EE.A.2c)

1. What is the area of the regular hexagon?

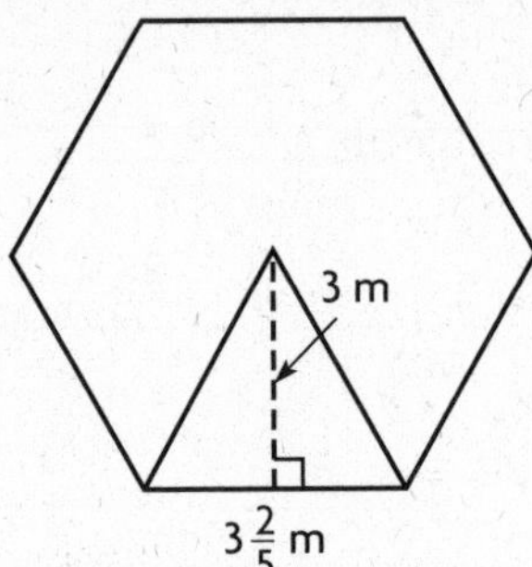

2. A regular 7-sided figure is divided into 7 congruent triangles, each with a base of 12 inches and a height of 12.5 inches. What is the area of the 7-sided figure?

Spiral Review (6.EE.A.2c, 6.EE.B.5, 6.EE.C.9, 6.G.A.1)

3. Which inequalities have $b = 4$ as one of its solutions?

$2 + b \geq 2$	$3b \leq 14$
$8 - b \leq 15$	$b - 3 \geq 5$

4. Each song that Tara downloads costs \$1.25. She graphs the relationship that gives the cost y in dollars of downloading x songs. Name one ordered pair that is a point on the graph of the relationship.

5. What is the area of triangle ABC?

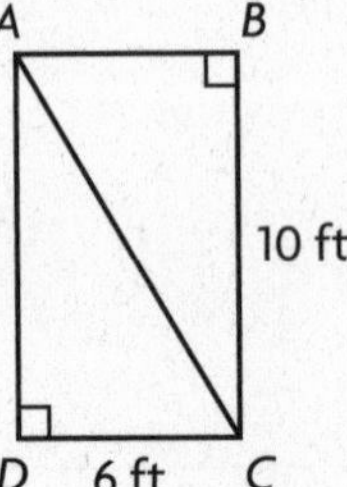

6. Marcia cut a trapezoid out of a large piece of felt. The trapezoid has a height of 9 cm and bases of 6 cm and 11 cm. What is the area of Marcia's felt trapezoid?

FOR MORE PRACTICE GO TO THE Personal Math Trainer

Name ______________________________

Composite Figures

Essential Question How can you find the area of composite figures?

Common Core **Geometry—6.G.A.1**
Also 6.EE.A.2c
MATHEMATICAL PRACTICES
MP1, MP6

A **composite figure** is made up of two or more simpler figures, such as triangles and quadrilaterals.

Unlock the Problem

The new entryway to the fun house at Happy World Amusement Park is made from the shapes shown in the diagram. It will be painted bright green. Juanita needs to know the area of the entryway to determine how much paint to buy. What is the area of the entryway?

4 ft
4 ft
10 ft
4 ft 4 ft

FUNHOUSE

Find the area of the entryway.

STEP 1 Find the area of the rectangles.

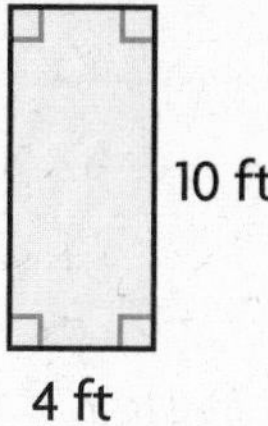

Write the formula. $A = lw$

Substitute the values for l and w and evaluate. $A = 10 \times$ ______ $=$ ______

Find the total area of two rectangles. $2 \times$ ______ $=$ ______ ft^2

STEP 2 Find the area of the triangles.

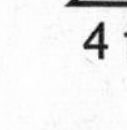

Write the formula. $A = \frac{1}{2}bh$

Substitute the values for b and h and evaluate. $A = \frac{1}{2} \times 4 \times$ ______ $=$ ______

Find the total area of two triangles. $2 \times$ ______ $=$ ______ ft^2

STEP 3 Find the area of the square.

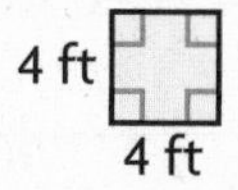

Write the formula. $A = s^2$

Substitute the value for s. $A = ($ ______ $)^2 =$ ______ ft^2

STEP 4 Find the total area of the composite figure.

Add the areas. $A = 80\ ft^2 +$ ______ $ft^2 +$ ______ $ft^2 =$ ______ ft^2

So, Juanita needs to buy enough paint to cover ______ ft^2.

MATHEMATICAL PRACTICES 1

Describe other ways you could divide up the composite figure.

Example 1 **Find the area of the composite figure shown.**

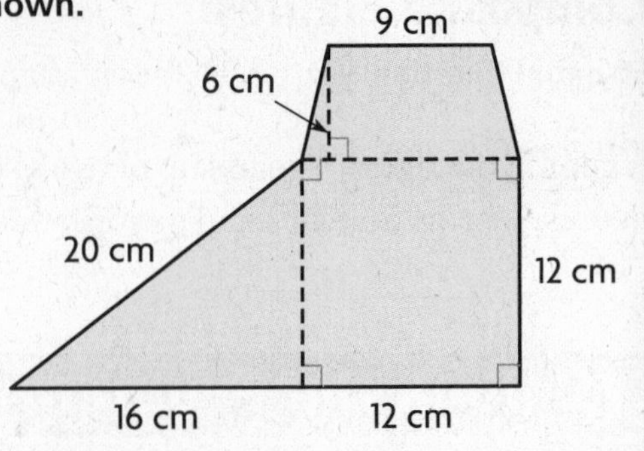

STEP 1 Find the area of the triangle, the square, and the trapezoid.

area of triangle $A = \frac{1}{2}bh = \frac{1}{2} \times 16 \times$ ______

$=$ ______ cm^2

area of square $A = s^2 = ($______$)^2$

$=$ ______ cm^2

area of trapezoid $A = \frac{1}{2}(b_1 + b_2)h = \frac{1}{2} \times ($______ $+$ ______$) \times$ ______

$= \frac{1}{2} \times$ ______ $\times 6$

$=$ ______ cm^2

STEP 2 Find the total area of the figure.

total area $A =$ ______ $\text{cm}^2 +$ ______ $\text{cm}^2 +$ ______ cm^2

$=$ ______ cm^2

So, the area of the figure is ______ cm^2.

Example 2 **Find the area of the shaded region.**

3 in.
3 in.
6 in.
1 ft

STEP 1 Find the area of the rectangle and the square.

area of rectangle (1 ft = 12 in.) $A = lw =$ ______ $\times$ ______

$A =$ ______ in.^2

area of square $A = s^2 = ($______$)^2$

$A =$ ______ in.^2

STEP 2 Subtract the area of the square from the area of the rectangle.

area of shaded region $A =$ ______ $\text{in.}^2 -$ ______ in.^2

$A =$ ______ in.^2

So, the area of the shaded region is ______ in.^2

Name ______________________________

Share and Show 

1. Find the area of the figure.

4 ft
3 ft
10 ft
5 ft 5 ft

area of one rectangle $A = lw$

$A = \_\_\_\_ \times \_\_\_\_ = \_\_\_\_ \text{ ft}^2$

area of two rectangles $A = 2 \times \_\_\_\_ = \_\_\_\_ \text{ ft}^2$

length of base of triangle $b = \_\_\_\_ \text{ ft} + \_\_\_\_ \text{ ft} + \_\_\_\_ \text{ ft}$

$= \_\_\_\_ \text{ ft}$

area of triangle $A = \frac{1}{2}bh$

$A = \frac{1}{2} \times \_\_\_\_ \times \_\_\_\_ = \_\_\_\_ \text{ ft}^2$

area of composite figure $A = \_\_\_\_ \text{ ft}^2 + \_\_\_\_ \text{ ft}^2 = \_\_\_\_ \text{ ft}^2$

Find the area of the figure.

2.

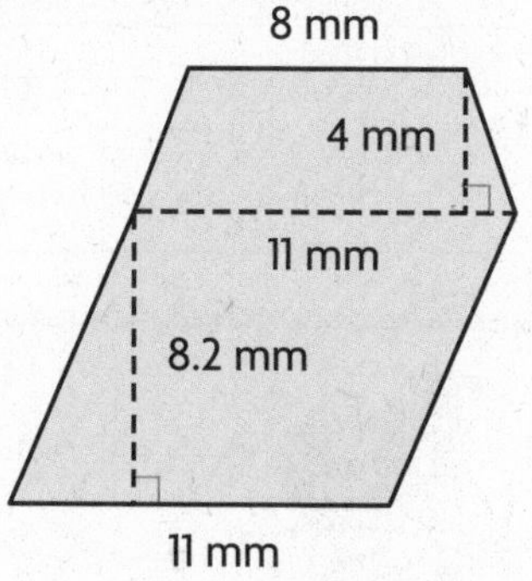

____

**3.**

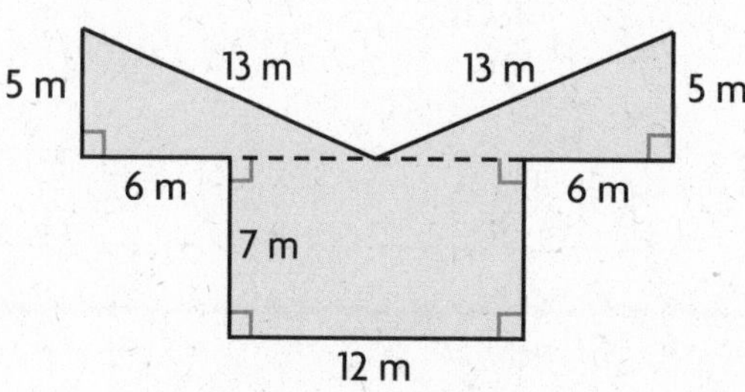

____

Math Talk MATHEMATICAL PRACTICES 6

Explain how to find the area of a composite figure.

On Your Own

4. Find the area of the figure.

8 in.
10 in.
6 in.
8 in. 16 in.

____

5. MATHEMATICAL PRACTICE 6 **Attend to Precision** Find the area of the shaded region.

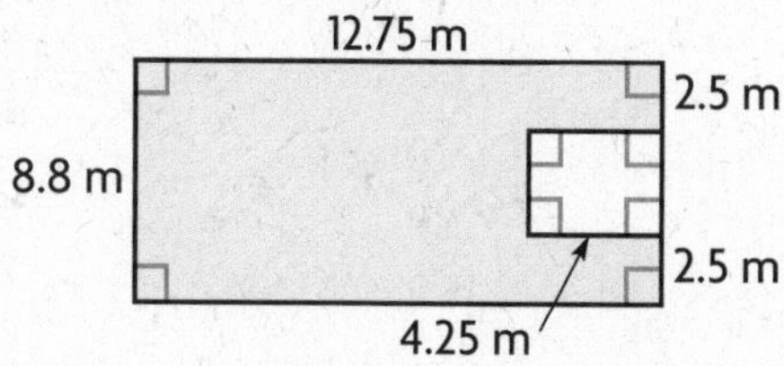

____

Unlock the Problem

6. GO DEEPER Marco made the banner shown at the right. What is the area of the yellow shape?

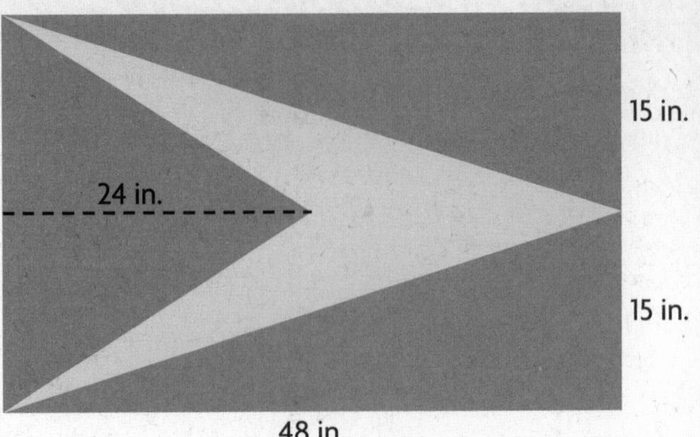

a. Explain how you could find the area of the yellow shape if you knew the areas of the green and red shapes and the area of the entire banner.

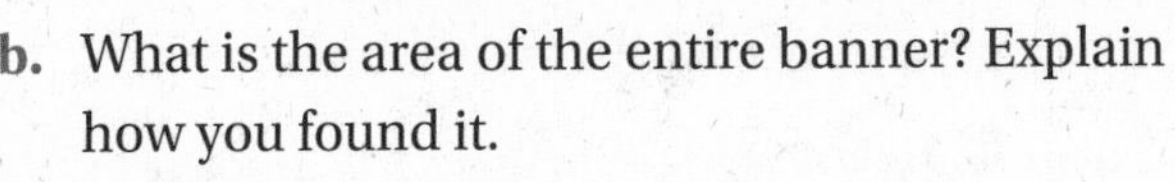

b. What is the area of the entire banner? Explain how you found it.

c. What is the area of the red shape? What is the area of each green shape?

d. What equation can you write to find A, the area of the yellow shape?

e. What is the area of the yellow shape?

7. There are 6 rectangular flower gardens each measuring 18 feet by 15 feet in a rectangular city park measuring 80 feet by 150 feet. How many square feet of the park are not used for flower gardens?

Personal Math Trainer

8. THINK SMARTER+ Sabrina wants to replace the carpet in a few rooms of her house. Select the expression she can use to find the total area of the floor that will be covered. Mark all that apply.

Ⓐ $8 \times 22 + 130 + \frac{1}{2} \times 10 \times 9$

Ⓑ $18 \times 22 - \frac{1}{2} \times 10 \times 9$

Ⓒ $18 \times 13 + \frac{1}{2} \times 10 \times 9$

Ⓓ $\frac{1}{2} \times (18 + 8) \times 22$

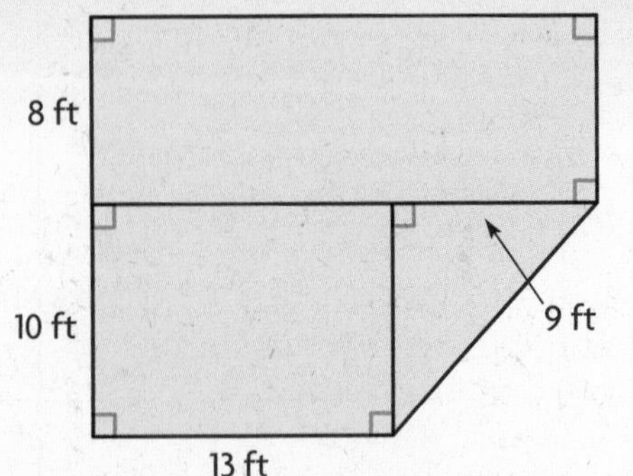

Name ______________________

Composite Figures

Common Core — **COMMON CORE STANDARD—6.G.A.1** *Solve real-world and mathematical problems involving area, surface area, and volume.*

Find the area of the figure.

1. 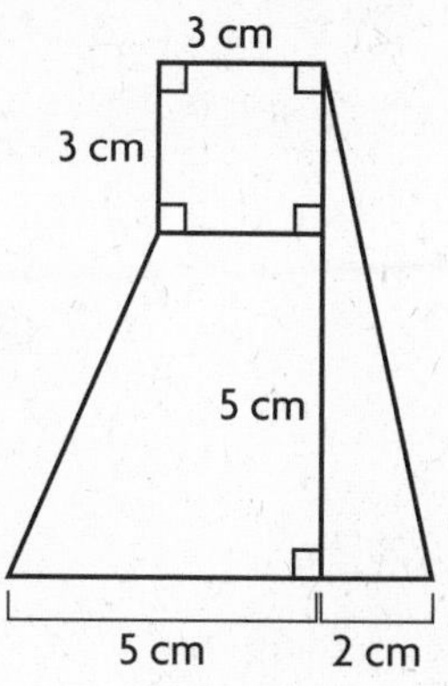

area of square $A = s \times s$

$= \underline{3} \times \underline{3} = \underline{9}\ \text{cm}^2$

area of triangle $A = \frac{1}{2}bh$

$= \frac{1}{2} \times \underline{2} \times \underline{8} = \underline{8}\ \text{cm}^2$

area of trapezoid $A = \frac{1}{2}(b_1 + b_2)h$

$= \frac{1}{2} \times (\underline{5} + \underline{3}) \times \underline{5} = \underline{20}\ \text{cm}^2$

area of composite figure $A = \underline{9}\ \text{cm}^2 + \underline{8}\ \text{cm}^2 + \underline{20}\ \text{cm}^2$

$= \underline{37}\ \text{cm}^2$

2. 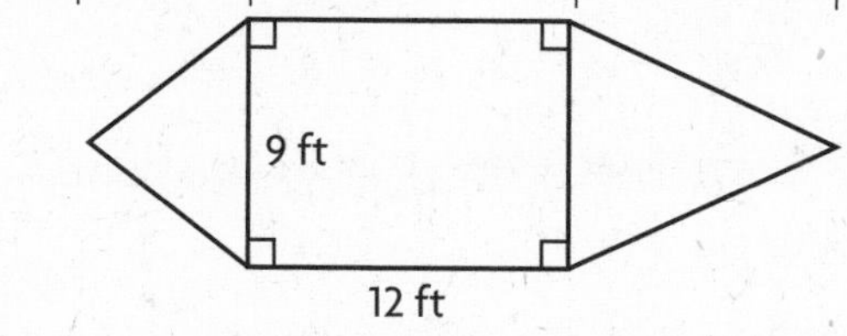

____

3. 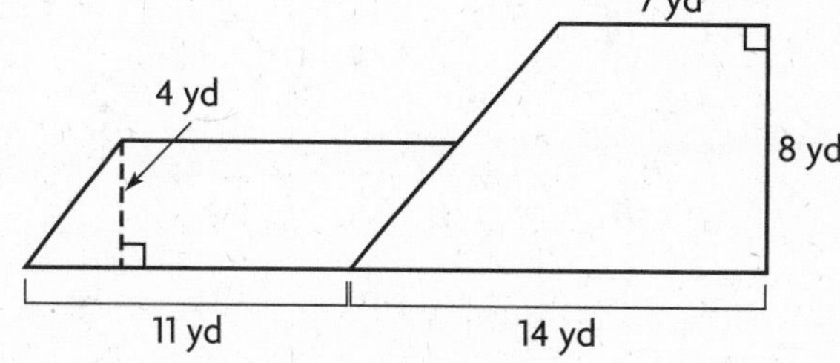

____

Problem Solving Real World

4. Janelle is making a poster. She cuts a triangle out of poster board. What is the area of the poster board that she has left?

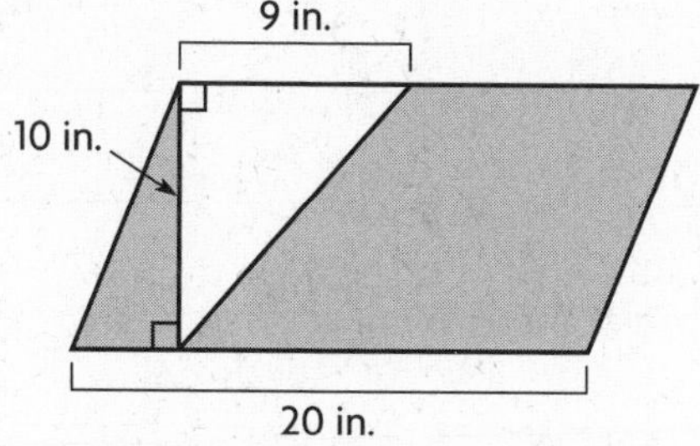

____

5. Michael wants to place grass on the sides of his lap pool. Find the area of the shaded regions that he wants to cover with grass.

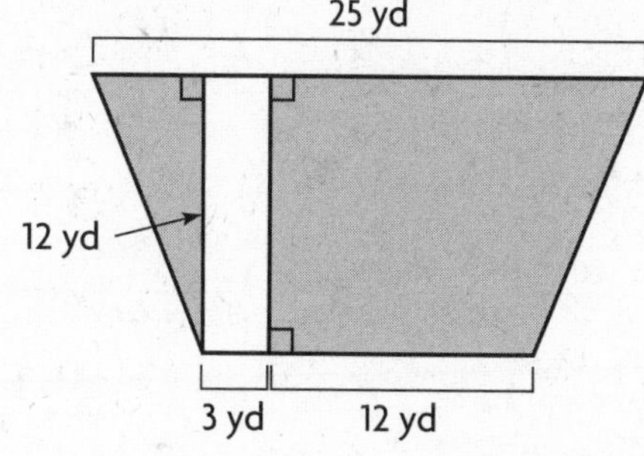

____

6. WRITE Math Describe one or more situations in which you need to subtract to find the area of a composite figure.

____

____

Lesson Check (6.G.A.1, 6.EE.A.2c)

1. What is the area of the composite figure?

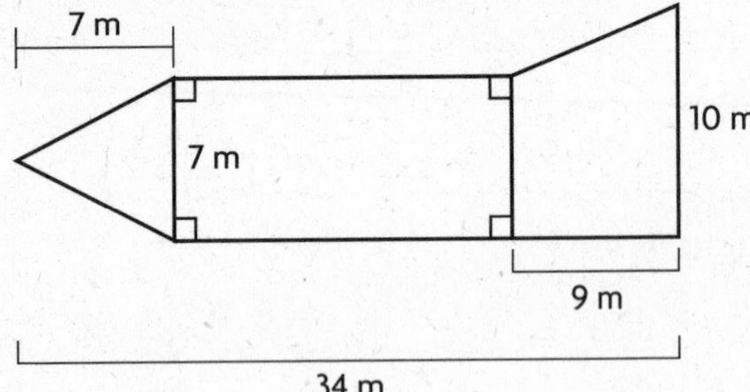

2. What is the area of the shaded region?

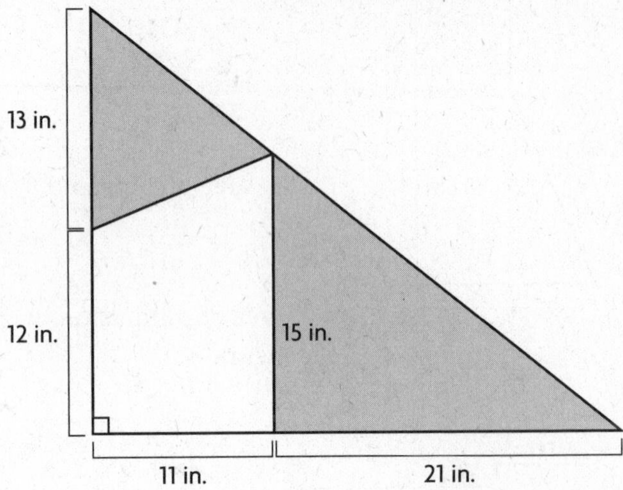

Spiral Review (6.EE.A.2c, 6.EE.B.8, 6.EE.C.9, 6.G.A.1)

3. In Maritza's family, everyone's height is greater than 60 inches. Write an inequality that represents the height h, in inches, of any member of Maritza's family.

4. The linear equation $y = 2x$ represents the cost y for x pounds of apples. Which ordered pair lies on the graph of the equation?

5. Two congruent triangles fit together to form a parallelogram with a base of 14 inches and a height of 10 inches. What is the area of each triangle?

6. A regular hexagon has sides measuring 7 inches. If the hexagon is divided into 6 congruent triangles, each has a height of about 6 inches. What is the approximate area of the hexagon?

FOR MORE PRACTICE GO TO THE **Personal Math Trainer**

Name ______________________________

Problem Solving • Changing Dimensions

Essential Question How can you use the strategy *find a pattern* to show how changing dimensions affects area?

Geometry—
6.G.A.1

MATHEMATICAL PRACTICES
MP2, MP4, MP8

Unlock the Problem

Jason has created a 3-in. by 4-in. rectangular design to be made into mouse pads. To manufacture the pads, the dimensions will be multiplied by 2 or 3. How will the area of the design be affected?

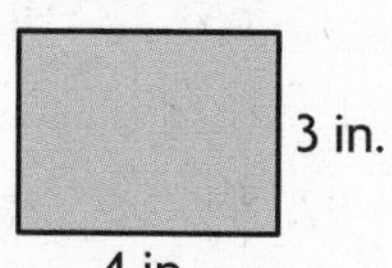

Use the graphic organizer to help you solve the problem.

Read the Problem

What do I need to find?

I need to find how ______________________ will be affected by changing the ______________.

What information do I need to use?

I need to use ______________ of the original design and ______________ ______________ ______________.

How will I use the information?

I can draw a sketch of each rectangle and calculate ______________ of each. Then I can look for ______________ in my results.

Solve the Problem

Sketch	Dimensions	Multiplier	Area
	3 in. by 4 in.	1	$A = 3 \times 4 = 12$ in.^{2}
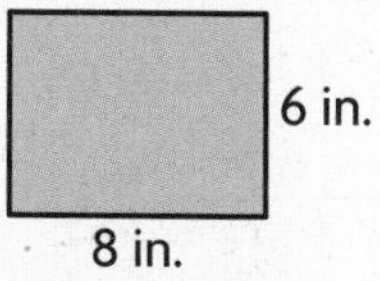 6 in. by 8 in. rectangle (6 in., 8 in.)	6 in. by 8 in.	2	$A =$ ______ $\times$ ______ $=$ ______ in.^{2}
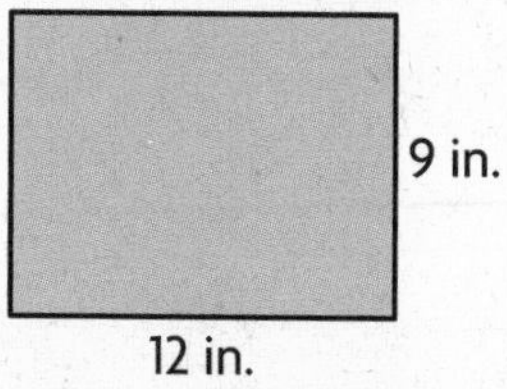 9 in. by 12 in. rectangle (9 in., 12 in.)			

So, when the dimensions are multiplied by 2, the area is multiplied by ______. When the dimensions are multiplied by 3, the area is multiplied by ______.

MATHEMATICAL PRACTICES 2

Reasoning What would happen to the area of a rectangle if the dimensions were multiplied by 4?

Try Another Problem

A stained-glass designer is reducing the dimensions of an earlier design. The dimensions of the triangle shown will be multiplied by $\frac{1}{2}$ or $\frac{1}{4}$. How will the area of the design be affected? Use the graphic organizer to help you solve the problem.

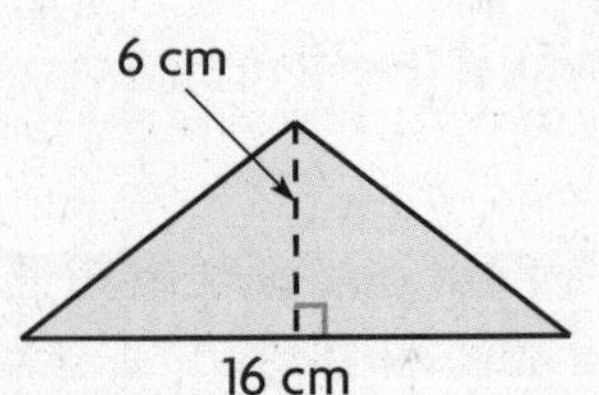

Read the Problem

What do I need to find?	What information do I need to use?	How will I use the information?

Solve the Problem

Sketch	Multiplier	Area
	1	$A = \frac{1}{2} \times 16 \times$ ______ $=$ ______ cm^2
3 cm 8 cm	$\frac{1}{2}$	

So, when the dimensions are multiplied by $\frac{1}{2}$, the area is multiplied by ______. When the dimensions are multiplied by ______, the area is multiplied by ______.

MATHEMATICAL PRACTICES 8

Generalize What happens to the area of a triangle when the dimensions are multiplied by a number n?

Name ______________________

Share and Show

1. The dimensions of a 2-cm by 6-cm rectangle are multiplied by 5. How is the area of the rectangle affected?

First, find the original area:

____

Next, find the new area:

____

So, the area is multiplied by ______.

2. THINKSMARTER **What if** the dimensions of the original rectangle in Exercise 1 had been multiplied by $\frac{1}{2}$? How would the area have been affected?

____

____

____

____

3. Evan bought two square rugs. The larger one measured 12 ft square. The smaller one had an area equal to $\frac{1}{4}$ the area of the larger one. What fraction of the side lengths of the larger rug were the side lengths of the smaller one?

____

4. GO DEEPER On Silver Island, a palm tree, a giant rock, and a buried treasure form a triangle with a base of 100 yd and a height of 50 yd. On a map of the island, the three landmarks form a triangle with a base of 2 ft and a height of 1 ft. How many times the area of the triangle on the map is the area of the actual triangle?

____

Unlock the Problem

- √ Plan your solution by deciding on the steps you will use.
- √ Find the original area and the new area, and then compare the two.
- √ Look for patterns in your results.

WRITE Math • Show Your Work

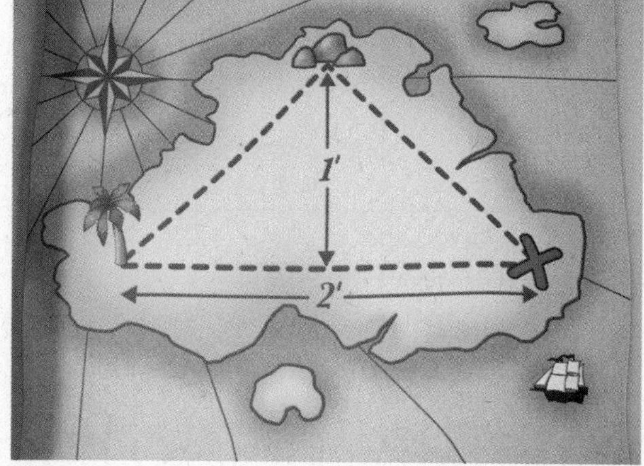

On Your Own

Show Your Work

5. A square game board is divided into smaller squares, each with sides one-ninth the length of the sides of the board. Into how many squares is the game board divided?

____

6. THINKSMARTER Flynn County is a rectangle measuring 9 mi by 12 mi. Gibson County is a rectangle with an area 6 times the area of Flynn County and a width of 16 mi. What is the length of Gibson County?

____

7. MATHEMATICAL PRACTICE 4 **Use Diagrams** Carmen left her house and drove 10 mi north, 15 mi east, 13 mi south, 11 mi west, and 3 mi north. How far was she from home?

____

8. GO DEEPER Bernie drove from his house to his cousin's house in 6 hours at an average rate of 52 mi per hr. He drove home at an average rate of 60 mi per hr. How long did it take him to drive home?

____

Personal Math Trainer

9. THINKSMARTER+ Sophia wants to enlarge a 5-inch by 7-inch rectangular photo by multiplying the dimensions by 3.

Find the area of the original photo and the enlarged photo. Then explain how the area of the original photo is affected.

____

____

____

Name ______________________________

Problem Solving • Changing Dimensions

Common Core **COMMON CORE STANDARD—6.G.A.1**
Solve real-world and mathematical problems involving area, surface area, and volume.

Read each problem and solve.

1. The dimensions of a 5-in. by 3-in. rectangle are multiplied by 6. How is the area affected?

new dimensions: $l = 6 \times 5 = 30$ in.
$w = 6 \times 3 = 18$ in.

original area: $A = 5 \times 3 = 15$ in.^{2}

new area: $A = 30 \times 18 = 540$ in.^{2}

$\frac{\text{new area}}{\text{original area}} = \frac{540}{15} = 36$

The area was multiplied by 36.

2. The dimensions of a 7-cm by 2-cm rectangle are multiplied by 3. How is the area affected?

multiplied by ____________

3. The dimensions of a 3-ft by 6-ft rectangle are multiplied by $\frac{1}{3}$. How is the area affected?

multiplied by ____________

4. The dimensions of a triangle with base 10 in. and height 4.8 in. are multiplied by 4. How is the area affected?

multiplied by ____________

5. The dimensions of a 1-yd by 9-yd rectangle are multiplied by 5. How is the area affected?

multiplied by ____________

6. The dimensions of a 4-in. square are multiplied by 3. How is the area affected?

multiplied by ____________

7. The dimensions of a triangle are multiplied by $\frac{1}{4}$. The area of the smaller triangle can be found by multiplying the area of the original triangle by what number?

____

8. WRITE ▸ *Math* Write and solve a word problem that involves changing the dimensions of a figure and finding its area.

____

____

Lesson Check (6.G.A.1)

1. The dimensions of Rectangle A are 6 times the dimensions of Rectangle B. How do the areas of the rectangles compare?

2. A model of a triangular piece of jewelry has an area that is $\frac{1}{4}$ the area of the jewelry. How do the dimensions of the triangles compare?

Spiral Review (6.RP.A.3c, 6.EE.A.2c, 6.EE.B.8, 6.G.A.1)

3. Gina made a rectangular quilt that was 5 feet wide and 6 feet long. She used yellow fabric for 30% of the quilt. What was the area of the yellow fabric?

4. Graph $y > 3$ on a number line.

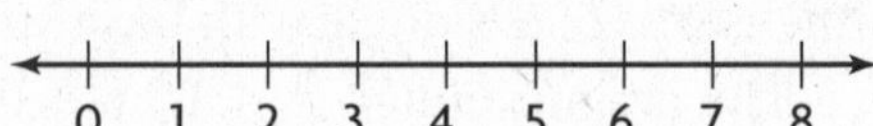

5. The parallelogram below is made from two congruent trapezoids. What is the area of the shaded trapezoid?

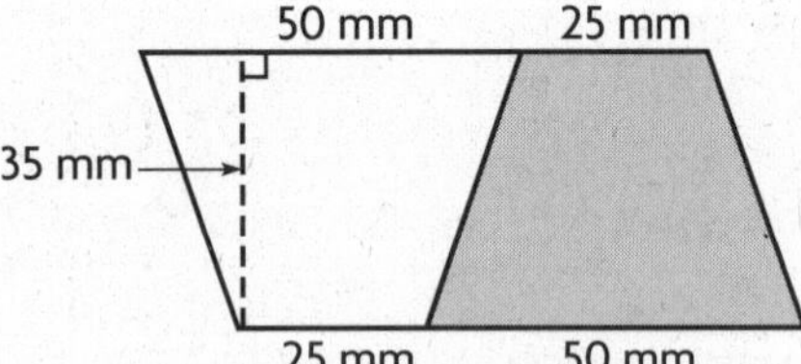

6. A rectangle has a length of 24 inches and a width of 36 inches. A square with side length 5 inches is cut from the middle and removed. What is the area of the figure that remains?

FOR MORE PRACTICE GO TO THE **Personal Math Trainer**

Name ______________________________

Figures on the Coordinate Plane

Geometry—6.G.A.3
Also 6.NS.C.8

MATHEMATICAL PRACTICES
MP4, MP6, MP8

Essential Question How can you plot polygons on a coordinate plane and find their side lengths?

Unlock the Problem (Real World)

The world's largest book is a collection of photographs from the Asian nation of Bhutan. A book collector models the rectangular shape of the open book on a coordinate plane. Each unit of the coordinate plane represents one foot. The book collector plots the vertices of the rectangle at $A(9, 3)$, $B(2, 3)$, $C(2, 8)$, and $D(9, 8)$. What are the dimensions of the open book?

- What two dimensions do you need to find?

____

____

Plot the vertices and find the dimensions of the rectangle.

STEP 1 Complete the rectangle on the coordinate plane.

Plot points $C(2, 8)$ and $D(9, 8)$.
Connect the points to form a rectangle.

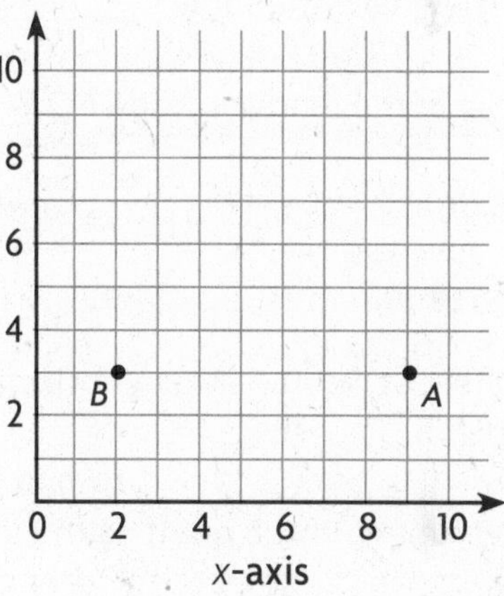

STEP 2 Find the length of the rectangle.

Find the distance between points $A(9, 3)$ and $B(2, 3)$.

The y-coordinates are the same, so the points lie on a ________ line.

Think of the horizontal line passing through A and B as a number line.

Horizontal distance of A from 0: $|9|$ = ______ ft

Horizontal distance of B from 0: $|2|$ = ______ ft

Subtract to find the distance from A to B: ______ − ______ = ______ ft.

STEP 3 Find the width of the rectangle.

Find the distance between points C (2, 8) and $B(2, 3)$.

The x-coordinates are the same, so the points lie on a ________ line.

Think of the vertical line passing through C and B as a number line.

Vertical distance of C from 0: $|8|$ = ______ ft

Vertical distance of B from 0: $|3|$ = ______ ft

Subtract to find the distance from C to B: ______ − ______ = ______ ft.

So, the dimensions of the open book are ______ ft by ______ ft.

Math Talk MATHEMATICAL PRACTICES 6

Explain How do you know whether to add or subtract the absolute values to find the distance between the vertices of the rectangle?

CONNECT You can use properties of quadrilaterals to help you find unknown vertices. The properties can also help you graph quadrilaterals on the coordinate plane.

Example Find the unknown vertex, and then graph.

Three vertices of parallelogram *PQRS* are *P*(4, 2), *Q*(3, $^-3$), and *R*($^-3$, $^-3$). Give the coordinates of vertex *S* and graph the parallelogram.

Math Idea

The name of a polygon, such as parallelogram *PQRS*, gives the vertices in order as you move around the polygon.

STEP 1

Plot the given points on the coordinate plane.

STEP 2

The opposite sides of a parallelogram are ____________.

They have the same ________________.

Since the length of side $\overline{RQ}$ is ______ units, the length of side ________________ must also be ______ units.

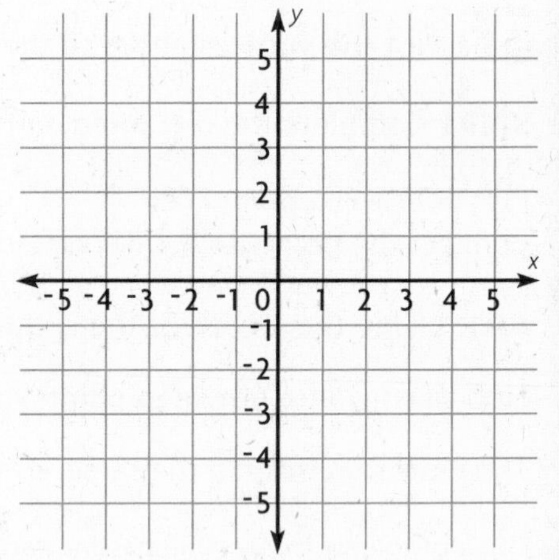

STEP 3

Start at point *P*. Move horizontally ______ units to the ________________ to find the location of the remaining vertex, *S*. Plot a point at this location.

STEP 4

Draw the parallelogram. Check that opposite sides are parallel and congruent.

So, the coordinates of the vertex *S* are ____________.

1. MATHEMATICAL PRACTICE 6 **Attend to Precision** Explain why vertex *S* must be to the left of vertex *P* rather than to the right of vertex *P*.

2. Describe how you could find the area of parallelogram *PQRS* in square units.

Name ______________________________

Share and Show

1. The vertices of triangle ABC are $A(^-1, 3)$, $B(^-4, ^-2)$, and $C(2, ^-2)$. Graph the triangle and find the length of side $\overline{BC}$.

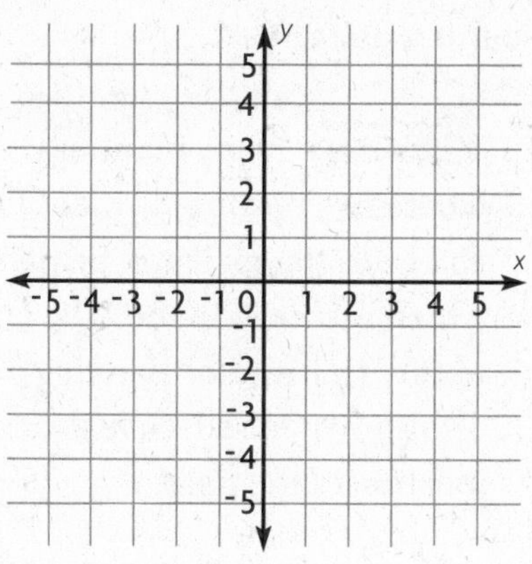

Horizontal distance of B from 0: $|^-4| =$ ______ units

Horizontal distance of C from 0: $|2| =$ ______ units

The points are in different quadrants, so add to find the

distance from B to C: ______ + ______ = ______ units.

Give the coordinates of the unknown vertex of rectangle *JKLM*, and graph.

2.

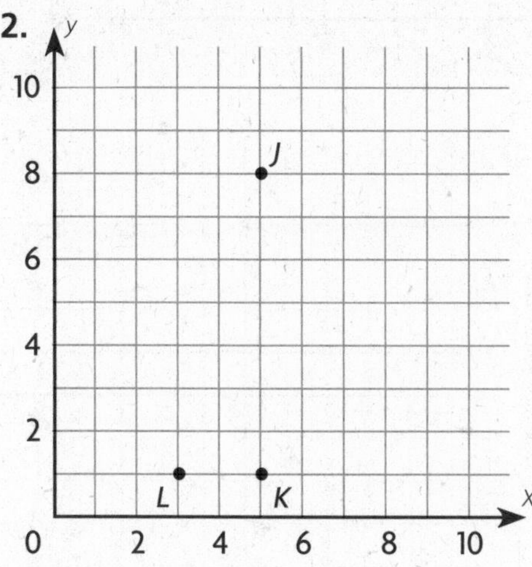

____

3.

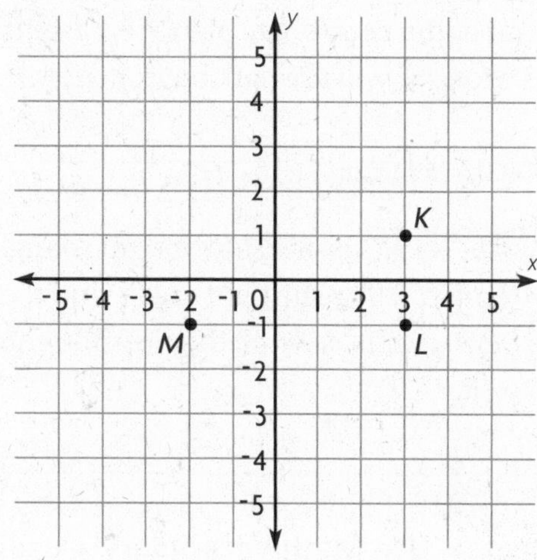

____

On Your Own

4. Give the coordinates of the unknown vertex of rectangle $PQRS$, and graph.

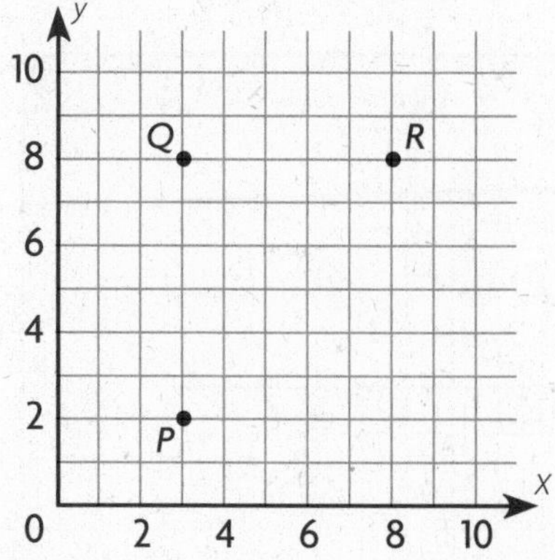

____

5. The vertices of pentagon $PQRST$ are $P(9, 7)$, $Q(9, 3)$, $R(3, 3)$, $S(3, 7)$, and $T(6, 9)$. Graph the pentagon and find the length of side $\overline{PQ}$.

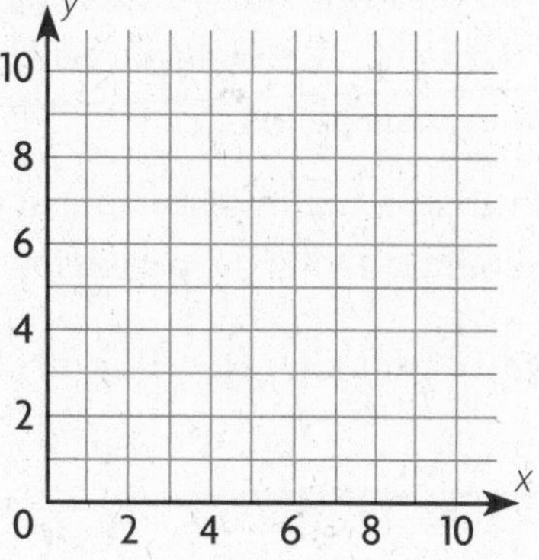

____

Problem Solving • Applications Real World

The map shows the location of some city landmarks. Use the map for 6–7.

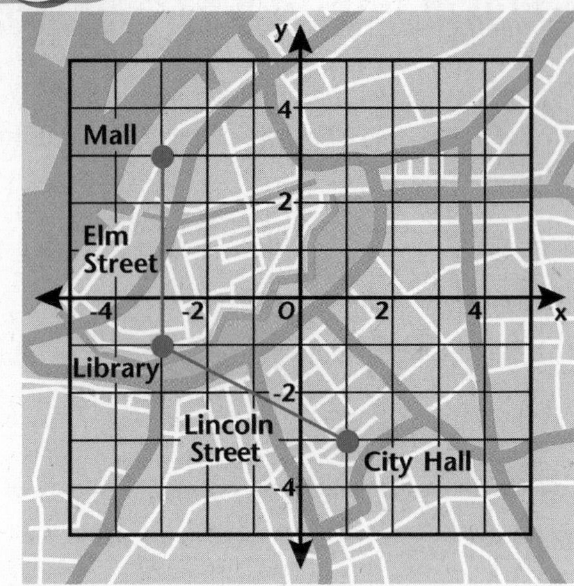

6. GO DEEPER A city planner wants to locate a park where two new roads meet. One of the new roads will go to the mall and be parallel to Lincoln Street which is shown in red. The other new road will go to City Hall and be parallel to Elm Street which is also shown in red. Give the coordinates for the location of the park.

____

7. Each unit of the coordinate plane represents 2 miles. How far will the park be from City Hall?

____

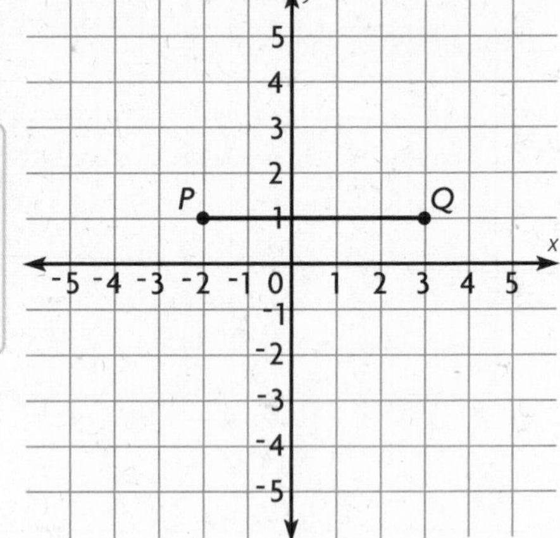

8. THINK SMARTER $\overline{PQ}$ is one side of right triangle PQR. In the triangle, $\angle P$ is the right angle, and the length of side $\overline{PR}$ is 3 units. Give all the possible coordinates for vertex R.

____

9. MATHEMATICAL PRACTICE 6 **Use Math Vocabulary** Quadrilateral $WXYZ$ has vertices with coordinates $W(^-4, 0)$, $X(^-2, 3)$, $Y(2, 3)$, and $Z(2, 0)$. Classify the quadrilateral using the most exact name possible and explain your answer.

____

____

10. THINK SMARTER Kareem is drawing parallelogram $ABCD$ on the coordinate plane.

Find and label the coordinates of the fourth vertex, D, of the parallelogram. Draw the parallelogram.

What is the length of side CD? How do you know?

____

____

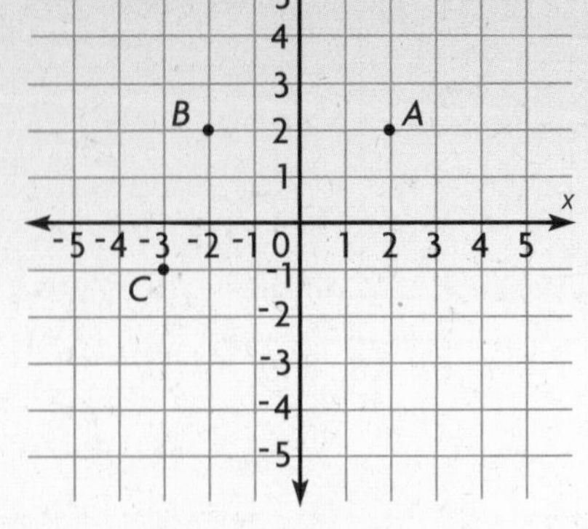

Name ___________________________

Figures on the Coordinate Plane

COMMON CORE STANDARD—6.G.A.3
Solve real-world and mathematical problems involving area, surface area, and volume.

1. The vertices of triangle *DEF* are $D(^{-}2, 3)$, $E(3, ^{-}2)$, and $F(^{-}2, ^{-}2)$. Graph the triangle, and find the length of side $\overline{DF}$.

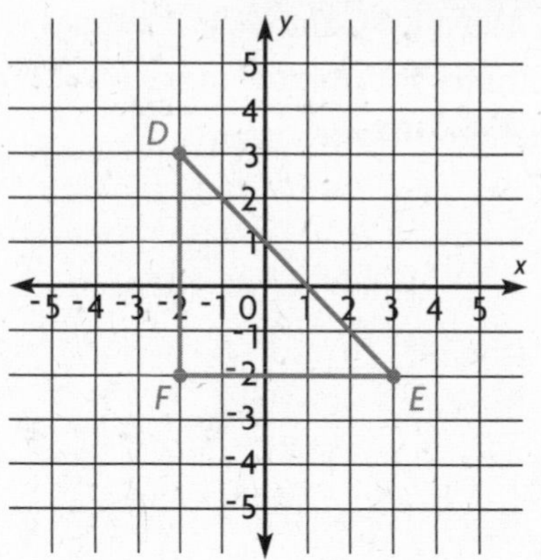

Vertical distance of *D* from 0: $|3|$ = <u>3</u> units

Vertical distance of *F* from 0: $|^{-}2|$ = <u>2</u> units

The points are in different quadrants, so add to find the distance from *D* to *F*: <u>3</u> + <u>2</u> = <u>5</u> units.

Graph the figure and find the length of side $\overline{BC}$.

2. $A(1, 4)$, $B(1, ^{-}2)$, $C(^{-}3, ^{-}2)$, $D(^{-}3, 3)$

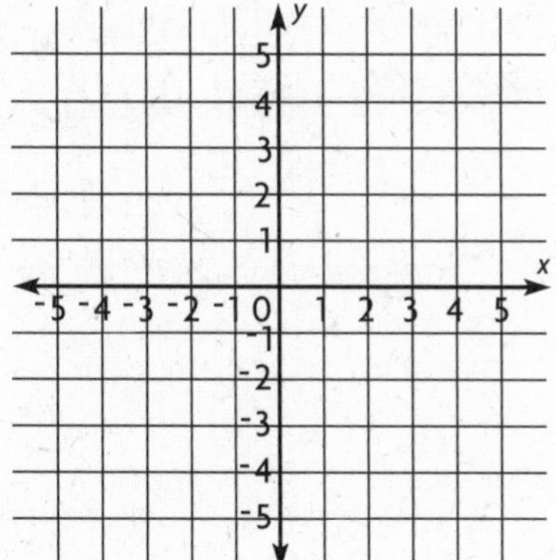

Length of $\overline{BC}$ = ______ units

3. $A(^{-}1, 4)$, $B(5, 4)$, $C(5, 1)$, $D(^{-}1, 1)$

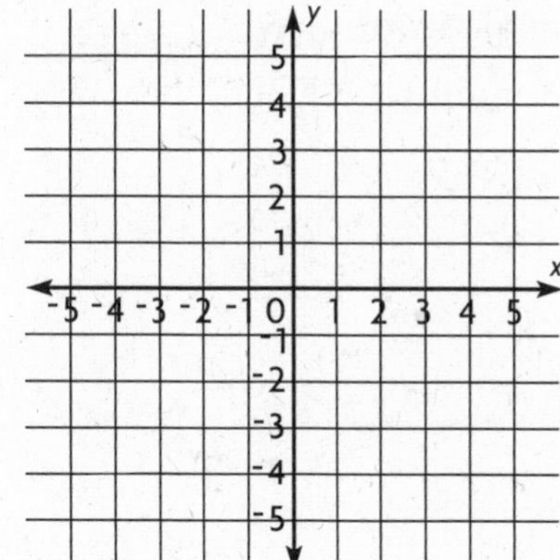

Length of $\overline{BC}$ = ______ units

Problem Solving Real World

4. On a map, a city block is a square with three of its vertices at $(^{-}4, 1)$, $(1, 1)$, and $(1, ^{-}4)$. What are the coordinates of the remaining vertex?

____

5. A carpenter is making a shelf in the shape of a parallelogram. She begins by drawing parallelogram *RSTU* on a coordinate plane with vertices $R(1, 0)$, $S(^{-}3, 0)$, and $T(^{-}2, 3)$. What are the coordinates of vertex *U*?

____

6. WRITE *Math* Explain how you would find the fourth vertex of a rectangle with vertices at $(2, 6)$, $(^{-}1, 4)$, and $(^{-}1, 6)$.

____

____

Lesson Check (6.G.A.3)

1. The coordinates of points M, N, and P are $M(^-2, 3)$, $N(4, 3)$, and $P(5, ^-1)$. What coordinates for point Q make $MNPQ$ a parallelogram?

2. Dirk draws quadrilateral $RSTU$ with vertices $R(^-1, 2)$, $S(4, 2)$, $T(5, ^-1)$, and $U(^-2, ^-1)$. Which is the best way to classify the quadrilateral?

Spiral Review (6.EE.A.2c, 6.EE.C.9, 6.G.A.1)

3. Marcus needs to cut a 5-yard length of yarn into equal pieces for his art project. Write an equation that models the length l in yards of each piece of yarn if Marcus cuts it into p pieces.

4. The area of a triangular flag is 330 square centimeters. If the base of the triangle is 30 centimeters long, what is the height of the triangle?

5. A trapezoid is $6\frac{1}{2}$ feet tall. Its bases are 9.2 feet and 8 feet long. What is the area of the trapezoid?

6. The dimensions of the rectangle below will be multiplied by 3. How will the area be affected?

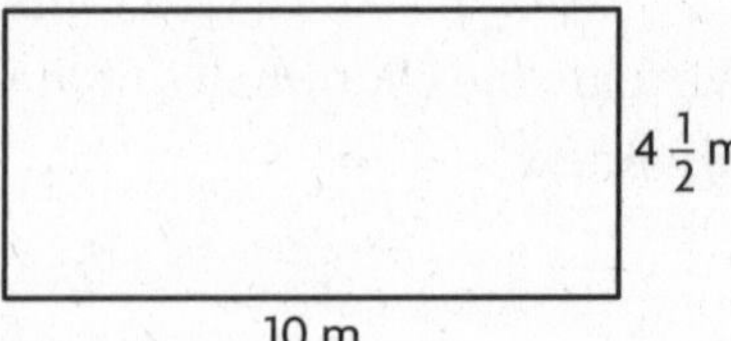

FOR MORE PRACTICE GO TO THE **Personal Math Trainer**

Name ___

Chapter 10 Review/Test

Personal Math Trainer
Online Assessment and Intervention

1. Find the area of the parallelogram.

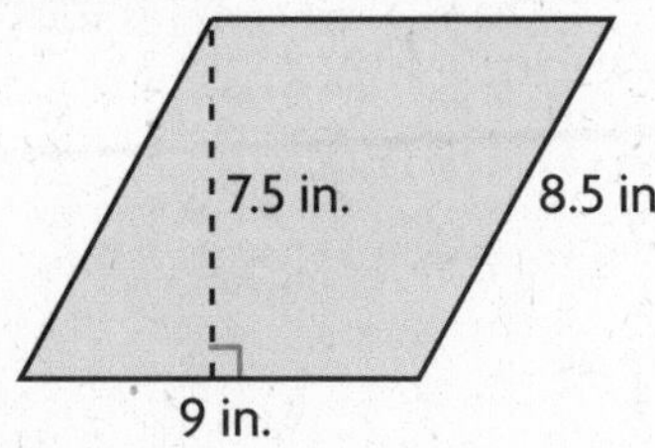

The area is ___ in.^{2}

2. A wall tile is two different colors. What is the area of the white part of the tile? Explain how you found your answer.

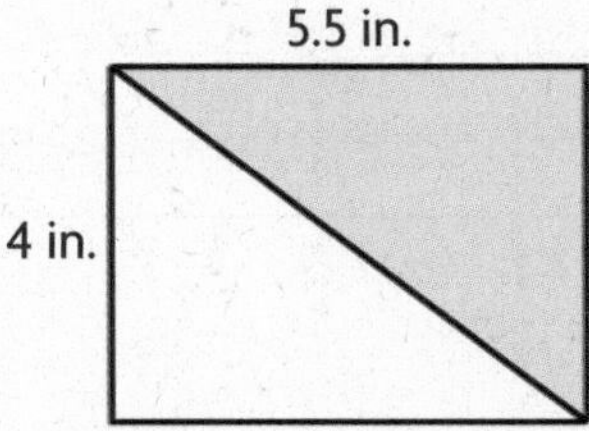

3. The area of a triangle is 36 ft^2. For numbers 3a–3d, select Yes or No to tell if the dimensions could be the height and base of the triangle.

3a.	$h = 3$ ft, $b = 12$ ft	○ Yes	○ No
3b.	$h = 3$ ft, $b = 24$ ft	○ Yes	○ No
3c.	$h = 4$ ft, $b = 18$ ft	○ Yes	○ No
3d.	$h = 4$ ft, $b = 9$ ft	○ Yes	○ No

4. Mario traced this trapezoid. Then he cut it out and arranged the trapezoids to form a rectangle. What is the area of the rectangle?

___ in.^{2}

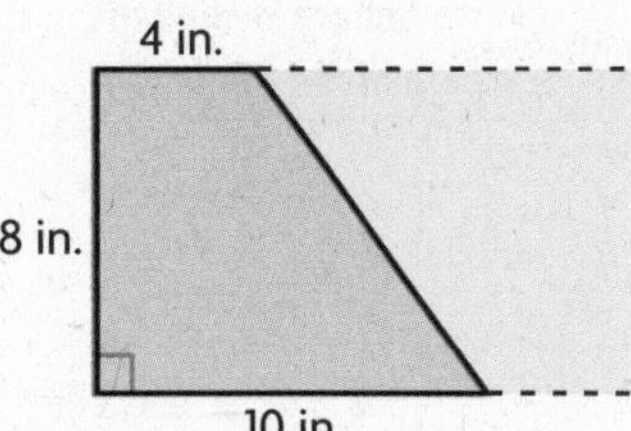

Assessment Options
Chapter Test

5. The area of the triangle is 24 ft^2. Use the numbers to label the height and base of the triangle.

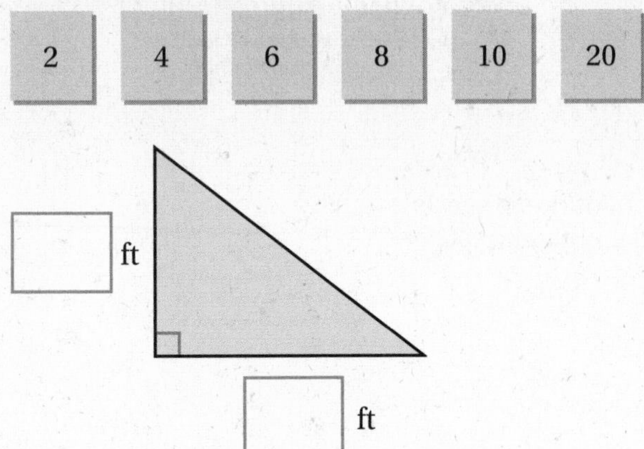

6. A rectangle has an area of 50 cm^2. The dimensions of the rectangle are multiplied to form a new rectangle with an area of 200 cm^2. By what number were the dimensions multiplied?

____

7. Sami put two trapezoids with the same dimensions together to make a parallelogram.

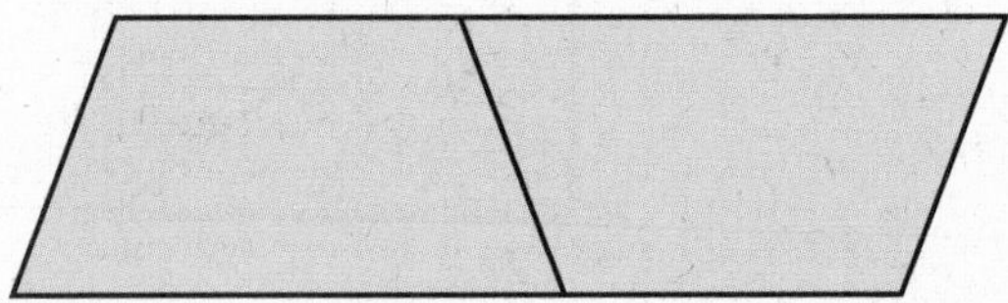

The formula for the area of a trapezoid is $A = \frac{1}{2}(b_1 + b_2)h$. Explain why the bases of a trapezoid need to be added in the formula.

8. GO DEEPER A rectangular plastic bookmark has a triangle cut out of it. Use the diagram of the bookmark to complete the table.

Area of Rectangle	Area of Triangle	Square Inches of Plastic in Bookmark

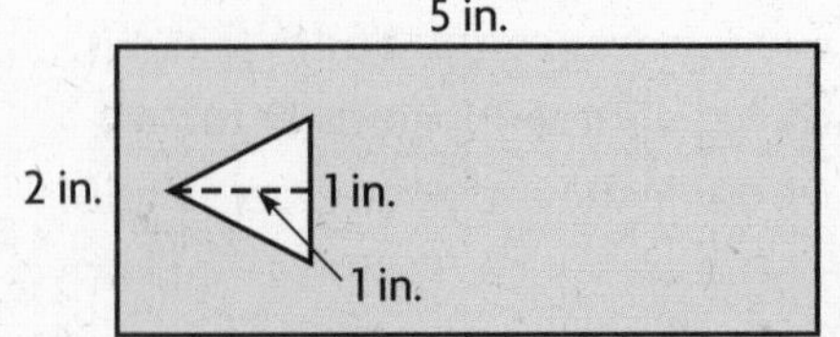

Name ___

9. A trapezoid has an area of 32 in.^{2}. If the lengths of the bases are 6 in. and 6.8 in., what is the height?

___ in.

10. A pillow is in the shape of a regular pentagon. The front of the pillow is made from 5 pieces of fabric that are congruent triangles. Each triangle has an area of 22 in.^{2}. What is the area of the front of the pillow?

___ in.^{2}

11. Which expressions can be used to find the area of the trapezoid? Mark all that apply.

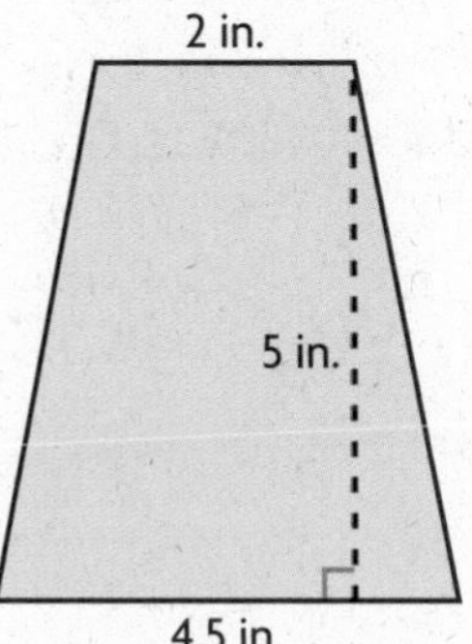

Ⓐ $\frac{1}{2} \times (5 + 2) \times 4.5$

Ⓑ $\frac{1}{2} \times (2 + 4.5) \times 5$

Ⓒ $\frac{1}{2} \times (5 + 4.5) \times 2$

Ⓓ $\frac{1}{2} \times (6.5) \times 5$

12. Name the polygon and find its area. Show your work.

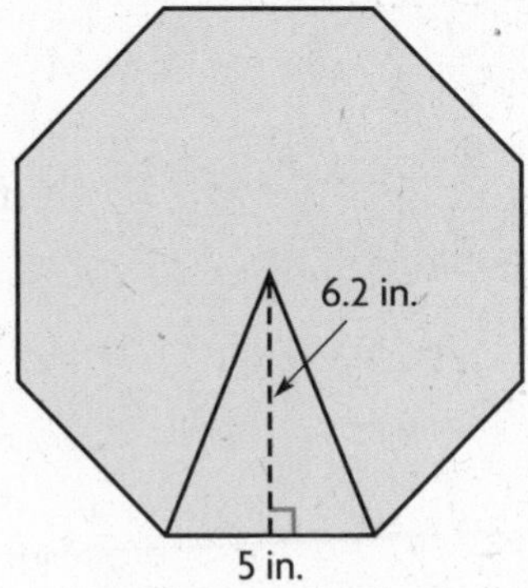

polygon: ___ area: ___

13. A carpenter needs to replace some flooring in a house.

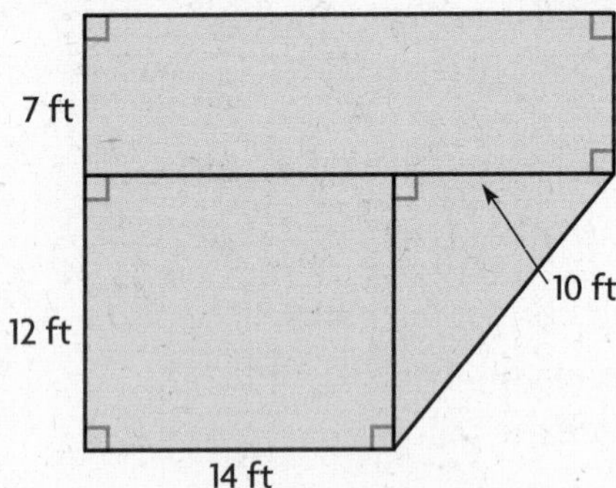

Select the expression that can be used to find the total area of the flooring to be replaced. Mark all that apply.

Ⓐ 19×14

Ⓑ $168 + 12 \times 14 + 60$

Ⓒ $19 \times 24 - \frac{1}{2} \times 10 \times 12$

Ⓓ $7 \times 24 + 12 \times 14 + \frac{1}{2} \times 10 \times 12$

14. Ava wants to draw a parallelogram on the coordinate plane. She plots these 3 points.

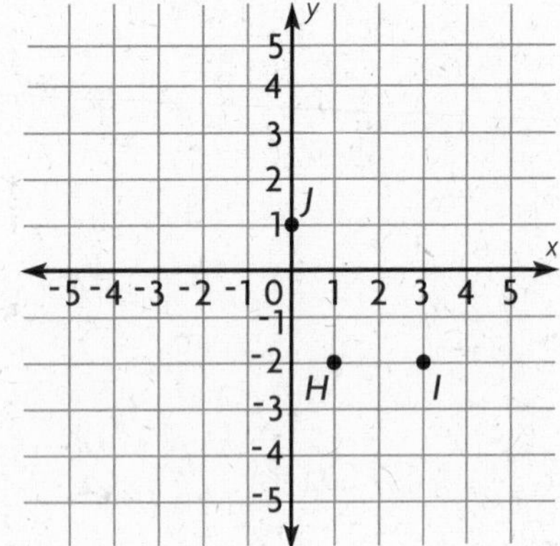

Part A

Find and label the coordinates of the fourth vertex, *K*, of the parallelogram. Draw the parallelogram.

Part B

What is the length of side *JK*? How do you know?

Name ____________________

15. Joan wants to reduce the area of her posters by one-third. Draw lines to match the original dimensions in the left column with the correct new area in the right column. Not all dimensions will have a match.

30 in. by 12 in.	20 in.^{2}
30 in. by 18 in.	60 in.^{2}
12 in. by 15 in.	180 in.^{2}
18 in. by 15 in.	360 in.^{2}

Personal Math Trainer

16. THINKSMARTER+ Alex wants to enlarge a 4-ft by 6-ft vegetable garden by multiplying the dimensions of the garden by 2.

Part A

Find each area.

Area of original garden: ____________

Area of enlarged garden: ____________

Part B

Explain how the area of the original garden will be affected.

17. Suppose the point (3, 2) is changed to (3, 1) on this rectangle. What other point must change so the figure remains a rectangle? What is the area of the new rectangle?

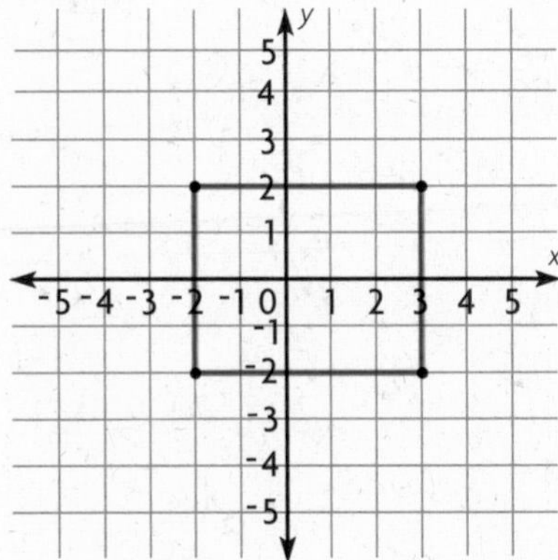

Point: ____________ would change to ____________.

The area of the new rectangle is ____________ square units.

18. Look at the figure below. The area of the parallelogram and the areas of the two congruent triangles formed by a diagonal are related. If you know the area of the parallelogram, how can you find the area of one of the triangles?

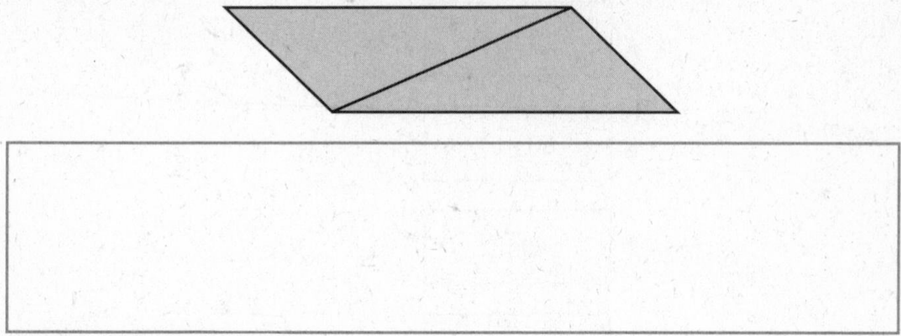

19. The roof of Kamden's house is shaped like a parallelogram. The base of the roof is 13 m and the area is 110.5 m^2. Choose a number and unit to make a true statement.

The height of the roof is

123.5
97.5
17
8.5

m.
m^2.
m^3.

20. Eliana is drawing a figure on the coordinate grid. For numbers 20a–20d, select True or False for each statement.

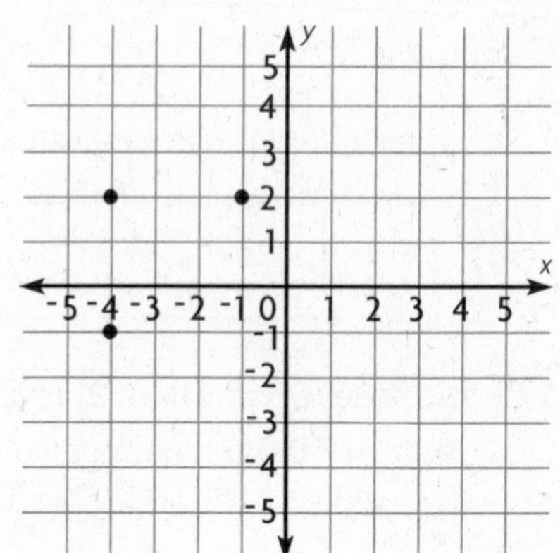

20a. The point $(^-1, 1)$ would be the fourth vertex of a square. ○ True ○ False

20b. The point $(1, 1)$ would be the fourth vertex of a trapezoid. ○ True ○ False

20c. The point $(2, ^-1)$ would be the fourth vertex of a trapezoid. ○ True ○ False

20d. The point $(^-1, ^-1)$ would be the fourth vertex of a square. ○ True ○ False

Chapter 11

Surface Area and Volume

Check your understanding of important skills.

Name ____________________

Estimate and Find Area Multiply to find the area. (4.MD.A.3)

1. ______

2. ______

Area of Squares, Rectangles, and Triangles Find the area. (6.G.A.1)

3. 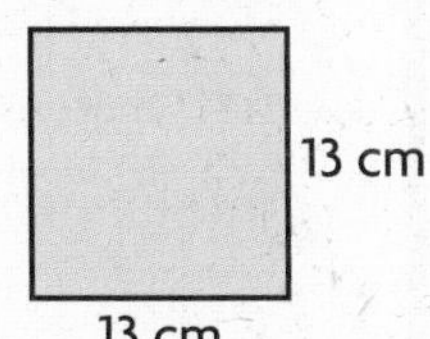

$A = s^2$

Area = ______

4. 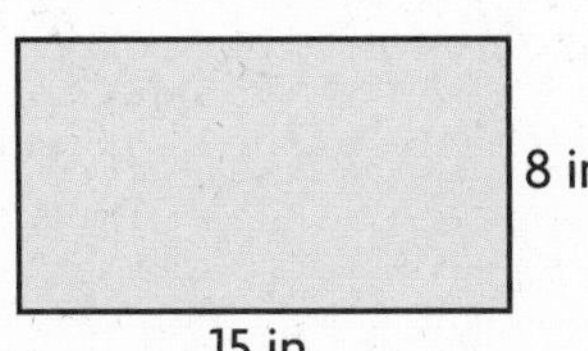

$A = lw$

Area = ______

5. 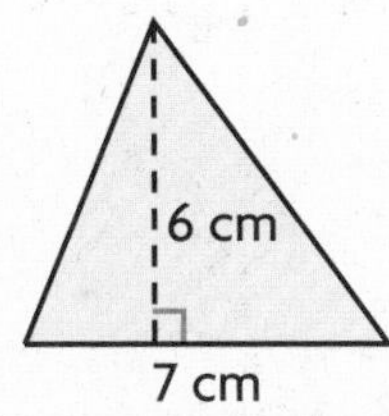

$A = \frac{1}{2}(b \times h)$

Area = ______

Evaluate Expressions Evaluate the expression. (6.EE.A.1)

6. $3 \times (2 + 4)$ ______

7. $6 + 6 \div 3$ ______

8. $4^2 + 4 \times 5 - 2$ ______

Jerry is building an indoor beach volleyball court. He has ordered 14,000 cubic feet of sand. The dimensions of the court will be 30 feet by 60 feet. Jerry needs to have a 10-foot boundary around the court for safety. How deep will the sand be if Jerry uses all the sand?

Vocabulary Builder

▶ Visualize It

Complete the bubble map. Use the review terms that name solid figures.

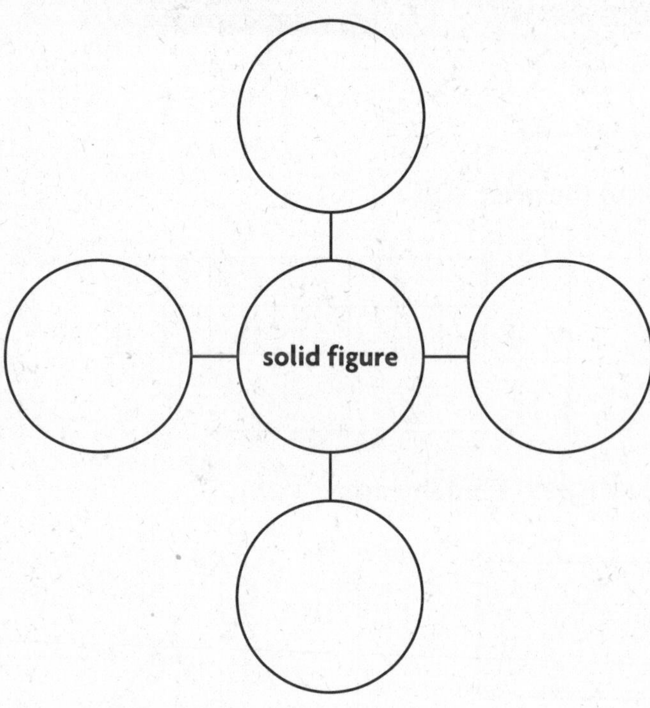

Review Words
base
cube
lateral face
polygon
polyhedron
prism
pyramid
vertex
edge

Preview Words
net
solid figure
surface area
volume

▶ Understand Vocabulary

Complete the sentences using the preview words.

1. A three-dimensional figure having length, width, and height is called a(n) ________________.

2. A two-dimensional pattern that can be folded into a three-dimensional figure is called a(n) ________________.

3. ________________ is the sum of the areas of all the faces, or surfaces, of a solid figure.

4. ________________ is the measure of space a solid figure occupies.

GO DIGITAL
• Interactive Student Edition
• Multimedia eGlossary

Chapter 11 Vocabulary

base (geometry)

base

7

lateral area

área lateral

47

net

plantilla

65

prism

prisma

79

pyramid

pirámide

81

solid figure

cuerpo geométrico

93

surface area

área total

100

volume

volumen

106

The sum of the areas of the lateral faces of a solid

Example:

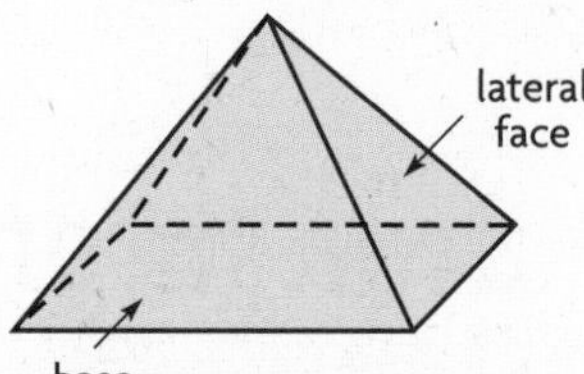

In two dimensions, one side of a triangle or parallelogram which is used to help find the area. In three dimensions, a plane figure, usually a polygon or circle, which is used to partially describe a solid figure and to help find the volume of some solid figures.

A solid figure that has two congruent, polygon-shaped bases, and other faces that are all rectangles

Examples:

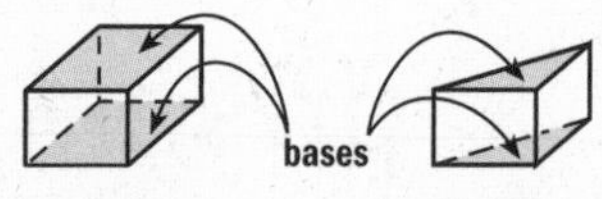

A two-dimensional pattern that can be folded into a three-dimensional polyhedron

Example:

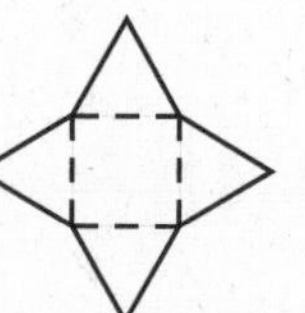

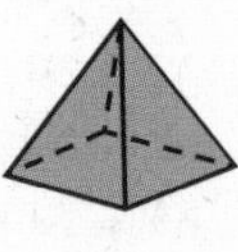

A three-dimensional figure having length, width, and height

Examples:

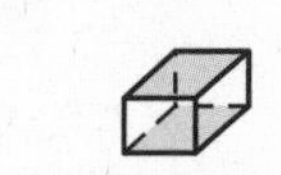

Sphere

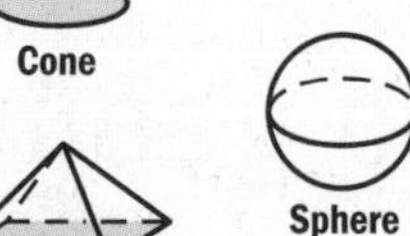

A solid figure with a polygon base and all other faces as triangles that meet at a common vertex

Example:

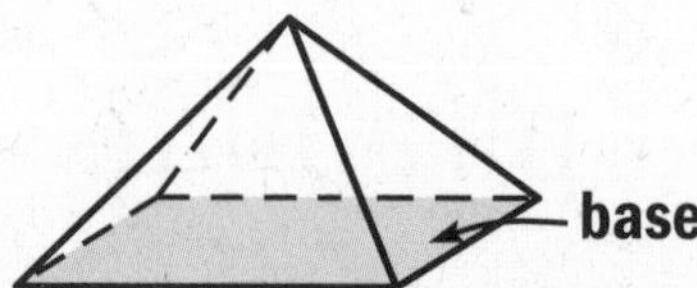

The measure of the space a solid figure occupies

The sum of the areas of all the faces, or surfaces, of a solid figure

Example:

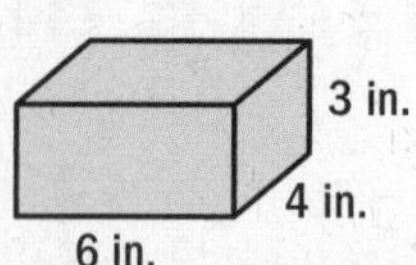

Surface area $= 2(6 \times 4) + 2(6 \times 3) + 2(4 \times 3)$

$= 180 \text{ in.}^2$

Bingo

Word Box
base
lateral area
net
prism
pyramid
solid figure
surface area
volume

For 3–6 players

Materials

- 1 set of word cards
- 1 Bingo board for each player
- game markers

How to Play

1. The caller chooses a card and reads the definition. Then the caller puts the card in a second pile.
2. Players put a marker on the word that matches the definition each time they find it on their Bingo boards.
3. Repeat Steps 1 and 2 until a player marks 5 boxes in a line going down, across, or on a slant and calls "Bingo."
4. To check the answers, the player who said "Bingo" reads the words aloud while the caller checks the definitions.

The Write Way

Reflect

Choose one idea. Write about it.

- Define *net* and explain how nets can be used to understand solid figures.
- Explain and illustrate two ways to find the surface area of a cube. Use a separate piece of paper for your drawing.
- Write two questions you have about finding a lateral area. Tell how you would start to find the answers to those questions.
- Write a creative story about a person who needs to find the volume of something.

Name ______________________________

Three-Dimensional Figures and Nets

Essential Question How do you use nets to represent three-dimensional figures?

MATHEMATICAL PRACTICES
MP1, MP6

A **solid figure** is a three-dimensional figure because it has three dimensions—length, width, and height. Solid figures can be identified by the shapes of their bases, the number of bases, and the shapes of their lateral faces.

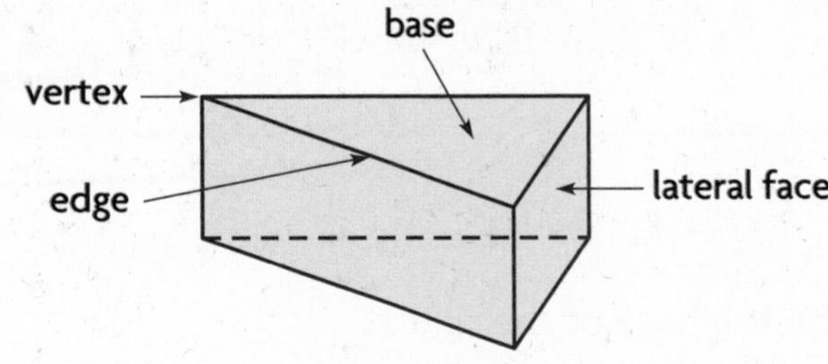

Triangular Prism

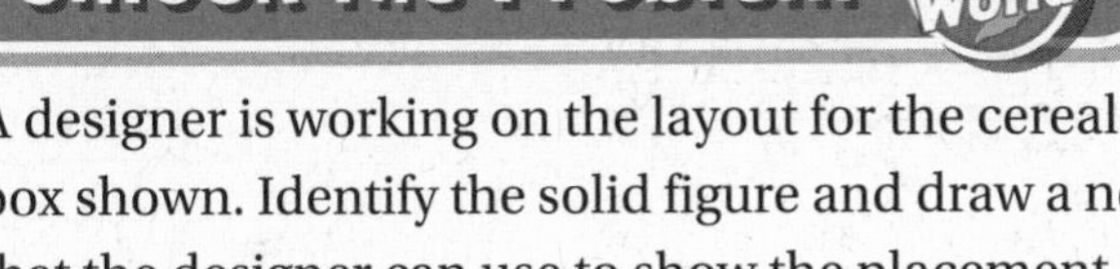

A designer is working on the layout for the cereal box shown. Identify the solid figure and draw a net that the designer can use to show the placement of information and artwork on the box.

- How many bases are there? ____________
- Are the bases congruent? ____________
- What shape are the bases? ____________

Identify the solid figure.

Recall that a prism is a solid figure with two congruent, parallel bases. Its lateral faces are rectangles. It is named for the shape of its bases.

Is the cereal box a prism? ____________

What shape are the bases? ____________

So, the box is a ______________________.

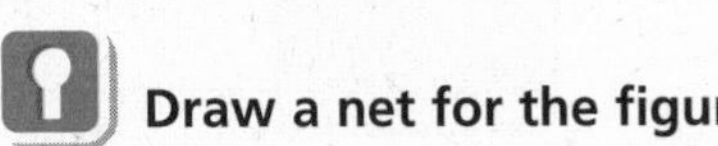
Draw a net for the figure.

A **net** is a two-dimensional figure that can be folded into a solid figure.

STEP 1

Make a list of the shapes you will use.

top and bottom bases: ____________

left and right faces: ____________

front and back faces: ____________

STEP 2

Draw the net using the shapes you listed in Step 1. One possible net is shown.

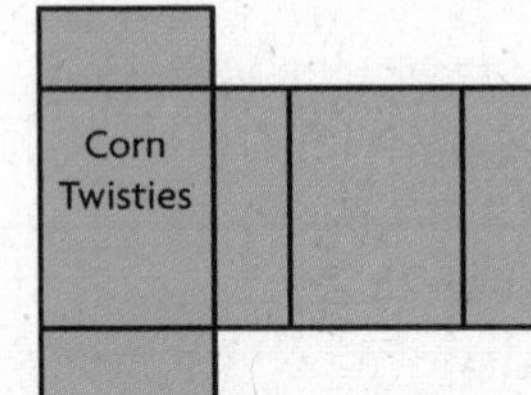

A *pyramid* is a solid figure with a polygon-shaped base and triangles for lateral faces. Like prisms, pyramids are named by the shape of their bases. A pyramid with a rectangle for a base is called a rectangular pyramid.

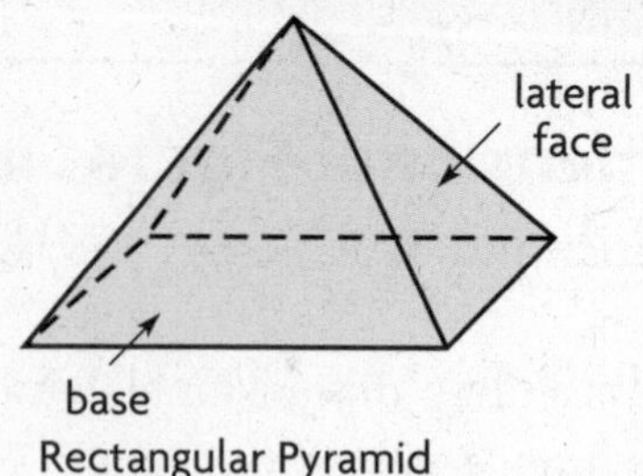

Rectangular Pyramid

Example 1 Identify and draw a net for the solid figure.

Describe the base of the figure.

____

Describe the lateral faces.

____

The figure is a ______________.

<u>Shapes to use in the net:</u>

base: __________

lateral faces: __________

<u>Net:</u>

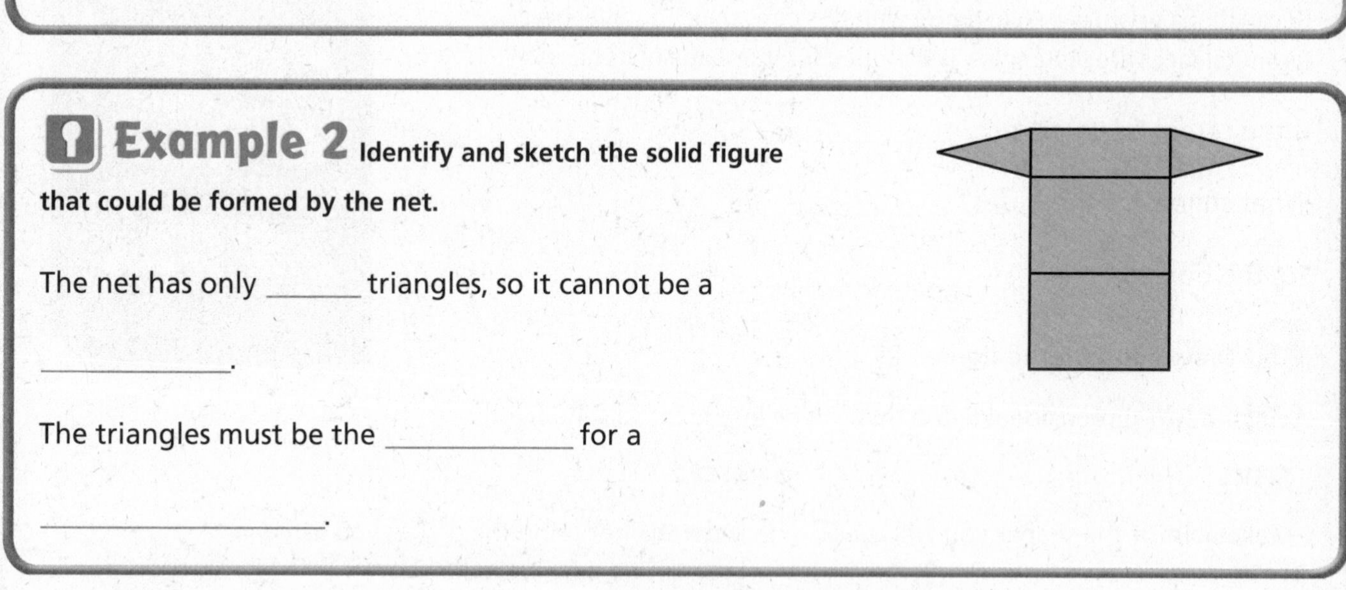

Example 2 Identify and sketch the solid figure that could be formed by the net.

The net has only _____ triangles, so it cannot be a __________.

The triangles must be the __________ for a __________.

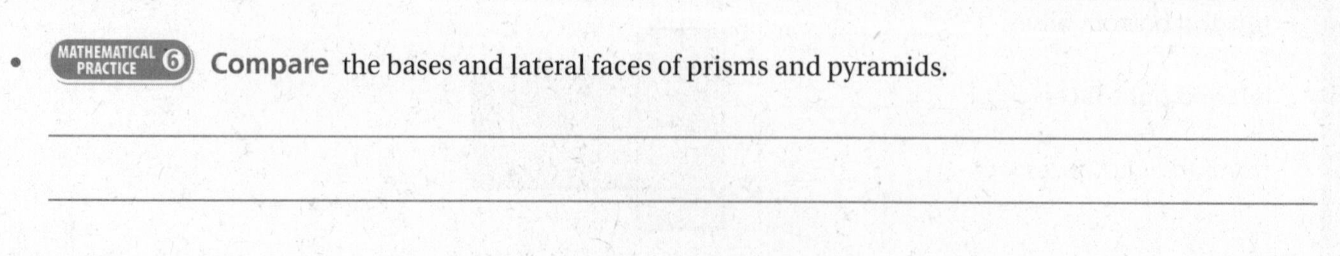

- **MATHEMATICAL PRACTICE 6** **Compare** the bases and lateral faces of prisms and pyramids.

____

____

____

Name ______________________

Identify and draw a net for the solid figure.

1. 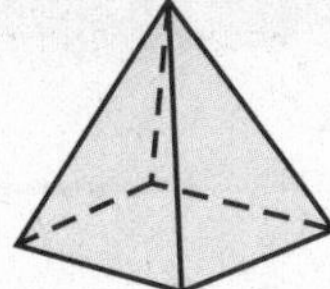

Net:

base: ______________

lateral faces: ______________

figure: ______________

 2. 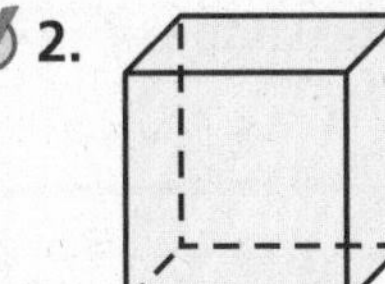

____

Identify and sketch the solid figure that could be formed by the net.

3. 

____

4. 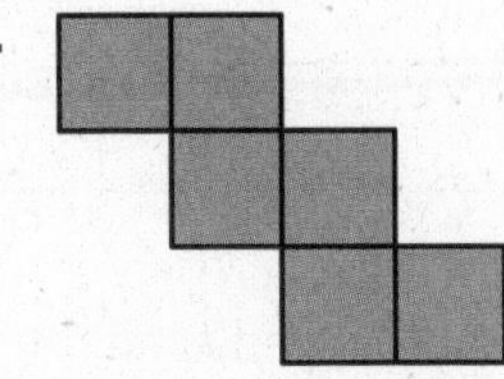

____

MATHEMATICAL PRACTICES 1

Describe What characteristics of a solid figure do you need to consider when making its net?

On Your Own

Identify and draw a net for the solid figure.

5. 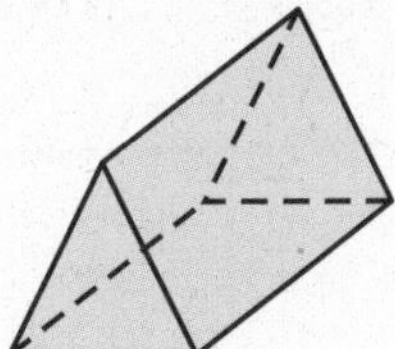

____

6. 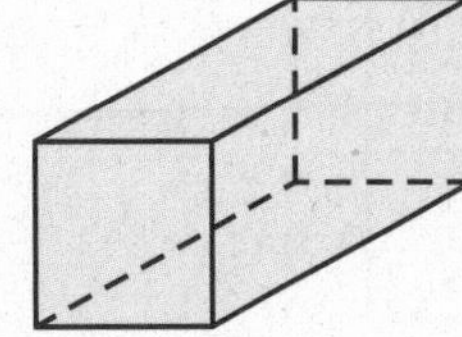

____

Problem Solving • Applications 

Solve.

7. The lateral faces and bases of crystals of the mineral galena are congruent squares. Identify the shape of a galena crystal.

____

8. THINK SMARTER Rhianon draws the net below and labels each square. Can Rhianon fold her net into a cube that has letters A through G on its faces? Explain.

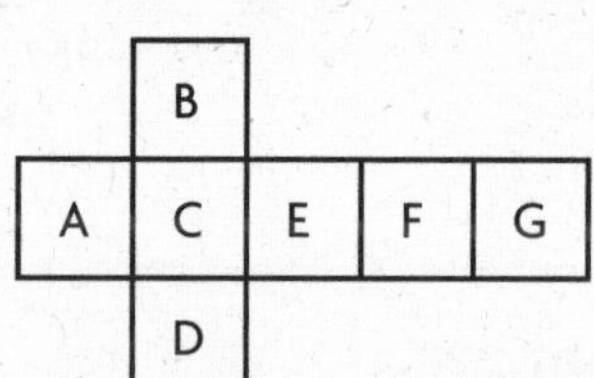

____

____

WRITE Math
Show Your Work

9. MATHEMATICAL PRACTICE 1 **Describe** A diamond crystal is shown. Describe the figure in terms of the solid figures you have seen in this lesson.

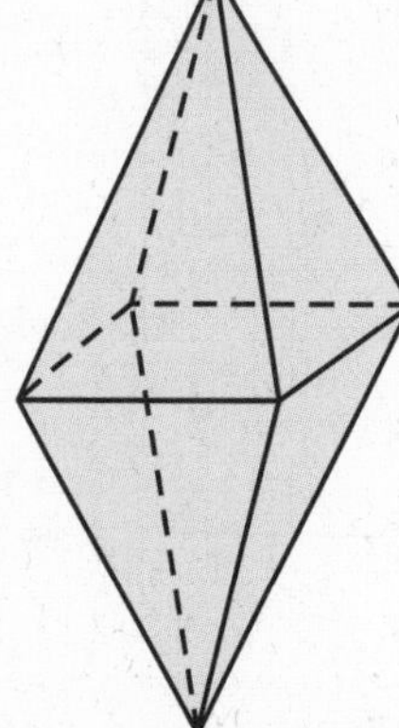

____

____

____

____

10. THINK SMARTER Sasha makes a triangular prism from paper.

The bases are [rectangles. / squares. / triangles.]

The lateral faces are [rectangles. / squares. / triangles.]

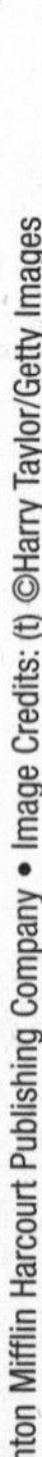

Name ____________________

Three-Dimensional Figures and Nets

Common Core **COMMON CORE STANDARD—6.G.A.4**
Solve real-world and mathematical problems involving area, surface area, and volume.

Identify and draw a net for the solid figure.

1. 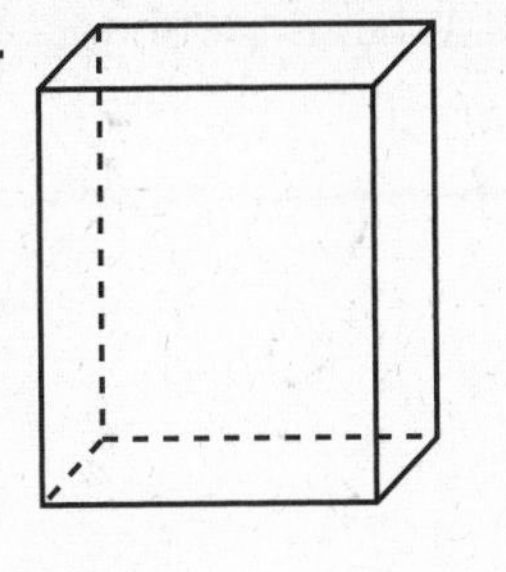

Net

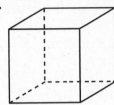

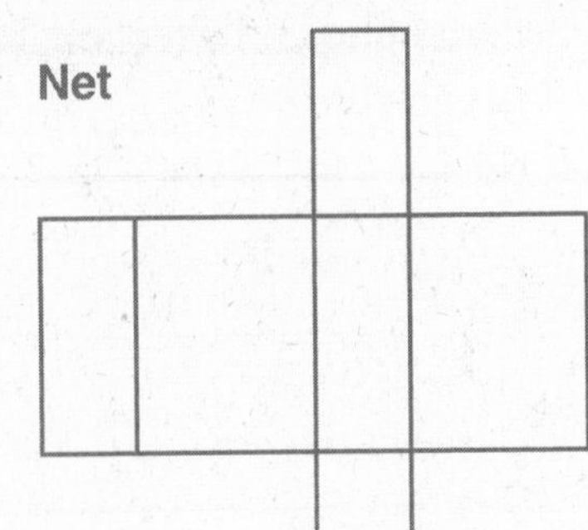

figure: rectangular prism

2. 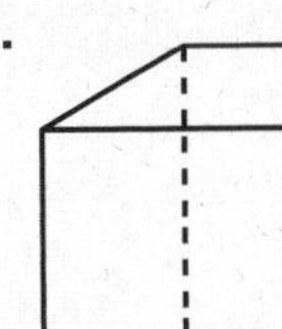

figure: ____________________

3. 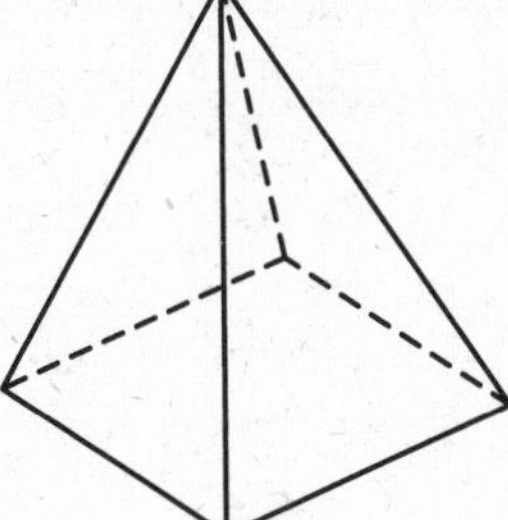

figure: ____________________

4.  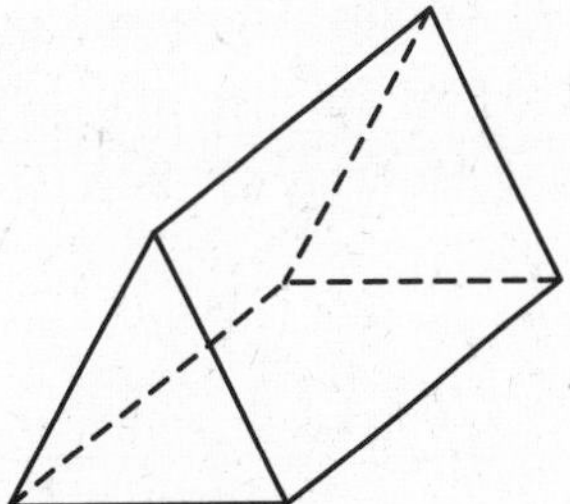

figure: ____________________

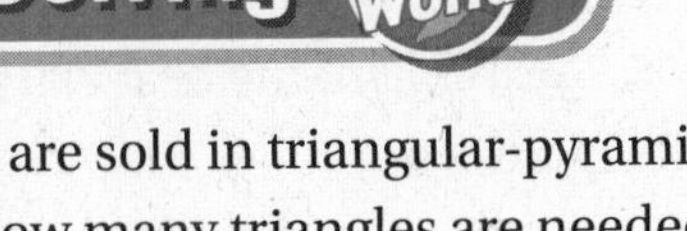

5. Hobie's Candies are sold in triangular-pyramid-shaped boxes. How many triangles are needed to make one box?

____

6. Nina used plastic rectangles to make 6 rectangular prisms. How many rectangles did she use?

____

7. WRITE ▸ *Math* Describe how you could draw more than one net to represent the same three-dimensional figure. Give examples.

____

____

Lesson Check (6.G.A.4)

1. How many vertices does a square pyramid have?

2. Each box of Fred's Fudge is constructed from 2 triangles and 3 rectangles. What is the shape of each box?

Spiral Review (6.EE.B.7, 6.EE.C.9, 6.G.A.1, 6.G.A.3)

3. Bryan jogged the same distance each day for 7 days. He ran a total of 22.4 miles. The equation $7d = 22.4$ can be used to find the distance d in miles he jogged each day. How far did Bryan jog each day?

4. A hot-air balloon is at an altitude of 240 feet. The balloon descends 30 feet per minute. What equation gives the altitude y, in feet, of the hot-air balloon after x minutes?

5. A regular heptagon has sides measuring 26 mm and is divided into 7 congruent triangles. Each triangle has a height of 27 mm. What is the area of the heptagon?

6. Alexis draws quadrilateral $STUV$ with vertices $S(1, 3)$, $T(2, 2)$, $U(2, ^{-}3)$, and $V(1, ^{-}2)$. What name best classifies the quadrilateral?

FOR MORE PRACTICE GO TO THE **Personal Math Trainer**

Name ______________________________

Explore Surface Area Using Nets

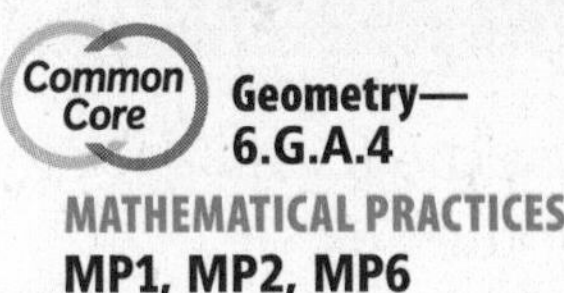

MATHEMATICAL PRACTICES
MP1, MP2, MP6

Essential Question What is the relationship between a net and the surface area of a prism?

CONNECT The **surface area** of a solid figure is the sum of the areas of all the faces or surfaces of the figure. Surface area is measured in square units. You can use a net to help you find the surface area of a solid figure.

Investigate

Hands On

Materials ■ centimeter grid paper, ruler, scissors

A box is shaped like a rectangular prism. The box is 8 cm long, 6 cm wide, and 4 cm high. What is the surface area of the box?

Find the surface area of the rectangular prism.

A. Draw a net of the prism on centimeter grid paper.

B. Cut out the net.

C. Fold the net to confirm that it represents a rectangular prism measuring 8 cm by 6 cm by 4 cm.

D. Count the unit squares on each face of the net.

So, the surface area of the box is ____________ cm^2.

ERROR Alert

Make sure you include all surfaces in the net of a three-dimensional figure, not just the surfaces you can see in the diagram of the figure.

Draw Conclusions

1. Explain how you used the net to find the surface area of the box.

____

____

2. THINKSMARTER Describe how you could find the area of each face of the prism without counting unit squares on the net.

____

____

Make Connections

You can also use the formula for the area of a rectangle to find the surface area of the box.

Find the surface area of the box in the Investigate, which measures 8 cm by 6 cm by 4 cm.

STEP 1 Label the rectangles in the net A through F. Then label the dimensions.

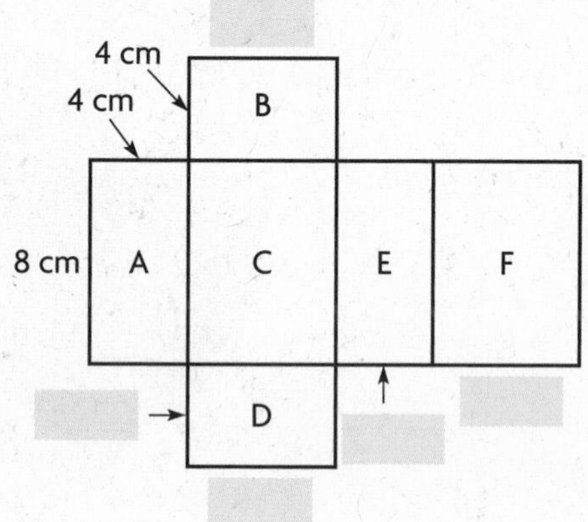

STEP 2 Find the area of each face of the prism.

Think: I can find the area of a rectangle by multiplying the rectangle's ______________

times its ______________.

Record the areas of the faces below.

Face A: $4 \times 8 = 32$ cm^2 Face B: ______ cm^2 Face C: ______ cm^2

Face D: ______ cm^2 Face E: ______ cm^2 Face F: ______ cm^2

STEP 3 Add the areas to find the surface area of the prism.

The surface area of the prism is ______ cm^2.

MATHEMATICAL PRACTICES 6

Compare What do you notice about the surface area you found by adding the areas of the faces and the surface area you found by counting grid squares? Explain.

3. MATHEMATICAL PRACTICE 2 **Use Reasoning** Identify any prism faces that have equal areas. How could you use that fact to simplify the process of finding the surface area of the prism?

____

____

____

4. Describe how you could find the surface area of a cube.

____

Name ______________________________

Share and Show MATH BOARD

Use the net to find the surface area of the prism.

1.

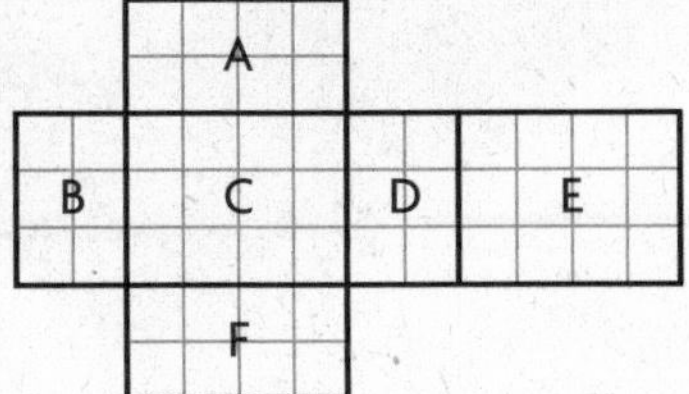

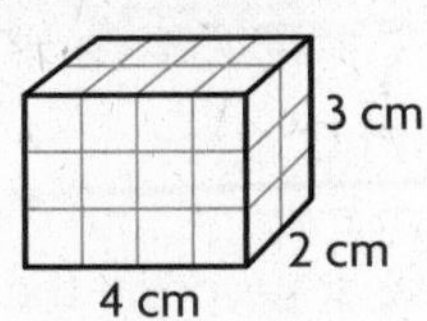

Face A: _______ cm^2 Face D: _______ cm^2

Face B: _______ cm^2 Face E: _______ cm^2

Face C: _______ cm^2 Face F: _______ cm^2

Surface area: _______ cm^2

Find the surface area of the rectangular prism.

2.

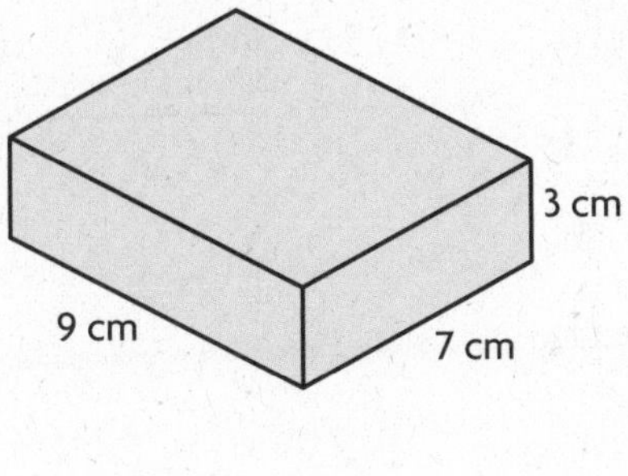

____

3.

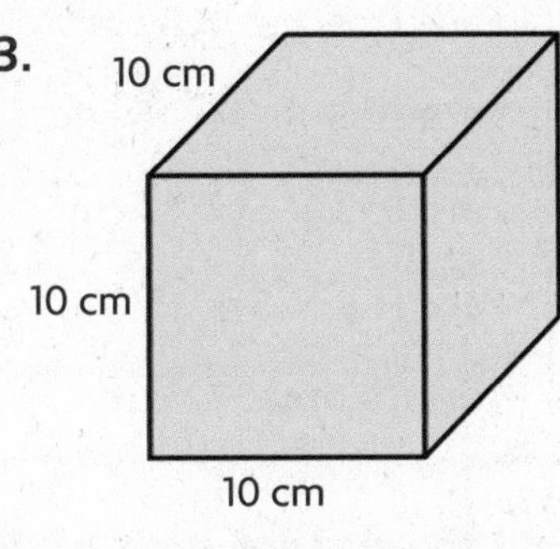

____

4.

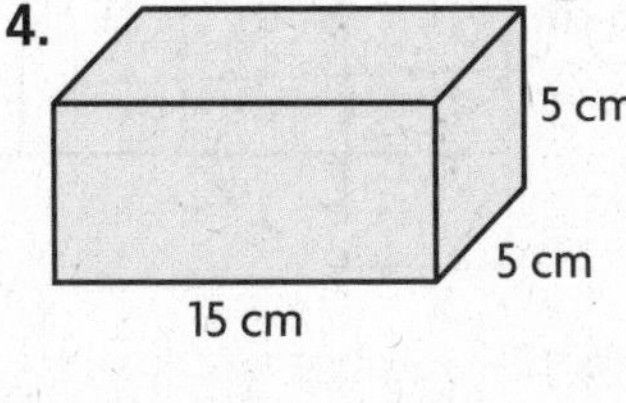

____

Problem Solving • Applications Real World

5. A cereal box is shaped like a rectangular prism. The box is 20 cm long by 5 cm wide by 30 cm high. What is the surface area of the cereal box?

____

6. MATHEMATICAL PRACTICE 1 Darren is painting a wooden block as part of his art project. The block is a rectangular prism that is 12 cm long by 9 cm wide by 5 cm high. Describe the rectangles that make up the net for the prism.

____

____

7.  In Exercise 6, what is the surface area, in square meters, that Darren has to paint?

____

What's the Error?

8. THINK SMARTER Emilio is designing the packaging for a new MP3 player. The box for the MP3 player is 5 cm by 3 cm by 2 cm. Emilio needs to find the surface area of the box.

Look at how Emilio solved the problem. Find his error.

STEP 1 Draw a net.

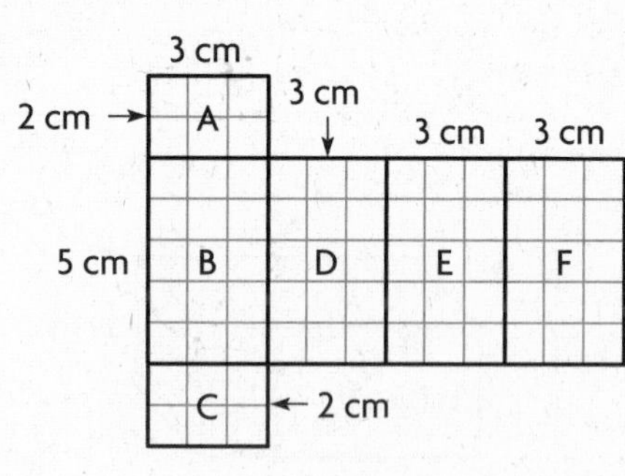

STEP 2 Find the areas of all the faces and add them.

Face A: $3 \times 2 = 6$ cm^2

Face B: $3 \times 5 = 15$ cm^2

Face C: $3 \times 2 = 6$ cm^2

Face D: $3 \times 5 = 15$ cm^2

Face E: $3 \times 5 = 15$ cm^2

Face F: $3 \times 5 = 15$ cm^2

Surface area: 72 cm^2

Correct the error. Find the surface area of the prism.

So, the surface area of the prism is ______________.

9. THINK SMARTER For numbers 9a–9d, select True or False for each statement.

9a. The area of face A is 10 cm^2. ○ True ○ False

9b. The area of face B is 10 cm^2. ○ True ○ False

9c. The area of face C is 40 cm^2. ○ True ○ False

9d. The surface area of the prism is 66 cm^2. ○ True ○ False

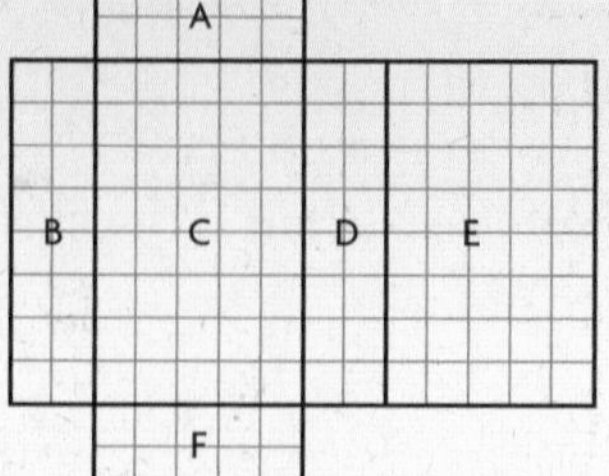

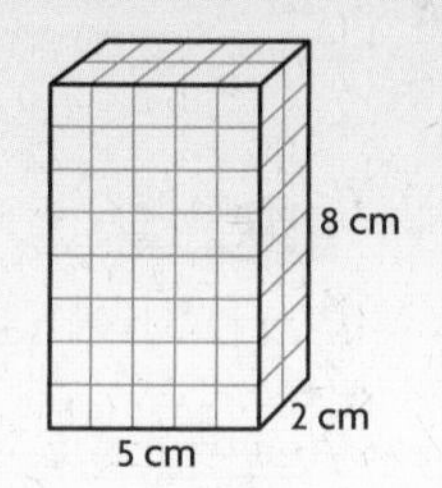

Name ______________________

Explore Surface Area Using Nets

Use the net to find the surface area of the rectangular prism.

COMMON CORE STANDARD—6.G.A.4
Solve real-world and mathematical problems involving area, surface area, and volume.

1.
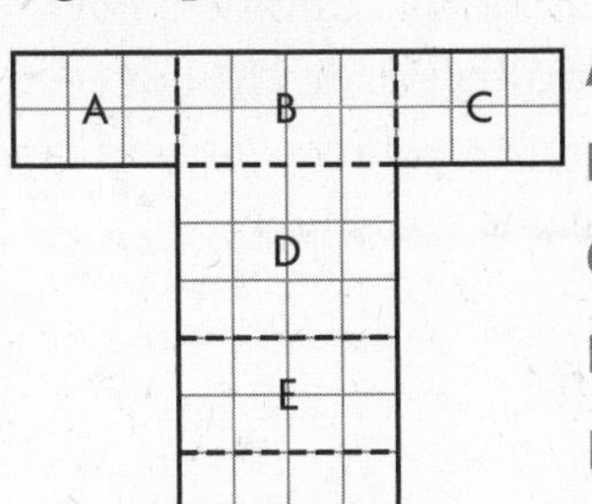

A: 6 squares
B: 8 squares
C: 6 squares
D: 12 squares
E: 8 squares
F: 12 squares

52 square units

2.
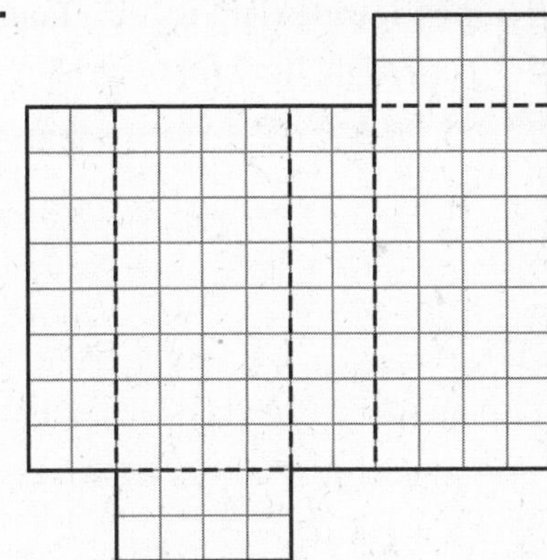

____

Find the surface area of the rectangular prism.

3.
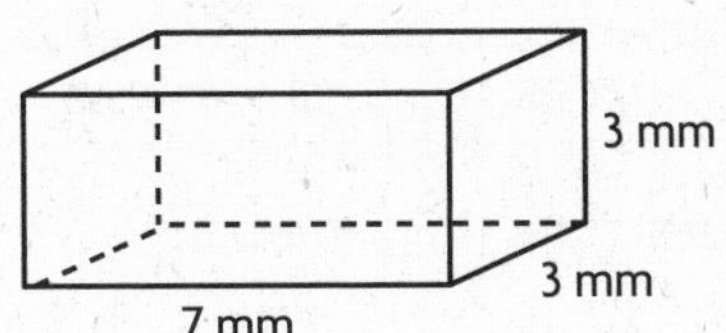

____

4.
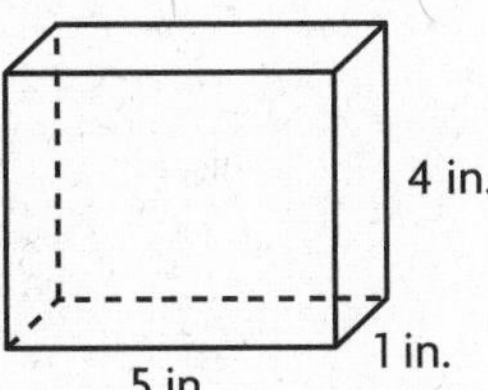

____

5.
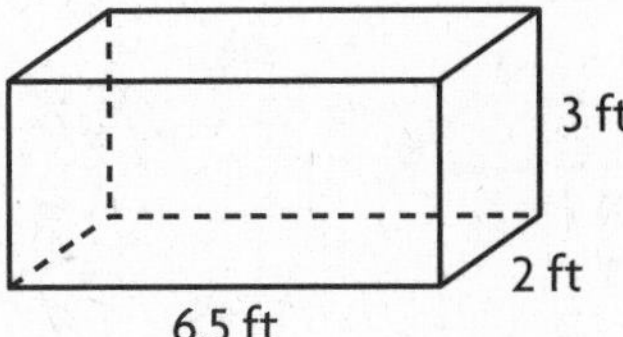

____

Problem Solving Real World

6. Jeremiah is covering a cereal box with fabric for a school project. If the box is 6 inches long by 2 inches wide by 14 inches high, how much surface area does Jeremiah have to cover?

____

7. Tia is making a case for her calculator. It is a rectangular prism that will be 3.5 inches long by 1 inch wide by 10 inches high. How much material (surface area) will she need to make the case?

____

8. WRITE *Math* Explain in your own words how to find the surface area of a rectangular prism.

____

____

Lesson Check (6.G.A.4)

1. Gabriela drew a net of a rectangular prism on centimeter grid paper. If the prism is 7 cm long by 10 cm wide by 8 cm high, how many grid squares does the net cover?

2. Ben bought a cell phone that came in a box shaped like a rectangular prism. The box is 5 inches long by 3 inches wide by 2 inches high. What is the surface area of the box?

Spiral Review (6.EE.B.5, 6.EE.C.9, 6.G.A.1, 6.G.A.4)

3. Katrin wrote the inequality $x + 56 < 533$. What is the solution of the inequality?

4. The table shows the number of mixed CDs y that Jason makes in x hours.

Mixed CDs				
Hours, x	2	3	5	10
CDs, y	10	15	25	50

Which equation describes the pattern in the table?

5. A square measuring 9 inches by 9 inches is cut from a corner of a square measuring 15 inches by 15 inches. What is the area of the L-shaped figure that is formed?

6. Boxes of Clancy's Energy Bars are rectangular prisms. How many lateral faces does each box have?

FOR MORE PRACTICE GO TO THE **Personal Math Trainer**

Name ______________________________

Surface Area of Prisms

Essential Question How can you find the surface area of a prism?

Common Core **Geometry—6.G.A.4**
Also 6.EE.A.2c
MATHEMATICAL PRACTICES
MP1, MP5, MP6

You can use a net to find the surface area of a solid figure, such as a prism.

Unlock the Problem

Alex is designing wooden boxes for his books. Each box measures 15 in. by 12 in. by 10 in. Before he buys wood, he needs to find the surface area of each box. What is the surface area of each box?

- What is the shape of each face?

  ____

- What are the dimensions of each face?

  ____

  ____

Use a net to find the surface area.

12 in.
10 in. A
10 in. 10 in. 12 in.
B C D E 15 in.
10 in. F

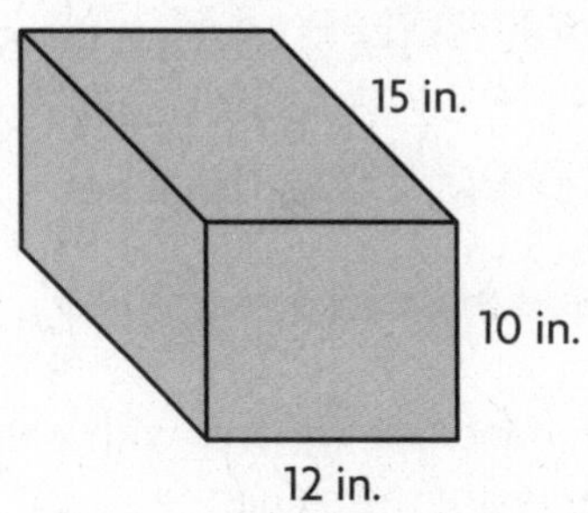

STEP 1 Find the area of each lettered face.

Face A: $12 \times 10 = 120$ in.^{2}

Face B: $15 \times 10 =$ ______ in.^{2}

Face C: ______ $\times$ ______ $=$ ______ in.^{2}

Face D: ______ $\times$ ______ $=$ ______ in.^{2}

Face E: ______ $\times$ ______ $=$ ______ in.^{2}

Face F: ______ $\times$ ______ $=$ ______ in.^{2}

STEP 2 Find the sum of the areas of the faces. ____________

So, the surface area of each box is ____________.

MATHEMATICAL PRACTICES 1

Describe What do you notice about the opposite faces of the box that could help you find its surface area?

Example 1 Use a net to find the surface area of the triangular prism.

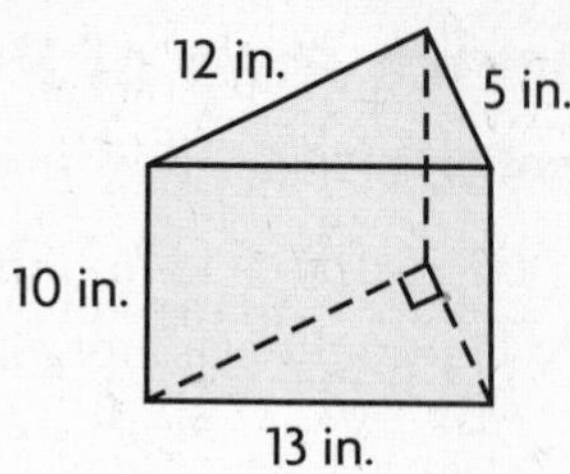

The surface area equals the sum of the areas of the three rectangular faces and two triangular bases. Note that the bases have the same area.

area of bases A and E: $A = \frac{1}{2}bh = \frac{1}{2} \times 12 \times$ ______ = ______

area of face B: $A = lw = 5 \times 10 =$ ______

area of face C: $A = lw =$ ______ $\times$ ______ = ______

area of face D: $A = lw =$ ______ $\times$ ______ = ______

Surface area: $2 \times$ ______ + ______ + ______ + ______ = ______

So, the surface area of the triangular prism is ______________.

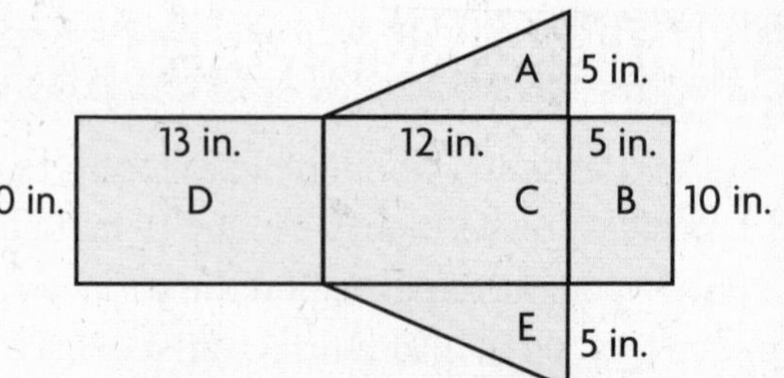

Math Talk MATHEMATICAL PRACTICES 6

Explain Why was the area of one triangular base multiplied by 2?

Example 2 Find the surface area of the cube.

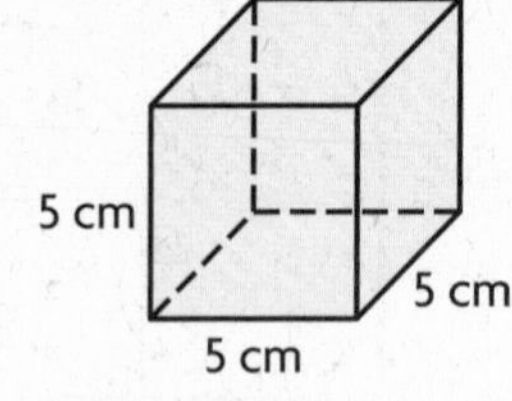

One Way Use a net.

STEP 1 Find the area of each face.

All of the faces are squares with a side length of __________, so the areas of all the squares are the same.

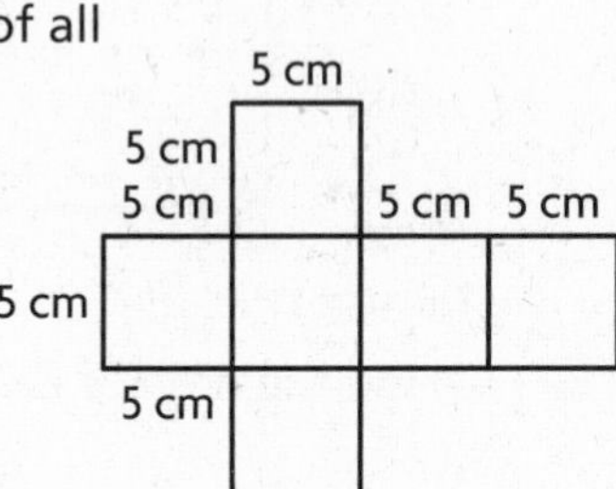

Area of one face: $A =$ ______ $\times$ ______ = __________

STEP 2 Find the sum of the areas of all ______ faces.

______ + ______ + ______ + ______ + ______ + ______ = __________

Another Way Use a formula.

You can also find the surface area of a cube using the formula $S = 6s^2$, where S is the surface area and s is the side length of the cube.

Write the formula. $S = 6s^2$

Replace s with 5. $S = 6($ ______ $)^2$

Simplify. $S = 6($ ______ $) =$ ______

The surface area of the cube is __________.

Name ______________________________

Share and Show

Use a net to find the surface area.

1.

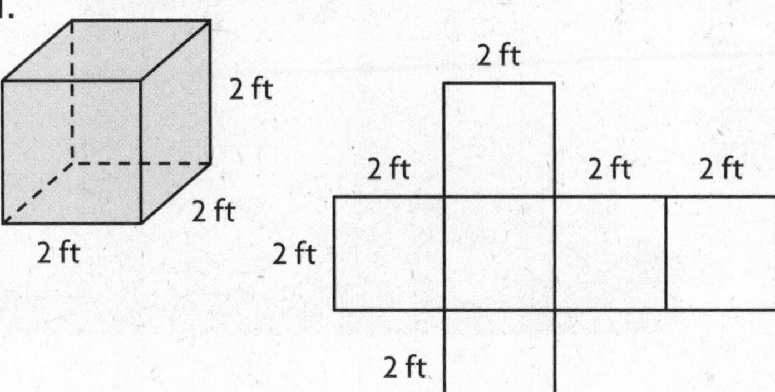

area of each face: ______ × ______ = ______

number of faces: ______

surface area = ______ × ______ = ______ ft^2

2.

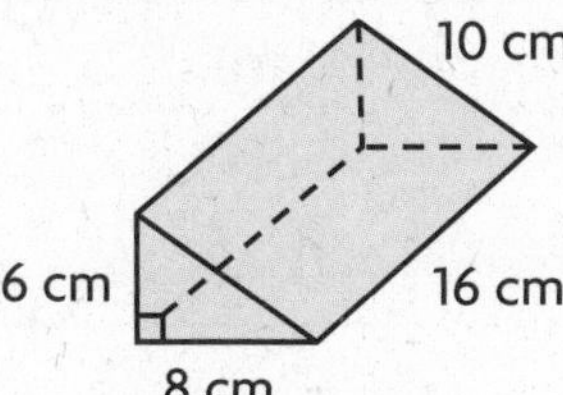

____

3.

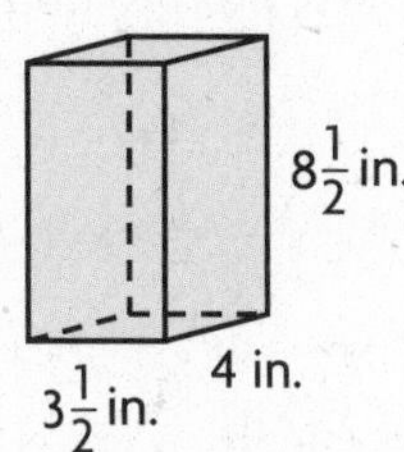

____

Math Talk MATHEMATICAL PRACTICES 5

Use Tools What strategy could you use to find the surface area of a rectangular prism with a length of 8 ft, a width of 2 ft, and a height of 3 ft?

On Your Own

Use a net to find the surface area.

4.

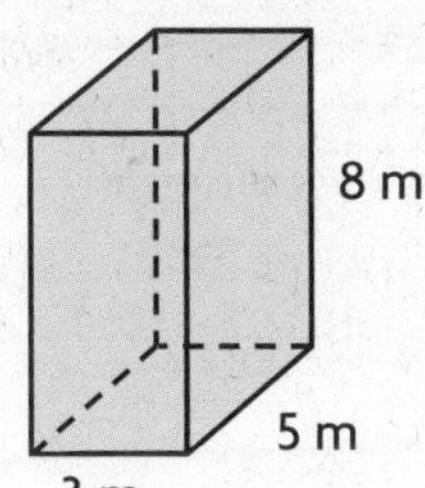

____

5.

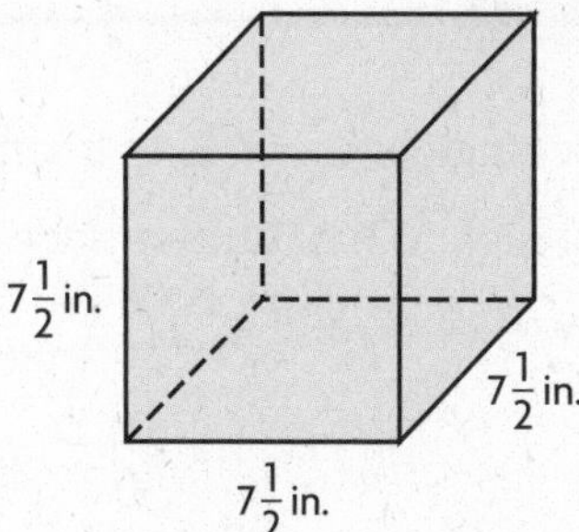

____

6. MATHEMATICAL PRACTICE 6 **Attend to Precision** Calculate the surface area of the cube in Exercise 5 using the formula $S = 6s^2$. Show your work.

____

Unlock the Problem Real World

7. THINK SMARTER The Vehicle Assembly Building at Kennedy Space Center is a rectangular prism. It is 218 m long, 158 m wide, and 160 m tall. There are four 139 m tall doors in the building, averaging 29 m in width. What is the building's outside surface area when the doors are open?

a. Draw each face of the building, not including the floor.

b. What are the dimensions of the 4 walls?

____

____

c. What are the dimensions of the roof?

____

d. Find the building's surface area (not including the floor) when the doors are closed.

____

e. Find the area of the four doors.

____

f. Find the building's surface area (not including the floor) when the doors are open.

____

8. GO DEEPER A rectangular prism is $1\frac{1}{2}$ ft long, $\frac{2}{3}$ ft wide, and $\frac{5}{6}$ ft high. What is the surface area of the prism in square inches?

____

9. THINK SMARTER A gift box is a rectangular prism. The box measures 8 inches by 10 inches by 3 inches. What is its surface area?

____

Name ____________________

Surface Area of Prisms

Common Core **COMMON CORE STANDARD—6.G.A.4**
Solve real-world and mathematical problems involving area, surface area, and volume.

Use a net to find the surface area.

1. 2 cm, 6 cm, 5 cm

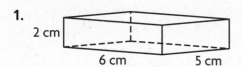

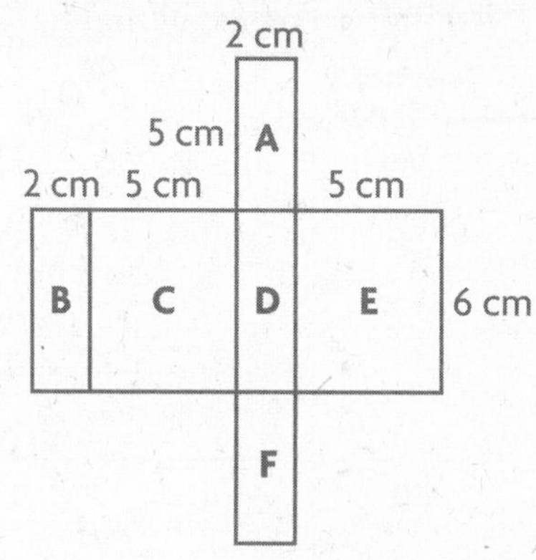

Area of A and F = $2 \times (5 \times 2) = 20 \text{ cm}^2$

Area of B and D = $2 \times (6 \times 2) = 24 \text{ cm}^2$

Area of C and E = $2 \times (6 \times 5) = 60 \text{ cm}^2$

S.A.= $20 \text{ cm}^2 + 24 \text{ cm}^2 + 60 \text{ cm}^2 = 104 \text{ cm}^2$

2.

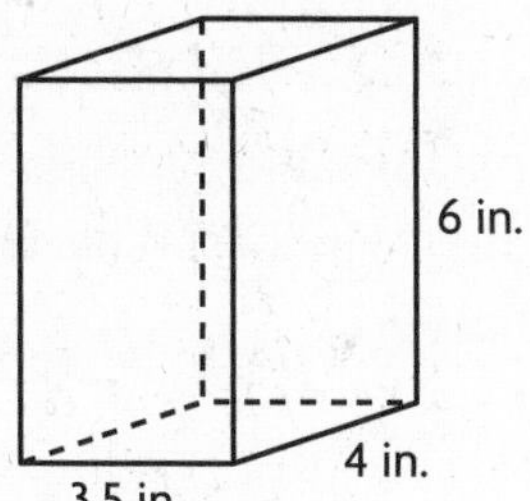

3.

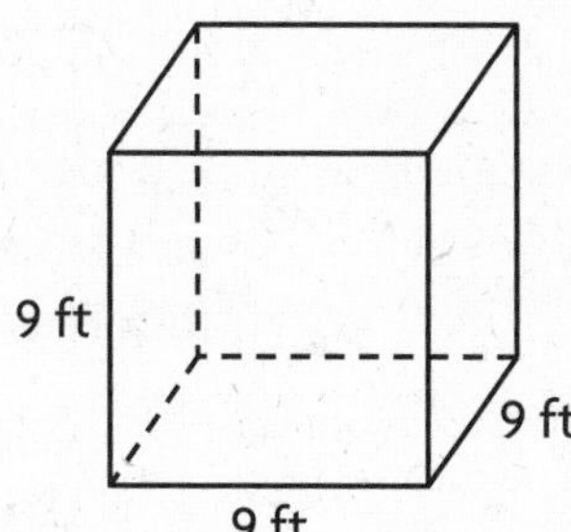

4.

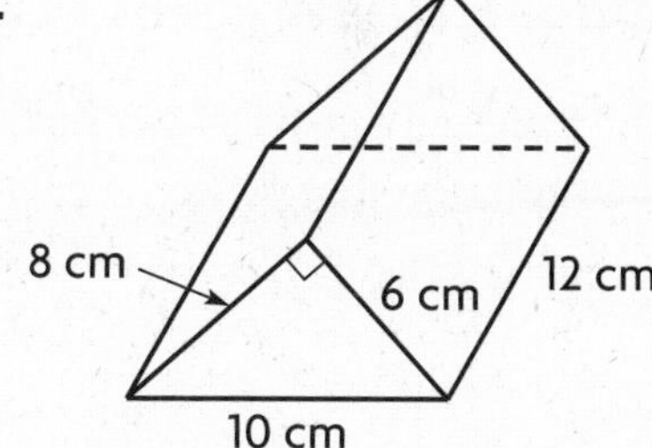

____________________ ____________________ ____________________

Problem Solving Real World

5. A shoe box measures 15 in. by 7 in. by $4\frac{1}{2}$ in. What is the surface area of the box?

____

6. Vivian is working with a styrofoam cube for art class. The length of one side is 5 inches. How much surface area does Vivian have to work with?

____

7. WRITE Math Explain why a two-dimensional net is useful for finding the surface area of a three-dimensional figure.

____

____

Lesson Check (6.G.A.4)

1. What is the surface area of a cubic box that contains a baseball that has a diameter of 3 inches?

2. A piece of wood used for construction is 2 inches by 4 inches by 24 inches. What is the surface area of the wood?

Spiral Review (6.EE.C.9, 6.G.A.1, 6.G.A.4)

3. Detergent costs $4 per box. Kendra graphs the equation that gives the cost y of buying x boxes of detergent. What is the equation?

4. A trapezoid with bases that measure 8 inches and 11 inches has a height of 3 inches. What is the area of the trapezoid?

5. City Park is a right triangle with a base of 40 yd and a height of 25 yd. On a map, the park has a base of 40 in. and a height of 25 in. What is the ratio of the area of the triangle on the map to the area of City Park?

6. What is the surface area of the prism shown by the net?

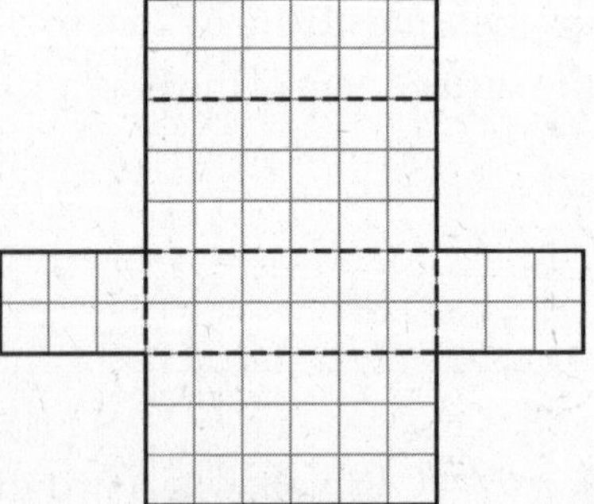

Name ____________________

Surface Area of Pyramids

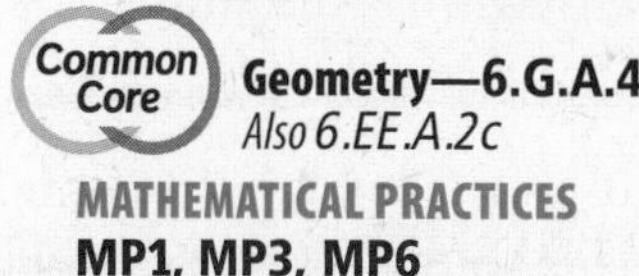

ALGEBRA Lesson 11.4

Essential Question How can you find the surface area of a pyramid?

Common Core **Geometry—6.G.A.4** *Also 6.EE.A.2c*

MATHEMATICAL PRACTICES MP1, MP3, MP6

Most people think of Egypt when they think of pyramids, but there are ancient pyramids throughout the world. The Pyramid of the Sun in Mexico was built around 100 C.E. and is one of the largest pyramids in the world.

Unlock the Problem (Real World)

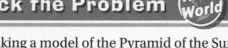

Cara is making a model of the Pyramid of the Sun for a history project. The base is a square with a side length of 12 in. Each triangular face has a height of 7 in. What is the surface area of Cara's model?

Find the surface area of the square pyramid.

STEP 1

Label the dimensions on the net of the pyramid.

STEP 2

Find the area of the base and each triangular face.

Base:

Write the formula for the area of a square. $A = s^2$

Substitute ______ for s and simplify. $A =$ ______ $=$ ______ in.^{2}

Face:

Write the formula for the area of a triangle. $A = \frac{1}{2}bh$

Substitute ______ for b and ______ for h and simplify. $A = \frac{1}{2}$(______)(______)

$=$ ______ in.^{2}

STEP 3

Add the areas to find the surface area of the pyramid.

$S =$ ______ $+ 4 \times$ ______ $=$ ______ $+$ ______ $=$ ______ in.^{2}

So, the surface area of Cara's model is ____________.

Math Talk **MATHEMATICAL PRACTICES 6**

Explain Why did you multiply the area of the triangular face by 4 when finding the surface area?

Sometimes you need to find the total area of the lateral faces of a solid figure, but you don't need to include the area of the base. The **lateral area** L of a solid figure is the sum of the areas of the lateral faces.

Example

Kwan is making a tent in the shape of a triangular pyramid. The three sides of the tent are made of fabric, and the bottom will be left open. The faces have a height of 10 ft and a base of 6 ft. What is the area of the fabric Kwan needs to make the tent?

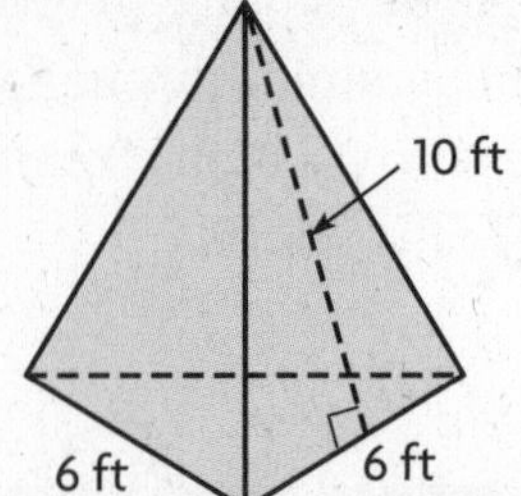

Find the lateral area of the triangular pyramid.

STEP 1

Draw and label a net for the pyramid.

STEP 2

Shade the lateral area of the net.

STEP 3

Find the area of one of the lateral faces of the pyramid.

Write the formula for the area of a triangle $A = \frac{1}{2}bh$

Substitute _______ for b and _______ for h. $A = \frac{1}{2}(\_\_\_\_\_\_)(\_\_\_\_\_\_)$

Simplify $A =$ _______ ft^2

STEP 4

To find the lateral area, find the area of all three lateral faces of the pyramid.

$L = 3 \times$ _______ $=$ _______ ft^2

So, the area of fabric Kwan needs is _______________.

1. MATHEMATICAL PRACTICE 6 **Compare** Explain the difference between finding the surface area and the lateral area of a three-dimensional figure.

2. Explain how you could find the amount of fabric needed if Kwan decided to make a fabric base for the tent. The height of the triangular base is about 5 ft.

Name ______________________________

Share and Show

1. Use a net to find the surface area of the square pyramid.

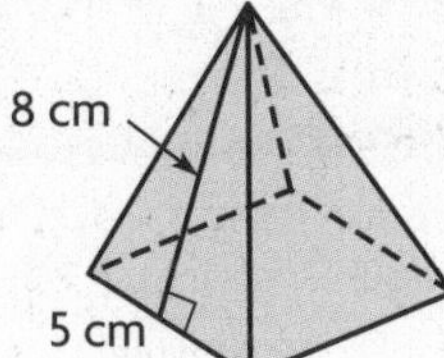

Base: $A =$ ______ $=$ ______ cm^2

Face: $A = \frac{1}{2}$(______)(______) $=$ ______ cm^2

Surface area of pyramid: $S =$ ______ $+ 4 \times$ ______

$=$ ______ $+$ ______ $=$ ______ cm^2

2. A triangular pyramid has a base with an area of 43 cm^2 and lateral faces with bases of 10 cm and heights of 8.6 cm. What is the surface area of the pyramid?

____

3. A square pyramid has a base with a side length of 3 ft and lateral faces with heights of 2 ft. What is the lateral area of the pyramid?

____

Math Talk MATHEMATICAL PRACTICES 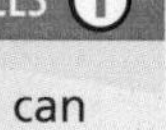

Describe What strategy can you use to find the surface area of a square pyramid if you know the height of each face and the perimeter of the base?

On Your Own

Use a net to find the surface area of the square pyramid.

4.

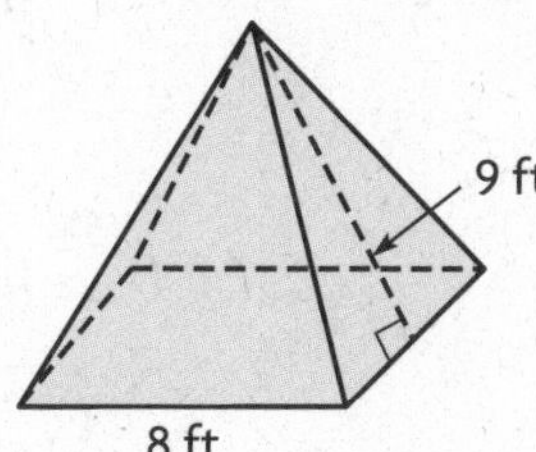

____

5.

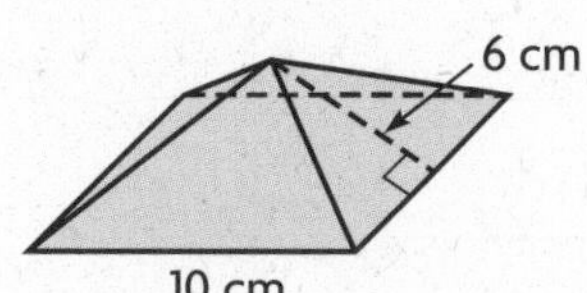

____

6.

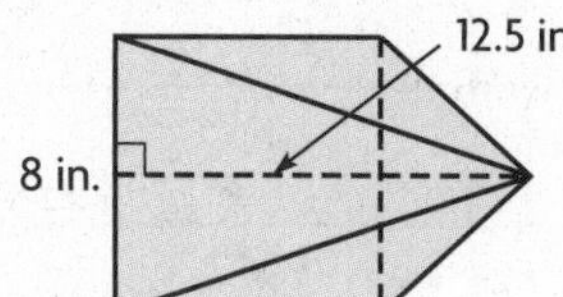

____

7. The Pyramid Arena is located in Memphis, Tennessee. It is in the shape of a square pyramid, and the lateral faces are made almost completely of glass. The base has a side length of about 600 ft and the lateral faces have a height of about 440 ft. What is the total area of the glass in the Pyramid Arena?

____

Problem Solving • Applications 

Use the table for 8–9.

8. The Great Pyramids are located near Cairo, Egypt. They are all square pyramids, and their dimensions are shown in the table. What is the lateral area of the Pyramid of Cheops?

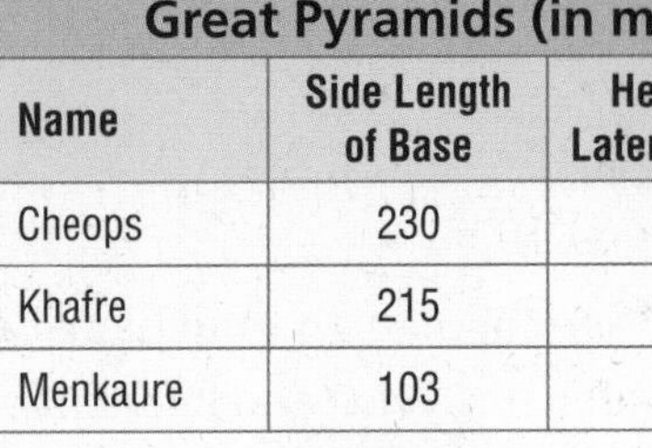

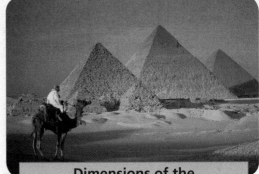

Dimensions of the Great Pyramids (in m)

Name	Side Length of Base	Height of Lateral Faces
Cheops	230	180
Khafre	215	174
Menkaure	103	83

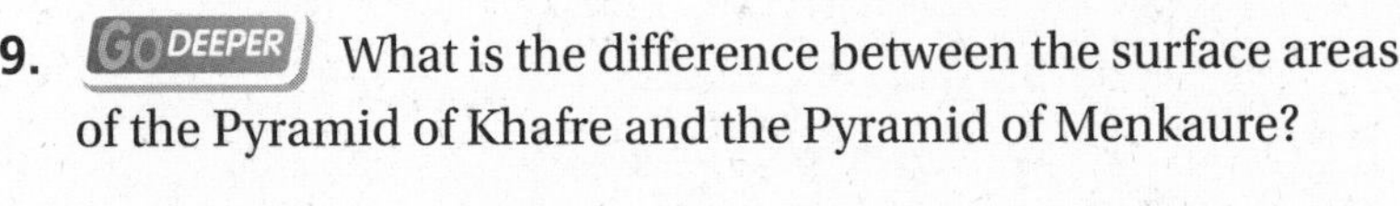

9. GO DEEPER What is the difference between the surface areas of the Pyramid of Khafre and the Pyramid of Menkaure?

10. THINK SMARTER Write an expression for the surface area of the square pyramid shown.

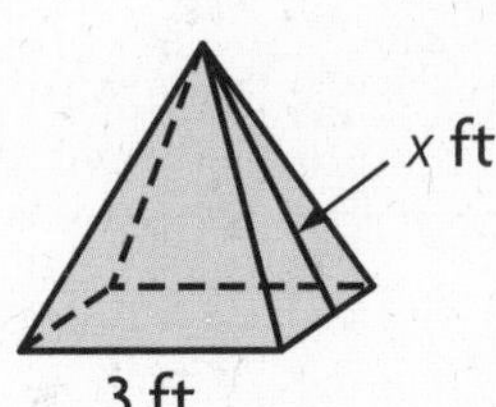

11. MATHEMATICAL PRACTICE 3 **Make Arguments** A square pyramid has a base with a side length of 4 cm and triangular faces with a height of 7 cm. Esther calculated the surface area as $(4 \times 4) + 4(4 \times 7) = 128$ cm^2. Explain Esther's error and find the correct surface area.

Personal Math Trainer

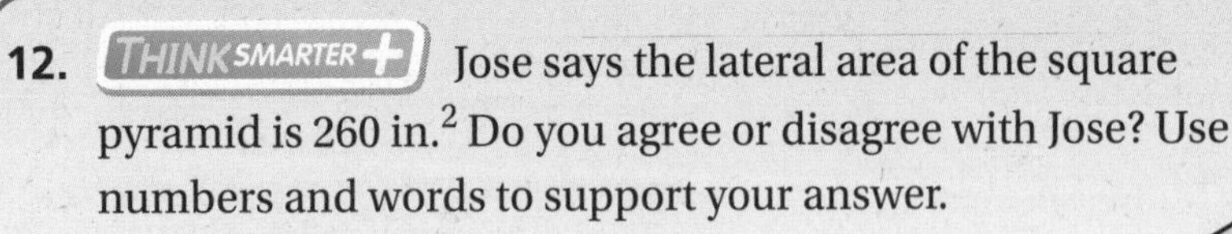

12. THINK SMARTER + Jose says the lateral area of the square pyramid is 260 in.^{2} Do you agree or disagree with Jose? Use numbers and words to support your answer.

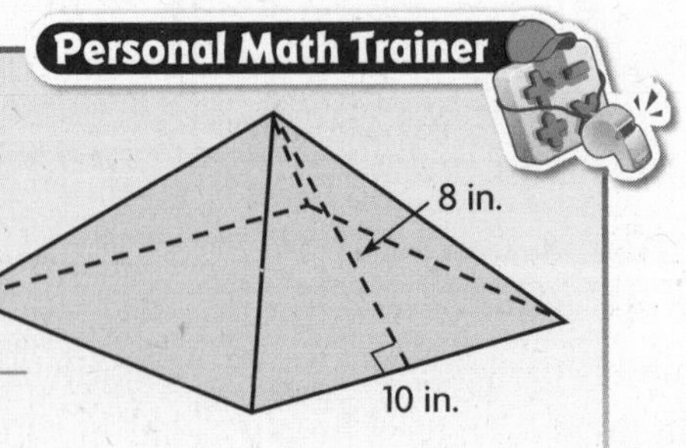

Name ______________________________

Surface Area of Pyramids

Practice and Homework
Lesson 11.4

Common Core

COMMON CORE STANDARD—6.G.A.4
Solve real-world and mathematical problems involving area, surface area, and volume.

Use a net to find the surface area of the square pyramid.

1.

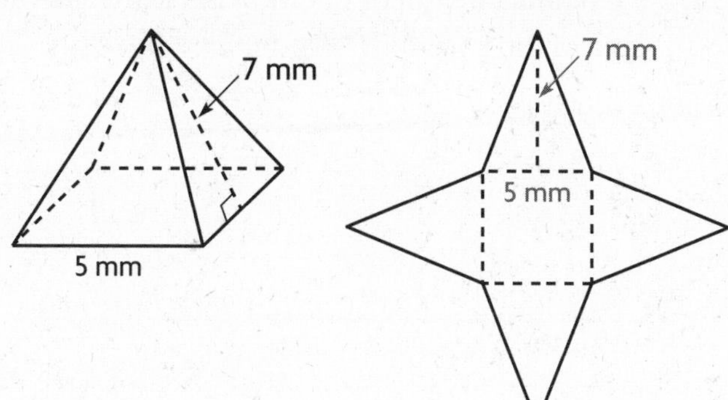

Base: $A = 5^2 = 25 \text{ mm}^2$

Face: $A = \frac{1}{2}(5)(7)$

$= 17.5 \text{ mm}^2$

$S.A. = 25 + 4 \times 17.5$

$= 25 + 70$

$= 95 \text{ mm}^2$

2.

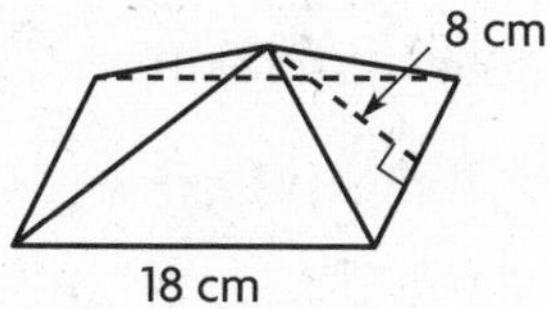

____

3.

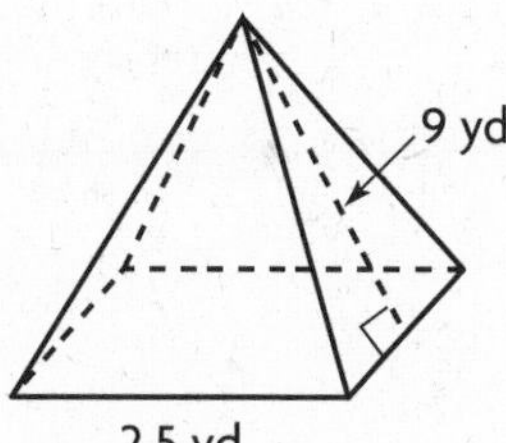

____

4.

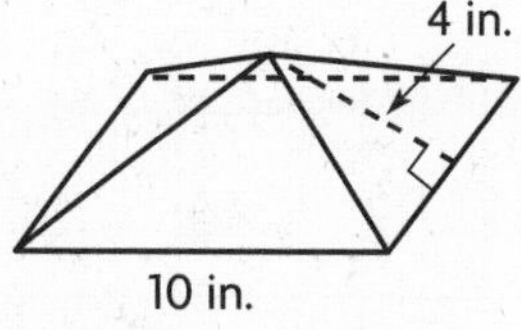

____

Problem Solving (Real World)

5. Cho is building a sandcastle in the shape of a triangular pyramid. The area of the base is 7 square feet. Each side of the base has a length of 4 feet and the height of each face is 2 feet. What is the surface area of the pyramid?

____

6. The top of a skyscraper is shaped like a square pyramid. Each side of the base has a length of 60 meters and the height of each triangle is 20 meters. What is the lateral area of the pyramid?

____

7. **WRITE** *Math* Write and solve a problem finding the lateral area of an object shaped like a square pyramid.

____

____

Lesson Check (6.G.A.4)

1. A square pyramid has a base with a side length of 12 in. Each face has a height of 7 in. What is the surface area of the pyramid?

2. The faces of a triangular pyramid have a base of 5 cm and a height of 11 cm. What is the lateral area of the pyramid?

Spiral Review (6.EE.C.9, 6.G.A.1, 6.G.A.3, 6.G.A.4)

3. What is the linear equation represented by the graph?

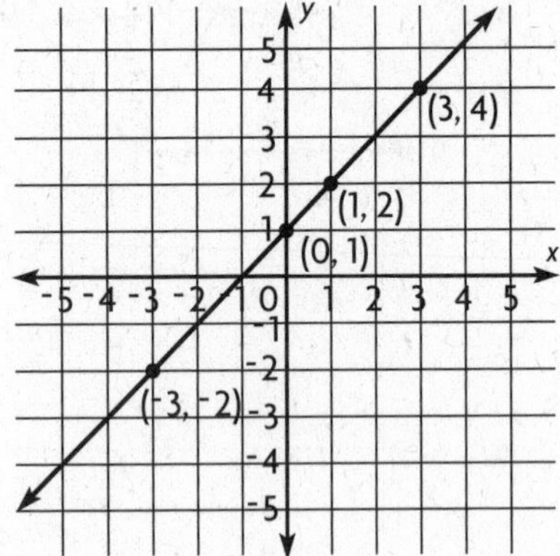

4. A regular octagon has sides measuring about 4 cm. If the octagon is divided into 8 congruent triangles, each has a height of 5 cm. What is the area of the octagon?

5. Carly draws quadrilateral *JKLM* with vertices $J(^-3, 3)$, $K(3, 3)$, $L(2, ^-1)$, and $M(^-2, ^-1)$. What is the best way to classify the quadrilateral?

6. A rectangular prism has the dimensions 8 feet by 3 feet by 5 feet. What is the surface area of the prism?

FOR MORE PRACTICE GO TO THE Personal Math Trainer

Name ________________________________

Mid-Chapter Checkpoint

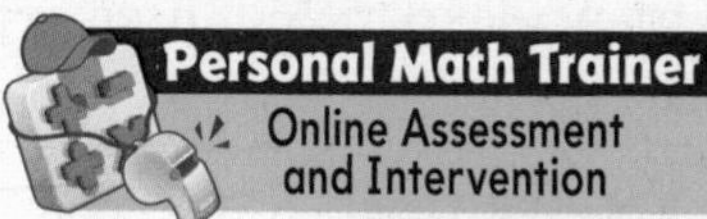

Vocabulary

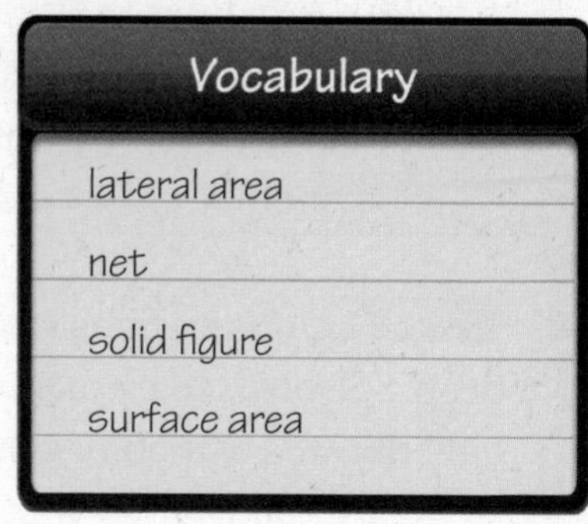

Choose the best term from the box to complete the sentence.

1. ________________ is the sum of the areas of all the faces, or surfaces, of a solid figure. (p. 603)

2. A three-dimensional figure having length, width, and height is called a(n) ________________. (p. 597)

3. The ________________ of a solid figure is the sum of the areas of its lateral faces. (p. 616)

Concepts and Skills

4. Identify and draw a net for the solid figure. (6.G.A.4)

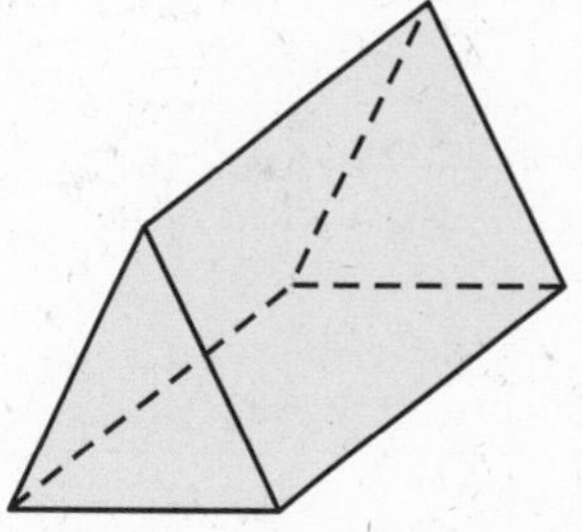

____

5. Use a net to find the lateral area of the square pyramid. (6.G.A.4)

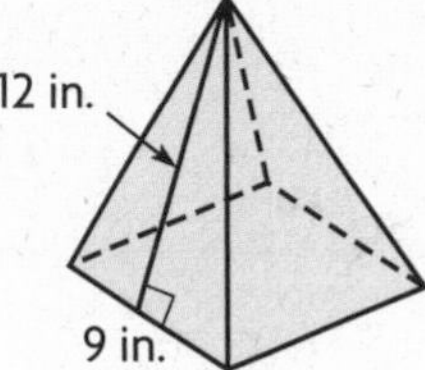

____

6. Use a net to find the surface area of the prism. (6.G.A.4)

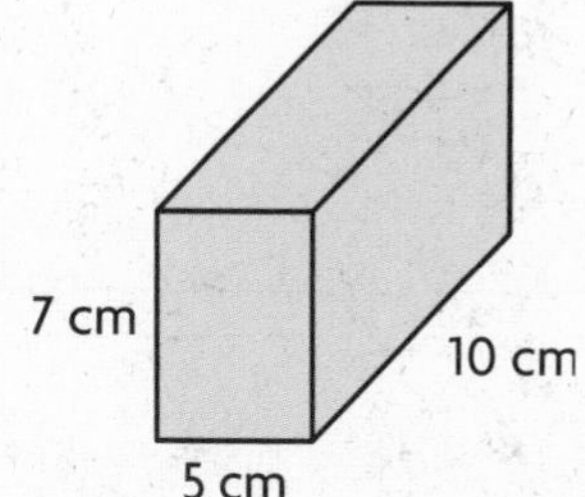

____

7. A machine cuts nets from flat pieces of cardboard. The nets can be folded into triangular pyramids used as pieces in a board game. What shapes appear in the net? How many of each shape are there? (6.G.A.4)

8. GO DEEPER Fran's filing cabinet is 6 feet tall, $1\frac{1}{3}$ feet wide, and 3 feet deep. She plans to paint all sides except the bottom of the cabinet. Find the area of the sides she intends to paint. (6.G.A.4)

9. A triangular pyramid has lateral faces with bases of 6 meters and heights of 9 meters. The area of the base of the pyramid is 15.6 square meters. What is the surface area of the pyramid? (6.G.A.4)

10. What is the surface area of a storage box that measures 15 centimeters by 12 centimeters by 10 centimeters? (6.G.A.4)

11. A small refrigerator is a cube with a side length of 16 inches. Use the formula $S = 6s^2$ to find the surface area of the cube. (6.EE.A.2c)

Name ______________________________

Fractions and Volume

Essential Question What is the relationship between the volume and the edge lengths of a prism with fractional edge lengths?

Common Core Geometry—6.G.A.2
MATHEMATICAL PRACTICES
MP5, MP6, MP7, MP8

CONNECT **Volume** is the measure of the number of unit cubes needed to occupy a given space without gaps or overlaps. You can find the volume of a rectangular prism by seeing how many unit cubes it takes to fill the prism. Recall that a unit cube is a cube with a side length of 1 and has a volume of 1 cubic unit.

Investigate

Hands On

Materials net of a rectangular prism, cubes, scissors, tape

A jewelry box has a length of $3\frac{1}{2}$ units, a width of $1\frac{1}{2}$ units, and a height of 2 units. What is the volume of the box in cubic units?

A. Each of the cubes in this activity has a side length of $\frac{1}{2}$ unit.

How many cubes with side length $\frac{1}{2}$ does it take to form a unit cube? _______

So, each smaller cube represents _______ of a unit cube.

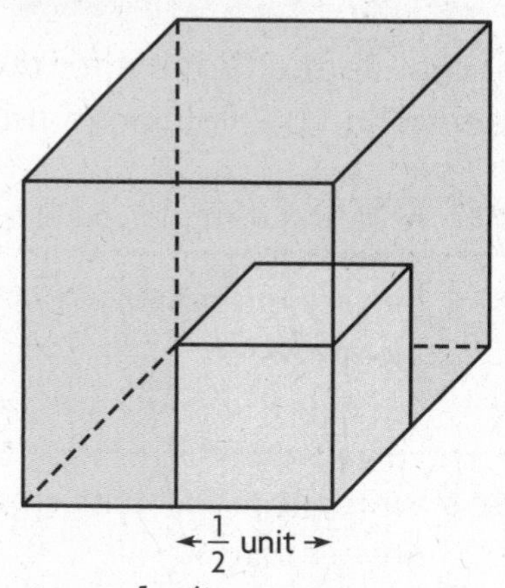

B. Cut out the net. Then fold and tape the net into a rectangular prism. Leave one face open so you can fill the prism with cubes.

C. Fill the prism with cubes.

How many cubes with side length $\frac{1}{2}$ does it take to fill the prism?

____

D. To find the volume of the jewelry box in cubic units, determine how many unit cubes you could make from the smaller cubes you used to fill the prism.

Think: It takes 8 smaller cubes to make 1 unit cube.

Divide the total number of smaller cubes by 8. Write the remainder as a fraction. _______ $\div 8 =$ _______ $=$ _______

So, the volume of the jewelry box is _______ cubic units.

MATHEMATICAL PRACTICES 2

Reasoning How did you determine the number of cubes with side length $\frac{1}{2}$ it takes to form a unit cube?

Draw Conclusions

1. MATHEMATICAL PRACTICE 8 **Draw Conclusions** Could you use the method of packing cubes to find the volume of a triangular prism? Explain.

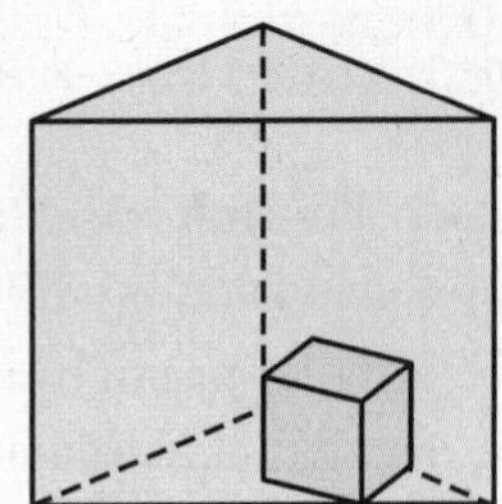

____

____

____

____

2. THINKSMARTER How many cubes with a side length of $\frac{1}{2}$ unit do you need to form 3 unit cubes? Explain how you know.

____

____

____

Make Connections

You can use the formula for the volume of a rectangular prism to find the volume of the jewelry box.

Remember

The volume of a rectangular prism is the product of the length, the width, and the height: $V = l \times w \times h$, or lwh.

STEP 1 Write the formula you will use. $V = lwh$

STEP 2 Replace the variables using the values you know. $V = 3\frac{1}{2} \times \square \times \square$

STEP 3 Write the mixed numbers as fractions greater than 1. $V = \frac{\square}{\square} \times \frac{3}{2} \times 2$

STEP 4 Multiply. $V = \frac{\square}{\square}$

STEP 5 Write the fraction as a mixed number. $V = \square\frac{2}{4} = \square$

So, the volume of the jewelry box is ______ cubic units.

Math Talk MATHEMATICAL PRACTICES 6

Compare What do you notice about the volume you found by using the formula and the volume you found by packing the prism with cubes?

Name ___________________________

Share and Show

1. A prism is filled with 38 cubes with a side length of $\frac{1}{2}$ unit. What is the volume of the prism in cubic units?

   $38 \div 8 =$ ______ $=$ ______

   volume = ______ cubic units

2. A prism is filled with 58 cubes with a side length of $\frac{1}{2}$ unit. What is the volume of the prism in cubic units?

   ____

Find the volume of the rectangular prism.

3. 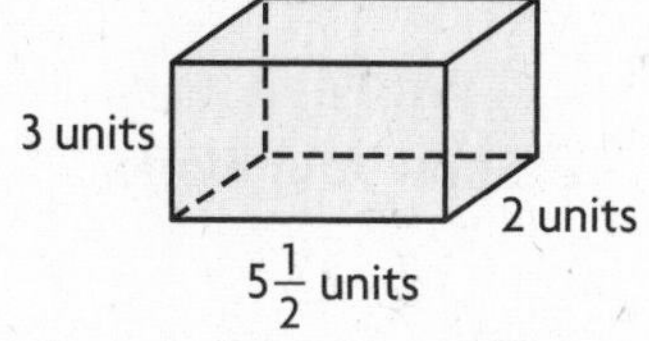

   ____

4. 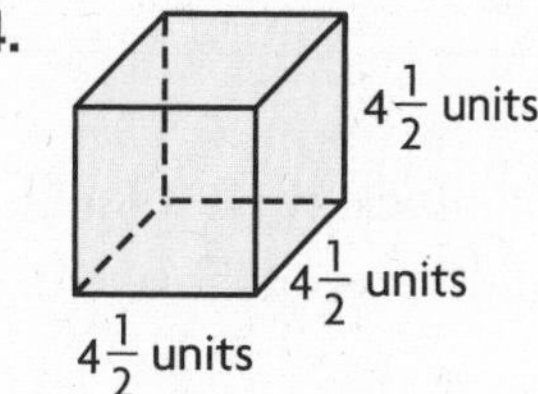

   ____

5. GO DEEPER Theodore wants to put three flowering plants in his window box. The window box is shaped like a rectangular prism that is 30.5 in. long, 6 in. wide, and 6 in. deep. The three plants need a total of 1,200 in.^{3} of potting soil to grow well. Is the box large enough? Explain.

____

____

____

6. WRITE Math Explain how use the formula $V = l \times w \times h$ to verify that a cube with a side length of $\frac{1}{2}$ unit has a volume of $\frac{1}{8}$ of a cubic unit.

____

____

____

Problem Solving • Applications

Use the diagram for 7–10.

A
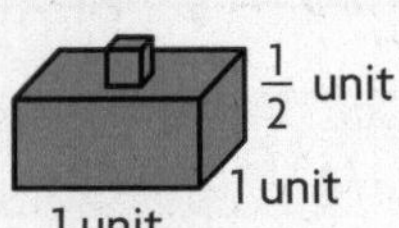

B
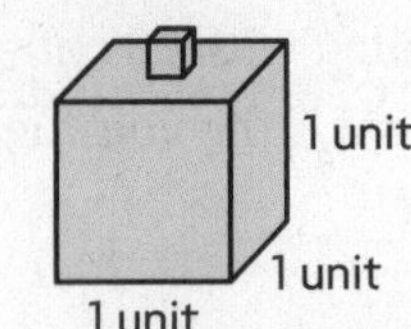

C
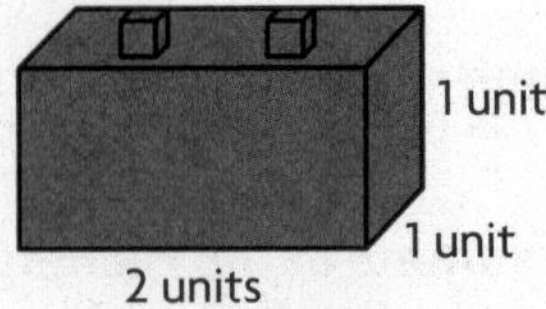

7. Karyn is using a set of building blocks shaped like rectangular prisms to make a model. The three types of blocks she has are shown at right. What is the volume of an A block? (Do not include the pegs on top.)

____

8. How many A blocks would you need to take up the same amount of space as a C block?

____

WRITE Math
Show Your Work

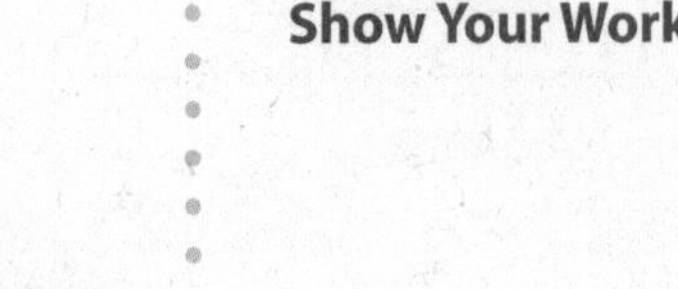

9. GO DEEPER Karyn puts a B block, two C blocks, and three A blocks together. What is the total volume of these blocks?

____

10. THINK SMARTER Karyn uses the blocks to make a prism that is 2 units long, 3 units wide, and $1\frac{1}{2}$ units high. The prism is made of two C blocks, two B blocks, and some A blocks. What is the total volume of A blocks used?

____

Math on the Spot

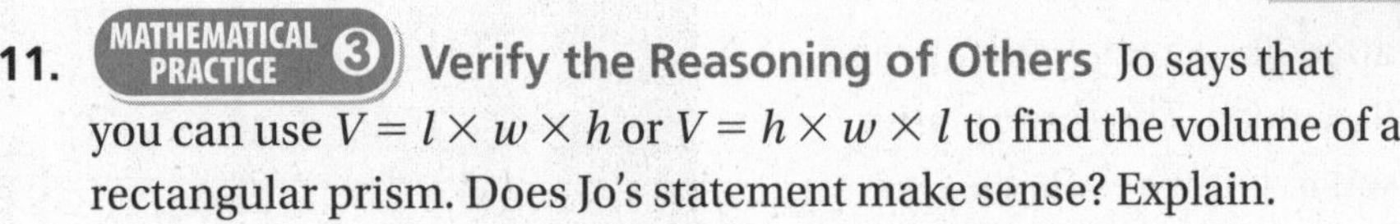

11. MATHEMATICAL PRACTICE 3 **Verify the Reasoning of Others** Jo says that you can use $V = l \times w \times h$ or $V = h \times w \times l$ to find the volume of a rectangular prism. Does Jo's statement make sense? Explain.

____

____

____

12. THINK SMARTER A box measures 5 units by 3 units by $2\frac{1}{2}$ units. For numbers 12a–12b, select True or False for the statement.

12a. The greatest number of cubes with a side length of $\frac{1}{2}$ unit that can be packed inside the box is 300. ○ True ○ False

12b. The volume of the box is $37\frac{1}{2}$ cubic units. ○ True ○ False

Name ______________________________

Fractions and Volume

COMMON CORE STANDARD—6.G.A.2
Solve real-world and mathematical problems involving area, surface area, and volume.

Find the volume of the rectangular prism.

1.

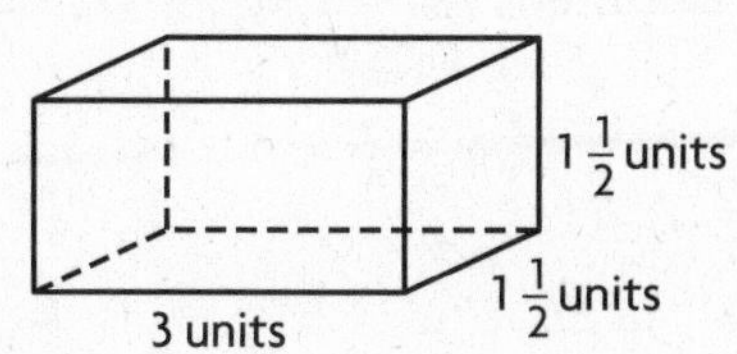

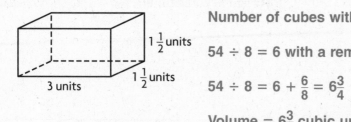

Number of cubes with side length $\frac{1}{2}$ unit: 54

$54 \div 8 = 6$ with a remainder of 6

$54 \div 8 = 6 + \frac{6}{8} = 6\frac{3}{4}$

Volume $= 6\frac{3}{4}$ cubic units

2.

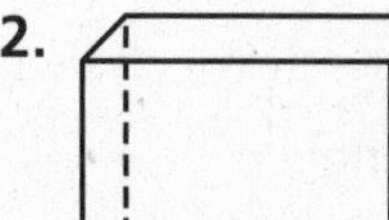

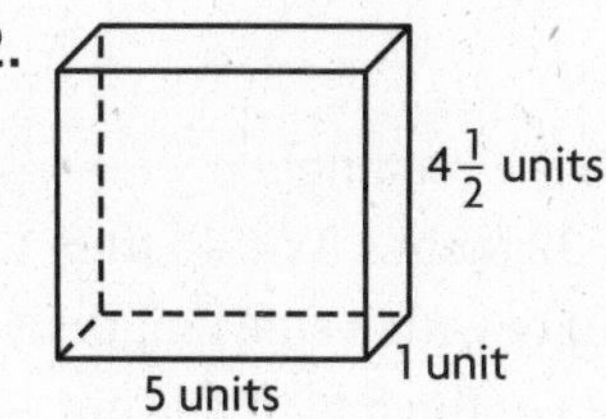

____

3.

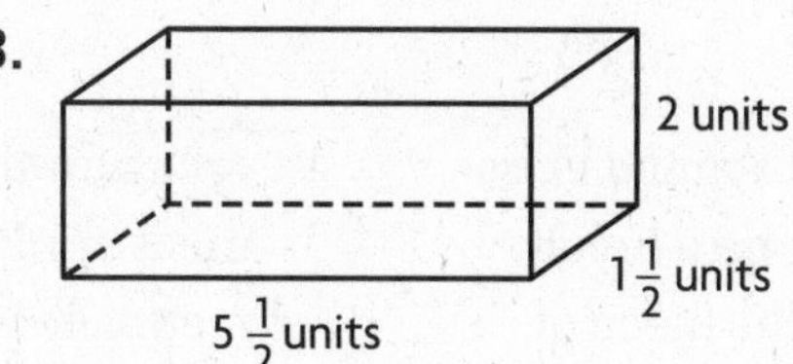

____

4.

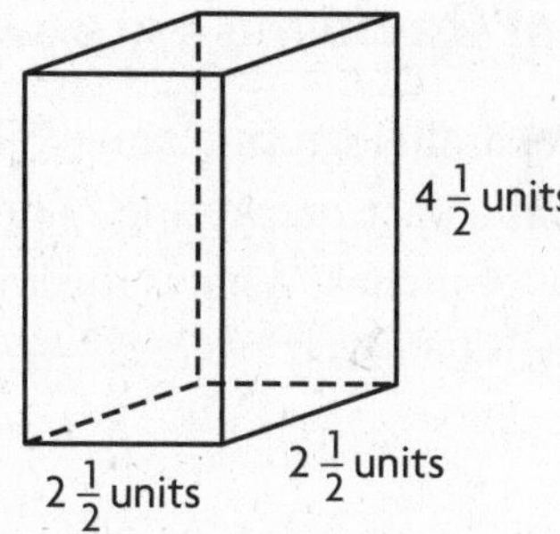

____

Problem Solving (Real World)

5. Miguel is pouring liquid into a container that is $4\frac{1}{2}$ inches long by $3\frac{1}{2}$ inches wide by 2 inches high. How many cubic inches of liquid will fit in the container?

____

6. A shipping crate is shaped like a rectangular prism. It is $5\frac{1}{2}$ feet long by 3 feet wide by 3 feet high. What is the volume of the crate?

____

7. **WRITE** *Math* How many cubes with a side length of $\frac{1}{4}$ unit would it take to make a unit cube? Explain how you determined your answer.

____

____

Lesson Check (6.G.A.2)

1. A rectangular prism is 4 units by $2\frac{1}{2}$ units by $1\frac{1}{2}$ units. How many cubes with a side length of $\frac{1}{2}$ unit will completely fill the prism?

2. A rectangular prism is filled with 196 cubes with $\frac{1}{2}$-unit side lengths. What is the volume of the prism in cubic units?

Spiral Review (6.G.A.1, 6.G.A.4)

3. A parallelogram-shaped piece of stained glass has a base measuring $2\frac{1}{2}$ inches and a height of $1\frac{1}{4}$ inches. What is the area of the piece of stained glass?

4. A flag for the sports club is a rectangle measuring 20 inches by 32 inches. Within the rectangle is a yellow square with a side length of 6 inches. What is the area of the flag that is not part of the yellow square?

5. What is the surface area of the rectangular prism shown by the net?

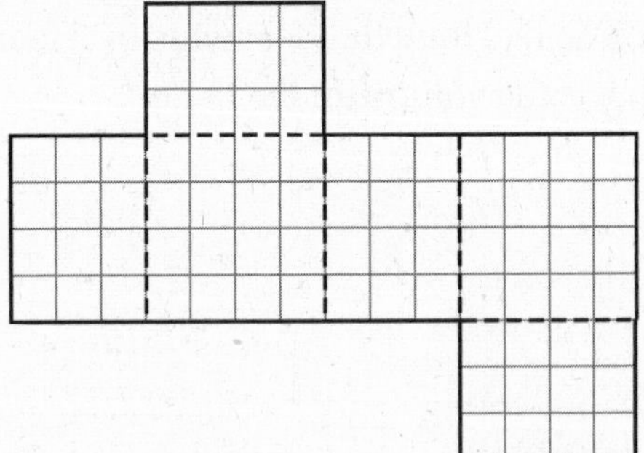

6. What is the surface area of the square pyramid?

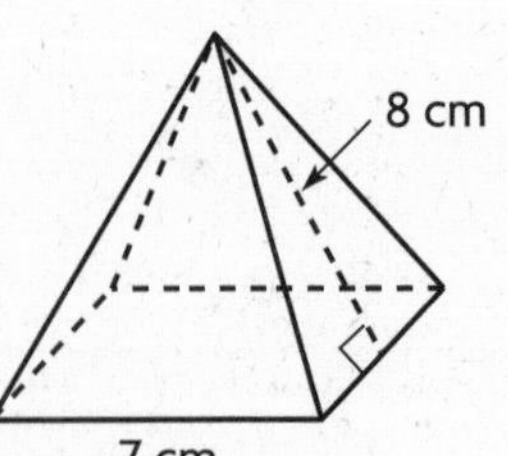

FOR MORE PRACTICE GO TO THE Personal Math Trainer

Name ________________________________

Volume of Rectangular Prisms

Essential Question How can you find the volume of rectangular prisms with fractional edge lengths?

Geometry— 6.G.A.2
Also 6.EE.A.2c

MATHEMATICAL PRACTICES
MP1, MP2, MP3, MP4

You can use the formula $V = l \times w \times h$ to find the volume of a rectangular prism when you know the length, width, and height of the prism.

Unlock the Problem (Real World)

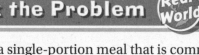

An obento is a single-portion meal that is common in Japan. The meal is usually served in a box. A small obento box is a rectangular prism that is 5 inches long, 4 inches wide, and $2\frac{1}{2}$ inches high. How much food fits in the box?

- Underline the sentence that tells you what you are trying to find.
- Circle the numbers you need to use.

Find the volume of a rectangular prism

You can use the formula $V = l \times w \times h$ to find the volume of a rectangular prism when you know the length, width, and height of the prism.

STEP 1

Sketch the rectangular prism.

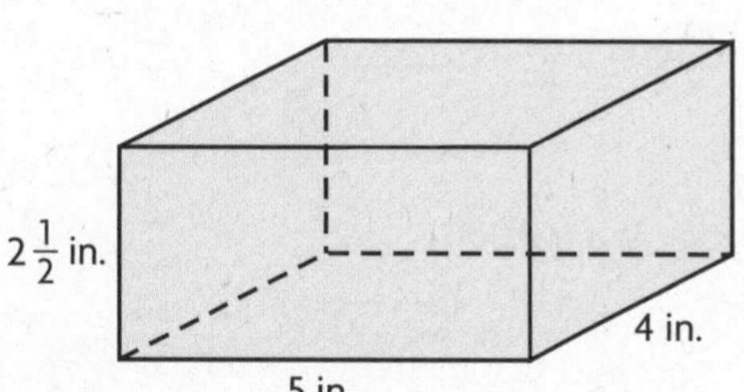

STEP 2 Identify the value for each variable.

The length l is 5 in.

The width w is ________ in.

The height h is ________ in.

STEP 3 Evaluate the formula.

Write the formula.	$V = l \times w \times h$
Replace l with 5, w with ______, and h with ______.	$V =$ ______ $\times$ ______ $\times$ ______
Multiply.	$V =$ ______ in.^{3}

So, ________ in.^{3} of food fits in the box.

MATHEMATICAL PRACTICES 2

Reasoning How do you know what units to use for the volume of the box?

CONNECT You know that the volume of a rectangular prism is the product of its length, width, and height. Since the product of the length and width is the area of one base, the volume is also the product of the area of one base and the height.

Volume of a Prism

Volume = area of one base × height | $V = Bh$

Example 1 Find the volume of the prism.

STEP 1 Identify the value for each variable.

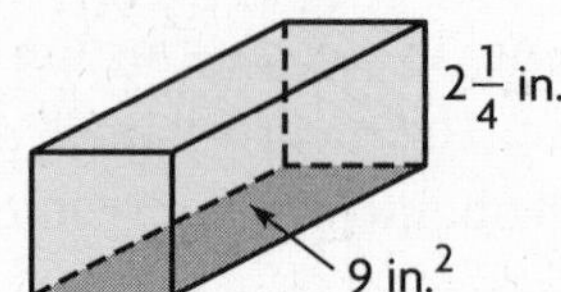

The height h is ________ in.

The area of the base B is ________ in.²

STEP 2 Evaluate the formula.

Write the formula. $V = Bh$

Replace B with ______ and h with ______. $V = \square \times \square$

Write the mixed number as a fraction greater than 1. $V = \square \times \frac{\square}{4}$

Multiply and write the product as a mixed number. $V = \square = \square\frac{1}{4}$ in.³

So, the volume of the prism is ____________.

Example 2 Find the volume of the cube.

Write the formula. The area of the square base is s^2. The height of a cube is also s, so $V = Bh = s^3$. $V = s^3$

$3\frac{1}{2}$ ft, $3\frac{1}{2}$ ft, $3\frac{1}{2}$ ft

Substitute ______ for s. $V = \left(\square\right)^3$

Write the mixed number as a fraction greater than 1. Then use repeated multiplication.

$V = \left(\square\right)^3 = \left(\square\right)\left(\square\right)\left(\square\right)$

Simplify.

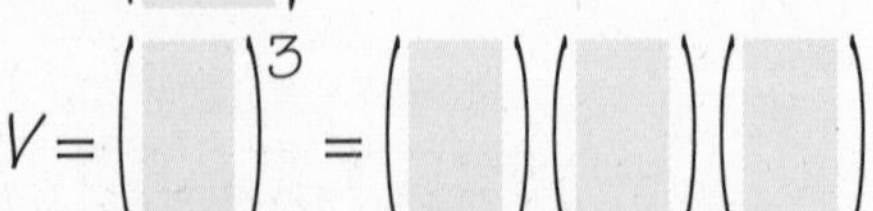

$V = \frac{\square}{8} = 42\frac{\square}{8}$ ft³

So, the volume of the cube is ____________.

Name ________________________________

Share and Show

MATH BOARD

Find the volume.

1. 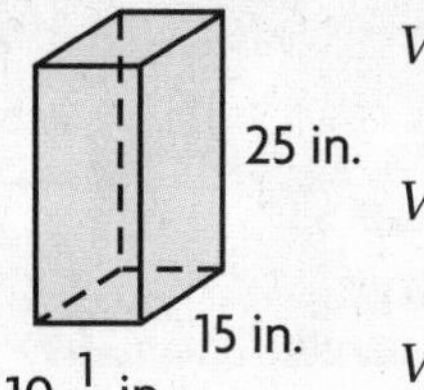

$V = lwh$

$V =$ ______ $\times$ ______ $\times$ ______

$V =$ __________ in.^{3}

2. 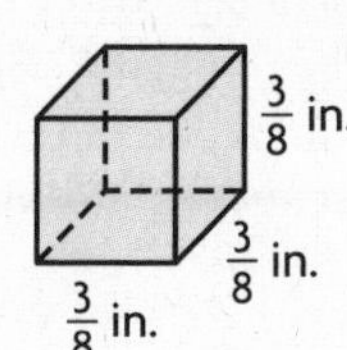

____

Math Talk MATHEMATICAL PRACTICES 1

Describe the steps for finding the volume of a cube.

On Your Own

Find the volume of the prism.

3. 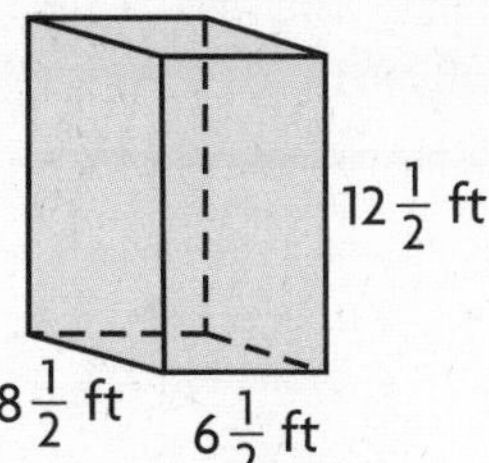

____

4. 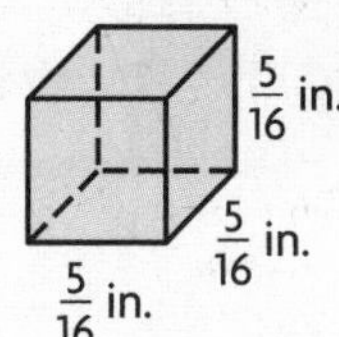

____

5. $1\frac{1}{3}$ yd $3\frac{1}{3}$ yd^2 6 yd

____

6. GO DEEPER Wayne's gym locker is a rectangular prism with a width and height of $14\frac{1}{2}$ inches. The length is 8 inches greater than the width. What is the volume of the locker?

____

7. THINK SMARTER Abraham has a toy box that is in the shape of a rectangular prism.

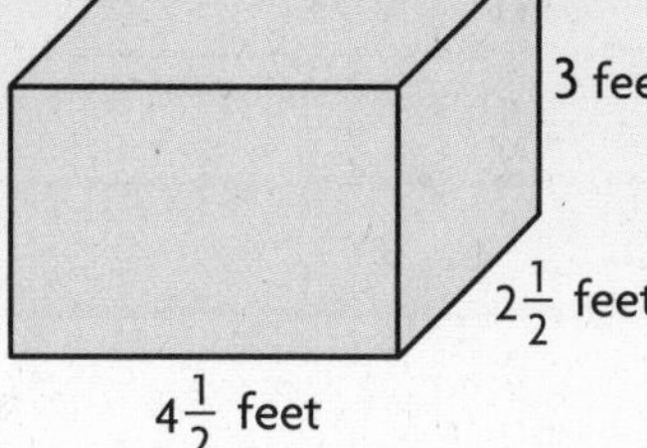

The volume is
- $33\frac{3}{4}$ ft^3.
- $35\frac{1}{2}$ ft^3.
- $64\frac{1}{2}$ ft^3.

Connect to Science

Aquariums

Large public aquariums like the Tennessee Aquarium in Chattanooga have a wide variety of freshwater and saltwater fish species from around the world. The fish are kept in tanks of various sizes.

The table shows information about several tanks in the aquarium. Each tank is a rectangular prism.

Find the length of Tank 1.

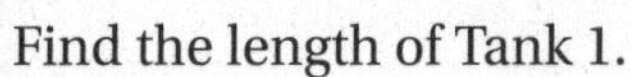

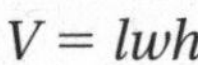

$V = lwh$

$52{,}500 = l \times$ ______ $\times$ ______

$52{,}500 = l \times$ ____________

$\frac{52{,}500}{\quad} = l$

______ $= l$

So, the length of Tank 1 is ____________.

Aquarium Tanks

	Length	Width	Height	Volume
Tank 1		30 cm	35 cm	52,500 cm^3
Tank 2	12 m		4 m	384 m^3
Tank 3	18 m	12 m		2,160 m^3
Tank 4	72 cm	55 cm	40 cm	

Solve.

8. Find the width of Tank 2 and the height of Tank 3.

____

9. THINK SMARTER To keep the fish healthy, there should be the correct ratio of water to fish in the tank. One recommended ratio is 9 L of water for every 2 fish. Find the volume of Tank 4. Then use the equivalencies 1 cm^3 = 1 mL and 1,000 mL = 1 L to find how many fish can be safely kept in Tank 4.

____

10. MATHEMATICAL PRACTICE 2 **Use Reasoning** Give another set of dimensions for a tank that would have the same volume as Tank 2. Explain how you found your answer.

____

____

Name ____________________

Volume of Rectangular Prisms

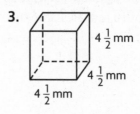

Common Core **COMMON CORE STANDARD—6.G.A.2**
Solve real-world and mathematical problems involving area, surface area, and volume.

Find the volume.

1. 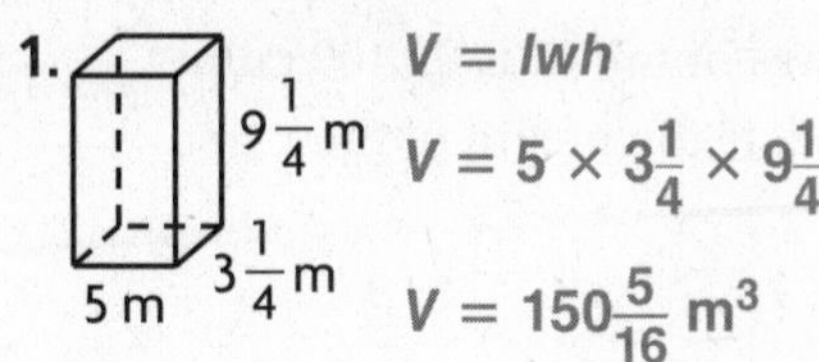

$V = lwh$

$V = 5 \times 3\frac{1}{4} \times 9\frac{1}{4}$

$V = 150\frac{5}{16}$ m^3

2. 2 in.; $2\frac{1}{2}$ in.; $5\frac{1}{2}$ in.

____

3. $4\frac{1}{2}$ mm; $4\frac{1}{2}$ mm; $4\frac{1}{2}$ mm

____

4. 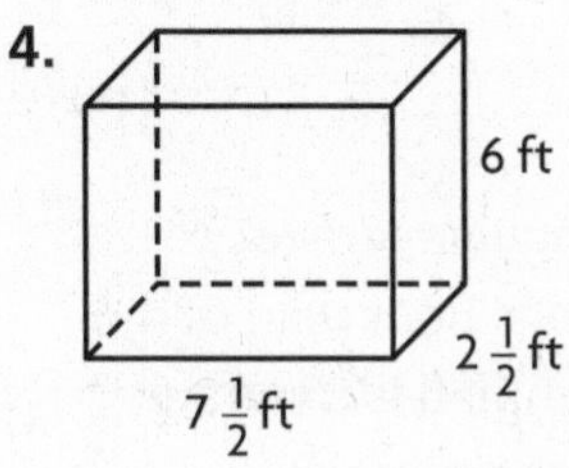

____

5. 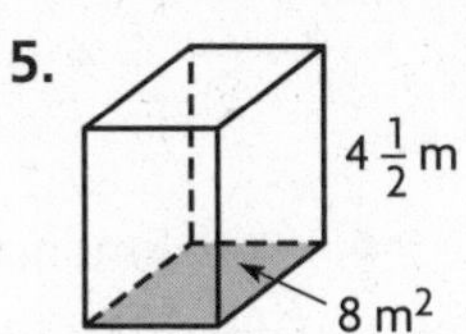

____

6. 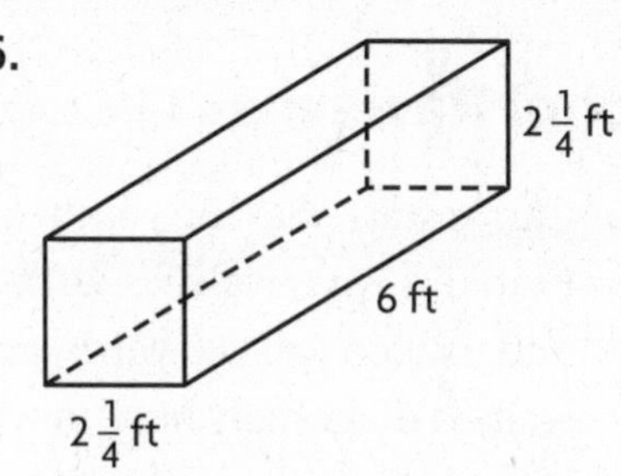

____

Problem Solving Real World

7. A cereal box is a rectangular prism that is 8 inches long and $2\frac{1}{2}$ inches wide. The volume of the box is 200 in.^{3}. What is the height of the box?

____

8. A stack of paper is $8\frac{1}{2}$ in. long by 11 in. wide by 4 in. high. What is the volume of the stack of paper?

____

9. WRITE ▸ *Math* Explain how you can find the side length of a rectangular prism if you are given the volume and the two other measurements. Does this process change if one of the measurements includes a fraction?

____

____

____

Lesson Check (6.G.A.2)

1. A kitchen sink is a rectangular prism with a length of $19\frac{7}{8}$ inches, a width of $14\frac{3}{4}$ inches, and height of 10 inches. Estimate the volume of the sink.

2. A storage container is a rectangular prism that is 65 centimeters long and 40 centimeters wide. The volume of the container is 62,400 cubic centimeters. What is the height of the container?

Spiral Review (6.G.A.1, 6.G.A.2, 6.G.A.4)

3. Carrie started at the southeast corner of Franklin Park, walked north 240 yards, turned and walked west 80 yards, and then turned and walked diagonally back to where she started. What is the area of the triangle enclosed by the path she walked?

4. The dimensions of a rectangular garage are 100 times the dimensions of a floor plan of the garage. The area of the floor plan is 8 square inches. What is the area of the garage?

5. Shiloh wants to create a paper-mâché box shaped like a rectangular prism. If the box will be 4 inches by 5 inches by 8 inches, how much paper does she need to cover the box?

6. A box is filled with 220 cubes with a side length of $\frac{1}{2}$ unit. What is the volume of the box in cubic units?

FOR MORE PRACTICE GO TO THE Personal Math Trainer

Name ________________

Problem Solving • Geometric Measurements

Essential Question How can you use the strategy *use a formula* to solve problems involving area, surface area, and volume?

Geometry—6.G.A.4 *Also 6.G.A.1, 6.G.A.2*

MATHEMATICAL PRACTICES
MP1, MP3, MP4, MP6

Unlock the Problem

Shedd Aquarium in Chicago has one of the country's few full-scale animal hospitals linked to an aquarium. One tank for sick fish is a rectangular prism measuring 75 cm long, 60 cm wide, and 36 cm high along the outside. The glass on the tank is 2 cm thick. How much water can the tank hold? How much water is needed to fill the tank?

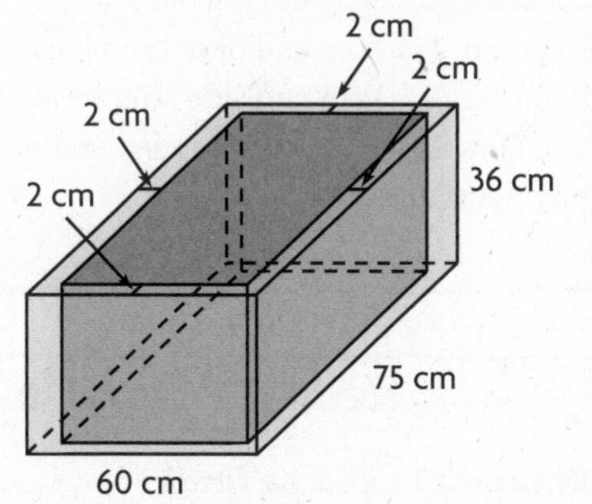

Use the graphic organizer to help you solve the problem.

Read the Problem

What do I need to find?

I need to find ________________ and ________________.

What information do I need to use?

I need to use ________________ and ________________.

How will I use the information?

First I will decide ________________. Then I will choose a ________________ I can use to calculate the measure. Finally, I will substitute the values for the ________________, and I will ________________ the formula.

Solve the Problem

- Choose the measure that specifies the amount of water that will fill a tank.

____

- Choose an appropriate formula.

____

- Subtract the width of the glass twice from the length and width and once from the height to find the inner dimensions.

Find the length. 75 cm − 4 cm = ______ cm

Find the width. 60 cm − 4 cm = ______ cm

Find the height. 36 cm − 2 cm = ______ cm

- Substitute and evaluate.

$V = 71 \times$ ______ = ______ = ______ cm^3

So, the volume of the tank is ________________.

MATHEMATICAL PRACTICES 6

Explain Why is volume the correct measure to use to solve the problem?

Try Another Problem

Alexander Graham Bell, the inventor of the telephone, also invented a kite made out of "cells" shaped like triangular pyramids.

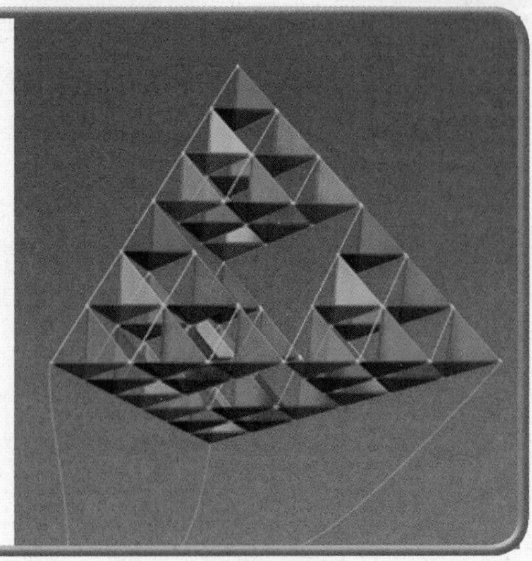

A kite is made of triangular pyramid-shaped cells with fabric covering one face and the base of the pyramid. The face and base both have heights of 17.3 cm and side lengths of 20 cm. How much fabric is needed to make one pyramid cell?

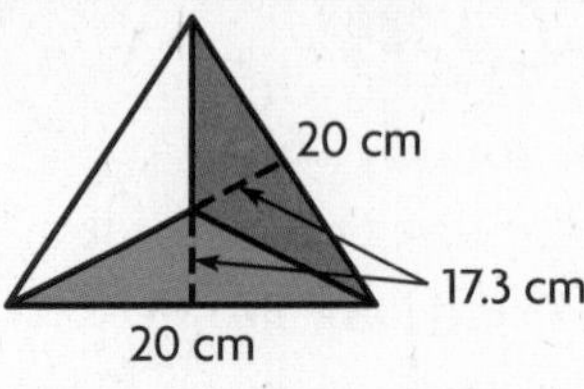

Read the Problem	Solve the Problem
What do I need to find?	
What information do I need to use?	
How will I use the information?	

So, _______ cm^2 of fabric is needed.

- Explain how you knew which units to use for your answer.

____

Math Talk — MATHEMATICAL PRACTICES 1

Analyze How did the strategy of using a formula help you solve the problem?

Name ________________________________

Share and Show 

1. An aquarium tank in the shape of a rectangular prism is 60 cm long, 30 cm wide, and 24 cm high. The top of the tank is open, and the glass used to make the tank is 1 cm thick. How much water can the tank hold?

First identify the measure and choose an appropriate formula.

____

Next find the inner dimensions and replace the variables with the correct values.

____

Finally, evaluate the formula.

____

So, the tank can hold ______________ of water.

2. THINKSMARTER **What if**, to provide greater strength, the glass bottom were increased to a thickness of 4 cm? How much less water would the tank hold?

____

3. An aquarium tank in the shape of a rectangular prism is 40 cm long, 26 cm wide, and 24 cm high. If the top of the tank is open, how much tinting is needed to cover the glass on the tank? Identify the measure you used to solve the problem.

____

4. The Louvre Museum in Paris, France, has a square pyramid made of glass in its central courtyard. The four triangular faces of the pyramid have bases of 35 meters and heights of 27.8 meters. What is the area of glass used for the four triangular faces of the pyramid?

____

Unlock the Problem

- ✓ Draw a diagram.
- ✓ Identify the measure needed.
- ✓ Choose an appropriate formula.

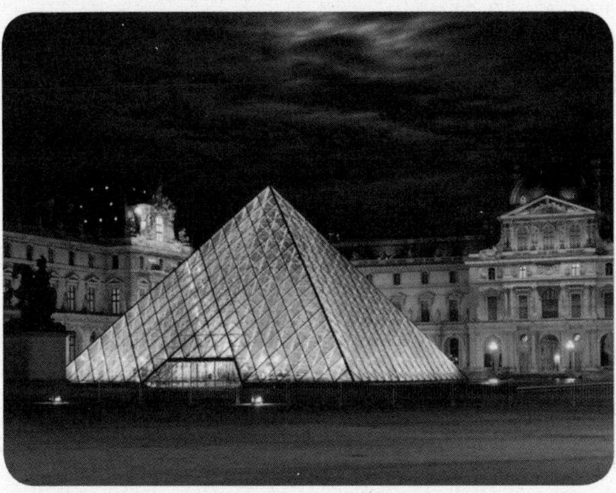

The Louvre Museum in Paris, France

WRITE Math • **Show Your Work**

On Your Own

5. THINK SMARTER A rectangular prism-shaped block of wood measures 3 m by $1\frac{1}{2}$ m by $1\frac{1}{2}$ m. How much of the block must a carpenter carve away to obtain a prism that measures 2 m by $\frac{1}{2}$ m by $\frac{1}{2}$ m?

____

6. GO DEEPER The carpenter (Problem 5) varnished the outside of the smaller piece of wood, all except for the bottom, which measures $\frac{1}{2}$ m by $\frac{1}{2}$ m. Varnish costs $2.00 per square meter. What was the cost of varnishing the wood?

____

7. A wax candle is in the shape of a cube with a side length of $2\frac{1}{2}$ in. What volume of wax is needed to make the candle?

____

8. MATHEMATICAL PRACTICE 1 **Describe** A rectangular prism-shaped box measures 6 cm by 5 cm by 4 cm. A cube-shaped box has a side length of 2 cm. How many of the cube-shaped boxes will fit into the rectangular prism-shaped box? Describe how you found your answer.

____

____

____

____

____

Personal Math Trainer

9. THINK SMARTER+ Justin is covering the outside of an open shoe box with colorful paper for a class project. The shoe box is 30 cm long, 20 cm wide, and 13 cm high. How many square centimeters of paper are needed to cover the outside of the open shoe box? Explain your strategy.

____

____

____

____

____

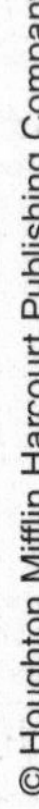

Name ____________________

Problem Solving • Geometric Measurements

Common Core

COMMON CORE STANDARD—6.G.A.4
Solve real-world and mathematical problems involving area, surface area, and volume.

Read each problem and solve.

1. The outside of an aquarium tank is 50 cm long, 50 cm wide, and 30 cm high. It is open at the top. The glass used to make the tank is 1 cm thick. How much water can the tank hold?

   $l = 50 - 2 = 48$, $w = 50 - 2 = 48$, $h = 30 - 1 = 29$

   $V = l \times w \times h$

   $= 48 \times 48 \times 29$

   $= 66{,}816$

   $66{,}816 \text{ cm}^3$

2. Arnie keeps his pet snake in an open-topped glass cage. The outside of the cage is 73 cm long, 60 cm wide, and 38 cm high. The glass used to make the cage is 0.5 cm thick. What is the inside volume of the cage?

   ____

3. A display number cube measures 20 in. on a side. The sides are numbered 1–6. The odd-numbered sides are covered in blue fabric and the even-numbered sides are covered in red fabric. How much red fabric was used?

   ____

4. The caps on the tops of staircase posts are shaped like square pyramids. The side length of the base of each cap is 4 inches. The height of the face of each cap is 5 inches. What is the surface area of the caps for two posts?

   ____

5. A water irrigation tank is shaped like a cube and has a side length of $2\frac{1}{2}$ feet. How many cubic feet of water are needed to completely fill the tank?

   ____

6. **WRITE** *Math* Write and solve a problem for which you use part of the formula for the surface area of a triangular prism.

   ____

   ____

Lesson Check (6.G.A.4)

1. Maria wants to know how much wax she will need to fill a candle mold shaped like a rectangular prism. What measure should she find?

2. The outside of a closed glass display case measures 22 inches by 15 inches by 12 inches. The glass is $\frac{1}{2}$ inch thick. How much air is contained in the case?

Spiral Review (6.G.A.1, 6.G.A.2, 6.G.A.3, 6.G.A.4)

3. A trapezoid with bases that measure 5 centimeters and 7 centimeters has a height of 4.5 centimeters. What is the area of the trapezoid?

4. Sierra has plotted two vertices of a rectangle at (3, 2) and (8, 2). What is the length of the side of the rectangle?

5. What is the surface area of the square pyramid?

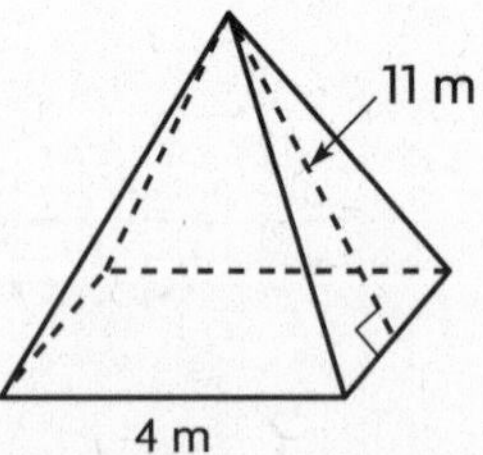

6. A shipping company has a rule that all packages must be rectangular prisms with a volume of no more than 9 cubic feet. What is the maximum measure for the height of a box that has a width of 1.5 feet and a length of 3 feet?

Name ______________________________

Chapter 11 Review/Test

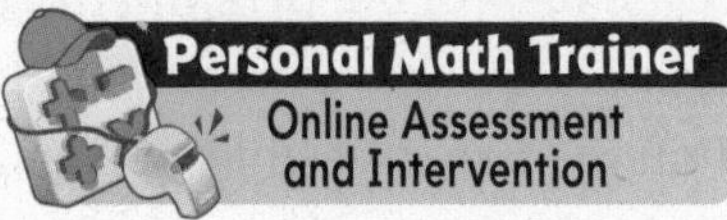

1. Elaine makes a rectangular pyramid from paper.

The base is a [rectangle. / pentagon. / triangle.] The lateral faces are [rectangles. / squares. / triangles.]

2. Darrell paints all sides except the bottom of the box shown below.

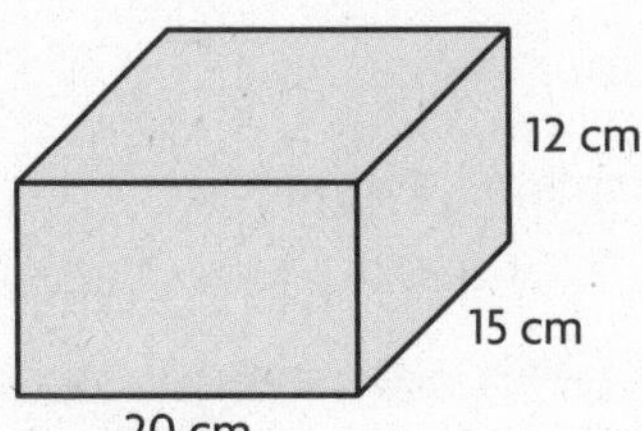

Select the expressions that show how to find the surface area that Darrell painted. Mark all that apply.

Ⓐ $240 + 240 + 180 + 180 + 300 + 300$

Ⓑ $2(20 \times 12) + 2(15 \times 12) + (20 \times 15)$

Ⓒ $(20 \times 12) + (20 \times 12) + (15 \times 12) + (15 \times 12) + (20 \times 15)$

Ⓓ $20 \times 15 \times 12$

3. A prism is filled with 44 cubes with $\frac{1}{2}$-unit side lengths. What is the volume of the prism in cubic units?

______ cubic units

4. A triangular pyramid has a base with an area of 11.3 square meters, and lateral faces with bases of 5.1 meters and heights of 9 meters.

Write an expression that can be used to find the surface area of the triangular pyramid.

____

GO DIGITAL Assessment Options Chapter Test

5. Jeremy makes a paperweight for his mother in the shape of a square pyramid. The base of the pyramid has a side length of 4 centimeters, and the lateral faces have heights of 5 centimeters. After he finishes, he realizes that the paperweight is too small and decides to make another one. To make the second pyramid, he doubles the length of the base in the first pyramid.

For numbers 5a–5c, choose Yes or No to indicate whether the statement is correct.

5a.	The surface area of the second pyramid is 144 cm^2.	○ Yes	○ No
5b.	The surface area doubled from the first pyramid to the second pyramid.	○ Yes	○ No
5c.	The lateral area doubled from the first pyramid to the second pyramid.	○ Yes	○ No

6. Identify the figure shown and find its surface area. Explain how you found your answer.

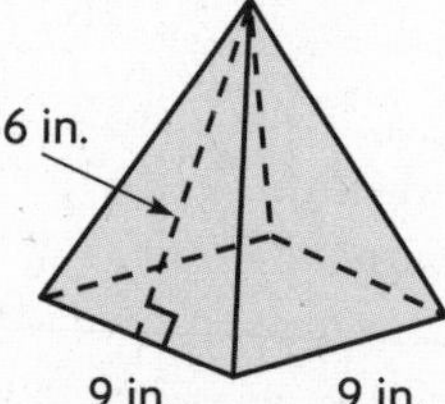

7. Dominique has a box of sewing buttons that is in the shape of a rectangular prism.

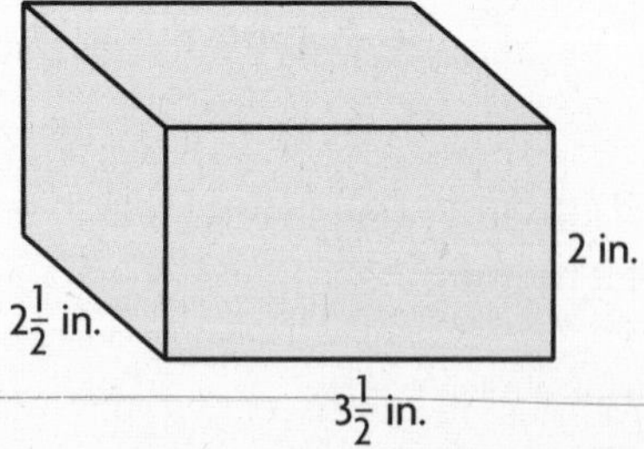

The volume of the box is $2\frac{1}{2}$ in. × $3\frac{1}{2}$ in. × [2 in. / $2\frac{1}{2}$ in. / $3\frac{1}{2}$ in.] = [8 $in.^3$ / $17\frac{1}{2}$ $in.^3$ / 35 $in.^3$]

Name ______________________________

8. Emily has a decorative box that is shaped like a cube with a height of 5 inches. What is the surface area of the box?

______ in.^{2}

9. Albert recently purchased a fish tank for his home. Match each question with the geometric measure that would be most appropriate for each scenario.

Question		Measure
How much water can the fish tank hold?	• •	The area of the base of the fish tank
How much material would it take to cover the entire fish tank?	• •	The surface area of the fish tank
How much space would the fish tank occupy on the table?	• •	The volume of the fish tank

10. Select the expressions that show the volume of the rectangular prism. Mark all that apply.

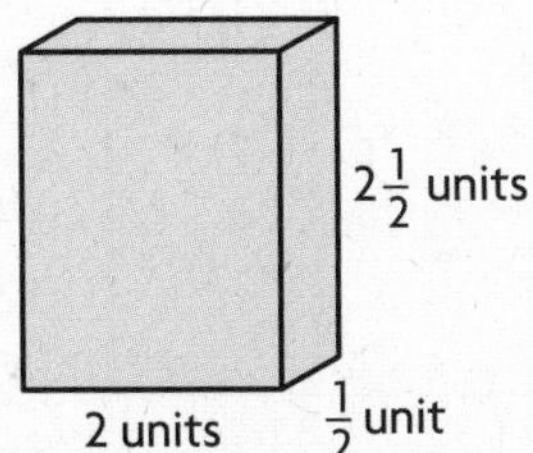

Ⓐ 2(2 units × $2\frac{1}{2}$ units) + 2(2 units × $\frac{1}{2}$ unit) + 2($\frac{1}{2}$ unit × $2\frac{1}{2}$ units)

Ⓑ 2(2 units × $\frac{1}{2}$ unit) + 4(2 units × $2\frac{1}{2}$ units)

Ⓒ 2 units × $\frac{1}{2}$ unit × $2\frac{1}{2}$ units

Ⓓ 2.5 cubic units

11. For numbers 11a–11d, select True or False for the statement.

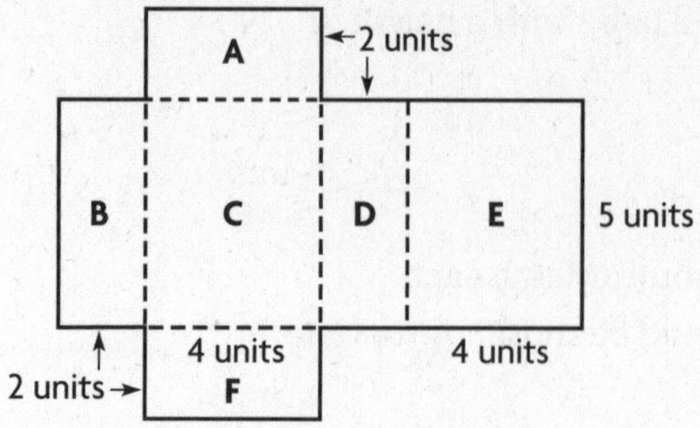

11a. The area of face A is 8 square units. ○ True ○ False

11b. The area of face B is 10 square units. ○ True ○ False

11c. The area of face C is 8 square units. ○ True ○ False

11d. The surface area of the prism is 56 square units. ○ True ○ False

12. Stella received a package in the shape of a rectangular prism. The box has a length of $2\frac{1}{2}$ feet, a width of $1\frac{1}{2}$ feet, and a height of 4 feet.

Part A

Stella wants to cover the box with wrapping paper. How much paper will she need? Explain how you found your answer.

Part B

Can the box hold 16 cubic feet of packing peanuts? Explain how you know.

Name ______________________________

13. A box measures 6 units by $\frac{1}{2}$ unit by $2\frac{1}{2}$ units.

For numbers 13a–13b, select True or False for the statement.

13a. The greatest number of cubes with a side length of $\frac{1}{2}$ unit that can be packed inside the box is 60. ○ True ○ False

13b. The volume of the box is $7\frac{1}{2}$ cubic units. ○ True ○ False

14. Bella says the lateral area of the square pyramid is 1,224 in.^{2} Do you agree or disagree with Bella? Use numbers and words to support your answer. If you disagree with Bella, find the correct answer.

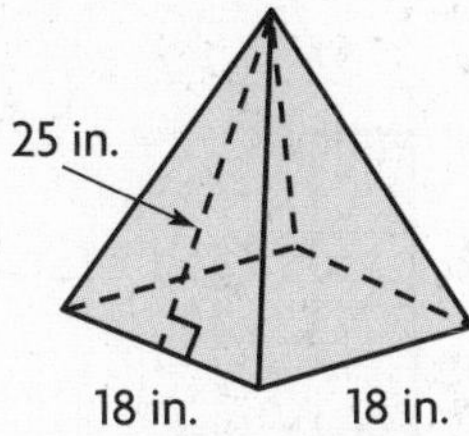

15. GO DEEPER Lourdes is decorating a toy box for her sister. She will use self-adhesive paper to cover all of the exterior sides except for the bottom of the box. The toy box is 4 feet long, 3 feet wide, and 2 feet high. How many square feet of adhesive paper will Lourdes use to cover the box?

____

16. Gary wants to build a shed shaped like a rectangular prism in his backyard. He goes to the store and looks at several different options. The table shows the dimensions and volumes of four different sheds.

Use the formula $V = l \times w \times h$ to complete the table.

	Length (ft)	Width (ft)	Height (ft)	Volume (ft^3)
Shed 1		10	8	960
Shed 2	18		10	2,160
Shed 3	12	4		288
Shed 4	10	12	10	

17. Tina cut open a cube-shaped microwave box to see the net. How many square faces does this box have?

______ square faces

18. Charles is painting a treasure box in the shape of a rectangular prism.

Which nets can be used to represent Charles' treasure box?
Mark all that apply.

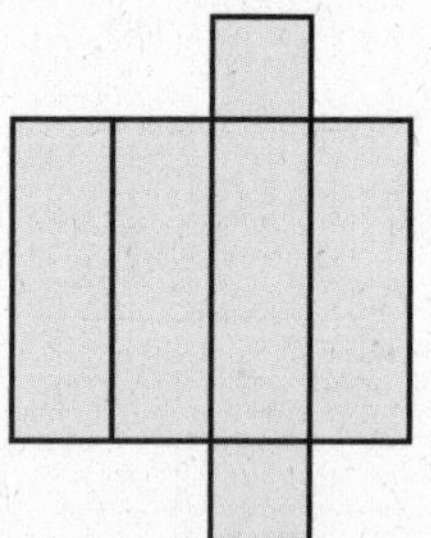

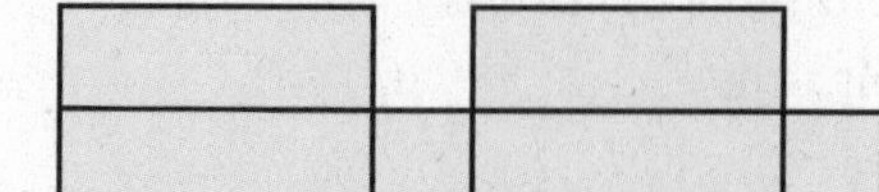

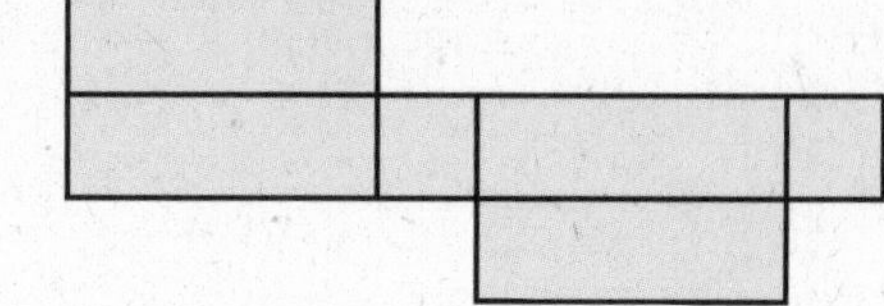

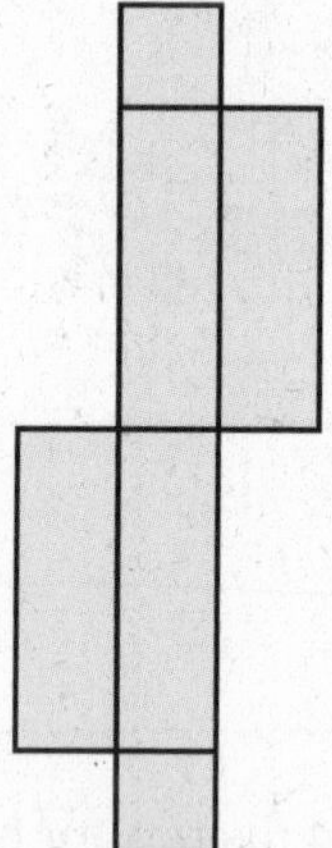

Personal Math Trainer

19. THINKSMARTER+ Julianna is lining the inside of a basket with fabric. The basket is in the shape of a rectangular prism that is 29 cm long, 19 cm wide, and 10 cm high. How much fabric is needed to line the inside of the basket if the basket does not have a top? Explain your strategy.

Data Displays and Measures of Center

Show What You Know

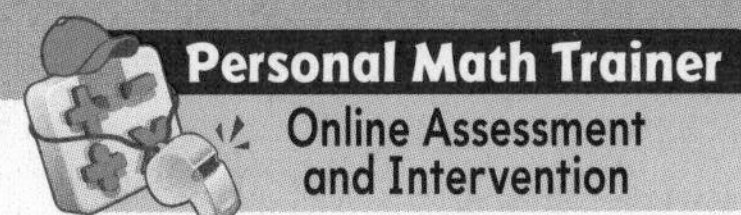

Check your understanding of important skills.

Name ______________________

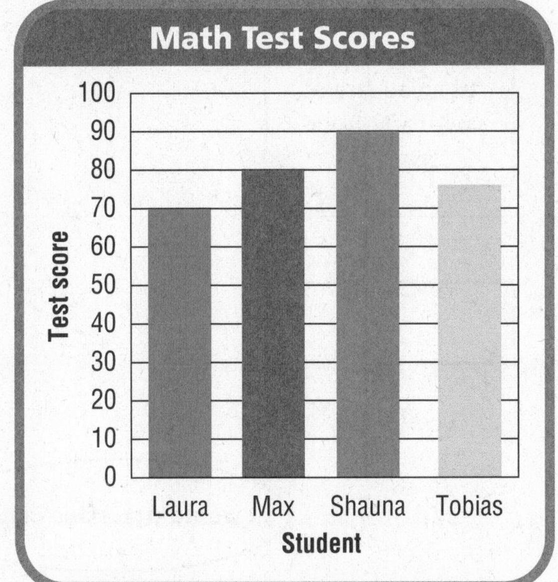

▶ **Read a Bar Graph** **Use the bar graph to answer the questions.** (3.MD.B.3)

1. Who has the highest test score?

   ____

2. Who has a score between 70 and 80?

   ____

3. What is the difference between the highest and lowest scores?

   ____

▶ **Division** **Find the quotient.** (6.NS.B.2)

4. $35\overline{)980}$
5. $16\overline{)352}$
6. $24\overline{)3{,}456}$
7. $42\overline{)3{,}276}$

▶ **Compare Decimals** **Compare. Write <, >, or =.** (5.NBT.A.3b)

8. 2.48 ◯ 2.53
9. 0.3 ◯ 0.04
10. 4.63 ◯ 4.3
11. 1.7 ◯ 1.70

Kayla scored 110 in the first game she bowled, but she can't remember her score from the second game. The average of the two scores is 116. Help Kayla figure out what her second score was.

____

Vocabulary Builder

▶ Visualize It

Sort the review words into the chart.

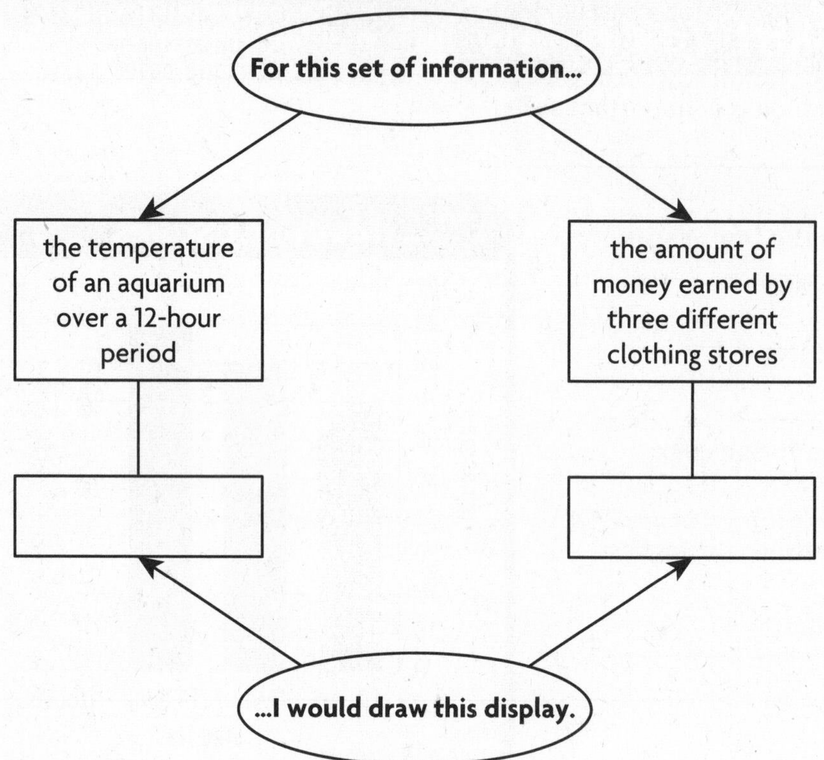

Review Words

- bar graph
- line graph

Preview Words

- dot plot
- frequency
- histogram
- mean
- median
- mode
- outlier
- statistical question

▶ Understand Vocabulary

Complete the sentences using the preview words.

1. A(n) __________________ is a bar graph that shows the frequency of data in specific intervals.
2. The __________________ is the middle value when a data set with an odd number of values is ordered from least to greatest.
3. A(n) __________________ is a value that is much less or much greater than the other values in a data set.
4. A(n) __________________ is a number line with dots that show the __________________ of the values in a data set.
5. You can calculate the __________________ of a data set by adding the values and then dividing the sum by the number of values.
6. The item(s) that occurs most often in a data set is called the __________________ of the data.

- Interactive Student Edition
- Multimedia eGlossary

Chapter 12 Vocabulary

bar graph

gráfica de barras

5

data

datos

18

dot plot

diagrama de puntos

26

frequency

frecuencia

36

frequency table

tabla de frecuencia

37

histogram

histograma

39

line graph

gráfica lineal

50

mean

media

55

Information collected about people or things, often to draw conclusions about them

© Houghton Mifflin Harcourt Publishing Company

A graph that uses horizontal or vertical bars to display countable data

Example:

Annual Sales at an Automobile Dealership

Number of Automobiles: 0, 100, 200, 300, 400

Cars Trucks SUVs

© Houghton Mifflin Harcourt Publishing Company

The number of times an event occurs

Joe's Reading Times (minutes)				
30	60	30	90	60
90	60	45	30	60
60	45	60	60	60
45	30	45	60	45

Joe's Reading Times	
Minutes	**Frequency**
30	4
45	5
60	9
90	2

© Houghton Mifflin Harcourt Publishing Company

A graph that shows frequency of data along a number line

Example:

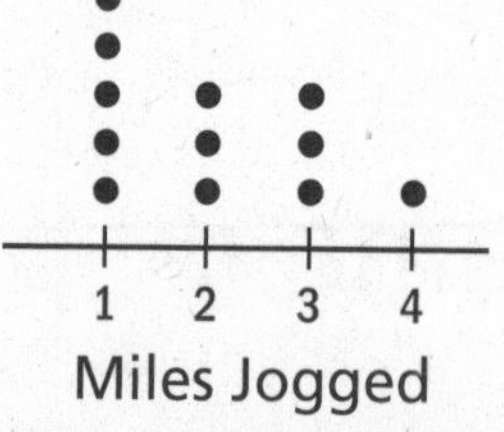

© Houghton Mifflin Harcourt Publishing Company

A type of bar graph that shows the frequencies of data in intervals

Example:

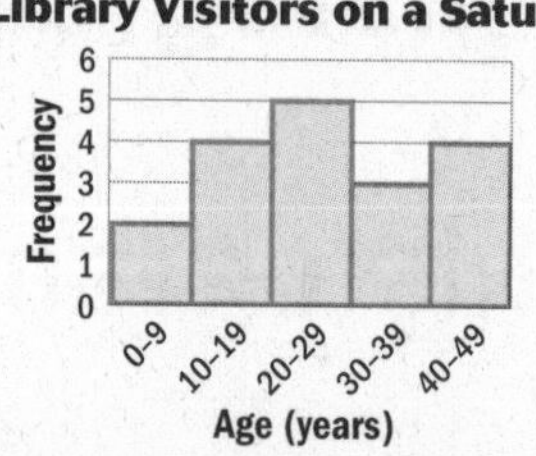

© Houghton Mifflin Harcourt Publishing Company

A table that uses numbers to record data about how often an event occurs

Joe's Reading Times (minutes)				
30	60	30	90	60
90	60	45	30	60
60	45	60	60	60
45	30	45	60	45

Joe's Reading Times	
Minutes	**Frequency**
30	4
45	5
60	9
90	2

© Houghton Mifflin Harcourt Publishing Company

The sum of a set of data items divided by the number of data items

Example:

The mean of the data set 85, 59, 97, 71 is

$$\frac{85 + 59 + 97 + 71}{4} = \frac{312}{4} = 78.$$

© Houghton Mifflin Harcourt Publishing Company

A graph that uses line segments to show how data change over time

Example:

measure of center

medida de tendencia central

57

median

mediana

59

mode

moda

61

outlier

valor atipico

72

relative frequency table

tabla de frecuencia relativa

91

statistical question

pregunta estadística

97

The middle value when a data set is written in order from least to greatest, or the mean of the two middle values when there is an even number of items

Example:

8, 17, 21, 23, 26, 29, 34, 40, 45

A single value used to describe the middle of a data set

Examples: mean, median, mode

A value much higher or much lower than the other values in a data set

Example:

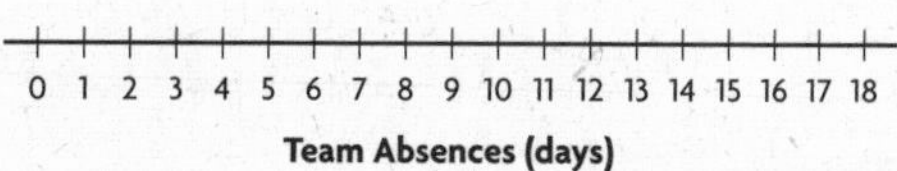

The value(s) in a data set that occurs the most often

Example: The mode of the data set 73, 42, 55, 77, 61, 55, 68 is 55.

A question that asks about a set of data that can vary

Example:

How many desks are in each classroom in my school?

A table that shows the percent of time each piece of data occurs

Macy's Biking		
Number of Miles	Frequency	Relative Frequency
1–5	4	20%
6–10	6	30%
11–15	7	35%
16–20	3	15%

Picture It

For 3 to 4 players

Materials

- timer
- sketch pad

How to Play

1. Take turns to play.
2. To take a turn, choose a math term from the Word Box. Do not say the term.
3. Set the timer for 1 minute.
4. Draw pictures and numbers on the sketch pad to give clues about the term.
5. The first player to guess the term before time runs out gets 1 point. If he or she can use the word in a sentence, they get 1 more point. Then that player gets a turn.
6. The first player to score 10 points wins.

Word Box
bar graph
data
dot plot
frequency
frequency table
histogram
line graph
mean
measure of center
median
mode
outlier
relative frequency table
statistical question

The Write Way

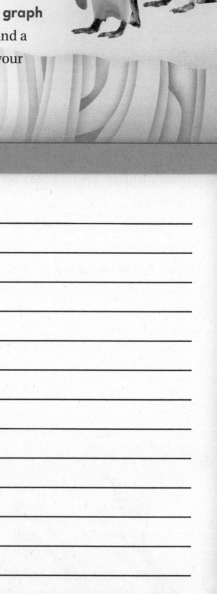

Reflect

Choose one idea. Write about it.

- Write a statistical question and explain why your question is a statistical one.
- Write a paragraph that uses at least three of these words or phrases.
  bar graph **data** **frequency table** **histogram** **line graph**
- Work with a partner to explain and illustrate three different ways to find a measure of center for a set of data. Use a separate piece of paper for your drawing.
- Explain what is most important to understand about an outlier.

Name ______________________________

Recognize Statistical Questions

Essential Question How do you identify a statistical question?

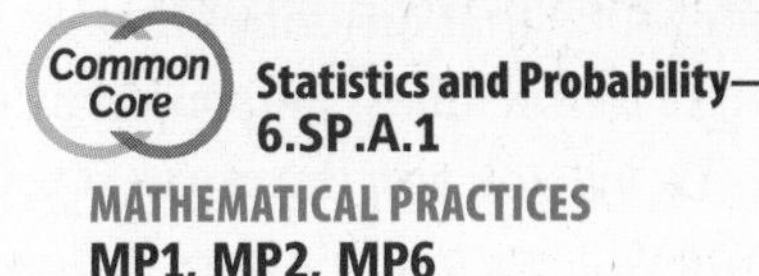

If you measure the heights of your classmates, you are collecting data. A set of **data** is a set of information collected about people or things. A question that asks about a set of data that can vary is called a **statistical question**.

"What are the heights of my classmates on July 1?" is a statistical question because height usually varies in a group of people. "What is Sasha's height on July 1?" is not a statistical question because it asks for only one piece of information at one time.

Unlock the Problem (Real World)

The New England Aquarium in Boston is home to over 80 penguins. Which of the following is a statistical question a biologist could ask about the penguins? Explain your reasoning.

A **How much does the penguin named Pip weigh this morning?**

B **How much does the penguin named Pip weigh each morning on 30 different days?**

Identify the statistical question.

Question A asks for Pip's weight at ____________ time(s),

so it ____________ ask about a set of data that varies.

Question A ____________ a statistical question.

Question B asks for Pip's weight at ____________ time(s), and it is

likely that Pip's weight ____________ vary during this period.

Question B asks about a set of data that can vary, so it ____________ a statistical question.

- Another biologist asks how old the penguin named Royal Pudding is. Is this a statistical question? Explain your reasoning.

____

____

A statistical question can ask about an entire set of data that can vary or a value that describes that set of data. For example, "What is the height of the tallest person in my class?" is a statistical question because it will tell you the greatest value in a set of data that can vary. You will learn other ways to describe a set of data later in this chapter.

Example

Bongos are a kind of antelope that live in central Africa. Bongos are unusual because both males and females have horns. Write two statistical questions a biologist could ask about a group of bongos.

1. What is the ____________ in inches of the horns on the bongo that has the ____________ horns in the group?

Different bongos will have different horn lengths. This question asks about a value in a set of data that ______ vary, so it ______ a statistical question.

2. What is the weight of the ____________ bongo in the group?

Different bongos will have different weights. This question asks about a value in a set of data that ______ vary, so it ______ a statistical question.

Math Talk MATHEMATICAL PRACTICES 2

Reasoning Give a different statistical question you could ask about the heights of students in your class.

Try This! **Write a statistical question you could ask in the situations described below.**

A **A researcher knows the amount of electricity used in 20 different homes on a Monday.**

____

____

____

____

____

B **A museum director records the number of students in each tour group that visits the museum during one week.**

____

____

____

____

____

Name ____________________

Share and Show

MATH BOARD

Identify the statistical question. Explain your reasoning.

1. **A.** What was the low temperature in Chicago each day in March?

   B. What was the low temperature in Chicago on March 7?

   Question A asks for the low temperature at ______ time(s),

   and it is likely the temperature ____________.

   Question B asks for the low temperature at ______ time(s).

   Question ______ is a statistical question.

2. **A.** How long did it take you to get to school this morning?

   B. How long did it take you to get to school each morning this week?

   ____

   ____

Write a statistical question you could ask in the situation.

3. A student recorded the number of pets in the households of 50 sixth-graders.

   ____

Math Talk — MATHEMATICAL PRACTICES 6

Explain How can you determine whether a question is a statistical question?

On Your Own

Identify the statistical question. Explain your reasoning.

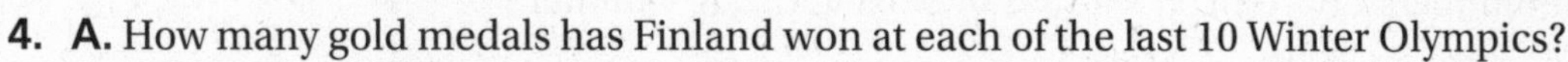

4. **A.** How many gold medals has Finland won at each of the last 10 Winter Olympics?

   B. How many gold medals did Finland win at the 2008 Winter Olympics?

   ____

   ____

Write a statistical question you could ask in the situation.

5. A wildlife biologist measured the length of time that 17 grizzly bears hibernated.

   ____

6. A doctor recorded the birth weights of 48 babies.

   ____

Problem Solving • Applications Real World

Use the table for 7 and 8.

Roller Coaster Data

Name	Height (ft)	Maximum Speed (mi/hr)
Rocket	256	83
Thunder Dolphin	281	87
Varmint	240	81
Screamer	302	92

7. Give a statistical question that you could ask about the data recorded in the table.

____

____

8. THINKSMARTER What statistical question could "92 mi/hr" be the answer to?

____

____

9. MATHEMATICAL PRACTICE 6 **Explain** A video game company will make a new game. The manager must choose between a role-playing game and an action game. He asks his sales staff which of the last 10 released games sold the most copies. Explain why this is a statistical question.

____

____

____

10. GO DEEPER Think of a topic. Record a set of data for the topic. Write a statistical question that you could ask about your data.

11. THINKSMARTER For numbers 11a–11d, choose Yes or No to indicate whether the question is a statistical question.

11a. How many minutes did it take Ethan to complete his homework last night? ○ Yes ○ No

11b. How many minutes did it take Madison to complete her homework each night this week? ○ Yes ○ No

11c. How many more minutes did Andrew spend on homework on Tuesday than on Thursday? ○ Yes ○ No

11d. What was the longest amount of time Abigail spent on homework this week? ○ Yes ○ No

Name ______________________

Recognize Statistical Questions

Common Core **COMMON CORE STANDARD—6.SP.A.1**
Develop understanding of statistical variability.

Identify the statistical question. Explain your reasoning.

1. **A.** How many touchdowns did the quarterback throw during the last game of the season?

   B. How many touchdowns did the quarterback throw each game of the season?

   B; the number of touchdowns in each game can vary.

2. **A.** What was the score in the first frame of a bowling game?

   B. What are the scores in 10 frames of a bowling game?

   ____

3. **A.** How many hours of television did you watch each day this week?

   B. How many hours of television did you watch on Saturday?

   ____

Write a statistical question you could ask in the situation.

4. A teacher recorded the test scores of her students.

   ____

5. A car salesman knows how many of each model of a car was sold in a month.

   ____

Problem Solving Real World

6. The city tracked the amount of waste that was recycled from 2000 to 2007. Write a statistical question about the situation.

   ____

7. The daily low temperature is recorded for a week. Write a statistical question about the situation.

   ____

8. WRITE Math Write three statistical questions that you could use to gather data about your family. Explain why the questions are statistical.

   ____

Lesson Check (6.SP.A.1)

1. Elise says that the question "Do you have any siblings?" is a statistical question. Mark says that "How many siblings do you have?" is a statistical question. Who is correct?

2. Kate says that "What was the lowest amount of precipitation in one month last year?" is a statistical question. Mike says that "What is the speed limit?" is a statistical question. Who is correct?

Spiral Review (6.G.A.1, 6.G.A.2, 6.G.A.4)

3. A regular decagon has side lengths of 4 centimeters long. If the decagon is divided into 10 congruent triangles, each has an approximate height of 6.2 centimeters. What is the approximate area of the decagon?

4. Mikki uses the net shown to make a solid figure.

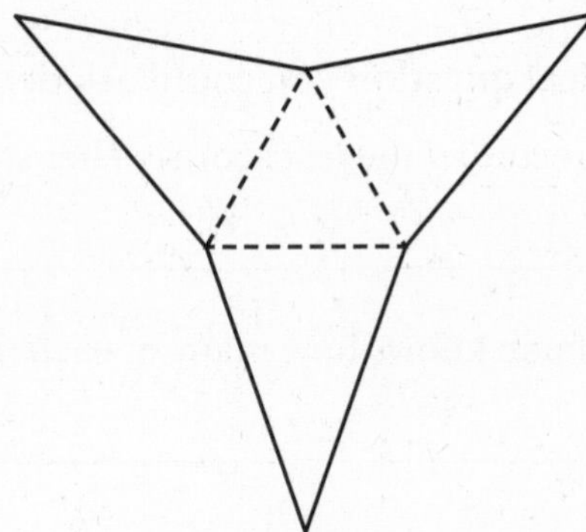

What solid figure does Mikki make?

5. A prism is filled with 30 cubes with $\frac{1}{2}$-unit side lengths. What is the volume of the prism in cubic units?

6. A tank in the shape of a rectangular prism has a length of 22 inches, a width of 12 inches, and a height of 15 inches. If the tank is filled halfway with water, how much water is in the tank?

FOR MORE PRACTICE GO TO THE Personal Math Trainer

Name ____________________

Describe Data Collection

Essential Question How can you describe how a data set was collected?

Common Core **Statistics and Probability—6.SP.B.5a, 6.SP.B.5b**

MATHEMATICAL PRACTICES
MP1, MP3, MP6

Unlock the Problem

One way to describe a set of data is by stating the number of *observations*, or measurements, that were made. Another way is by listing the attributes that were measured. An *attribute* is a property or characteristic of the item being measured, such as its color or length.

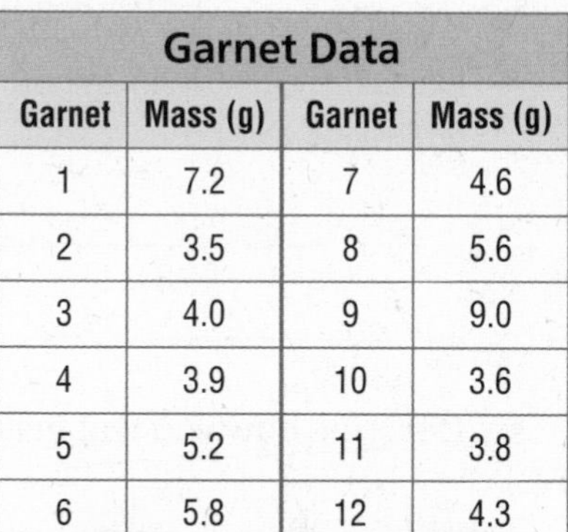

Garnet Data			
Garnet	Mass (g)	Garnet	Mass (g)
1	7.2	7	4.6
2	3.5	8	5.6
3	4.0	9	9.0
4	3.9	10	3.6
5	5.2	11	3.8
6	5.8	12	4.3

Jeffrey's hobby is collecting rocks and minerals. The chart gives data on garnets he found during a recent mineral-hunting trip. Identify:

- The attribute being measured
- The unit of measure
- The likely means by which measurements were made
- The number of observations

Describe the data set.

Think: What property or characteristic of the garnets did Jeffrey measure?

- The attribute Jeffrey measured was the __________ of the garnets.
- The unit used to measure the mass of the garnets was __________.
- To measure mass in grams, Jeffrey probably used a ______________.
- The number of observations Jeffrey made was __________.

1. Would Jeffrey likely have gotten the same data set if he had measured a different group of garnets? Explain.

____

____

2. What other attributes of the garnets could Jeffrey have measured?

____

____

Hands On

Activity Collect a data set.

Materials ■ ruler

In this activity, you will work with other students to collect data on the length of the students' index fingers in your group. You will present the data in a chart.

- Describe the attribute you will measure. What unit will you use?

____

____

- Describe how you will make your measurements.

____

____

____

- Describe the data you will record in your chart.

____

____

____

- In the space at the right, make a chart of your data.
- How many observations did you make?

____

____

____

MATHEMATICAL PRACTICES 6

Explain What statistical question does your data set in the Activity answer?

3. MATHEMATICAL PRACTICE 3 **Make Arguments** One of your classmates made 3 observations and another made 10 observations to answer a statistical question. Who do you think arrived at a better answer to the statistical question? Explain.

____

____

____

Name ____________________

Share and Show MATH BOARD

Describe the data set by listing the attribute measured, the unit of measure, the likely means of measurement, and the number of observations.

1. Greg's 100-meter race results

attribute: ____________

unit of measure: ____________

likely means by which measurements were taken: ____________

number of observations: ______

100-Meter Run Data			
Race	Time (sec)	Race	Time (sec)
1	12.8	5	13.5
2	12.5	6	13.7
3	12.9	7	12.6
4	13.4		

2. The Andrews family's water use

____

____

____

Daily Water Use (gal)				
153.7	161.8	151.5	153.7	160.1
161.9	155.5	152.3	166.7	158.3
155.8	167.5	150.8	154.6	

Math Talk MATHEMATICAL PRACTICES 3

Apply Why do you think it is important to make more than one observation when attempting to answer a statistical question?

On Your Own

3. **Practice: Copy and Solve** Collect data on one of the topics listed below. You may wish to work with other students. Make a chart of your results. Then describe the data set.

- Weights of cereal boxes, soup cans, or other items
- Numbers of family members
- Lengths of time to multiply two 2-digit numbers
- Numbers of pets in families
- Lengths of forearm (elbow to fingertip)
- Numbers of pages in books

4. THINK SMARTER Describe the data set by writing the attribute measured, the unit of measure, the likely means of measurement, and the number of observations in the correct location on the chart.

Heights of 6th Graders (in.)						
50	58	56	60	58	52	50
53	54	61	48	59	48	59
55	59	62	49	57	56	61

- 21
- yardstick
- inches
- heights of 6th graders

Attribute	Unit of Measure	Likely Means of Measurement	Number of Observations

Connect to Reading

Summarize

When you *summarize* a reading passage, you restate the most important information in a shortened form. This allows you to understand more easily what you have read. Read the following passage:

A biologist is studying green anacondas. The green anaconda is the largest snake in the world. Finding the length of any snake is difficult because the snake can curl up or stretch out while being measured. Finding the length of a green anaconda is doubly difficult because of the animal's great size and strength. The standard method for measuring a green anaconda is to calm the snake, lay a piece of string along its entire length, and then measure the length of the string. The table at the right gives data collected by the biologist using the string method.

Green Anaconda Lengths (cm)

357.2	407.6	494.5	387.0
417.6	305.3	189.4	267.7
441.3	507.5	413.2	469.8
168.9	234.0	366.2	499.1
370.0	488.8	219.2	

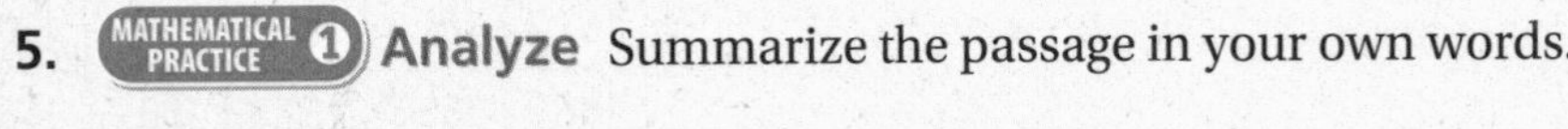

5. MATHEMATICAL PRACTICE 1 **Analyze** Summarize the passage in your own words.

____

____

____

____

6. THINKSMARTER Use your summary to name the attribute the biologist was measuring. Describe how the biologist measured this attribute.

____

____

____

7. Give any other information that is important for describing the data set.

____

____

8. GO DEEPER Write the greatest green anaconda length that the biologist measured in feet. Round your answer to the nearest foot. (Hint: 1 foot is equal to about 30 centimeters.)

____

Name ______________________

Describe Data Collection

Practice and Homework
Lesson 12.2

Common Core **COMMON CORE STANDARDS—6.SP.B.5a, 6.SP.B.5b** *Summarize and describe distributions.*

Describe the data set by listing the attribute measured, the unit of measure, the likely means of measurement, and the number of observations.

1. Daily temperature

Daily High Temperature (°F)				
78	83	72	65	70
76	75	71	80	75
73	74	81	79	69
81	78	76	80	82
70	77	74	71	73

Attribute: daily temperature; unit of measure: degrees Fahrenheit; means of measurement: thermometer; number of observations: 25

2. Plant heights

Height of Plants (inches)				
10.3	9.7	6.4	8.1	11.2
5.7	11.7	7.5	9.6	6.9

____

3. Cereal in boxes

Amount of Cereal in Boxes (cups)							
8	7	8.5	5	5	5	6.5	6
8	8.5	7	7	9	8	8	9

____

4. Dog weights

Weight of Dogs (pounds)							
22	17	34	23	19	18	20	20

____

Problem Solving Real World

5. The table below gives the amount of time Preston spends on homework. Name the likely means of measurement.

Amount of Time Spent on Homework (hours)							
5	3	1	2	4	1	3	2

____

6. The table below shows the speed of cars on a highway. Name the unit of measure.

Speeds of Cars (miles per hour)							
71	55	53	65	68	61	59	62
70	69	57	50	56	66	67	63

____

7. WRITE *Math* Gather data about the heights of your family members or friends. Then describe how you collected the data set.

____

Lesson Check (6.SP.B.5a, 6.SP.B.5b)

1. What is the attribute of the data set shown in the table?

Mass of Produce (grams)				
2.4	1.7	3.2	1.1	2.6
3.3	1.3	2.6	2.7	3.1

2. What is the number of observations of the data set shown below?

Swim Times (min)		
1.02	1.12	1.09
1.01	1.08	1.03

Spiral Review (6.G.A.1, 6.G.A.2, 6.G.A.4, 6.SP.A.1)

3. What is the area of the figure shown below?

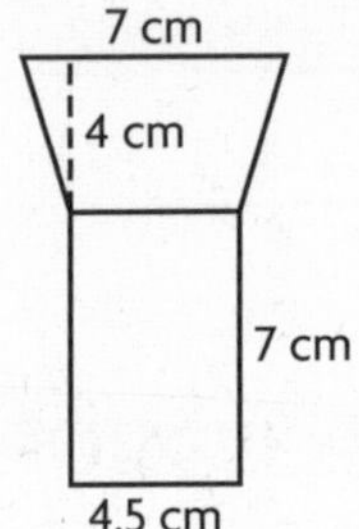

4. Each base of a triangular prism has an area of 43 square centimeters. Each lateral face has an area of 25 square centimeters. What is the surface area of the prism?

5. How much sand can this container hold?

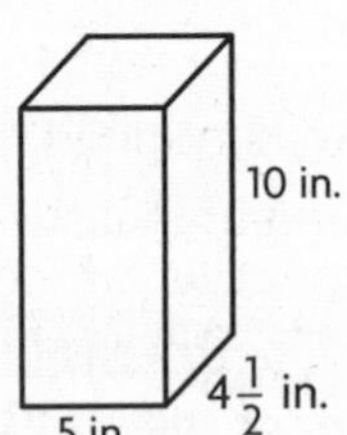

6. Jay says that "How much does Rover weigh today?" is a statistical question. Kim says that "How long are the puppies' tails in the pet store?" is a statistical question. Who is NOT correct?

FOR MORE PRACTICE GO TO THE **Personal Math Trainer**

Name ______________________

Dot Plots and Frequency Tables

Essential Question How can you use dot plots and frequency tables to display data?

Statistics and Probability—6.SP.B.4

MATHEMATICAL PRACTICES
MP1, MP4, MP5

A **dot plot** is a number line with marks that show the frequency of data. **Frequency** is the number of times a data value occurs.

Unlock the Problem — Real World

Hannah is training for a walkathon. The table shows the number of miles she walks each day. She has one day left in her training. How many miles is she most likely to walk on the last day?

- What do you need to find?

____

Distance Hannah Walked (mi)				
4	2	9	3	3
5	5	1	6	2
5	2	5	4	5
4	9	3	2	4

Make a dot plot.

STEP 1

Draw a number line with an appropriate scale.

Numbers vary from ______ to ______, so use a scale from 0 to 10.

STEP 2

For each piece of data, plot a dot above the number that corresponds to the number of miles Hannah walked.

Complete the dot plot by making the correct number of dots above the numbers 5 through 10.

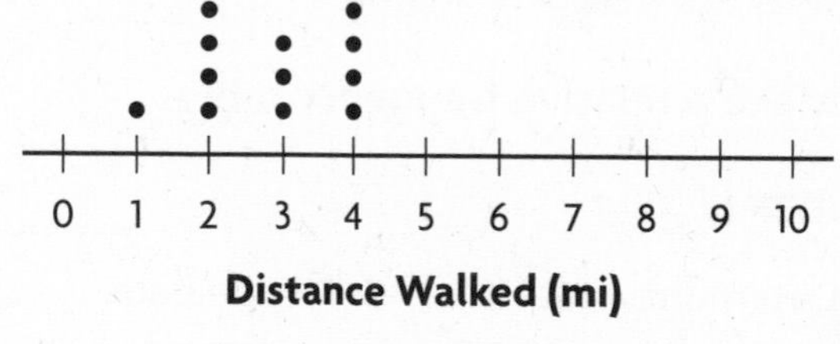

The number of miles Hannah walked most often is the value with the tallest stack of dots. The tallest stack in this dot plot is for

______________________.

So, the number of miles Hannah is most likely to walk on the last day of her training is

______________.

Math Idea
A dot plot is sometimes called a line plot.

- **MATHEMATICAL PRACTICE 5** **Communicate** Explain why a dot plot is useful for solving this problem.

____

____

A **frequency table** shows the number of times each data value or range of values occurs. A **relative frequency table** shows the percent of time each piece of data or group of data occurs.

Example 1

Jill kept a record of her workout times. How many of Jill's workouts lasted exactly 90 minutes?

Jill's Workout Times (minutes)						
30	60	30	90	60	30	60
90	60	120	30	60	90	90
60	120	60	60	60	30	30
120	30	120	60	120	60	120

Make a frequency table.

STEP 1

List the workout times in the first column.

STEP 2

Record the frequency of each time in the Frequency column.

Jill's Workout Times

Minutes	Frequency
30	7
60	
90	
120	

Complete the frequency table.

So, ________ of Jill's workouts lasted exactly 90 minutes.

Example 2

The table shows the number of laps Ricardo swam each day. What percent of the days did Ricardo swim 18 or more laps?

Ricardo's Lap Swimming				
10	10	15	5	12
12	5	19	3	19
16	14	17	18	13
6	17	16	11	8

Make a relative frequency table.

STEP 1

Determine equal intervals for the data. List the intervals in the first column.

STEP 2

Count the number of data values in each interval. Record this in the Frequency column.

STEP 3

Divide each frequency by the total number of data values. Write the result as a percent in the Relative Frequency column.

Ricardo's Lap Swimming

Number of Laps	Frequency	Relative Frequency
3–7	4	20%
8–12	6	30%
13–17	7	
18–22	3	

There are 20 data values.

$\frac{4}{20} = 0.2 = 20\%$

$\frac{6}{20} = 0.3 = 30\%$

Complete the relative frequency table.

So, Ricardo swam 18 or more laps on ____________ of the days.

Math Talk — MATHEMATICAL PRACTICES 1

Describe How could you find the percent of days on which Ricardo swam 13 or more laps?

Name ________________________________

Share and Show 

For 1–4, use the data at right.

Daily Distance Lionel Biked (km)				
3	5	12	2	1
8	5	8	6	3
11	8	6	4	10
10	9	6	6	6
5	2	1	2	3

✓ **1.** Complete the dot plot.

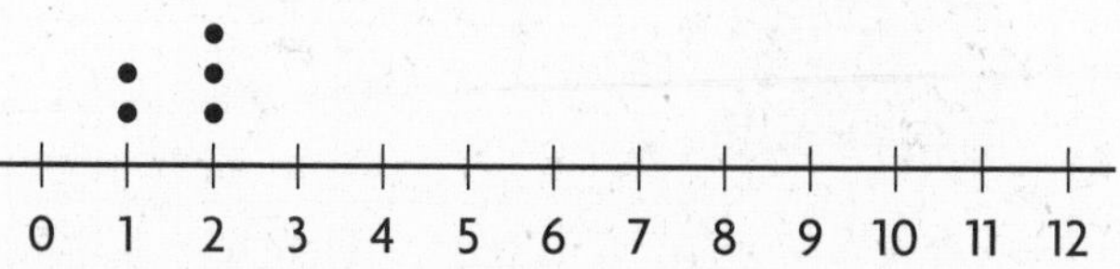

2. What was the most common distance Lionel biked? How do you know?

____

____

✓ **3.** Make a frequency table. Use the intervals 1–3 km, 4–6 km, 7–9 km, and 10–12 km.

4. Make a relative frequency table. Use the same intervals as in Exercise 3.

On Your Own

Practice: Copy and Solve **For 5–9, use the table.**

Gloria's Daily Sit-Ups				
13	3	14	13	12
12	13	4	15	12
15	13	14	3	11
13	13	12	14	15
11	14	13	15	11

5. Make a dot plot of the data.

6. Make a frequency table of the data with three intervals.

7. Make a relative frequency table of the data with three intervals.

8. MATHEMATICAL PRACTICE 1 **Describe** how you decided on the intervals for the frequency table.

____

9. THINKSMARTER Could someone use the information in the frequency table to make a dot plot? Explain.

____

Unlock the Problem

10. THINKSMARTER The manager of a fitness center asked members to rate the fitness center. The results of the survey are shown in the frequency table. What percent of members in the survey rated the center as excellent or good?

Fitness Center Survey	
Response	**Frequency**
Excellent	18
Good	15
Fair	21
Poor	6

a. What do you need to find?

____

b. How can you use relative frequency to help you solve the problem?

____

____

c. Show the steps you use to solve the problem.

d. Complete the sentences.

The percent of members who rated the center as excellent is _______.

The percent of members who rated the center as good is _______.

The percent of members who rated the center as excellent or good is _______.

11. GO DEEPER Use the table above. What is the difference in percent of the members in the survey that rated the fitness center as poor versus excellent?

____

Personal Math Trainer

12. THINKSMARTER+ Julie kept a record of the number of minutes she spent reading for 20 days. Complete the frequency table by finding the frequency and the relative frequency (%).

Julie's Reading Times (min)				
15	30	15	30	30
30	60	15	60	45
15	45	30	45	15
60	45	30	30	30

Julie's Reading Times		
Minutes	**Frequency**	**Relative Frequency (%)**
15	5	25
30		
45		
60		

Name ______________________________

Dot Plots and Frequency Tables

For 1–4, use the chart.

Common Core **COMMON CORE STANDARD—6.SP.B.4**
Summarize and describe distributions.

1. The chart shows the number of pages of a novel that Julia reads each day. Complete the dot plot using the data in the table.

Pages Read				
12	14	12	18	20
15	15	19	12	15
14	11	13	18	15
15	17	12	11	15

10 11 12 13 14 15 16 17 18 19 20

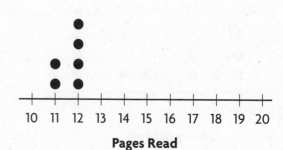

Pages Read

2. What number of pages does Julia read most often? Explain.

____

3. Make a frequency table in the space below. Use the intervals 10–13, 14–17, and 18–21.

4. Make a relative frequency table in the space below.

Problem Solving Real World

5. The frequency table shows the ages of the actors in a youth theater group. What percent of the actors are 10 to 12 years old?

____

Actors in a Youth Theater Group	
Age	**Frequency**
7–9	8
10–12	22
13–15	10

6. WRITE Math Explain how dot plots and frequency tables are alike and how they are different.

____

____

Lesson Check (6.SP.B.4)

1. The dot plot shows the number of hours Mai babysat each week. How many hours is Mai most likely to babysit?

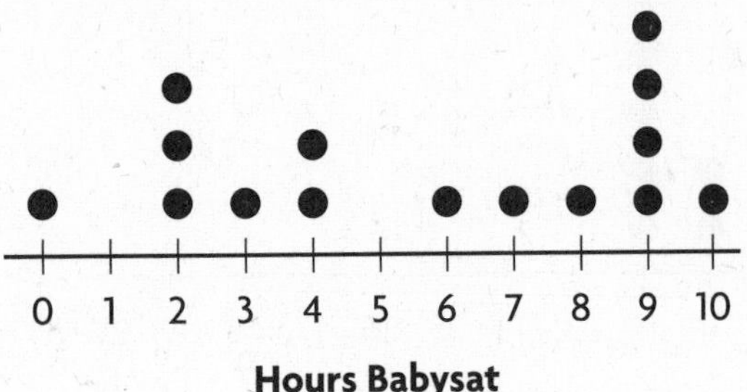

2. The frequency table shows the ratings that a movie received from online reviewers. What percent of the reviewers gave the movie a 4-star rating?

Movie Ratings	
Rating	Frequency
1 star	2
2 stars	5
3 stars	7
4 stars	6

Spiral Review (6.G.A.1, 6.G.A.2, 6.G.A.4, 6.SP.B.5b)

3. The dimensions of a rectangular playground are 50 times the dimensions of a scale drawing of the playground. The area of the scale drawing is 6 square feet. What is the area of the actual playground?

4. A square pyramid has a base side length of 8 feet. The height of each lateral face is 12 feet. What is the surface area of the pyramid?

5. A gift box is in the shape of a rectangular prism. The box has a length of 24 centimeters, a width of 10 centimeters, and a height of 13 centimeters. What is the volume of the box?

6. For a science experiment, Juanita records the height of a plant every day in centimeters. What is the attribute measured in her experiment?

FOR MORE PRACTICE GO TO THE Personal Math Trainer

Name ____________________

Histograms

Essential Question How can you use histograms to display data?

Common Core Statistics and Probability—6.SP.B.4
MATHEMATICAL PRACTICES
MP1, MP4, MP5, MP6

When there is a large number of data values, it is helpful to group the data into intervals. A **histogram** is a bar graph that shows the frequency of data in intervals. Unlike a bar graph, there are no gaps between the bars in a histogram.

Unlock the Problem Real World

The histogram shows the ages of winners of the Academy Award for Best Actor from 1990 to 2009. How many winners were under 40 years old?

Ages of Best Actor Winners, 1990–2009

Age	Frequency
20–29	1
30–39	6
40–49	8
50–59	3
60–69	2

Interpret the histogram.

The height of each bar shows how many data values are in the interval the bar represents.

How many winners were 20–29 years old?

____

Which other bar represents people under 40?

____

How many winners were 30–39 years old? __________

To find the total number of winners who were under 40 years old, add the frequencies for the intervals 20–29 and 30–39.

______ + ______ = ______

So, ______ of the winners were under 40 years old.

1. MATHEMATICAL PRACTICE 4 **Use Graphs** Explain whether it is possible to know from the histogram if any winner was 37 years old.

____

Example

The table shows the ages of winners of the Academy Award for Best Actress from 1986 to 2009. How many of the winners were under 40 years old?

Ages of Best Actress Winners					
45	21	41	26	80	42
29	33	36	45	49	39
34	26	25	33	35	35
28	30	29	61	32	33

Make a histogram.

STEP 1

Make a frequency table using intervals of 10.

Interval	20–29	30–39	40–49	50–59	60–69	70–79	80–89
Frequency	7			0			1

STEP 2

Set up the intervals along the

_______________ axis of the graph. The intervals must be all the same size. In this case, every interval includes 10 years.

Write a scale for the frequencies on

the _______________ axis.

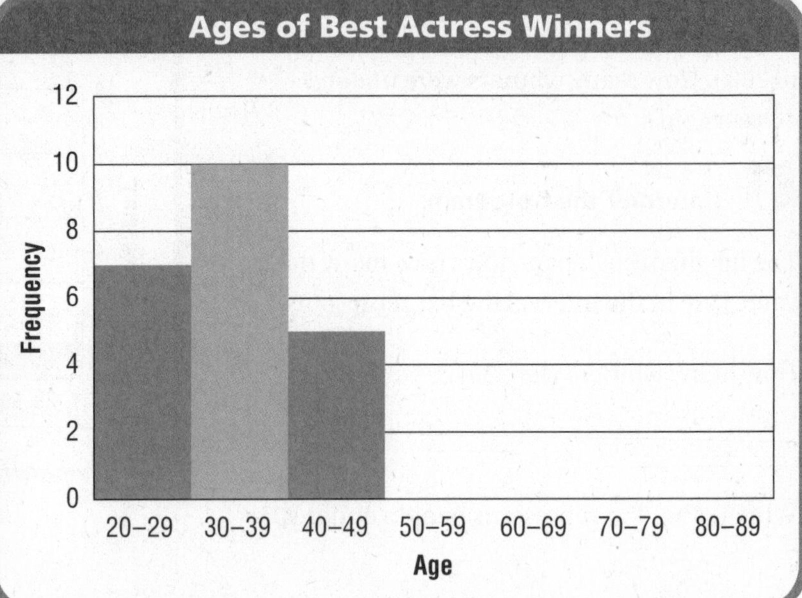

STEP 3

Graph the number of winners in each interval.

STEP 4

Give the graph a title and label the axes.

Complete the histogram by drawing the bars for the intervals 60–69, 70–79, and 80–89.

To find the number of winners who were under 40 years old, add the frequencies for the intervals 20–29 and 30–39.

_______ + _______ = _______

So, _______ of the winners were under 40 years old.

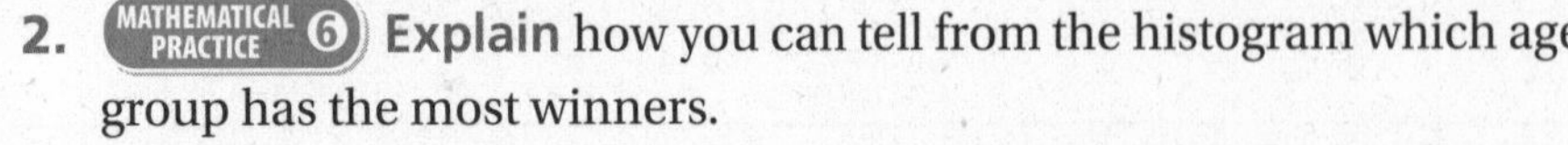

2. MATHEMATICAL PRACTICE 6 **Explain** how you can tell from the histogram which age group has the most winners.

____

____

Name ______________________________

Share and Show

For 1–4, use the data at right.

Ages of People at a Health Club (yr)				
21	25	46	19	33
38	18	22	30	29
26	34	48	22	31

1. Complete the frequency table for the age data in the table at right.

Interval	10–19	20–29	30–39	40–49
Frequency	2			

2. Complete the histogram for the data.

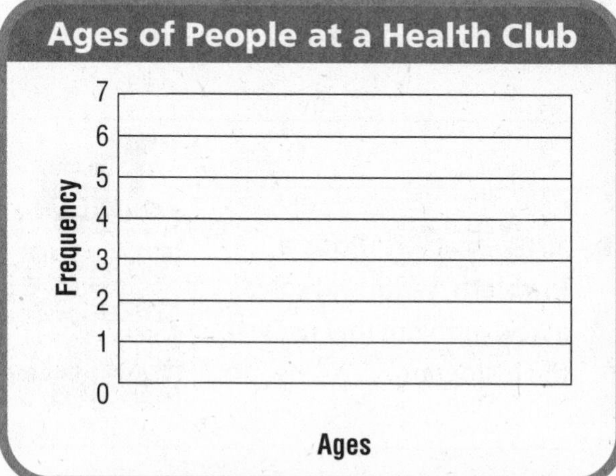

3. Use your histogram to find the number of people at the health club who are 30 or older.

____

4. GO DEEPER Use your histogram to determine the percent of the people at the health club who are 20–29 years old.

____

Math Talk MATHEMATICAL PRACTICES 5

Use Tools Explain whether you could use the histogram to find the number of people who are 25 or older.

On Your Own

Practice: Copy and Solve For 5–7, use the table.

Weights of Dogs (lb)				
16	20	15	24	32
33	26	30	15	21
21	12	19	21	37
10	39	21	17	35

5. Make a histogram of the data using the intervals 10–19, 20–29, and 30–39.

6. Make a histogram of the data using the intervals 10–14, 15–19, 20–24, 25–29, 30–34, and 35–39.

7. MATHEMATICAL PRACTICE 6 **Compare** Explain how using different intervals changed the appearance of your histogram.

____

____

____

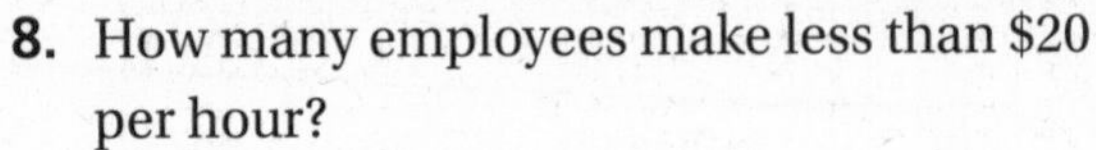

Problem Solving • Applications

The histogram shows the hourly salaries, to the nearest dollar, of the employees at a small company. Use the histogram to solve 8–11.

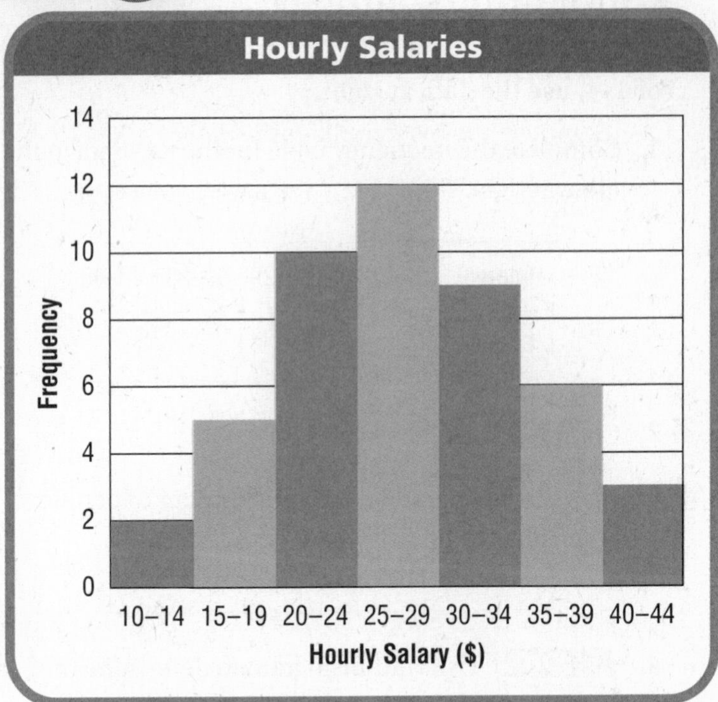

8. How many employees make less than $20 per hour?

____

9. GO DEEPER How many employees work at the company? Explain how you know.

____

____

10. THINKSMARTER **Pose a Problem** Write and solve a new problem that uses the histogram.

____

____

11. MATHEMATICAL PRACTICE 1 **Analyze** Describe the overall shape of the histogram. What does this tell you about the salaries at the company?

____

____

Personal Math Trainer

12. THINKSMARTER+ The frequency table shows the TV ratings for the show American Singer. Complete the histogram for the data.

TV ratings	
Rating	**Frequency**
14.1-14.5	2
14.6-15.0	6
15.1-15.5	6
15.6-16.0	5
16.1-16.5	1

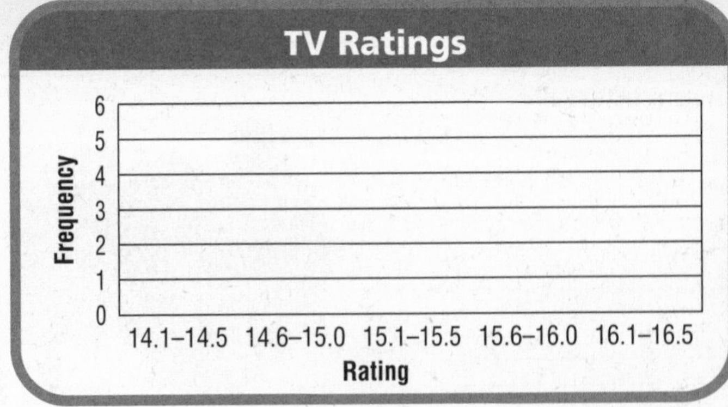

Name ______________________

Histograms

COMMON CORE STANDARD—6.SP.B.4
Summarize and describe distributions.

For 1–4 use the data at right.

Scores on a Math Test									
85	87	69	90	82	75	74	76	84	87
99	65	75	76	83	87	91	83	92	69

1. Complete the histogram for the data.

2. What do the numbers on the y-axis represent?

____

3. How many students scored from 60 to 69?

____

4. Use your histogram to find the number of students who got a score of 80 or greater. Explain.

____

____

____

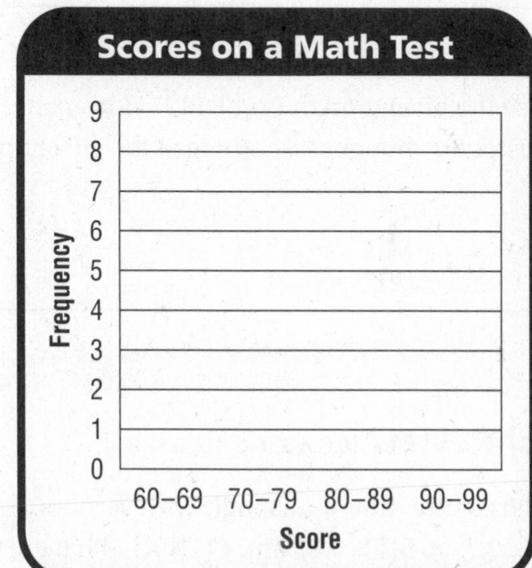

Problem Solving

For 5–6, use the histogram.

5. For which two age groups are there the same number of customers?

____

6. How many customers are in the restaurant? How do you know?

____

____

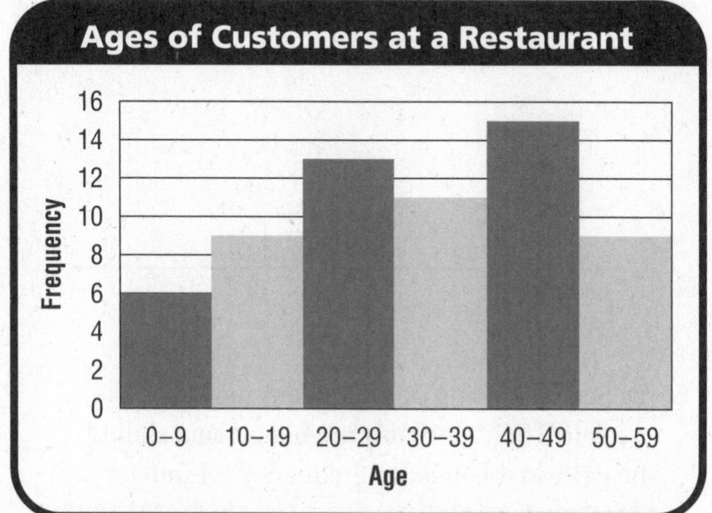

7. WRITE Math Write a letter to another student that explains how to make a histogram and what type of data a histogram displays.

____

____

Lesson Check (6.SP.B.4)

1. The histogram shows the amount, to the nearest dollar, that customers spent at a museum gift shop. How many customers spent less than $20?

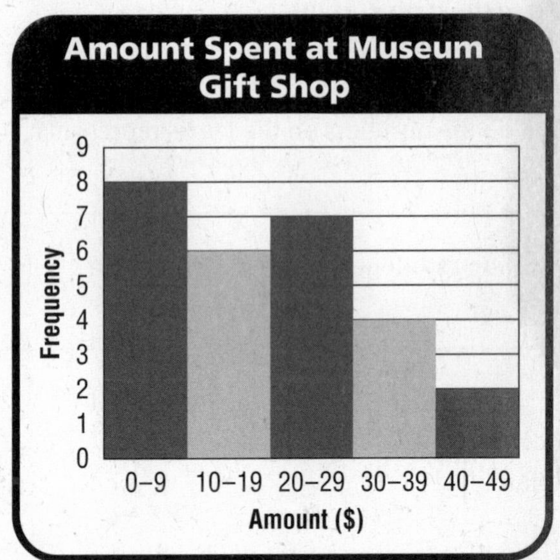

____

2. Use the histogram in Problem 1. How many customers bought something at the gift shop?

____

Spiral Review (6.G.A.2, 6.G.A.3, 6.SP.B.4)

3. Marguerite drew a rectangle with vertices $A(^-2, ^-1)$, $B(^-2, ^-4)$, and $C(1, ^-4)$. What are the coordinates of the fourth vertex?

____

4. A rectangular swimming pool can hold 1,408 cubic feet of water. The pool is 22 feet long and has a depth of 4 feet. What is the width of the pool?

____

5. DeShawn is using this frequency table to make a relative frequency table. What percent should he write in the Relative Frequency column for 5 to 9 push-ups?

DeShawn's Daily Push-Ups

Number of Push-Ups	Frequency
0–4	3
5–9	7
10–14	8
15–19	2

____

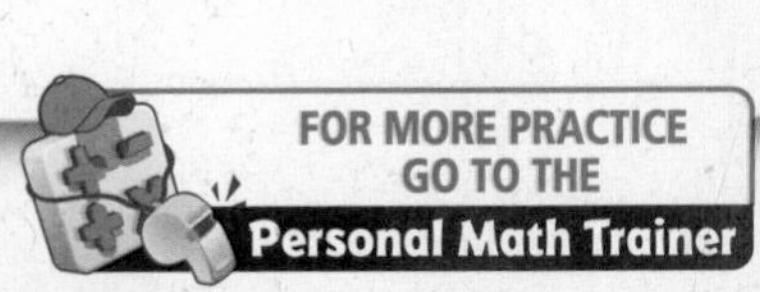

Name ______________________________

Mid-Chapter Checkpoint

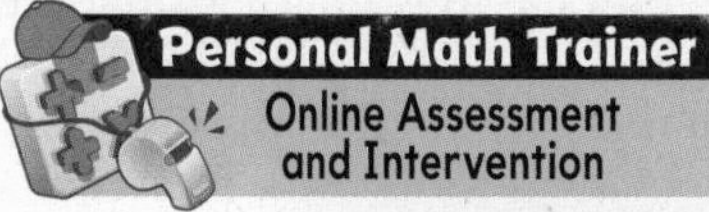

Vocabulary

Vocabulary
dot plot
histogram
statistical question

Choose the best term from the box to complete the sentence.

1. A ____________________ is a kind of bar graph that shows the frequency of data grouped into intervals. (p. 667)

2. A question that asks about a set of data that varies is called a ____________________. (p. 649)

Concepts and Skills

3. A sports reporter records the number of touchdowns scored each week during the football season. What statistical question could the reporter ask about the data? (6.SP.A.1)

____

____

4. Flora records her pet hamster's weight once every week for one year. How many observations does she make? (6.SP.B.5a)

____

5. GO DEEPER The number of runs scored by a baseball team in 20 games is given below. Draw a dot plot of the data and use it to find the most common number of runs scored in a game. (6.SP.B.4)

Runs Scored									
3	1	4	3	4	2	1	7	2	3
5	3	2	9	4	3	2	1	1	4

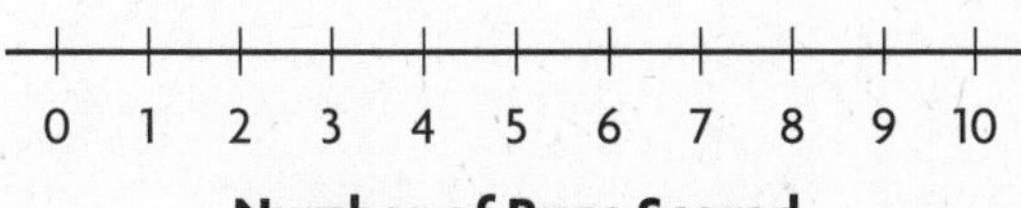

Number of Runs Scored

____

6. Write a statistical question you could ask about a set of data that shows the times visitors arrived at an amusement park. (6.SP.A.1)

7. A school principal is trying to decide how long the breaks should be between periods. He plans to time how long it takes several students to get from one classroom to another. Name a tool he could use to collect the data. (6.SP.B.5b)

8. The U.S. Mint uses very strict standards when making coins. On a tour of the mint, Casey asks, "How much copper is in each penny?" Lenny asks, "What is the value of a nickel?" Who asked a statistical question? (6.SP.A.1)

9. Chen checks the temperature at dawn and at dusk every day for a week for a science project. How many observations does he make? (6.SP.B.5a)

10. The table shows the lengths of the songs played by a radio station during a 90-minute period. Alicia is making a histogram of the data. What frequency should she show for the interval 160–169 seconds? (6.SP.B.4)

Song Lengths (sec)				
166	157	153	194	207
150	175	168	209	206
151	201	187	162	152
209	194	168	165	156

Name ______________________________

Mean as Fair Share and Balance Point

Essential Question How does the mean represent a fair share and balance point?

Common Core Statistics and Probability—6.SP.B.5c
MATHEMATICAL PRACTICES
MP3, MP4, MP8

Investigate

Hands On

Materials ■ counters

On an archaeological dig, five students found 1, 5, 7, 3, and 4 arrowheads. The students agreed to divide the arrowheads evenly. How many arrowheads should each student get?

A. Use counters to show how many arrowheads each of the five students found. Use one stack of counters for each student.

B. Remove a counter from the tallest stack and move it to the shortest. Keep moving counters from taller stacks to shorter stacks until each stack has the same height.

C. Count the number of counters in each stack.

The number of counters in each stack is the *mean*, or average, of the data. The mean represents the number of arrowheads each student should get if the arrowheads are shared equally.

There are 5 stacks of ______ counters.

So, each student should get ______ arrowheads.

MATHEMATICAL PRACTICES 8

Generalize What is the mean of the data set 3, 3, 3, 3, 3? Explain how you know.

Draw Conclusions

1. Explain what is "fair" about a fair share of a group of items.

____

____

____

2. THINKSMARTER How could you find the fair share of arrowheads using the total number of arrowheads and division?

____

____

Make Connections

The mean can also be seen as a kind of balance point.

Ms. Burnham's class holds a walk-a-thon to help raise money to update the computer lab. Five of the students walked 1, 1, 2, 4, and 7 miles. The mean distance walked is 3 miles.

Complete the dot plot of the data set.

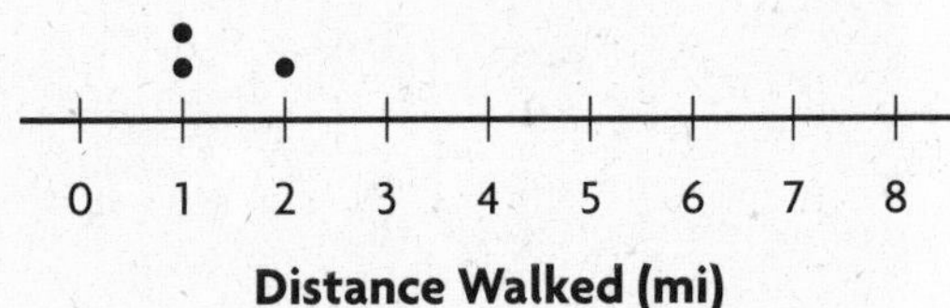

Circle the number that represents the mean.

Complete the table to find the distances of the data points from the mean.

	Values Less than the Mean			Values Greater than the Mean	
Data point	1 mi	1 mi	mi	4 mi	mi
Distance from the mean	2 mi	mi	mi	mi	mi

The total distance from the mean for values less than the mean is:

2 miles + 2 miles + 1 mile = ______ miles

The total distance from the mean for values greater than the mean is:

______ mile + ______ miles = ______ miles

The total distance of the data values less than the mean is ____________ the total distance of the data values greater than the mean. The mean represents a balance point for data values less than the mean and greater than the mean.

3. Explain how you found the distance of each data value from the mean.

____

____

4. MATHEMATICAL PRACTICE 8 **Generalize** Can all of the values in a data set be greater than the mean? Explain why or why not.

____

____

Name ____________________

Share and Show

MATH BOARD

Use counters to find the mean of the data set.

1. On the first day of a school fundraiser, five students sell 1, 1, 2, 2, and 4 gift boxes of candy.

   Make ______ stacks of counters with heights 1, 1, 2, 2, and 4.

   Rearrange the counters so that all ______ stacks have the same height.

   After rearranging, every stack has ______ counters.

   So, the mean of the data set is ______.

Make a dot plot for the data set and use it to check whether the given value is a balance point for the data set.

2. Rosanna's friends have 0, 1, 1, 2, 2, and 12 pets at home. Rosanna says the mean of the data is 3. Is Rosanna correct?

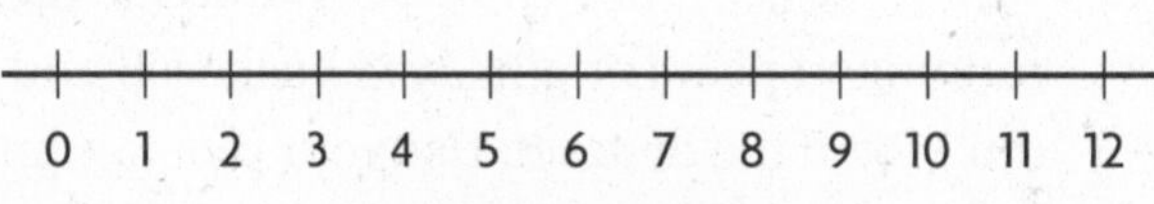

   The total distance from 3 for data values less than 3 is ______.

   The total distance from 3 for data values greater than 3 is ______.

   The mean of 3 __________ a balance point.

   So, Rosanna __________ correct.

Problem Solving • Applications

3. GO DEEPER Four people go to lunch, and the costs of their orders are $6, $9, $10, and $11. They want to split the bill evenly. Find each person's fair share. Explain your work.

____

____

____

Use the table for 4–6.

Fruit Baskets			
Basket	**Apples**	**Oranges**	**Pears**
A	4	2	2
B	1	2	1
C	4	2	5

4. A grocer is preparing fruit baskets to sell as holiday presents. If the grocer rearranges the apples in baskets A, B, and C so that each has the same number, how many apples will be in each basket? Use counters to find the fair share.

____

5. MATHEMATICAL PRACTICE 3 **Make Arguments** Can the pears be rearranged so that there is an equal whole number of pears in each basket? Explain why or why not.

____

____

____

____

6. THINKSMARTER Use counters to find the mean of the number of pears originally in baskets B and C. Draw a dot plot of the data set. Use your plot to explain why the mean you found is a balance point.

____

____

____

____

7. THINKSMARTER Four friends go to breakfast and the costs of their breakfasts are $5, $8, $9, and $10. Select True or False for each statement.

7a. The mean of the cost of the breakfasts can be found by adding each of the costs and dividing that total by 4. ○ True ○ False

7b. The mean cost of the four breakfasts is $10. ○ True ○ False

7c. The difference between the greatest cost and the mean is $2. ○ True ○ False

7d. The difference between the least cost and the mean is $2. ○ True ○ False

Name ______________________

Mean as Fair Share and Balance Point

Use counters to find the mean of the data set.

COMMON CORE STANDARD—6.SP.B.5c
Summarize and describe distributions.

1. Six students count the number of buttons on their shirts. The students have 0, 4, 5, 2, 3, and 4 buttons.

   Make ___6___ stacks of counters with heights 0, 4, 5, 2, 3, and 4.

   Rearrange the counters so that all ___6___ stacks have the same height.

   After rearranging, every stack has ___3___ counters.

   So, the mean of the data set is ___3___.

2. Four students completed 1, 2, 2, and 3 chin-ups. __________

Make a dot plot for the data set and use it to check whether the given value is a balance point for the data set.

3. Sandy's friends ate 0, 2, 3, 4, 6, 6, and 7 pretzels. Sandy says the mean of the data is 4. Is Sandy correct?

   0 1 2 3 4 5 6 7 8 9 10

   The total distance from 4 for values less than 4 is ________. The total distance from 4 for values greater than 4 is ________. The mean of 4 ________ a balance point.

   So, Sandy ________ correct.

Problem Solving (Real World)

4. Three baskets contain 8, 8, and 11 soaps. Can the soaps be rearranged so that there is an equal whole number of soaps in each basket? Explain why or why not.

5. Five pages contain 6, 6, 9, 10, and 11 stickers. Can the stickers be rearranged so that there is an equal whole number of stickers on each page? Explain why or why not.

6. WRITE Math Describe how to use counters to find the mean of a set of data. Give a data set and list the steps to find the mean.

Lesson Check (6.SP.B.5c)

1. What is the mean of 9, 12, and 15 stamps?

2. Four friends spent $9, $11, $11, and $17 on dinner. If they split the bill equally, how much does each person owe?

Spiral Review (6.G.A.4, 6.SP.B.5b)

3. What figure does the net below represent?

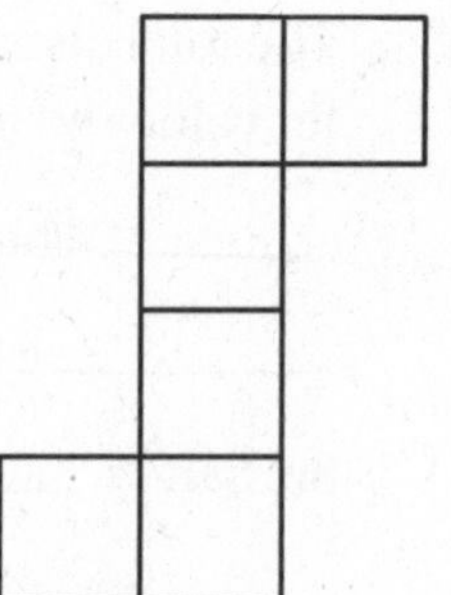

4. Sarah paints the box below. She paints the whole box except for the front face. What area of the box does she paint?

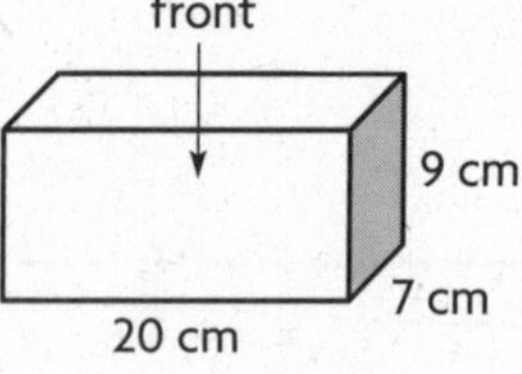

5. Chloe collected data and then displayed her results in the table to the right. What is the unit of measure of the data?

Temperature at Noon	
Monday	80°F
Tuesday	84°F
Wednesday	78°F
Thursday	90°F
Friday	80°F

FOR MORE PRACTICE GO TO THE **Personal Math Trainer**

Name ______________________

Measures of Center

Essential Question How can you describe a set of data using mean, median, and mode?

Common Core **Statistics and Probability—6.SP.B.5c** *Also 6.SP.A.2, 6.SP.A.3*

MATHEMATICAL PRACTICES **MP2, MP5, MP6**

A **measure of center** is a single value used to describe the middle of a data set. A measure of center can be a useful way to summarize a data set, especially when the data set is large.

Unlock the Problem

Kara made a paper airplane. She flew her airplane 6 times and recorded how long it stayed in the air during each flight. The times in seconds for the flights are 5.8, 2.9, 6.7, 1.6, 2.9, and 4.7. What are the mean, median, and mode of the data?

What unit of time is used in the problem?

____

How many flight times are given?

____

Find the mean, median, and mode.

The **mean** is the sum of the data items divided by the number of data items.

Mean $= \dfrac{5.8 + 2.9 + 6.7 + 1.6 + 2.9 + 4.7}{\square} = \dfrac{\square}{\square} = \square$

The **median** is the middle value when the data are written in order. If the number of data items is even, the median is the mean of the two middle values.

Order the values from least to greatest.

1.6, 2.9, 2.9, 4.7, 5.8, 6.7

The data set has an ______________ number of values, so the median is the mean of the two middle values. Circle the two middle values of the data set.

Now find the mean of the two middle values.

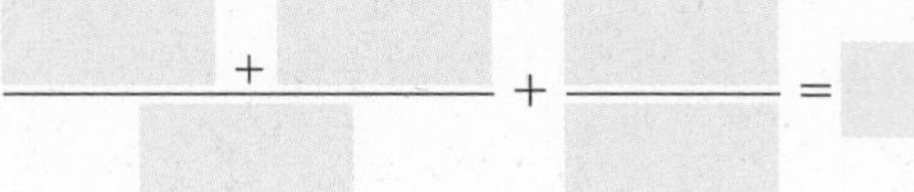

$\dfrac{\square + \square}{\square} + \dfrac{\square}{\square} = \square$

The **mode** is the data value or values that occur most often.

______ occurs twice, and all the other values occur once.

______________ is the mode.

MATHEMATICAL PRACTICES 5

Use Tools How could you use a dot plot and the idea of a balance point to check your answer for the mean?

Try This! In 2009, an engineer named Takuo Toda set a world record for flight time for a paper airplane. His plane flew for 27.9 sec. If Toda's time was included in Kara's set of times, what would the median be?

____

Example 1

Mrs. O'Donnell's class has a fundraiser for a field trip to a wildlife preservation. Five of the donations are $15, $25, $30, $28, and $27. Find the mean, median, and mode of the donations.

Mean = $\frac{\square + \square + \square + \square + \square}{\square}$

= $\frac{\square}{\square}$ = $\square$

Order the data from least to greatest to find the median.

______, ______, ______, ______, ______

Median = ______

If all of the values in a data set occur with equal frequency, then the data set has no mode.

The data set has no repeated values, so there is no ____________.

Example 2

Keith surveys his classmates about how many brothers and sisters they have. Six of the responses were 1, 3, 1, 2, 2, and 0. Find the mean, median, and mode of the data.

Mean = $\frac{\square + \square + \square + \square + \square + \square}{\square}$ = $\frac{\square}{\square}$ = $\square$

Order the data from least to greatest to find the median.

______, ______, ______, ______, ______, ______

The number of data values is even, so find the mean of the two middle values.

Median = $\frac{\square + \square}{\square}$ = $\frac{\square}{\square}$ = $\square$

The data values ______ and ______ appear twice in the set. If two or more values appear in the data set the most number of times, then the data set has two or more modes.

Modes = ______ and ______

Name ______________________________

Share and Show

1. Terrence records the number of e-mails he receives per day. During one week, he receives 7, 3, 10, 5, 5, 6, and 6 e-mails. What are the mean, median, and mode of the data?

Mean = __________ Median = __________ Mode(s) = __________

2. Julie goes to several grocery stores and researches the price of a 12 oz bottle of juice. Find the mean, median, and mode of the prices shown.

Juice Prices		
$0.95	$1.09	$0.99
$1.25	$0.99	$1.99

Mean = __________ Median = __________ Mode(s) = __________

MATHEMATICAL PRACTICES 6

Explain how you can find the median of a set of data with an even number of values.

On Your Own

3. T.J. is training for the 200-meter dash event for his school's track team. Find the mean, median, and mode of the times shown in the table.

T.J.'s Times (sec)		
22.3	22.4	23.3
24.5	22.5	

Mean = __________ Median = __________ Mode(s) = __________

4. MATHEMATICAL PRACTICE 6 **Make Connections Algebra** The values of a data set can be represented by the expressions x, $2x$, $4x$, and $5x$. Write the data set for $x = 3$ and find the mean.

____

5. GO DEEPER In the last six months, Sonia's family used 456, 398, 655, 508, 1,186, and 625 minutes on their cell phone plan. In an effort to spend less time on the phone each month, Sonia's family wants to try and keep the mean cell phone usage at 600 minutes or less. Over the last 6 months, by how many minutes did the mean number of minutes exceed their goal?

____

Problem Solving • Applications

THINKSMARTER **Sense or Nonsense?**

6. Jeremy scored 85, 90, 72, 88, and 92 on five math tests, for a mean of 85.4. On the sixth test he scored a 95. He calculates his mean score for all 6 tests as shown below, but Deronda says he is incorrect. Whose answer makes sense? Whose answer is nonsense? Explain your reasoning.

Jeremy's Work

The mean of my first 5 test scores was 85.4, so to find the mean of all 6 test scores, I just need to find the mean of 85.4 and 95.

$$\text{Mean} = \frac{85.4 + 95}{2} = \frac{180.4}{2} = 90.2$$

So, my mean score for all 6 tests is 90.2.

Deronda's Work

To find the mean of all 6 test scores, you need to add up all 6 scores and divide by 6.

$$\text{Mean} = \frac{85 + 90 + 72 + 88 + 92 + 95}{6}$$

$$= \frac{522}{6} = 87$$

So, Jeremy's mean score for all 6 tests is 87.

7. THINKSMARTER Alex took a standardized test 4 times. His test scores were 16, 28, 24, and 32.

The mean of the test scores is
- 24.
- 25.
- 26.

The median of the test scores is
- 24.
- 26.
- 28.

The mode of the test scores is
- 16.
- 32.
- no mode.

Name ______________________

Measures of Center

Common Core

COMMON CORE STANDARD—6.SP.B.5c
Summarize and describe distributions.

Use the table for 1–4.

Number of Points Blaine Scored in Five Basketball Games	
Game	**Points Scored**
1	10
2	8
3	11
4	12
5	6

1. What is the mean of the data?

$$\frac{10 + 8 + 11 + 12 + 6}{5} = \frac{47}{5} = 9.4$$

9.4 points

2. What is the median of the data?

____

3. What is the mode(s) of the data?

____

4. Suppose Blaine played a sixth game and scored 10 points during the game. Find the new mean, median, and mode.

____

____

Problem Solving Real World

5. An auto manufacturer wants their line of cars to have a median gas mileage of 25 miles per gallon or higher. The gas mileage for their five models are 23, 25, 26, 29, and 19. Do their cars meet their goal? Explain.

____

____

____

6. A sporting goods store is featuring several new bicycles, priced at \$300, \$250, \$325, \$780, and \$350. They advertise that the average price of their bicycles is under \$400. Is their ad correct? Explain.

____

____

____

7. WRITE *Math* Explain how to find the mean of a set of data.

____

____

Lesson Check (6.SP.B.5c)

1. The prices for a video game at 5 different stores are $39.99, $44.99, $29.99, $35.99, and $31.99. What is the mode(s) of the data?

2. Manuel is keeping track of how long he practices the saxophone each day. The table gives his practice times for the past five days. What is the mean of his practice times?

Manuel's Practice Time	
Day	**Minutes Practiced**
Monday	25
Tuesday	45
Wednesday	30
Thursday	65
Friday	30

Spiral Review (6.G.A.4, 6.SP.B.4, 6.SP.B.5c)

3. What is the surface area of the triangular prism shown below?

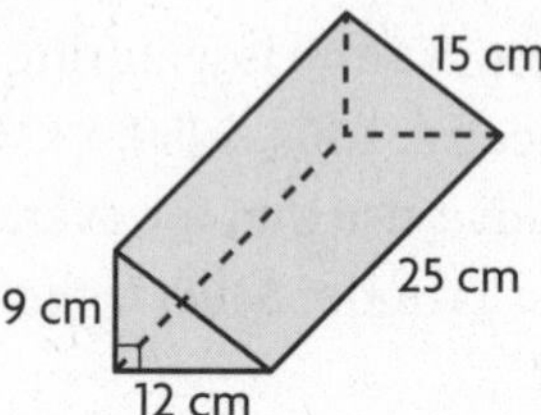

4. Kate records the number of miles that she bikes each day. She displayed the number of daily miles in the dot plot below. Each dot represents the number of miles she biked in one day. How many days did she bike 4–7 miles?

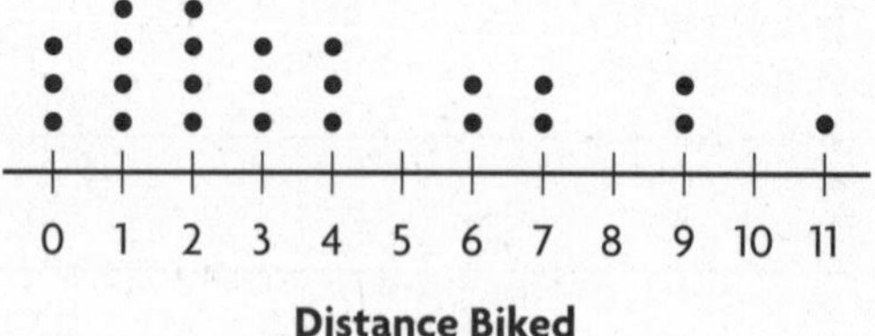

5. Six people eat breakfast together at a restaurant. The costs of their orders are $4, $5, $9, $8, $6, and $10. If they want to split the check evenly, how much should each person pay?

FOR MORE PRACTICE GO TO THE Personal Math Trainer

Name ______________________

Effects of Outliers

Essential Question How does an outlier affect measures of center?

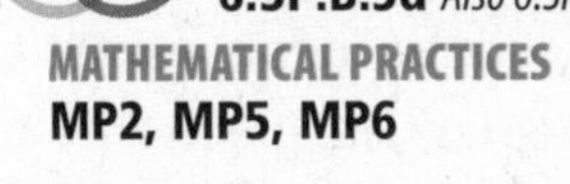

Common Core Statistics and Probability—6.SP.B.5d Also 6.SP.B.5c

MATHEMATICAL PRACTICES
MP2, MP5, MP6

An **outlier** is a value that is much less or much greater than the other values in a data set. An outlier may greatly affect the mean of a data set. This may give a misleading impression of the data.

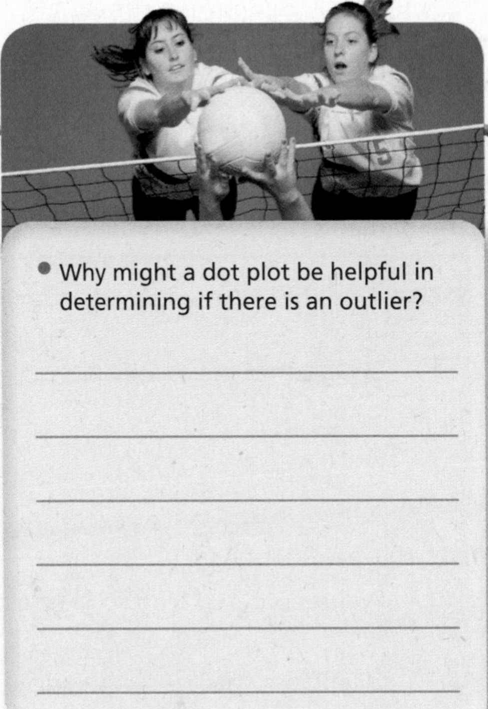

Unlock the Problem

The table gives the number of days that the 24 members of the Garfield Middle School volleyball team were absent from school last year.

Volleyball Team Absences (days)							
4	6	7	4	5	5	3	6
6	7	3	5	8	16	5	4
5	6	5	7	6	4	5	4

- Why might a dot plot be helpful in determining if there is an outlier?

____

Does the data set contain any outliers?

Use a dot plot to find the outlier(s).

STEP 1 Plot the data on the number line.

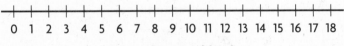

0 1 2 3 4 5 6 7 8 9 10 11 12 13 14 15 16 17 18

Team Absences (days)

STEP 2 Find any values that are much greater or much less than the other values.

Most of the data values are between ______ and ______.

The value ______ is much greater than the rest, so ______ is an outlier.

1. MATHEMATICAL PRACTICE 6 **Explain** What effect do you think an outlier greater than the other data would have on the mean of the data set? Justify your answer.

____

Example The high temperatures for the week in Foxdale, in degrees Fahrenheit, were 43, 43, 45, 42, 26, 43, and 45. The mean of the data is 41°F, and the median is 43°F. Identify the outlier and describe how the mean and median are affected by it.

STEP 1 Draw a dot plot of the data and identify the outlier.

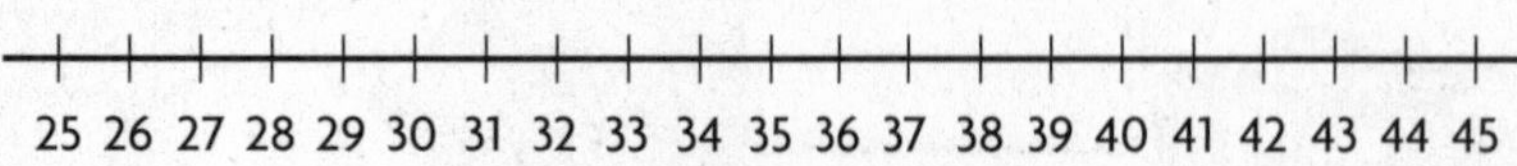

High Temperatures (°F)

The outlier is ______ °F.

STEP 2 Find the mean and median of the temperatures *without* the outlier.

$$\text{Mean} = \frac{43 + \square + \square + \square + \square + \square}{\square}$$

$$= \frac{\square}{6} = \square \text{ °F}$$

Values ordered least to greatest: 42, ______, ______, ______, ______, ______

$$\text{Median} = \frac{43 + \square}{2} = \square \text{ °F}$$

The mean with the outlier is ______ °F, and the mean without the outlier is ______ °F.

The outlier made the mean ____________.

The median with the outlier is ______ °F, and the median without the outlier is ______ °F.

The outlier ____________ affect the median.

2. MATHEMATICAL PRACTICE 2 **Use Reasoning** Explain why the mean without the outlier could be a better description of the data set than the mean with the outlier.

3. If the outlier had been 59°F rather than 26°F, how would the mean have been affected by the outlier? Explain your reasoning.

Name ____________________

Share and Show

MATH BOARD

1. Find the outlier by drawing a dot plot of the data.

Foul Shots Made						
2	3	1	3	2	2	1
15	2	1	3	1	3	

0 1 2 3 4 5 6 7 8 9 10 11 12 13 14 15 16 17 18

Foul Shots Made

The outlier is ______.

2. The prices of the X-40 Laser Printer at five different stores are \$99, \$68, \$98, \$105, and \$90. The mean price is \$92, and the median price is \$98. Identify the outlier and describe how the mean and median are affected by it.

The outlier is ______.

without the outlier: Mean = \$______

Median = \$______

____

Math Talk MATHEMATICAL PRACTICES 2

Reasoning The mean of a certain data set is much greater than the median. Explain how this can happen.

On Your Own

3. Identify the outlier in the data set of melon weights. Then describe the effect the outlier has on the mean and median.

Melon Weights (oz)					
47	45	48	45	49	47
14	45	51	46	47	

The outlier is ______ oz.

____

____

4. MATHEMATICAL PRACTICE 2 **Use Reasoning** In a set of Joanne's test scores, there is an outlier. On the day of one of those tests, Joanne had the flu. Do you think the outlier is greater or less than the rest of her scores? Explain.

____

____

Problem Solving • Applications

Baseball All-Time Stolen Base Leaders	
Player	**Stolen Bases**
Rickey Henderson	1,406
Lou Brock	938
Billy Hamilton	914
Ty Cobb	897
Tim Raines	808

▲ Ty Cobb steals a base.

Use the table for 5–7.

5. Which player's number of stolen bases is an outlier?

6. GO DEEPER What effect does the outlier have on the median of the data set?

7. THINK SMARTER Miguel wrote that the mean of the data set is 992.6. Is this the mean with or without the outlier? Explain how you can tell without doing a calculation.

8. THINK SMARTER Does an outlier have any effect on the mode of a data set? Explain.

9. THINK SMARTER The prices of mesh athletic shorts at five different stores are \$9, \$16, \$18, \$20, and \$22. The mean price is \$17 and the median price is \$18. Identify the outlier and describe how the mean and median are affected by it.

WRITE Math • Show Your Work

Name ____________________

Effects of Outliers

Common Core **COMMON CORE STANDARD—6.SP.B.5d**
Summarize and describe distributions.

1. Identify the outlier in the data set of students in each class. Then describe the effect the outlier has on the mean and median.

Students in Each Class				
30	22	26	21	24
28	23	26	28	12

12; Possible answer: The outlier decreases the mean from about 25.3 to 24. The outlier decreases the median from 26 to 25.

2. Identify the outlier in the data set of pledge amounts. Then describe the effect the outlier has on the mean and median.

Pledge Amounts			
$100	$10	$15	$20
$17	$20	$32	$40

____

____

Problem Solving Real World

3. Duke's science quiz scores are 99, 91, 60, 94, and 95. Describe the effect of the outlier on the mean and median.

____

____

____

____

4. The number of people who attended an art conference for five days was 42, 27, 35, 39, and 96. Describe the effect of the outlier on the mean and median.

____

____

____

5. WRITE *Math* Find or create a set of data that has an outlier. Find the mean and median with and without the outlier. Describe the effect of the outlier on the measures of center.

____

____

Lesson Check (6.SP.B.5d)

1. What is the outlier for the data set?

   19, 19, 27, 21, 77, 18, 23, 29

2. The number of counties in several states is 64, 15, 42, 55, 41, 60, and 52. How does the outlier change the median?

Spiral Review (6.G.A.4, 6.SP.B.4, 6.SP.B.5b, 6.SP.B.5c)

3. Hector covers each face of the pyramid below with construction paper. The area of the base of the pyramid is 28 square feet. What area will he cover with paper?

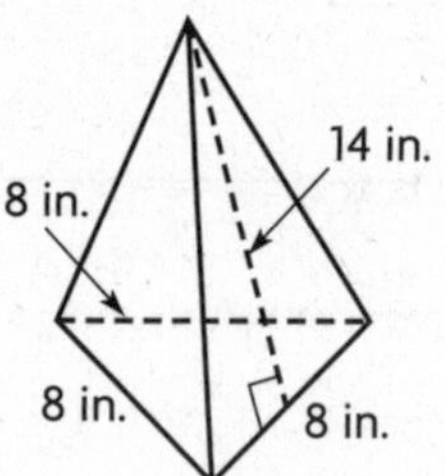

4. Mr. Stevenson measured the heights of several students and recorded his findings in the chart below. How many observations did he complete?

Heights of Students (cm)						
160	138	148	155	159	154	155
140	135	144	142	162	170	171

5. Kendra is making a histogram for the data in the chart. She uses the intervals 0–4, 5–9, 10–14, and 15–19. What should be the height of the longest bar in her histogram?

Lengths of Lizards (cm)				
8	3	12	12	15
19	4	16	9	5
5	10	14	15	8

6. Sharon has 6 photo files on her computer. The numbers below are the sizes of the files in kilobytes. What is the median number of kilobytes for the files?

   69.7, 38.5, 106.3, 109.8, 75.6, 89.4

FOR MORE PRACTICE GO TO THE **Personal Math Trainer**

Name ______________________

Problem Solving • Data Displays

Common Core Statistics and Probability—6.SP.B.4
MATHEMATICAL PRACTICES
MP1, MP3, MP5, MP6

Essential Question How can you use the strategy *draw a diagram* to solve problems involving data?

Unlock the Problem

The 32 students in the History Club are researching their family histories so they can draw family trees. The data set at the right shows the numbers of aunts and uncles the students have. What is the most common number of aunts and uncles among the students in the club?

Use the graphic organizer to help you solve the problem.

Number of Aunts and Uncles							
4	3	2	4	5	7	0	3
1	4	2	4	6	3	5	1
2	5	0	6	3	2	4	5
4	1	3	0	4	2	8	3

Read the Problem

What do I need to find?

I need to find the ______________ number of aunts and uncles among students in the club.

The most common number in the data is the __________.

What information do I need to use?

I need to use the number of ______________ each student has from the table.

How will I use the information?

I can draw a diagram that shows the __________ of each value in the data set. A good way to show the frequency of each value in a data set is a __________.

Solve the Problem

- Make a dot plot of the data.

  Check: Are there the same number of dots on the plot as there are data values?

- Use the plot to determine the mode. The mode is the data value with the ________ dots. The data value with the most dots is _____.

0 1 2 3 4 5 6 7 8 9 10

Number of Aunts and Uncles

So, the most common number of aunts and uncles is _____.

Math Talk MATHEMATICAL PRACTICES 3

Make Arguments Explain why displaying the data in a dot plot is a better choice for solving this problem than displaying the data in a histogram.

Try Another Problem

The table shows the attendance for the Pittsburgh Pirates' last 25 home games of the 2009 baseball season. What percent of the games were attended by at least 25,000 people?

Attendance at 25 Pittsburgh Pirates Games (in thousands)				
12	13	23	33	21
17	17	24	15	27
19	15	18	11	26
20	24	13	16	16
16	19	36	27	17

Read the Problem

What do I need to find?	What information do I need to use?	How will I use the information?

Solve the Problem

So, _______ of the last 25 home games were attended by at least 25,000 people.

Math Talk

MATHEMATICAL PRACTICES 1

Analyze What other type of display might you have used to solve this problem? Explain how you could have used the display.

Name ________________________________

Share and Show

1. The table shows the number of goals scored by the Florida Panthers National Hockey League team in the last 20 games of the 2009 season. What was the most common number of goals the team scored?

Goals Scored									
1	3	3	2	1	1	2	2	2	1
4	5	1	3	3	3	0	2	4	2

First, draw a dot plot of the data.

Next, use the plot to find the mode of the data: The value ______ appears ______ times.

So, the most common number of goals the Panthers scored was ______.

2. Draw a histogram of the hockey data. Use it to find the percent of the games in which the Panthers scored more than 3 goals.

____

3. MATHEMATICAL PRACTICE 5 **Use Appropriate Tools** If you needed to find the mean of a data set, which data display—dot plot or histogram—would you choose? Explain your reasoning.

____

____

____

Unlock the Problem

- √ Read the question carefully to be sure you understand what you need to find.
- √ Check that you plot every data value exactly once.
- √ Check that you answered the question.

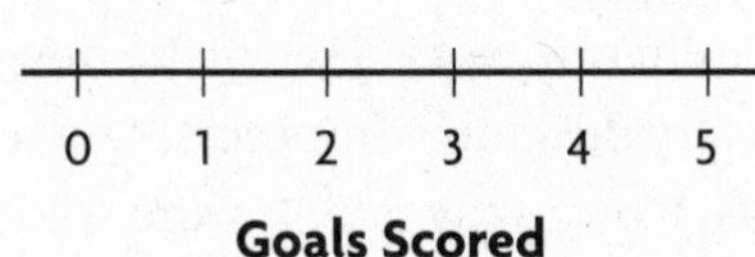

Goals Scored

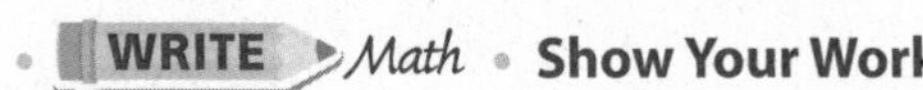

Show Your Work

On Your Own

4. THINK SMARTER Corey collected data on the ages of the parents of his classmates. Make a data display and use it to find the percent of parents at least 30 years old but under 50 years old.

42, 36, 35, 49, 52, 43, 41, 32, 45, 39, 50, 38, 27, 29, 37, 39

___

5. What is the mode of the data in Exercise 4?

___

6. MATHEMATICAL PRACTICE 6 **Explain** An online retail store sold 500 electronic devices in one week. Half of the devices were laptop computers and 20% were desktop computers. The remaining devices sold were tablets. How many tablets were sold? Explain how you found your answer.

___

___

7. GO DEEPER A recipe for punch calls for apple juice and cranberry juice. The ratio of apple juice to cranberry juice is 3:2. Tyrone wants to make at least 20 cups of punch, but no more than 30 cups of punch. Describe two different ways he can use apple juice and cranberry juice to make the punch.

___

___

8. THINK SMARTER The data set shows the total points scored by the middle school basketball team in the last 14 games. What is the most common number of points scored in a game? Explain how to find the answer using a dot plot.

Total Points Scored						
42	36	35	49	52	43	41
32	45	39	50	38	37	39

___

___

Name ___________________________

Problem Solving • Data Displays

COMMON CORE STANDARD—6.SP.B.4
Summarize and describe data distributions.

Read each problem and solve.

1. Josie collected data on the number of siblings her classmates have. Make a data display and determine the percent of Josie's classmates that have more than 2 siblings.

   5, 1, 2, 1, 2, 4, 3, 2, 2, 6

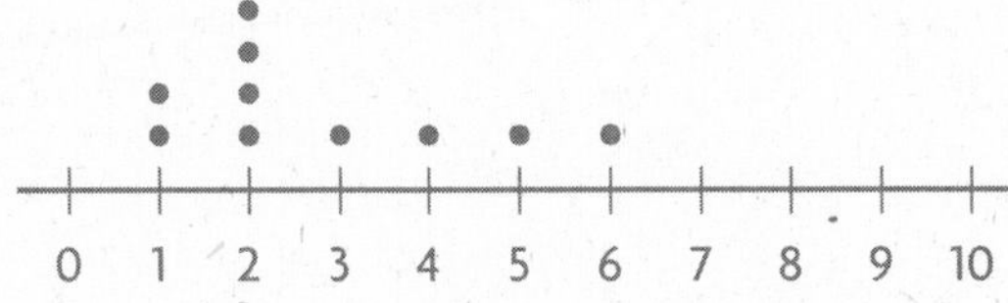

40%

2. The following data show the number of field goals a kicker attempted each game. Make a data display and tell which number of field goals is the mode.

   4, 6, 2, 1, 3, 1, 2, 1, 5, 2, 2, 3

   ____

3. The math exam scores for a class are shown below. Make a data display. What percent of the scores are 90 and greater?

   91, 68, 83, 75, 81, 99, 97, 80, 85, 70, 89, 92, 77, 95, 100, 64, 88, 96, 76, 88

   ____

4. The heights of students in a class are shown below in inches. Make a data display. What percent of the students are taller than 62 inches?

   63, 57, 60, 64, 59, 62, 65, 58, 63, 65, 58, 61, 63, 64

   ____

5. WRITE *Math* Write and solve a problem for which you would use a dot plot or histogram to answer questions about given data.

   ____

   ____

   ____

Lesson Check (6.SP.B.4)

1. The number of student absences is shown below. What is the mode of the absences?

   2, 1, 3, 2, 1, 1, 3, 2, 2, 10, 4, 5, 1, 5, 1

2. Kelly is making a histogram of the number of pets her classmates own. On the histogram, the intervals of the data are 0–1, 2–3, 4–5, 6–7. What is the range of the data?

Spiral Review (6.G.A.2, 6.SP.B.4, 6.SP.B.5c, 6.SP.B.5d)

3. The area of the base of the rectangular prism shown below is 45 square millimeters. The height is $5\frac{1}{2}$ millimeters. What is the volume of the prism?

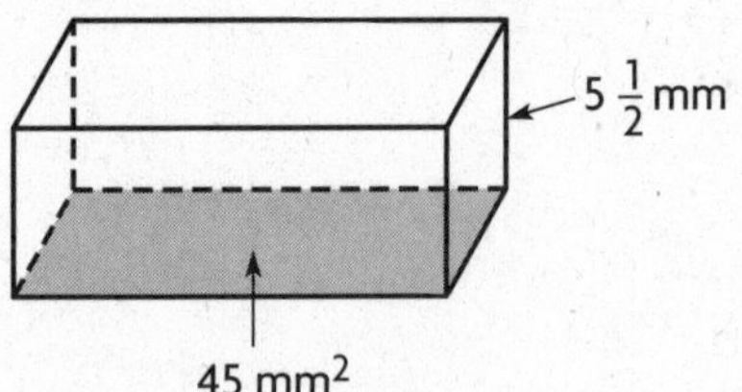

4. The frequency table shows the number of runs scored by the Cougars in 20 of their baseball games. In what percent of the games did they score 5 or fewer runs?

Runs Scored by the Cougars

Number of Runs	Frequency
0–2	14
3–5	3
6–8	2
9–11	1

5. There are 5 plates of bagels. The numbers of bagels on the plates are 8, 10, 9, 10, and 8. Shane rearranges the bagels so that each plate has the same amount. How many bagels are now on each plate?

6. By how much does the median of the data set 12, 9, 9, 11, 14, 28 change if the outlier is removed?

FOR MORE PRACTICE GO TO THE Personal Math Trainer

Name ______________________________

Chapter 12 Review/Test

Personal Math Trainer
Online Assessment and Intervention

1. The data set shows the total number of sandwiches sold each day for 28 days. What is the most common number of sandwiches sold in a day?

Number of sandwiches sold each day						
10	14	11	12	19	13	24
12	12	18	9	17	15	20
20	21	10	13	13	16	19
21	22	18	13	15	14	10

____

2. Michael's teacher asks, "How many items were sold on the first day of the fund raiser?" Explain why this is not a statistical question.

3. Describe the data set by writing the attribute measured, the unit of measure, the likely means of measurement, and the number of observations in the correct location on the chart.

Daily Temperature (°F)						
64	53	61	39	36	43	48

7 | thermometer | degrees Fahrenheit | daily temperature

Attribute	Unit of Measure	Likely Means of Measurement	Number of Observations

GO DIGITAL Assessment Options Chapter Test

4. The numbers of points scored by a football team in 7 different games are 26, 38, 33, 20, 27, 3, and 28. For numbers 4a–4c, select True or False to indicate whether the statement is correct.

4a. The outlier in the data set is 3. ○ True ○ False

4b. The difference between the outlier and the median is 24. ○ True ○ False

4c. The outlier in this set of data affects the mean by increasing it. ○ True ○ False

5. Mr. Jones gave a quiz to his math class. The students' scores are listed in the table. Make a dot plot of the data.

Math Test Scores				
100	90	40	70	70
90	80	50	70	60
90	70	60	80	100
70	50	80	90	90
80	70	80	90	70

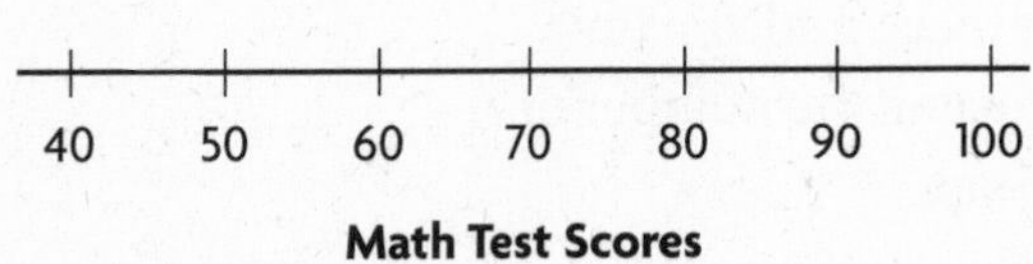

6. Melanie scored 10, 10, 11, and 13 points in her last 4 basketball games.

The mean of the test scores is [10. / 11. / 13.]

The median of the test scores is [10. / 10.5. / 11.]

The mode of the test scores is [10. / 11. / no mode.]

Name ___________________________

7. The Martin family goes out for frozen yogurt to celebrate the last day of school. The costs of their frozen yogurts are \$1, \$1, \$2, and \$4. Select True or False for each statement.

7a. The mean cost for the frozen yogurts can be found by adding each cost and dividing that total by 4. ○ True ○ False

7b. The mean cost of the four frozen yogurts is \$2. ○ True ○ False

7c. The difference between the greatest cost and the mean is \$1. ○ True ○ False

7d. The difference between the least cost and the mean is \$1. ○ True ○ False

8. The histogram shows the amount of time students spent on homework for the week. For numbers 8a–8d, choose True or False to indicate whether the statement is correct.

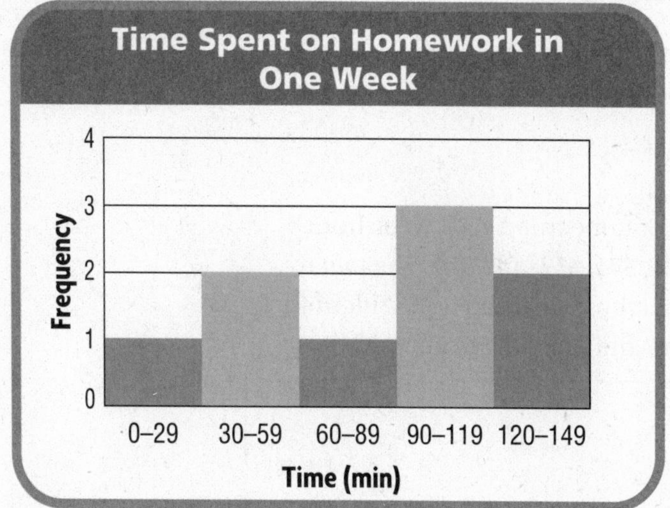

8a. The number of students that spent between 30 minutes and 59 minutes on homework is 2. ○ True ○ False

8b. The greatest number of students spent between 90 minutes and 119 minutes on homework. ○ True ○ False

8c. Five of the students spent less than 60 minutes on homework for the week. ○ True ○ False

8d. Six of the students spent 60 minutes or more on homework for the week. ○ True ○ False

9. The dot plot shows how many games of chess 8 different members of the chess club played in one month. If Jackson is a new member of the chess club, how many games of chess is he likely to play in one month? Explain how the dot plot helped you find the answer.

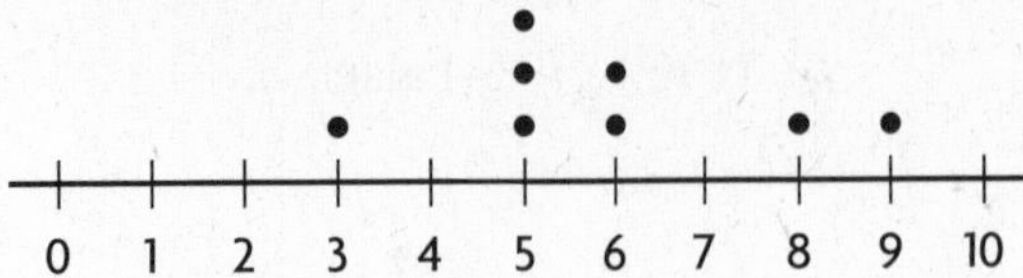

Number of Games Played in One Month

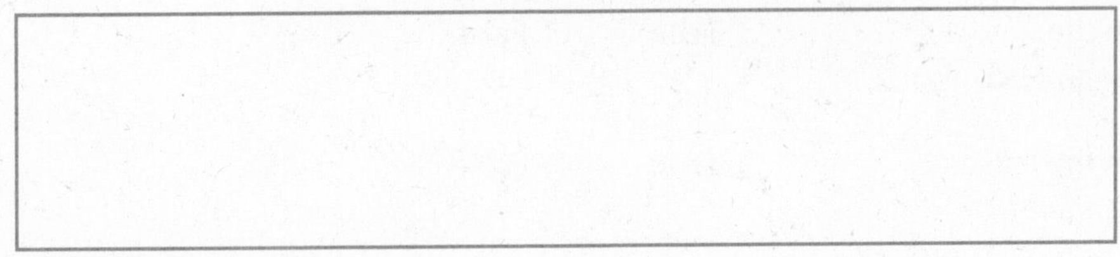

10. Larry is training for a bicycle race. He records how far he rides each day. Find the mode of the data.

Miles Larry Rides each Day					
Monday	Tuesday	Wednesday	Thursday	Friday	Saturday
15	14	12	16	15	15

______

11. GO DEEPER The amounts of money Connor earned each week from mowing lawns for 5 weeks are \$12, \$61, \$71, \$52, and \$64. The mean amount earned is \$52 and the median amount earned is \$61. Identify the outlier and describe how the mean and median are affected by it.

12. The frequency table shows the height, in inches, of 12 basketball players. What fraction of the players are 70 inches or taller?

Heights of Basketball Players	
Inches	Frequency
60-69	3
70-79	6
80-89	3

______

Name ______________________________

13. A teacher surveys her students to find out how much time the students spent eating lunch on Monday.

She uses [hours / minutes / seconds] as the unit of measure.

Monday Lunch Time (min)			
15	18	18	14
15	20	16	15
15	19	15	19

14. For numbers 14a–14d, choose Yes or No to indicate whether the question is a statistical question.

14a. What are the heights of the trees in the park? ○ Yes ○ No

14b. How old are the trees in the park? ○ Yes ○ No

14c. How tall is the cypress tree on the north side of the lake this morning? ○ Yes ○ No

14d. What are the diameters of the trees in the park? ○ Yes ○ No

15. Five friends have 8, 6, 5, 2, and 4 baseball cards to divide equally among themselves.

Each friend will get [4 / 5 / 6] cards.

16. The data set shows the ages of the members of the cheerleading squad. What is the most common age of the members of the squad? Explain how to find the answer using a dot plot.

Ages of Cheerleaders (years)				
8	11	13	12	14
12	10	11	9	11

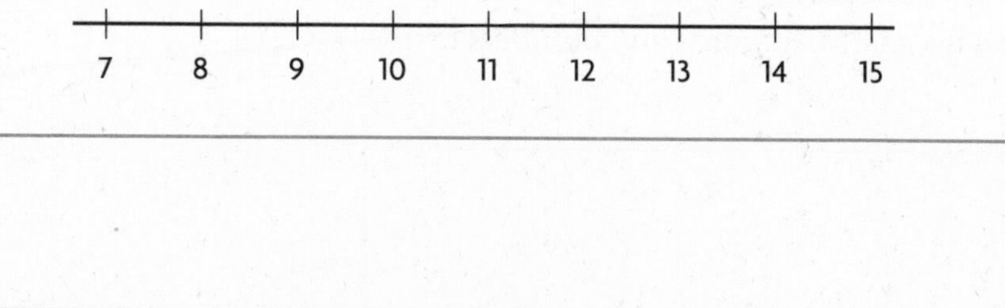

17. THINK SMARTER + The band director kept a record of the number of concert tickets sold by 20 band members. Complete the frequency table by finding the frequency and the relative frequency.

Number of Concert Tickets Sold				
4	6	6	7	7
8	8	9	9	9
8	11	12	11	13
15	14	18	20	19

Number of Concert Tickets Sold

Number of Tickets Sold	Frequency	Relative Frequency (%)
1-5	1	5
6-10		
11-15		
16-20		

18. Gilbert is training for a marathon by running each week. The table shows the distances, in miles, that he ran each week during the first 7 weeks.

Week	1	2	3	4	5	6	7
Distance (miles)	8	10	9	10	15	18	21

Part A

Gilbert set a goal that the mean number of miles he runs in 7 weeks is at least 14 miles. Did Gilbert reach his goal? Use words and numbers to support your answer.

Part B

Suppose Gilbert had run 18 miles during week 5 and 22 miles during week 6. Would he have reached his goal? Use words and numbers to support your answer.

Chapter 13

Variability and Data Distributions

Show What You Know

Personal Math Trainer
Online Assessment and Intervention

Check your understanding of important skills.

Name ____________________

Place the First Digit Tell where to place the first digit. Then divide. (4.NBT.B.6)

1. $4\overline{)872}$ __________ place

2. $8\overline{)256}$ __________ place

Order of Operations Evaluate the expression. (6.EE.A.2)

3. $9 + 4 \times 8$ __________

4. $2 \times 7 + 5$ __________

5. $6 \div (3 - 2)$ __________

6. $(12 - 3^2) \times 5$ __________

7. $2^3 \times (22 \div 2)$ __________

8. $(8 - 2)^2 - 9$ __________

9. $(9 - 2^3) + 8$ __________

10. $(27 + 9) \div 3$ __________

Mean Find the mean for the set of data. (6.SP.B.5c)

11. 285, 420, 345, 390 __________

12. 0.2, 0.23, 0.16, 0.21, 0.2 __________

13. \$33, \$48, \$55, \$52 __________

14. 8.1, 7.2, 8.4 __________

Raina watched two of her friends play a game of darts. She has to pick one of them to be her partner in a tournament. Help Raina figure out which of her friends is a more consistent dart player.

____

____

Dart Scores						
Hector	15	5	7	19	3	19
Marin	12	10	11	11	10	14

Vocabulary Builder

▶ Visualize It

Sort the review words into the chart.

Measures of Center

How Do I Find It?

Find the sum of all the data values and divide the sum by the number of data values.	Order the data and find the middle value or the mean of the two middle values if the number of values is even.	Find the data value(s) that occurs most often.

Review Words

- histogram
- mean
- median
- mode

Preview Words

- box plot
- lower quartile
- interquartile range
- measure of variability
- range
- upper quartile

▶ Understand Vocabulary

Complete the sentences using the preview words.

1. The median of the upper half of a data set is the ____________________.

2. The ____________________ is the difference between the greatest value and the least value in a data set.

3. A(n) ____________________ is a graph that shows the median, quartiles, least value, and greatest value of a data set.

4. A data set's ____________________ is the difference between its upper and lower quartiles.

5. You can describe how spread out a set of data is using a(n) ____________________.

- Interactive Student Edition
- Multimedia *e*Glossary

Chapter 13 Vocabulary

English	Spanish	Page
box plot	diagrama de caja	8
interquartile range	rango intercuartil	45
lower quartile	primer cuartil	54
mean absolute deviation	desviación absoluta respecto a la media	56
measure of variability	medida de dispersión	58
median	mediana	59
range	rango	85
upper quartile	tercer cuartil	107

The difference between the upper and lower quartiles of a data set

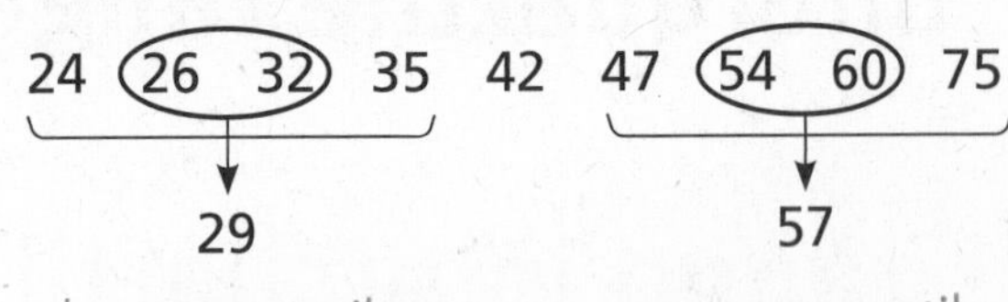

lower quartile upper quartile

The interquartile range is 57 − 29 = 28.

A graph that shows how data are distributed using the median, quartiles, least value, and greatest value

Example:

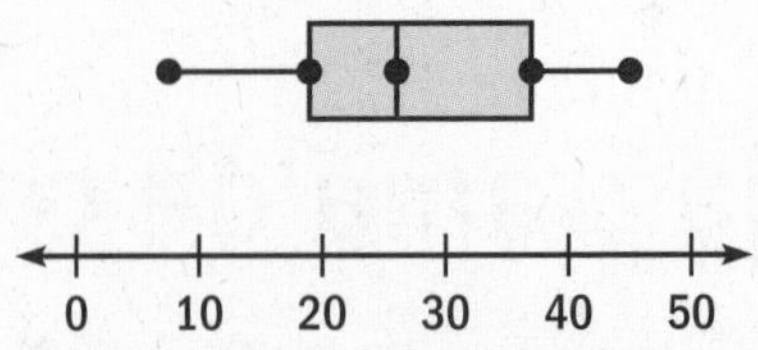

The mean of the distances from each data value in a set to the mean of the set

The median of the lower half of a data set

Example:

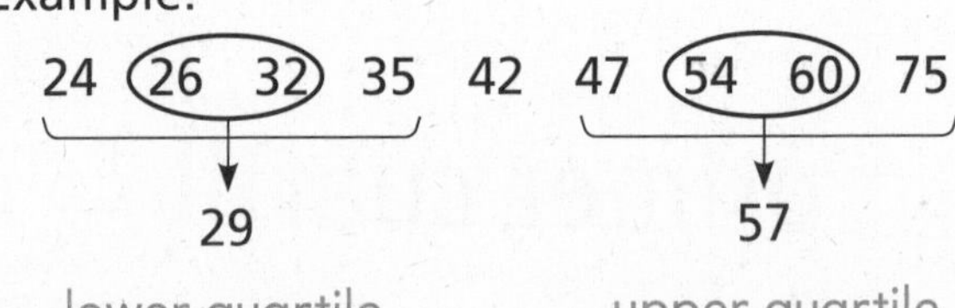

lower quartile upper quartile

The middle value when a data set is written in order from least to greatest, or the mean of the two middle values when there is an even number of items

Example:

8, 17, 21, 23, 26, 29, 34, 40, 45

A single value used to describe how the values in a data set are spread out

Examples: range, interquartile range, mean absolute deviation

The median of the upper half of a data set

Example:

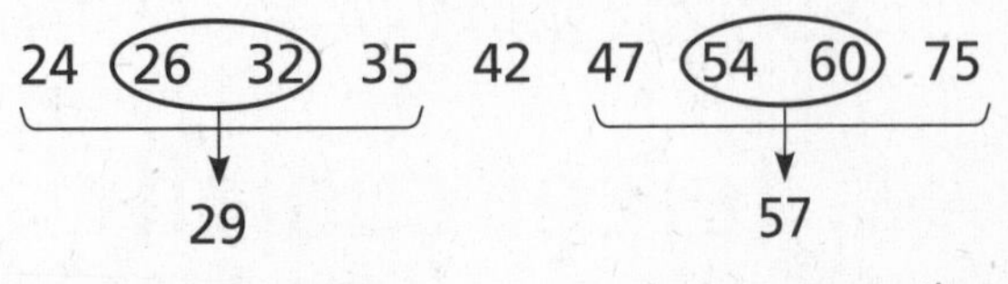

lower quartile upper quartile

The difference between the greatest and least numbers in a data set

Example: The range of the data set 60, 35, 22, 46, 81, 39 is 81 − 22 = 59.

Matchup

Word Box
box plot
interquartile range
lower quartile
mean absolute deviation
measure of variability
median
range
upper quartile

For 2–3 players

Materials

- 1 set of word cards

How to Play

1. Place the cards face-down on a table in even rows. Take turns to play.
2. Choose two cards and turn them face-up.
   - If the cards show a word and its meaning, it's a match. Keep the pair and take another turn.
   - If the cards do not match, turn them over again.
3. The game is over when all cards have been matched. The players count their pairs. The player with the most pairs wins.

The Write Way

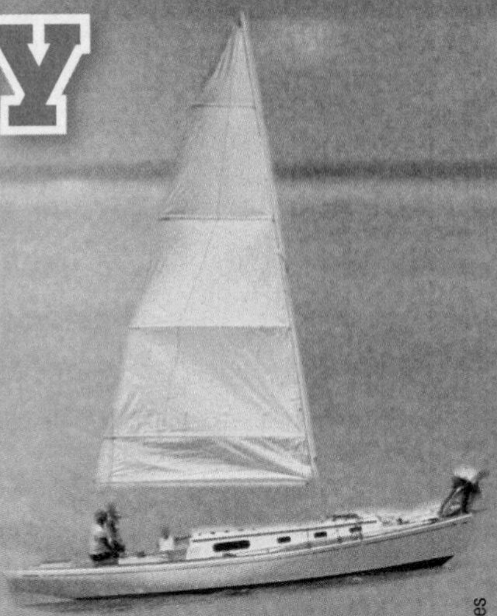

Reflect

Choose one idea. Write about it.

- Summarize the information represented in a box plot.
- Explain in your own words what the *mean absolute deviation* is.
- Joe says that the median for a set of data is a measure of variability. Yossi says that the range is. Identify who is correct and explain why.
- Describe how to calculate the interquartile range for a set of data.

Name ______________________________

Patterns in Data

Essential Question How can you describe overall patterns in a data set?

Common Core **Statistics and Probability—6.SP.B.5c** *Also 6.SP.A.2*

MATHEMATICAL PRACTICES
MP7, MP8

CONNECT Seeing data sets in graphs, such as dot plots and histograms, can help you find and understand patterns in the data.

Unlock the Problem

Many lakes and ponds contain freshwater fish species such as bass, pike, bluegill, and trout. Jacob and his friends went fishing at a nearby lake. The dot plot shows the sizes of the fish that the friends caught. The lengths are rounded to the nearest inch. What patterns do you see in the data?

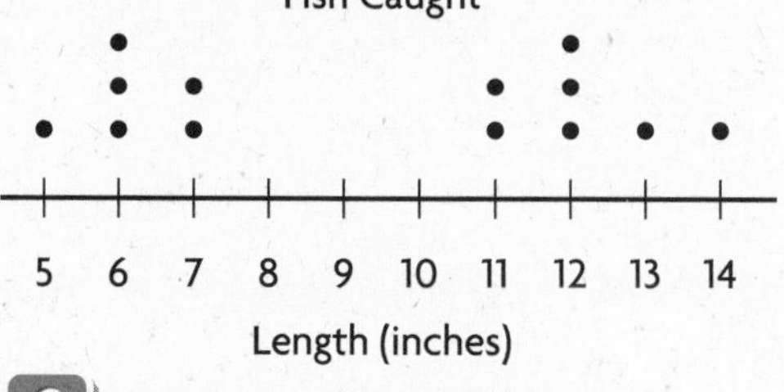

- Circle any spaces with no data.
- Place a box around any groups of data.

Analyze the dot plot.

A *gap* is an interval that contains no data.

Does the dot plot contain any gaps?

If so, where? ______________________

A *cluster* is a group of data points that lie within a small interval.

There is a cluster from ______ to ______ and another cluster from ______ to ______.

So, there were no fish from ______ to ______ inches long,

and there were two clusters of fish measuring from ______

to ______ inches long and from ______ to ______ inches long.

MATHEMATICAL PRACTICES 7

Look for Structure What is the mode(s) of the data? Explain how you know.

1. Summarize the information shown in the dot plot.

____

____

2. MATHEMATICAL PRACTICE 8 **Draw Conclusions** What conclusion can you draw about why the data might have this pattern?

____

____

You can also analyze patterns in data that are displayed in histograms. Some data sets have symmetry about a peak, while others do not.

Example Analyze a histogram.

Erica made this histogram to show the weights of the pumpkins grown at her father's farm in October. What patterns do you see in the data?

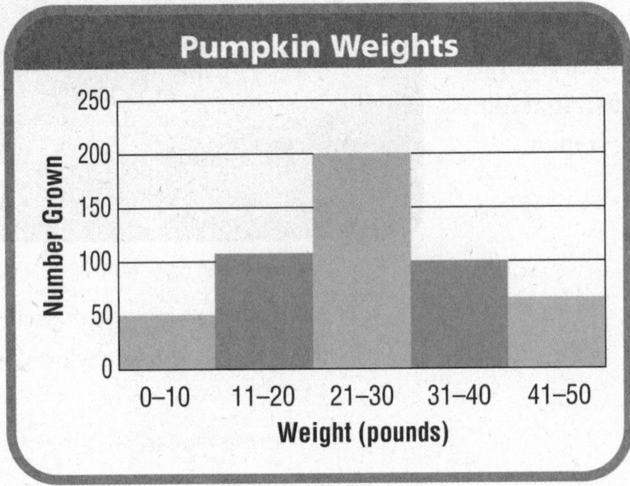

STEP 1 Identify any peaks in the data.

The histogram has ______ peak(s).

The interval representing the greatest number of pumpkins is for weights between ______ and ______ pounds.

STEP 2 Describe how the data changes across the intervals.

The number of pumpkins increases from 0 to ______ pounds and ____________ from 31 to 50 pounds.

STEP 3 Describe any symmetry the graph has.

If I draw a vertical line through the interval for ______ to ______ pounds, the left and right sides of the histogram are very close to being mirror images. The histogram ____________ symmetry.

Math Idea

A graph can have symmetry if you can draw a line through it so that the two sides of the graph are almost mirror images of each other.

So, the data values increase to one peak in the interval for ______ to ______ pounds and then decrease. The data set ____________ symmetry about the peak.

Name ______________________________

Share and Show MATH BOARD

For 1–3, use the dot plot.

1. The dot plot shows the number of paintings students in the art club displayed at the art show. Does the dot plot contain any gaps?

   If so, where? ______________________________

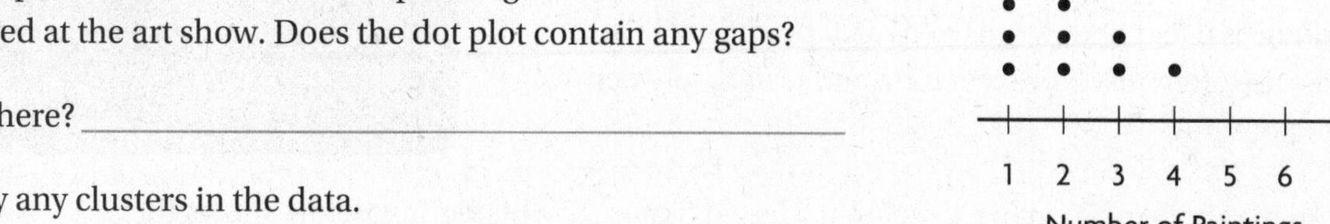

2. Identify any clusters in the data.

   ____

3. Summarize the information in the dot plot.

   ____

   ____

On Your Own

4. GO DEEPER What patterns do you see in the histogram data?

   ____

   ____

   ____

   ____

   ____

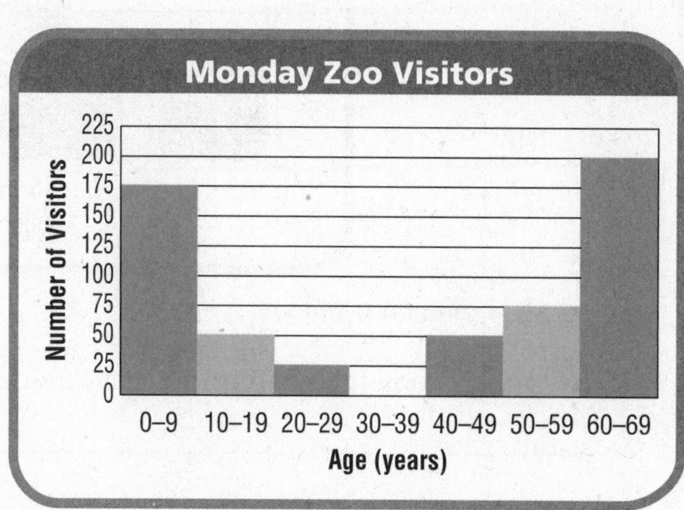

5. THINK SMARTER The dot plot shows the number of errors made by a baseball team in the first 16 games of the season. For numbers 5a-5e, choose Yes or No to indicate whether the statement is correct.

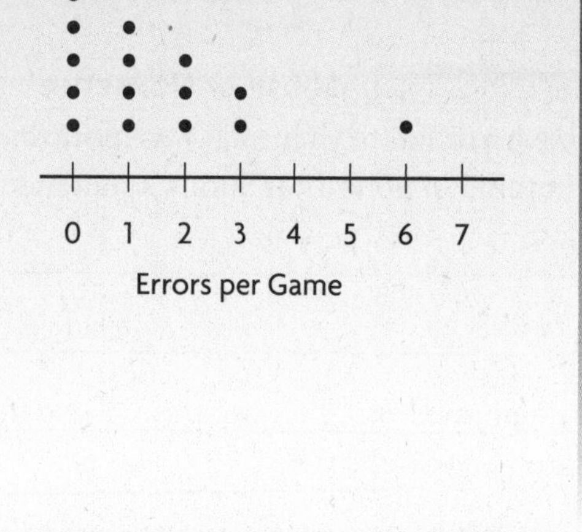

5a. There is a gap from 4 to 5. ○ Yes ○ No

5b. There is a peak at 0. ○ Yes ○ No

5c. The dot plot has symmetry. ○ Yes ○ No

5d. There are two modes. ○ Yes ○ No

5e. There is one cluster. ○ Yes ○ No

Connect to Science

Big Cats

There are 41 species of cats living in the world today. Wild cats live in places as different as deserts and the cold forests of Siberia, and they come in many sizes. Siberian tigers may be as long as 9 feet and weigh over 2,000 pounds, while bobcats are often just 2 to 3 feet long and weigh between 15 and 30 pounds.

You can find bobcats in many zoos in the United States. The histogram below shows the weights of several bobcats. The weights are rounded to the nearest pound.

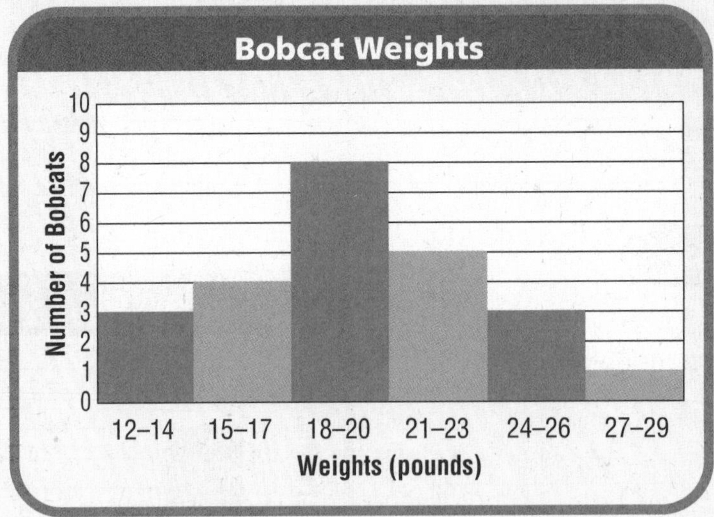

Use the histogram for 6 and 7.

6. MATHEMATICAL PRACTICE 7 **Look for a Pattern** Describe the overall shape of the histogram.

7. THINKSMARTER **Sense or Nonsense?** Sunny says that the graph might have a different shape if it was redrawn as a bar graph with one bar for each number of pounds. Is Sunny's statement sense or nonsense? Explain.

Name ______________________

Patterns in Data

Common Core **COMMON CORE STANDARD—6.SP.B.5c**
Summarize and describe distributions.

For 1–2, use the dot plot.

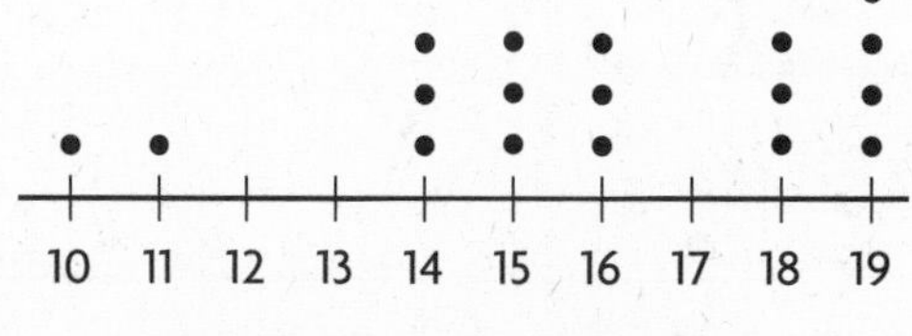

Omelets Ordered Per Day

1. The dot plot shows the number of omelets ordered at Paul's Restaurant each day. Does the dot plot contain any gaps?

   Yes; from 12 to 13, and at 17

2. Identify any clusters in the data.

   ____

For 3–4, use the histogram.

3. The histogram shows the number of people that visited a local shop each day in January. How many peaks does the histogram have?

   ____

4. Describe how the data values change across the intervals.

   ____

Problem Solving Real World

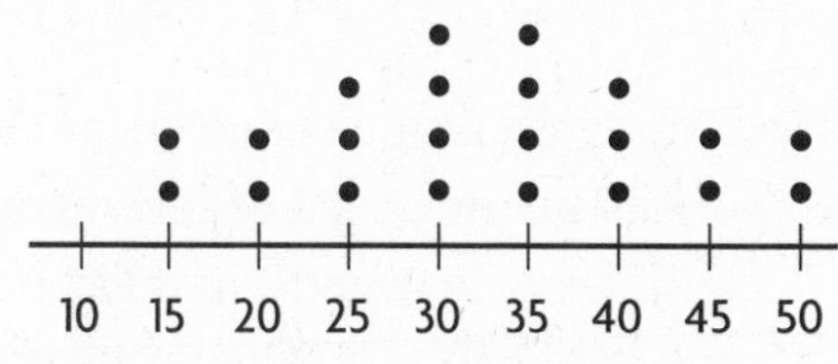

Gift Cards Purchased This Week

5. Look at the dot plot at the right. Does the graph have symmetry? Explain.

   ____

6. WRITE ▸ *Math* A histogram that shows the ages of students at a library has intervals 1–5, 6–10, 11–15, 16–20, and 21–25. There is a peak at 11–15 years and the graph is symmetric. Sketch what the histogram could look like and describe the patterns you see in the data.

   ____

Lesson Check (6.SP.B.5c)

1. What interval in the histogram has the greatest frequency?

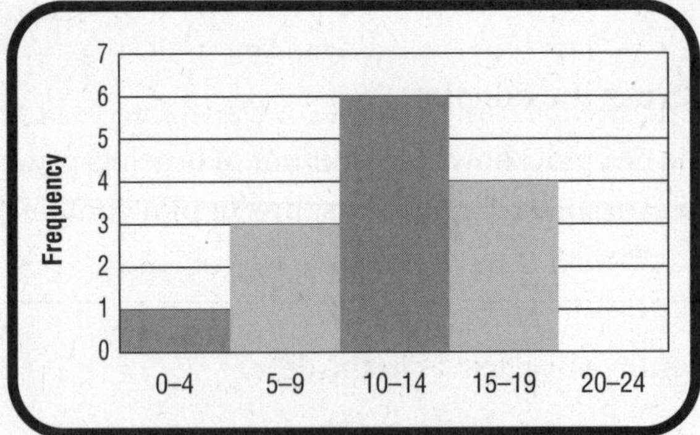

2. Meg makes a dot plot for the data 9, 9, 4, 5, 5, 3, 4, 5, 3, 8, 8, 5. Where does a gap occur?

Spiral Review (6.G.A.2, 6.SP.B.4, 6.SP.B.5c)

3. A rectangular fish tank is 20 inches long, 12 inches wide, and 20 inches tall. If the tank is filled halfway with water, how much water is in the tank?

4. Look at the histogram below. How many students scored an 81 or higher on the math test?

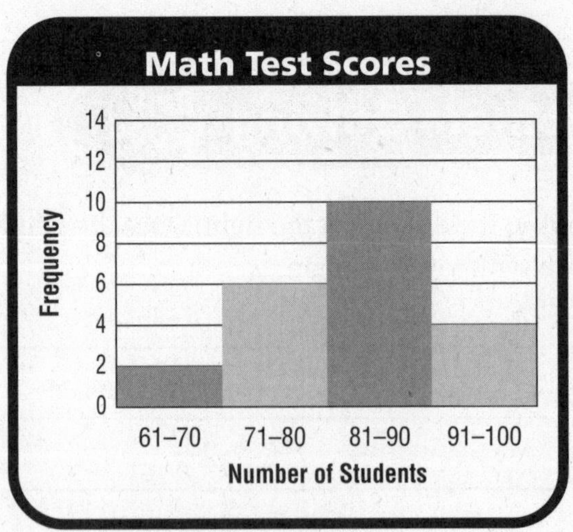

5. The Little League coach uses a radar gun to measure the speed of several of Kyle's baseball pitches. The speeds, in miles per hour, are 52, 48, 63, 47, 47. What is the median of Kyle's pitch speeds?

FOR MORE PRACTICE GO TO THE **Personal Math Trainer**

Name ______________________

Box Plots

Essential Question How can you use box plots to display data?

Statistics and Probability—6.SP.B.4

MATHEMATICAL PRACTICES
MP1, MP3, MP6

The median is the middle value, or the mean of the two middle values, when data is written in order. The **lower quartile** is the median of the lower half of a data set, and the **upper quartile** is the median of the upper half of a data set.

Unlock the Problem — Real World

In 1885, a pair of jeans cost $1.50. Today, the cost of jeans varies greatly. The chart lists the prices of jeans at several different stores. What are the median, lower quartile, and upper quartile of the data?

Prices of Jeans								
\$35	\$28	\$42	\$50	\$24	\$75	\$47	\$32	\$60

Find the median, lower quartile, and upper quartile.

STEP 1 Order the numbers from least to greatest. — \$24 \$28 \$32 \$35 \$42 \$47 \$50 \$60 \$75

STEP 2 Circle the middle number, or the median. — The median is \$______.

STEP 3 Calculate the upper and lower quartiles.

Find the median of each half of the data set.

Think: If a data set has an even number of values, the median is the mean of the two middle values.

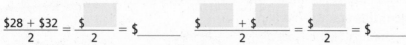

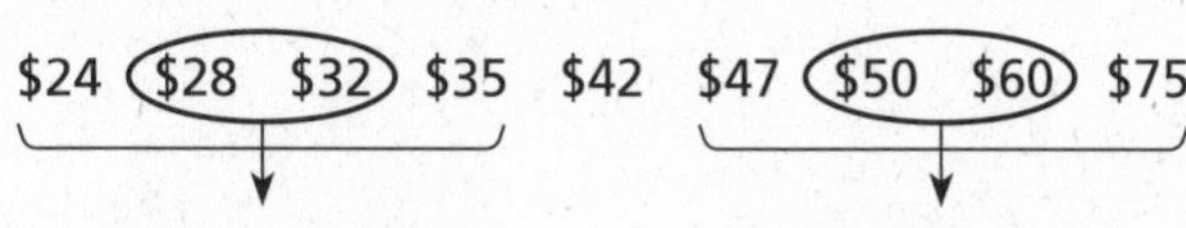

lower quartile — upper quartile

$\frac{\$28 + \$32}{2} = \frac{\$\_\_\_}{2} = \$\_\_\_\_\_\_$ $\frac{\$\_\_\_ + \$\_\_\_}{2} = \frac{\$\_\_\_}{2} = \$\_\_\_\_\_\_$

ERROR Alert

When a data set has an odd number of values, do not include the median when finding the lower and upper quartiles.

So, the median is \$______, the lower quartile is \$______, and the upper quartile is \$______.

A **box plot** is a type of graph that shows how data are distributed by using the least value, the lower quartile, the median, the upper quartile, and the greatest value. Below is a box plot showing the data for jean prices from the previous page.

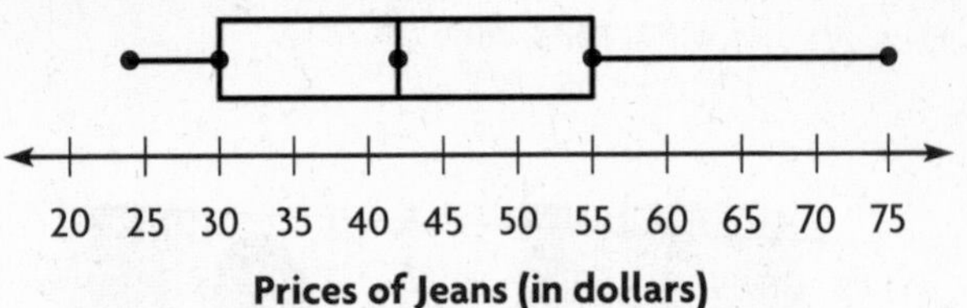

Example Make a box plot.

The data set below represents the ages of the top ten finishers in a 5K race. Use the data to make a box plot.

Ages of Top 10 Runners (in years)									
33	18	21	23	35	19	38	30	23	25

STEP 1 Order the data from least to greatest. Then find the median and the lower and upper quartiles.

18, ______, ______, ______, ______, ______, ______, ______, ______, ______

Median = $\frac{\square + \square}{2}$ = ______ years

Lower quartile = ______ years The lower quartile is the median of the lower half of the data set, which includes the values from 18 to 23.

Upper quartile = ______ years The upper quartile is the median of the upper half of the data set, which includes the values from 25 to 38.

STEP 2 Draw a number line. Above the number line, plot a point for the least value, the lower quartile, the median, the upper quartile, and the greatest value.

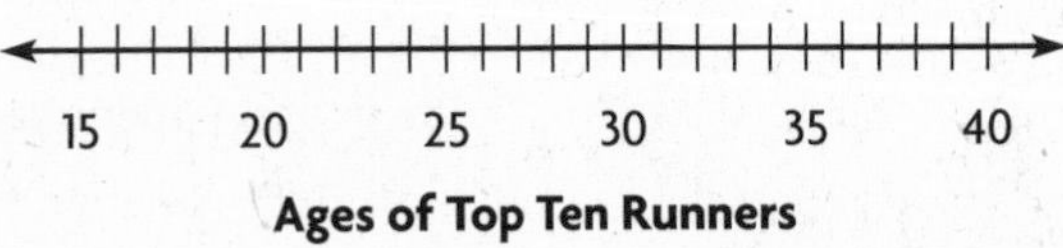

STEP 3 Draw a box from the lower to upper quartile. Inside the box, draw a vertical line segment through the median. Then draw line segments from the box to the least and greatest values.

MATHEMATICAL PRACTICES 6

Describe the steps for making a box plot.

- MATHEMATICAL PRACTICE 6 **Explain** Would the box plot change if the data point for 38 years were replaced with 40 years? Explain.

______

Name ______________________

Find the median, lower quartile, and upper quartile of the data.

1. the scores of 11 students on a geography quiz:
87, 72, 80, 95, 86, 80, 78, 92, 88, 76, 90

Order the data from least to greatest. 72, 76, 78, 80, 80, 86, 87, 88, 90, 92, 95

median: ______ lower quartile: ______ upper quartile: ______

2. the lengths, in seconds, of 9 videos posted online:
50, 46, 51, 60, 62, 50, 65, 48, 53

median: ______ lower quartile: ______ upper quartile: ______

3. Make a box plot to display the data set in Exercise 2.

45 50 55 60 65 70

Lengths of Online Videos (seconds)

MATHEMATICAL PRACTICES 6

Compare How are box plots and dot plots similar? How are they different?

Find the median, lower quartile, and upper quartile of the data.

4. 13, 24, 37, 25, 56, 49, 43, 20, 24

median: ______

lower quartile: ______

upper quartile: ______

5. 61, 23, 49, 60, 83, 56, 51, 64, 84, 27

median: ______

lower quartile: ______

upper quartile: ______

6. The chart shows the height of trees in a park. Display the data in a box plot.

Tree Heights (feet)											
8	12	20	30	25	18	18	8	10	28	26	29

5 10 15 20 25 30 35

Tree Heights (feet)

7. MATHEMATICAL PRACTICE 1 **Analyze** Eric made this box plot for the data set below. Explain his error.

Number of Books Read								
5	13	22	8	31	37	25	24	10

____

Problem Solving • Applications

Pose a Problem

8. The box plots show the number of flights delayed per day for two different airlines. Which data set is more spread out?

Find the distance between the least and greatest values for each data set.

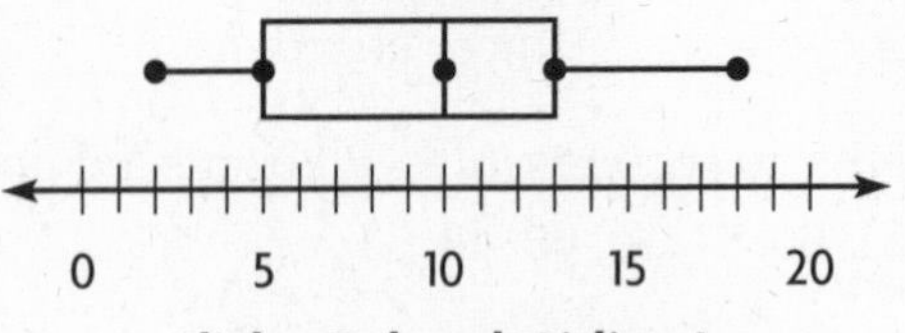

Flights Delayed: Airline A

Airline A: greatest value − least value =

______ − ______ = ______

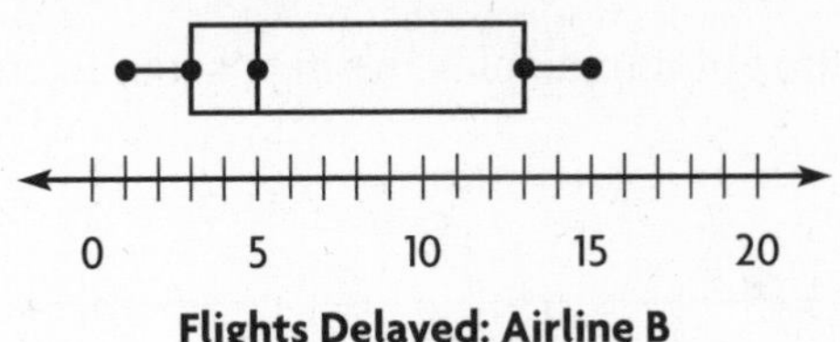

Flights Delayed: Airline B

Airline B: greatest value − least value =

______ − ______ = ______

So, the data for __________ is more spread out.

Write a new problem that can be solved using the data in the box plots.

Pose a Problem

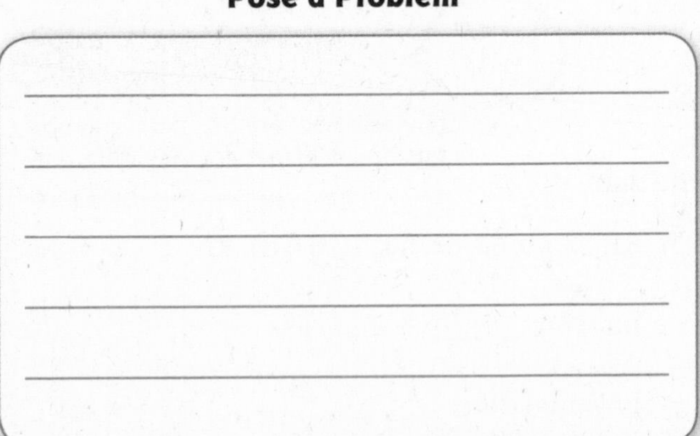

Solve Your Problem

9. THINKSMARTER The data set shows the cost of the dinner specials at a restaurant on Friday night.

Cost of Dinner Specials ($)										
30	24	24	16	24	25	19	28	18	19	26

The median is [19. / 24. / 25.] The lower quartile is [16. / 18. / 19.] The upper quartile is [26. / 28. / 30.]

Name ____________________

Box Plots

Common Core **COMMON CORE STANDARD—6.SP.B.4**
Summarize and describe distributions.

Find the median, lower quartile, and upper quartile of the data.

1. the amounts of juice in 12 glasses, in fluid ounces:

11, 8, 4, 9, 12, 14, 9, 16, 15, 11, 10, 7

Order the data from least to greatest: 4, 7, 8, 9, 9, 10, 11, 11, 12, 14, 15, 16

median: 10.5 lower quartile: 8.5 upper quartile: 13

2. the lengths of 10 pencils, in centimeters:

18, 15, 4, 9, 14, 17, 16, 6, 8, 10

median: ______ lower quartile: ______ upper quartile: ______

3. Make a box plot to display the data set in Exercise 2.

Lengths of Pencils (centimeters)

4. The numbers of students on several teams are 9, 4, 5, 10, 11, 9, 8, and 6. Make a box plot for the data.

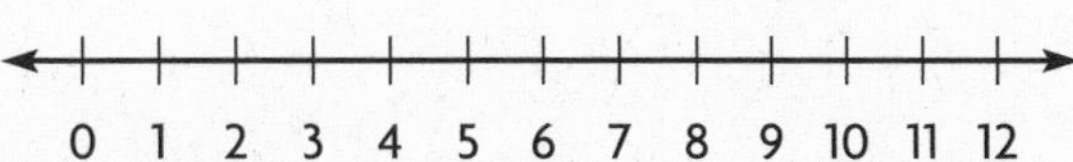

Number of Students on a Team

Problem Solving Real World

5. The amounts spent at a gift shop today are \$19, \$30, \$28, \$22, \$20, \$26, and \$26. What is the median? What is the lower quartile?

____

6. The weights of six puppies in ounces are 8, 5, 7, 5, 6, and 9. What is the upper quartile of the data?

____

7. WRITE Math Draw a box plot to display this data: 81, 22, 34, 55, 76, 20, 56.

____

____

Lesson Check (6.SP.B.4)

1. The values in a data set are 15, 7, 11, 12, 6, 3, 10, and 6. Where would you draw the box in a box plot for the data?

2. What is the lower quartile of the following data set?

   22, 27, 14, 21, 22, 26, 18

Spiral Review (6.SP.A.1, 6.SP.B.5c, 6.SP.B.5d)

3. Jenn says that "What is the average number of school lunches bought per day?" is a statistical question. Lisa says that "How many lunches did Mark buy this week?" is a statistical question. Who is NOT correct?

4. The prices of several chairs are $89, $76, $81, $91, $88, and $70. What is the mean of the chair prices?

5. By how much does the mean of the following data set change if the outlier is removed?

   13, 19, 16, 40, 12

6. Where in the dot plot does a cluster occur?

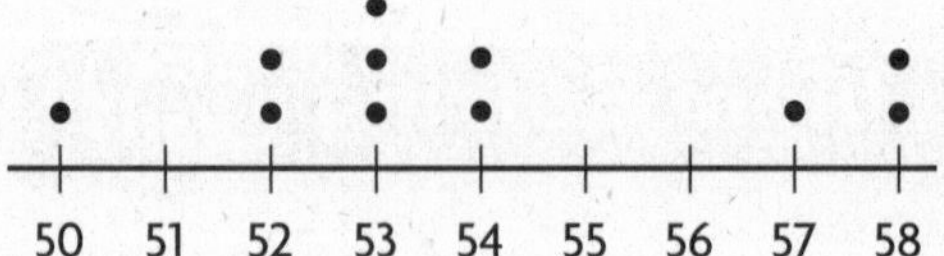

Name ______________________

Mean Absolute Deviation

Essential Question How do you calculate the mean absolute deviation of a data set?

Common Core **Statistics and Probability—6.SP.B.5c**

MATHEMATICAL PRACTICES
MP2, MP3, MP4, MP6

One way to describe a set of data is with the mean. However, two data sets may have the same mean but look very different when graphed. When interpreting data sets, it is important to consider how far away the data values are from the mean.

Investigate

Hands On

Materials ■ counters, large number line from 0–10

The number of magazine subscriptions sold by two teams of students for a drama club fundraiser is shown below. The mean number of subscriptions for each team is 4.

Team A				
3	3	4	5	5

Team B				
0	1	4	7	8

A. Make a dot plot of each data set using counters for the dots. Draw a vertical line through the mean.

B. Count to find the distance between each counter and the mean. Write the distance underneath each counter.

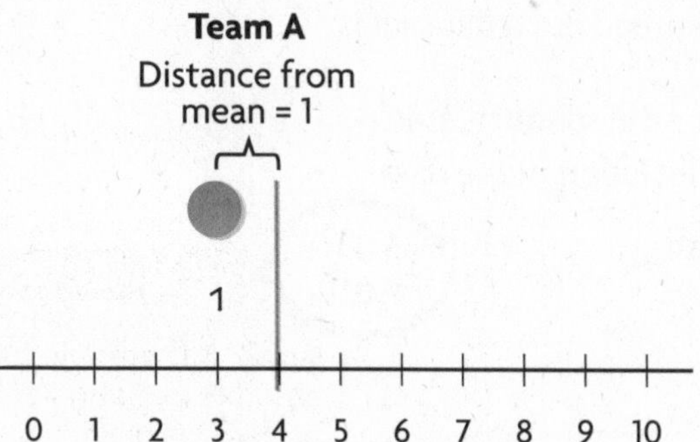

C. Find the mean of the distances for each data set.

Team A

$$\frac{1 + \_\_\_ + \_\_\_ + \_\_\_ + \_\_\_}{5} = \frac{\_\_\_}{5} = \_\_\_$$

Team B

$$\frac{\_\_\_ + \_\_\_ + \_\_\_ + \_\_\_ + \_\_\_}{\_\_\_} = \frac{\_\_\_}{\_\_\_} = \_\_\_$$

Draw Conclusions

1. THINKSMARTER Which data set, Team A or B, looks more spread out in your dot plots? Which data set had a greater average distance from the mean? Explain how these two facts are connected.

____

____

2. MATHEMATICAL PRACTICE 2 **Reason Quantitatively** The table shows the average distance from the mean for the heights of players on two basketball teams. Tell which set of heights is more spread out. Explain how you know.

Heights of Players

Team	Average Distance from Mean (in.)
Chargers	2.8
Wolverines	1.5

____

____

____

Make Connections

The mean of the distances of data values from the mean of the data set is called the **mean absolute deviation**. As you learned in the Investigation, mean absolute deviation is a way of describing how spread out a data set is.

The dot plot shows the ages of gymnasts registered for the school team. The mean of the ages is 10. Find the mean absolute deviation of the data.

STEP 1 Label each dot with its distance from the mean.

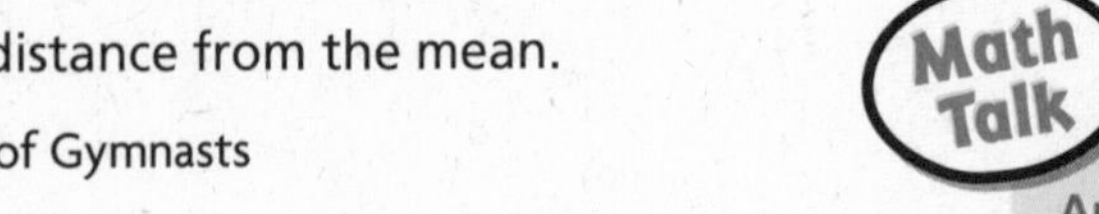

MATHEMATICAL PRACTICES 3

Apply Is it possible for the mean absolute deviation of a data set to be zero? Explain.

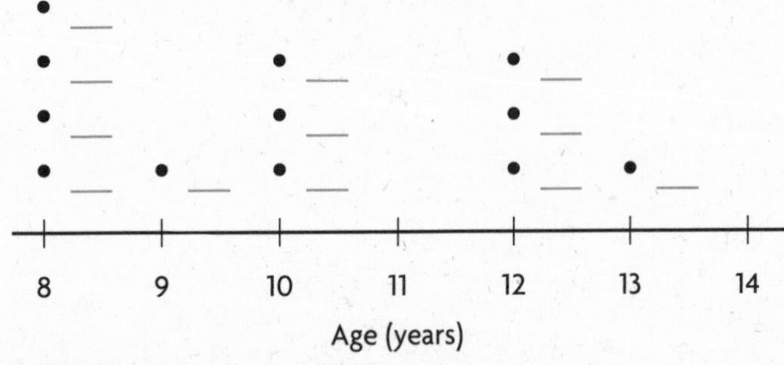

STEP 2 Find the mean of the distances.

$\dfrac{\square + \square + \square + \square + \square + \square + \square + \square + \square + \square + \square + \square}{\square} = \dfrac{\square}{\square} = \square$

So, the mean absolute deviation of the data is ______ years.

Name ________________

Share and Show MATH BOARD

Use counters, a dot plot, or *i*Tools to find the mean absolute deviation of the data.

1. Find the mean absolute deviation for both data sets. Explain which data set is more spread out.

the number of laps Shawna swam on 5 different days:

5, 6, 6, 8, 10

mean = 7

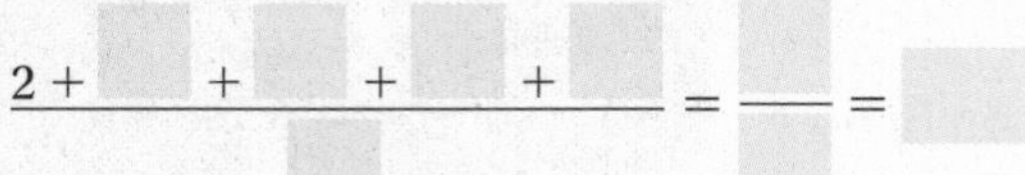

mean absolute deviation = ______ laps

the number of laps Lara swam on 5 different days:

1, 3, 7, 11, 13

mean = 7

mean absolute deviation = ______ laps

The data set of ____________ laps is more spread out because the mean absolute deviation of her data is ____________.

Use the dot plot to find the mean absolute deviation of the data.

2. mean = 7 books

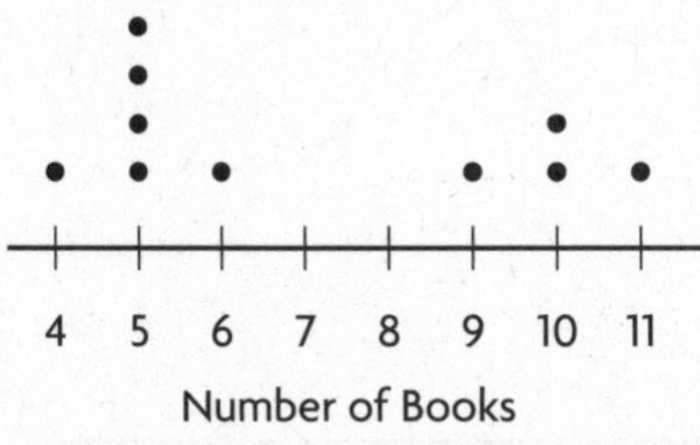

mean absolute deviation = ____________

3. mean = 29 pounds

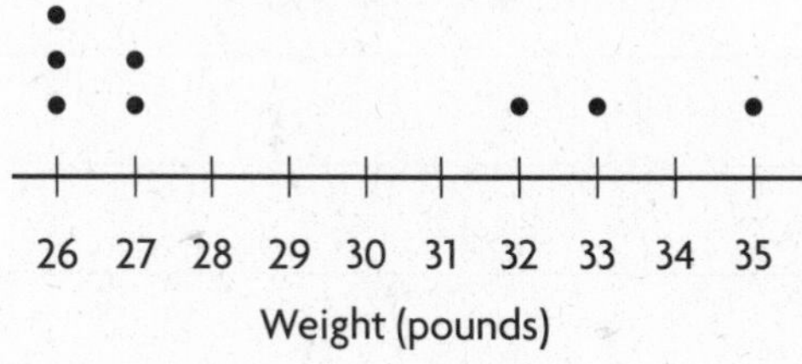

mean absolute deviation = ____________

4. WRITE Math The mean absolute deviation of the number of daily visits to Scott's website for February is 167.7. In March, the absolute mean deviation is 235.9. In which month did the number of visits to Scott's website vary more? Explain how you know.

____

5. MATHEMATICAL PRACTICE 4 **Write an Inequality** **Algebra** In April, the data for Scott's website visits are less spread out than they were in February. Use a to represent the mean absolute deviation for April. Write an inequality to describe the possible values of a.

____

Problem Solving • Applications

6. GO DEEPER Use the table.

Days of Precipitation											
Jan	Feb	Mar	Apr	May	Jun	Jul	Aug	Sep	Oct	Nov	Dec
10	12	13	18	10	8	7	6	16	14	8	10

The mean of the data is 11. What is the mean absolute deviation of the data?

____

7. THINK SMARTER Suppose all of the players on a basketball team had the same height. Explain how you could use reasoning to find the mean absolute deviation of the players' heights.

____

____

____

8. MATHEMATICAL PRACTICE 6 **Explain** Tell how an outlier that is much greater than the mean would affect the mean absolute deviation of the data set. Explain your reasoning.

____

____

____

9. THINK SMARTER The data set shows the number of soccer goals scored by players in 3 games.

Number of Goals Scored			
Player A	1	2	1
Player B	2	2	2
Player C	3	2	1

For numbers 9a–9c, choose Yes or No to indicate whether the statement is correct.

9a. The mean absolute deviation of Player A is 1. ○ Yes ○ No

9b. The mean absolute deviation of Player B is 0. ○ Yes ○ No

9c. The mean absolute deviation of Player C is greater than the mean absolute deviation of Player A. ○ Yes ○ No

Name ______________________________

Mean Absolute Deviation

Common Core **COMMON CORE STANDARD—6.SP.B.5c**
Summarize and describe distributions.

Use counters and a dot plot to find the mean absolute deviation of the data.

1. the number of hours Maggie spent practicing soccer for 4 different weeks:

9, 6, 6, 7

mean = 7 hours

$\frac{2 + 1 + 1 + 0}{4} = \frac{4}{4} = 1$

mean absolute deviation = 1 hour

2. the heights of 7 people in inches:

60, 64, 58, 60, 70, 71, 65

mean = 64 inches

mean absolute deviation = ______________

Use the dot plot to find the mean absolute deviation of the data.

3. mean = 10

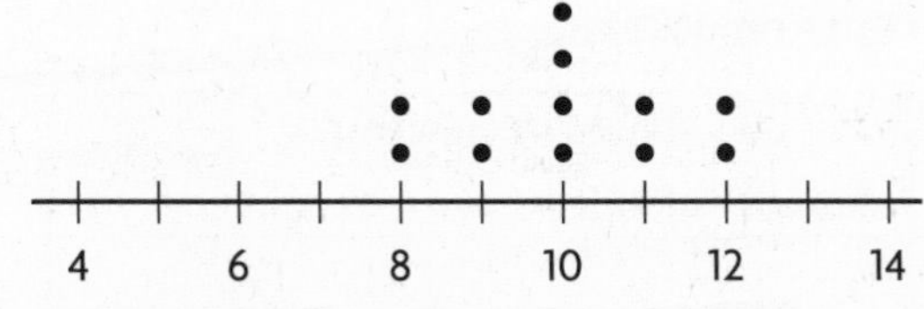

Ages of Students in Dance Class

mean absolute deviation = ______________

4. mean = 8

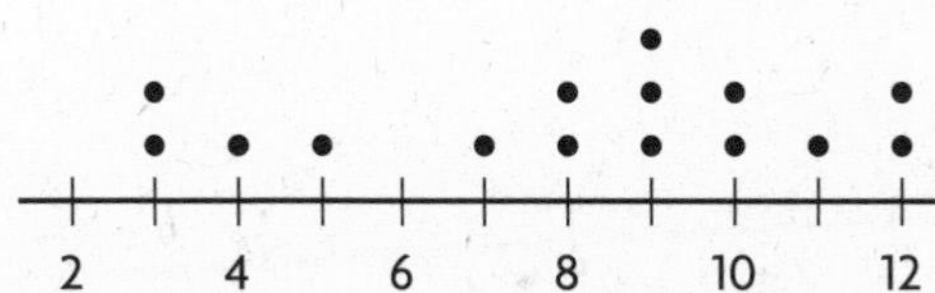

Weekly Hours Spent Doing Homework

mean absolute deviation = ______________

Problem Solving Real World

5. In science class, Troy found the mass, in grams, of 6 samples to be 10, 12, 7, 8, 5, and 6. What is the mean absolute deviation?

____

6. Five recorded temperatures are 71°F, 64°F, 72°F, 81°F, and 67°F. What is the mean absolute deviation?

____

7. WRITE *Math* Make a dot plot of the following data: 10, 10, 11, 12, 12, 13, 13, 15. Use the dot plot to find the mean absolute deviation.

____

____

Lesson Check (6.SP.B.5c)

1. Six test grades are 86, 88, 92, 90, 82, and 84. The mean of the data is 87. What is the mean absolute deviation?

2. Eight heights in inches are 42, 36, 44, 46, 48, 42, 48, and 46. The mean of the data is 44. What is the mean absolute deviation?

Spiral Review (6.G.A.2, 6.SP.B.4)

3. What is the volume of a rectangular prism with dimensions 4 meters, $1\frac{1}{2}$ meters, and 5 meters?

4. Carrie is making a frequency table showing the number of miles she walked each day during the 30 days of September. What value should she write in the Frequency column for 9 to 11 miles?

Carrie's Daily Walks	
Number of Miles	Frequency
0–2	17
3–5	8
6–8	4
9–11	?

5. The following data shows the number of laps each student completed. What number of laps is the mode?

9, 6, 7, 8, 5, 1, 8, 10

6. What is the upper quartile of the following data?

43, 48, 55, 50, 58, 49, 38, 42, 50

FOR MORE PRACTICE GO TO THE **Personal Math Trainer**

Name ______________________________

Measures of Variability

Essential Question How can you summarize a data set by using range, interquartile range, and mean absolute deviation?

Common Core Statistics and Probability— 6.SP.B.5c *Also 6.SP.A.2, 6.SP.A.3*
MATHEMATICAL PRACTICES
MP6, MP7

CONNECT A **measure of variability** is a single value used to describe how spread out a set of data values are. The mean absolute deviation is a measure of variability.

Unlock the Problem

In gym class, the students recorded how far they could jump. The data set below gives the distances in inches that Manuel jumped. What is the mean absolute deviation of the data set?

Manuel's Jumps (in inches)					
54	58	56	59	60	55

Find the mean absolute deviation.

STEP 1 Find the mean of the data set.

Add the data values and divide the sum by the number of data values.

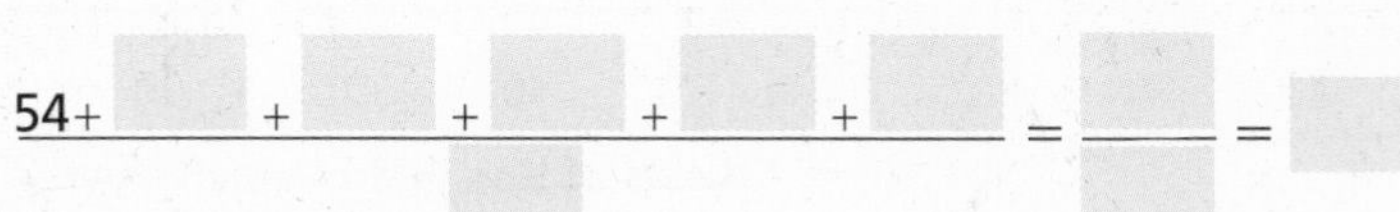

The mean of the data set is ______ inches.

STEP 2 Find the distance of each data value from the mean.

Subtract the lesser value from the greater value.

Data Value	Subtract (Mean = 57)	Distance between data value and the mean
54	57 − 54 =	3
58	58 − 57 =	
56	57 − 56 =	
59	59 − 57 =	
60	60 − 57 =	
55	57 − 55 =	
Total of distances from the mean:		

STEP 3 Add the distances.

STEP 4 Find the mean of the distances.

Divide the sum of the distances by the number of data values.

______ ÷ 6 = ______

So, the mean absolute deviation of the data is ______ inches.

MATHEMATICAL PRACTICES 7

Look for Structure Give an example of a data set that has a small mean absolute deviation. Explain how you know that the mean absolute deviation is small without doing any calculations.

Range is the difference between the greatest value and the least value in a data set. **Interquartile range** is the difference between the upper quartile and the lower quartile of a data set. Range and interquartile range are also measures of variability.

Example Use the range and interquartile range to compare the data sets.

The box plots show the price in dollars of the handheld game players at two different electronic stores. Find the range and interquartile range for each data set. Then compare the variability of the prices of the handheld game players at the two stores.

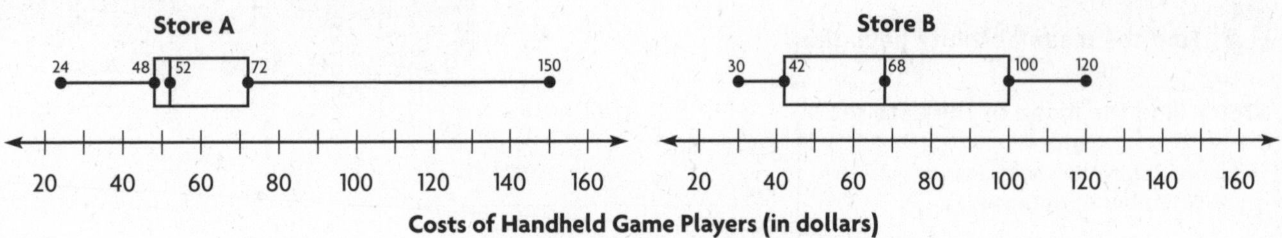

	STORE A	STORE B
Calculate the range. Find the difference between the greatest and least values.	150 − 24 = ______ The range for Store A is ______.	120 − ______ = ______ The range for Store B is ______.
Calculate the interquartile range. Find the difference between the upper quartile and lower quartile.	72 − 48 = ______ The interquartile range for Store A is ______.	100 − ______ = ______ The interquartile range for Store B is ______.

So, Store A has a greater ____________, but

Store B has a greater ________________.

Math Talk MATHEMATICAL PRACTICES 6

Compare Explain how range and interquartile range are alike and how they are different.

Name ______________________________

Share and Show

MATH BOARD

1. Find the range and interquartile range of the data in the box plot.

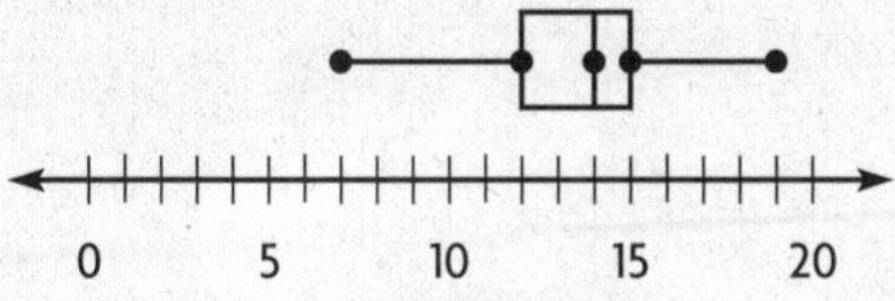

For the range, find the difference between the greatest and least values.

_____ − _____ = _____

range: $ _____

For the interquartile range, find the difference between the upper and lower quartiles.

_____ − _____ = _____

interquartile range: $ _____

Practice: Copy and Solve **Find the mean absolute deviation for the data set.**

2. heights in inches of several tomato plants:

16, 18, 18, 20, 17, 20, 18, 17

mean absolute deviation: __________

3. times in seconds for students to run one lap:

68, 60, 52, 40, 64, 40

mean absolute deviation: __________

MATHEMATICAL PRACTICES 6

Explain how you can find the mean absolute deviation of a data set.

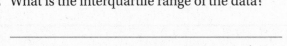

On Your Own

Use the box plot for 4 and 5.

4. What is the range of the data? _____

5. What is the interquartile range of the data?

____

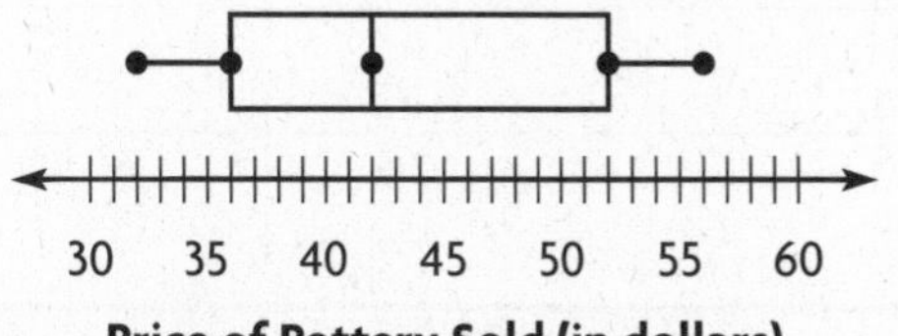

Practice: Copy and Solve **Find the mean absolute deviation for the data set.**

6. times in minutes spent on a history quiz

35, 35, 32, 34, 34, 32, 34, 36

mean absolute deviation: __________

7. number of excused absences for one semester:

1, 2, 1, 10, 9, 9, 10, 6, 1, 1

mean absolute deviation: __________

8. The chart shows the price of different varieties of dog food at a pet store. Find the range, interquartile range, and the mean absolute deviation of the data set.

Cost of Bag of Dog Food ($)									
18	24	20	26	24	20	32	20	16	20

____

____

Problem Solving • Applications Real World

9. GO DEEPER Hyato's family began a walking program. They walked 30, 45, 25, 35, 40, 30, and 40 minutes each day during one week. At the right, make a box plot of the data. Then find the interquartile range.

____

10. MATHEMATICAL PRACTICE 6 **Compare** Jack recorded the number of minutes his family walked each day for a month. The range of the data is 15. How does this compare to the data for Hyato's family?

____

____

____

11. THINK SMARTER **Sense or Nonsense?** Nathan claims that the interquartile range of a data set can never be greater than its range. Is Nathan's claim sense or nonsense? Explain.

____

____

____

12. THINK SMARTER The box plot shows the heights of corn stalks from two different farms.

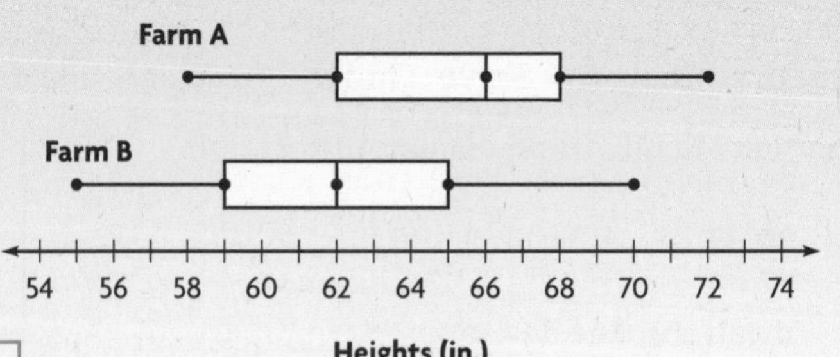

The range of Farm A's heights is [the same as / less than / greater than] the range of Farm B's heights.

Name ____________________

Measures of Variability

Common Core **COMMON CORE STANDARD—6.SP.B.5c**
Summarize and describe distributions.

1. Find the range and interquartile range of the data in the box plot.

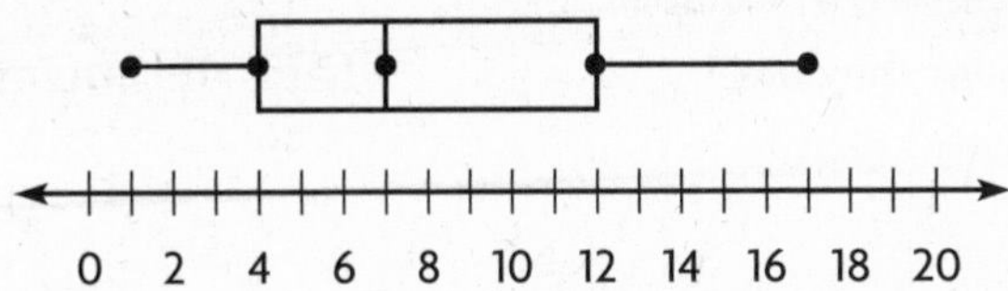

For the range, find the difference between the greatest and least values.

17 − 1 = 16

range: 16 miles

For the interquartile range, find the difference between the upper and lower quartiles.

12 − 4 = 8

interquartile range: 8 miles

Use the box plot for 2 and 3.

2. What is the range of the data?

____

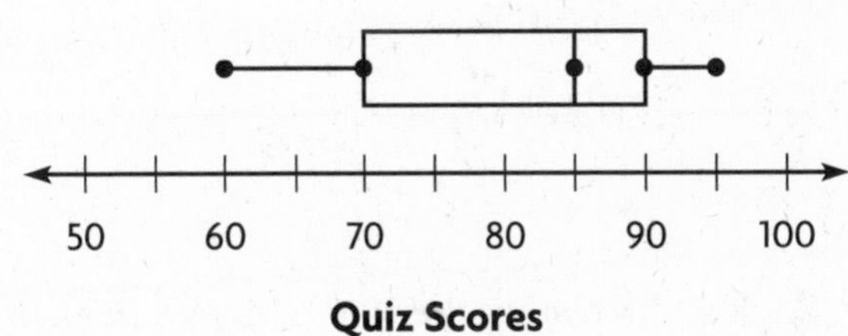

3. What is the interquartile range of the data?

____

Find the mean absolute deviation for the set.

4. heights in centimeters of several flowers:

14, 7, 6, 5, 13

mean absolute deviation: ____________

5. ages of several children:

5, 7, 4, 6, 3, 5, 3, 7

mean absolute deviation: ____________

Problem Solving Real World

6. The following data set gives the amount of time, in minutes, it took five people to cook a recipe. What is the mean absolute deviation for the data?

33, 38, 31, 36, 37

____

7. The prices of six food processors are \$63, \$59, \$72, \$68, \$61, and \$67. What are the range, interquartile range, and mean absolute deviation for the data?

____

8. WRITE Math Find the range, interquartile range, and mean absolute deviation for this data set: 41, 45, 60, 61, 61, 72, 80.

____

Lesson Check (6.SP.B.5c)

1. Daily high temperatures recorded in a certain city are 65°F, 66°F, 70°F, 58°F, and 61°F. What is the mean absolute deviation for the data?

2. Eight different cereals have 120, 160, 135, 144, 153, 122, 118, and 134 calories per serving. What is the interquartile range for the data?

Spiral Review (6.SP.B.4, 6.SP.B.5c)

3. Look at the histogram. How many days did the restaurant sell more than 59 pizzas?

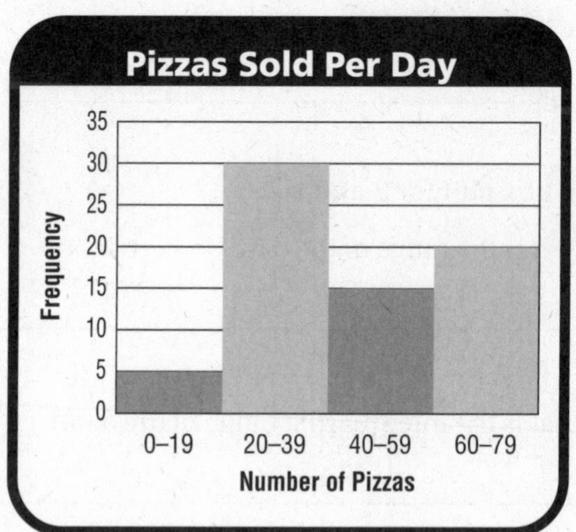

4. Look at the histogram. Where does a peak in the data occur?

5. What is the mode of the data set?

   14, 14, 18, 20

6. The data set below lists the ages of people on a soccer team. The mean of the data is 23. What is the mean absolute deviation?

   24, 22, 19, 19, 23, 23, 26, 27, 24

FOR MORE PRACTICE GO TO THE Personal Math Trainer

Name ______________________________

Mid-Chapter Checkpoint

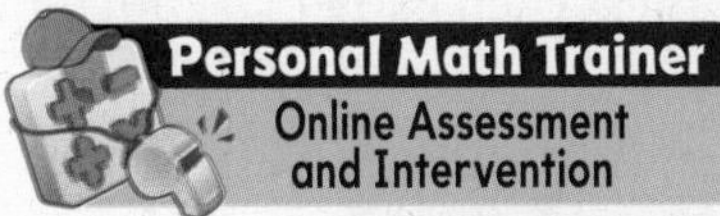

Vocabulary

Vocabulary
box plot
interquartile range
mean absolute deviation
measure of variability
range

Choose the best term from the box to complete the sentence.

1. The ____________ is the difference between the upper quartile and the lower quartile of a data set. (p. 726)

2. A graph that shows the median, quartiles, and least and greatest values of a data set is called a(n) ____________. (p. 714)

3. The difference between the greatest value and the least value in a data set is the ____________. (p. 726)

4. The ____________ is the mean of the distances between the values of a data set and the mean of the data set. (p. 720)

Concepts and Skills

5. Make a box plot for this data set: 73, 65, 68, 72, 70, 74. (6.SP.B.4)

Find the mean absolute deviation of the data. (6.SP.B.5c)

6. 43, 46, 48, 40, 38

7. 26, 20, 25, 21, 24, 27, 26, 23

8. 99, 70, 78, 85, 76, 81

Find the range and interquartile range of the data. (6.SP.B.5c)

9. 2, 4, 8, 3, 2

10. 84, 82, 86, 87, 88, 83, 84

11. 39, 22, 33, 45, 42, 40, 28

12. Yasmine keeps track of the number of hockey goals scored by her school's team at each game. The dot plot shows her data.

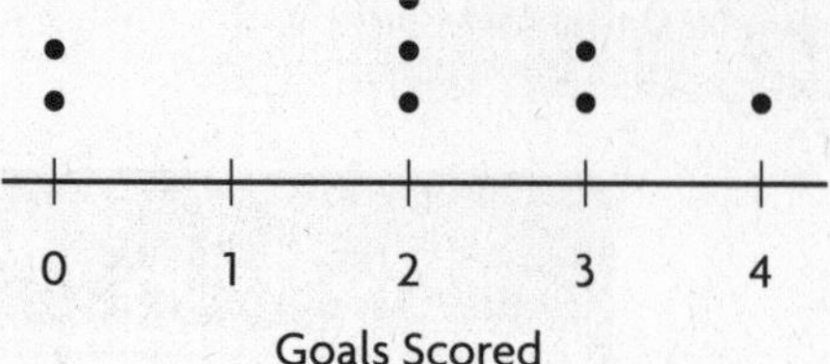

Where is there a gap in the data? (6.SP.B.5c)

---

13. What is the interquartile range of the data shown in the dot plot with Question 12? (6.SP.B.5c)

---

14. GO DEEPER Randall's teacher added up the class scores for the quarter and used a histogram to display the data. How many peaks does the histogram have? Explain how you know. (6.SP.B.5c)

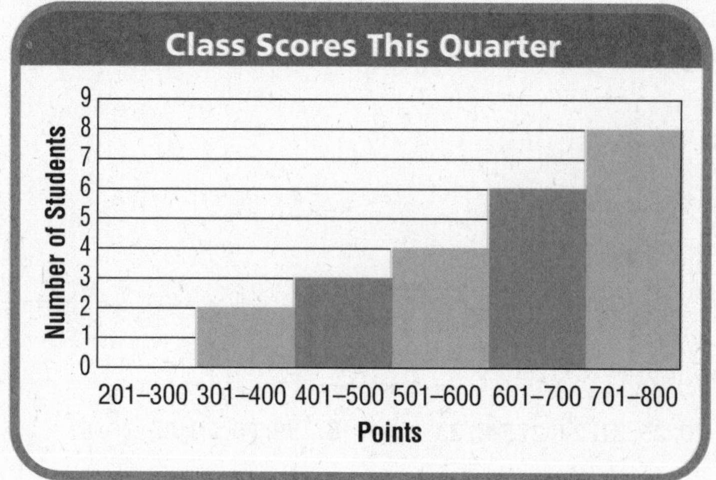

---

15. In a box plot of the data below, where would the box be drawn? (6.SP.B.4)

55, 37, 41, 62, 50, 49, 64

Name ______________________________

Choose Appropriate Measures of Center and Variability

Common Core Statistics and Probability—6.SP.B.5d
MATHEMATICAL PRACTICES MP2, MP4, MP6

Essential Question How can you choose appropriate measures of center and variability to describe a data set?

Outliers, gaps, and clusters in a set of data can affect both the measures of center and variability. Some measures of center and variability may describe a particular set of data better than others.

Unlock the Problem Real World

Thomas is writing an article for the school newsletter about a paper airplane competition. In the distance category, Kara's airplanes flew 17 ft, 16 ft, 18 ft, 15 ft, and 2 ft. Should Thomas use the mean, median, or mode to best describe Kara's results? Explain your reasoning.

- Do you need to order the numbers?

____
____
____
____

Find the mean, median, and mode and compare them.

Mean = $\frac{\square + \square + \square + \square + \square}{\square}$

$= \frac{\square}{\square} = \square$

Order the data from least to greatest to find the median.

_____, _____, _____, _____, _____

Median = _____

The data set has no repeated values so there is no __________.

The mean is __________ than 4 of the 5 values, so it is not a good description of the center of the data. The __________ is closer to most of the values, so it is the best way to describe Kara's results.

So, Thomas should use the __________ to describe Kara's results.

Math Idea

The measures of center for some data sets may be very close together. If that is the case, you can list more than one measure as the best way to describe the data.

1. Explain why the two modes may be a better description than the mean or median of the data set 2, 2, 2, 2, 7, 7, 7, 7.

____

____

Example

Mr. Tobin is buying a book online. He compares prices of the book at several different sites. The table shows his results. Make a box plot of the data. Then use the plot to find the range and interquartile range. Which measure better describes the data? Explain your reasoning.

Prices of Book

Site	Price ($)
1	15
2	35
3	17
4	18
5	5
6	16
7	17

STEP 1 Make a box plot.

Write the data in order from least to greatest. ______, ______, ______, ______, ______, ______, ______

Find the median of the data. median = ______

Find the lower quartile—the median of the lower half of the data. lower quartile = ______

Find the upper quartile—the median of the upper half of the data. upper quartile = ______

Make the plot.

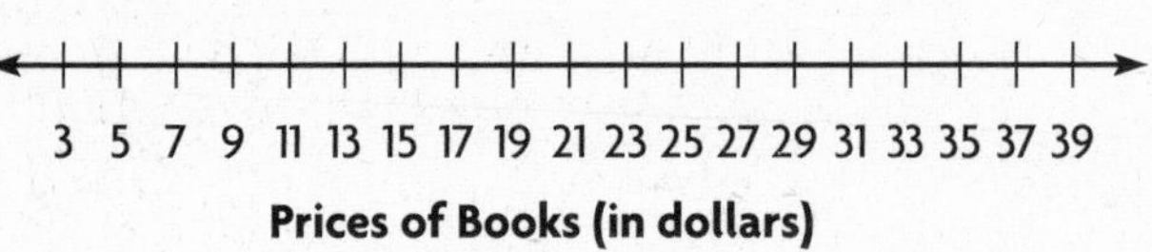

Prices of Books (in dollars)

MATHEMATICAL PRACTICES 2

Reasoning Describe a data set for which the range is a better description than the interquartile range.

STEP 2 Use the box plot to find the range and the interquartile range.

range = ______ − ______ = ______

interquartile range = ______ − ______ = ______

__________ of the seven prices are within the ______________.
The other two prices are much higher or lower.

So, the ______________ better describes the data because the

______________ makes it appear that the data values vary more than they actually do.

2. THINKSMARTER How can you tell from the box plot how varied the data are? Explain.

____

____

Name ______________________________

Share and Show

1. The distances in miles students travel to get to school are 7, 1, 5, 9, 9, and 8. Decide which measure(s) of center best describes the data set. Explain your reasoning.

mean = ____________

median = ____________

mode = ____________

The ____________ is less than 4 of the 6 data points, and the ____________ describes only 2 of the greatest data points. So, the ____________ best describes the data.

2. MATHEMATICAL PRACTICE 4 **Use Graphs** The numbers of different brands of orange juice carried in several stores are 2, 1, 3, 1, 12, 1, 2, 2, and 5. Make a box plot of the data and find the range and interquartile range. Decide which measure better describes the data set and explain your reasoning.

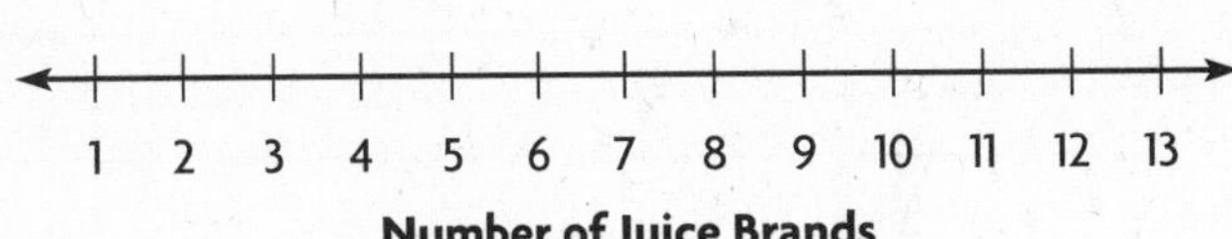

range = ______

interquartile range = ______

____

____

Math Talk MATHEMATICAL PRACTICES 6

Explain How does an outlier affect the range of a data set?

On Your Own

3. MATHEMATICAL PRACTICE 2 **Use Reasoning** The ages of students in a computer class are 14, 13, 14, 15, 14, 35, 14. Decide which measure of center(s) best describes the data set. Explain your reasoning.

mean = ____________

median = ____________

mode = ____________

____

____

4. GO DEEPER Mateo scored 98, 85, 84, 80, 81, and 82 on six math tests. When a seventh math test score is added, the measure of center that best describes his scores is the median. What could the seventh test score be? Explain your reasoning.

____

____

Unlock the Problem 

5. THINKSMARTER Jaime is on the community swim team. The table shows the team's results in the last 8 swim meets. Jaime believes they can place in the top 3 at the next swim meet. Which measure of center should Jaime use to persuade her team that she is correct? Explain.

Swim Team Results

Meet	Place
Meet 1	1
Meet 2	2
Meet 3	3
Meet 4	18
Meet 5	1
Meet 6	2
Meet 7	3
Meet 8	2

a. What do you need to find?

____

b. What information do you need to solve the problem?

____

c. What are the measures of center?

____

d. Which measure of center should Jaime use? Explain.

____

Personal Math Trainer

6. THINKSMARTER+ The numbers of sit-ups students completed in one minute are 10, 42, 46, 50, 43, and 49. The mean of the data values is 40 and the median is 44.5. Which measure of center better describes the data, the mean or median? Use words and numbers to support your answer.

____

Name ____________________

Choose Appropriate Measures of Center and Variability

COMMON CORE STANDARD—6.SP.B.5d
Summarize and describe distributions.

1. The distances, in miles, that 6 people travel to get to work are 14, 12, 2, 16, 16, and 18. Decide which measure(s) of center best describes the data set. Explain your reasoning.

mean = 13 miles

median = 15 miles

mode = 16 miles

The ____________ is less than 4 of the data points, and the ____________ describes only 2 of the data points. So, the ____________ best describes the data.

2. The numbers of pets that several children have are 2, 1, 2, 3, 4, 3, 10, 0, 1, and 0. Make a box plot of the data and find the range and interquartile range. Decide which measure better describes the data set and explain your reasoning.

range = ______ interquartile range = ______

____

____

____

Problem Solving

3. Brett's history quiz scores are 84, 78, 92, 90, 85, 91, and 0. Decide which measure(s) of center best describes the data set. Explain your reasoning.

mean = ____________ median = ____________

mode = ____________

____

____

____

4. Eight students were absent the following number of days in a year: 4, 8, 0, 1, 7, 2, 6, and 3. Decide if the range or interquartile range better describes the data set, and explain your reasoning.

range = ______ interquartile range = ______

____

____

____

5. WRITE *Math* Create two sets of data that would be best described by two different measures of center.

____

____

Lesson Check (6.SP.B.5d)

1. Chloe used two box plots to display some data. The box in the plot for the first data set is wider than the box for the second data set. What does this say about the data?

2. Hector recorded the temperature at noon for 7 days in a row. The temperatures are 20°F, 20°F, 20°F, 23°F, 23°F, 23°F, and 55°F. Which measure of center would best describe the data?

Spiral Review (6.SP.B.4, 6.SP.B.5c, 6.SP.B.5d)

3. By how much does the median of the following data set change if the outlier is removed?

   13, 20, 15, 19, 22, 26, 42

4. What percent of the people surveyed spent at least an hour watching television?

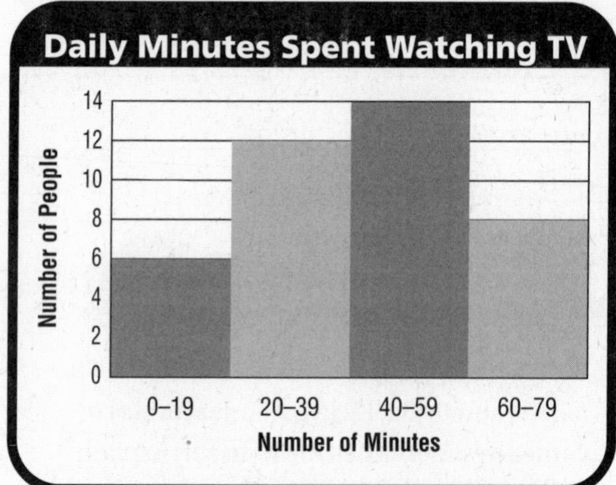

5. What is the lower quartile of the following data?

   12, 9, 10, 8, 7, 12

6. What is the interquartile range of the data shown in the box plot?

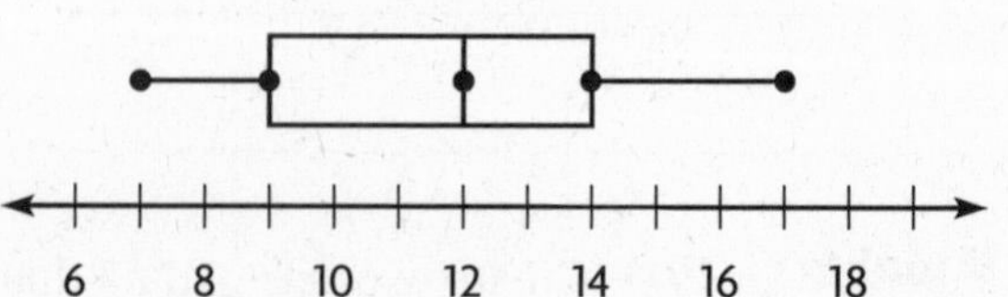

FOR MORE PRACTICE GO TO THE Personal Math Trainer

Name ______________________________

Apply Measures of Center and Variability

Statistics and Probability— 6.SP.A.3
Also 6.SP.A.2

MATHEMATICAL PRACTICES
MP2, MP4, MP6

Essential Question What do measures of center and variability indicate about a data set?

Unlock the Problem Real World

Julia is collecting data on her favorite sports teams for a report. The table shows the median and interquartile range of the heights of the players on her favorite baseball and basketball teams. How do the heights of the two teams compare?

Sports Team Data

	Median	Interquartile Range
Baseball Team Heights	70 in.	6 in.
Basketball Team Heights	78 in.	4 in.

Compare the medians and interquartile ranges of the two teams.

Median

The median of the ____________ players' heights is ______ inches greater than the median of the ____________ players' heights.

Interquartile Range

The interquartile range of the baseball team is ____________ the interquartile range of the basketball team, so the heights of the baseball players vary ____________ the heights of the basketball team.

So, the players on the ____________ team are typically taller than the players on the ____________ team, and the heights of the ____________ team vary more than the those of the ____________ team.

Math Talk

MATHEMATICAL PRACTICES 2

Reasoning What if the mean of the heights of players on the baseball team is 75 in.? Explain what this could tell you about the data.

1. Julia randomly picks one player from the basketball team and one player from the baseball team. Given data in the table, can you say that the basketball player will definitely be taller than the baseball player? Explain your reasoning.

____

____

____

Example Compare the means and ranges of the two data sets.

Kamira and Joey sold T-shirts during lunch to raise money for a charity. The table shows the number of T-shirts each student sold each day for two weeks. Find the mean and range of each data set, and use these measures to compare the data.

T-Shirts Sold	
Kamira	5, 1, 2, 1, 3, 3, 1, 4, 5, 5
Joey	0, 1, 2, 13, 2, 1, 3, 4, 4, 0

STEP 1 Find the mean of each data set.

Kamira:

Mean = $\dfrac{\_\_ + \_\_ + \_\_ + \_\_ + \_\_ + \_\_ + \_\_ + \_\_ + \_\_ + \_\_}{\_\_}$

$= \dfrac{\_\_}{\_\_} = \_\_$

Joey:

Mean = $\dfrac{\_\_ + \_\_ + \_\_ + \_\_ + \_\_ + \_\_ + \_\_ + \_\_ + \_\_ + \_\_}{\_\_}$

$= \dfrac{\_\_}{\_\_} = \_\_$

ERROR Alert

Make sure you include zeroes when you count the total number of data values.

STEP 2 Find the range of each data set.

Kamira:

Range = ___ − ___ = ___

Joey:

Range = ___ − ___ = ___

STEP 3 Compare the mean and range.

The mean of Joey's sales is ___ the mean of Kamira's sales.

The range of Joey's sales is ___ the range of Kamira's sales.

So, the typical number of shirts Joey sold each day was ___ the typical number of shirts Kamira sold. However, since the range of Joey's data was ___ than Kamira's, the number of shirts Joey sold varied ___ from day to day than the number of shirts Kamira sold.

2. MATHEMATICAL PRACTICE 6 **Explain** Which measure of center would better describe Joey's data set? Explain.

___

___

Name ______________________________

Share and Show

1. Zoe collected data on the number of points her favorite basketball players scored in several games. Use the information in the table to compare the data.

Points Scored		
	Mean	Interquartile Range
Player 1	24	8
Player 2	33	16

The mean of Player 1's points is ____________ the mean of Player 2's points.

The interquartile range of Player 1's points is ____________ the interquartile range of Player 2's points.

So, Player 2 typically scores ____________ points than Player 1, but

Player 2's scores typically vary ____________ Player 1's scores.

2. Mark collected data on the weights of puppies at two animal shelters. Find the median and range of each data set, and use these measures to compare the data.

Puppy Weight, in pounds
Shelter A: 7, 10, 5, 12, 15, 7, 7
Shelter B: 4, 11, 5, 11, 15, 5, 13

____

____

____

____

On Your Own

Kwan analyzed data about the number of hours musicians in her band practice each week. The table shows her results. Use the table for Exercises 3–5.

3. Which two students typically practiced the same amount each week, with about the same variation in practice times?

____

4. Which two students typically practiced the same number of hours, but had very different variations in their practice times?

____

5. Which two students had the same variation in practice times, but typically practiced a different number of hours per week?

____

Hours of Practice per Week		
	Mean	Range
Sally	5	2
Matthew	9	12
Tim	5	12
Jennifer	5	3

Problem Solving • Applications 

Miles Run
Week 1 2, 1, 5, 2, 3, 3, 4
Week 2 3, 8, 1, 8, 1, 3, 1

6. MATHEMATICAL PRACTICE 6 **Compare** The table shows the number of miles Johnny ran each day for two weeks. Find the median and the interquartile range of each data set, and use these measures to compare the data sets.

____

____

____

7. THINKSMARTER **Sense or Nonsense?** Yashi made the box plots at right to show the data he collected on plant growth. He thinks that the variation in bean plant growth was about the same as the variation in tomato plant growth. Does Yashi's conclusion make sense? Why or why not?

____

____

____

____

____

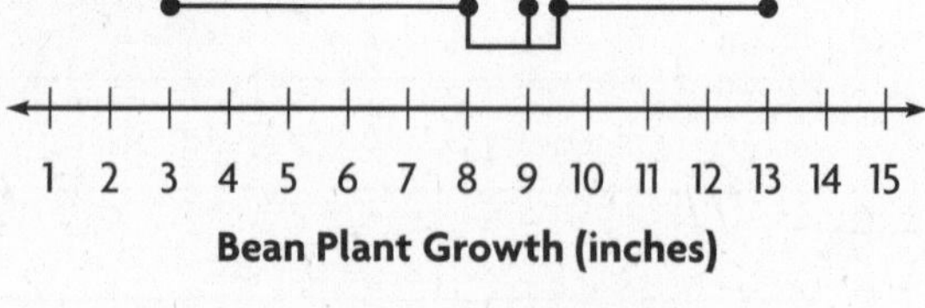

Bean Plant Growth (inches)

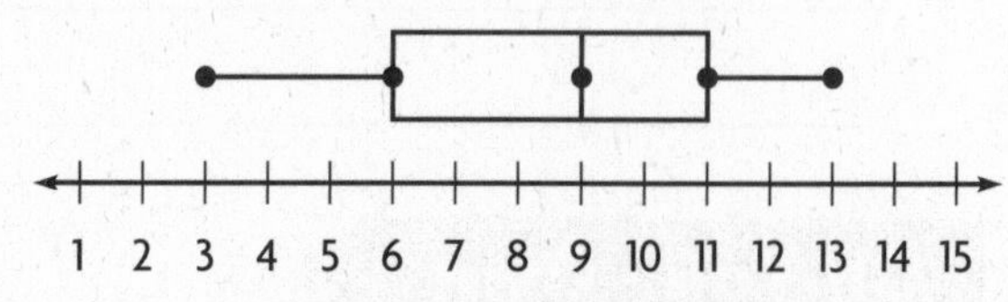

Tomato Plant Growth (inches)

Personal Math Trainer

8. THINKSMARTER+ Kylie's teacher collected data on the heights of boys and girls in a sixth-grade class. Use the information in the table to compare the data.

Heights (in.)							
Girls	55	60	56	51	60	63	65
Boys	72	68	70	56	58	62	64

The mean of the boys' heights is [the same as / less than / greater than] the mean of the girls' heights.

The range of the boys' heights is [the same as / less than / greater than] the range of the girls' heights.

Name ______________________________

Apply Measures of Center and Variability

Common Core **COMMON CORE STANDARD—6.SP.A.3**
Develop understanding of statistical variability.

Solve.

1. The table shows temperature data for two cities. Use the information in the table to compare the data.

Daily High Temperatures (°F)		
	Mean	Interquartile Range
City 1	60	7
City 2	70	15

The mean of City 1's temperatures is **less than** the mean of City 2's temperatures.

The **interquartile range** of City 1's temperatures is **less than** the **interquartile range** of City 2's temperatures.

So, City 2 is typically **warmer than** City 1, but City 2's temperatures vary **more than** City 1's temperatures.

2. The table shows weights of fish that were caught in two different lakes. Find the median and range of each data set, and use these measures to compare the data.

Fish Weight (pounds)
Lake A: 7, 9, 10, 4, 6, 12
Lake B: 6, 7, 4, 5, 6, 4

____

____

____

____

Problem Solving Real World

3. Mrs. Mack measured the heights of her students in two classes. Class 1 has a median height of 130 cm and an interquartile range of 5 cm. Class 2 has a median height of 134 cm and an interquartile range of 8 cm. Write a statement that compares the data.

____

____

____

4. Richard's science test scores are 76, 80, 78, 84, and 80. His math test scores are 100, 80, 73, 94, and 71. Compare the medians and interquartile ranges.

____

____

____

____

5. **WRITE** *Math* Write a short paragraph to a new student that explains how you can compare data sets by examining the mean and the interquartile range.

____

____

Lesson Check (6.SP.A.3)

1. Team A has a mean of 35 points and a range of 8 points. Team B has a mean of 30 points and a range of 7 points. Write a statement that compares the data.

2. Jean's test scores have a mean of 83 and an interquartile range of 4. Ben's test scores have a mean of 87 and an interquartile range of 9. Compare the students' scores.

Spiral Review (6.SP.A.3, 6.SP.B.4, 6.SP.B.5d)

3. Look at the box plots below. What is the difference between the medians for the two groups of data?

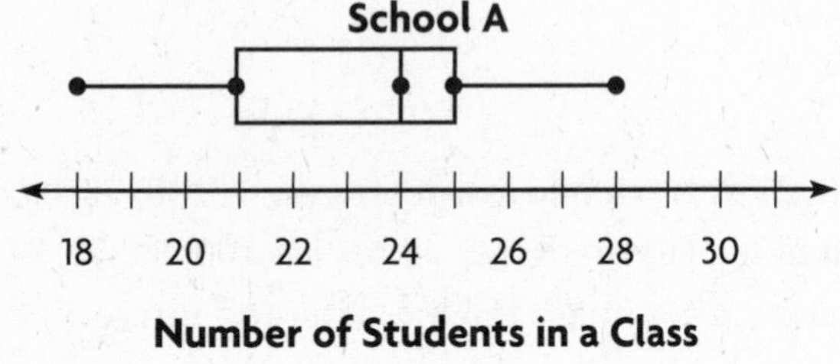

School B

18 20 22 24 26 28 30

Number of Students in a Class

4. The distances in miles that 6 people drive to get to work are 10, 11, 9, 12, 9, and 27. What measure of center best describes the data set?

5. Which two teams typically practice the same number of hours, but have very different variations in their practice times?

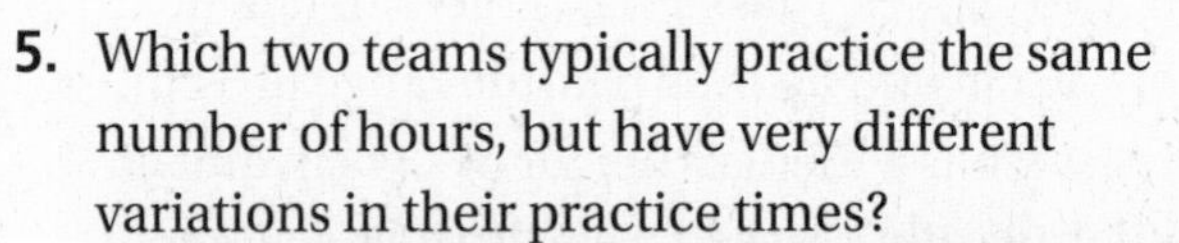

Hours of Practice Per Week		
Team	Mean	Range
A	7	1.5
B	10.5	1.5
C	7.5	5
D	10	2

FOR MORE PRACTICE GO TO THE Personal Math Trainer

Name ______________________

Describe Distributions

Essential Question How can you describe the distribution of a data set collected to answer a statistical question?

Common Core **Statistics and Probability— 6.SP.A.2** *Also 6.SP.B.5d*

MATHEMATICAL PRACTICES
MP1, MP3, MP5, MP6

Activity

Ask at least 20 students in your school how many pets they have. Record your results in a frequency table like the one shown.

Pet Survey	
Number of Pets	**Frequency**
0	
1	
2	
3	
4	

- What statistical question could you use your data to answer?

____

____

Unlock the Problem

You can graph your data set to see the center, spread, and overall shape of the data.

Make a dot plot or a histogram of your data.

- What type of graph will you use?

____

- How will you label your graph?

____

____

Math Talk MATHEMATICAL PRACTICES 5

Use Tools Explain why you chose the display you used.

Think about the **distribution**, or overall shape of your data.

- Are there any clusters?
- Are there peaks in the data?
- Are there gaps in the data?
- Does the graph have symmetry?

1. MATHEMATICAL PRACTICE 6 **Use Math Vocabulary** Describe the overall distribution of the data. Include information about clusters, gaps, peaks, and symmetry.

____

____

Example

Find the mean, median, mode, interquartile range, and range of the data you collected.

STEP 1 Find the mean, median, and mode.

Mean: ____________ Median: ____________

Mode: ____________

STEP 2 Draw a box plot of your data and use it to find the interquartile range and range.

Interquartile range: ____________ Range: ____________

2. Which measure of center do you think best describes your data? Why?

____

____

3. Does the interquartile range or range best describe your data? Why?

____

____

4. What is the answer to the statistical question you wrote on the previous page?

____

____

MATHEMATICAL PRACTICES 6

Describe Compare your data set to the data set of one of your classmates. How are the data sets similar and how they are different?

Name ______________________________

Share and Show 

Connie asked people their ages as they entered the food court at the mall. Use the histogram of the data she collected for 1–5.

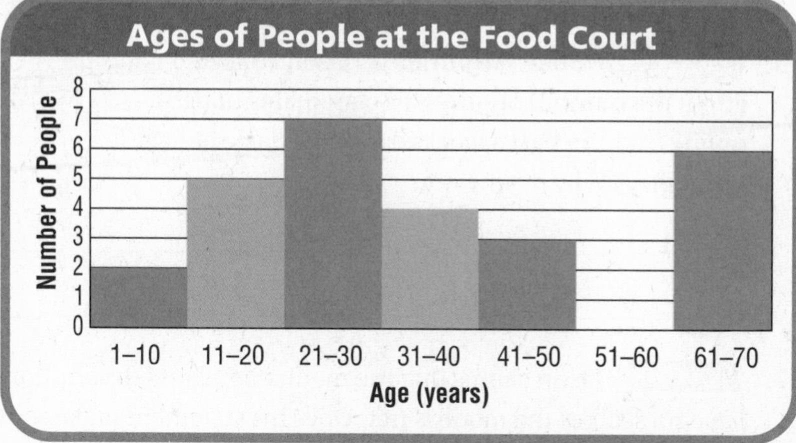

1. What statistical question could Connie ask about her data?

____

____

____

2. Describe any peak or gap in the data.

____

____

3. Does the graph have symmetry? Explain your reasoning.

____

____

On Your Own

4. The lower quartile of the data set is 16.5 years, and the upper quartile is 51.5 years. Find the interquartile range. Is it a better description of the data than the range? Explain your reasoning.

____

____

____

____

____

MATHEMATICAL PRACTICES 1

Analyze Explain what, if any, information you would need to answer the statistical question you wrote in Exercise 1 and what calculations you would need to do.

5. MATHEMATICAL PRACTICE 3 **Make Arguments** The mode of the data is 16 years old. Is the mode a good description of the center of the data? Explain.

____

____

Problem Solving • Applications 

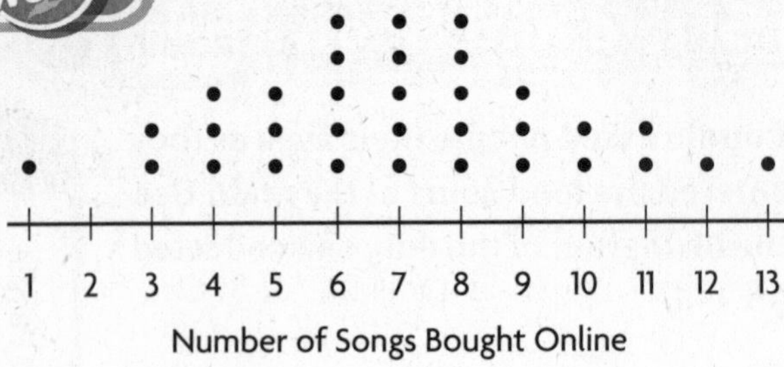

Use the dot plot for 6–8.

6. MATHEMATICAL PRACTICE 3 **Make Arguments** Jason collected data about the number of songs his classmates bought online over the past 3 weeks. Does the data set have symmetry? Why or why not?

____

____

7. GO DEEPER Jason claims that the median is a good description of his data set, but the mode is not. Does his statement make sense? Explain.

____

____

8. THINK SMARTER Trinni surveyed her classmates about how many siblings they have. A dot plot of her data increases from 0 siblings to a peak at 1 sibling, and then decreases steadily as the graph goes to 6 siblings. How is Trinni's dot plot similar to Jason's? How is it different?

____

____

____

9. THINK SMARTER Diego collected data on the number of movies seen last month by a random group of students.

Number of Movies Seen Last Month												
0	1	3	2	1	0	5	12	2	3	2	2	3

Draw a box plot of the data and use it to find the interquartile range and range.

Interquartile range ______

Range ______

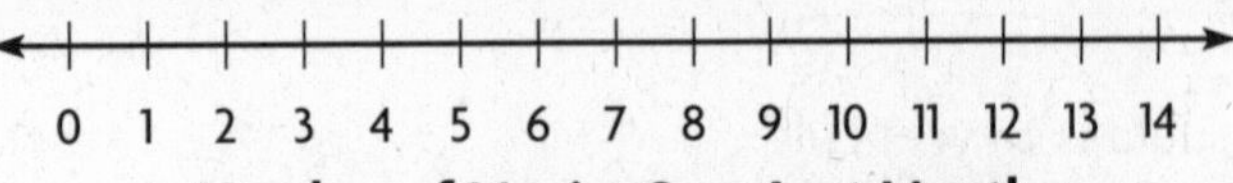

Number of Movies Seen Last Month

Name ________________________________

Describe Distributions

Practice and Homework
Lesson 13.7

COMMON CORE STANDARD—6.SP.A.2
Develop understanding of statistical variability.

Chase asked people how many songs they have bought online in the past month. Use the histogram of the data he collected for 1–4.

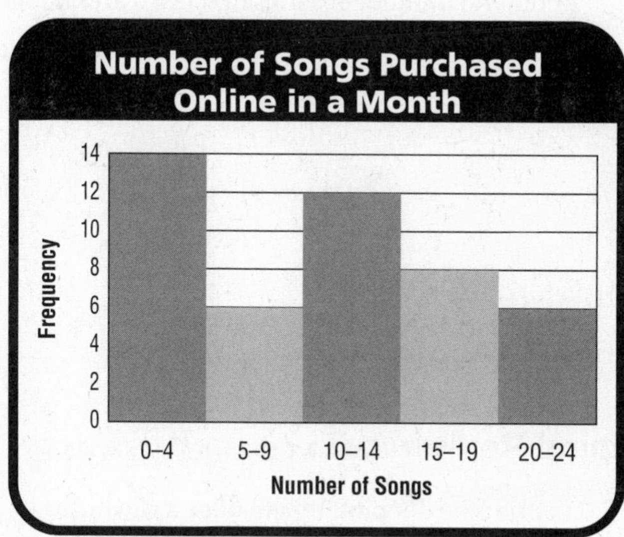

1. What statistical question could Chase ask about the data?
   Possible answer: What is the median number of songs purchased?

2. Describe any peaks in the data.
   ____
   ____

3. Describe any gaps in the data.
   ____
   ____

4. Does the graph have symmetry? Explain your reasoning.
   ____
   ____

Problem Solving

5. Mr. Carpenter teaches five classes each day. For several days in a row, he kept track of the number of students who were late to class and displayed the results in a dot plot. Describe the data.

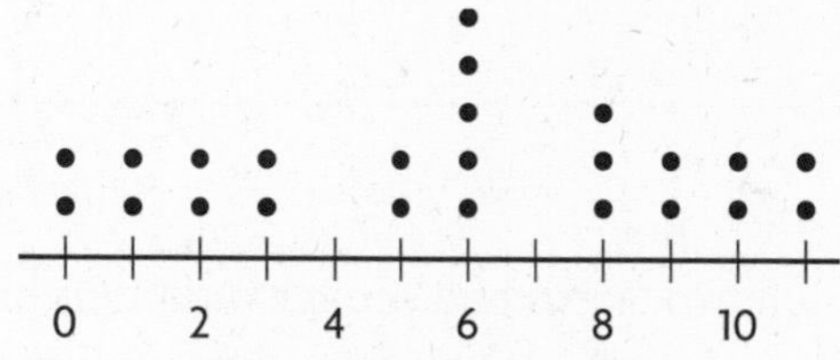

Number of Students Late to Class Each Day

   ____
   ____
   ____
   ____

6. WRITE Math Describe how a graph of a data set can be used to understand the distribution of the data.
   ____
   ____

Lesson Check (6.SP.A.2)

1. The ages of people in a restaurant are 28, 10, 44, 25, 18, 8, 47, and 30. What is the median age of the people in the restaurant?

____

2. What is the median in the dot plot?

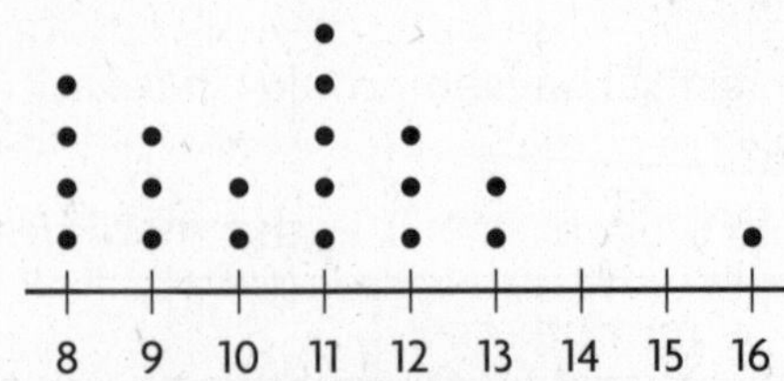

____

Spiral Review (6.SP.A.2, 6.SP.A.3, 6.SP.B.5c, 6.SP.B.5d)

3. Look at the dot plot. Where does a gap occur in the data?

____

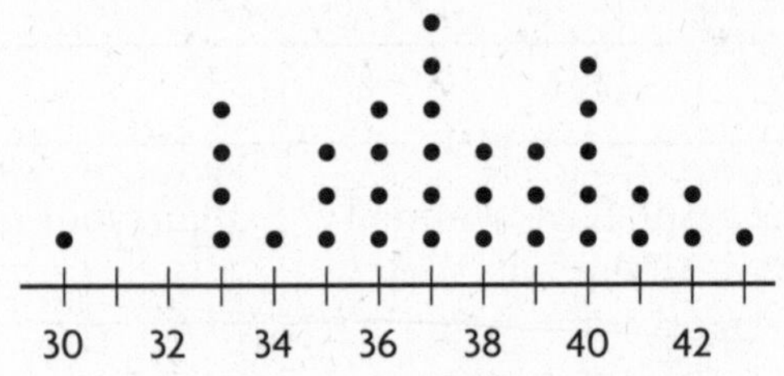

4. Look at the dot plot. Where does a peak occur in the data?

____

5. Which two teams had similar variations in points earned, but typically earned a different number of points per game?

Points Earned Per Game		
Team	Mean	Range
Red	20	8
Blue	28	8
Green	29	4
Orange	28	4

____

6. Manny's monthly electric bills for the past 6 months are $140, $165, $145, $32, $125, and $135. What measure of center best represents the data?

____

FOR MORE PRACTICE GO TO THE **Personal Math Trainer**

Name ______________________________

Problem Solving • Misleading Statistics

Essential Question How can you use the strategy *work backward* to draw conclusions about a data set?

Statistics and Probability—6.SP.A.2 *Also 6.SP.B.5c*

MATHEMATICAL PRACTICES
MP2, MP6, MP7

Unlock the Problem

Mr. Owen wants to move to a town where the daily high temperature is in the 70s most days. A real estate agent tells him that the mean daily high temperature in a certain town is 72°. Other statistics about the town are given in the table. Does this location match what Mr. Owen wants? Why or why not?

Town Statistics for the Past Year (Daily High Temperature)	
Minimum	62°
Maximum	95°
Median	69°
Mean	72°

Use the graphic organizer to help you solve the problem.

Read the Problem

What do I need to find?	What information do I need?	How will I use the information?
I need to decide if the daily high temperature in the town ______________.	I need the __________ in the table.	I will work backward from the statistics to draw conclusions about the __________ of data.

Solve the Problem

The minimum high temperature is ______. **Think:** The high temperature is sometimes __________ than 70°.

The maximum high temperature is ______. **Think:** The high temperature is sometimes __________ than 80°.

The median of the data set is ______. **Think:** The median is the middle value in the data set.

Because the median is 69°, at least half of the days must have high temperatures less than or equal to 69°.

So, the location does not match what Mr. Owen wants. The median indicates that most days __________ have a high temperature in the 70s.

MATHEMATICAL PRACTICES 6

Explain Why is the mean temperature misleading in this example?

Try Another Problem

Ms. Garcia is buying a new car. She would like to visit a dealership that has a wide variety of cars for sale at many different price ranges. The table gives statistics about one dealership in her town. Does the dealership match Ms. Garcia's requirements? Explain your reasoning.

Statistics for New Car Prices	
Lowest Price	$12,000
Highest Price	$65,000
Lower Quartile Price	$50,000
Median Price	$55,000
Upper Quartile Price	$60,000

Read the Problem

What do I need to find?	What information do I need?	How will I use the information?

Solve the Problem

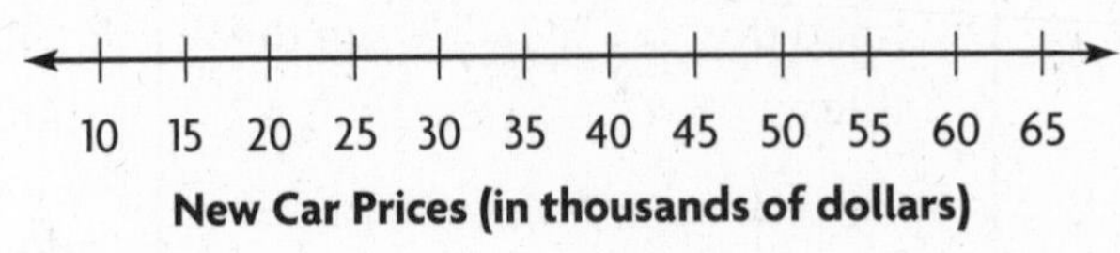

- What would the box plot look like for a dealership that does meet Ms. Garcia's requirements?

Name ___________________________

Share and Show

1. Josh is playing a game at the carnival. If his arrow lands on a section marked 25 or higher, he gets a prize. Josh will only play if most of the players win a prize. The carnival worker says that the average (mean) score is 28. The box plot shows other statistics about the game. Should Josh play the game? Explain your reasoning.

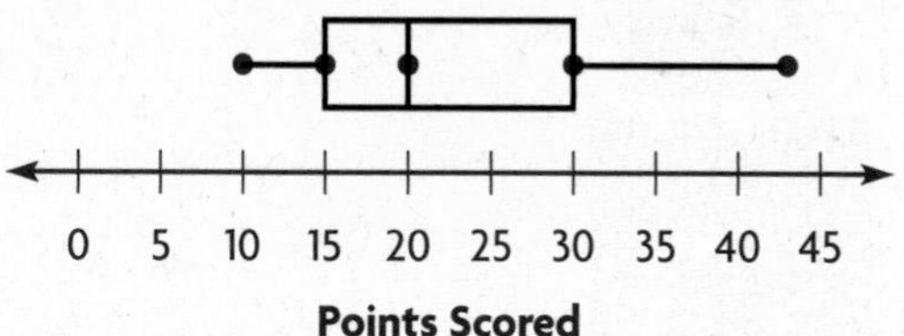

First, look at the median. The median is ______ points.

Next, work backward from the statistics.

The median is the ____________ value of the data.

So, at least ____________ of the values are scores

less than or equal to ______.

Finally, use the statistics to draw a conclusion.

____

____

Unlock the Problem

- ✓ Circle important facts.
- ✓ Organize the information.
- ✓ Choose a strategy.
- ✓ Check to make sure you answered the question.

2. THINKSMARTER **What if** a score of 15 or greater resulted in a prize? How would that affect Josh's decision? Explain.

____

____

3. GO DEEPER A store collects data on the sales of DVD players each week for 3 months. The manager determines that the data has a range of 62 players and decides that the weekly sales were very inconsistent. Use the statistics in the table to decide if the manager is correct. Explain your answer.

Weekly DVD Player Sales	
Minimum	16
Maximum	78
Lower quartile	58
Upper quartile	72

____

____

____

On Your Own

4. GO DEEPER Gerard is fencing in a yard that is 21 feet by 18 feet. How many yards of fencing material does Gerard need? Explain how you found your answer.

____

____

5. THINK SMARTER Susanna wants to buy a fish that grows to be about 4 in. long. Mark suggests she buys the same type of fish he has. He has five of these fish with lengths of 1 in., 1 in., 6 in., 6 in., and 6 in., with a mean length of 4 in. Should Susanna buy the type of fish that Mark suggests? Explain.

____

____

____

6. MATHEMATICAL PRACTICE 7 **Look for a Pattern** The graph shows the number of stamps that Luciano collected over several weeks. If the pattern continues, how many stamps will Luciano collect in Week 8? Explain.

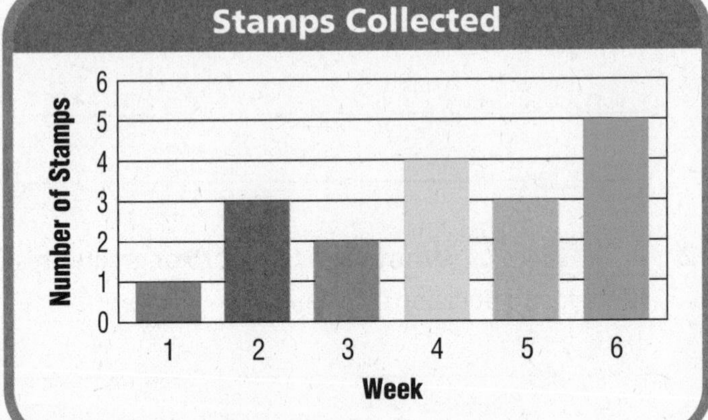

____

____

____

____

____

7. THINK SMARTER The data set shows the number of hours Luke plays the piano each week. Luke says he usually plays the piano 3 hours per week. Why is Luke's statement misleading?

Hours Playing the Piano						
1	2	1	3	2	10	2

____

____

Name ______________________

Problem Solving · Misleading Statistics

Practice and Homework
Lesson 13.8

Common Core **COMMON CORE STANDARD—6.SP.A.2**
Develop understanding of statistical variability.

Mr. Jackson wants to make dinner reservations at a restaurant that has most meals costing less than $16. The Waterside Inn advertises that they have meals that average $15. The table shows the menu items.

Menu Items	
Meal	**Price**
Potato Soup	$6
Chicken	$16
Steak	$18
Pasta	$16
Shrimp	$18
Crab Cake	$19

1. What is the minimum price and maximum price?

min = $6

max = $19

2. What is the mean of the prices?

______

3. Construct a box plot for the data.

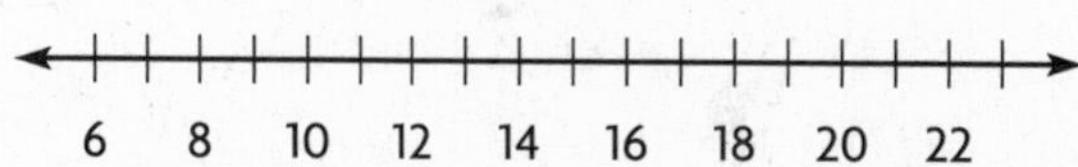

4. What is the range of the prices?

______

5. What is the interquartile range of the prices?

______

6. Does the menu match Mr. Jackson's requirements? Explain your reasoning.

______

______

______

7. WRITE *Math* Give an example of a misleading statistic. Explain why it is misleading.

______

______

Lesson Check (6.SP.A.2)

1. Mary's science test scores are 66, 94, 73, 81, 70, 84, and 88. What is the range of Mary's science test scores?

2. The heights in inches of students on a team are 64, 66, 60, 68, 69, 59, 60, and 70. What is the interquartile range?

Spiral Review (6.SP.B.4, 6.SP.B.5c, 6.SP.B.5d)

3. By how much does the median of the following data set change if the outlier is removed?

   26, 21, 25, 18, 0, 28

4. Look at the box plot. What is the interquartile range of the data?

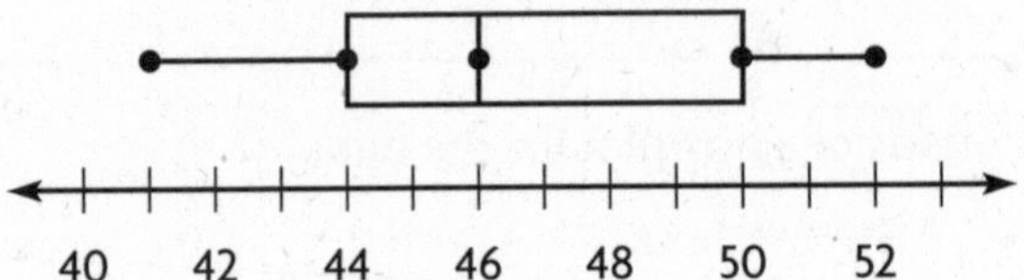

5. Erin is on the school trivia team. The table shows the team's scores in the last 8 games. Erin wants to build confidence in her team so that they will do well in the last game. If a score of 20 is considered a good score, what measure of center would be best for Erin to use to motivate her teammates?

Trivia Game Results

Game	Score
Game 1	20
Game 2	20
Game 3	18
Game 4	19
Game 5	23
Game 6	40
Game 7	22
Game 8	19

FOR MORE PRACTICE GO TO THE **Personal Math Trainer**

Name ____________________

Chapter 13 Review/Test

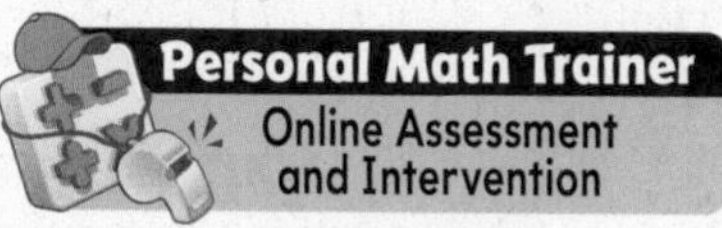

1. The dot plot shows the number of chin-ups done by a gym class.

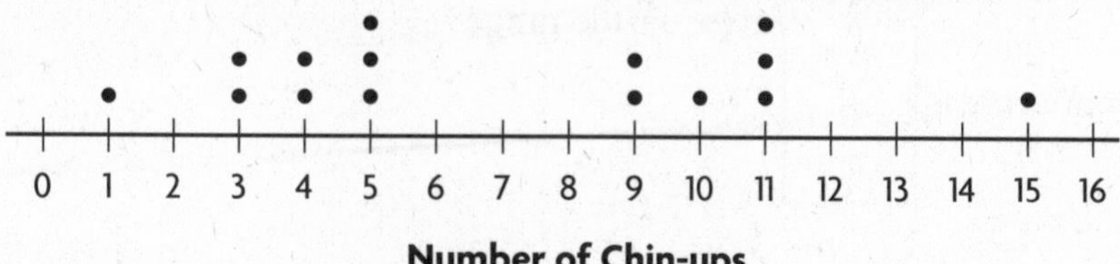

For numbers 1a–1e, choose Yes or No to indicate whether the statement is correct.

1a. There are two peaks. ○ Yes ○ No

1b. There are no clusters. ○ Yes ○ No

1c. There is a gap from 6 to 8. ○ Yes ○ No

1d. The most chin-ups anyone did was 15. ○ Yes ○ No

1e. The modes are 3, 4, and 9. ○ Yes ○ No

2. The histogram shows the high temperatures in degrees Fahrenheit of various cities for one day in March.

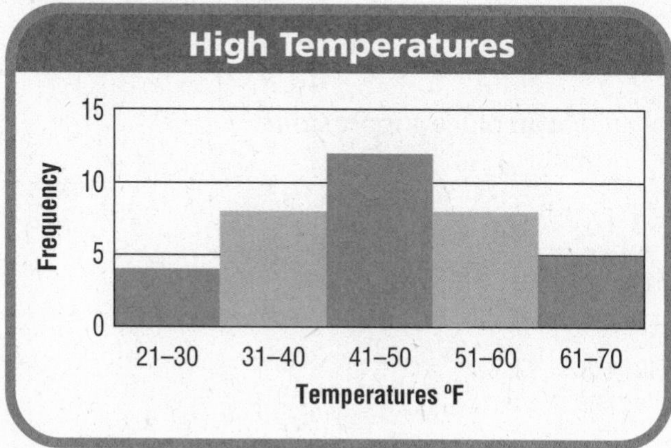

Select the best word to complete each sentence.

The histogram has [zero / one / two] peak(s). The histogram [has / does not have] symmetry.

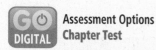

GO DIGITAL Assessment Options Chapter Test

3. The data set shows the scores of the players on the winning team of a basketball game.

Scores of Players on Winning Team												
0	17	47	13	4	1	22	0	5	6	9	1	30

The median is [6. / 9. / 13.] The lower quartile is [0. / 1. / 4.]

The upper quartile is [15 / 19.5 / 26]

4. The data set shows the number of desks in 12 different classrooms.

Classroom Desks											
24	21	18	17	21	19	17	20	21	22	20	16

Find the values of the points on the box plot.

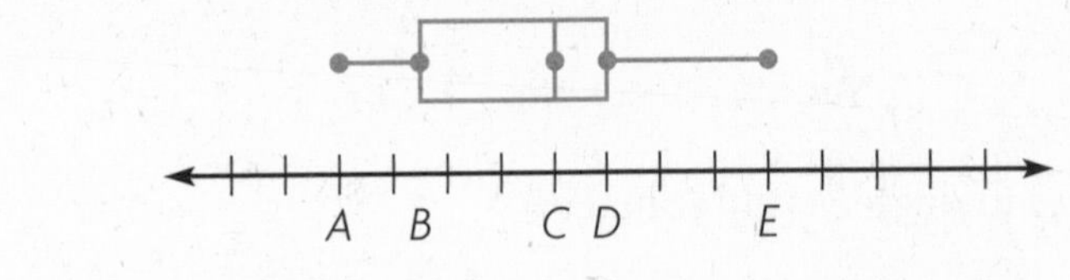

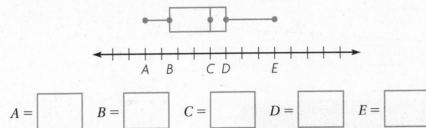

$A =$ ☐ $B =$ ☐ $C =$ ☐ $D =$ ☐ $E =$ ☐

5. The box plot shows the number of boxes sold at an office supply store each day for a week.

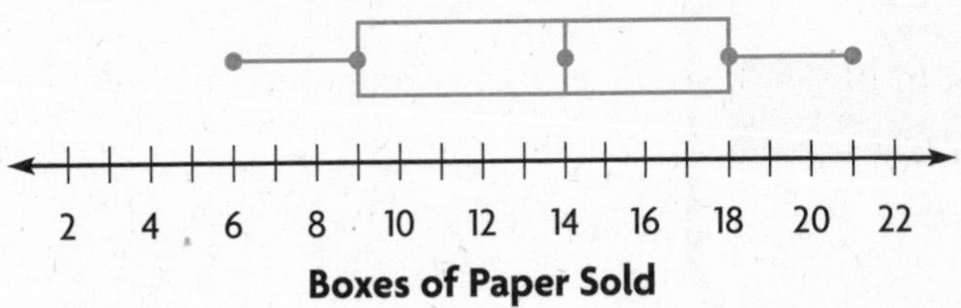

For numbers 5a–5d, select True or False for each statement.

5a. The median is 18. ○ True ○ False

5b. The range is 15. ○ True ○ False

5c. The interquartile range is 9. ○ True ○ False

5d. The upper quartile is 18. ○ True ○ False

Name ______________________

6. The data set shows the number of glasses of water Dalia drinks each day for a week.

Glasses of Water						
6	7	9	9	8	7	10

Part A

What is the mean number of glasses of water Dalia drinks each day?

____

Part B

What is the mean absolute deviation of the number of glasses of water Dalia drinks each day? Round your answer to the nearest tenth. Use words and numbers to support your answer.

7. The numbers of emails Megan received each hour are 9, 10, 9, 8, 7, and 2. The mean of the data values is 7.5 and the median is 8.5. Which measure of center better describes the data, the mean or median? Use words and numbers to support your answer.

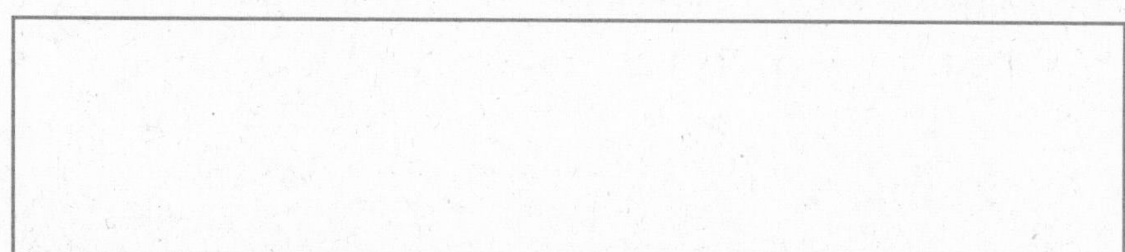

8. The number of miles Madelyn drove between stops was 182, 180, 181, 184, 228, and 185. Which measure of center best describes the data?

Ⓐ mean

Ⓑ median

Ⓒ mode

9. The histogram shows the weekly earnings of part-time workers. What interval(s) represents the most common weekly earnings?

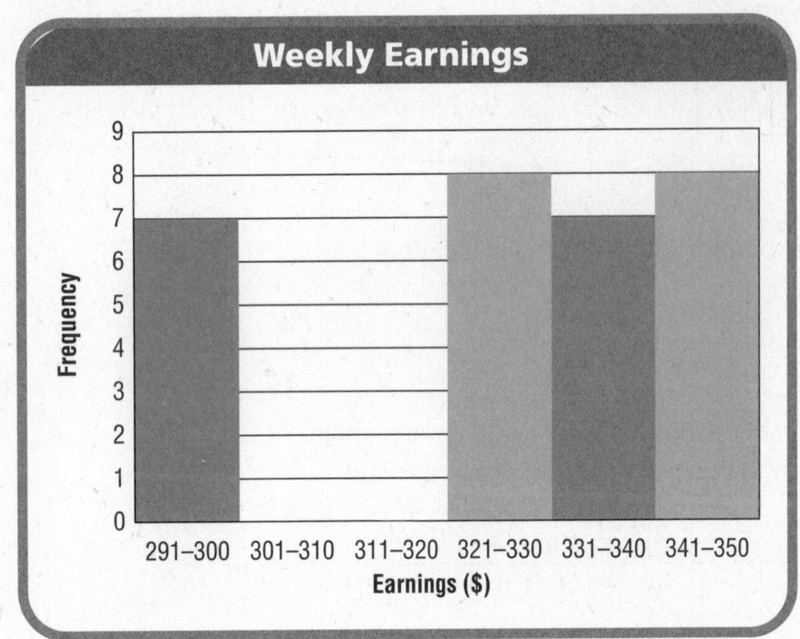

---

10. Jordan surveyed a group of randomly selected smartphone users and asked them how many applications they have downloaded onto their phones. The dot plot shows the results of Jordan's survey. Select the statements that describe patterns in the data. Mark all that apply.

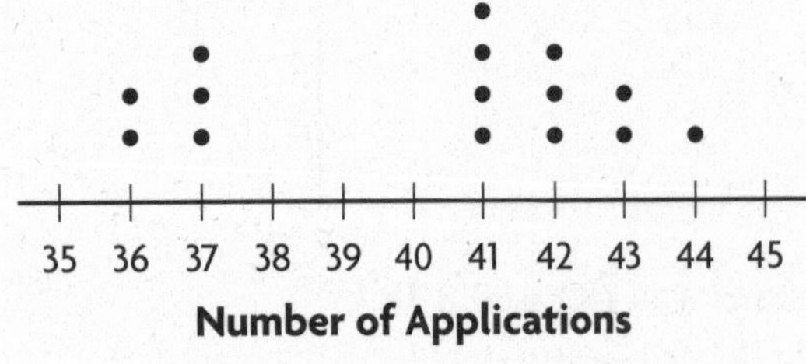

Ⓐ The modes are 37 and 42.

Ⓑ There is a gap from 38 to 40.

Ⓒ There is a cluster from 41 to 44.

Ⓓ There is a cluster from 35 to 36.

Name ______________________________

11. Mrs. Gutierrez made a histogram of the birth month of the students in her class. Describe the patterns in the histogram by completing the chart.

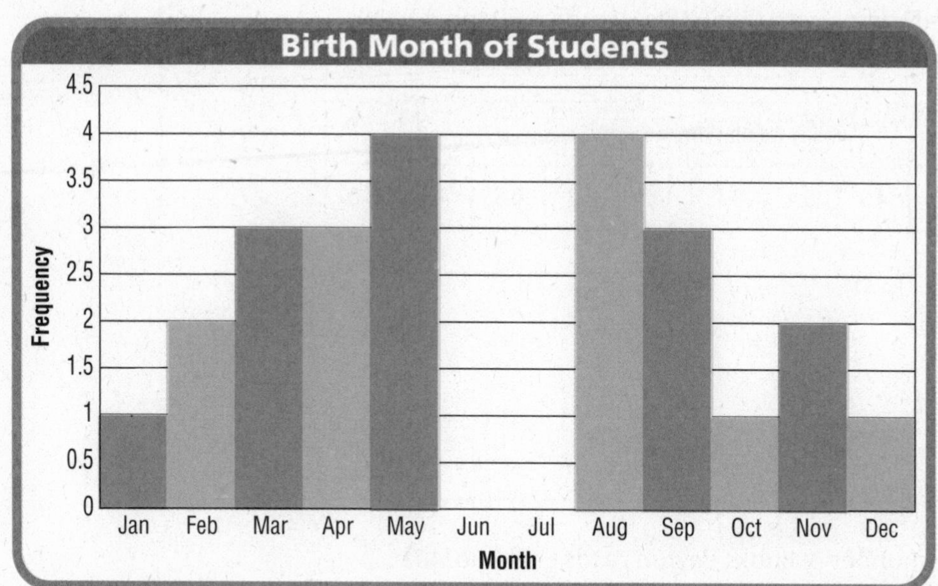

Identify any peaks.	Identify any increases across the intervals.	Identify any decreases across the intervals.

12. GO DEEPER Ian collected data on the number of children in 13 different families.

Number of Children												
1	2	4	3	2	1	0	8	1	1	0	2	3

Draw a box plot of the data and use it to find the interquartile range and range.

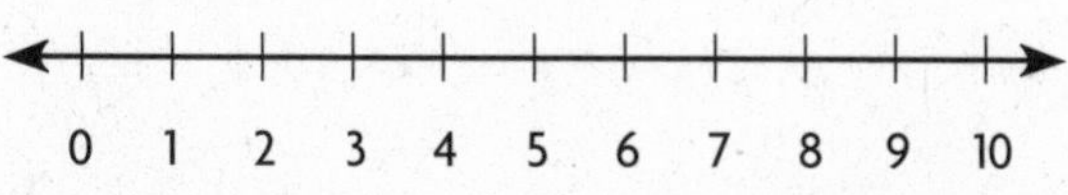

Interquartile range: ______ Range: ______

Personal Math Trainer

13. THINKSMARTER+ Gavin wants to move to a county where it rains about 5 inches every month. The data set shows the monthly rainfall in inches for a county. The mean of the data is 5 and the median is 4.35. After analyzing the data, Gavin says that this county would be a good place to move. Do you agree or disagree with Gavin? Use words and numbers to support your answer.

Monthly Rainfall (in.)											
4.4	3.7	6	2.9	4.3	5.4	6.1	14.1	4.3	0.5	4.5	3.8

14. The data set shows the number of books Peyton reads each month. Peyton says she usually reads 4 books per month. Why is Peyton's statement misleading?

Books Read						
2	3	2	4	3	11	3

15. The data set shows the scores of three players for a board game.

Board Game Scores			
Player A	90	90	90
Player B	110	100	90
Player C	95	100	95

For numbers 15a–15d, choose Yes or No to indicate whether the statement is correct.

15a. The mean absolute deviation of Player B's scores is 0. ○ Yes ○ No

15b. The mean absolute deviation of Player A's scores is 0. ○ Yes ○ No

15c. The mean absolute deviation of Player B's scores is greater than the mean absolute deviation of Player C's scores. ○ Yes ○ No

Glossary

Pronunciation Key

a	add, map	f	fit, half	n	nice, tin	p	pit, stop	û(r)	burn, term
ā	ace, rate	g	go, log	ng	ring, song	r	run, poor	yo͞o	fuse, few
â(r)	care, air	h	hope, hate	o	odd, hot	s	see, pass	v	vain, eve
ä	palm, father	i	it, give	ō	open, so	sh	sure, rush	w	win, away
b	bat, rub	ī	ice, write	ô	order, jaw	t	talk, sit	y	yet, yearn
ch	check, catch	j	joy, ledge	oi	oil, boy	th	thin, both	z	zest, muse
d	dog, rod	k	cool, take	ou	pout, now	t̲h̲	this, bathe	zh	vision, pleasure
e	end, pet	l	look, rule	o͝o	took, full	u	up, done		
ē	equal, tree	m	move, seem	o͞o	pool, food	ů	pull book		

ə the schwa, an unstressed vowel representing the sound spelled *a* in **a**bove, *e* in sick**e**n, *i* in poss**i**ble, *o* in mel**o**n, *u* in circ**u**s

Other symbols:
- • separates words into syllables
- ′ indicates stress on a syllable

absolute value [ab′sə•lo͞ot val′yo͞o] **valor absoluto** The distance of an integer from zero on a number line (p. 165)

acute angle [ə•kyo͞ot′ ang′gəl] **ángulo agudo** An angle that has a measure less than a right angle (less than 90° and greater than 0°)
Example:

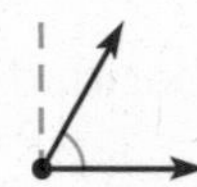

acute triangle [ə•kyo͞ot′ trī′ang•gəl] **triángulo acutángulo** A triangle that has three acute angles

addend [ad′end] **sumando** A number that is added to another in an addition problem

addition [ə•dish′ən] **suma** The process of finding the total number of items when two or more groups of items are joined; the inverse operation of subtraction

Addition Property of Equality [ə•dish′ən präp′ər•tē əv ē•kwôl′ə•tē] **propiedad de suma de la igualdad** The property that states that if you add the same number to both sides of an equation, the sides remain equal

additive inverse [ad′ə•tiv in′v ûrs] **inverso aditivo** The number which, when added to the given number, equals zero

algebraic expression [al•jə•brā′ik ek•spresh′ən] **expresión algebraica** An expression that includes at least one variable (p. 369)
Examples: $x + 5$, $3a - 4$

angle [ang′gəl] **ángulo** A shape formed by two rays that share the same endpoint
Example:

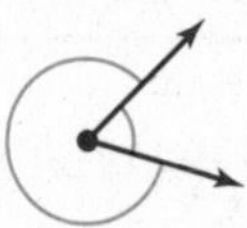

area [âr′ē•ə] **área** The measure of the number of unit squares needed to cover a surface (p. 533)

array [ə•rā′] **matriz** An arrangement of objects in rows and columns
Example:

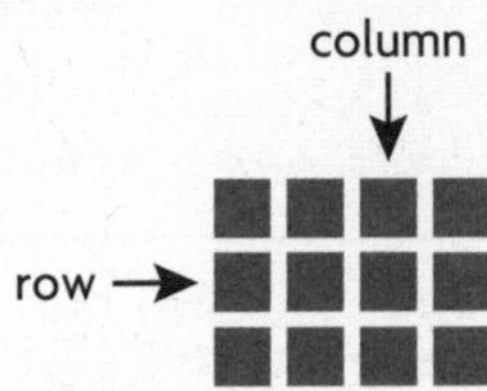

Associative Property of Addition [ə•sō′shē•ə•āt•iv präp′ər•tē əv ə•dish′ən] **propiedad asociativa de la suma** The property that states that when the grouping of addends is changed, the sum is the same
Example: (5 + 8) + 4 = 5 + (8 + 4)

Associative Property of Multiplication [ə•sō′shē•ə•tiv präp′ər•tē əv mul•tə•pli•kā′shən] **propiedad asociativa de la multiplicación** The property that states that when the grouping of factors is changed, the product is the same
Example: (2 × 3) × 4 = 2 × (3 × 4)

bar graph [bär graf] **gráfica de barras** A graph that uses horizontal or vertical bars to display countable data
Example:

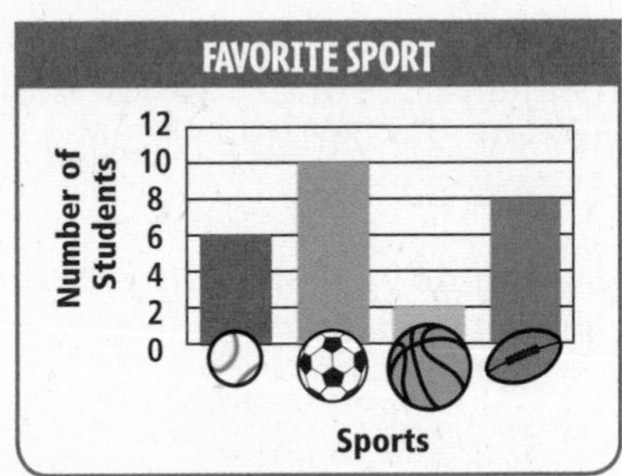

base [bās] (arithmetic) **base** A number used as a repeated factor (p. 357)
Example: $8^3 = 8 \times 8 \times 8$. The base is 8.

base [bās] (geometry) **base** In two dimensions, one side of a triangle or parallelogram which is used to help find the area. In three dimensions, a plane figure, usually a polygon or circle, which is used to partially describe a solid figure and to help find the volume of some solid figures. See also *height.*
Examples:

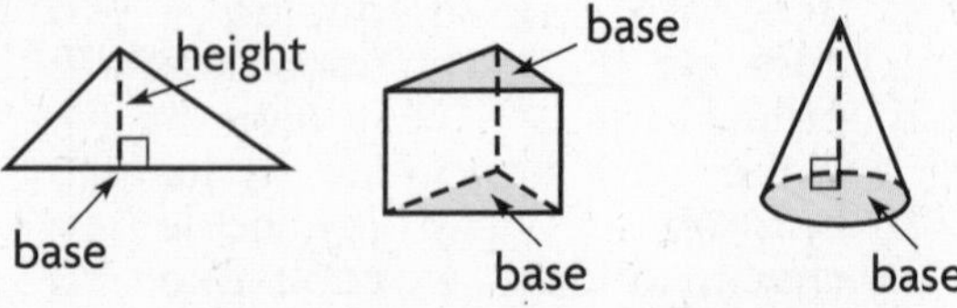

benchmark [bench′märk] **punto de referencia** A familiar number used as a point of reference

billion [bil′yən] **millardo** 1,000 millions; written as 1,000,000,000

box plot [bäks plät] **diagrama de caja** A graph that shows how data are distributed using the median, quartiles, least value, and greatest value (p. 714)
Example:

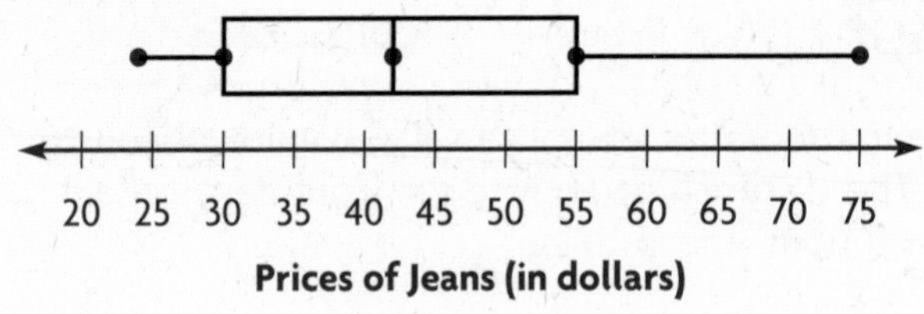

capacity [kə•pas′i•tē] **capacidad** The amount a container can hold (p. 321)
Examples: $\frac{1}{2}$ gallon, 2 quarts

Celsius (°C) [sel′sē•əs] **Celsius (°C)** A metric scale for measuring temperature

closed figure [klōzd fig′yər] **figura cerrada** A figure that begins and ends at the same point

coefficient [kō•ə•fish′ənt] **coeficiente** A number that is multiplied by a variable (p. 376)
Example: 6 is the coefficient of x in $6x$

common denominator [käm′ən dē•näm′ə•nāt•ər] **denominador común** A common multiple of two or more denominators
Example: Some common denominators for $\frac{1}{4}$ and $\frac{5}{6}$ are 12, 24, and 36.

common factor [käm′ən fak′tər] **factor común** A number that is a factor of two or more numbers (p. 23)

common multiple [käm′ən mul′tə•pəl] **múltiplo común** A number that is a multiple of two or more numbers

Commutative Property of Addition [kə•myōōt′ ə•tiv präp′ər•tē əv ə•dish′ən] **propiedad conmutativa de la suma** The property that states that when the order of two addends is changed, the sum is the same
Example: $4 + 5 = 5 + 4$

Commutative Property of Multiplication [kə•myōōt′ə•tiv präp′ər•tē əv mul•tə•pli•kāsh′ən] **propiedad conmutativa de la multiplicación** The property that states that when the order of two factors is changed, the product is the same
Example: $4 \times 5 = 5 \times 4$

compatible numbers [kəm•pat′ə•bəl num′bərz] **números compatibles** Numbers that are easy to compute with mentally

composite figure [kəm•päz′it fig′yər] **figura compuesta** A figure that is made up of two or more simpler figures, such as triangles and quadrilaterals (p. 571)
Example:

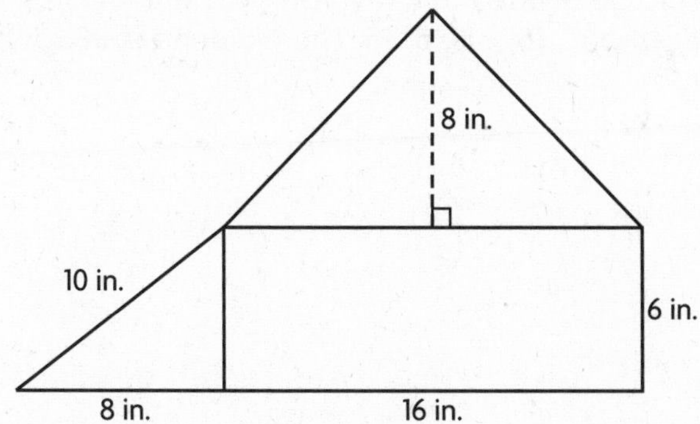

composite number [kəm•päz′it num′bər] **número compuesto** A number having more than two factors
Example: 6 is a composite number, since its factors are 1, 2, 3, and 6.

cone [kōn] **cono** A solid figure that has a flat, circular base and one vertex
Example:

congruent [kən•grōō′ənt] **congruente** Having the same size and shape (p. 539)
Example:

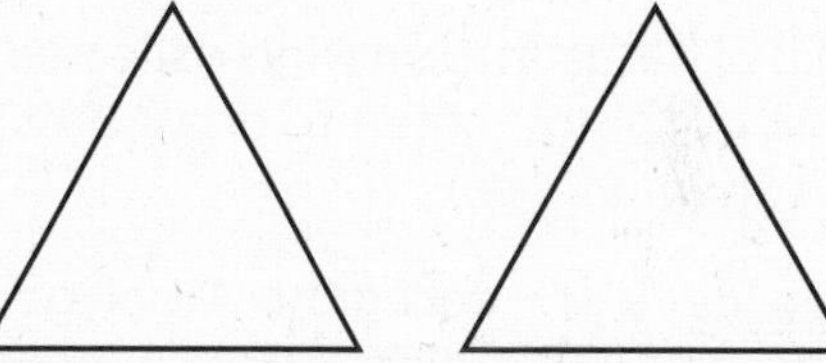

conversion factor [kən•vûr′zhən fak′tər] **factor de conversión** A rate in which two quantities are equal, but use different units (p. 315)

coordinate plane [kō•ôrd′n•it plān] **plano cartesiano** A plane formed by a horizontal line called the x-axis and a vertical line called the y-axis (p. 177)
Example:

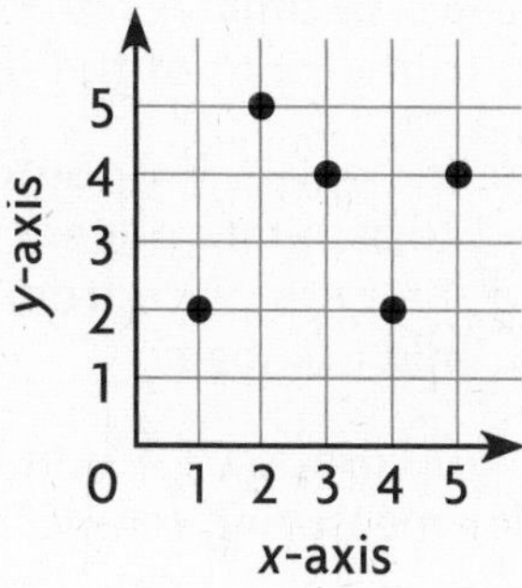

cube [kyo͞ob] **cubo** A solid figure with six congruent square faces
Example:

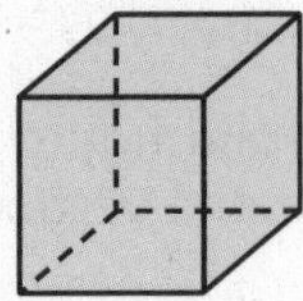

cubic unit [kyo͞o′bik yo͞o′nit] **unidad cúbica** A unit used to measure volume such as cubic foot (ft^3), cubic meter (m^3), and so on

data [dāt′ə] **datos** Information collected about people or things, often to draw conclusions about them (p. 649)

decagon [dek′ə•gän] **decágono** A polygon with 10 sides and 10 angles
Examples:

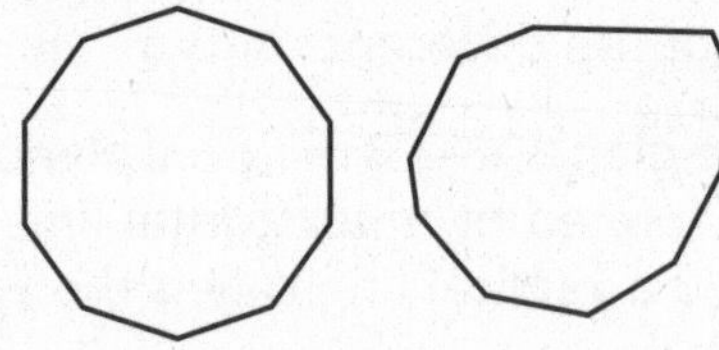

decimal [des′ə•məl] **decimal** A number with one or more digits to the right of the decimal point

decimal point [des′ə•məl point] **punto decimal** A symbol used to separate dollars from cents in money, and the ones place from the tenths place in decimal numbers

degree (°) [di•grē′] **grado (°)** A unit for measuring angles or for measuring temperature

degree Celsius (°C) [di•grē′ sel′sē•əs] **grado Celsius** A metric unit for measuring temperature

degree Fahrenheit (°F) [di•grē′ fâr′ən•hīt] **grado Fahrenheit** A customary unit for measuring temperature

denominator [dē•näm′ə•nāt•ər] **denominador** The number below the bar in a fraction that tells how many equal parts are in the whole or in the group

Example: $\frac{3}{4}$ ← denominator

dependent variable [dē•pen′dənt vâr′ē•ə•bəl] **variable dependiente** A variable whose value depends on the value of another quantity (p. 491)

difference [dif′ər•əns] **diferencia** The answer to a subtraction problem

digit [dij′it] **dígito** Any one of the ten symbols 0, 1, 2, 3, 4, 5, 6, 7, 8, 9 used to write numbers

dimension [də•men′shən] **dimensión** A measure in one direction

distribution [dis•tri•byo͞o′shən] **distribución** The overall shape of a data set

Distributive Property [di•strib′yo͞o•tiv präp′ər•tē] **propiedad distributiva** The property that states that multiplying a sum by a number is the same as multiplying each addend in the sum by the number and then adding the products (p. 24)
Example: $3 \times (4 + 2) = (3 \times 4) + (3 \times 2)$
$3 \times 6 = 12 + 6$
$18 = 18$

divide [də•vīd′] **dividir** To separate into equal groups; the inverse operation of multiplication

dividend [div′ə•dend] **dividendo** The number that is to be divided in a division problem
Example: $36 \div 6$; $6\overline{)36}$ The dividend is 36.

divisible [də•viz′ə•bəl] **divisible** A number is divisible by another number if the quotient is a counting number and the remainder is zero
Example: 18 is divisible by 3.

division [də•vizh′ən] **división** The process of sharing a number of items to find how many groups can be made or how many items will be in a group; the operation that is the inverse of multiplication

Division Property of Equality [də•vizh′ən präp′ər•tē əv ē•kwôl′ə•tē] **propiedad de división de la igualdad** The property that states that if you divide both sides of an equation by the same nonzero number, the sides remain equal

divisor [də•vī′zər] **divisor** The number that divides the dividend
Example: $15 \div 3$; $3\overline{)15}$ The divisor is 3.

dot plot [dot plät] **diagrama de puntos** A graph that shows frequency of data along a number line (p. 661)
Example:

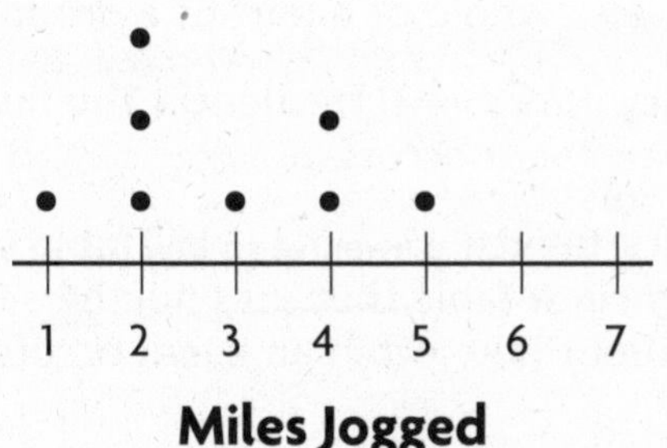

edge [ej] **arista** The line where two faces of a solid figure meet
Example:

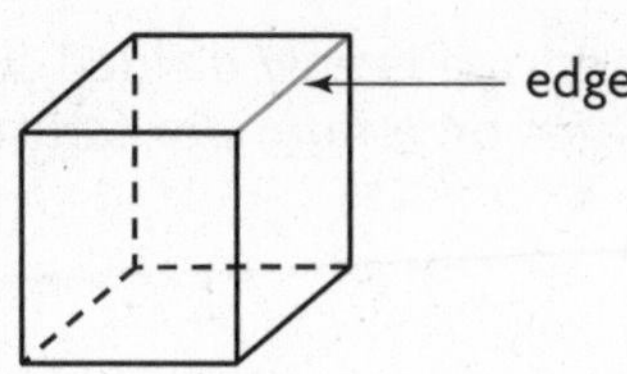

equation [i•kwā′zhən] **ecuación** An algebraic or numerical sentence that shows that two quantities are equal (p. 421)

equilateral triangle [ē•kwi•lat′ər•əl trī′ang•gəl] **triángulo equilátero** A triangle with three congruent sides
Example:

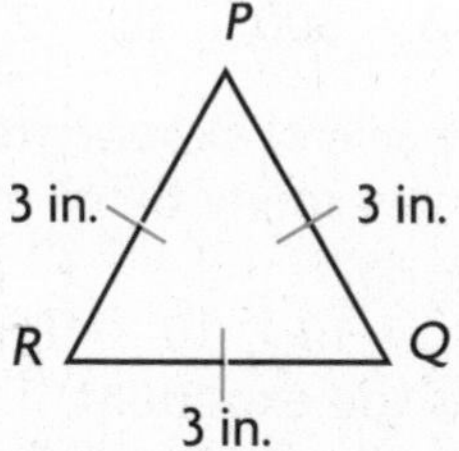

equivalent [ē•kwiv′ə•lənt] **equivalente** Having the same value

equivalent decimals [ē•kwiv′ə•lənt des′ə•məlz] **decimales equivalentes** Decimals that name the same number or amount
Example: $0.4 = 0.40 = 0.400$

equivalent expressions [ē•kwiv′ə•lənt ek•spresh′ənz] **expresiones equivalentes** Expressions that are equal to each other for any values of their variables (p. 401)
Example: $2x + 4x = 6x$

equivalent fractions [ē•kwiv′ə•lənt frak′shənz] **fracciones equivalentes** Fractions that name the same amount or part
Example: $\frac{3}{4} = \frac{6}{8}$

equivalent ratios [ē•kwiv′ə•lənt rā′shē•ōz] **razones equivalentes** Ratios that name the same comparison (p. 223)

estimate [es′tə•mit] *noun* **estimación (s)** A number close to an exact amount

estimate [es′tə•māt] *verb* **estimar (v)** To find a number that is close to an exact amount

evaluate [ē•val′yo͞o•āt] **evaluar** To find the value of a numerical or algebraic expression (p. 363)

even [ē′vən] **par** A whole number that has a 0, 2, 4, 6, or 8 in the ones place

expanded form [ek•span′did fôrm] **forma desarrollada** A way to write numbers by showing the value of each digit
Example: 832 = 800 + 30 + 2

exponent [eks′pōn•ənt] **exponente** A number that shows how many times the base is used as a factor (p. 357)
Example: $10^3 = 10 \times 10 \times 10$;
3 is the exponent.

Word History

Exponent comes from the combination of the Latin roots *ex* ("out of") + *ponere* ("to place"). In the 17th century, mathematicians began to use complicated quantities. The idea of positioning a number by raising it "out of place" is traced to René Descartes.

expression [ek•spresh′ən] **expresión** A mathematical phrase or the part of a number sentence that combines numbers, operation signs, and sometimes variables, but does not have an equal or inequality sign

face [fās] **cara** A polygon that is a flat surface of a solid figure
Example:

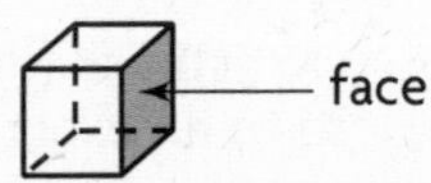

fact family [fakt fam′ə•lē] **familia de operaciones** A set of related multiplication and division, or addition and subtraction, equations
Example: $7 \times 8 = 56$; $8 \times 7 = 56$;
$56 \div 7 = 8$; $56 \div 8 = 7$

factor [fak′tər] **factor** A number multiplied by another number to find a product

factor tree [fak′tər trē] **árbol de factores** A diagram that shows the prime factors of a number
Example:

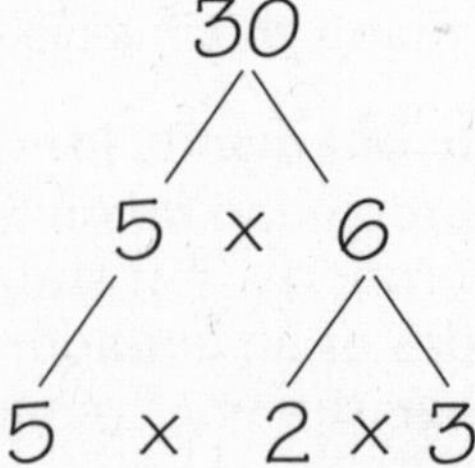

Fahrenheit (°F) [fâr′ən•hīt] **Fahrenheit (°F)** A customary scale for measuring temperature

formula [fôr′myo͞o•lə] **fórmula** A set of symbols that expresses a mathematical rule
Example: $A = b \times h$

fraction [frak′shən] **fracción** A number that names a part of a whole or a part of a group

frequency [frē′kwən•sē] **frecuencia** The number of times an event occurs (p. 661)

frequency table [frē′kwən•sē tā′bəl] **tabla de frecuencia** A table that uses numbers to record data about how often an event occurs (p. 662)

greatest common factor (GCF) [grāt′est käm′ən fak′tər] **máximo común divisor (MCD)** The greatest factor that two or more numbers have in common (p. 23)
Example: 6 is the GCF of 18 and 30.

grid [grid] **cuadrícula** Evenly divided and equally spaced squares on a figure or flat surface

height [hīt] **altura** The length of a perpendicular from the base to the top of a plane figure or solid figure
Example:

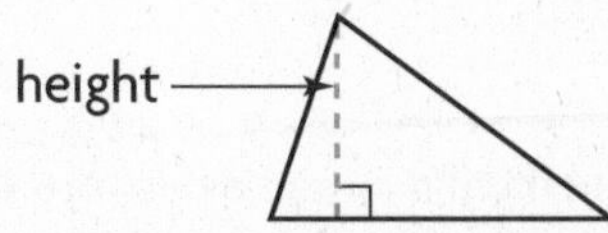

hexagon [hek′sə•gän] **hexágono** A polygon with six sides and six angles
Examples:

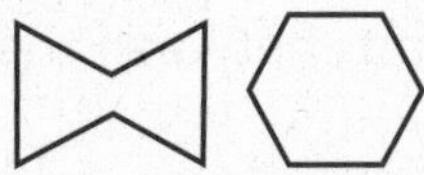

histogram [his′tə•gram] **histograma** A type of bar graph that shows the frequencies of data in intervals. (p. 667)
Example:

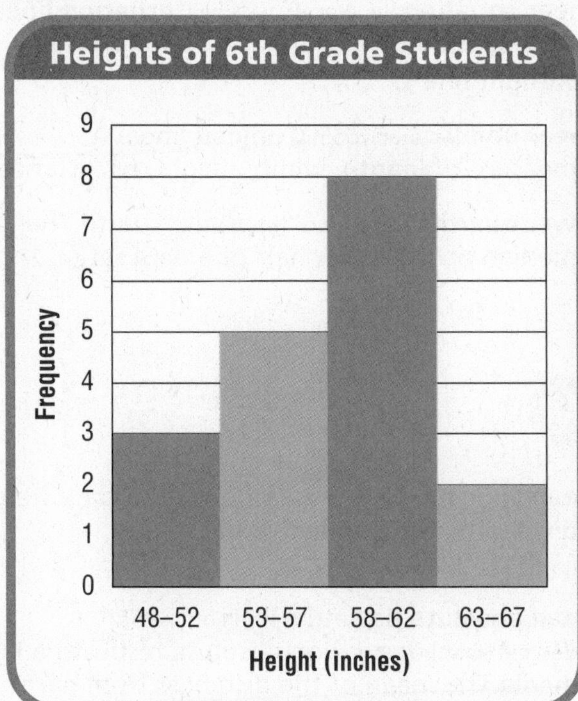

horizontal [hôr•i•zänt′əl] **horizontal** Extending left and right

hundredth [hun′drədth] **centésimo** One of one hundred equal parts
Examples: 0.56, $\frac{56}{100}$, fifty-six hundredths

Identity Property of Addition [ī•den′tə•tē präp′ər•tē əv ə•dish′ən] **propiedad de identidad de la suma** The property that states that when you add zero to a number, the result is that number

Identity Property of Multiplication [ī•den′tə•tē präp′ər•tē əv mul•tə•pli•kāsh′ən] **propiedad de identidad de la multiplicación** The property that states that the product of any number and 1 is that number

independent variable [in•dē•pen′dənt′ vâr′ē•ə•bəl] **variable independiente** A variable whose value determines the value of another quantity (p. 491)

inequality [in•ē•kwôl′ə•tē] **desigualdad** A mathematical sentence that contains the symbol $<$, $>$, $\leq$, $\geq$, or $\neq$ (p. 465)

integers [in′tə•jərz] **enteros** The set of whole numbers and their opposites (p. 139)

interquartile range [in′tûr•kwôr′tīl rānj] **rango intercuartil** The difference between the upper and lower quartiles of a data set (p. 726)

intersecting lines [in•tər•sekt′ing līnz] **líneas secantes** Lines that cross each other at exactly one point
Example:

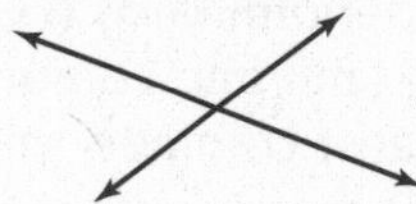

inverse operations [in′vûrs äp•pə•rā′shənz] **operaciones inversas** Opposite operations, or operations that undo each other, such as addition and subtraction or multiplication and division (p. 439)

key [kē] **clave** The part of a map or graph that explains the symbols

kite [kīt] **cometa** A quadrilateral with exactly two pairs of congruent sides that are next to each other; no two sides are parallel
Example:

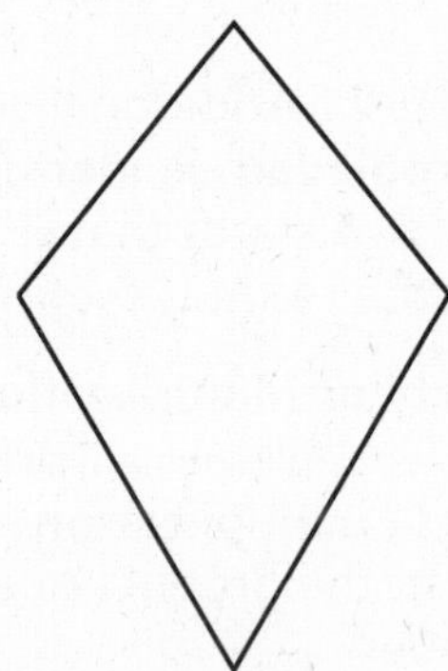

ladder diagram [lad′ər dī′ə•gram] **diagrama de escalera** A diagram that shows the steps of repeatedly dividing by a prime number until the quotient is 1

lateral area [lat′ər•əl âr′ē•ə] **área lateral** The sum of the areas of the lateral faces of a solid (p. 616)

lateral face [lat′ər•əl fās] **cara lateral** Any surface of a polyhedron other than a base

least common denominator (LCD) [lēst käm′ən dē•näm′ə•nāt•ər] **mínimo común denominador (m.c.d.)** The least common multiple of two or more denominators

Example: The LCD for $\frac{1}{4}$ and $\frac{5}{6}$ is 12.

least common multiple (LCM) [lēst käm′ən mul′tə•pəl] **mínimo común múltiplo (m.c.m.)** The least number that is a common multiple of two or more numbers (p. 17)

like terms [līk tûrmz] **términos semejantes** Expressions that have the same variable with the same exponent (p. 395)

line [līn] **línea** A straight path in a plane, extending in both directions with no endpoints
Example:

line graph [līn graf] **gráfica lineal** A graph that uses line segments to show how data change over time

line of symmetry [līn əv sim′ə•trē] **eje de simetría** A line that divides a figure into two halves that are reflections of each other (p. 184)

line segment [līn seg′mənt] **segmento** A part of a line that includes two points called endpoints and all the points between them
Example:

line symmetry [līn sim′ə•trē] **simetría axial** A figure has line symmetry if it can be folded about a line so that its two parts match exactly. (p. 184)

linear equation [lin′ē•ər ē•kwā′zhən] **ecuación lineal** An equation that, when graphed, forms a straight line (p. 517)

linear unit [lin′ē•ər yo͞o′nit] **unidad lineal** A measure of length, width, height, or distance

lower quartile [lō′ər kwôr′tīl] **primer cuartil** The median of the lower half of a data set (p. 713)

mean [mēn] **media** The sum of a set of data items divided by the number of data items (p. 681)

mean absolute deviation [mēn ab′sə•lo͞ot dē•vē•ā′shən] **desviación absoluta respecto a la media** The mean of the distances from each data value in a set to the mean of the set (p. 720)

measure of center [mezh′ər əv sent′ər] **medida de tendencia central** A single value used to describe the middle of a data set (p. 681)
Examples: mean, median, mode

measure of variability [mezh′ər əv vâr′ē•ə•bil′ə•tē] **medida de dispersión** A single value used to describe how the values in a data set are spread out (p. 725)
Examples: range, interquartile range, mean absolute deviation

median [mē′dēən] **mediana** The middle value when a data set is written in order from least to greatest, or the mean of the two middle values when there is an even number of items (p. 681)

midpoint [mid′point] **punto medio** A point on a line segment that is equally distant from either endpoint

million [mil′yən] **millón** 1,000 thousands; written as 1,000,000

mixed number [mikst num′bər] **número mixto** A number that is made up of a whole number and a fraction
Example: $1\frac{5}{8}$

mode [mōd] **moda** The value(s) in a data set that occurs the most often (p. 681)

multiple [mul′tə•pəl] **múltiplo** The product of two counting numbers is a multiple of each of those numbers

multiplication [mul•tə•pli•kā′shən] **multiplicación** A process to find the total number of items made up of equal-sized groups, or to find the total number of items in a given number of groups; It is the inverse operation of division.

Multiplication Property of Equality [mul•tə•pli•kā′shən präp′ər•tē əv ē•kwôl′ə•tē] **propiedad de multiplicación de la igualdad** The property that states that if you multiply both sides of an equation by the same number, the sides remain equal

multiplicative inverse [mul′tə•pli•kāt•iv in′vûrs] **inverso multiplicativo** A reciprocal of a number that is multiplied by that number resulting in a product of 1 (p. 108)

multiply [mul′tə•plī] **multiplicar** When you combine equal groups, you can multiply to find how many in all; the inverse operation of division

negative integer [neg′ə•tiv in′tə•jər] **entero negativo** Any integer less than zero
Examples: $^-4$, $^-5$, and $^-6$ are negative integers.

net [net] **plantilla** A two-dimensional pattern that can be folded into a three-dimensional polyhedron (p. 597)
Example:

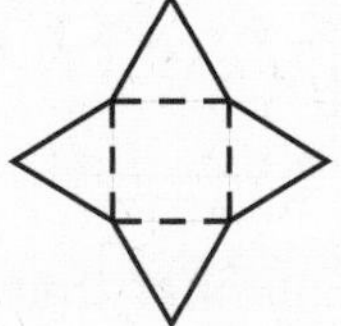
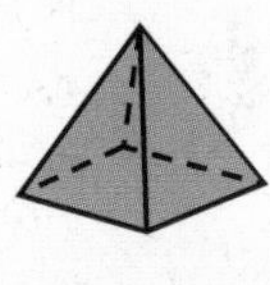

not equal to (≠) [not ē′kwəl to͞o] **no igual a** A symbol that indicates one quantity is not equal to another

number line [num′bər līn] **recta numérica** A line on which numbers can be located
Example:

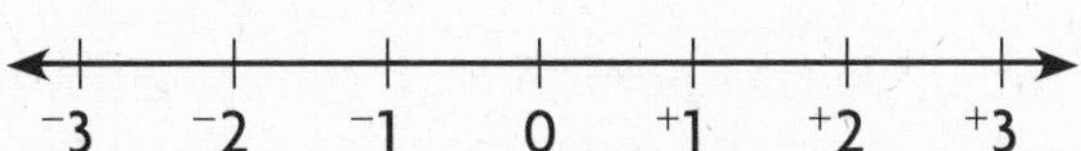

numerator [no͞o′mər•āt•ər] **numerador** The number above the bar in a fraction that tells how many equal parts of the whole are being considered
Example: $\frac{3}{4}$ ← numerator

numerical expression [no͞o•mer′i•kəl ek•spresh′ən] **expresión numérica** A mathematical phrase that uses only numbers and operation signs (p. 363)

O

obtuse angle [äb•to͞os′ ang′gəl] **ángulo obtuso** An angle whose measure is greater than 90° and less than 180°
Example:

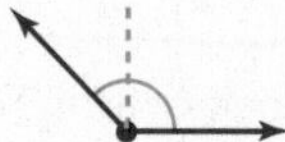

obtuse triangle [äb•to͞os′ trī′ang•gəl] **triángulo obtusángulo** A triangle that has one obtuse angle

octagon [äk′tə•gän] **octágono** A polygon with eight sides and eight angles
Examples:

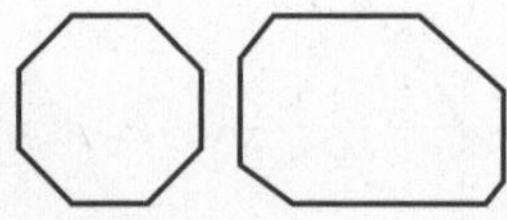

odd [od] **impar** A whole number that has a 1, 3, 5, 7, or 9 in the ones place

open figure [ō′pən fig′yər] **figura abierta** A figure that does not begin and end at the same point

opposites [äp′ə•zits] **opuestos** Two numbers that are the same distance, but in opposite directions, from zero on a number line (p. 139)

order of operations [ôr′dər əv äp•ə•rā′shənz] **orden de las operaciones** A special set of rules which gives the order in which calculations are done in an expression (p. 363)

ordered pair [ôr′dərd pâr] **par ordenado** A pair of numbers used to locate a point on a grid. The first number tells the left-right position and the second number tells the up-down position. (p. 177)

origin [ôr′ə•jin] **origen** The point where the two axes of a coordinate plane intersect; (0,0) (p. 177)

outlier [out′lī•ər] **valor atípico** A value much higher or much lower than the other values in a data set (p. 687)

overestimate [ō′vər•es•tə•mit] **sobrestimar** An estimate that is greater than the exact answer

P

parallel lines [pâr′ə•lel līnz] **líneas paralelas** Lines in the same plane that never intersect and are always the same distance apart
Example:

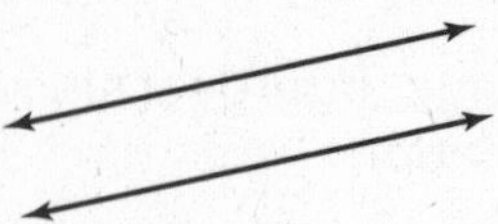

parallelogram [pâr•ə•lel′ə•gram] **paralelogramo** A quadrilateral whose opposite sides are parallel and congruent
Example:

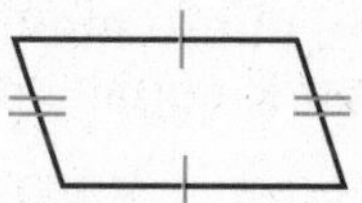

parentheses [pə•ren′thə•sēz] **paréntesis** The symbols used to show which operation or operations in an expression should be done first

partial product [pär′shəl präd′əkt] **producto parcial** A method of multiplying in which the ones, tens, hundreds, and so on are multiplied separately and then the products are added together

pattern [pat′ərn] **patrón** An ordered set of numbers or objects; the order helps you predict what will come next
Examples: 2, 4, 6, 8, 10

pentagon [pen′tə•gän] **pentágono** A polygon with five sides and five angles
Examples:

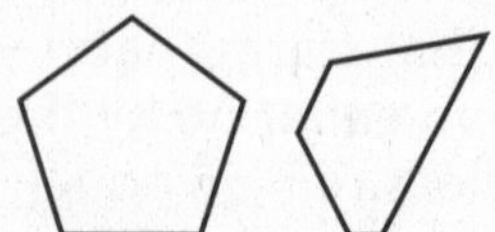

percent [pər•sent′] **porcentaje** The comparison of a number to 100; percent means "per hundred" (p. 269)

perimeter [pə•rim′ə•tər] **perímetro** The distance around a closed plane figure

period [pir′ē•əd] **período** Each group of three digits separated by commas in a multidigit number
Example: 85,643,900 has three periods.

perpendicular lines [pər•pən•dik′yo͞o•lər līnz] **líneas perpendiculares** Two lines that intersect to form four right angles
Example:

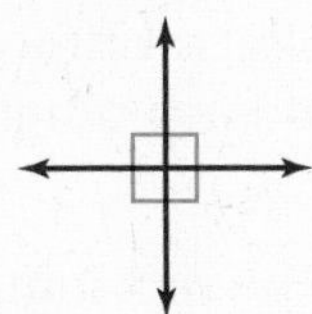

pictograph [pik′tə•graf] **pictografía** A graph that displays countable data with symbols or pictures
Example:

HOW WE GET TO SCHOOL	
Walk	❋ ❋ ❋
Ride a Bike	❋ ❋ ❋ ❋
Ride a Bus	❋ ❋ ❋ ❋ ❋ ◖
Ride in a Car	❋ ❋

Key: Each ❋ = 10 students

place value [plās val′yo͞o] **valor posicional** The value of each digit in a number based on the location of the digit

plane [plān] **plano** A flat surface that extends without end in all directions
Example:

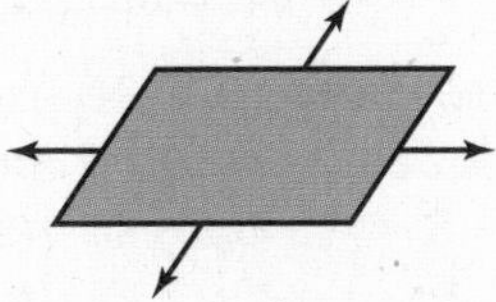

plane figure [plān fig′yər] **figura plana** A figure that lies in a plane; a figure having length and width

point [point] **punto** An exact location in space

polygon [päl′i•gän] **polígono** A closed plane figure formed by three or more line segments
Examples:

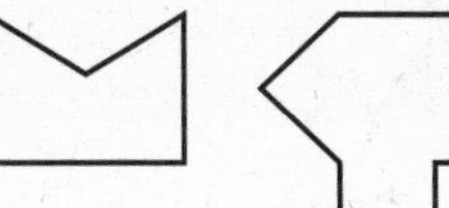
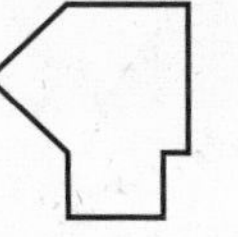

Polygons

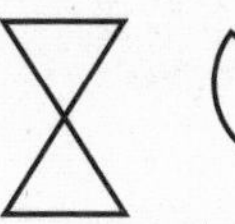

Not Polygons

polyhedron [päl•i•hē′drən] **poliedro** A solid figure with faces that are polygons
Examples:

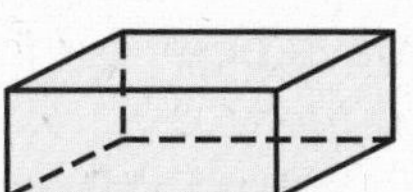
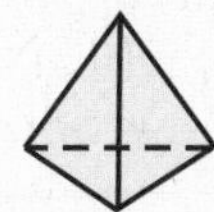

positive integer [päz′ə•tiv in′tə•jər] **entero positivo** Any integer greater than zero

prime factor [prīm fak′tər] **factor primo** A factor that is a prime number

prime factorization [prīm fak•tə•rə•zā′shən] **descomposición en factores primos** A number written as the product of all its prime factors (p. 11)

prime number [prīm num′bər] **número primo** A number that has exactly two factors: 1 and itself
Examples: 2, 3, 5, 7, 11, 13, 17, and 19 are prime numbers. 1 is not a prime number.

prism [priz′əm] **prisma** A solid figure that has two congruent, polygon-shaped bases, and other faces that are all rectangles
Examples:

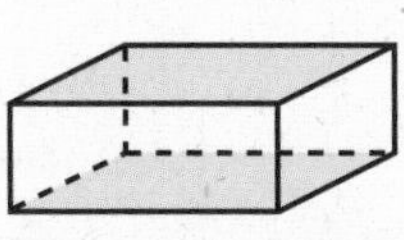
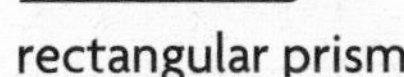

rectangular prism

triangular prism

product [präd′əkt] **producto** The answer to a multiplication problem

pyramid [pir′ə•mid] **pirámide** A solid figure with a polygon base and all other faces as triangles that meet at a common vertex
Example:

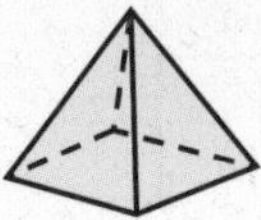

Word History

A fire is sometimes in the shape of a pyramid, with a point at the top and a wider base. This may be how *pyramid* got its name. The Greek word for fire was *pura*, which may have been combined with the Egyptian word *mer*.

quadrants [kwä′drənts] **cuadrantes** The four regions of the coordinate plane separated by the *x*- and *y*-axes (p. 183)

quadrilateral [kwä•dri•lat′ər•əl] **cuadrilátero** A polygon with four sides and four angles
Example:

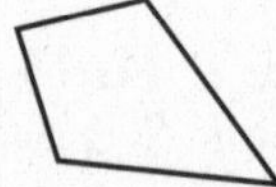

quotient [kwō′shənt] **cociente** The number that results from dividing
Example: 8 ÷ 4 = 2. The quotient is 2.

range [rānj] **rango** The difference between the greatest and least numbers in a data set (p. 726)

rate [rāt] **tasa** A ratio that compares two quantities having different units of measure (p. 218)

ratio [rā′shē•ō] **razón** A comparison of two numbers, *a* and *b*, that can be written as a fraction $\frac{a}{b}$ (p. 211)

rational number [rash′•ən•əl num′bər] **número racional** Any number that can be written as a ratio $\frac{a}{b}$ where *a* and *b* are integers and $b \neq 0$. (p. 151)

ray [rā] **semirrecta** A part of a line; it has one endpoint and continues without end in one direction
Example:

reciprocal [ri•sip′rə•kəl] **recíproco** Two numbers are reciprocals of each other if their product equals 1. (p. 108)

rectangle [rek′tang•gəl] **rectángulo** A parallelogram with four right angles
Example:

rectangular prism [rek•tang′gyə•lər priz′əm] **prisma rectangular** A solid figure in which all six faces are rectangles
Example:

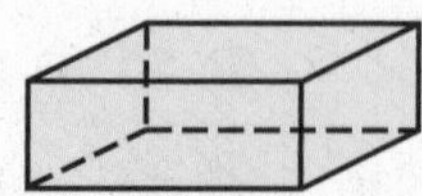

reflection [ri•flek′shən] **reflexión** A movement of a figure to a new position by flipping it over a line; a flip
Example:

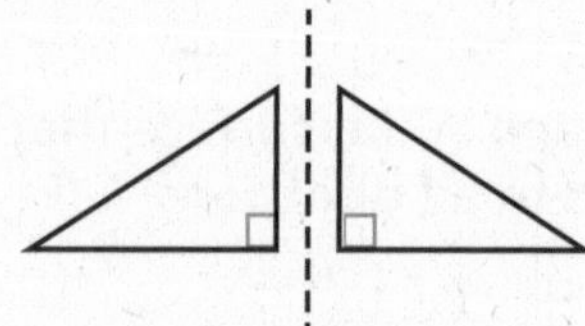

regroup [rē•grōōp′] **reagrupar** To exchange amounts of equal value to rename a number
Example: 5 + 8 = 13 ones or 1 ten 3 ones

regular polygon [reg′yə•lər päl′i•gän] **polígono regular** A polygon in which all sides are congruent and all angles are congruent (p. 565)

relative frequency table [rel′ə•tiv frē′kwən•sē tā′bəl] **tabla de frecuencia relativa** A table that shows the percent of time each piece of data occurs (p. 662)

remainder [ri•mān′dər] **residuo** The amount left over when a number cannot be divided equally

rhombus [räm′bəs] **rombo** A parallelogram with four congruent sides
Example:

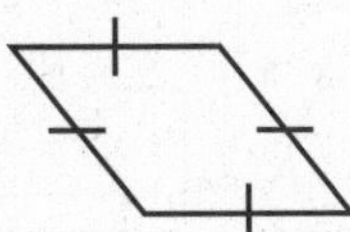

Word History

Rhombus is almost identical to its Greek origin, *rhombos.* The original meaning was "spinning top" or "magic wheel," which is easy to imagine when you look at a rhombus, an equilateral parallelogram.

right triangle [rīt trī′ang•gəl] **triángulo rectángulo** A triangle that has a right angle
Example:

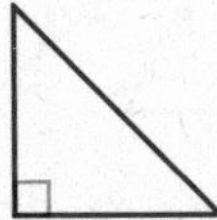

round [round] **redondear** To replace a number with one that is simpler and is approximately the same size as the original number
Example: 114.6 rounded to the nearest ten is 110 and to the nearest unit is 115.

sequence [sē′kwəns] **secuencia** An ordered set of numbers

simplest form [sim′pləst fôrm] **mínima expresión** A fraction is in simplest form when the numerator and denominator have only 1 as a common factor

simplify [sim′plə•fī] **simplificar** The process of dividing the numerator and denominator of a fraction or ratio by a common factor

solid figure [sä′lid fig′yər] **cuerpo geométrico** A three-dimensional figure having length, width, and height (p. 597)

solution of an equation [sə•lo͞o′shən əv an ē•kwā′zhən] **solución de una ecuación** A value that, when substituted for the variable, makes an equation true (p. 421)

solution of an inequality [sə•lo͞o′shən əv an in•ē•kwôl′ə•tē] **solución de una desigualdad** A value that, when substituted for the variable, makes an inequality true (p. 465)

square [skwâr] **cuadrado** A polygon with four equal, or congruent, sides and four right angles

square pyramid [skwâr pir′ə•mid] **pirámide cuadrada** A solid figure with a square base and with four triangular faces that have a common vertex
Example:

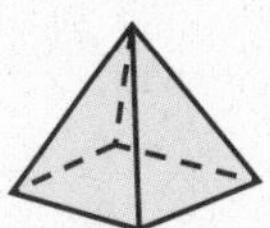

square unit [skwâr yo͞o′nit] **unidad cuadrada** A unit used to measure area such as square foot (ft^2), square meter (m^2), and so on

standard form [stan′dərd fôrm] **forma normal** A way to write numbers by using the digits 0–9, with each digit having a place value
Example: 456 ← standard form

statistical question [stə•tis′ti•kəl kwes′chən] **pregunta estadística** A question that asks about a set of data that can vary (p. 649)
Example: How many desks are in each classroom in my school?

Substitution Property of Equality [sub•stə•to͞o′shən präp′ər•tē əv ē•kwôl′ə•tē] **propiedad de sustitución de la igualdad** The property that states that if you have one quantity equal to another, you can substitute that quantity for the other in an equation

subtraction [səb•trak′shən] **resta** The process of finding how many are left when a number of items are taken away from a group of items; the process of finding the difference when two groups are compared; the inverse operation of addition

Subtraction Property of Equality [səb•trak′shən präp′ər•tē əv ē•kwôl′ə•tē] **propiedad de resta de la igualdad** The property that states that if you subtract the same number from both sides of an equation, the sides remain equal

sum [sum] **suma o total** The answer to an addition problem

surface area [sûr′fis âr′ē•ə] **área total** The sum of the areas of all the faces, or surfaces, of a solid figure (p. 603)

tally table [tal′ē tā′bəl] **tabla de conteo** A table that uses tally marks to record data

tenth [tenth] **décimo** One of ten equal parts
Example: 0.7 = seven tenths

terms [tûrmz] **términos** The parts of an expression that are separated by an addition or subtraction sign (p. 376)

thousandth [thou′zəndth] **milésimo** One of one thousand equal parts
Example: 0.006 = six thousandths

three-dimensional [thrē də•men′shə•nəl] **tridimensional** Measured in three directions, such as length, width, and height

three-dimensional solid [thrē də•men′shə•nəl säl′id] **figura tridimensional** See *solid figure*

trapezoid [trap′i•zoid] **trapecio** A quadrilateral with at least one pair of parallel sides (p. 551)
Examples:

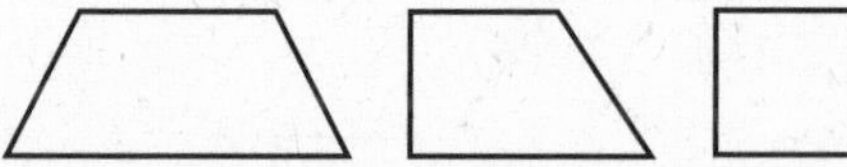

tree diagram [trē dī′ə•gram] **diagrama de árbol** A branching diagram that shows all possible outcomes of an event

trend [trend] **tendencia** A pattern over time, in all or part of a graph, where the data increase, decrease, or stay the same

triangle [trī′ang•gəl] **triángulo** A polygon with three sides and three angles
Examples:

triangular prism [trī•ang′gyə•lər priz′əm] **prisma triangular** A solid figure that has two triangular bases and three rectangular faces

two-dimensional [to͞o də•men′shə•nəl] **bidimensional** Measured in two directions, such as length and width

two-dimensional figure [to͞o də•men′shə•nəl fig′yər] **figura bidimensional** See *plane figure*

U

underestimate [un•dər•es′tə•mit] **subestimar** An estimate that is less than the exact answer

unit cube [yo͞o′nit kyo͞ob] **cubo unitaria** A cube that has a length, width, and height of 1 unit

unit fraction [yo͞o′nit frak′shən] **fraccion unitaria** A fraction that has 1 as a numerator

unit rate [yo͞o′nit rāt] **tasa por unidad** A rate expressed so that the second term in the ratio is one unit (p. 218)
Example: 55 mi per hr

unit square [yo͞o′nit skwâr] **cuadrado de una unidad** A square with a side length of 1 unit, used to measure area

unlike fractions [un′līk frak′shənz] **fracciones no semejantes** Fractions with different denominators

upper quartile [up′ər kwôr′tīl] **tercer cuartil** The median of the upper half of a data set (p. 713)

variable [vâr′ē•ə•bəl] **variable** A letter or symbol that stands for an unknown number or numbers (p. 369)

Venn diagram [ven dī′ə•gram] **diagrama de Venn** A diagram that shows relationships among sets of things
Example:

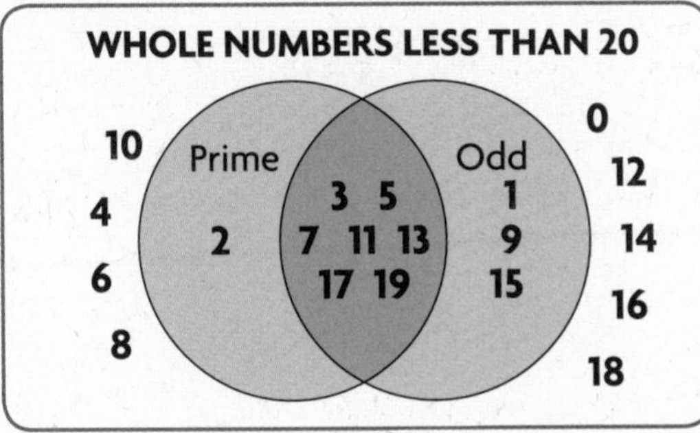

vertex [vûr′teks] **vértice** The point where two or more rays meet; the point of intersection of two sides of a polygon; the point of intersection of three (or more) edges of a solid figure; the top point of a cone; the plural of *vertex* is *vertices*
Examples:

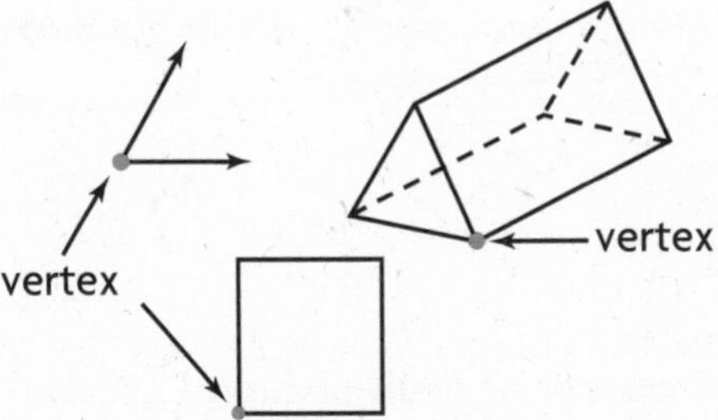

vertical [vûr′ti•kəl] **vertical** Extending up and down

volume [väl′yo͞om] **volumen** The measure of the space a solid figure occupies (p. 623)

weight [wāt] **peso** How heavy an object is

whole number [hōl num′bər] **número entero** One of the numbers 0, 1, 2, 3, 4, . . . ; the set of whole numbers goes on without end

x*-axis** [eks ak′sis] **eje de la *x The horizontal number line on a coordinate plane (p. 177)

x*-coordinate** [eks kō•ôrd′n•it] **coordenada *x The first number in an ordered pair; tells the distance to move right or left from (0,0) (p. 177)

y-axis [wī ak′sis] **eje de la y** The vertical number line on a coordinate plane (p. 177)

y-coordinate [wī kō•ôrd′•n•it] **coordenada y** The second number in an ordered pair; tells the distance to move up or down from (0,0) (p. 177)

Zero Property of Multiplication [zē′rō präp′ər•tē əv mul•tə•pli•kā′shən] **propiedad del cero de la multiplicación** The property that states that when you multiply by zero, the product is zero

Correlations

COMMON CORE STATE STANDARDS

Standards You Will Learn

Mathematical Practices		Some examples are:
MP1	Make sense of problems and persevere in solving them.	Lessons 1.1, 2.6, 2.9, 6.3, 6.5, 7.6, 8.7, 12.8, 13.2, 13.7
MP2	Reason abstractly and quantitatively.	Lessons 1.1, 2.3, 3.1, 7.3, 7.4, 7.9, 11.2, 12.7, 13.5
MP3	Construct viable arguments and critique the reasoning of others.	Lessonss 1.2, 2.3, 3.5, 6.4, 7.7, 8.1, 11.4, 12.5, 13.7
MP4	Model with mathematics.	Lessons 1.4, 2.5, 2.8, 6.3, 7.2, 8.2, 10.4, 12.4, 13.3
MP5	Use appropriate tools strategically.	Lessons 2.8, 3.4, 5.1, 6.3, 8.3, 9.2, 12.3, 12.8, 13.7
MP6	Attend to precision.	Lessons 1.6, 2.9, 3.5, 7.4, 7.9, 8.1, 13.6, 13.7, 13.8
MP7	Look for and make use of structure.	Lessons 1.2, 2.9, 3.1, 5.2, 6.5, 8.6, 13.1, 13.4, 13.8
MP8	Look for and express regularity in repeated reasoning.	Lessons 1.9, 2.7, 3.2, 4.5, 6.1, 7.1, 10.2, 12.5, 13.1
Domain: Ratios and Proportional Relationships		**Student Edition Lessons**
Understand ratio concepts and use ratio reasoning to solve problems.		
6.RP.A.1	Understand the concept of a ratio and use ratio language to describe a ratio relationship between two quantities.	Lessons 4.1, 4.2
6.RP.A.2	Understand the concept of a unit rate *a*/*b* associated with a ratio *a*:*b* with $b \neq 0$, and use rate language in the context of a ratio relationship.	Lessons 4.2, 4.6

Standards You Will Learn

Student Edition Lessons

Domain: Ratios and Proportional Relationships *(Continued)*		
6.RP.A.3	Use ratio and rate reasoning to solve real-world and mathematical problems, e.g., by reasoning about tables of equivalent ratios, tape diagrams, double number line diagrams, or equations.	
	a. Make tables of equivalent ratios relating quantities with whole-number measurements, find missing values in the tables, and plot the pairs of values on the coordinate plane. Use tables to compare ratios.	Lessons 4.3, 4.4, 4.5, 4.8
	b. Solve unit rate problems including those involving unit pricing and constant speed.	Lessons 4.6, 4.7
	c. Find a percent of a quantity as a rate per 100 (e.g., 30% of a quantity means 30/100 times the quantity); solve problems involving finding the whole, given a part and the percent.	Lessons 5.1, 5.2, 5.3, 5.4, 5.5, 5.6
	d. Use ratio reasoning to convert measurement units; manipulate and transform units appropriately when multiplying or dividing quantities.	Lessons 6.1, 6.2, 6.3, 6.4, 6.5

Standards You Will Learn

		Student Edition Lessons
Domain: The Number System		
Apply and extend previous understandings of multiplications and division to divide fractions by fractions.		
6.NS.A.1	Interpret and compute quotients of fractions, and solve word problems involving division of fractions by fractions, e.g., by using visual fraction models and equations to represent the problem.	Lessons 2.5, 2.6, 2.7, 2.8, 2.9, 2.10
Compute fluently with multi-digit numbers and find common factors and multiples.		
6.NS.B.2	Fluently divide multi-digit numbers using the standard algorithm.	Lesson 1.1
6.NS.B.3	Fluently add, subtract, multiply, and divide multi-digit decimals using the standard algorithm for each operation.	Lessons 1.6, 1.7, 1.8, 1.9
6.NS.B.4	Find the greatest common factor of two whole numbers less than or equal to 100 and the least common multiple of two whole numbers less than or equal to 12. Use the distributive property to express a sum of two whole numbers 1–100 with a common factor as a multiple of a sum of two whole numbers with no common factor.	Lessons 1.2, 1.3, 1.4, 1.5, 2.3, 2.4

Standards You Will Learn

Standards You Will Learn		Student Edition Lessons
Apply and extend previous understandings of numbers to the system of rational numbers.		
6.NS.C.5	Understand that positive and negative numbers are used together to describe quantities having opposite directions or values (e.g., temperature above/below zero, elevation above/below sea level, credits/ debits, positive/negative electric charge); use positive and negative numbers to represent quantities in real-world contexts, explaining the meaning of 0 in each situation.	Lesson 3.1, 3.3
6.NS.C.6	Understand a rational number as a point on the number line. Extend number line diagrams and coordinate axes familiar from previous grades to represent points on the line and in the plane with negative number coordinates.	
	a. Recognize opposite signs of numbers as indicating locations on opposite sides of 0 on the number line; recognize that the opposite of the opposite of a number is the number itself, e.g., $-(-3) = 3$, and that 0 is its own opposite.	Lessons 3.1, 3.3
	b. Understand signs of numbers in ordered pairs as indicating locations in quadrants of the coordinate plane; recognize that when two ordered pairs differ only by signs, the locations of the points are related by reflections across one or both axes.	Lesson 3.8
	c. Find and position integers and other rational numbers on a horizontal or vertical number line diagram; find and position pairs of integers and other rational numbers on a coordinate plane.	Lessons 2.1, 3.1, 3.3, 3.7

Standards You Will Learn

Standards You Will Learn		Student Edition Lessons
Apply and extend previous understandings of numbers to the system of rational numbers. *(Continued)*		
6.NS.C.7	Understand ordering and absolute value of rational numbers.	
	a. Interpret statements of inequality as statements about the relative position of two numbers on a number line diagram.	Lessons 2.2, 3.2, 3.4
	b. Write, interpret, and explain statements of order for rational numbers in real-world contexts.	Lessons 3.2, 3.4
	c. Understand the absolute value of a rational number as its distance from 0 on the number line; interpret absolute value as magnitude for a positive or negative quantity in a real-world situation.	Lesson 3.5
	d. Distinguish comparisons of absolute value from statements about order.	Lesson 3.6
6.NS.C.8	Solve real-world and mathematical problems by graphing points in all four quadrants of the coordinate plane. Include use of coordinates and absolute value to find distances between points with the same first coordinate or the same second coordinate.	Lessons 3.9, 3.10

Standards You Will Learn

Standards You Will Learn		Student Edition Lessons
Domain: Expressions and Equations		
Apply and extend previous understandings of arithmetic to algebraic expressions.		
6.EE.A.1	Write and evaluate numerical expressions involving whole-number exponents.	Lessons 7.1, 7.2
6.EE.A.2	Write, read, and evaluate expressions in which letters stand for numbers.	
	a. Write expressions that record operations with numbers and with letters standing for numbers.	Lesson 7.3
	b. Identify parts of an expression using mathematical terms (sum, term, product, factor, quotient, coefficient); view one or more parts of an expression as a single entity.	Lesson 7.4
	c. Evaluate expressions at specific values of their variables. Include expressions that arise from formulas used in real-world problems. Perform arithmetic operations, including those involving whole-number exponents, in the conventional order when there are no parentheses to specify a particular order (Order of Operations).	Lessons 7.5, 10.1, 10.3, 10.5, 10.6, 10.7, 11.3, 11.4, 11.6
6.EE.A.3	Apply the properties of operations to generate equivalent expressions.	Lessons 7.7, 7.8

Standards You Will Learn

Standards You Will Learn		Student Edition Lessons
Apply and extend previous understandings of arithmetic to algebraic expressions. *(Continued)*		
6.EE.A.4	Identify when two expressions are equivalent (i.e., when the two expressions name the same number regardless of which value is substituted into them). *For example, the expressions y + y + y and 3y are equivalent because they name the same number regardless of which number y stands for.*	Lesson 7.9
Reason about and solve one-variable equations and inequalities.		
6.EE.B.5	Understand solving an equation or inequality as a process of answering a question: which values from a specified set, if any, make the equation or inequality true? Use substitution to determine whether a given number in a specified set makes an equation or inequality true.	Lessons 8.1, 8.8
6.EE.B.6	Use variables to represent numbers and write expressions when solving a real-world or mathematical problem; understand that a variable can represent an unknown number, or, depending on the purpose at hand, any number in a specified set.	Lesson 7.6
6.EE.B.7	Solve real-world and mathematical problems by writing and solving equations of the form $x + p = q$ and $px = q$ for cases in which p, q and x are all nonnegative rational numbers.	Lessons 8.2, 8.3, 8.4, 8.5, 8.6, 8.7, 10.1
6.EE.B.8	Write an inequality of the form $x > c$ or $x < c$ to represent a constraint or condition in a real-world or mathematical problem. Recognize that inequalities of the form $x > c$ or $x < c$ have infinitely many solutions; represent solutions of such inequalities on number line diagrams.	Lessons 8.9, 8.10

Standards You Will Learn		**Student Edition Lessons**
Represent and analyze quantitative relationships between dependent and independent variables.		
6.EE.C.9	Use variables to represent two quantities in a real-world problem that change in relationship to one another; write an equation to express one quantity, thought of as the dependent variable, in terms of the other quantity, thought of as the independent variable. Analyze the relationship between the dependent and independent variables using graphs and tables, and relate these to the equation. *For example, in a problem involving motion at constant speed, list and graph ordered pairs of distances and times, and write the equation* $d = 65t$ *to represent the relationship between distance and time.*	Lessons 9.1, 9.2, 9.3, 9.4, 9.5
Domain: Geometry		
Solve real-world and mathematical problems involving area, surface area, and volume.		
6.G.A.1	Find the area of right triangles, other triangles, special quadrilaterals, and polygons by composing into rectangles or decomposing into triangles and other shapes; apply these techniques in the context of solving real-world and mathematical problems.	Lessons 10.1, 10.2, 10.3, 10.4, 10.5, 10.6, 10.7, 10.8, 11.7
6.G.A.2	Find the volume of a right rectangular prism with fractional edge lengths by packing it with unit cubes of the appropriate unit fraction edge lengths, and show that the volume is the same as would be found by multiplying the edge lengths of the prism. Apply the formulas $V = lwh$ and $V = bh$ to find volumes of right rectangular prisms with fractional edge lengths in the context of solving real-world and mathematical problems.	Lessons 11.5, 11.6, 11.7

Standards You Will Learn		Student Edition Lessons
Solve real-world and mathematical problems involving area, surface area, and volume. *(Continued)*		
6.G.A.3	Draw polygons in the coordinate plane given coordinates for the vertices; use coordinates to find the length of a side joining points with the same first coordinate or the same second coordinate. Apply these techniques in the context of solving real-world and mathematical problems.	Lesson 10.9
6.G.A.4	Represent three-dimensional figures using nets made up of rectangles and triangles, and use the nets to find the surface area of these figures. Apply these techniques in the context of solving real-world and mathematical problems.	Lessons 11.1, 11.2, 11.3, 11.4, 11.7
Domain: Statistics and Probability		
Develop understanding of statistical variability.		
6.SP.A.1	Recognize a statistical question as one that anticipates variability in the data related to the question and accounts for it in the answers. *For example, "How old am I?" is not a statistical question, but "How old are the students in my school?" is a statistical question because one anticipates variability in students' ages.*	Lesson 12.1
6.SP.A.2	Understand that a set of data collected to answer a statistical question has a distribution which can be described by its center, spread, and overall shape.	Lessons 12.6, 13.1, 13.4, 13.6, 13.7, 13.8
6.SP.A.3	Recognize that a measure of center for a numerical data set summarizes all of its values with a single number, while a measure of variation describes how its values vary with a single number.	Lessons 12.6, 13.4, 13.6

Standards You Will Learn

		Student Edition Lessons
Summarize and describe distributions.		
6.SP.B.4	Display numerical data in plots on a number line, including dot plots, histograms, and box plots.	Lessons 12.3, 12.4, 12.8, 13.2
6.SP.B.5	Summarize numerical data sets in relation to their context, such as by:	
	a. Reporting the number of observations.	Lesson 12.2
	b. Describing the nature of the attribute under investigation, including how it was measured and its units of measurement.	Lesson 12.2
	c. Giving quantitative measures of center (median and/or mean) and variability (interquartile range and/or mean absolute deviation), as well as describing any overall pattern and any striking deviations from the overall pattern with reference to the context in which the data were gathered.	Lessons 12.5, 12.6, 12.7, 13.1, 13.3, 13.4, 13.8
	d. Relating the choice of measures of center and variability to the shape of the data distribution and the context in which the data were gathered.	Lessons 12.7, 13.5, 13.7

Index

A

D

E

G

Q

S

V

Table of Measures

METRIC	CUSTOMARY
Length	
1 meter (m) = 1,000 millimeters (mm)	1 foot (ft) = 12 inches (in.)
1 meter = 100 centimeters (cm)	1 yard (yd) = 3 feet
1 meter = 10 decimeters (dm)	1 yard = 36 inches
1 dekameter (dam) = 10 meters	1 mile (mi) = 1,760 yards
1 hectometer (hm) = 100 meters	1 mile = 5,280 feet
1 kilometer (km) = 1,000 meters	
Capacity	
1 liter (L) = 1,000 milliliters (mL)	1 cup (c) = 8 fluid ounces (fl oz)
1 liter = 100 centiliters (cL)	1 pint (pt) = 2 cups
1 liter = 10 deciliters (dL)	1 quart (qt) = 2 pints
1 dekaliter (daL) = 10 liters	1 quart = 4 cups
1 hectoliter (hL) = 100 liters	1 gallon (gal) = 4 quarts
1 kiloliter (kL) = 1,000 liters	
Mass/Weight	
1 gram (g) = 1,000 milligrams (mg)	1 pound (lb) = 16 ounces (oz)
1 gram = 100 centigrams (cg)	1 ton (T) = 2,000 pounds
1 gram = 10 decigrams (dg)	
1 dekagram (dag) = 10 grams	
1 hectogram (hg) = 100 grams	
1 kilogram (kg) = 1,000 grams	

TIME	
1 minute (min) = 60 seconds (sec)	1 year (yr) = about 52 weeks
1 hour (hr) = 60 minutes	1 year = 12 months (mo)
1 day = 24 hours	1 year = 365 days
1 week (wk) = 7 days	1 decade = 10 years
	1 century = 100 years
	1 millennium = 1,000 years

SYMBOLS

$=$	is equal to	10^2	ten squared
$\neq$	is not equal to	10^3	ten cubed
$\approx$	is approximately equal to	2^4	the fourth power of 2
$>$	is greater than	$\lvert {}^{-}4 \rvert$	the absolute value of $^{-}4$
$<$	is less than	%	percent
$\geq$	is greater than or equal to	(2, 3)	ordered pair (x, y)
$\leq$	is less than or equal to	$^\circ$	degree

FORMULAS

Perimeter and Circumference		Area	
Polygon	$P =$ sum of the lengths of sides	Rectangle	$A = lw$
Rectangle	$P = 2l + 2w$	Parallelogram	$A = bh$
Square	$P = 4s$	Triangle	$A = \frac{1}{2}bh$
		Trapezoid	$A = \frac{1}{2}(b_1 + b_2)h$
		Square	$A = s^2$

Volume		Surface Area	
Rectangular Prism	$V = lwh$ or Bh	Cube	$S = 6s^2$
Cube	$V = s^3$		

Made in the USA
Middletown, DE
22 December 2021